Conflict in the Holy Land

Conflict in the Holy Land

From Ancient Times to the Arab-Israeli Conflicts

Robert C. DiPrizio, Editor

BLOOMSBURY ACADEMIC
NEW YORK • LONDON • OXFORD • NEW DELHI • SYDNEY

BLOOMSBURY ACADEMIC
Bloomsbury Publishing Inc
1385 Broadway, New York, NY 10018, USA
50 Bedford Square, London, WC1B 3DP, UK
29 Earlsfort Terrace, Dublin 2, Ireland

BLOOMSBURY, BLOOMSBURY ACADEMIC and the Diana logo
are trademarks of Bloomsbury Publishing Plc

First published in the United States of America by ABC-CLIO 2020
Paperback edition published by Bloomsbury Academic 2025

Copyright © Bloomsbury Publishing Inc, 2025

For legal purposes the Acknowledgments on p. xiii constitute an extension of this copyright page.

COVER PHOTO: Tear gas canisters are fired by Israeli forces at Palestinian protesters
during clashes along the Israel-Gaza border, May 14, 2018.
(dpa picture alliance/Alamy Stock Photo)

All rights reserved. No part of this publication may be reproduced
or transmitted in any form or by any means, electronic or mechanical,
including photocopying, recording, or any information storage or retrieval
system, without prior permission in writing from the publishers.

Bloomsbury Publishing Inc does not have any control over, or responsibility for,
any third-party websites referred to or in this book. All internet addresses given
in this book were correct at the time of going to press. The author and publisher
regret any inconvenience caused if addresses have changed or sites have
ceased to exist, but can accept no responsibility for any such changes.

Library of Congress Cataloging- in- Publication Data
Names: DiPrizio, Robert C., 1968– editor.
Title: Conflict in the Holy Land : from ancient times to the Arab-Israeli conflicts /
Robert C. DiPrizio, editor.
Description: Santa Barbara, California : ABC-CLIO, [2020] | Includes bibliographical references and index.
Identifiers: LCCN 2019033036 (print) | LCCN 2019033037 (ebook) | ISBN 9781440867477 (cloth) |
ISBN 9781440867484 (ebook) Subjects: LCSH: Arab-Israeli conflict—Encyclopedias. |
Jewish-Arab relations—Encyclopedias. | Israel—Ethnic relations—Encyclopedias.
Classification: LCC DS119.7 .C6524 2020 (print) | LCC DS119.7 (ebook) | DDC 956.0403—dc23

LC record available at https://lccn.loc.gov/2019033036
LC ebook record available at https://lccn.loc.gov/2019033037

ISBN: HB: 978-1-4408-6747-7
PB: 979-8-7651-4011-6
ePDF: 978-1-4408-6748-4
eBook: 979-8-2160-6476-3

To find out more about our authors and books visit www.bloomsbury.com
and sign up for our newsletters.

For Sarah and Julio

Contents

List of Entries   ix

Acknowledgments   xiii

Introduction   xv

Chronology   xix

A–Z Entries   1

Bibliography   341

About the Editor and Contributor List   345

Index   349

List of Entries

Abbas, Mahmoud
Abdullah II, King of Jordan
Absentee Landlords
Adalah
Al-Aqsa Martyrs Brigades
Aliya
Aliya Bet
Allon Plan
American Israel Public Affairs Committee (AIPAC)
American Jewish Congress (AJC)
American Palestine Committee (APC)
Arab Boycott of Israel
Arab Higher Committee (AHC)
Arab-Islamic Conquest of Palestine
Arab-Israeli War, 1948
Arab-Israeli War, 1956
Arab-Israeli War, 1967
Arab-Israeli War, 1973
Arab-Jewish Clashes in Palestine, Pre-1947
Arab-Jewish Communal War, 1947
Arab League
Arab Peace Plan
Arab Revolt, 1916
Arab Revolt, 1936
Arab Spring
Arab Spring, Effects on Israel
Arab Spring, Effects on Palestine
Arafat, Yasser
Ashrawi, Hanan
Assad, Bashar al-
Assad, Hafez al-
Assyrian Conquest of Israel
B'Tselem
Babylonian Conquest of Judah
Balfour Declaration
Barghouti, Marwan
Bedouins
Begin, Menachem
Ben-Gurion, David
Ben-Yehuda, Eliezer
Bernadotte, Count Folke
Bethlehem
Black September
Boycott, Divestment, and Sanctions (BDS) Movement
Breaking the Silence
British Mandate for Palestine
British White Paper
Camp David Accords
Camp David Summit, 2000
Canaanites
Cave of the Patriarchs Massacre
Christian Zionism
Christianity

List of Entries

Church of the Holy Sepulcher
Closed Military Zones
Crusades in the Holy Land
Dahlan, Mohammed
David
Dayan, Moshe
Deir Yassin Massacre
Democratic Front for the Liberation of Palestine (DFLP)
Demographics in Israel and Palestine
Diaspora, Jewish
Diaspora, Palestinian
Druze
Egypt
Egyptian Conquest of Canaan
Entebbe Raid
Erekat, Saeb
Eretz Israel
Fatah
Faysal-Weizmann Agreement
First and Second Temple Periods
Gaza Raid, 1955
Gaza Strip
Gaza Strip Blockade
Gaza Strip Disengagement
Geneva Accord, 2003
Golan Heights
Grand Mufti of Jerusalem
Great March of Return
Gush Emunim
Habash, George
Haganah
Hamas
Haram al-Sharif/Temple Mount
Hattin, Battle of
Hebron
Herod the Great
Herzl, Theodor
Hezbollah
Holy War Army (HWA)
Husayn ibn Ali, Sharif of Mecca
Husayn, King of Jordan
Intifada, First
Intifada, Second
Irgun Tsvai Leumi
Islam
Israel
Israel Defense Forces (IDF)
Israel-Hezbollah War, 2006
Israeli Occupations
Israelis
Israeli Security Barrier
Israelite Conquest of Canaan
Izz al-Din al-Qassam Brigade
Jabotinsky, Ze'ev
Jerusalem
Jerusalem, Old City of
Jewish Agency
Jewish Defense League (JDL)
Jewish Emigration from Arab Countries
Jewish Legion
Jewish National Fund (JNF)
Jewish Revolts
Jewish Underground
Jordan
Judaism
Judea and Samaria
Kahane, Meir
Katyusha Rockets
Khartoum Resolution
Kibbutz
King David Hotel Bombing
Kingdom of Israel
Kingdom of Judah

Knesset
Kook, Avraham Yitzhak
Labor Party
Lavon Affair
Law of Return
Lawrence, T. E.
League of Nations
Lebanon
Lebanon, Israeli Invasion of
Likud Party
Lydda and Ramle
Madrid Conference
Masada
McMahon-Husayn Correspondence
Meir, Golda
Middle East Quartet
Mishal, Khalid
Mossad
Mubarak, Hosni
Muhammad, Prophet of Islam
Munich Olympics
Nakba
Nasser, Gamal Abdel
Netanyahu, Benjamin
One-State Solution
Operation Nickel Grass
Oslo Accords
Ottoman Conquest of Palestine
Pale of Settlement
Palestine
Palestine Liberation Army (PLA)
Palestine Liberation Front (PLF)
Palestine Liberation Organization (PLO)
Palestinian Authority (PA)
Palestinian Authority Security Forces (PASF)
Palestinian Hijackings
Palestinian Islamic Jihad (PIJ)
Palestinian National Council (PNC)
Palestinian Refugee Camps
Palestinian Refugees
Palestinians
Palmach
Peace Now
Peres, Shimon
Permanent Status Issues
Persian Conquest of Palestine
Pinsker, Leon
Plan Dalet
Popular Front for the Liberation of Palestine (PFLP)
Qassam, Izz al-Din al-
Rabin, Yitzhak
Ramallah
Right of Return
Roman Conquest of Judea
Sadat, Anwar
Saladin
Saul
Settlements
Settler Violence
Shamir, Yitzhak
Sharon, Ariel
Shin Bet
Solomon
Stern Gang
Suicide Bombings
Supreme Muslim Council (SMC)
Sykes-Picot Agreement
Syria
Tanzim

Tel Aviv
Third Temple Movement
Two-State Solution
United Kingdom of Israel
UN Partition Plan for Palestine
UN Relief and Works Agency for Palestine Refugees in the Near East (UNRWA)
UN Security Council Resolution 242
UN Security Council Resolution 338
U.S. Aid to Israel
U.S. Involvement in Israeli-Palestinian Affairs

USS *Liberty*
War of Attrition
Water Security
Weizmann, Chaim
West Bank
World Zionist Organization (WZO)
Yassin, Sheikh Ahmed
Yishuv
Zealots
Zionism
Zionist Organization of America (ZOA)

Acknowledgments

I would like to thank the many authors from around the world who contributed to this volume—without their expertise and hard work, this encyclopedia would not exist. Special thanks go out to a number of colleagues at Air Command and Staff College at Maxwell Air Force Base, Alabama. Jim Forsyth and Ron Dains afforded me the time and flexibility to concentrate on writing, while Paul Springer and Jonathan Zartman offered sage advice that helped me navigate the complexities of such a large project. Special thanks also go to Lieutenant Colonel Hugh "Buck" Gardenier, for both his contributions to the book and his moral support. Finally, I would like to thank the many people at ABC-CLIO who have worked on this encyclopedia, especially Padraic (Pat) Carlin, for entrusting me with the project; and Barbara Patterson, Bridget Austiguy-Preschel, and Jitendra Kumar, for seeing it through to fruition.

Introduction

The Holy Land. Israel. Palestine. No place on Earth evinces as much emotion, or has seen as much conflict, as this tiny sliver of land between the Jordan River and Mediterranean Sea. Revered by Jews, Christians, and Muslims, and fought over for millennia, it remains the epicenter of one of the world's most vexing and enduring conflicts. This encyclopedia surveys the record of violence across the Holy Land from ancient times to the ongoing Arab-Israeli conflicts.

While some have sought to control the Holy Land for its geostrategic value as a land bridge between Africa, Asia, and Europe, others seek to monopolize its sacred value. Jews built their historical identity around their conquest of the land, and then their return after the Babylonian captivity. They retained their devotion to the land after their dispersion by the Romans. After Christianity became a religion of the state in the Roman and Byzantine empires, Christians came on pilgrimages to strengthen their faith. Centuries after the Arab Muslim conquest, when the Seljuk Turks inhibited pilgrimage, the Roman Catholic Church authorized numerous Crusades to reclaim the Holy Land. After 100 years of conquest and occupation by the Crusaders, Muslims regrouped and reclaimed Jerusalem and its environs.

Even today, religious attachments to the land inform the clash between Arabs and Israelis. Most Arabs are Muslim and consider Jerusalem their third-holiest city, behind Mecca and Medina. It was once the *qibla* (direction of prayer), and the Prophet Muhammad is believed to have traveled to Jerusalem during his Night Journey to heaven, an event commemorated by the world-famous Dome of the Rock and al-Aqsa Mosque in the Old City of Jerusalem. For their part, many Jews believe that God granted them the Holy Land 4,000 years ago as part of a special covenant. They trace their history as a people back to the ancient Jewish kingdoms that stood there for hundreds of years. Jerusalem holds special significance as the location of a great religious temple in two different time periods, making it the spiritual center of Judaism. Today, the Western (Wailing) Wall and Temple Mount stand out as the most important of many Jewish holy sites in the area. Even tens of millions of Christians today view the Arab-Israeli conflict through a religious lens. For example, many Christian Zionists believe that God commands them to favor Jews as his "chosen people" in their struggle to control the Holy Land, and that the Jewish people must return to Zion before the second coming of Christ can occur.

In addition to religion, the conflict between Israelis and Palestinians represents a clash between competing national movements. From this perspective, the

Arab-Israeli conflict only began in the late nineteenth century, with the development of modern Zionism. As nationalist movements spread throughout Europe, some European Jews concluded that persistent anti-Semitism and periodic pogroms (organized massacres of Jews) required the Jewish people to establish a state of their own. In 1897, the first Zionist Congress met in Switzerland and created the World Zionist Organization (WZO). Over the next few decades, the WZO and other Zionist groups pursued the creation of a Jewish state in Palestine. At the time, the Ottoman Empire controlled Palestine and allowed a small number of Jewish migrants into the area, but it opposed the creation of a Jewish homeland there.

Following World War I, Britain took control of Palestine and allowed greater amounts of Jewish immigration. The 1917 Balfour Declaration committed Britain to "the establishment in Palestine of a national home for the Jewish people." Britain reiterated this goal in 1920, when it received mandate authority over Palestine from the League of Nations. Despite the anger and opposition of the Arab inhabitants, Britain allowed hundreds of thousands of Jewish migrants into Palestine until the eve of World War II. During the war, fear of provoking greater regional Arab unrest caused the British to reverse course and restrict Jewish migration. Still, many Jews kept coming, and by 1948, Zionists had become one-third of the population in Palestine.

Faced with ongoing violence between Arabs and Jews, and suffering from increasingly deadly attacks by Zionist militants who resented London's about-face, the British referred the matter to the newly formed United Nations (UN). In 1947, UN member-states voted to partition Palestine into two states—one for Jews and another for Arabs. Jews were to receive about 56 percent of the land, despite representing only a third of the population; and Jerusalem was to be an international city administered by the United Nations. Arabs in Palestine rejected partition and waged war for several months, but the Jews gained territory in the months-long Communal War.

When Israel declared independence in May 1948, its Arab neighbors immediately invaded, expanding the communal conflict into an international war. When the dust settled on the first Arab-Israeli war, Israel had secured control over 78 percent of Palestine. Hundreds of thousands of Palestinians fled or were forced from their homes during the war and prevented from returning. Egypt and Jordan took control of those parts of the stillborn Palestinian state that Israel did not acquire. As a result of another major war in 1967, Israel took the Gaza Strip and Sinai Desert from Egypt, the Golan Heights from Syria, and the West Bank (including East Jerusalem) from Jordan. Israel eventually returned the Sinai to Egypt as part of a peace treaty, but it still controls the remaining territories.

The Arab-Israeli conflict evolved again in the 1980s. The 1981 peace treaty between Israel and Egypt reduced the possibility that any coalition of Arab states could pose an existential threat to Israel. The following year, Israel invaded Lebanon and drove the Palestine Liberation Organization (PLO) to Tunis, where it became increasingly marginalized. In December 1987, Palestinians living under Israeli military occupation took matters into their own hands and launched the First Intifada (Uprising), thus reigniting the Palestinian nationalist movement. Within months, the PLO asserted its leadership on the uprising and declared an independent Palestine, claiming sovereignty over the Gaza Strip, East Jerusalem, and the West Bank. Thus, the center of gravity of the Arab-Israeli conflict once again became the struggle between Arabs and Jews for control of Palestine.

In 1993, Israel and the PLO signed the Oslo Accords, which many hoped would lead to real Palestinian statehood. However, rejectionists on both sides derailed the peace train, and by the end of 2000, a very bloody Second Intifada erupted. Since then, Israel-Palestinian relations have suffered periodic spikes in violence and intermittent negotiations that have failed to generate any major agreements.

From the Israelite conquest of Canaan to the ongoing violence between Israelis and Palestinians, conflict in the Holy Land is unique in both its staggering persistence and its global importance. This encyclopedia offers readers comprehensive yet concise coverage of the many conflicts in the Holy Land over the past 4,000 years. It begins with a chronology of events, and then presents a set of entries in alphabetical order. These entries cover major historical events, as well as important leaders, locations, groups, movements, and ideas. Each entry includes a list of further readings, and the sources are augmented by a bibliography at the end of the book.

A note on terminology: For topics known by many names, entry titles use neutral language, such as "Arab-Israeli War of 1973" rather than "Yom Kippur War" or "Ramadan War." Similarly, the "Lebanon, Israeli Invasion of" entry discusses what Israel calls "Operation Peace for Galilee." Finally, for the purposes of standardization, the spelling of names, places, and events uses transliterations commonly adopted in English publications.

Chronology

c.3000–900 BCE
Canaanites inhabit Palestine west of the Jordan River, coastal Lebanon, and southern Syria

c.1450–1150 BCE
Egypt rules Canaan

c.1200–1100 BCE
Philistines and Jews settle in the Palestine region of Canaan

c.1050 BCE
United Kingdom of Israel established; first Jewish temple built in Jerusalem

c.930 BCE
United Kingdom of Israel splits into the northern Kingdom of Israel and southern Kingdom of Judah

722 BCE
Assyrian Empire conquers the Kingdom of Israel

586 BCE
Babylonian Empire conquers the Kingdom of Judah; Jews exiled to Babylon

539–140 BCE
Persians conquer Babylon, permit Jews to return to southern Palestine; Jewish Temple rebuilt; Palestine ruled by Persian and Greek dynasties until the revolt of the Maccabees in 140 BCE

140–63 BCE
Maccabees create the Hasmonean dynasty and restore Jewish independence until the Roman conquest in 63 BCE, when Palestine is incorporated into the province of Judea

63 BCE–638 CE
Palestine ruled by the Roman or Byzantine Empire

66–73 CE
Jewish Zealots rebel against Romans, hold out at Masada until 73; Romans destroy Jerusalem and Jewish Temple in the process of restoring rule

132–135
Bar Kokhba revolt put down by Romans, who then expel most Jews from Palestine

622–632
Emigration of Prophet Muhammad to Medina; forming of a community and subjugation of Mecca

632
Muhammad dies

630–730
Arab-Islamic empire expands to Spain in the west, across North Africa and the Middle East, and to India in the east; Middle East is Islamized and Arabized

638
Jerusalem and Palestine incorporated into Arab-Islamic rule

661–750
Umayyad caliphate rules Islamic empire from Damascus

750–1258
Abbasid caliphate rules Islamic empire from Baghdad

1097–1291
Christian Crusades in the Holy Land

1250–1517
Period of Mumluk dynasties, centered in Damascus and Cairo

1453
Ottoman Turks conquer Constantinople; end of Byzantine Empire

1516–1918
Ottomans rule Palestine

1790–1791
Russia passes laws restricting Jews to Pale of Settlement

1869
Suez Canal opens

1875
Britain buys Egyptian ruler Ismail Pasha's shares of the Suez Canal Company

1881
Y(ehudah). L(eib). Pinsker's *Auto-Emancipation* published

1882
Britain occupies Egypt; remains until 1956

1882–1904
First Aliya (mass immigration of Jews to Palestine)

1896
Theodor Herzl's *Der Judenstaat* published

1897
World Zionist Organization (WZO) founded

1901
Jewish National Fund (JNF) established

1904–1914
Second Aliya

1908
Young Turk Revolution in the Ottoman Empire

1914–1918
World War I

1914
Ottomans enter the war on the German side; British declares a protectorate over Egypt

1915–1916
McMahon-Husayn correspondence

1916
Britain and France sign Sykes-Picot Agreement; Sharif Husayn declares Arab Revolt against Ottomans; British officer T. E. Lawrence assists in Arab Revolt

1917
Balfour Declaration issued by Britain; Bolshevik revolution in Russia (Russia leaves war); British forces capture Jerusalem

1918
Woodrow Wilson declares Fourteen Points (including right to self-determination); World War I ends

1919
Paris Peace Conference determines the fate of Ottoman-controlled lands; Faysal-Weizmann agreement

1919–1923
Third Aliya

1920
Kingdom of Syria declared under Faysal Husayn but is short-lived, as France occupies Damascus within months; San Remo Conference grants Britain mandate powers over Palestine; Arab anti-Zionist riots break out in Palestine; Haganah established

1921
Britain splits Mandate Palestine into two—Palestine west of the Jordan River and Transjordan in the east; installs Abdullah as emir in Transjordan; Britain appoints Hajj Amin al-Husayn as Grand Mufti of Jerusalem

1922
Supreme Muslim Council (SMC) in Palestine established; League of Nations formally approves British Mandate for Palestine

1923
Jewish Agency for Palestine established

1924–1928
Fourth Aliya

1925
Ze'ev Jabotinsky founds the Revisionist Party

1929
Western (Wailing) Wall riots leave over 200 Jews and Arabs dead, many hundreds injured

1933
Adolf Hitler becomes German chancellor

1935
Palestinian Islamist leader Izz al-Din al-Qassam killed by the British

1936
Arab Revolt in Palestine begins

1937
Peel Commission advises partition of Palestine between Jews and Arabs; Irgun is formed

1938–1939
British and Haganah forces cooperate to put down Arab Revolt

1939
British White Paper greatly restricts Jewish migration to Palestine in effort to assuage Arab opinion in the region on the eve of World War II, which begins in September

1940
Stern Gang (later Lehi) formed

1942
Biltmore Conference takes place in New York City

1944
Lehi assassinates Lord Moyne in Cairo

1945
Arab League created; World War II ends

1946
British-Zionist tensions simmer; British raid Jewish Agency for Palestine; Irgun blows up King David Hotel in Jerusalem

1947
Britain submits the Palestinian question to United Nations (UN); UN General Assembly approves UN Special Commission on Palestine (UNSCOP) partition plan; war breaks out between Arabs and Jews in Palestine

1948
Deir Yassin Massacre; Palestinians take revenge on Jewish medical convoy; Israel declares independence and Arab neighbors invade; Lehi assassinates UN mediator Count Folke Bernadotte

1949
Armistice between Israel and Arab neighbors leaves Israel in control of 78 percent of Palestine; Egypt controls Gaza Strip; Jordan controls West Bank and East Jerusalem; Israelis elect first Knesset; David Ben-Gurion becomes prime minister

1951
Palestinian assassinates King Abdullah of Jordan in East Jerusalem

1952
Gamal Abdel Nasser leads a coup of Egyptian officers, ousting King Farouk

1954
Nasser secures control of the Egyptian government; Israeli defense minister Pinhas Lavon authorizes agents to plant bombs in Cairo; Britain agrees to pull out of Suez Canal zone

1955
Two Israeli spies executed in Cairo in Lavon Affair; Ben-Gurion returns as prime minister; Israel launches raid into Gaza

1956
Nasser nationalizes Suez Canal; Israel invades Egypt in coordination with France and Britain; France and Britain withdraw by end of year

1957
Israel withdraws from Egypt; Eisenhower doctrine proffered

1958
Fatah established; the Hashemite king Faysal II overthrown in Iraq; U.S. troops land in Lebanon

1963
Levi Eshkol replaces Ben-Gurion as prime minister in Israel

1964
Palestine Liberation Organization (PLO) created

1965
Fatah initiates raids against Israel

1966
Israel attacks Syrian water-diversion projects

1967

Israel and Syria clash along Golan Heights; Israel warns of military action against Syria; Nasser evicts UN peacekeepers from Sinai and closes the Tiran Strait to Israeli shipping; Jordan enters a mutual defense pact with Egypt; Israel launches a surprise attack on June 5; Israel sinks USS *Liberty* during war; Israel captures Golan Heights from Syria, Sinai Desert and Gaza Strip from Egypt, and West Bank and East Jerusalem from Jordan; war ends in six days; Arab League Khartoum Conference follows end of war; UN Security Council approves Resolution 242

1968

Israeli and Palestinian forces clash in Jordan, elevating Yasser Arafat's profile

1969

Golda Meir installed as Israeli prime minister; Arafat elected head of PLO; War of Attrition begins

1970

Israeli-Egyptian cease-fire along Suez Canal; Jordan and PLO clash in what becomes known as "Black September"; Nasser dies and is succeeded by Anwar Sadat; Hafiz al-Assad takes power in Syria

1972

Palestinian terrorists kill eleven Israeli athletes and coaches during the Munich Summer Olympics

1973

Egypt and Syria launch a surprise attack on Israel during Yom Kippur; Operation Nickel Grass helps Israel win the war; UN Security Council passes Resolution 338

1974

First Israeli-Egyptian disengagement agreement; Gush Emunim formed in Israel; Meir resigns as prime minister and is replaced by Yitzhak Rabin; Israeli-Syrian disengagement agreement; Arab League recognizes the PLO as "the sole legitimate representative of the Palestinian people"; PLO chairman Arafat addresses the UN General Assembly

1975

Second Israeli-Egyptian disengagement agreement; first Lebanon civil war lasts eighteen months

1977

Likud ends four decades of Labor Party rule in Israel by winning Knesset (parliamentary) elections; Menachem Begin becomes Israeli prime minister; Sadat addresses Israel's Knesset, initiating Israeli-Egyptian peace talks

1978

Israel invades south Lebanon and withdraws in months; U.S. president Jimmy Carter brokers Camp David Accords, which result in a peace agreement between Israel and Egypt

1981
Sadat assassinated and succeeded by Hosni Mubarak; Israel annexes Golan Heights

1982
Israel invades Lebanon, occupies southern Lebanon for next eighteen years; Maronite massacre of Palestinians at Sabra and Shatila; PLO relocates from Lebanon to Tunisia; United States sends peacekeeping troops to Lebanon

1983
Begin replaced by Yitzhak Shamir as Israeli prime minister; a suicide bomber kills 241 U.S. Marines in Beirut; Hezbollah emerges as a major political force in Lebanon

1984
U.S. troops withdraw from Lebanon

1985
PLO assassinates three Israelis in Cyprus; Israel bombs PLO headquarters

1987
First Intifada begins in December

1988
PLO takes control of Intifada leadership; Hamas is founded; King Husayn of Jordan renounces any claim to West Bank and East Jerusalem; Palestinian National Council (PNC) accepts two-state solution formula

1990
Israeli forces kill seven Palestinians, triggering riots that leave seventeen Palestinians dead and 600 wounded; Palestinian terror attack, initiated from Baghdad, intercepted by Israel; United States suspends dialogue with PLO; Iraq invades Kuwait; PLO supports Iraq

1991
U.S.-led coalition liberates Kuwait; Arab-Israeli peace talks begin in Madrid; Soviet Union dissolves

1992
Rabin becomes Israeli prime minister again; secret Israeli-PLO negotiations take place

1993
Oslo Accords signed in Washington, D.C.

1994
Israeli settler Baruch Goldstein kills twenty-nine Arabs at the Mosque of Abraham in Hebron; Palestinian self-rule begins in Gaza and Jericho; Israel-Jordan peace treaty signed

1995
Hamas suicide bombers kill ten Israelis and leave more than 100 injured; Oslo II Accords signed; Prime Minister Rabin assassinated by an Israeli extremist;

Shimon Peres becomes prime minister; Israel withdraws from areas A and B of West Bank, in accordance with Oslo II

1996
Hamas bombmaker Yahya Ayyash assassinated by Israel's Shin Bet; Palestinians elect Arafat president; Hamas suicide bombers avenge Ayyash's assassination by killing fifty-nine Israelis and wounding 200; Israel launches Operation Grapes of Wrath in response to clashes with Hezbollah; Benjamin Netanyahu elected prime minister of Israel

1998
Wye Memorandum between Israel and Palestinians signed; PLO officially removes clause in charter calling for Israel's destruction

1999
Ehud Barak elected prime minister of Israel; Israel-Syria negotiations over Golan Heights fail

2000
Hafiz al-Assad of Syria dies, replaced as president by his son Bashir; Camp David Summit fails; Ariel Sharon visits Temple Mount/Haram al-Sharif; Second Intifada begins

2001
Sharon elected prime minister of Israel, launches Operation Defensive Shield, destroying much of the Palestinian Authority (PA) infrastructure; al-Qaeda attacks the United States on September 11; United States invades Afghanistan in response

2002
Saudi Arabia offers Arab Peace Plan; U.S. president George W. Bush formally adopts the two-state solution as U.S. policy

2003
United States invades Iraq; Bush administration issues "Road Map to Peace"

2004
Israel assassinates multiple Hamas leaders; Arafat dies of causes that are still debated

2005
Mahmoud Abbas elected president of PA; Israel unilaterally withdraws from Gaza Strip

2006
Sharon suffers a stroke and falls into a coma; Hamas wins Palestinian parliamentary elections; Israel-Hamas tensions lead to Israel's invasion of Gaza; Israel-Hezbollah war erupts weeks later

2007
Annapolis conference fails to produce an agreement between Israel and the Palestinians

2008
Israel-Hamas truce lasts for six months beginning in June; the first Gaza war begins in December

2009
The Gaza war ends in January; U.S. president Barack Obama takes office; Netanyahu becomes prime minister of Israel for a second time and offers conditional support for a two-state solution

2010
Arab Spring erupts in Tunisia; United States orchestrates direct Israeli-Palestinian negotiations that quickly falter

2011
Widespread protests in Egypt result in Mubarak's removal from power and election of the Muslim Brotherhood; a Syrian civil war begins; Palestinians fail to secure UN Security Council recognition of statehood

2012
Israel and Hamas fight a one-week war in November; United Nations upgrades status of Palestine to "non-Member observer status"

2013
Netanyahu reelected Israeli prime minister; Obama administration pushes to restart Israeli-Palestinian peace negotiations

2014
Israeli-Palestinian talks falter again; Israel and Hamas fight a six-week war during July and August

2015
Netanyahu is reelected again, after declaring that Palestinian independence will not happen while he is in power

2016
Obama agrees to give Israel $38 billion in military aid over the next ten years

2017
U.S. president Donald Trump takes office and appoints pro-Israel advisors to develop what he calls the "deal of the century" to resolve the Israel-Palestinian dispute; Trump recognizes Jerusalem as Israel's capital; in response, Palestinian leaders refuse to meet with U.S. officials

2018
Great March of Return begins; United States moves its embassy from Tel Aviv to Jerusalem and cuts funding to Palestinians; Israel passes the Nation-State Law, declaring Israel the nation-state of the Jewish people

2019
United States recognizes Israel's claim to sovereignty over Golan Heights; Netanyahu is reelected as prime minister for a record fifth term despite facing

indictment on multiple charges of corruption; however, new elections were called when Netanyahu could not form a coalition government. On July 20, Netanyahu becomes Israel's longest-serving prime minister; however, in the new elections in September, he comes in second to the Blue and White Party's Benny Gantz, but neither wins a majority; to date, negotiations over forming a new government were in progress

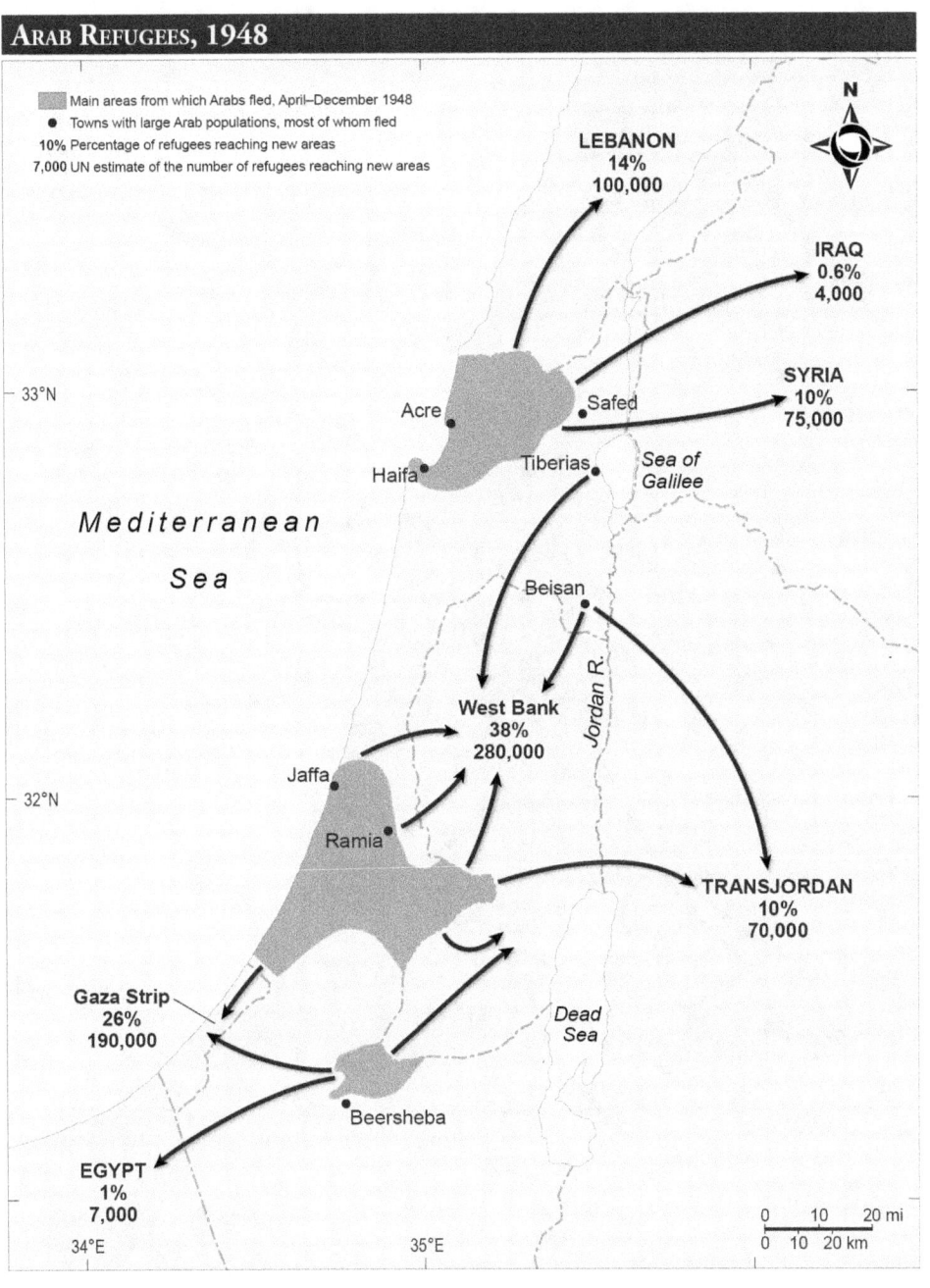

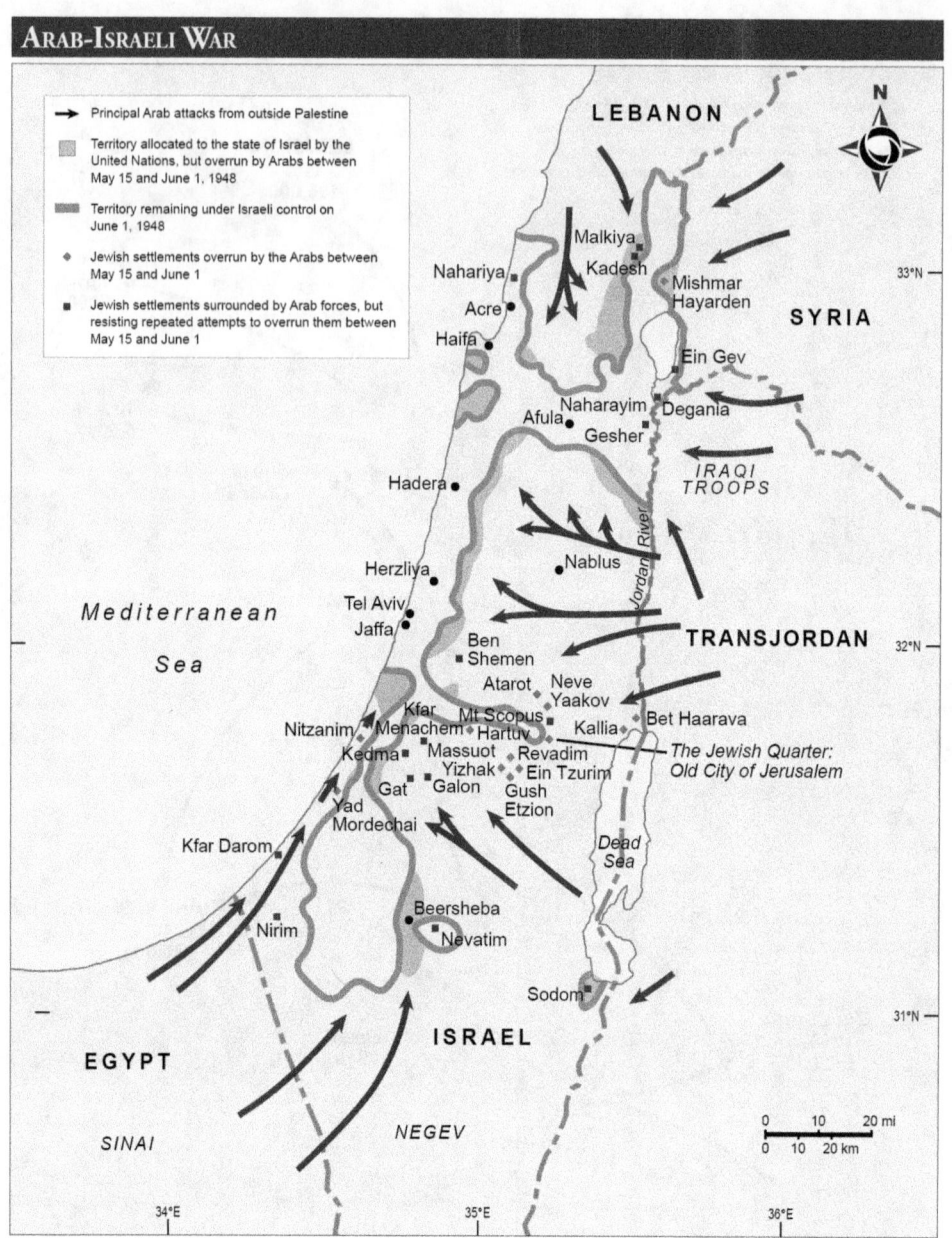

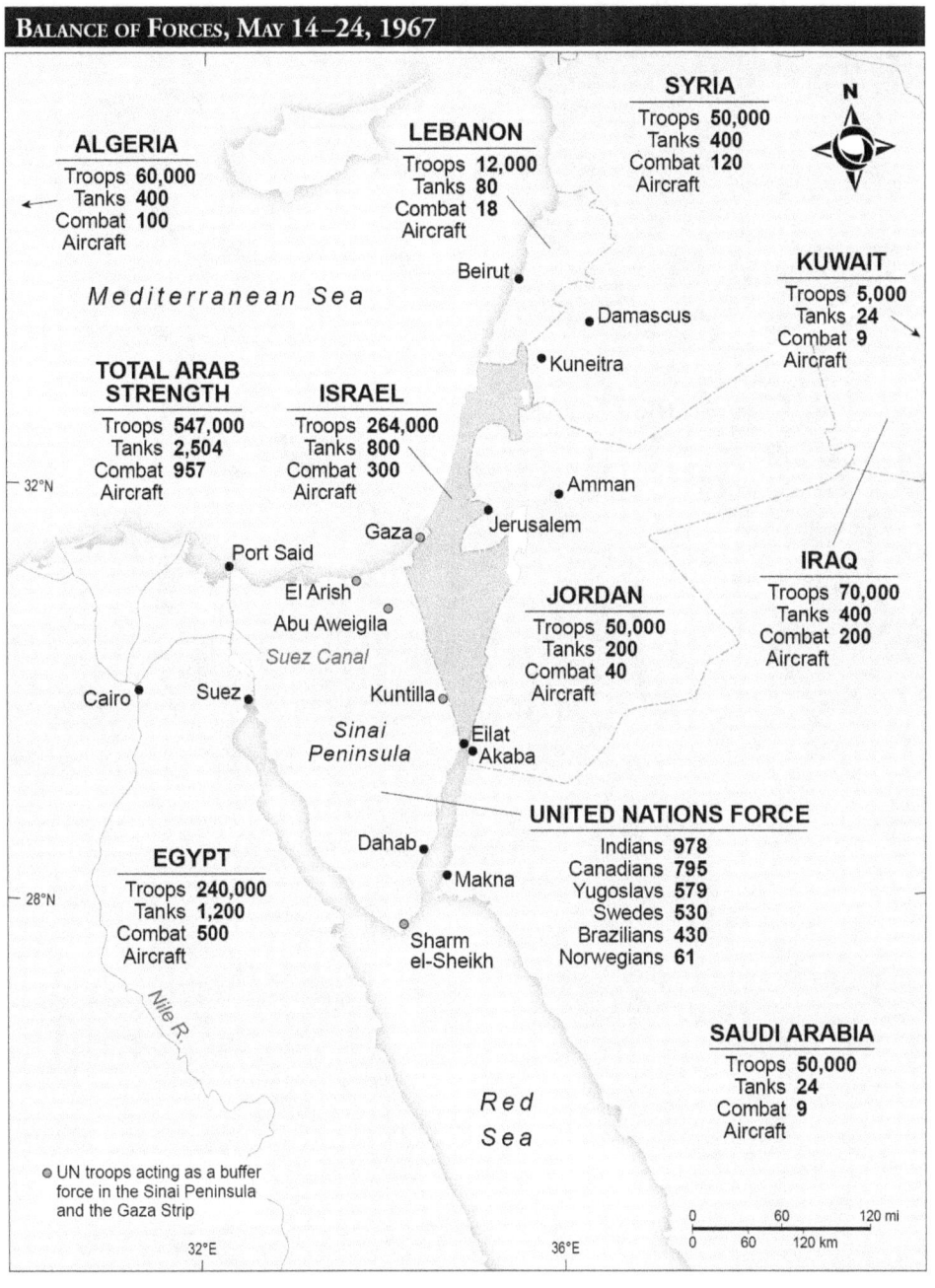

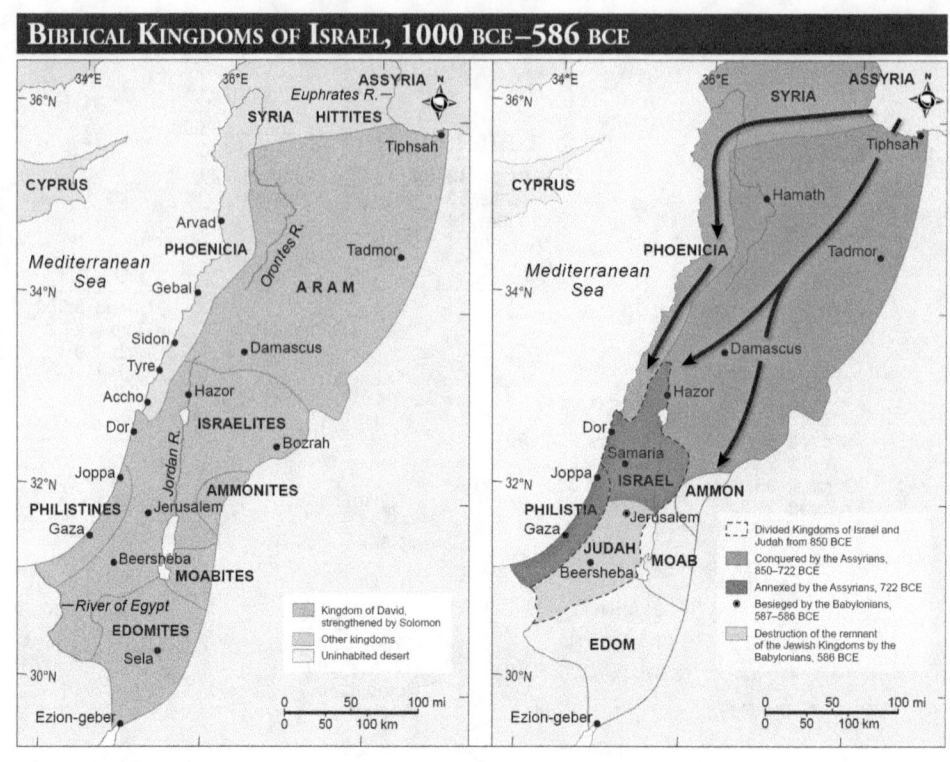

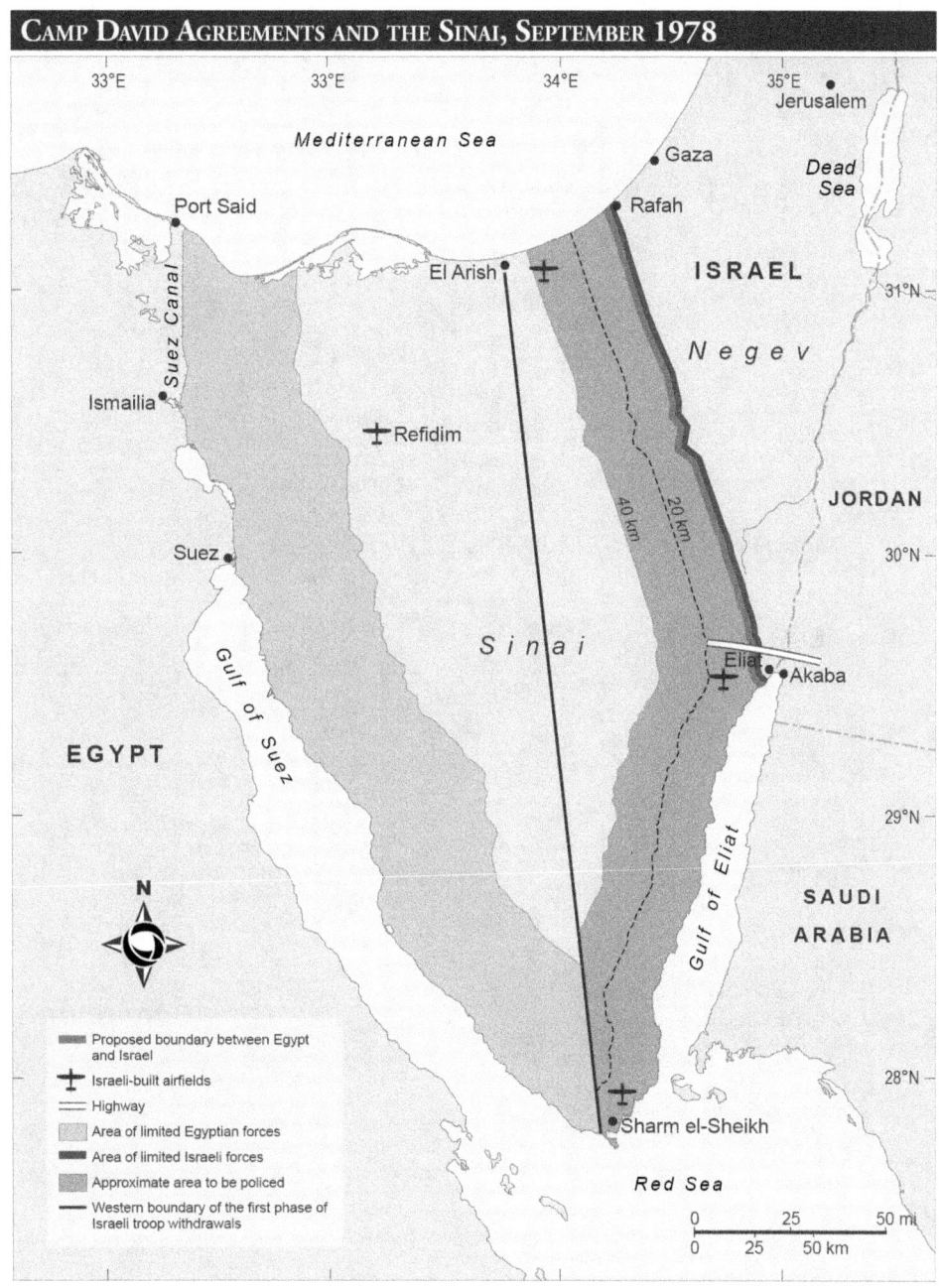

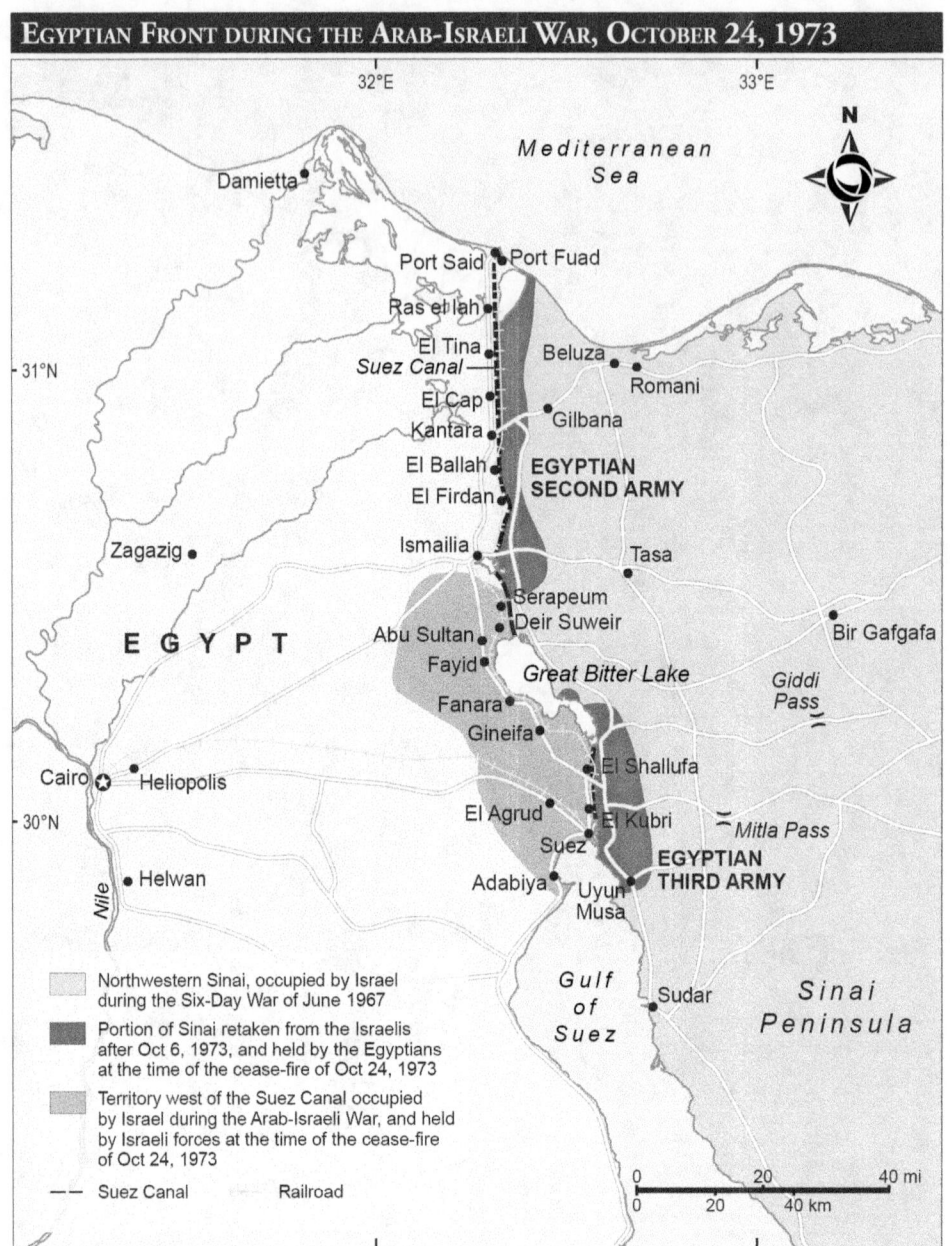

Golan Heights Campaign, June 6–10, 1967

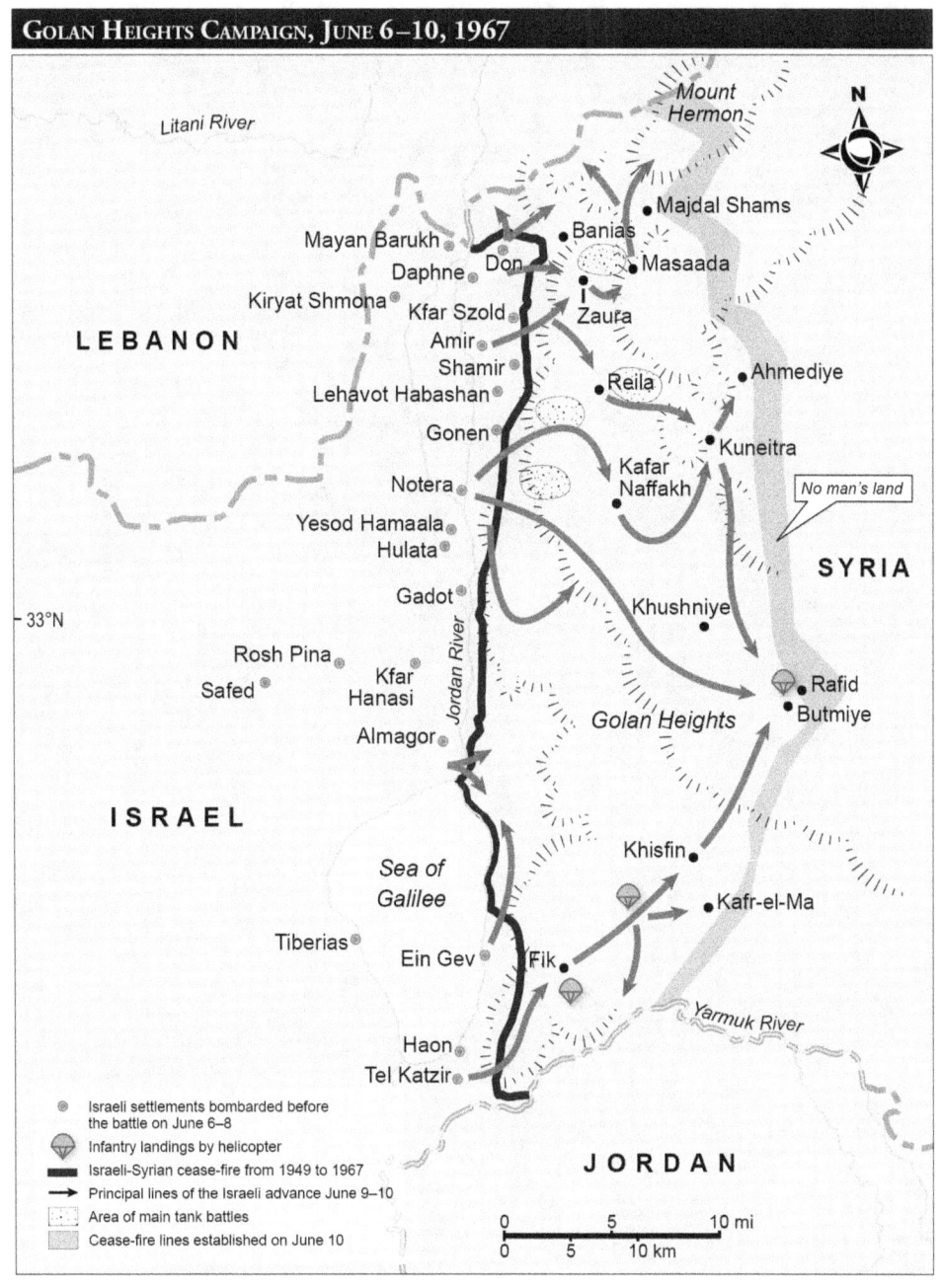

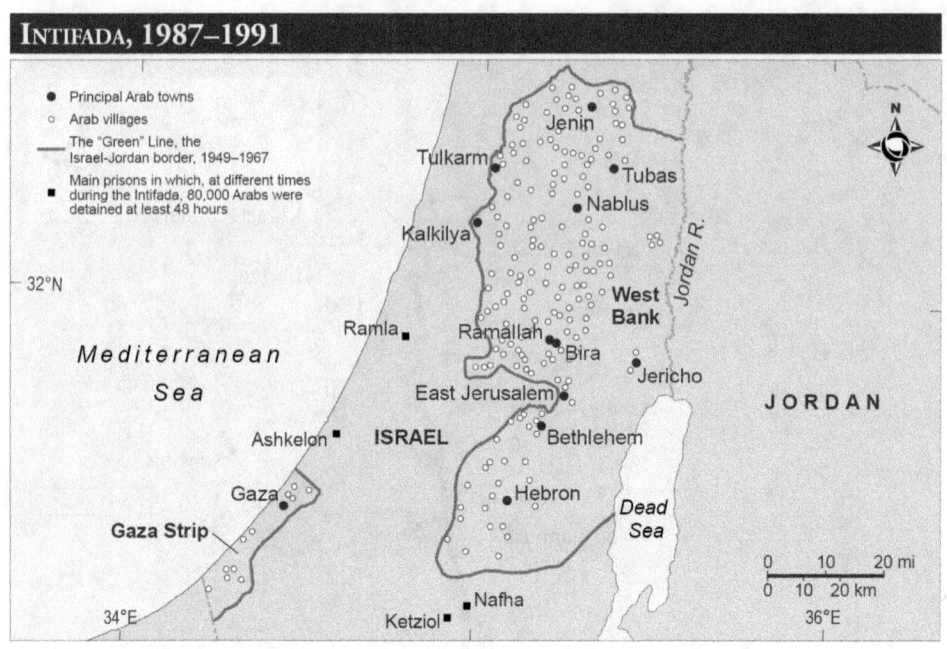

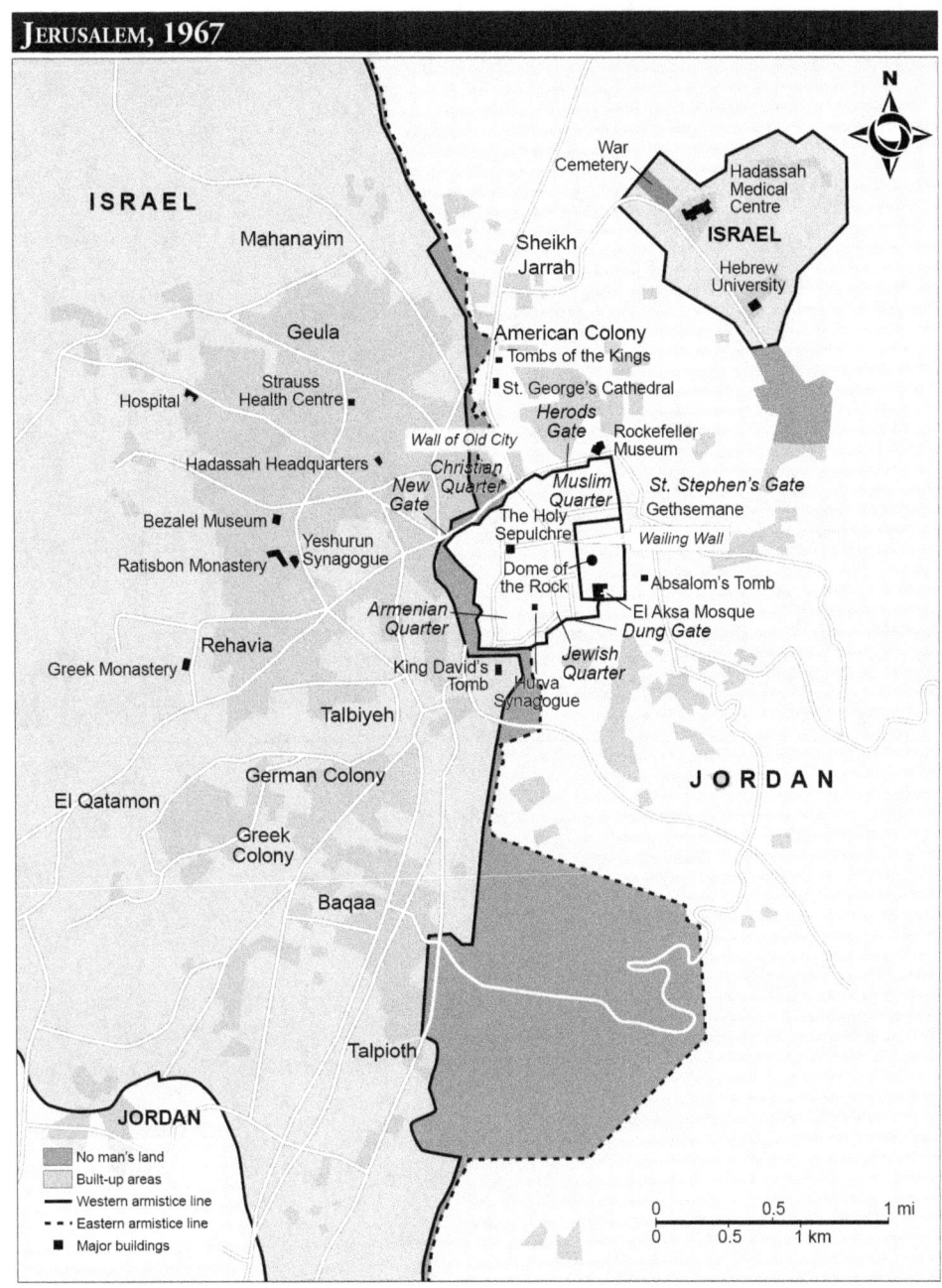

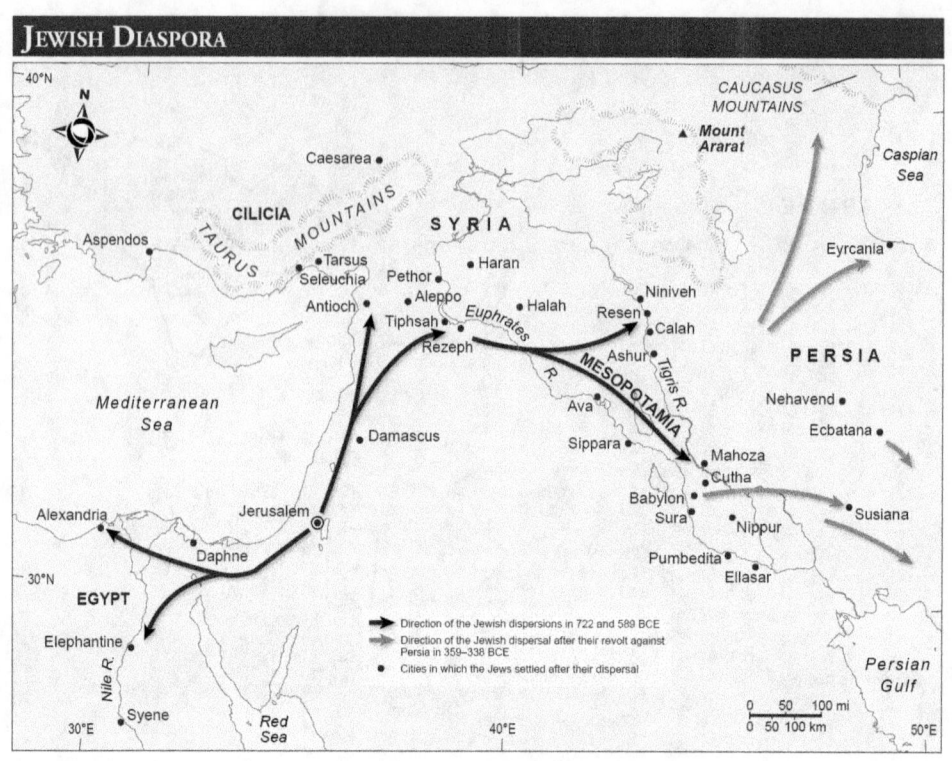

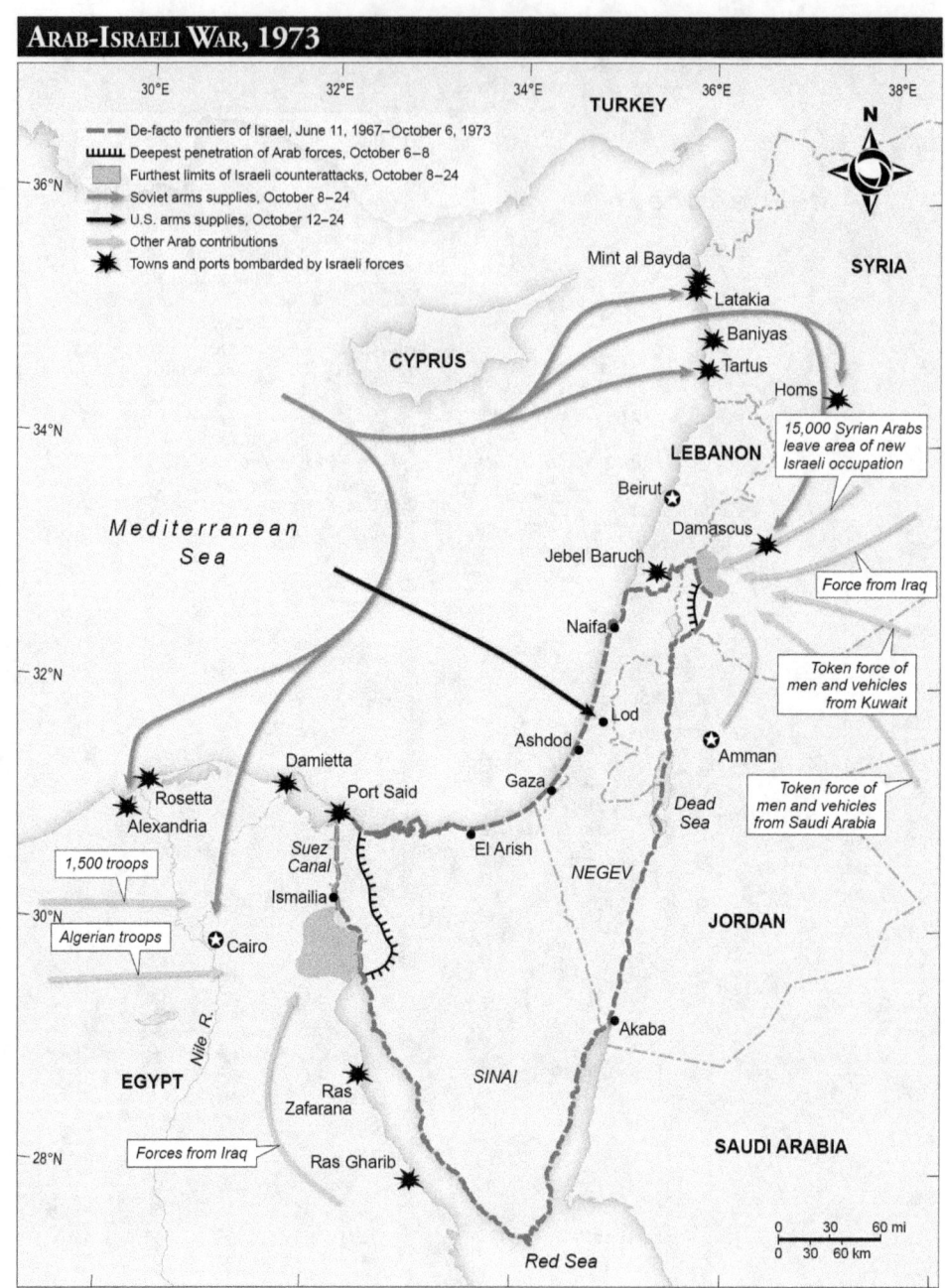

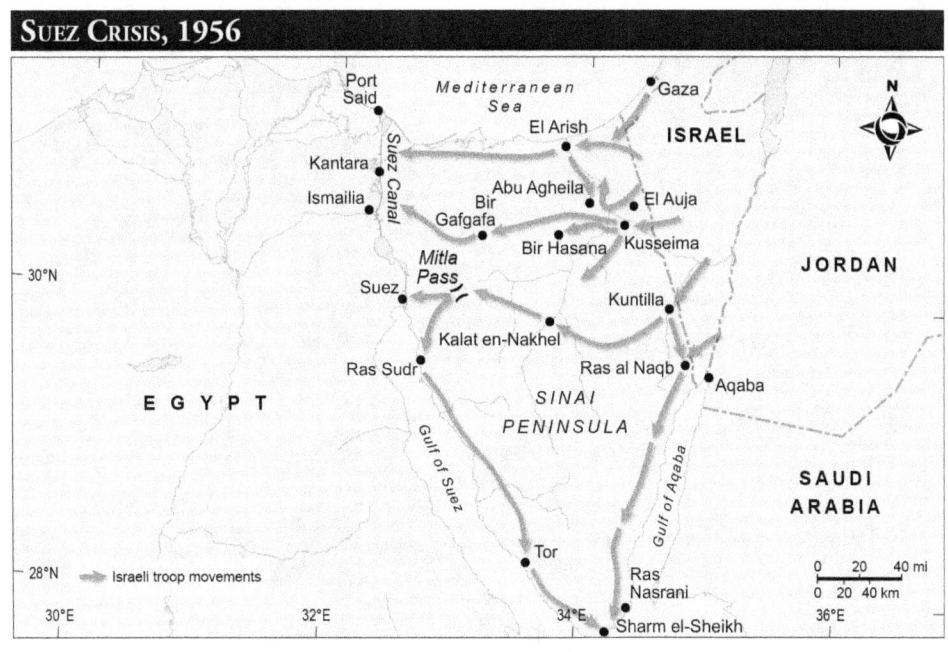

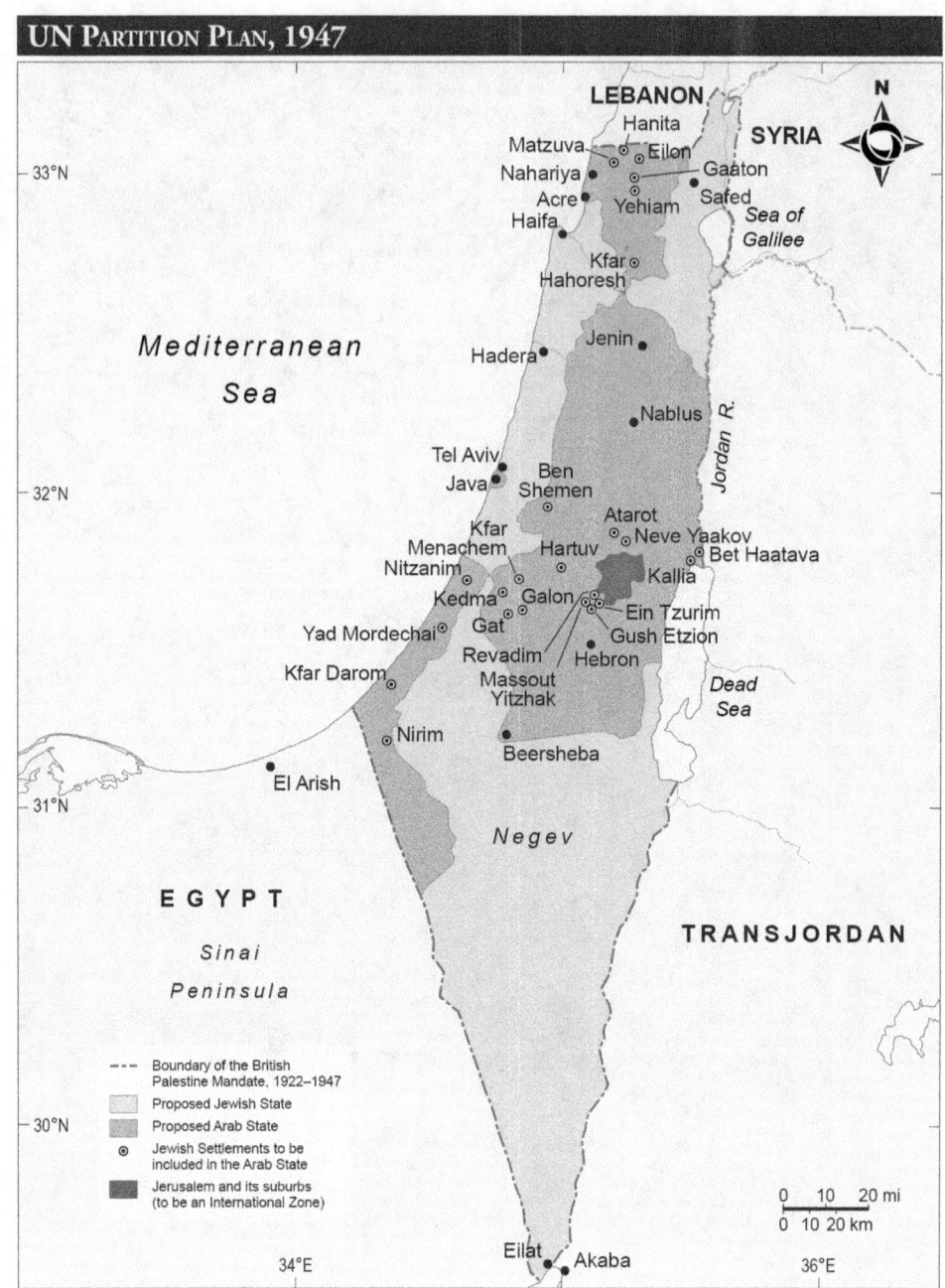

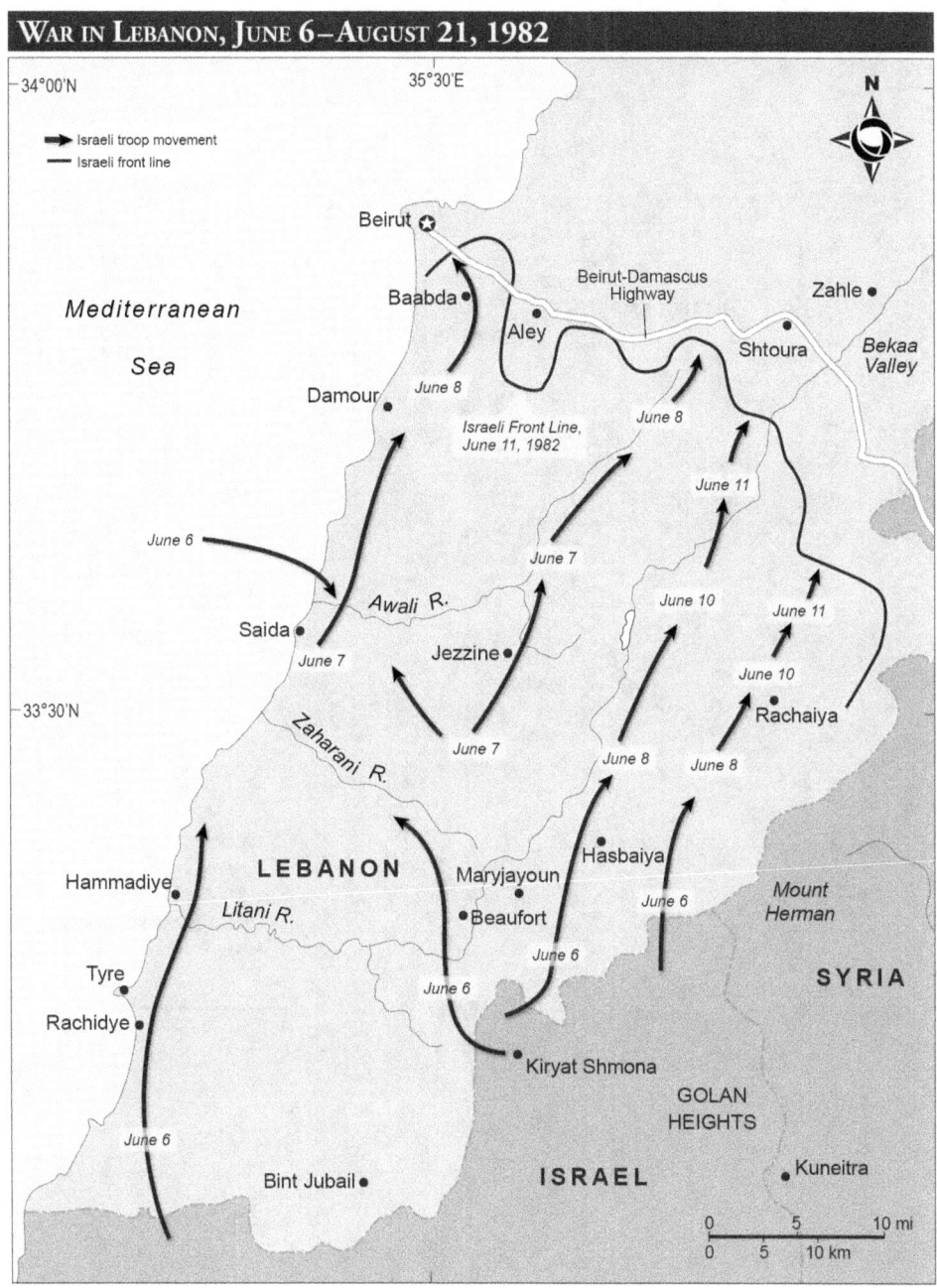

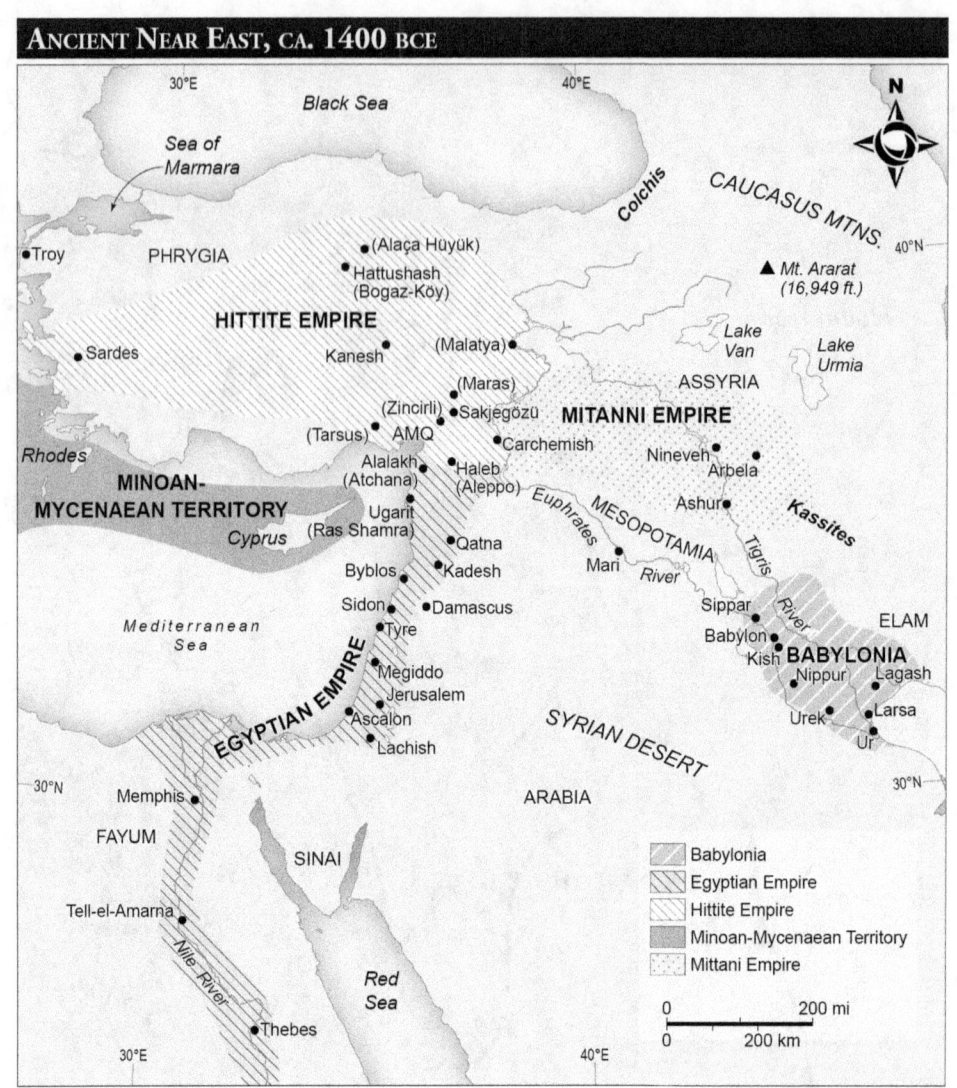

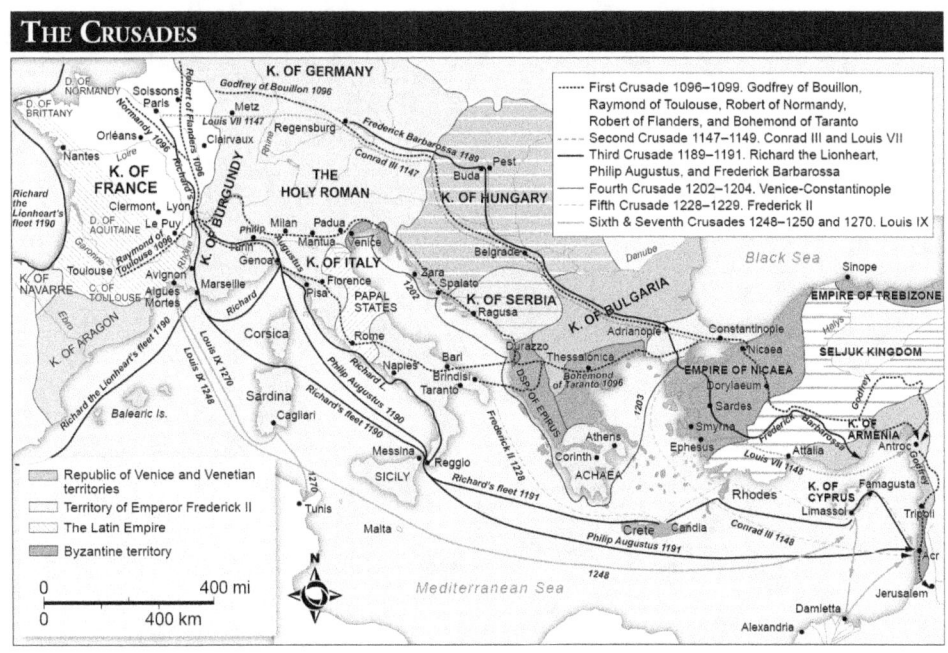

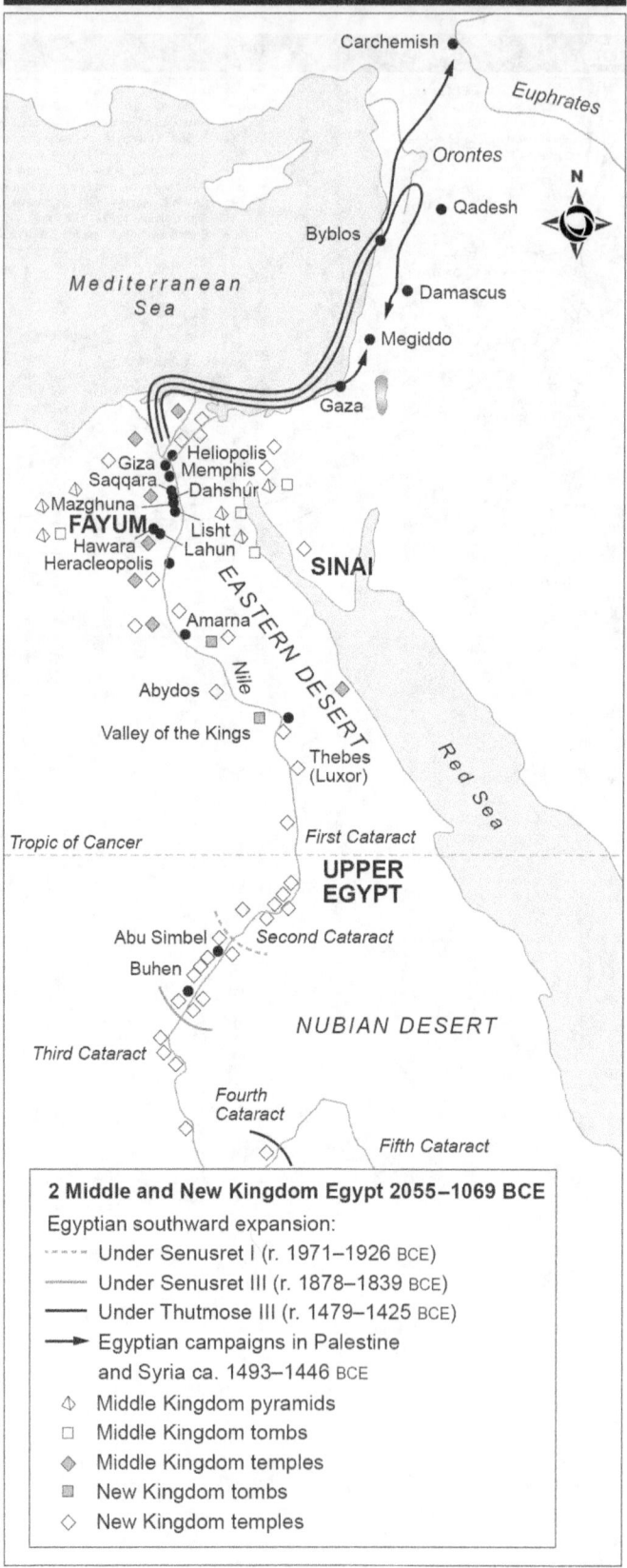

Abbas, Mahmoud

The second president of the Palestinian Authority (PA). Mahmoud Abbas was born March 26, 1935, in Safed, British Mandatory Palestine. During the 1948 Arab-Israeli War, his family fled Palestine and settled in Syria. Abbas became an early member of Fatah and steadily rose through the ranks of the Palestine Liberation Organization (PLO). He was a major architect of the 1993 Oslo Accords between the PLO and Israel.

On March 19, 2003, President Yasser Arafat appointed Abbas as the first prime minister of the PA. Abbas resigned months later due to Arafat's unwillingness to share power, persistent conflicts with militant Palestinian groups such as Hamas and Palestinian Islamic Jihad, Israeli targeted assignations of Palestinian militants, and a perceived lack of support from the United States. Following Arafat's death in late 2004, Abbas became chairman of the PLO and on January 15, 2005, he was elected president of the PA. In January 2006 elections, Hamas won a majority of the seats in the PA Parliament and reduced Abbas's Fatah to minority status. Though Abbas remained PA president, Hamas controlled the parliament, governmental services, and security forces. Israel, the United States, and many European states refused to acknowledge Hamas's new position because they viewed (and still view) the group as a terrorist organization. In 2007, Hamas took control of the Gaza Strip, limiting Abbas's authority to the autonomous areas of the West Bank.

Widely seen as a moderate and supporter of nonviolent efforts to secure a two-state solution, Abbas has had limited success advancing the Palestinian nationalist agenda. While his government's security forces have closely coordinated with Israel for over a decade to quell anti-Israel violence in the West Bank, the occupation continues and Israeli settlements continue to grow. He has garnered some international support for the Palestinian cause, most notably an upgrade to "nonmember observer state" status for Palestine at the United Nations (UN) in November 2012, which allows it to join international organizations like the International Criminal Court (ICC) and Interpol, which it did in 2015 and 2017, respectively. But Abbas's attempts to achieve full membership in the United Nations have been blocked by the United States and Israel.

Abbas has also proved ineffective at overcoming internal Palestinian divisions, due in part to domestic political intrigue and international pressure from the United States and Israel undermining such efforts. In early 2018, Abbas cut the salaries of PA officials in Gaza, restricted social welfare payments to the enclave, and even coordinated with Israel to restrict the supply of electricity—all in an effort to force Hamas to release all governing power to the PA. Abbas enjoys little support among Palestinians, many of whom consider his government corrupt, ineffective, and coopted. He has not allowed a presidential election since taking office and rules in an autocratic manner. There is no clearly established process for selecting his successor.

Richard M. Edwards

See also: Arafat, Yasser; Fatah; Gaza Strip; Hamas; Palestinian Authority; Palestine Liberation Organization; West Bank

Further Reading
Abbas, Mahmoud. *Through Secret Channels: The Road to Oslo: Senior PLO Leader Abu Mazen's Revealing Story of the Negotiations with Israel*. Reading, UK: Garnet Publishing, 1997.
Smith, Charles D. *Palestine and the Arab-Israeli Conflict: A History with Documents*, 9th ed. New York: Bedford/St. Martin's, 2017.

Abdullah II, King of Jordan

Fourth king of Jordan. Born in Amman, Jordan, on January 30, 1962, Abdullah bin Husayn was the eldest son of King Husayn and Princess Muna Husayn. He is a forty-third-generation direct descendant of the Prophet Muhammad. Abdullah attended schools in England and the United States. He became king following the death of his father in 1999.

Since his accession, Abdullah has continued his father's efforts to negotiate a solution to the Arab-Israeli conflict. Toward that end, he has maintained close relations with Israel and met frequently with world leaders, but he has been unable to push the peace process forward. Abdullah have focused much of his attention on domestic matters since the 2011 Arab Spring triggered widespread protests against economic privation, governmental corruption, and Jordan's relations with Israel. Abdullah has suppressed some dissenters while pursuing high-profile corruption cases and reshuffling his cabinet ministers numerous times. Protests picked up again in 2018, demanding economic and governmental reform.

Jordan joined the World Trade Organization (WTO) in 2000 and has ratified free trade agreements with a number of countries, including the United States, but a series of constitutional amendments have significantly increased Abdullah's power. In late 2015, he declared that the Islamic State had initiated a "third world war against humanity" and hijacked Islam. Over 2 million refugees from Iraq and Syria have created extensive economic and security challenges for Jordan.

Spencer C. Tucker

See also: Arab-Israeli War, 1967; Arab Spring; Jordan; Palestinian Refugees; Syria

Further Reading
Bar'el, Zvi. "Jordan's King at Critical Juncture as Public Unrest Boils over into Mass Protests." *Haaretz*, June 5, 2018.
Wagner, Heather Lehr. *King Abdullah II*. New York: Chelsea House, 2005.

Absentee Landlords

Owners of large sections of land in Palestine who often live in Cairo, Kuwait, Beirut, or Istanbul and who sold land to Jewish immigrants and became the targets of great anger from the tenant farmers displaced from their source of livelihood. Arab resistance to Jewish immigration places great significance on the enabling role of these absentee landlords.

Palestinian portrayals of Ottoman rule describe a few landowning families who control extremely large estates and rule over a large number of very poor peasants. The Ottoman legal classification of land included four main categories: state land, private property, land held by charitable endowments, and undeveloped so-called wasteland, such as deserts and swampy areas available for shared community use. A process of integrating Palestine into global markets, exporting agricultural produce, which began in the early 1800s, strengthened the market for land. The 1858 Ottoman Land Code sought to protect small peasant holdings and state property, as well as to restrain the formation of large estates, but establishing legal protections on property rights further increased the market for land.

In 1867, the Ottoman government began allowing foreigners to acquire land in their own name. The Ottoman use of tax farmers and exploitation by new urban elites drove many peasants into poverty and debt, which compelled them to sell their land, thus enabling the creation and development of larger estates. Because peasants justifiably feared that land registration might trigger tax collection and military conscription, they often allowed village notables and tribal sheikhs to sign on their behalf, who thus acquired title to huge blocks of land.

Jewish immigrants primarily bought large sections of land in the coastal plain and the more fertile areas of Palestine, rather than in the densely populated hilly areas. When organizations like the Jewish National Fund and other Zionist groups bought land from the large landowners, they displaced many Arabs. The Zionist project, which sought to employ Jewish labor at the expense of Arab labor, created a distinctive, largely separate economic system, with a large wage differential between the two classes. People excluded from the land on which they formerly earned their livelihood by farming or caring for livestock moved into the urban areas and greatly struggled to find employment, creating strong grievances against the Jewish immigrant population.

Jonathan K. Zartman

See also: Aliya; British Mandate for Palestine; Zionism

Further Reading

Kramer, Gudrun. *A History of Palestine: From the Ottoman Conquest to the Founding of the State of Israel.* Trans. Graham Karman and Gudrun Kramer. Princeton, NJ: Princeton University Press, 2008.

Tamari, Salim. "Who Rules Palestine?" *Institute of Palestinian Studies* 31, no. 4 (Summer 2002): 102–113.

Weinstock, Nathan. "The Impact of Zionist Colonization of Palestinian Arab Society Before 1948." *Journal of Palestinian Studies* 2, no. 2 (Winter 1973): 49–63.

Adalah

An Israeli human rights organization. Adalah, The Legal Center for Arab Minority Rights in Israel, is a prominent nonprofit organization that works to advance the human rights of Palestinians living under Israeli rule. It was founded in 1996 by Hassan Jabareen, who today serves as the organization's director. Adalah is based out of the mixed Israeli city of Haifa and has around twenty staff members, most of whom are Palestinian citizens of Israel. Its stated mission is to "promote human rights in Israel in general and the rights of the Palestinian minority, citizens of Israel, in particular." The organization notes that this mandate includes individuals living in the Occupied Palestinian Territories (OPT). As such, Adalah is unique, in that it is a Palestinian-run organization that works to protect the rights of Palestinians, with and without Israeli citizenship, through Israeli courts. It employs a mix of litigation and advocacy strategies and has brought hundreds of cases to Israeli courts on issues such as political and civil rights, land and planning rights, and social and economic rights. Many of these cases have resulted in precedent-setting decisions.

In addition, Adalah has been at the forefront of the legal battle to protect the right of Bedouins in the Naqab to remain on their land. It also offers legal consultation services and trains emerging legal leaders in the area of human rights. Adalah works in the public sphere to disseminate information and analyses that raise awareness about the injustices that Palestinians living in Israel and the OPT face today.

Emily Schneider

See also: Bedouins; Gaza Strip; Israeli Occupations; Settlements; Settler Violence; West Bank

Further Reading

Adalah. "About." https://www.adalah.org/en/content/view/7189.

Haklai, Oded. "Palestinian NGOs in Israel: A Campaign for Civic Equality or 'Ethnic Civil Society'?" *Israel Studies* 9, no. 3 (2004): 157–168.

Weizman, E. "Cause Lawyering and Resistance in Israel: The Legal Strategies of Adalah." *Social & Legal Studies* 25, no. 1 (2016): 43–68.

Al-Aqsa Intifada (see Intifada, Second)

Al-Aqsa Martyrs Brigades

A Palestinian nationalist group, formed to force Israel from the West Bank and Gaza Strip through suicide bombings and other terrorist actions. Unlike Hamas and the Palestinian Islamic Jihad, al-Aqsa is not rooted in political Islam, the al-Aqsa Martyrs Brigades are strictly secular.

The al-Aqsa Martyrs Brigades were born out of the turbulent violence of the Second Intifada (also known as the *al-Aqsa Intifada*). The uprising was triggered partly by the breakdown in the Arab-Israeli peace process in the late 1990s. The actual fuse was lit, however, by Likud Party leader Ariel Sharon's controversial visit in September 2000 to the Haram al-Sharif, home to the holy al-Aqsa Mosque. Sharon's actions enraged Palestinians, and the al-Aqsa Martyrs Brigades arose from this outrage. They became one of the most active players in the al-Aqsa Intifada, which erupted shortly after Sharon's visit.

Initially, the group's strategy was to target Israeli military outposts and Jewish settlers within the West Bank and the Gaza Strip. However, in response to increased Israeli retaliation, the Martyrs Brigades stepped up their activities to include targets in Israel itself. Their tactics began to shift in early 2002. The Martyrs Brigades cite Lebanon's militant Hezbollah group as the inspiration for its style of violence. They sometimes collaborate with other terrorist organizations, such as Hamas. Many of the group's members are from Fatah's militant youth group, Tanzim, while the Brigades' purported leader—the now-jailed Marwan Barghouti—was formerly Fatah's general secretary.

Typically, the al-Aqsa Martyrs Brigades' attacks were carried out via shootings and suicide bombings, including women and children as suicide bombers. The Brigades have also resorted to rocket attacks on Israel launched from Palestinian territory. Among the worst of these attacks were twin suicide bombings in downtown Tel Aviv in January 2003 that killed 23 and wounded 100; a March 2002 suicide bombing of a Jerusalem café that killed 11 and wounded 50; and a sniper assault at an Israeli checkpoint in the West Bank that killed 10 Israelis in March 2002.

Since the end of the Second Intifada, the activities of the al-Aqsa Martyrs Brigades have been limited. Many members were folded into the Palestinian Authority (PA) security forces in 2007, but Brigade members have continued periodic terror attacks on Israelis, including in 2014 and 2017.

Sherifa Zuhur

See also: Fatah; Gaza Strip; Intifada, Second; Suicide Bombings; West Bank

Further Reading

Jones, Clive, and Ami Pedahzur, eds. *Between Terrorism and Civil War: The Al-Aqsa Intifada.* London: Routledge, 2005.

Oknio, Yasser, and Hashavua, Maarive. "Fatah-Splinter Group Claims Responsibility for Rocket Attack," *Jerusalem Post*, March 10, 2017. https://www.jpost.com/Arab-Israeli-Conflict/Fatah-claims-responsibility-for-rocket-attack-for-first-time-since-Op-Protective-Edge-483836.

Parsons, Nigel. *The Politics of the Palestinian Authority: from Oslo to Al-Aqsa.* London: Routledge, 2005.

Aliya

Hebrew for "going up" or "ascending," referring to Jewish immigration rights. There were five major waves of Jewish immigration to Palestine prior to 1948. Aliya is an integral part of Zionism holding that any Jew in the world has the right of return to Palestine. This belief is enshrined in Israeli law, which holds that any Jew may legally establish residency in and attain citizenship rights from Israel. This policy is intended to increase the numbers of Jews in Israel.

A Jewish immigration camp in what would become Tel Aviv, the first all-Jewish city in Palestine. One of the great achievements of the Second Aliya, Tel Aviv was founded in 1909. It rapidly grew from a neighborhood of sixty Jewish families into a modern city. (Library of Congress)

The First Aliya (1882–1904) was the first wave of immigration specifically associated with the Zionist movement. It established the cultural and economic tenor of the Yishuv (Jewish community in Palestine) for nearly a generation. First Aliya pioneers introduced many uniquely Jewish experiments, such as *moshavim* (cooperative farms). Most of these immigrants came from Russia after Czar Alexander II's 1881 assassination, which many Russians blamed on a Jewish conspiracy. This event set off a spasm of violence against Jews, aimed mainly at the large Jewish population in the Pale of Settlement, a Jewish ghetto of sorts in western Russia where most Russian Jews were forced to live. Thus, beginning in 1882, Russian Jews began seeking refuge in Palestine, which was not met with much enthusiasm by the Ottoman Turk authorities, who would rule Palestine until 1917.

The Second Aliya (1904–1914) saw the immigration of approximately 40,000 Jews to Palestine. Most came from czarist Russia and had left because of pogroms, rising anti-Semitism, and the abortive Russian Revolution of 1905. A sizable number were socialists seeking the overthrow of the capitalist-imperialist world order. Because of depressed economic conditions in Palestine, however, almost half of these migrants later left. The Jews of the Second Aliya were social as well as cultural pioneers, and the glimmer of an autonomous Jewish nation-state first took hold with them. Indeed, the Second Aliya saw the formation of the first kibbutz (Degania), the beginnings of the first all-Jewish city (Tel Aviv), the creation of Jewish self-defense forces, the adoption of Hebrew as the de facto language of the

Yishuv (although the First Aliya actually had set the precedent for this), and the advancement of education. The Second Aliya created nearly all the institutions necessary to organize and run a modern nation and provided many of the philosophical and political constructs of modern Zionism.

The Third Aliya (1919–1923) saw an influx of about 35,000 Jews to Palestine. Immigrants from the Second Aliya reached out to the new arrivals in unprecedented ways, making their transition to a new life in Palestine far easier than it had been for those who came before. Most were from Russia and Poland. This immigration influx made many key contributions to the Yishuv. Not only did it augment the Jewish population there by some 60 percent, but its youth, vitality, and pioneering spirit lent new purpose and urgency to the Zionist ideal. These immigrants helped form *kibbutzim* and *moshavim*, made important contributions to the organized labor movement, and in 1920 founded and staffed Haganah, a Jewish defense group in Palestine. And during the Arab uprising in 1921, many members of the Third Aliya played crucial roles in protecting Jewish lives and property. The sheer number of *moshavim* and *kibbutzim* that they founded greatly advanced Jewish settlement in the region. It is no exaggeration to say that the Third Aliya fundamentally altered the Yishuv's outlook and character with its youthful enthusiasm, pioneering spirit, and dutiful work habits.

The Fourth Aliya (1924–1928) is associated most directly with political and economic crises in Poland and Hungary, from which the majority came, and restrictive new immigration policies passed by the U.S. Congress. For many, moving to the United States made the most sense, but a nativist backlash in the United States after World War I compelled Congress to severely restrict immigration beginning in 1924. Thus, most Poles went to Palestine instead. In total, the number of Jews who went to Palestine during this period is estimated at about 60,000.

The Fifth Aliya (1929–1939) saw as many as 250,000 Jews pour into Palestine, making it the largest of the pre-1948 immigration waves. About 230,000 Jews arrived in Palestine legally, while some 20,000 came illegally. The Fifth Aliya came on the immediate heels of a sharp economic downturn in Europe, lasting from 1926 to 1928. From 1929 to 1931, the influx of immigrants was relatively small—just 15,000 or so. The majority of these were part of the Zionist youth movement.

By 1933, with the rise of Adolf Hitler and a marked increase in anti-Semitism in Eastern Europe, the *aliya* took on a dramatic new urgency that saw the trickle of immigrants turn into a flood. Between 1933 and 1936 alone, about 170,000 Jews came to Palestine. Many were German Jews, while most of the remaining were from Poland, Lithuania, Hungary, Romania, and other areas of central and Eastern Europe. Beginning in 1936, the British tightened restrictions on Jewish immigration to Palestine. After this last immigration wave, the Yishuv remained largely stable until after the 1948 creation of Israel, which precipitated a massive *aliya* that commenced in 1949.

Paul G. Pierpaoli Jr.

See also: Aliya Bet; British Mandate for Palestine; Haganah; Israelis; Kibbutz; Tel Aviv; Zionism

Further Reading

Pappe, Ilan. *A History of Modern Palestine: One Land, Two Peoples*. Cambridge: Cambridge University Press, 2003.

Sachar, Howard M. *A History of Israel: From the Rise of Zionism to Our Time*. New York: Knopf, 2007.

Segev, Tom. *One Palestine, Complete: Jews and Arabs under the British Mandate*. New York: Owl Books, 2001.

Aliya Bet

The illegal immigration of Jews from Europe to the British Mandate for Palestine. The word *aliya* means "immigration" in Hebrew, while *Bet* is the letter *B*. The translation of "Immigration B" implied nonofficial immigration. The operation was part of the Berihah underground operation during 1944–1948, which moved Jews from the displaced persons (DP) camps in Europe to Palestine. Jews were not supposed to leave the DP camps, and the British had severely limited immigration since 1939, even to the point of stationing warships off the coast to intercept immigrant ships. At times, though, American authorities provided unofficial support, allowing the Jews to cross through their occupation zones.

Led by Abba Kovner, Berihah was established in Warsaw in late 1944. It soon merged with similar undertakings by Haganah, led by Shaul Avigur, and the Jewish Brigade.

Operating primarily in Czechoslovakia, Hungary, Poland, Romania, and Yugoslavia, the illegal efforts moved more than 250,000 Holocaust survivors through extensive smuggling networks into Austria and Germany, and then to Italy and France. The Italians had great sympathy for the plight of the DPs and some resentment against the British who were in occupation. The French were especially helpful, in part because of anger at being pushed out of the Levant by the British during the war and in part because of influential French Jews such as Léon Blum, Jules Moch, and Daniel Mayer. Despite daunting odds, the illegal immigration operation continued until the establishment of the state of Israel, when immigration became legal.

Spencer C. Tucker

See also: Aliya; British Mandate for Palestine; British White Paper; Haganah; Zionism

Further Reading

Hadari, Ze'ev V. *Second Exodus: The Full Story of Jewish Illegal Immigration to Palestine, 1945–1948*. London: Valentine Mitchell, 1991.

Sachar, Howard M. *A History of Israel: From the Rise of Zionism to Our Time*. New York: Knopf, 2007.

Allon Plan

A peace plan authored by the Israeli military officer and politician Yigal Allon. The Allon Plan was a proposal to negotiate the partitioning of West Bank territories between Israel and Jordan in the immediate aftermath of the 1967 Arab-Israeli

War. Allon hoped to establish safe and defensible borders for Israel, while at the same time extending an olive branch of sorts to Jordan.

Under the terms of the plan, the Israelis would turn over to Jordan the heavily populated areas of the West Bank. Meanwhile, Israel was to control a strip of relatively unpopulated territory along the Jordan River stretching from near the Syrian border in the north through the Jordan River Valley and south to the Negev Desert. Included in this land was a sliver of territory along the western shore of the Dead Sea and a large area surrounding Jerusalem.

Allon reasoned that this territory, in the eastern part of the West Bank, would provide the Israelis with a buffer zone against a concerted Arab attack. Under the proposed plan, Israel would ultimately retain control over some 700 square miles in the West Bank, or approximately 35 percent of the entire land mass. For the Israeli-controlled areas, Allon proposed the building of settlements and military installations. In other areas, local leaders would be involved in the creation of a semiautonomous Palestinian-Jordanian region that would maintain close economic ties to Israel. The Israelis would retain sole control of an expanded Jerusalem, with the possibility of a Jordanian-administered Muslim section within the Old City of Jerusalem.

In September 1968, Israeli officials presented the Allon Plan to King Husayn of Jordan in secret talks. But Husayn rejected it as an infringement of Jordan's sovereignty. The proposal was never formally adopted as a plan of action by any Israeli government, but it shaped settlement policies until 1977. Since then, successive Israeli governments have allowed settlements well beyond the confines of the Allon Plan, undermining the possibility of creating a Palestinian state. Modern military analysts have argued that control of the West Bank would afford virtually no protection from attack in the age of ballistic missiles and rockets.

Paul G. Pierpaoli Jr.

See also: Arab-Israeli War, 1967; Husayn, King of Jordan; Jerusalem, Old City of; Jordan

Further Reading

Hillel, Frisch. *Countdown to Statehood: Palestinian State Formation in the West Bank and Gaza.* Ithaca, NY: SUNY Press, 1998.

Parker, Richard B., ed. *The Six-Day War: A Retrospective.* Gainesville: University Press of Florida, 1996.

Smith, Charles D. *Palestine and the Arab-Israeli Conflict: A History with Documents,* 9th ed. New York: Bedford/St. Martin's, 2017.

American Israel Public Affairs Committee (AIPAC)

A large, pro-Israeli political lobbying group located in the United States. The American Israel Public Affairs Committee (AIPAC) was founded in 1953 by I. L. "Si" Kenen under the name of American Zionist Committee for Public Affairs. The main thrust of AIPAC's efforts is to lobby members of the U.S. Congress, with the goal of influencing legislation and policymaking that affect Israel and Israeli-American relations and the larger Middle East region. AIPAC is believed to be among the most influential lobbying organizations in the United States. The group closely

Attendees at the annual conference of the American Israel Public Affairs Committee in Washington, D.C. This conference regularly attracts high ranking Democratic and Republican politicians as well as nearly 20,000 members. AIPAC is considered by many to be one of the most influential lobby groups in the United States. (Laurence Agron/Dreamstime.com)

monitors and compiles the voting records of U.S. representatives and senators on Israel-related issues.

To date, AIPAC boasted a membership of more than 100,000 (mostly Jews and so-called Christian Zionists) living in all fifty U.S. states. Through more than 2,000 meetings with members of the U.S. Congress, the organization helps to ensure the passage of some 100 legislative bills each year that affect U.S.-Israeli relations. AIPAC has a high-profile public relations function as well, which involves interacting with journalists and other opinion makers to promote pro-Israel positions. The group has regional offices all across the United States that monitor politics, public opinion, and public events at the local level, as well as sponsoring a variety of political and educational functions.

In its early years, AIPAC had rather strained relations with President Dwight D. Eisenhower's administration, particularly after the 1956 Suez Crisis, when Eisenhower exerted great pressure on Britain, France, and Israel to withdraw their forces from Egypt. Over the years, AIPAC has boasted many successes, including successful lobbying for increased U.S.-Israeli cooperation on defense issues, arms sales to the Israelis, and direct and indirect aid to Israel worth well over $100 billion.

AIPAC has also attracted its share of controversy. In 1982, the group managed to convince the majority in Congress and President Ronald Reagan's administration to veto the proposed United Nations (UN) resolution condemning Israel's invasion of Lebanon that same year. This brought much criticism that the United States was unwilling to take appropriate measures to halt the violence in Lebanon. In 1992, David Steiner, AIPAC's president, courted trouble when he was recorded bragging that he had "cut a deal" with President George H. W. Bush's administration for major new aid initiatives to Israel. Steiner also claimed that he was already lobbying the incoming administration of President Bill Clinton to the same ends. The resultant firestorm of public exposure led to charges that AIPAC was too influential in Washington. In 2005, allegations surfaced that a U.S. Department of Defense employee had knowingly divulged top-secret information to several AIPAC members. A few months later, two top-level AIPAC employees were accused of having conspired to receive top-secret information and pass it to the Israelis.

AIPAC enjoys fairly broad bipartisan support. On the other hand, a number of politicians have complained that the organization has torpedoed the reelection efforts of several legislators whose voting records were deemed anti-Israel. Others have charged that AIPAC tends to support the political right wing in Israel. Some allege that the group has become so powerful that its influence may be detrimental to U.S. interests in the Middle East.

As of 2018, AIPAC has raised over $100 million a year from donors, according to tax returns. In 2016, it had an endowment of some $250 million. Throughout 2014 and into 2015, AIPAC campaigned vigorously against a diplomatic deal with Iran that would permit that country to continue any level of nuclear activity. At the time, the United States, Russia, France, and several other nations were engaged in grueling talks with Iranian diplomats in an effort to reach a nuclear agreement that would limit Iran's nuclear programs and alleviate the need for them to undertake military action against Iran. Despite reservations from many quarters, a deal was reached in July 2015. AIPAC and the Israeli government promptly condemned it, however, asserting that it was not strict enough. When Donald J. Trump was elected president in 2016, it pressed his new administration to scuttle the Iran deal, recognize Jerusalem as Israel's capital, move the U.S. embassy there, and recognize Israel's claim of sovereignty over the Golan Heights, which Israel captured from Syria in 1967. The Trump administration did all these things between 2017 and 2019.

Paul G. Pierpaoli Jr.

See also: Christian Zionism; U.S. Aid to Israel; U.S. Involvement in Israeli-Palestinian Affairs; Zionism

Further Reading

Chomsky, Noam. *Fateful Triangle: The United States, Israel, and the Palestinians.* Cambridge, MA: South End Press, 2002.

Dershowitz, Alan M. *The Case for Israel.* New York: Wiley, 2004.

Mearsheimer, John, and Walt, Stephen. *The Israel Lobby and US Foreign Policy.* New York: Farrar, Straus and Giroux, 2007.

Terry, Janice. *U.S. Foreign Policy in the Middle East: The Role of Lobbies and Special Interest Groups.* London: Pluto, 2005.

American Jewish Congress (AJC)

A Jewish-American civic and advocacy organization founded in 1918 and dedicated to the creation and security of Israel. Formally convened in 1918, the chief and immediate goal of the American Jewish Congress (AJC) was to provide U.S. Jews a united voice at the upcoming Paris Peace Conference (1919) and to advocate on behalf of Jews in Europe. Its members have included such Jewish luminaries as Supreme Court justices Louis D. Brandeis and Felix Frankfurter and Israeli prime minister Golda Meyerson (Meir).

The AJC claims to be the first organization in the United States to embrace Zionism and to call for a boycott of products made in Nazi Germany in the 1930s. In 1936, it played a key role in organizing the World Jewish Congress, which met amid the pall of Nazi oppression. It also worked to help safeguard Jews in central and Eastern Europe during and after World War II.

By 2009, the AJC had grown to about 50,000 members. It is headquartered in New York City and maintains a permanent office in Jerusalem; it also has had offices in several other nations over the years. In 2010, the AJC endured a severe financial crisis precipitated by the Bernie Madoff Ponzi scheme, which depleted much of its investments and resources. It suspended operations in July 2010 but regrouped in 2013. The AJC strongly opposed the July 2015 nuclear deal with Iran and supported President Donald J. Trump's decision to abrogate the agreement in 2017. It also supported President Trump's recognition of Jerusalem as Israel's capital.

Paul G. Pierpaoli Jr.

See also: U.S. Aid to Israel; World Zionist Organization; Zionism

Further Reading

Farber, Roberta Rosenberg, and Chaim I. Waxman, eds. *Jews in America: A Contemporary Reader.* Waltham, MA: Brandeis University Press, 1999.

Sachar, Howard M. *A History of the Jews in America.* New York: Knopf, 1992.

American Palestine Committee (APC)

An organization intended to promote the goals of Zionism among the non-Jewish population of the United States. The American Palestine Committee (APC) was established in 1932 by Emanuel Neumann, who believed that Christian political leaders would see the inherent value in the establishment of an independent Jewish state in the territory of Palestine.

Neumann emigrated from the United States to Palestine in 1932, virtually destroying his nascent organization, which was ineffective without his charismatic leadership. He returned in 1941 and revived the APC, and he also formed the Christian Council on Palestine (CCP), an organization designed to draw support for Zionism from Christian clergy. The APC quickly gathered support from national and state politicians as well as academics. It raised awareness of the Zionist cause and served as a fund-raising organ for other Zionist organizations.

When the war ended in 1945, the APC and the CCP merged into a single entity, the American Christian Palestine Committee (ACPC), as a means of streamlining fund-raising and enhancing the ties between pro-Zionist clergy and laypersons. When the Zionist dream was realized in May 1948 with the proclamation of the state of Israel, the fundamental purpose of the ACPC shifted from the creation of a Zionist state to the preservation and assistance of Israel. It was quickly superseded by other pro-Israeli organizations in the United States and formally disbanded in 1961.

Paul J. Springer

See also: U.S. Aid to Israel; World Zionist Organization; Zionism

Further Reading
Cohn-Sherbok, Dan, and Dawoud El-Alami. *The Palestine-Israeli Conflict: A Beginner's Guide.* Oxford, UK: Oneworld, 2001.
Laqueur, Walter. *A History of Zionism.* New York: Holt, Rinehart and Winston, 1972.

Arab Boycott of Israel

A collective and national Arab economic boycott of Jewish-owned and Israeli businesses. In 1945, the newly formed Arab League initiated an economic boycott of Jewish goods and services to help Palestinians combat Zionism. After Israel's creation, the boycott prohibited direct trade between Arab states and Israel. A secondary boycott prohibits dealing with firms that do business with Israel, which are blacklisted by the Arab League. A tertiary boycott also prohibits doing business with entities that have done business with blacklisted firms.

The Arab League does not enforce the boycotts itself, and its declarations are not binding. Indeed, several Arab states have chosen not to follow the secondary and tertiary boycotts. Even the primary boycotts have weakened over time. In 1979, Egypt and Israel made peace and normalized trade relations. In the 1990s, the Gulf States, the Palestinian Authority (PA), and Jordan all abandoned or limited their boycotts of Israel in order to advance the peace process.

The impact of the boycotts on Israel has not been great because they have been only sporadically enforced. To get around them, Israeli products are often shipped to a third party, which then exports the goods to various Arab states. Few countries adhere closely to the boycotts anymore, although they remain of symbolic importance to many. Accordingly, Israel chooses not to file complaints against fellow Arab members of the World Trade Organization (WTO). Instead, it works behind the scenes to liberalize trade relations. The United States regularly presses Arab states to formally abandon their boycotts, and Congress prohibits American corporations from participating.

Keith A. Leitich

See also: Camp David Accords; Egypt; Israel; Jordan

Further Reading
Feiler, Gil. *From Boycott to Economic Cooperation: The Political Economy of the Arab Boycott of Israel.* London: Frank Cass, 1998.
Weiss, Martin A. *Arab Boycott of Israel.* Washington, DC: Congressional Research Service, Library of Congress, 2017.

Arab Higher Committee (AHC)

A principal political organization of the Arabs of Palestine that took a leading role in the Arab Revolt (1936–1939). Also known as the Fourth Higher Committee of the Arab League, the Arab Higher Committee (AHC) was formed on April 25, 1936. Haj Amin al-Husayni, the Grand Mufti of Jerusalem, took the lead in forming the AHC and became its president. The AHC was able to unite Arab religious and political leaders and political parties.

Staunchly opposed to Jewish immigration into Palestine, the AHC took the lead in the general strike and rebellions against British Mandate authorities, beginning in April 1936, that became the Arab Revolt of 1936–1939. The British banned the AHC outright in 1937 and arrested a number of its leaders, including Dr. Husayn al-Khalidi, the mayor of Jerusalem. All were deported to the Seychelles Islands.

The AHC subsequently split into the Arab Higher Committee under al-Husayni and a new organization, the Arab Higher Front. The British government ordered the release of AHC leaders from the Seychelles so that they might participate in the London Round Table Conference in Palestine in 1939. The AHC sent a delegation to the United Nations (UN) upon the latter's formation, but it rejected the subsequent UN plan for the partition of Palestine.

Spencer C. Tucker

See also: Arab Revolt, 1936; British Mandate for Palestine; Grand Mufti of Jerusalem

Further Reading

Khalaf, Ossa. *Politics in Palestine: Arab Factionalism and Social Disintegration, 1939–1948*. New York: SUNY Press, 1991.

Levenberg, Haim. *Military Preparations of the Arab Community in Palestine, 1945–1948*. London: Routledge, 1993.

Arab-Islamic Conquest of Palestine

Conquest of the Palestine region by the Arab-Islamic Empire in the seventh century. Palestine, and more specifically the city of Jerusalem, have long been places of importance in Islam. Behind the cities of Mecca and Medina, Jerusalem stands as a location of holy significance. Like Jews and Christians, Muslims see Jerusalem as a city of promise and prophecy. Jerusalem was the first Qibla, the place toward which they turn in prayer. Islamic tradition holds that the Prophet Muhammad ascended to heaven from Jerusalem during his night journey with the angel Gabriel.

Reverence for Palestine inspired early efforts made by Muslim forces to gain control of the region. In 630 CE, the Prophet Muhammad's focus was on consolidating and organizing his followers, but he authorized the start of efforts to secure control of Palestine. During this period, the region was largely under Byzantine authority, but the Sasanian Empire also vied for dominance. Initial forays were made by loosely organized Muslim bands and made little progress. Following Muhammad's death, his uncle, Abu Bakr, became the first caliph. Although Abu Bakr focused on consolidated control of contentious factions on the Arabian Peninsula, he maintained the seeds of the campaign started by Muhammad in

Palestine. Abu Bakr lived for only two years after he became caliph, and it was left to his successor, Umar ibn Al-Khattab, to press the Palestine campaign.

Under Umar's overall direction, the now-more-organized Muslim army began to gain momentum on the battlefield. Umar's field commanders were able to consolidate their gains by 636 CE and began direct attacks on Jerusalem. Just one year after the offensive started, the city was under the control of the fledgling Arab empire. Three important contributing factors helped ensure the success of Umar's forces. First, the Byzantine Empire was trying to recover from a wave of the plague that devastated much of the population in Palestine. Second, the Byzantine ruler, Emperor Heraclius, had just waged a bloody war with the Sasanian Empire for control of the region. By 630 CE, Heraclius regained supremacy over Palestine, but the price was a war-weary and sick population who owed little allegiance to his empire. Third, in contrast to the Byzantine Empire, the nascent Muslim empire benefited from a shared purpose shaped by their perception of divine destiny. After the loss of Jerusalem, the Byzantines were never able to recover fully. While sporadic fighting continued for another fourteen years, the Muslim conquest of the region was mostly complete. In 640 CE, the Muslim army captured the coastal city of Ascalon, the last bastion of opposition to complete Arab-Islamic rule over Palestine. As with the rest of the Middle East, Palestine thus became Arabized and Islamized. Except for brief periods during the Crusades, Palestine remained under Muslim rulers until the early 20th century.

Sean N. Blas

See also: Islam; Jerusalem; Jerusalem, Old City of; Muhammad, Prophet of Islam

Further Reading
Gil, Moshe. *A History of Palestine 634–1099.* Cambridge: Cambridge University Press, 1997.
Kennedy, Hugh. *The Great Arab Conquests: How the Spread of Islam Changed the World We Live In.* Boston: Da Capo Press, 2007.

Arab-Israeli War, 1948

A conflict between the newly created state of Israel and its Arab neighbors that occurred between May 1948 and May 1949; also known as the Israeli War for Independence and referred to as *nakba,* or "catastrophe," by Palestinians. When the Ottoman Empire was dismantled in the wake of World War I, Great Britain received a mandate from the League of Nations over Palestine. Much of the British Mandate period (1922–1948) was spent maintaining peace among the Muslim, Jewish, and Christian populations in the region.

In the 1920s and 1930s, the region received a large influx of Zionists (Jews determined to establish a Jewish state in Palestine). Many were fleeing persecution in Europe. The rising number of Jewish residents spawned a violent backlash from Palestinian Arabs. This often took the form of demonstrations against British policies, including a series of riots centered in Jerusalem. During the Arab Revolt of 1936, Arab insurgents attacked Jewish settlements and businesses. They also boycotted British-owned businesses. Riots swept Palestine and were put down by British forces, which sometimes were augmented by Jewish auxiliary police.

Thousands of Palestinians were killed, wounded, or imprisoned during the revolt. After British forces successfully quelled the rebellion, the mandate administration adopted a decidedly pro-Jewish stance, turning a blind eye to Jewish militia forces such as Haganah, which were officially outlawed. These militia forces would prove vital when open fighting erupted between Arabs and Jews in 1948. At the same time, in an attempt to placate Arab sentiment on the eve of World War II, the British reversed their position on Jewish migration, trying to apply more strict immigration quotas after decades of supporting large-scale Zionist migration. Increasingly, Jewish paramilitary forces such as the Irgun Tsvai Leumi (National Military Organization) battled the British occupiers, who arrested a number of them. The British seemed unable to please either side as the violence escalated.

World War II marked the end of colonialism in the Middle East and elsewhere. Lebanon became independent in 1943, although French troops did not leave that country until 1946, when they also departed from the French Mandate for Syria. British-controlled Transjordan and Iraq also gained independence in 1946, under King Abdullah and his half-brother, King Faysal, respectively. The British remained in Palestine until November 29, 1947, when the United Nations (UN) approved a partition plan that would have created two states, one Jewish and the other Arab. Jewish and Arab leaders each criticized aspects of the partition. However, the Jewish populace of Palestine mostly supported the UN resolution as the key to an independent Jewish state. The Arabs roundly rejected the plan.

On November 30, 1947, seven Jewish inhabitants of Palestine died in three separate attacks by Arabs. Jewish militia forces retaliated, and British authorities proved unable to halt the escalating violence in the region. The British became increasingly unwilling to intervene in the growing conflict as the date of complete British withdrawal drew near. In December 1947 and January 1948, almost 1,000 Palestinian residents died in the fighting, which continued to escalate in early 1948.

Although Arabs outnumbered Jews in Palestine two to one, Jewish forces proved better armed and organized. Arab military efforts focused on cutting communications between Jewish settlements and isolating the city of Jerusalem. Jewish counterattacks sought to control roads linking Jewish towns but could rarely open routes to Jerusalem.

Jewish leaders declared the independence of the state of Israel on May 14, 1948, the day that the British Mandate expired. Israel promptly received diplomatic recognition from the United States and the Soviet Union but was also immediately invaded by troops from surrounding Arab nations. The Arab forces included regular units from Egypt, Iraq, Lebanon, Syria, and Transjordan, augmented by Libyan, Saudi Arabian, and Yemeni volunteers. Officially, the troops cooperated under the auspices of the Arab League, which had formed in 1945. Nominally, King Abdullah of Transjordan was the commander-in-chief of the Arab armies, although cooperation among the Arab forces remained almost nonexistent throughout the war.

On May 15, 1948, the Arab League announced its intention to create the United State of Palestine, encompassing the Jewish and Arab regions created by the UN partition plan. Although the Arab invasion was denounced by the United States, the Soviet Union, and UN secretary-general Trygve Lie, it found support from the Republic of China (Taiwan) and other UN member states.

On May 26, 1948, the Israeli government created the Israel Defense Forces (IDF), primarily by incorporating the irregular Jewish militias that had existed under the British Mandate, including Haganah, the Palmach, and Irgun. Although the IDF numbered fewer than 30,000 troops at its formation, by mid-July 1948, it had more than doubled in size. It continued to grow exponentially, and by the end of 1948, Israel could place more than 100,000 troops in the field. The vast majority of those troops, however, were recently arrived immigrants from the concentration camps and displaced person camps of Europe who had little or no military training. In comparison, the combined Arab armies, which began the conflict with approximately 23,500 troops, increased to only 40,000 by July 1948 and 55,000 that October.

Despite the rapid growth in the IDF's personnel, the Arab armies had a significant superiority in heavy weapons at the beginning of the conflict. Worldwide observers opined that the Jewish state would be quickly overrun because of its almost complete lack of armored vehicles, artillery, and warplanes. The new Israeli government quickly moved to purchase weapons, however, beginning with a shipment of twenty-five Czechoslovakian aircraft that arrived in late May 1948. Czechoslovakia continued to provide weapons to the IDF for the remainder of the war, even during UN-mandated cease-fires that prohibited the sale of arms to any belligerent.

In the first phase of the fighting, Arab armies from Transjordan and Iraq advanced on Jerusalem with the aim of driving all Jewish inhabitants from the city. Abdullah ordered an assault on Jerusalem to begin on May 17, 1948. Two weeks of brutal house-to-house fighting followed, partially negating the Arab Legion's advantage in mobility and heavier weapons. Transjordanian troops succeeded in driving back IDF forces, but Iraqi attacks were ineffective, and soon the Iraqi force shifted to a defensive posture in the regions of Jenin and Nablus. A Syrian attack along the northern front of the war, supported by tanks and artillery, was defeated by Jewish settlers at Degania, the oldest kibbutz in Palestine. The settlers there had only light weapons, but they skillfully used terrain features and night attacks to halt the Syrian advance.

Only in the south did Arab forces make significant territorial gains. Egyptian forces captured several kibbutzim but took heavy losses in the process and bogged down near Ashdod. The first phase of the war ended when a UN-declared truce came into effect on June 11, 1948. Although the truce included an arms embargo for all belligerents, the Israelis successfully smuggled in munitions from Czechoslovakia while the four-week truce was in effect. The UN mediator, Folke Bernadotte, also proposed a new partition plan that was immediately rejected by both sides. When Egyptian forces resumed their attacks on July 8, the truce collapsed.

In the second phase of the war, the IDF assumed the offensive. Its primary objective was to restore Israeli command of the Tel Aviv–Jerusalem corridor. This it secured by a massive assault against Lod, which included the first Israeli use of bomber aircraft. The city, defended by Transjordanian troops augmented by Palestinian irregulars and the Arab Liberation Army (ALA), surrendered on July 11. The next day, the IDF captured Ramla, also in the vital corridor, but it failed to take Latrun.

With the Jerusalem sector fairly stable, the IDF launched Operation DEKEL, a major push against Syrian and Lebanese troops in lower Galilee. The IDF captured Nazareth on July 16. Only against Egyptian forces in the south did the IDF fail to make significant progress in the July fighting.

Another UN-brokered truce went into effect on July 18. Bernadotte presented yet another partition plan, this time calling for Transjordan to annex the Arab regions, the creation of an independent Jewish state, and the establishment of Jerusalem as an international city. All belligerents again rejected the plan, and the day after Bernadotte presented his latest solution to the conflict, he was assassinated by members of the Zionist militia Lehi. The truce remained in effect, however, until October 15, when Israel ended the cease-fire with a series of offensives designed to drive out the Arab armies completely.

In the third phase of the war, the Israelis began their offensives with an assault against Egyptian forces in the Negev Desert, forcing the Egyptian army to abandon its forward positions and evacuate the northern Negev. On October 24, IDF forces pushed into the upper Galilee region, virtually destroyed the remnants of the ALA, and pushed several miles into Lebanon, driving Lebanese forces completely out of Israel. A renewed assault against the Egyptians started on December 22, when IDF troops encircled Egyptian units in the Gaza Strip and attacked their positions in the Sinai Peninsula. The Egyptians withdrew from and accepted a cease-fire effective January 7, 1949.

Once the truce went into effect, IDF troops withdrew from the Sinai and Gaza. In December 1948, the United Nations passed Resolution 194, which declared that refugees from the Arab-Israeli conflict should have the opportunity to return to their homes and live in peace. Those who chose not to return were to be offered compensation for their property by the government in control of that territory at the end of the conflict. The resolution never achieved its goals, and the huge population of Palestinian refugees (approximately 700,000) became a lasting legal and diplomatic problem for the region.

In 1949, Israel concluded separate armistices with each of the Arab belligerents, with the exception of Iraq. On February 24, Egypt and Israel signed a cease-fire, which left Egyptian troops in occupation of the Gaza Strip. On March 23, Lebanon and Israel concluded an armistice and the IDF withdrew from Lebanese territory. The Transjordan-Israel armistice, signed on April 3, left Transjordanian troops in control of the West Bank. On July 20, Syria agreed to a cease-fire and the creation of a demilitarized zone along the Israeli-Syrian border.

The new state of Israel now covered three-fourths of the former British Mandate for Palestine and was 50 percent larger than the land area offered in Bernadotte's original partition proposal. Israel's independence cost 6,000 Israelis their lives, one-third of which were civilians. Arab losses were higher; most estimates place the number of Arabs killed at approximately 10,000.

Paul J. Springer

See also: Arab-Jewish Communal War, 1947; Bernadotte, Count Folke; British Mandate for Palestine; British White Paper; Deir Yassin Massacre; Haganah; Irgun; Israel Defense Forces; Lydda and Ramle; *Nakba;* Palestinian Refugees; Palmach; Stern Gang; UN Partition Plan for Palestine

Further Reading

Herzog, Chaim. *The Arab-Israeli Wars: War and Peace in the Middle East.* New York: Random House, 1982.

Lustick, Ian. *From War to War: Israel vs. the Arabs, 1948–1967.* New York: Garland, 1983.

Morris, Benny. *1948: A History of the First Arab-Israeli War.* New Haven, CT: Yale University Press, 2008.

Pappé, Ilan. *A History of Modern Palestine: One Nation, Two Peoples.* 2nd ed. Cambridge: Cambridge University Press, 2006.

Arab-Israeli War, 1956

A brief invasion of Egypt by Israeli, French, and British forces, stemming in part from the nationalization of the Suez Canal; also known as the Suez Crisis or Suez War. In 1952, the charismatic Gamal Abdel Nasser led a bloodless coup in Egypt, overthrowing King Faruq. He consolidated his power by 1954 and negotiated an agreement with Great Britain to remove their troops from the Suez Canal zone by 1956. Nasser's rhetoric toward Israel was often violent, but the border remained quiet while he focused on domestic issues.

This changed in the aftermath of the Lavon Affair, in which Israeli spies (mostly Egyptian Jews) were caught planting bombs in Cairo; and the Gaza Raid, in which Israel launched a surprise attack that killed forty-eight Egyptian soldiers. In response, Nasser actively sponsored Palestinian *fedeyeen* attacks into Israel and sought to purchase massive supplies of modern equipment from Czechoslovakia, then a Soviet satellite. Nasser supported Arab revolutionary movements throughout the Arab world, putting him at odds with the Western powers. He gained great prestige in the Arab world by nationalizing the Suez Canal in July 1956, the revenues from which he said would be used to pay for the Aswan Dam project, which he considered crucial for his country's economic development. For a number of reasons (most notably his increasingly cozy relationship with the Soviets and his Arab nationalist, anti-Israeli rhetoric), the United States and Britain refused to aid the project and blocked international funding of the dam by the World Bank. Nasser also closed the canal and the Straits of Tiran to Israeli shipping.

France and Great Britain reacted to the nationalization of the canal by planning an invasion of Egypt. Israel, concerned about Nasser's repeated threats and growing military capabilities, was already planning an invasion of its own. It readily accepted an Anglo-French invitation to participate, gaining an influx of French arms in return. The Anglo-French-Israeli alliance counted on the United States and the Soviet Union not intervening because of the current tensions over Hungary and Poland.

Israeli forces conquered the Sinai Peninsula quickly. However, muddling by the British and French leadership and the surprisingly vehement disapproval of the United States and the Soviet Union resulted in a complete fiasco. The French and British forces, late in arriving, were forced to withdraw. Israel had to give up the territory that it had conquered in the Sinai in return for promises of free passage of its shipping in certain Arab waters.

Despite the overwhelming defeat of his forces at the hands of the Israelis, Nasser gained even greater stature as a result of his defiance of France and Britain. Israel realized through the Sinai Campaign that it could not rely on foreign assistance to achieve its own security. The machinations of the superpowers would always take precedence over any guarantees to the fledgling Jewish state. As such, Israel embarked on a massive effort to develop its own weapons industry, military education system, and compulsory service for all its citizens.

Walter Boyne and Paul J. Springer

See also: Egypt; Gaza Raid, 1955; Lavon Affair; Nasser, Gamal Abdel

Further Reading

Goldschmidt, Arthur. *Modern Egypt: The Formation of a Nation State.* 2nd ed. Boulder, CO: Westview Press, 2004.

Gorst, Anthony, and Lewis Johnman. *The Suez Crisis.* New York: Routledge, 1997.

Ochsenwald, William, and Sydney Nettleton Fisher. *The Middle East: A History.* 6th ed. New York: McGraw-Hill, 2004.

Varble, Derek. *The Suez Crisis—1956.* London: Osprey Publishing, 2003.

Arab-Israeli War, 1967

A war between Israel and its neighbors that reshaped the Arab-Israeli conflict; also known as the Six-Day War. Military setbacks in 1948 and 1956 left Arab leaders reluctant to engage Israel directly in war. Instead, they allowed the conflict to proceed via low-intensity, state-sponsored terrorism. Operating from Syria's Golan Heights, Palestinian militants staged daily attacks against Israeli farmers living in the north.

Israel staged its own overt and covert strikes on guerrilla camps and villages in the Golan Heights and in Jordan. Many were disproportionate responses aimed at deterring future violence. An Arab attempt to divert the flow of the Jordan River resulted in a series of attacks by the Israel Defense Forces (IDF) against the diversion sites in Syria in 1965.

On November 13, 1966, the IDF launched a large-scale attack against Es Samu in Jordan, a Palestinian refugee village that the Israelis believed was a base for terrorists. On April 7, 1967, a major aerial battle over the Golan Heights resulted in the downing of six Syrian MiG-21s. By late spring of 1967, a cycle of violence across the border had taken hold.

With the United States heavily engaged in Vietnam, the leaders of the Soviet Union saw an opportunity to alter the balance of power in the Middle East to favor their own client-states, Egypt and Syria. On May 13, 1967, the Soviets provided the Egyptians an intelligence report falsely indicating that Israeli forces were building up along the Syrian border.

Egyptian president Gamal Abdel Nasser announced he would stand alongside Syria in the crisis. Israel's protestations that the Soviet report was untrue fell on deaf ears, as there was little reason for the Egyptians to believe the Israelis. Scholars disagree over whether Nasser actually intended to go to war. Most believe that he thought he could bluff his way through the crisis without actual recourse to arms, extricating himself diplomatically while bolstering his prestige.

On May 16, Nasser ordered the United Nations Emergency Force (UNEF) to leave the Sinai, which it soon did. Formed at the conclusion of the Suez Crisis in 1956, the UNEF had maintained a relatively demilitarized Sinai for more than 10 years. On May 22, Nasser closed the Straits of Tiran to Israeli shipping and ordered his military to prepare for war. Hoping to find an international solution to the crisis, Israel sent Foreign Minister Abba Eban to Washington on May 26. President Lyndon B. Johnson pressed the Israelis to resist attacking while he sought an international coalition to reopen the straits.

Jordan's King Husayn arrived in Cairo on May 30, 1967, to finalize a tripartite alliance among Egypt, Jordan, and Syria. The alliance strengthened Egypt's position, but the Soviet Union now urged Nasser to show restraint. The Soviets were responding to a direct hot-line message sent to the Kremlin by President Johnson. Nasser countered that a surprise first strike by Israel could neutralize Egypt's numerical superiority, but the Soviets remained firm.

Egypt and Israel both subsequently played a waiting game. Each day brought the Israeli economy closer to the brink of disaster. The mobilization for war alone had a catastrophic impact on Israel's economy, which ground to a near-halt as all males between the ages of 16 and 55 entered active service. The prospect of war was also destabilizing to Egypt, whose economy was in difficult times, with peasant complaints, riots, and inconclusive reforms. A failed war could mean the end of the regime.

An Israeli gun boat passes through the Straits of Tiran near Sharm El Sheikh, June 8, 1967. Egypt closed the straits to Israeli shipping on May 22nd. Securing passage through this vital waterway was one of Israel's major military objectives during the 1967 war. (Israel Government Press Office/Yaacov Agor)

On June 2, 1967, Israel sent another envoy to Washington. By now, the hope of an international flotilla capable of keeping the Straits of Tiran open had disappeared. To reassure their Israeli allies, U.S. officials insisted that Israel could defeat Egypt, Jordan, and Syria within two to three weeks, even if it was caught off guard. Israel, however, refused to wait for its enemies to strike first; finally, on June 4, Israeli prime minister Levi Eshkol authorized a preemptive strike against Egypt.

At dawn on June 5, 180 Israeli aircraft launched against targets in Egypt and the Sinai. The Israeli strike force caught the Egyptians by surprise. Within minutes, all Egypt's airfields were under attack. By noon, Egypt had lost more than 300 aircraft and 100 pilots. The Israelis lost 19 aircraft. The loss of Egypt's air force had a dramatic impact on the war. Although Egypt outnumbered the Israelis on the ground, the absence of air support left Egyptian armor vulnerable to Israel's air force. By the end of the fighting in the Sinai, Egypt had lost 80 percent of its military equipment and 11,500 troops killed, 20,000 wounded, and 5,500 captured. By contrast, the IDF lost 338 personnel.

Shortly after the surprise attack on the Egyptian airfields, Israel notified Jordan's King Husayn that its conflict lay with Egypt, and that it had no interest in Jordan so long as Husayn kept his forces out of the fray. Simultaneously, however, Husayn received Egyptian state-run radio broadcasts, claiming staggering victories and predicting the destruction of Israel. Husayn decided that the Israeli communiqué was a desperate ploy and ordered his forces to attack West Jerusalem. Only then did Nasser admit to his ally what actually was occurring in the Sinai. By then, it was too late for Husayn to withdraw from the conflict. On June 6, Israeli prime minister Eshkol ordered the IDF to seize East Jerusalem and force the Jordanian military completely out of the West Bank.

Israeli air superiority was decisive once more. Within days, Israel pushed the Jordanian forces across the Jordan River. Israeli paratroopers entered the Old City of Jerusalem on June 7. The defeat was a staggering blow to Jordan, which lost almost 7,000 troops and suffered more than 12,000 wounded. The Israelis lost about 300. King Husayn called upon Nasser for help, but the Egyptian president could offer little more than a ruse that, if successful, might bring the Soviet Union to the rescue.

Nasser assured Husayn that the Soviet Union would waste no time intervening if it believed that the United States already had done so. In calling for Soviet support, Nasser alleged that the Americans had led the initial air strikes against Egypt. King Husayn supported Nasser's claim and the war appeared on the verge of becoming a major Cold War superpower confrontation. The Soviets were disappointed that their plans to change the Middle East balance of power had failed. Israel now controlled the Sinai Peninsula, the Gaza Strip, and the West Bank and had sent its forces north to the Golan Heights. Initially giving credence to the Egyptian claim that the Americans had been involved, the Soviet Union planned to defend Syria. Soviet help in retaking the West Bank and Sinai would soon arrive.

When the Johnson administration learned that the Soviets were mobilizing air units, President Johnson ordered the *Independence* carrier group in the Mediterranean to head for Israel. Then, in one of the most controversial incidents of the war, IAF aircraft attacked the USS *Liberty*, an American electronic intelligence ship operating just outside of Egypt's territorial waters, on June 8. The attack killed thirty-four U.S. sailors. The Israelis later claimed that they had committed a tragic error amid the fog of war, but much about the incident remains unclear.

Still, the U.S. message to the Soviets was unequivocal: If they sought to raise the stakes, the United States would match them. Neither superpower relished the prospect of direct confrontation, but neither wanted to be perceived as weak. For the United States, that meant standing firm against the Soviets publicly while pursuing diplomacy through the United Nations (UN).

While the Israeli ambassador to the United Nations had little trouble justifying Israel's actions against Egypt, the United Nations demanded an immediate withdrawal from the West Bank and an end to hostilities with Syria in the Golan Heights. Arab delegates demanded an Israeli withdrawal on all fronts of the war. For Israel, however, the opportunity to seize control of the strategic Golan Heights was irresistible. Eshkol ordered his country's UN ambassador to stall for time and to falsely claim that Israel had no further designs on Arab territory. When President Johnson demanded that the Israeli ambassador convey the American insistence to withdraw from the Golan Heights, Eshkol claimed to be unable to understand the message because of problems with the phone lines.

As the situation stabilized on the IDF's southern and central fronts, Moshe Dayan was able to turn his attention to the Golan Heights and Syria. The IAF had already destroyed two-thirds of the Syrian Air Force on the evening of June 5. By the morning of June 10, Israel controlled the Golan Heights, having lost only 141 soldiers. The Syrians lost 2,500, and another 5,000 were wounded.

Having occupied the Sinai, the Gaza Strip, the West Bank, and the Golan Heights, Israel prepared to face the United Nations. With the fighting over, the United States and the Soviet Union pulled back from the brink. By this point, Soviet intelligence had concluded that the United States had not participated in the early-morning attacks of June 5, 1967, as Nasser had claimed. A series of cease-fires officially ended the 1967 conflict, but the first formal peace treaty between Israel and an Arab nation remained twelve years in the future.

By the end of 1967, the United Nations passed Resolution 242, which called upon the Israelis to return the captured territories. The resolution also stipulated that the Arab nations should negotiate and sign peace treaties with Israel. Neither side, however, was interested in compromise. Israel argued that because of its national security requirements, it should not be required to return the territories. By more than doubling the territory under its control, Israel now had viable geographic buffer zones between it and most of its Arab enemies for the first time. Israel insisted that peace treaties would have to precede any discussion of territorial returns. For their part, the Arab states insisted that they would not consider peace treaties until Israel returned their territories—a catch-22.

Israel's occupation of the West Bank and Gaza greatly complicated their long-term prospects for peace with the Palestinians. For security and religious reasons, many Israelis insisted that abandoning these territories—part of biblical Israel—was out of the question. Indeed, every Israeli government since 1967 has supported the building of Jewish settlements in occupied lands, and the settler movement has become a major force in Israeli domestic politics. But the occupation also has made it difficult for Israel to retain its identity as both a Jewish and democratic state because an indefinite occupation is undemocratic, but affording full political rights to Palestinians would alter the Jewish character of Israel. Half a century after the Six-Day War, there is no end in sight to Israel's occupation and no peace between Israelis and Palestinians.

Bryan Vizzini and David T. Zabecki

See also: Arab-Israeli War, 1948; Gaza Strip; Golan Heights; Israel Defense Forces; Israeli Occupations; Jerusalem, Old City of; USS *Liberty*; West Bank

Further Reading

Finkelstein, Norman G. *The Rise and Fall of Palestine: A Personal Account of the Intifada Years.* Minneapolis: University of Minnesota Press, 1996.

Friedman, Thomas L. *From Beirut to Jerusalem.* New York: Anchor, 1990.

Morris, Benny. *Righteous Victims: A History of the Zionist-Arab Conflict, 1881–2001.* New York: Vintage Books, 2002.

Ochsenwald, William, and Sydney Nettleson Fisher. *The Middle East: A History.* Boston: McGraw-Hill, 2004.

Oren, Michael B. *Six Days of War: June 1967 and the Making of the Modern Middle East.* New York: Oxford University Press, 2002.

Arab-Israeli War, 1973

A war between Israel and its Arab neighbors in October 1973; also known as the Yom Kippur War because it began with a coordinated Egyptian-Syrian surprise attack against Israel on the Jewish holy day of Yom Kippur. Arabs often call it the "Ramadan War" because it began during the holy month of Ramadan.

In addition to the long-standing issues of the Arab-Israeli conflict dating to 1948, the more pressing causes of the Yom Kippur War were inherent in the results of the Six-Day War in June 1967. During that campaign, the Israel Defense Forces (IDF) humiliated the Arab armies and seized large portions of Syrian, Jordanian, and Egyptian territory. Although possession of the Golan Heights and the Sinai Peninsula gave Israel much-needed strategic depth, this was absolutely intolerable to the highly nationalistic regimes in Damascus and Cairo. Israel's continued occupation of these lands transformed the abstract grievances of Palestinian rights into a deeply resented insult to the Arab governments and armies involved.

Paradoxically, therefore, Israel's very success in 1967 had made it more difficult, both politically and emotionally, for Arab leaders to reach a negotiated settlement with the Israelis. Israel insisted on peace as a prerequisite for any withdrawal, whereas its opponents demanded complete evacuation before negotiations. In addition, these Israeli-held territories caused a constant drain on the reservist Israeli military, which had to provide forces to defend large sectors that it had never previously possessed. In particular, the thirty-five positions of the so-called Bar-Lev Line along the Suez Canal required garrisons to provide early warning and deter Egyptian infiltrations. Moreover, the distance between Israel proper and the canal meant that in the event of war, Israeli reserve units would take several days to mobilize and reach the southern front. For Egypt's part, a constant state of semimobilization in combination with the loss of revenues from the Suez Canal placed enormous strains on the economy, increasing pressure to resolve the situation at all costs.

Renewed warfare was therefore inevitable, waiting only until the frontline Arab states had rearmed and reorganized their forces. The question in 1973 was how the Arabs could overcome the enormous advantages possessed by the IDF. The 1956 Suez Crisis and Sinai Campaign, and especially the 1967 Six-Day War, had shown the IDF to be a master of flexible, offensive warfare reminiscent of World War II blitzkrieg tactics. Arab armies could not easily match the Israelis' mechanized maneuvers, and few Arab pilots had the experience of their Israeli counterparts.

The problem for the Egyptians was further complicated by the fact that they had to begin their offensive by crossing the Suez Canal, whose concrete-lined banks and adjacent sand walls made it difficult to breach with heavy vehicles. To span the Suez Canal, the Egyptians decided to use high-pressure water cannon to cut through the huge sand walls that Israel had built on the eastern side. During the event, 450 British- and German-made pumps enabled the attackers to create sixty gaps in the sand wall during the first six hours of the campaign.

At a time when most of his contemporaries still sought a single war of annihilation against Israel, Lieutenant General Saad el-Shazly (Egypt's armed forces chief of staff and primary architect of Egypt's military strategy) decided to conduct a limited offensive—one that would capitalize on the abilities of his troops and shake the IDF's confidence in their own invincibility. Thus, Operation High Minarets intended to penetrate no more than six miles east of the Suez Canal. This meant that to attack the Egyptians, the Israeli air force would have to fly through a battery of air defense missiles located on the banks of the canal. As they crossed the canal, Egyptian units would take with them antitank guided missiles and a variety of mobile air defense weapons. Working together, these Soviet-supplied weapons posed an integrated air defense capability that would degrade or neutralize the Israeli advantage in fighter-bombers.

Although there was general agreement on this first phase of the operation, most Egyptian officials expected far more from the war. Some had promised their Syrian allies that they would quickly move forward to the Sinai passes, denying Israel any defensible terrain in the desert. General el-Shazly consistently opposed such plans because a deep advance would leave behind the air defense umbrella and tightly coordinated defensive positions that gave the Egyptians their initial advantages. Instead, el-Shazly envisaged forcing Israel to choose between a long, stalemated war that it could not afford, unacceptably high casualties to retake the canal, or peace negotiations.

For its part, the Syrian plan was more conventional, relying on multiple attack echelons to overwhelm the IDF in the occupied Golan Heights before Israeli reserves could arrive. From the beginning, Damascus was pushing for a total victory, which was a serious divergence from the Egyptian plans. Again, an integrated Soviet-manufactured air defense system would shelter the Syrian ground advance. Given the shallow (approximately 12.5-mile) depth of the IDF enclave on the Golan Heights, this plan appeared more feasible than an equivalent Egyptian effort to retake the entire Sinai.

Preparations for the attack included unprecedented secrecy and deception efforts. During the final weeks of intensive preparations, all concerned continued routine activities in public. Egypt in particular desensitized the Israelis by a series of field exercises and no fewer than twenty-two practice mobilizations and demobilizations of reservists during 1973. A major Egyptian troop concentration had passed without incident in the spring of 1973, further desensitizing observers. Meanwhile, the Egyptian General Staff maintained secrecy to the point that it did not inform its division commanders until three days before the attack.

Israel's lack of strategic warning has been the subject of much debate. With few exceptions, the Israeli leaders were convinced that the Arab states did not intend to launch a war, because in their eyes, Syria knew that it could not win alone and Egypt supposedly felt too vulnerable to Israeli air attacks on its economy and population. Israeli leaders assumed that their opponents shared the IDF's views about the likely outcome of an immediate war. Indeed, the Israeli director of military intelligence was so convinced of this interpretation that he repeatedly delayed reporting key information to his superiors and downplayed the significance of the reports that he did present.

During the final twenty-four hours before the war began, sufficient intelligence indications appeared to make the threat of attack seem real. In particular, after Anwar Sadat and Hafez al-Assad informed their Soviet military advisers that an attack was imminent, Soviet aircraft urgently evacuated the families of their personnel from both countries during October 4–6. King Husayn of Jordan provided several specific warnings, as did one of Israel's highest human intelligence sources in Egypt. By the morning of October 6, therefore, the IDF belatedly began mobilization. The Israeli air force also prepared a preemptive strike against Arab targets, but low clouds made it impossible to strike the Golan Heights, and eventually Prime Minister Golda Meir cancelled the attack. She reportedly told the U.S. ambassador to Israel, Kenneth Keating, that Israel wanted to avoid any accusation that it was responsible for the war.

As a result, the IDF began the conflict flatfooted. It was gravely outmanned on its borders with Syria and Egypt. The initial Arab attack began on both fronts with air strikes at 2:00 p.m. on October 6, followed immediately by brief artillery barrages to suppress the defenders in fortified positions. Within hours, the Egyptians had crossed the Suez Canal, established a beachhead on its western bank, and hunkered down under the protection of their Soviet air defense systems. Thus, the Egyptians had effectively achieved General el-Shazly's main objective in the first days of fighting and then largely paused their offensive. This pause allowed Israel to shift its focus to the Golan Heights, where it had suffered early defeats and were desperately holding the line against Syrian forces. By October 10, Israel had turned the tide in the Golan, retaking its prewar positions except for Mount Hermon. Still, the Syrian army had withdrawn in good order. Fearing that an early cease-fire would leave Israel with a net loss in territory, Prime Minister Meir ordered an offensive into Syria to begin on October 11.

This offensive, in combination with Israeli air attacks against Syrian command and infrastructure targets, changed the course of the war. Damascus appealed to Cairo to divert Israeli attention with a renewed attack, and President Sadat overruled his field commanders, ordering the Egyptian army to leave its air defense umbrella and advance to the Sinai passes on the morning of October 14. This attack was a predictable disaster, and soon Israeli troops crossed the Suez Canal, fanned out, and disrupted the Egyptian air defense network.

The Egyptian failure was compounded by continued defeats in Syria, where the IDF continued to push toward Damascus while defeating other Arab auxiliary forces, including armored brigades from Iraq and Jordan.

From the beginning of the conflict, the Soviet Union had attempted to impose a cease-fire, at first because it expected the Arabs to be defeated, and later to preserve their gains. Sadat had refused such initiatives until the Israeli crossing endangered his forces. Meanwhile, U.S. secretary of state Henry Kissinger tried to delay cease-fire negotiations in order to give Israel time to regain its initial positions. By mid-October, such a cease-fire appeared imminent, accelerating IDF offensives in the Sinai and Golan Heights.

At the same time, Kissinger had to persuade his own government (and especially Secretary of Defense James R. Schlesinger) that Israel urgently needed replacement tanks, aircraft, and ammunition. Many officials suspected a trick, but Kissinger argued that an IDF defeat would appear to be an American defeat as well. President Richard Nixon decisively supported Kissinger. Beginning on October 13, the United States launched Operation Nickel Grass to help resupply Israel's dwindling arsenal. The Soviet Union responded with an airlift of its own to replace the losses of its client states.

On October 22 the United Nations Security Council approved a cease-fire, but the agreement failed, as each side accused the other of violations. The IDF used this excuse to push southward on the western bank of the canal, cutting off the Third Egyptian Army from its supplies. In defeat, the Egyptians continued to fight in a disciplined manner, and a combination of soldiers and local militia thwarted Israeli efforts to seize Suez City, at the southern end of the canal, on October 23 and 25.

The continued fighting, with the Third Army stranded and the IDF approaching Damascus, provoked a superpower confrontation at the end of the war. The Soviet Union had alerted some of its forces at the start of hostilities and reportedly increased the readiness of certain airborne units after an Israeli victory became apparent. On October 24, Soviet leader Leonid Brezhnev sent President Nixon a note threatening unilateral action if the Israelis were not curbed. Kissinger had already told Meir that further incursions violated the spirit of his agreements with Moscow, but this new message prompted the United States to alert its nuclear forces to Defense Condition 3 at 11:41 p.m. on October 24. Although Brezhnev's true intentions have never been established, the situation was defused peacefully when, after repeated Security Council resolutions, the fighting finally halted on October 26. Even then, Israel refused to permit resupply of the stricken Third Army until Egypt returned all prisoners.

Overall, Israel suffered at least 2,687 killed and 7,251 wounded. Some 314 more were taken prisoner. This compares to combined Arab losses, which exceeded 15,400 dead, 42,000 wounded, and 8,400 captured. Although the Yom Kippur War ended with Israeli victories, General el-Shazly's larger objectives were clearly accomplished. Egypt and Syria proved to be much more formidable than the 1967 war suggested. Egypt in particular had demonstrated that Israel could not occupy the Sinai indefinitely, thereby establishing the psychological preconditions for successful peace negotiations in 1978.

The conflict also contributed to Middle Eastern disenchantment with the superpowers. The Soviet Union had shown itself unwilling or unable to give the Arabs weapons equal in quality to those that the United States had provided to Israel. However, the open U.S. support for Israel offended many Arab governments and led directly to the crippling oil embargo by Arab nations during late 1973 and early 1974. That imbroglio wreaked havoc on already-weak U.S. and West European economies and saw the near-quadrupling of petroleum prices in the span of only a few months.

Jonathan M. House

See also: Meir, Golda; Operation Nickel Grass; Sadat, Anwar; UN Security Council Resolution 338

Further Reading

Adan, Avraham. *On the Banks of the Suez: An Israeli General's Personal Account of the Yom Kippur War.* Novato, CA: Presidio Press, 1980.

Dunstan, Simon. *The Yom Kippur War 1973 (I): The Golan Heights and (II): The Sinai.* Oxford, UK: Osprey Publishing, 2003.

Morris, Benny. *Righteous Victims: A History of the Zionist-Arab Conflict, 1881–2001.* New York: Vintage Books, 2002.

Smith, Charles D. *Palestine and the Arab-Israeli Conflict: A History with Documents.* New York: Bedford/St. Martin's, 2017.

Arab-Jewish Clashes in Palestine, Pre-1947

Early confrontations between Arabs and Jews in Palestine in the early twentieth century. These early altercations followed a pattern of increasing Jewish control and waning Arab influence in Palestine. The British military took over Palestine shortly after the Ottoman Empire's capitulation in World War I. The British Mandate intended to keep the peace, but the military struggled to manage the conflicting interests of Zionists and Arabs in Palestine. As the situation deteriorated, British officials were forced to make concessions between strong Zionist pressure from political leaders back in England and the realities present on the ground in Palestine. Early clashes between the Arabs and Jews cemented a deep divide and created a pattern of conflict that is still observable today.

As the Zionist movement gained steam, tensions between Arabs and Jews in Palestine intensified and often spilled over into violence. One of the first incidents was the 1920 Nebi Musa riots in Jerusalem. The riots occurred during the Nebi Musa festival, at which Arab religious leaders gave speeches expressing discontent with the growing Zionist influence in Palestine. Simmering tensioned exploded into violence in various parts of the city. Fighting continued until April 7. In the end, nine people were killed, and several hundred were wounded.

The next year, Jaffa and Tel-Aviv experienced violent confrontations. Between 1919 and 1921, a new wave of young and motivated European Jews arrived in the region with strong cultural identities that clashed with the existing Arab residents.

Many of these immigrants came with strong socialist beliefs, and a majority moved into towns and cities. The communal tension previously seen primarily in rural areas now moved into urban middle-class areas. In May 1921, violence erupted in Tel Aviv and Jaffa when Jewish immigrant workers and Arabs began fighting in the streets. By the end, ninety Jews and sixty-two Arabs had died in the fighting and the subsequent British response to restore order.

In 1929, riots broke out again, this time in Jerusalem and Safad. This new spate of violence flared over disagreements concerning access to the West Wall in old Jerusalem. While the dispute was over access to religious sites, economic hardships and perceptions of British favoritism to Jews were the real catalysts. From 1924 to 1926, a fourth wave of Jewish migration arrived, comprised of wealthy families, which also settled in urban areas. These immigrants initially triggered an economic upturn, but a two-year depression soon reversed the increases. The depression deeply affected many Arab families, leading to further tensions between the two groups. Additionally, the Balfour Declaration played a significant part in inflaming tensions and was used by Palestinian leaders as a salient example of British favoritism. The riots of 1929 resulted in the death of 133 Jews and 116 Arabs. The violence exhibited in the street fighting further solidified British commitment to Zionist policies, and in many cases, Arab organizers earned the stigma of being troublemakers.

That same year, sixty-seven Jews were massacred in Hebron. On August 24, 1929, as fighting continued throughout the British Mandate, Arab rioters, spurred on by rumors that Jews were attempting to gain control of the Temple Mount, precipitated a series of deadly attacks against Jews in Hebron. Initially, these clashes resulted in a few deaths, but as authorities did little to quell the violence, the rioters turned to widespread attacks in largely Jewish communities. The more violent aspects of the riot did not end until British authorities forcibly removed Jews from the city.

In the face of what appeared to be inescapable tension and violence, the Jewish community in Palestine sought to acquire arms as a means of defense. In October 1933, a Zionist shipment of arms in Jaffa led to Arab riots and violent British response. When information leaked that authorities discovered a secret weapons cache, large numbers of Arab Palestinians took to the streets in protest. While these protests were initially only disruptive, the dynamics changed when authorities fired into large crowds to disperse the rioters. Estimates indicate that nineteen were killed and over seventy were injured. The Jaffa Massacre became the catalyst for a weeklong general strike and running gunfighting throughout the city.

Intercommunal violence decreased in the wake of the failed 1936 Arab Revolt and the outbreak of World War II. It returned with a vengeance, however, with the Arab-Jewish Communal War in 1947, which erupted after the United Nations decided to partition Palestine.

Sean N. Blas

See also: Aliya; Arab-Revolt, 1936; Balfour Declaration; British Mandate for Palestine; Hebron; Zionism

Further Reading

Grinberg, Lev Luis. *Movements of Resistance: Politics, Economy and Society in Israel/Palestine 1931–2013*. Boston: Academic Studies Press, 2014.

Nashif, Taysir. "Palestinian Arab and Jewish Leadership in the Mandate Period." *Journal of Palestine Studies* 6, no 4 (Summer 1977), 113–121.

Smith, Charles. *Palestine and the Arab-Israeli Conflict: A History with Documents*. 9th ed. Boston: Bedford/St. Martin's, 2017.

Arab-Jewish Communal War, 1947

Organized violence between Arabs and Jews in Palestine just prior to Israel's declaration of independence. Fighting between Arabs and Jews in Palestine erupted on November 30, 1947, immediately following announcement of the United Nations General Assembly vote approving the partition plan for Palestine. The Arab Palestinian population was assisted by irregular Arab forces from the neighboring states, but their efforts were only loosely coordinated.

When the fighting began, the principal Jewish military force was the Haganah. Illegally constituted during the British Mandate, this self-styled self-defense force consisted of a small, fully mobilized nucleus and a larger militia element. It could count on about 45,000 fighters and had secret arms workshops producing Stern submachine guns, hand grenades, and other explosives. Two other Jewish organizations of importance were the Irgun Tsvai Leumi (National Military Organization), of about 5,000 members, and Lohamei Herut Israel (Fighters for the Freedom of Israel), also known as Lehi or the Stern Gang, with about 1,000 men. These two elements operated very much on their own at the start of the fighting. Indeed, there was no love lost between them and the Haganah, and there had even been armed clashes among them.

The early Arab military attacks took the form of hit-and-run raids against isolated Jewish settlements. The attacks were mounted entirely by Palestinian Arabs, but their efforts were handicapped by ongoing tensions between the Nashashibi and Husayni families. In late 1947, the leaders of the surrounding Arab states formed the Arab Liberation Army (ALA), and within months, some 7,000 ALA members infiltrated Palestine. Soon after Arab forces launched a series of attacks on the Jewish quarters of major cities and cut key supply lines, including those between Tel Aviv and Jerusalem. The Jewish farms in the Negev were also soon isolated.

The difficulty of the military situation facing the Jews was compounded by the decision to defend every bit of territory allocated to the future Jewish state under the partition plan, as well as Jewish settlements allocated to the Arab state. This decision meant that already meager Haganah resources would have to be dispersed throughout Palestine in a defensive stance, making impossible the concentration into larger units for offensive operations. Resupply operations of isolated Jewish settlements Jewish enclaves in the cities would be particularly difficult.

In March, the Arabs decided to concentrate the bulk of their military effort against Jewish road traffic. By the end of March, the Jewish section of Jerusalem was cut off from the coast, and settlements near the city were isolated. The Negev and settlements of western Galilee were similarly cut off. On the other hand, Jewish forces were now more fully mobilized, and progress had also been made in manufacturing light weapons and explosives, as well as importing additional weapons from Czechoslovakia.

From April 6–15, fighting along the supply route to Jerusalem was intense, especially at Kastel, which changed hands several times before the Arabs finally abandoned it on April 10. Abd el-Kadr al-Husayni, the Palestinian commander of the Jerusalem area, was killed at Kastel on April 8, one day before Jewish forces massacred over 100 Palestinians in the town of Deir Yassin. By April 15, three large Jewish convoys reached the besieged Jerusalem. Jewish forces also cleared Arab villages around Tel Aviv–Jaffa in April. By the end of the month, they had encircled Jaffa, which was to be included in the Arab part of Palestine under the partition plan. Many of Jaffa's 70,000 Arab residents fled.

Emboldened by its successes, the Haganah stepped up its offensive, forcing Arab evacuations of Tiberias and Haifa. Success there made possible the resupply of Jewish settlements in Upper Galilee, and contact was reestablished with Safed, which the Jews took on May 10. The Arab inhabitants fled the city and the surrounding areas with the result that by mid-May, all the Jewish settlements in Upper Galilee were connected. Jewish forces also consolidated their grip on West Jerusalem but were unable to create a supply corridor to the Jewish quarter of the Old City. Meanwhile, isolated Jewish settlements near Jerusalem were abandoned as indefensible.

In six weeks of heavy fighting before the proclamation of the state of Israel and the invasion by regular Arab armies, Jewish fighters had secured Haifa, Jaffa, Safed, and Tiberias. They had also captured about 100 Arab villages and had surrounded Akko. Most of the main roads were again open to Jewish traffic. For all practical purposes, the Palestinian Arab military forces had been defeated. The ALA had suffered heavy losses, and the Jewish armed forces had now increased to 30,000 men. The arms shipments from Czechoslovakia had filled many deficiencies, including antitank and antiaircraft weapons, but the Jews still lacked fighter aircraft, field artillery, and tanks. On May 15, 1948, regular Arab armies invaded Israel, beginning the Israeli War of Independence.

Spencer C. Tucker

See also: Arab-Israeli War, 1948; British Mandate for Palestine; Haganah; Irgun; Stern Gang; UN Partition Plan for Palestine

Further Reading

Lucas, Noah. *The Modern History of Israel*. New York: Praeger, 1975.

Sachar, Howard M. *A History of Israel: From the Rise of Zionism to Our Time*. New York: Knopf, 2007.

Smith, Charles D. *Palestine and the Arab-Israeli Conflict,* 9th ed. Boston: Bedford/St. Martin's, 2017.

Arab League

A voluntary political organization of Arabic-speaking nations. The Arab League was founded after World War II with the stated purposes of improving conditions in Arab countries, liberating Arab states still under foreign domination, and preventing the formation of a Jewish state in Palestine. The league's pact also stated that all members would represent the Palestinians together, so long as Palestine was not an independent state.

In 1945, the Arab League organized an economic boycott of Jewish goods and services to help Palestinians combat Zionism. After Israel's creation, the boycott prohibited direct trade between Arab states and Israel. During the 1950s, Egypt effectively led the Arab League. In 1954, Gamal Abdel Nasser took control of Egypt as a strong proponent of Arab unity. In 1956, Egypt nationalized the Suez Canal and closed it to Israeli shipping. The failure of British, French, and Israeli troops to overthrow Nasser in the 1956 Suez War increased his stature in the Arab world and raised the visibility of Pan-Arabism and of the Arab League.

In 1964, the Arab League provided support for the creation of the Palestine Liberation Organization (PLO), and in 1967, it issued the Khartoum Resolution, which vowed members would not recognize, negotiate with, or enter into peace with Israel. Egypt was suspended in the wake of the 1978 Camp David Accord. Egypt was readmitted in 1989. The league continues its efforts to resolve the Israel-Palestine dispute in Palestine's favor.

Amy Hackney Blackwell

See also: Arab Boycott of Israel; Arab-Israeli War, 1956; Camp David Accords; Egypt; Khartoum Resolution; Nasser, Gamal Abdel; Palestine Liberation Organization

Further Reading
Hourani, Albert. *A History of the Arab Peoples.* New York: Warner, 1992.
Smith, Charles D. *Palestine and the Arab-Israeli Conflict: A History with Documents,* 9th ed. New York: Bedford/St. Martin's, 2017.

Arab Peace Plan

A plan to settle the Arab-Israeli conflict, proposed by the Arab League. Saudi Arabia proposed the plan, and the Arab League signed off on it in 2002. The Arab Peace Plan was an attempt to address the differences between Israel and the Arab states with whom it did not already have peace agreements (namely, Egypt and Jordan). This effort was motivated by the belief that a comprehensive peace among all the Middle Eastern countries was the best strategic option for the region. An end to the Arab-Israeli conflict would also allow open coordination and cooperation between Israel and Arab states to counter growing Iranian influence in the Middle East. Based on United Nations Security Council Resolutions 242 and 338, the plan calls on Israel to end its occupation of all territories occupied since June 1967, allow the establishment of an independent Palestinian state with East Jerusalem as its capital, and pursue a just solution to the Palestinian Refugee problem in accordance with United Nations General Assembly Resolution 194, which states that Palestinian refugees should be allowed to return to their homes or be compensated for losses incurred in the 1948 Arab-Israeli War. In return, members of the Arab League agreed to establish normal relations with Israel and consider the Arab-Israeli conflict ended. While this plan continues to garner the support of Arab states, it has been rejected by successive Israeli governments.

Hugh Gardenier

See also: Arab-Israeli War, 1948; Arab League; Palestinian Refugees; Two-State Solution

Further Reading

Quandt, William B. *Peace Process: American Diplomacy and the Arab-Israeli Conflict Since 1967*, Washington, DC: Brookings Institution, 2005.

Smith, Charles D. *Palestine and the Arab-Israeli Conflict,* 9th ed. New York: St. Martin's Press, 2017.

Arab Revolt, 1916

An uprising during World War I by the Arab peoples of Arabia against Ottoman rule. Since the sixteenth century, the Ottoman government had controlled the area of present-day Syria, Palestine, and Iraq, as well as the western provinces of Saudi Arabia and part of Yemen. In 1908, the Young Turks came to power and promoted Turkish nationalism, sent troops into Arab lands, and introduced conscription, all of which angered Arabs.

The center of the Arab nationalist movement was the Hejaz region of central Arabia, which contained the holy cities of Mecca and Medina. The region was connected to Anatolia by the Damascus-Medina (Hejaz) Railway. Husayn ibn Ali ibn Mohammed, sharif of Mecca, was the nominal head of the Hejaz. He was a direct descendant of the Prophet Muhammad. Husayn saw the railway as an infringement on his control and hoped for an independent Arab kingdom under his rule.

Bedouin tribal leaders on the way to Arabia to offer Prince Faysal support during the Arab Revolt. The revolt freed Arab lands from the Ottoman Turks and spurred Arab nationalism but failed to create the Arab super state envisioned by the revolt's architects. (Library of Congress)

As early as February 1914, Husayn, through his son Abdullah, had communicated with British authorities in Cairo, including the British high commissioner in Egypt, Field Marshal Horatio Kitchener, and told him that the Arabs were prepared to rebel in return for British support. The British were skeptical, but the entrance of the Ottoman Empire into the war on the side of the Central Powers changed their attitude. Sir Henry McMahon, Kitchener's successor, remained in contact with Husayn.

In the spring of 1915, Husayn sent his third son, Emir Faysal, to Damascus to reassure Ottoman authorities there of his loyalty and to sound out Arab opinion. Faysal had favored the Turks, but the profound discontent that he discovered there among Arabs reversed this view.

Husayn entered into active negotiations with McMahon in Cairo, promising to declare war on the Ottoman Empire and raise an Arab army to assist Britain in return for British support for him as king of a postwar pan-Arab state. The British agreed and soon provided rifles and ammunition. Meanwhile, the Turks were combating Arab nationalism in Damascus, where they executed a number of Arab nationalist leaders. Many other Arab patriots fled south to Mecca, where they urged Husayn to take up arms. The actual revolt was triggered by the dispatch of Turkish troops to reinforce their garrison at Medina. Outside Medina, on June 5, 1916, Husayn's eldest son Ali and Faysal officially proclaimed the start of the Arab Revolt.

Joined by 30,000 tribesmen, Faysal immediately led an assault on the Ottoman garrison at Medina, but the Turks drove them off. The Arabs, however, cut the railway to the north of the city. To the south, Husayn led an attack on the 1,000-man Turkish garrison at Mecca, taking the city after three days of street fighting. Another Arab attack shortly thereafter, against the port city of Jiddah, was also successful. In September, the 3,000-man garrison at Taif, the last city in southern Hejaz held by the Turks, surrendered to Arab forces supported by British-supplied artillery.

On November 2, Husayn proclaimed himself "King of the Arab Countries." This created some embarrassment for the British government with the French. Finally, the Allies worked out a compromise by which they addressed Husayn as "King of the Hejaz." Husayn largely left leadership of the revolt to his four sons. A number of Arabs serving in the Ottoman Army who were taken prisoner in the fighting helped provide leadership for the so-called Arab Army. The military strength of its four main forces commanded by Husayn's sons fluctuated greatly, and few of the men involved were trained.

In October 1916, the Turks managed to drive the Arab Army south of Medina and reopened the railway. The British sent a party of advisers to Husayn. Captain T. E. Lawrence, an Arabist, became Faysal's official adviser and successfully urged him to resume the offensive. Rather than meet Turkish power head on, the two men initiated a series of hit-and-run raids over northern Arabia that took advantage of the support of the local populations and forced the Turks to divert increasing numbers of troops to the region.

In July 1917, Lawrence led an attack that captured Aqaba, which then became Faysal's chief base, while forces under Abdullah and Ali contained the Turkish garrison at Medina and protected Mecca. Faysal's northern wing of the Arab Army was the revolt's chief military force and acted on the right flank of Lieutenant

General Edmund Allenby's British forces in Palestine. In the autumn of 1917, Lawrence, who understood and effectively practiced guerrilla warfare, led a series of successful attacks on Turkish rail traffic. Allenby's calls for diversionary attacks by the Arab Army produced a series of raids that diverted some 23,000 Ottoman troops from the fighting in Palestine. Faysal also cooperated closely with Allenby in the Megiddo Offensive and, with 30,000 men, led the revolt's climactic action—the entrance into Damascus in October 1918.

The Arab Revolt fueled Arab nationalism. It helped free Arab lands from Turkish rule and led to the formation of Arab states. But the victorious Allies thwarted Husayn's ambitions. McMahon's pledge to Husayn preceded by six months the 1916 Sykes-Picot Agreement between the British and French governments, a breach of promises made to the Arabs that in effect set up British and French spheres of influence in the Middle East. Ultimately, much of the territory was awarded as mandates to Great Britain and France under the League of Nations. Faysal received Syria but was deposed and became king of Iraq under British protection. Abdullah became king of the newly created Transjordan. Husayn declared himself caliph of Islam in March 1924 but was forced to abdicate as king of the Hejaz to his son Ali when Abd al-Aziz al-Saud (Ibn Saud) conquered most of the Hejaz.

Spencer C. Tucker

See also: Balfour Declaration; British Mandate for Palestine; Lawrence, T. E.; League of Nations; McMahon-Husayn Correspondence; Sykes-Picot Agreement

Further Reading

Fromkin, David. *A Peace to End All Peace: The Fall of the Ottoman Empire and the Creation of the Modern Middle East.* New York: Avon, 1989.

Hourani, Albert. *A History of the Arab Peoples.* Cambridge, MA: Harvard University Press, 1991.

Tauber, Eliezer. *The Arab Movements in World War I.* London: Frank Cass, 1993.

Arab Revolt, 1936

A general revolt among Arabs in the British Mandate of Palestine. Although the Arab Revolt of 1936 was aimed primarily at British interests, attacks against Jews were not uncommon. The revolt was the culmination of growing Arab unrest over Jewish immigration and land purchases in Palestine and economic dislocation resulting from increased urbanization and industrialization. It was the most severe of a number of communal disturbances between Jews and Arabs dating from the early 1920s. Despite its failure, the Great Revolt marked the dawn of a distinctive Palestinian Arab nationalism.

The unrest was triggered in part by events outside the region. Growing anti-Semitism in Eastern Europe and Nazi control of Germany from 1933 led to an increase in Jewish immigration into Palestine. At the same time, growing land purchases by Zionists brought the expulsion of large numbers of Arab peasants from lands on which they had been tenant farmers. This was part of a deepening economic crisis as Palestinian agricultural exports to Europe and the United States declined during the worldwide Great Depression.

The revolt was centered on landless Arabs, often forced into slums around the cities. Its leaders came from the more politically conscious Arab elite, dominated by the Husayni family, led by Haj Amin al-Husayni, Grand Mufti of Jerusalem; and their rivals, the Nashashibis, represented by Fakhri al-Nashashibi. The revolt's true leadership, however, came from local Arab committees in Jerusalem and other population centers.

Tensions among Arabs, Jews, and British administrators in Palestine had been building for several months prior to the revolt's outbreak in April 1936, thanks not only to economic conditions but also to a surge of Islamic extremism led by Sheikh Izz al-Din al-Qassam, a Syrian-born, Egyptian-educated cleric who had been preaching fundamentalist Islam and calling for a jihad (holy war) against both Britons and Jews. His followers murdered a Jewish policeman near Gilboa, and al-Qassam was killed in a subsequent shootout with British troops on November 20, 1935. His death triggered Arab nationalist demonstrations throughout Palestine. At the same time, the discovery by the British of an arms cache in a shipment of cement barrels intended for a Jewish importer fed rumors that the Jews were arming for war against the Arabs. These developments pushed a tense atmosphere into outright rebellion. The revolt officially began in April 1936 in the hill country around Tulkarm and spread rapidly. The first six months claimed the lives of 200 Arabs, 80 Jews, and 28 British soldiers and policemen.

The initial British reaction was restrained. London hoped that the disturbances would blow over without scarring Anglo-Arab relations. Only in September 1936 did British authorities impose martial law. Eventually the government sent 20,000 troops from Britain and Egypt and recruited 2,700 Jewish supernumeraries to deal with the disturbances.

The Jewish Agency for Palestine worked to strengthen the Haganah, its self-defense force, and fortify Jewish settlements, leaving suppression of the revolt to the British. As the uprising continued and attacks on Jewish settlements increased, however, Palestinian Jews resorted to aggressive self-defense, including ambushes of rebel Arab bands and reprisals against neighboring Arab villages suspected of harboring guerrillas. This doctrine of disproportionate retaliation developed by the Zionist leadership during the revolt became a permanent fixture of Zionist military policy.

In the first months of the revolt, the British succeeded—through the use of night curfews, patrols, searches, and ambushes—in pushing Arab rebels out of the towns. By mid-May 1936, rural Palestine had become the center of gravity of the revolt and would remain so until its end in 1939. Leadership remained with the local committees. The Arab Higher Committee (AHC) was increasingly paralyzed by rivalries between the Husayni and Nashashibi clans but did provide money, arms, and rhetorical support.

By the autumn of 1937, some 9,000–10,000 Palestinian fighters were roaming the countryside. Internecine violence among rival families resulted in more deaths among the Arabs than did actions by the British or Zionists. The rebels' practice of extorting food and other valuables from Arab peasants damaged the rural economy and increasingly alienated the rebels from their base of support. To pacify the countryside, the British shrewdly exploited Arab divisions and employed combined British-Zionist Special Night Squads to ambush rebel bands, launch retaliatory strikes against Arab villages suspected of harboring guerrillas, and carry out targeted assassinations of rebel leaders.

The Arab Revolt collapsed in 1939 in the face of eroding support in the countryside, the arrest or exile of the senior leaders, lack of cohesion in the revolt's organization and leadership, and mounting British pressure. Some 5,000 Arabs, 400 Jews, and 200 British soldiers and officials died in the uprising. The revolt had profound consequences for the mandate and Palestinian Arabs and Jews. The uprising led London to send a commission to Palestine chaired by Lord William Robert Peel in late 1936. The commission's report of July 1937 proposed the partition of Palestine into a Jewish area and a much larger Arab area—the first time that partition had been advanced as a solution. Both sides essentially rejected the suggestion, though, and the British eventually backed away from it.

Palestinian Jews were shocked by implementation of the British White Paper of May 1939, which restricted Jewish immigration and land purchases and promised an independent Palestinian Arab state in ten years if the rights of the Jewish community were protected. From the Jewish perspective, the White Paper represented a surrender to Arab violence and intimidation. The White Paper also closed Palestine to European Jews at a time when anti-Jewish violence in Germany and Eastern Europe was intensifying. Indeed, the measure permanently damaged relations between Britain and the Jews in Palestine.

The worst damage, however, was to Palestinian Arabs. Although the Arab Revolt gained a permanent place in Arab nationalist mythology, Palestinians were left with the consequences of a failed revolt. Most of the political leadership was in prison, had been exiled, or exited politics. Blood feuds between families that had supported the uprising and those that were opposed to it disrupted Palestinian society and paralyzed political life for years.

Walter F. Bell

See also: Arab Higher Committee; British Mandate for Palestine; British White Paper; Jewish Agency; Palestinians; Zionism

Further Reading

Gelvin, James L. *The Israel-Palestine Conflict: One Hundred Years of War.* New York: Cambridge University Press, 2005.

Morris, Benny. *Righteous Victims: A History of the Zionist-Arab Conflict, 1881–1999.* New York: Knopf, 1999.

Porath, Yehoshua. *The Palestinian National Movement, 1929–1939: From Riot to Rebellion.* London: Cass, 1974.

Swedenburg, Ted. *Memories of Revolt: The 1936–1939 Rebellion and the Palestinian National Past.* Minneapolis: University of Minnesota Press, 1995.

Arab Spring

A wave of protests in Arab states demanding political and economic reforms, sometimes resulting in violent uprisings. They began in Tunisia, when a food vendor, Mohamed Bouazizi, burned himself to death. Popular protests in January 2011 led to the overthrow of President Zine Ben-Ali, who had ruled the country since 1987. Similar popular uprisings soon spread to other countries in the Middle East. In

Egypt, mass protests ended the thirty-year reign of Hosni Mubarak. Egypt's first democratically elected government was dominated by Islamists, but it was overthrown a year later by the military. Since then, Egypt has been ruled by General Abdel Fattah Saeed Hussein Khalil El-Sisi, a coup leader, who won a suspiciously high 97 percent of the vote in new elections.

In Libya, protests were forcefully repressed by Muammar Gadhafi, who had ruled since 1969. Within weeks, rebels controlled a number of major cities. When Gadhafi was about to route the rebel stronghold of Benghazi, the United Nations authorized the North Atlantic Treaty Organization (NATO) to intervene. Gadhafi was captured and killed weeks later by rebel forces, but Libya has faced domestic instability ever since.

In early 2011, mass protests demanding economic and political reforms also broke out in Syria. President Bashir al-Assad responded with violent repression. Within weeks, civil war broke out, pitting the Assad regime, whose core supporters come from the country's minority Alawites, against a mix of opposition forces ranging from secularists to radical Islamists. As of mid-2019, Assad was poised to retain power. His success was made possible by the active military support of Hezbollah, Iran, and Russia. In time, the Islamic State of Iraq and Syria (ISIS) became the most formidable opposition force threatening Assad's regime. When ISIS established control over a large section of Syria and Iraq, the United States and others joined the fray to defeat it, helping the Assad regime to survive. Popular protests also occurred in Palestine, Jordan, Oman, Bahrain, Kuwait, and Saudi Arabia, but rulers there were able to either quickly repress or in other ways mitigate the dissent.

Robert C. DiPrizio

See also: Arab Spring, Effects on Israel; Arab Spring, Effects on Palestine; Egypt; Jordan; Lebanon; Syria

Further Reading

Danahar, Paul. *The New Middle East: The World After the Arab Spring.* New York: Bloomsbury Press, 2015.

Haas, Mark L., and Lesch, David W. *The Arab Spring: The Hope and Reality of the Uprisings.* 2nd ed. New York: Routledge, 2017.

Worth, Robert F. *A Rage for Order: The Middle East in Turmoil, from Tahrir Square to ISIS.* New York: Farrar, Straus and Giroux, 2016.

Arab Spring, Effects on Israel

The Arab Spring has greatly affected Israel's strategic position vis-à-vis neighboring Arab states, Iran, and the Palestinians. Initially, many assumed that the Arab Spring would usher in unwelcomed changes to Israel's security environment. The most obvious threat was the overthrow of the Hosni Mubarak regime in Egypt and the rise of the Islamist Muslim Brotherhood. For thirty years, Israel and Egypt had reaped the rewards of a peace treaty. Indeed, the 1979 treaty effectively removed any existential threat to Israel posed by the Arab world because without Egypt, no array of Arab states could destroy it. For its part, Egypt received tens of billions of dollars in U.S. military and economic aid. The peace between Israel and Egypt was a cold one on a societal level; anti-Semitic attitudes are still as prevalent in Egypt as anti-Arab attitudes are in Israel. Still, the governments cooperated on security issues. Their shared border remained stable, Israeli warships made regular use of the Suez Canal, Cairo and Jerusalem coordinated policies toward the Gaza Strip, and both worked to undermine Iran's regional influence. When the Muslim Brotherhood took power, all this was placed in jeopardy. Many feared that if the new Egyptian regime was to be more representative of the people's will, the peace treaty with Israel would be in peril. Few expected war, but many predicted that cooperation across a wide array of issues would decrease and Israel would be left more insecure. Some feared that the Muslim Brotherhood would actively support Hamas, a splinter organization. Such fears turned out to be overblown, however, because the Brotherhood's grip on power was short lived and did not fundamentally change Egypt's policies toward Israel. After a year in power, the Brotherhood was overthrown by the Egyptian military, which then installed one of its own as president.

The new regime quickly promised to meet all its obligations under the peace treaty with Israel. Still, Egypt's control over the Sinai Desert was dramatically undermined after Mubarak's overthrow, which opened up space for Islamist militants to operate. Moreover, the fall of the Libyan regime triggered a flood of weapons into the region, some of which have found their way into the hands of anti-Israeli forces in the Sinai and Gaza. Still, none of the security threats to Israel triggered by Egypt's political convulsions have amounted to much. Indeed, the two countries are cooperating more closely now than ever to combat mutual enemies in the Sinai and Gaza, and to undermine Iranian influence in the region.

Israel's strategic position with Jordan has changed little since the Arab Spring. These countries signed a peace treaty in 1994 and had cordial relations long before that. Initially, the Hashemite kingdom faced widespread unrest among some Palestinian tribes and Islamist groups protesting economic privation, governmental corruption, and Jordan's relations with Israel. Protesters have also called for more public input into the governing system. King Abdullah has cracked down on some dissenters while pursuing high-profile corruption cases and shuffling his cabinet ministers numerous times. Hundreds of thousands of Syrian and Iraqi refugees have proved to be a great economic burden on Jordan. Israel would be rightly concerned if Jordan's ruling family were to fall from power because the status quo is very much in Israel's favor; but there is little reason to believe that radical political change is imminent, despite ongoing protests pressing for political and economic reform.

Events on Israel's northern borders with Lebanon and Syria have been far more consequential. In 2011, protesters demanded economic and political reforms in Syria. President Assad violently repressed demonstrations, and within weeks, a civil war erupted which pitted the president, whose core supporters come from the country's minority Alawites, against a mishmash of opposition forces ranging from secularists to radical Islamists.

After nearly eight years of fighting, Assad is poised to retain power. His success was made possible by the active military support of Hezbollah, Iran, and Russia. Syria's longstanding relations with Hezbollah and Iran have grown closer during the civil war, making Syria a target of increased Israeli incursions. Iran has built military bases and stationed troops and missile systems throughout the country. It is also reportedly supplying Hezbollah with more capable weapons, including sophisticated missile guidance systems. Israel has launched hundreds of air strikes into Syria to disrupt the delivery of material to Hezbollah and to degrade Iran's growing military presence.

Israeli prime minister Benjamin Netanyahu has cultivated close relations with Russian president Vladimir Putin, who has sought to protect Russian interests in Syria by propping up the Assad regime. Netanyahu has repeatedly asked Putin to help reduce Iran's presence in Syria, but it is unclear how much Russia can and will do about the matter. Assad has even less control than Russia over Iran's presence in Syria, and for the moment, he still needs Tehran's support to stay in power. Thus, Israel's primary security concerns in mid-2019—Iran's growing presence in Syria and Hezbollah's increased fighting capabilities—are direct results of the instability wrought by the Arab Spring.

For some Israelis, the violence and unforeseen results of the Arab Spring reaffirm that the Middle East is too dangerous a neighborhood for them to give up territory. Israel captured the Golan Heights during the 1967 Arab-Israeli War and annexed it in 1981. In the 1990s, Israeli leaders flirted with returning the Golan to Syria in exchange for peace but negotiations failed. Some have noted that if Israel had returned the Golan Heights to Syria, Israel would have lost an important buffer zone protecting its northern cities from the mayhem of the Syrian civil war.

In 2019, the United States became the only country to recognize Israel's claim of sovereignty over the Golan, noting that by doing so, it is simply recognizing facts on the ground—that Israel controls the area and that its security requires maintaining that control indefinitely. Many have similarly argued the Arab Spring has created so much uncertainty along Israel's borders that Israel cannot be expected to negotiate a two-state solution with the Palestinians because it cannot accept the risks associated with giving up control of the West Bank. Indeed, ending the occupation and resolving conflict with the Palestinians have become far less pressing matters for Israeli governments. Instead, more and more prominent Israelis now call for annexation of all or large parts of the West Bank, and very few advocate for a two-state solution to the Israeli-Palestinian conflict anymore. During both of his reelection campaigns in 2019, Prime Minister Netanyahu promised to annex Israeli settlements in the West Bank.

The Palestinian issue used to be a high priority for most Arab countries, but since the U.S. invasion of Iraq in 2003 and the Arab Spring, many have become more concerned with Iran's spreading influence and have quietly been working with Israel to counter that threat. Israel has been encouraging these Arab states to pressure Palestinian leaders to accept a peace deal that is even less generous than previous offers. The Donald Trump administration has been applying similar pressure. It scuttled the Barack Obama–era nuclear deal with Iran, which was unpopular with many Arab leaders, and is encouraging these leaders to strong-arm Palestinians into accepting Trump's "deal of the century," which offers Palestinians far less than statehood. It remains to be seen if Arab leaders will publicly accept a plan that does not give Palestinians a viable state with East Jerusalem as its capital, because this issue still resonates in the Arab and Islamic world.

Robert C. DiPrizio

See also: Arab Spring; Arab Spring, Effects on Palestine; Egypt; Jordan; Lebanon; One-State Solution; Palestine; Syria; Two-State Solution

Further Reading

Beck, Martin. "'Watching and Waiting' and 'Much Ado About Nothing'? Making Sense of the Israeli Response to the Arab Uprisings." *Palgrave Communications* 2, no. 16079 (2016). https://www.nature.com/articles/palcomms201679.

Scheinmann, Gabriel. "The Real Big Winner of the Arab Spring." *The Tower Magazine*, no. 7 (October 2013). http://www.thetower.org/article/the-real-big-winner-of-the-arab-spring/.

Sharp, Jeremy M. "Egypt: Background and U.S. Relations." *Congressional Research Service*, updated March 12, 2019. https://fas.org/sgp/crs/mideast/RL33003.pdf.

Sharp, Jeremy M. "Jordan: Background and U.S. Relations." *Congressional Research Service*, updated April 9, 2019. https://fas.org/sgp/crs/mideast/RL33546.pdf.

Zanotti, Jim. "Israel: Background and U.S. Relations in Brief." *Congressional Research Service*, updated September 18, 2019. https://fas.org/sgp/crs/mideast/R44245.pdf.

Arab Spring, Effects on Palestine

In modern-day parlance, *Palestine* refers to the West Bank, East Jerusalem, and the Gaza Strip, an area in which 5 million Palestinians live under Israeli control. Israel captured these territories in the 1967 Arab-Israeli War. Palestinian leaders declared independence in 1988, and over 130 states recognize Palestine as a sovereign state. However, in fact it remains under Israeli occupation to this day.

Palestine has fared poorly since the Arab Spring, in part because Palestinian popular protests have been in vain, and in part because the Palestinian national cause has been eclipsed by other more pressing matters. Inspired by mass uprisings elsewhere, Palestinians in Gaza and the West Bank went to the streets in 2011 to call for reconciliation between rivals Hamas and Fatah. Another wave of demonstrations in 2012 railed against poor living conditions, inept governance, corruption, and Israel's continued occupation. These protests, and others since, have had few tangible effects. Hamas and Fatah, the two dominant factions in Palestine, remain unwilling to overcome or incapable of overcoming their differences, improving the living conditions of their constituents, or achieving Palestinian independence.

However, the most deleterious effect that the Arab Spring has had on Palestine has been the creation of regional instability. In the minds of many Arab leaders, maintaining internal security, combating militants, and restraining Iran's growing influence in the region have eclipsed Palestine as priority concerns. This insecurity has afforded Israel opportunities to pursue back-door diplomacy with its Arab neighbors and drive a wedge between Palestinians and their major Arab benefactors. Meanwhile, in Egypt, political upheavals, economic struggles, and rising terrorist threats at home have encouraged President Abdel Fattah Saeed Hussein Khalil El-Sisi to focus on internal affairs. The fall of the Hosni Mubarak regime, and the brief rule of the Muslim Brotherhood, weakened Egypt's grip on the Sinai Peninsula, where militants have moved in. Egypt now is working closely with Israel to combat these groups and restore stability to the Egyptian-Israeli border. This reliance on Israel hampers Egypt's ability to promote pro-Palestine policies.

Jordanian leaders too have focused much of their attention on domestic concerns since 2011, when prominent tribal leaders broke with tradition to criticize the monarchy publicly. Periodic mass protests, including in 2018, have decried corruption and demanded economic and governmental reforms. King Abdullah II also struggles to manage the economic and security challenges associated with hosting millions of refugees fleeing war-torn areas like Iraq, Yemen, and Syria, the latter of which deteriorated into civil war when mass protests in early 2011 were violently repressed by the government.

As of mid-2019, after eight years of fighting, the Assad regime in Syria has regained control of most of the country. This has been made possible in no small part by the active military support of Iran, the sworn enemy of Israel and many of its Arab neighbors. Israel has repeatedly struck Iranian arms transfers to Hezbollah, the Lebanese paramilitary organization that has been fighting Israel since it invaded Lebanon in 1982. Israel has also struck numerous sites where it believes that Iran is establishing permanent bases. For Israel, any expansion of Iranian influence is unacceptable. Many Arab countries also fear the spread of Iranian influence, in part because it promotes Shia Islam, while most Arabs embrace Sunni Islam. Saudi Arabia and other Gulf states have been actively supporting rebel forces in Syria, including radical Islamist groups. Israel has quietly been assisting Saudi Arabia and the United Arab Emirates (UAE) in their proxy wars against Iran in Syria and Yemen.

Many Israelis believe that Tehran is developing nuclear weapons to be used to destroy Israel. A nuclear-armed Iran also scares Arab governments. Israeli and Arab leaders have thus found common cause in pressing the Donald Trump administration to abandon the Barack Obama–era multilateral nuclear deal, which they believe did little to restrain Iran. Trump scuttled that deal in May 2018. Many Israelis now argue that progress on the Palestinian issue is no longer a prerequisite for normalizing relations with Arab states, which are growing increasingly reliant on Israel to fight their common enemies and to maintain good relations with Washington. Normalized relations with Israel could also afford Arab states' access to the most technologically advanced and dynamic economy in the region.

Israelis have long argued that they have no partner for peace among the Palestinians, as evidenced by the rejection of past "generous" offers and repeated Palestinian terrorist attacks. They also argue the divisions between Hamas and Fatah make negotiating a deal impossible. By creating enough strategic uncertainty in the region, events related to the Arab Spring convinced many that Israel cannot accept the risks associated with a two-state solution.

As of this writing, the Trump administration is preparing to unveil its "deal of the century," intended to finally settle the Israeli-Palestinian conflict. Palestinians have declared Trump unfit to serve as an interlocutor because of his extreme bias toward Israel, as evidenced by his decisions to recognize Jerusalem as the Israeli capital, to cut nearly all Palestinian aid, and to appoint pro-Israel partisans to head up his negotiating team. Palestinian leaders have already declared the Trump plan dead on arrival. Nonetheless, Israeli and U.S. officials have strongly encouraged Arab leaders (nearly all of whom depend on Jerusalem and Washington for security assistance in one form or another) to pressure Palestinians to accept the Trump plan, which does not offer Palestinians independence. It remains to be seen if Arab leaders will publicly advocate for a plan that does not call for a viable Palestinian state, with East Jerusalem as its capital because this issue still resonates among the masses in the Arab and Islamic world.

Robert C. DiPrizio

See also: Arab Spring, Effects on Israel; Egypt; Israel; Jordan; Lebanon; One-State Solution; Palestine; Syria; Two-State Solution

Further Reading

Batrawy, Aya, and Gambrell, Jon. "Gulf Arab states Support Palestinians, but Also Form Subtle Ties to Israel." *Christian Science Monitor*, May 16, 2018.

Entous, Adan. "Donald Trump's New World Order." *The New Yorker Magazine*, June 18, 2018.

Katz, Mark. "The Arab Spring and the Israeli/Palestinian Conflict: International Implications." April 15, 2013, http://eng.globalaffairs.ru/number/The-Arab-Spring-and-the-IsraeliPalestinian-Conflict-international-implications-15933.

Lovatt, Hugh. "Palestinian Issue and Israel in the Post Arab Uprisings Regional (Dis)Order." August 22, 2016. http://www.sharqforum.org/2016/08/22/palestinian-issue-and-israel-in-the-post-arab-uprisings-regional-disorder.

Arafat, Yasser

Palestinian nationalist and leader of the Palestine Liberation Organization (PLO) from 1969 to 2004. Yasser Arafat, officially named Mohammed Abdel Raouf Arafat al-Qudwa al-Husayni, was born on August 24, 1929 (though records differ on this point). Arafat always stated that he was born in Jerusalem, but Israeli officials began to claim in the 1970s that he was born in Cairo, in order to discredit him. He went by the name "Yasser" as a child.

Arafat's father was a Palestinian Egyptian textile merchant. Neither Arafat nor his siblings were close to their father. His mother, Zahwa, also a Palestinian, was a member of a family that had lived in Jerusalem for generations. She died when Arafat was five years old, and he then lived with his mother's brother in Jerusalem. Arafat vividly remembered British soldiers invading his uncle's house one night, destroying possessions and beating its residents. When Arafat was nine years old, his father brought him back to Cairo, where his older sister raised him.

As a teenager in Cairo, Arafat became involved in smuggling arms to Palestine to aid those struggling against both the British authorities and the Jews living there. He attended the Fuad I University (later Cairo University) in Cairo, but he left to fight in Gaza against Israel in the 1948 Arab-Israeli War (also known as the *Israeli War of Independence*). When the Arabs lost the war and Israel was firmly established, Arafat was inconsolable. He briefly attended the University of Texas, but then he returned to Cairo University to study engineering. He spent most of his time with fellow Palestinian students, spreading his hopes for a free Palestinian state.

Arafat became president of the Union of Palestinian Students, holding that position from 1952 to 1956. He joined the Muslim Brotherhood in 1952. He finally

A portrait of a young Yasser Arafat as seen on the Israeli separation wall in Kalandia, West Bank, on May 29, 2009. Arafat remains popular throughout Palestine for his contributions to the Palestinian cause. (Rrodrickbeiler/Dreamstime.com)

graduated from college in 1956 and spent a short time working in Egypt. During the 1956 Suez Crisis, he served as a second lieutenant in the Egyptian army. In 1957, he moved to Kuwait, where he worked as an engineer and formed his own contracting company. The next year he founded the Fatah organization, an underground guerrilla group dedicated to the liberation of Palestine. In 1964, he quit his job and moved to Jordan to devote all his energies to the promotion of Palestinian nationhood and to organize raids into Israel. The PLO was founded that same year.

In 1968, the Israel Defense Forces (IDF) attacked Fatah at the small Jordanian village of al-Karameh. The Palestinians eventually forced the Israelis back, and Arafat's face appeared on the cover of *Time* magazine as the leader of the Palestinian movement. In consequence, Palestinians embraced Fatah, and Arafat became their hero. He was appointed chairman of the PLO the next year, and within four years, he controlled both the military (the Palestine Liberation Army, or PLA) and political branches of the organization.

By 1970, Palestinians had assembled a well-organized unofficial state within Jordan. However, King Husayn of Jordan deemed them a threat to security and sent his army to evict them. Arafat enlisted the aid of Syria, while Jordan called on the United States for assistance. On September 24, 1970, the PLO agreed to a cease-fire and agreed to leave Jordan. Arafat moved the organization to Lebanon, which had a weak government that was not likely to restrict the PLO's operations. The PLO soon began launching occasional attacks across the Israeli border.

Arafat did not approve of overseas attacks because they gave the PLO a bad image abroad. He publicly dissociated the group from Black September, the organization that killed eleven Israeli athletes at the 1972 Munich Olympics, although there is now evidence of his involvement. In 1974, he limited the PLO's attacks to Israel, the Gaza Strip, and the West Bank. Although Israel claimed that Arafat was responsible for the numerous terrorist attacks that occurred within the country during the 1970s, he denied responsibility. In 1974, he spoke before the United Nations General Assembly as the leader of the PLO and appealed for help establishing independent statehood for Palestine.

During the Lebanese civil war, the PLO initially sided with the Lebanese National Front against the Lebanese forces, who were supported by Israel and backed by Defense Minister Ariel Sharon. As such, when Israeli forces invaded southern Lebanon, the PLO ended up fighting the Israelis and then the Syrian militia group Amal. Thousands of Palestinians, many of them civilians, were killed during the struggle, and the PLO was forced to leave Lebanon in 1982 and relocate to Tunisia, where it remained until 1993.

During the 1980s, Iraq and Saudi Arabia donated millions of dollars to Arafat to help him rebuild the PLO. Arafat approved the First Intifada (1987) against Israel. In 1988, the Palestinians declared Palestinian statehood at a meeting in Algiers. Arafat then announced that they would renounce terrorism and recognize the state of Israel. The Palestinian National Council elected Arafat president of this new, unrecognized state in 1989.

Arafat and the Israelis conducted peace negotiations at the Madrid Conference in 1991. Although negotiations were temporarily set back when the PLO supported Iraq in the 1991 Persian Gulf War, over the next two years, the two parties held a number of secret discussions. These negotiations led to the 1993 Oslo Peace Accords, in which Israel agreed to Palestinian self-rule in the Gaza Strip and the West Bank. Arafat also officially recognized the existence of the state of Israel. Despite the condemnation of many Palestinian nationalists, who viewed Arafat's moves as a sellout, the peace process appeared to be moving in a positive direction in the mid-1990s. Israeli troops withdrew from parts of the Gaza Strip and Jericho in May 1994. Arafat was elected leader of the new Palestinian Authority (PA) in January 1996, with 88 percent of the vote, in elections that were by all accounts free and fair (but with severely limited competition because Hamas and other opposition groups refused to participate).

Later that same year, Benjamin Netanyahu of the Likud Party became prime minister of Israel, and the peace process began to unravel. Netanyahu, a hardline conservative, blamed Palestinians for numerous suicide bombings against Israeli citizens. He also did not trust Arafat, who he charged was supporting terrorists. Arafat continued negotiations with the Israelis into 2000. That July, with Ehud Barak having replaced Netanyahu as Israeli prime minister, Arafat traveled to the United States to meet with Barak and President Bill Clinton at the Camp David Summit. Negotiations failed to produce an agreement, and soon the peace process collapsed and the Second (al-Aqsa) Intifada began.

From the beginning of the Second Intifada in 2000, Arafat was a besieged man who appeared to be losing influence and control within the Palestinian and larger

Arab communities. His inability or unwillingness to stop Palestinian terrorist attacks against Israel resulted in his virtual captivity at his Ramallah headquarters from 2002 onward. In declining health by 2004, the PLO leader was flown to France for medical treatment. Arafat died on November 11, 2004, at Percy Military Hospital outside Paris.

There has been much conspiratorial conjecture concerning his mysterious illness and death. Rumors persist that he was assassinated by poisoning. In November 2012, three teams of forensic investigators (from Russia, France, and Switzerland) conducted tests on Arafat's body and the soil from his grave, located at his former headquarters in the city of Ramallah. The Swiss team claimed to have found abnormally high traces of polonium, a radioactive element, in Arafat's body. Other experts, however, claim that the likelihood of contamination of the test results was high and that the findings did not definitely prove that Arafat died from polonium poisoning. A Russian expert later concluded that he died from natural causes. Despite these investigations, assassination theories persist.

Amy Hackney Blackwell

See also: Camp David Summit, 2000; Fatah; Intifada, First; Intifada, Second; Oslo Accords; Palestine; Palestinian Authority; Palestine Liberation Army; Palestine Liberation Organization

Further Reading

Aburish, Said K. *Arafat: From Defender to Dictator.* New York and London: Bloomsbury, 1998.

Hart, Alan. *Arafat: A Political Biography.* Rev. ed. London: Sidgwick & Jackson, 1994.

Peleg, Ilan, ed. *Middle East Peace Process: Interdisciplinary Perspectives.* Albany: State University of New York Press, 1998.

Sharif, Bassam Abu. *Arafat and the Dream of Palestine: An Insider's Account.* New York: St. Martin's Press, 2009.

Ashrawi, Hanan

Palestinian political leader and activist. Hanan Ashrawi was born Hanan Mikhail on October 8, 1946, in Ramallah, in what was then the British Mandate for Palestine (now the West Bank). A Christian Palestinian, she attended the Quakers' Friends Girls School and then the American University of Beirut in Lebanon, where she received a master's degree in English literature in 1970. Soon after, she earned her PhD in medieval studies at the University of Virginia. Returning home, she took a position at Birzeit University in the West Bank, where she worked until 1995, serving at times as the chair of the English department and as dean of the College of Arts.

In 1969, Ashrawi attended an international conference in Jordan, where she first met Palestine Liberation Organization (PLO) chairman Yasser Arafat. She subsequently formed an outspoken ideological commitment to the PLO. Politically active since her student days, Ashrawi joined the General Union of Palestinian Students and the General Union of Palestinian Women. Committed to improving the living conditions of her compatriots, which had deteriorated sharply since the 1967 Six-Day War, she actively entered the political arena following Israel's 1982 invasion of Lebanon, in which thousands of Palestinian refugees in Beirut were killed. She emerged as a principal voice of the Palestinian people on the international news circuit during the years of the First Intifada.

Articulate and eloquent, Ashrawi helped to dispel stereotypes about Palestinians. She made frequent appearances on American television during 1988–1991. Despite her ties to the PLO, Ashrawi used her strong connections with U.S. secretary of state James Baker III to override Israeli objections to her presence at Middle East peace talks in Madrid that October.

Despite having conflicts with Arafat regarding his autocratic leadership style, Ashrawi remained a committed and active spokesperson for the Palestinian struggle. She was elected as an independent candidate to the newly established Palestinian Legislative Council in 1996. She served briefly as higher education minister in Arafat's government, which she criticized as corrupt. Thus she parted ways with Arafat and left her post in 1998. She helped found the Ramallah-based nongovernmental organization (NGO) Miftah, the Palestinian Initiative for the Promotion of Global Dialogue and Democracy, which works to promote dialogue, Palestinian nation-building, democratic empowerment, and human rights. In July 2001, the Arab League appointed her as the organization's media commissioner, a newly established post. Ashrawi remains one of the best-known spokespersons for the Palestinian cause.

Spencer C. Tucker

See also: Arafat, Yasser; Intifada, First; Palestinian Authority; Palestine Liberation Organization

Further Reading

Ashrawi, Hanan. *This Side of Peace: A Personal Account.* New York: Simon and Schuster, 1996.

Victor, Barbara. *Voice of Reason: Hanan Ashrawi and Peace in the Middle East.* New York: Harcourt Brace, 1994.

Assad, Bashar al-

President of the Syrian Arab Republic (2000–present). Bashar al-Assad was born in Damascus, Syria, on September 11, 1965. His father was Hafez al-Assad, the strongman president of Syria from 1971 to 2000. The Alawi sect to which Assad belongs encompasses approximately 12 percent of the Syrian population. Bashar was not as well known to the Syrian public as his popular elder brother, Basil, who died in an automobile accident in 1994.

Bashar al-Assad continued a hardline position toward Israel, along with sympathies toward the Palestinian cause. Yet domestically, the public saw the president as maintaining an honorable cold peace with Israel, deemed necessary for economic development. Bashar and his father, Hafez, conditioned any formal peace deal with Israel on the latter returning all the Golan Heights, much of which Israel captured in 1967.

Various attempts to negotiate a peace deal have floundered, though, in part because of Israel has been unwilling relinquish all the Golan, a strategic plateau that overlooks much of northern Israel and from which important water sources flow into the country. Given the events of the Syrian civil war and the activity of Israel's enemies near its northern border, Israel is even more determined now to retain control of the Golan. Israel annexed the territory in 1981, but it took until 2019 for the United States to recognize Israel's claim to sovereignty over the Golan Heights. The rest of the international community still refuses to recognize Israel's annexation.

Syria used to be a power broker in Lebanon but when former Lebanese prime minister Rafik Hariri was assassinated in a bombing in February 2005, suspicions fell on Syria. Anti-Syrian Lebanese demonstrations led to a withdrawal of Syrian troops in April 2005, thereby ending a long period of direct and indirect influence over the country.

The Arab Spring revolts that erupted in Tunisia and Egypt quickly spread to Syria in 2011. Assad cracked down hard on protesters, and civil war broke out, complicated by the rapid rise of the Islamic State of Iraq and Syria (ISIS), which briefly took control of large swaths of the country. Assad repeatedly used chemical weapons against his own people, much as his father had decades earlier. With the help of Iran, Hezbollah, and Russia, Bashar al-Assad has managed to retain his grip on power. Estimates are that over 500,000 people have died since war broke out in March 2011.

Sherifa Zuhur

See also: Arab Spring; Arab Spring, Effects on Israel; Assad, Hafez al-; Hezbollah; Syria

Further Reading

Darraj, Susan Muaddi. *Bashar al-Assad*. New York: Chelsea House, 2005.

George, Alan. *Syria: Neither Bread nor Freedom*. London: Zed, 2003.

Leverett, Flynt. *Inheriting Syria: Bashar's Trial by Fire*. Washington, DC: Brookings Institution Press, 2005.

Assad, Hafez al-

Longtime president of Syria (1971–2000). Hafez al-Assad rose from an impoverished background to eventually become the president of Syria. He began his political career by joining the Ba'ath Party at age sixteen. He was an Alawite, a member of a small sect of Shia Islam. However, as a secular party, the Ba'ath Party actively recruited members from all sects and branches of Islam, as well as from Christian groups. Ba'athism also opposed imperialism and colonialism and espoused nonalignment except with Arab countries.

He graduated from the Syrian Military Academy as an Air Force pilot in early 1955 and received advanced fighter training by the Soviet military. Assad was exiled to Egypt (1959–1961) after he opposed the union of Syria and Egypt that created the United Arab Republic. Assad joined with other military officers to lead a Ba'athist coup (1963). He became the commander of the Syrian Air Force in 1964. A new ruling military junta removed the remaining Ba'ath Party founders after another coup in 1966, led by a group of Alawite military officers that included Assad. He was elevated to minister of defense in 1966 and then seized control of the government in November 1970. He remained president until his death in 2000. Under his rule, political dissenters were subject to arrest, torture, and execution.

Assad insisted throughout his presidency on the return of the whole of the Golan Heights as a condition for a peace deal with Israel, something that Israel consistently resisted. Still, Assad ensured that the Golan border remained largely quiet, instead working through proxies in Lebanon like Hezbollah and certain radical Palestinian groups to attack Israel periodically. He opposed all peace accords between Palestinians and Israelis, as well as the Israeli-Jordanian peace treaty of 1994.

Assad sent troops into Lebanon in 1976 to end the civil war there and assumed a permanent peacekeeping presence under the sponsorship of the Arab League. Israel's invasion and occupation of southern Lebanon (1982–2000) allowed Assad to impose changes in the constitution of Lebanon that granted Muslims equal representation with the minority Christian population in the Lebanese government, while securing Assad's virtual control of Lebanon. The only major internal threat that Assad faced was a 1982 rebellion in Hamah, which he suppressed by dispersing poison gas, killing 10,000–35,000 civilians. Assad died of a heart attack in 2000 and was succeeded by his son, Bashar.

Richard M. Edwards

See also: Arab-Israeli War, 1967; Assad, Bashar al-; Golan Heights; Hezbollah; Lebanon; Syria

Further Reading

George, Alan. *Syria: Neither Bread nor Freedom*. London: Zed, 2003.

Seale, Patrick. *Assad of Syria: The Struggle for the Middle East*. Berkeley: University of California Press, 1990.

Smith, Charles D. *Palestine and the Arab-Israeli Conflict: A History with Documents*, 9th ed. New York: Bedford/St. Martin's, 2017.

Assyrian Conquest of Israel

Conquest of the Kingdom of Israel by the Assyrian Empire, which culminated around 722 BCE and resulted in the mass deportation of Jews in the region. The Kingdom of Israel consisted of ten of the twelve tribes of Israel associated with the sons of Jacob listed in Genesis 49. These tribes were Reuben, Simeon, Dan, Naphtali, Gad, Asher, Issachar, Zebulun, Manasseh, and Ephraim. They split with the tribes of Judah and Levi after Solomon's son, Rehoboam, was rejected as king by the tribes living in the north of the country. The rejection came as a result of Rehoboam refusing to acquiesce to demands of the northern tribes for equitable working conditions. This split, depicted in 2 Chronicles 10, occurred around 930 BCE and resulted in two Hebrew kingdoms: the Kingdom of Israel, also referred to as the Northern Kingdom, and the Kingdom of Judah, also known as the Southern Kingdom.

At about the same time as the split in Israel, the Assyrian Empire was recovering from its Bronze Age decline and entering what is now considered the Neo-Assyrian period. Starting around 911 BCE and lasting until around 609 BCE, when the Assyrian Empire was defeated in the Medo-Babylonian War, the empire was ascendant and subjugated its neighbors in all directions. Assyrian dominance in this period was attributed to transportation, communication, weapons, and battlefield reforms that led to significant skill in siege warfare. Neither the Northern Kingdom nor the Southern Kingdom was immune to Assyrian aggression, but while the Assyrians completely conquered the Northern Kingdom during this period, they were unable to conquer Jerusalem, a fact that biblical accounts attribute to divine intervention.

The Assyrians, led by Tilglath-Pilneser III, established dominance over the Northern Kingdom starting in approximately 740 BCE through military conquest that resulted in the Kingdom of Israel being made an Assyrian vassal state. In line with Assyrian practice, parts of the tribes in the Northern Kingdom were deported to other areas of the empire to dissuade resistance by the conquered people. Almost twenty years later, King Hoshea betrayed the Assyrian king Shalmaneser by refusing to pay tribute and also by trying to establish an alliance with Egypt against Assyria. This resulted in a three-year siege of Samaria, the ruling city of the Northern Kingdom, by the Assyrians and after the city's fall, the rest of the Kingdom of Israel was deported and scattered throughout the Assyrian Empire as punishment for their rebellion. This event is documented in 2 Kings 17 and by artifacts found from the Assyrian Empire; it has become known as "the loss of ten tribes of Israel" because, unlike the Babylonian exile of the Kingdom of Judah, the ten tribes of Israel were not allowed to return to their lands. This has resulted in many claims of Jewish descent by groups attributed to the lost tribes and some religious traditions espousing a view that the tribes will return with the coming of the Messiah.

Hugh Gardenier

See also: Babylonian Conquest of Judah; Israelite Conquest of Canaan; Kingdom of Judah

Further Reading

Benite, Zvi Ben-Dor. *The Ten Lost Tribes: A World History.* Oxford: Oxford University Press, 2009.

Brereton, Gareth. *I Am Ashurbanipal: King of the World, King of Assyria.* New York: Thames & Hudson, 2018.

Genesis 49, 2 Chronicles 10, 2 Kings 17. *The Bible, English Standard Version.* Wheaton, IL: Good News Publishers, 2008.

Shavitsky, Ziva. *The Mystery of the Ten Lost Tribes: A Critical Survey of Historical and Archaeological Records Relating to the People of Israel in Exile in Syria, Mesopotamia and Persia up to ca. 300 BCE.* Newcastle, UK: Cambridge Scholars Publishing, 2012.

B

B'Tselem

Israeli human rights organization. B'Tselem, The Israeli Information Center for Human Rights in the Occupied Territories, aims to promote human rights, democracy, liberty, and equality through ending the occupation. The organization was founded in 1989 and is run today by executive director Hagai El-Ad, alongside thirty-eight staff-members. For most of its existence, B'Tselem has focused its activities on documenting Israeli violations of Palestinians' human rights in the Occupied Palestinian Territories (OPT; i.e., West Bank, East Jerusalem, and Gaza). As of 2018, however, B'Tselem has shifted toward demanding an unequivocal end to the occupation. The organization aims to achieve this goal through deconstructing the apparatuses that enable the occupation and by challenging its legitimacy, both in Israel and abroad. B'Tselem is internationally recognized for its work on behalf of human rights and has been awarded numerous honors, including the Carter-Menil Award for Human Rights (jointly with Al-Haq, a Palestinian human-rights organization); the Danish PL Foundation Human Rights Award (jointly with Al-Haq); and the Stockholm Human Rights Award.

Despite numerous smear campaigns that question B'Tselem's sources of funding, the organization is an independent, nonpartisan nongovernmental organization (NGO) that primarily receives funding from European and North American foundations, as well as individuals. B'Tselem disseminates information and media about a variety of issues affecting Palestinians' human rights in the OPT. It has recently issued reports on topics such as unlawful military strikes on civilians, land confiscation practices, torture, the Israeli military court system, the separation wall, settlements, repression of Palestinian popular protest, checkpoints, the permit regime, and the denial of Palestinians' freedom of movement.

Emily Schneider

See also: Gaza Strip; Israeli Occupations; Jerusalem, Old City of; West Bank

Further Reading

Felner, Eitan. "Human Rights Leaders in Conflict Situations: A Case Study of the Politics of 'Moral Entrepreneurs'." *Journal of Human Rights Practice*, 4, no. 1 (2012), 57–81.

Gordon, Neve. *Israel's Occupation: Sovereignty, Discipline, and Control*. Berkeley: University of California Press, 2008.

Babylonian Conquest of Judah

Conquest of the Kingdom of Judah, culminating in the temporary expulsion of Jews from the region. Following the death of Solomon in 931 BCE, the United Kingdom of Israel divided into two separate kingdoms, Israel in the north and Judah in the south. Israel's capital, Samaria, was destroyed by the Assyrians in 722, and the great bulk of the kingdom's population was taken captive and scattered throughout the Assyrian Empire. Following Assyrian policy in such circumstances, foreigners were imported into Israel, resulting eventually in a mixed ethnicity called *Samaritans*. All this, the Bible says, was God's punishment for Israel's infidelity (2 Kings 17:7–13). The southern Kingdom of Judah, under the more godly kings of the Davidic dynasty, held on for more years but then met the same fate as Israel. This time, the instrument of Yahweh's wrath was the Babylonians, who had overcome and replaced Assyria on the world stage by 626.

The first campaign was led by Nebuchadnezzar II in 605. He had overwhelmed the last remnants of the Assyrian hegemony at Haran in 609, then at Carchemish in 605, and then he swept into Judah to take a number of choice Jewish captives to Babylon. Judah at the time was ruled in rapid succession by three sons and one brother of the godly King Josiah: Jehoahaz (609), Jehoiakim (608–598), Jehoiachin (598–597), and Zedekiah (597–586). Jehoahaz ended up in Egypt because of his rebellion against Pharaoh Necho, the temporary lord of the Levant. Jehoiakim, an appointee of Necho, occupied Judah's throne in the last years of Egyptian suzerainty. Nebuchadnezzar subjected him to vassalage in 605, a state of affairs that continued under Jehoiachin.

By 597, the Babylonian king ran out of patience with the incessant attempts at rebellion by the Jewish rulers. He besieged Jerusalem, plundered the royal palace and temple, and took thousands of captives, including Jehoiachin. Nebuchadnezzar permitted Zedekiah, the uncle of the previous three kings, to occupy Judah's throne until he too rebelled. After a two-year siege (588–586), Nebuchadnezzar came once more, this time leveling the holy city to the ground and burning down its magnificent Solomonic temple. Zedekiah was captured, blinded, and taken to Babylon along with thousands of other prisoners of war. Meanwhile, Jehoiachin, the last surviving heir to the Davidic crown, was languishing under house arrest in Babylonia until the death of Nebuchadnezzar in 562, whose successor, Merodach-Baladan, released him and granted him a pension on which he lived for the rest of his days.

The Bible provides only a few glimpses into the affairs of the Jewish diaspora during the seventy years of the Babylonian exile, but after Cyrus the Great of Persia (550–530) destroyed the city of Babylon in 539, he issued a decree in which he gave permission for captives in the hitherto Babylonian Empire to return to their homelands, including Jews to Palestine.

Eugene H. Merrill

See also: Assyrian Conquest of Israel; Diaspora, Jewish; Israelite Conquest of Canaan; Kingdom of Judah; United Kingdom of Israel

Further Reading

Merrill, Eugene H. *Kingdom of Priests: A History of Old Testament Israel*. 2nd ed. Grand Rapids, MI: Baker, 2008.

Moore, Megan Bishop, and Brad E. Kelle. *Biblical History and Israel's Past*. Grand Rapids, MI: Eerdmans, 2011.

Wiseman, D. J. *Chronicles of Chaldaean Kings (626–556 B.C.)*. London: Trustees of the British Museum, 1961.

Balfour Declaration

A promise by the British government to support the creation of a national home for the Jewish people. The Balfour Declaration was issued in an effort to gain the support of Jews around the world for the Allied war effort. It apparently contradicted an earlier British promise to Arabs to support the establishment of an independent Arab state after World War I. The Balfour Declaration helped encourage Jewish immigration to Palestine during the 1920s and 1930s, but it alienated Arabs from the British Mandate government. Indirectly, the Balfour Declaration led to the creation of the state of Israel and the ongoing conflict between Arabs and Jews in the Middle East.

When World War I broke out, Zionists (Jewish nationalists seeking to create a state in Palestine) urged the various governments to support their movement as a way of gaining Jewish support around the world. The most fertile ground was in Great Britain. Although the total number of Jews in Britain was small, they included very influential people, such as Sir Herbert Samuel and the Rothschild banking family. The leader of the Zionists in Britain was Dr. Chaim Weizmann, a chemistry professor at Manchester University. Weizmann had discovered a revolutionary method of producing acetone, important to the munitions industry. Members of the British government understandably held Weizmann in high esteem. Others felt that Europe had a moral duty to Jews because of past injustices.

Events during the spring of 1917 aided Weizmann's campaign for British support for a Jewish homeland in Palestine. The first was the revolution going on in Russia. Some of the most prominent leaders of the revolution were Jews, and Weizmann argued that they were more likely to keep Russia in the war if an Allied goal was a Jewish homeland. Another important event was the entry of the United States into the war in April 1917. The relatively large Jewish population in the United States could campaign for more immediate and greater U.S. contributions to the war effort. Furthermore, Jewish financial contributions toward the war effort might be increased with support for a homeland. Weizmann also told his friends in the British government that support for a Jewish homeland might prevent German Jews from giving their full support to the Kaiser's war effort.

Arthur James Balfour was foreign secretary at the time. He supported a promise of a Jewish homeland after the war. On a trip to the United States, he conferred with Supreme Court justice Louis Brandeis, a Zionist. Brandeis was an advisor to President Woodrow Wilson, and he told Balfour that Wilson supported a homeland for Jews. At the time, however, Wilson was reluctant to offer public support because the United States was not at war with the Ottoman Empire, which had ruled Palestine for the past 400 years and opposed the creation of a Jewish state there. Other prominent Americans, such as former presidential candidate William Jennings Bryan, supported a Jewish homeland, and many Americans thought that this would fulfill biblical prophecies.

Members of the Zionist movement in Britain helped draft a declaration that was approved by the British cabinet and released by Balfour on November 2, 1917. The Balfour Declaration committed the British government to supporting a national home for the Jewish people, while insisting that the civil and religious rights of the existing non-Jewish majority in Palestine were not to be prejudiced. These commitments seemed incompatible to many. The French government gave the declaration its support on February 11, 1918. Wilson finally gave open approval in a letter to Rabbi Stephen Wise on October 29, 1918.

The declaration won Jewish support for the Allied war effort, but it had unintended effects as well. Correspondence between Henry McMahon, High Commissioner in Egypt, and Husayn ibn Ali, Sharif of Mecca, in 1915 had promised the establishment of an independent Arab state upon the defeat of the Ottomans. It was understood that this state would include Palestine. The apparent double-dealing by the British government alienated many Arabs.

At the end of World War I, the League of Nations granted a mandate over Palestine to Britain. Language from the Balfour Declaration was incorporated into the mandate's wording. In thirty years, the Jewish population of Palestine increased from 50,000 to 600,000. Rapid Jewish migration caused conflicts with Palestinians already living there. In 1920, 1921, 1929, and 1933, violence erupted between Jews and Palestinians. From 1936 to 1939, an Arab uprising occurred that required additional British forces.

The task of trying to keep conflicting promises to Arabs and Jews proved too much for the British. They gave up their mandate in 1948, and the state of Israel was created. The result has been hostility and sporadic wars between Jews and Arabs ever since.

Tim J. Watts

See also: British Mandate for Palestine; Herzl, Theodor; League of Nations; McMahon-Husayn Correspondence; Weizmann, Chaim; World Zionist Organization; Zionism

Further Reading

Lenczowski, George. *The Middle East in World Affairs*. Ithaca, NY: Cornell University Press, 1952.

Sanders, Ronald. *The High Walls of Jerusalem: A History of the Balfour Declaration and the Birth of the British Mandate for Palestine*. New York: Holt Rinehart & Winston, 1984.

Schneer, Jonathan. *The Balfour Declaration: The Origins of the Arab-Israeli Conflict*. New York: Random House, 2010.

Stein, Leonard. *The Balfour Declaration*. New York: Simon & Schuster, 1961.

Barghouti, Marwan

Palestinian leader, politician, and prominent member of Fatah. Marwan Barghouti was born on June 6, 1959, in Ramallah. He earned a master's degree in international relations from Birzeit University, where he was president of the student body. He was arrested numerous times, beginning in 1976, by Israeli authorities and spent six years in an Israeli prison for his political organizing. During the First Intifada (1987–1993), he was exiled to Jordan.

Barghouti returned to the West Bank in 1994 as part of the exchanges negotiated at the 1993 Oslo Accords. He became the general secretary of Fatah in 1996 and supported the peace process, although he opposed Israeli prime minister Ehud Barak's efforts at the 2000 Camp David Summit because of Israel's stated intent to maintain most of the settlements, control Jerusalem, and not recognize the right of return for Palestinian refugees.

During the Second Intifada (2000–2005), Barghouti was a member of the coordinating committee for the West Bank. He was also accused of being a leader in Fatah's military wing, Tanzim, and for creating the al-Aqsa Martyrs Brigades, which carried out suicide attacks in Israel. He was arrested in 2002 and tried in an Israeli civilian court for twenty-six deaths allegedly carried out under his supervision. He was sentenced to five life sentences for the killings of four Israelis and a Greek Orthodox monk. Barghouti denied establishing the al-Aqsa Martyrs Brigades and claimed that he had opposed attacks on civilians and attacks within Israeli territory. He refused to provide a defense at trial, insisting Israel was usurping jurisdiction from the Palestinian Authority (PA).

Despite his legal woes, Barghouti enjoyed popularity among many Palestinians when he criticized corruption in the PA and called for a more democratic leadership. From prison, he helped to negotiate a unilateral truce during the intifada in June 2003. In December 2005, Barghouti established a new Palestinian political party called al-Mustaqbal (the Future), which claims to represent the younger generation within Fatah. Barghouti was also influential in issuing the Document of National Reconciliation of Palestinian Prisoners in 2006, designed principally to heal the division between Hamas and Fatah.

Supporters call for Barghouti's release from prison, speculating that it might be negotiated in time. In 2011, Hamas insisted that he have input in prisoner exchange talks, despite his status as a prisoner. In 2017, Barghouti led nearly 1,600 prisoners in a hunger strike to demand improved living conditions. He is often portrayed as a Nelson Mandela–style figure—one of the few leaders with the nationalist credibility and charisma to bridge the gap between Fatah and Hamas and reinvigorate the Palestinian nationalist movement. Polls regularly suggest that he could win the next election for PA president, despite his incarceration.

Sherifa Zuhur

See also: Al-Aqsa Martyrs Brigades; Fatah; Hamas; Intifada, Second; Palestinian Authority; Tanzim

Further Reading

Barghouti, Marwan, with Lisa Hajjar. "Competing Political Cultures: An Interview with Marwan Barghouti and Introduction by Lisa Hajjar," in *The Struggle for Sovereignty: Palestine and Israel, 1993–2005*, ed. Joel Beinin and Rebecca Stein. Stanford, CA: Stanford University Press, 2006, 105–111.

Usher, Graham. *Dispatches from Palestine: The Rise and Fall of the Oslo Peace Process*. London: Pluto, 1999.

Usher, Graham. *Palestine in Crisis: The Struggle for Peace and Political Independence after Oslo*. London: Pluto, 1995.

Bedouins

Nomadic and seminomadic desert-dwelling peoples generally located in Arabia, North Africa, the Levant, Iraq, Israel, and Egypt. Bedouin are of Arab origin and practice Islam. For centuries, they have been nomads who engage in light agriculture, usually animal husbandry, and live off of the land. However, urban sprawl, government policies, and the shrinking of suitable grazing lands have pushed many Bedouin into sedentary, urban lifestyles. There may be only a million or so Bedouin left in the Middle East. While they are noted for their generous hospitality, they are also fiercely territorial and do not take violations of their land rights lightly. The Bedouin have their own tribal, or customary, laws, and thus disputes are often resolved according to those laws rather than resorting to state courts.

Currently, Bedouin make up about 12 percent of the total Arab citizen population in Israel. As part of the Arab minority, they face many of the same hurdles as their brethren, including institutional and societal discrimination, reduced socioeconomic opportunities, substandard education, and poor health care. However, they have come under additional pressure as the Israeli government has tried to impose settlement policies on them and reduce or eliminate their traditional land areas. A fair number of Bedouin (5–10 percent of Bedouin males) serve in the Israeli military. Their intricate knowledge of the local terrain makes them valuable rangers and trackers.

Bedouin face similar pressures in Arab states, as governments purposely adopt land-use and settlement policies that are at odds with traditional Bedouin culture and lifestyle. Nevertheless, Bedouin have held fast to their tribal and cultural identities, even after they have settled and adopted a modern, urbanized lifestyle.

Paul G. Pierpaoli Jr.

See also: Israel Defense Forces; Israelis

Further Reading

Alotaibi, Muhammad. *Bedouin: The Nomads of the Desert.* Vero Beach, FL: Rourke, 1989.

Ingham, Bruce. *The Bedouin of Northern Arabia.* London: Kegan Paul International, 1986.

Losleben, Elizabeth. *The Bedouin of the Middle East.* Minneapolis: Lerner, 2002.

Nevins, Edward, and Theon Wright. *World Without Time: The Bedouin.* New York: John Day, 1969.

Begin, Menachem

Zionist insurgent leader, and subsequently prime minister of Israel. Born in Brest-Litovsk, Poland, on August 16, 1913, Menachem Begin attended Warsaw University, where he received a law degree in 1935. An ardent Zionist, Begin became active in the Revisionist Zionist Movement, headed by Ze'ev Jabotinsky, in Eastern Europe, and then in Palestine. Begin was involved in the East European resistance effort against the German occupation and helped various Zionist groups to infiltrate British-controlled Palestine. After the German invasion of the Soviet Union in 1941, he joined the Polish army, was posted to the Middle East, and wound up in Palestine.

In 1943 Begin assumed command of the militantly Zionist Irgun Tsvai Leumi (National Military Organization), generally referred to as Irgun. Considered a terrorist organization by the British, Irgun was known for its harsh retaliatory attacks following violence against the Jewish community and for its advocacy of military action against the British. On July 22, 1946, Irgun bombed the British military, police, and civil headquarters at the King David Hotel in Jerusalem, killing ninety-one people. Begin and Irgun claimed to have issued three warnings in an attempt to limit casualties.

During the struggle that led to the establishment of Israel in 1948, Begin's militancy was at odds with mainstream Zionists headed by David Ben-Gurion. Begin and his partisans established the Herut Party in 1948 to foster the Revisionist Zionist program for a Greater Israel that included territories east of the Jordan River. The Herut Party was later broadened to include other political sentiments opposed to Ben-Gurion's so-called Labor Zionism. The party was renamed Likud in 1973.

The Likud Party won a majority of seats in the Knesset (parliamentary) elections of 1977 and formed a government with Begin as prime minister. Begin actively promoted immigration to Israel, particularly from the Soviet Union and Ethiopia, and sought to move the Israeli economy away from the centralized, command-style policies of the Labor Party. His six-year tenure as prime minister was marked by a number of important foreign policy events.

In 1977, he participated in the groundbreaking Camp David peace talks with Egyptian president Anwar Sadat, sponsored by U.S. president Jimmy Carter. The talks ultimately led to the 1978 Camp David Accords, followed by a formal Israeli-Egyptian peace treaty signed in 1979. In 1981, Begin ordered an air attack against an Iraqi nuclear power plant near Osirak that destroyed the facility. He also ordered the Israeli military to retaliate against Palestinian terrorist attacks, which led to Israeli invasions of Lebanon in 1977 and 1982. Begin retired in September 1983 to his home in Yafeh Nof, near Jerusalem, and died in Tel Aviv on March 9, 1992.

Daniel E. Spector

See also: Camp David Accords; Irgun Tsvai Leumi; Jabotinsky, Ze'ev; King David Hotel Bombing; Lebanon, Israeli Invasion of; Sadat, Anwar; Zionism

Further Reading

Hirschler, Gertrude, and Lester S. Eckman. *Menachem Begin: From Freedom Fighter to Statesman.* New York: Shengold, 1979.

Quandt, William B. *Camp David: Peacemaking and Politics.* Washington, DC: Brookings Institution Press, 1986.

Silver, Eric. *Begin: The Haunted Prophet.* New York: Random House, 1984.

Ben-Gurion, David

An important Zionist leader and Israel's first prime minister and defense minister. Celebrated as Israel's founding father, David Ben-Gurion was born David Grün in Plonsk, Poland, on October 16, 1886. Educated in his Zionist father's Hebrew school, as a teenager he joined the Zionist youth group Erza. He then taught at a Hebrew school in Warsaw and joined the Poalei Zion (Workers of Zion). Ben-Gurion believed that Zionism would be achieved by Jewish settlement in Palestine and by collective farming and industrialization of the land.

Putting his beliefs into action, Ben-Gurion moved to Jaffa, Palestine, in 1906 and established the first Jewish workers' commune there. He then began organizing other workers into unions. In Jerusalem in 1910, he began writing for the newspaper *Ahdut*, publishing his first article on Zionism under the name Ben-Gurion (which means "son of the lion" in Hebrew).

Ben-Gurion then moved to Jerusalem and joined the editorial staff of a Hebrew-language newspaper. He left Palestine in 1912 to earn a law degree from the University of Constantinople during 1912–1914. Returning to Palestine to take up his union work, he was expelled by the Ottomans—who still controlled Palestine—in March 1915 for his dangerous activities.

Settling in New York City, Ben-Gurion met Russian-born Paula Munweis, whom he married in 1917. Buoyed by the 1917 British Balfour Declaration, which proposed a Jewish homeland in Palestine, Ben-Gurion joined the Jewish Legion, a volunteer British military unit formed to help defeat the Turks. In 1920, he returned to union organizing. Indeed, he helped found the Histadrut, a powerful federation of Jewish labor unions. During 1921–1935, he served as its general secretary. The Histadrut became in effect a state within British-controlled Palestine. Ben-Gurion was also a driving force behind the establishment of the Haganah, the paramilitary force of the Zionist movement that helped facilitate illegal Jewish immigration to Palestine and protect the Jewish settlements there.

Within the Zionist movement in Palestine, however, he was known as a moderate who opposed the radical approach advocated by Ze'ev Jabotinsky and Menachem Begin. Briefly, Ben-Gurion cooperated with Begin's Irgun Tsvai Leumi (National Military Organization) but only rarely supported violence, and then only against military targets. While Ben-Gurion agreed to Begin's plan to bomb the King David Hotel, it was only with the aim of humiliating the British. When it became apparent that the effort would result in loss of life, Ben-Gurion ordered Begin to call off the bombing, which Begin refused to do.

When it became clear after World War II that Britain was no longer sympathetic to the establishment of a Jewish state in Palestine, Ben-Gurion pursued other avenues to achieve Jewish statehood. He supported the 1947 partition plan of the United Nations (UN) that called for separate Jewish and Arab states in Palestine. He did so knowing the Arabs would not accept partition and that war would offer Israel the opportunity to expand its borders. In May 1948, as the last of the British troops pulled out, Israel declared its independence.

Ben-Gurion was concurrently prime minister and defense minister of the new nation. As defense minister, he immediately consolidated all the Jewish paramilitary organizations into the Israel Defense Forces (IDF), enabling them to effectively fight both the Arab Palestinians and the surrounding Arab nations. As Israel's prime minister, Ben-Gurion promoted Jewish immigration from the Arab states. He also oversaw establishment of the Jewish state's governmental institutions, advocated compulsory primary education, and urged the creation of new Jewish towns and cities. Deeply involved in rural development projects, he urged the establishment of new Jewish settlements, especially in the Negev. He was also one of the founders of Mapai, the political party that held power in the first three decades of Israel's existence.

Ben-Gurion retired from politics in 1953, only to return as prime minister and defense minister in 1955. His second period as prime minister coincided with the 1956 Suez Crisis, during which the Israeli government worked secretly with the French and British governments to seize control of the Suez Canal and topple Egyptian president Gamal Abdel Nasser from power. Although the IDF performed admirably, heavy pressure from the U.S. government brought the withdrawal of the British, which in turn forced the French and Israelis to remove their own forces.

The last years of Ben-Gurion's premiership were marked by general Israeli prosperity and stalled secret peace talks with the Arabs. He resigned his posts in June 1963 but retained his seat in the Knesset (Israeli parliament). In 1965, he broke with the Mapai Party over Prime Minister Levi Eshkol's handling of the Lavon Affair. Ben-Gurion then formed a new party, Rafi. When it voted to merge with Mapai to form the Labor Party in 1968, he formed another new party, the State List. He resigned from the Knesset and left politics altogether in 1970. Among his books are *Israel: An Achieved Personal History* (1970) and *The Jews in Their Land* (1974). He spent his last years on his kibbutz. Ben-Gurion died in Tel Aviv–Jaffa on December 1, 1973.

Richard M. Edwards

See also: Arab-Israeli War, 1948; Arab-Israeli War, 1956; Arab-Jewish Communal War, 1947; Israel Defense Forces; King David Hotel Bombing; Lavon Affair; Yishuv; Zionism

Further Reading

Bar-Zohar, Michel. *Ben-Gurion: The Armed Prophet*. Trans. Len Ortzen. London: Barker, 1967.

Cohen, Eliot. *Supreme Command: Soldiers, Statesmen, and Leadership in Wartime*. New York: Free Press, 2002.

Kurzman, Dan. *Ben-Gurion: Prophet of Fire*. New York: Simon & Shuster, 1983.

Zweig, Ronald W., ed. *David Ben-Gurion: Politics and Leadership in Israel*. Jerusalem: Y. I. Ben-Zvi, 1991.

Ben-Yehuda, Eliezer

The individual most responsible for the resurrection of the Hebrew language in the twentieth century. Eliezer Ben-Yehuda (1858–1922), born Eliezer Yitzhak Perlman, was born in Belarus, where he studied Hebrew and the Torah at a yeshiva. After learning about the Zionist movement, he became convinced that reviving Hebrew in Israel might serve to unite the Jews of the world and undo the effects of the Jewish diaspora. He emigrated to Jerusalem and helped found the Committee of the Hebrew Language, a group that not only promoted the use of Hebrew in everyday conversation, but also coined new words to make it practical in the modern era, using the grammatical rules of the existing language.

Ben-Yehuda edited several Hebrew-language newspapers, which he used to promote his concept of reviving the language. He faced significant opposition from Jerusalem's ultra-Orthodox Jews, who outnumbered Zionists at the time and who felt that the holy tongue should be reserved for religious purposes. Ben-Yehuda raised his son, Ben-Zion Ben-Yehuda, to speak only Hebrew, making him the first modern native speaker of Hebrew. Ben-Yehuda died of tuberculosis at age 64 and was buried on the Mount of Olives in Jerusalem.

Paul J. Springer

See also: Israelis; Zionism

Further Reading

Fellman, Jack. *The Revival of a Classical Tongue: Eliezer Ben Yehuda and the Modern Hebrew Language.* The Hague: Mouton, 1973.

St. John, Robert. *Tongue of the Prophets: The Life Story of Eliezer Ben Yehuda.* Garden City, NY: Doubleday, 1952.

Bernadotte, Count Folke

United Nations (UN) diplomat assassinated by Israeli terrorists. A proven diplomat fluent in six languages, Count Folke Bernadotte was asked by the United Nations to mediate between Arabs and Jews during the war that erupted as soon as Israel declared independence on May 14, 1948. After conferences with Arab and Jewish leaders in Palestine, and Arab leaders in Cairo, Egypt, and Jordan, he succeeded in obtaining agreement to a thirty-day truce commencing June 11, 1948. Drawing upon his experience of Red Cross work, he also initiated the humanitarian relief program for Palestinian refugees.

Bernadotte considered the original partition plan unsuitable. He proposed that Arabs and Jews form a union consisting of a small Jewish entity and an enlarged Transjordan. Israel would receive the western Galilee, and Transjordan would control the Negev and Jerusalem. The union was rejected by both sides. Particularly appalling to Jews was that the Arabs would control Jerusalem, and it was perhaps this that sealed Bernadotte's fate.

One organization that saw Bernadotte's efforts as a threat was the Lohamei Herut Israel–Lehi (also known as the Stern Gang, or Fighters for the Freedom of Israel), a Jewish underground group that had waged a campaign of personal terror to force the British out of Palestine. Lehi considered Bernadotte a British agent and viewed his plan as a threat to Israel's ability to conquer both banks of the Jordan River.

The decision to assassinate Bernadotte was made by the Central Committee of the Lehi, which included Yitzhak Shamir, a future prime minister of Israel. On September 17, Bernadotte and Colonel André Serot of the French Air Force were assassinated in Jerusalem by a group led by Avraham Stern. Bernadotte's peace plan died soon thereafter.

Peter Overlack

See also: Shamir, Yitzhak; Stern Gang; UN Partition Plan for Palestine

Further Reading

Marton, Kati. *A Death in Jerusalem.* New York: Pantheon, 1994.

Persson, Sune O. *Mediation and Assassination: Count Bernadotte's Mission to Palestine in 1948.* London: Ithaca, 1979.

Bethlehem

Historic West Bank town important to Judaism, Christianity, and Islam. Bethlehem is home to about 28,000 Palestinians. Most residents are Muslim, but about 20 percent are Christian. Until fairly recently, Bethlehem boasted one of the largest Palestinian Christian communities in the Middle East.

To Jews, Bethlehem is known as the birthplace of King David, the second king of the Israelites, as told in the Old Testament (Torah). David was crowned king in Bethlehem by Samuel, who was the first major Jewish prophet. The city is also believed to be the birthplace of Jesus Christ and is therefore one of Christianity's holiest cities. The Church of the Nativity, perhaps the most revered church in all of Christendom, sits over a small cave where Jesus is said to have been born. Built by the Roman emperor Constantine around 330 CE, the Church of the Nativity may be the oldest Christian church in the world. For centuries since the early 1500s, the Roman Catholic Church and the Greek Orthodox Church have struggled to control the Church of the Nativity.

Bethlehem has significance for Muslims as well. The Prophet Muhammad, it is believed, stopped in Bethlehem and prayed en route to Jerusalem upon the instructions of the archangel Gabriel, who informed him that his "brother" and fellow prophet, Jesus, had been born there. Bethlehem has seen many invasions, violent occupations, and other calamities. Throughout, the Church of the Nativity was spared major damage. In 1099, the Christian Crusaders won control of Bethlehem, but it fell to Saladin in 1187. From 1517 until 1917, the Ottoman Empire ruled the city and its surrounding areas.

Beginning in 1947, Bethlehem witnessed a major influx of (mostly Muslim) Palestinian refugees fleeing advancing Jewish forces, first during the 1947–1948 Arab-Jewish Communal War, and then during the 1948–1949 Arab-Israeli War (the Israeli War of Independence). When the fighting finally stopped, Bethlehem and the West Bank were under Jordanian control. After the 1967 Arab-Israeli War, Israel occupied the West Bank.

Israel administered Bethlehem until December 1995, when the newly created Palestinian Authority took control. After the outbreak of the Second Intifada in 2000, the city witnessed several showdowns between Palestinians and Israelis. In 2002, Palestinian militants holed themselves up in the Church of the Nativity against invading Israeli troops. The crisis was diffused only after international intervention.

Most recently, the construction of the Israeli Security Barrier has cut off Palestinians who work in Bethlehem from their nearby homes. The barrier disrupted the city's economy and forced many to leave. Since 2005, there has been a mass exodus of Christians from Bethlehem, with their percentage of the population as whole shrinking markedly by 2016.

Paul G. Pierpaoli Jr.

See also: Intifada, Second; Israeli Occupations; Israeli Security Barrier; Palestinian Authority; West Bank

Further Reading
Mansour, Atallah. *Narrow Gate Churches: The Christian Presence in the Holy Land Under Muslim and Jewish Rule.* Carol Stream, IL: Hope Publishing House, 2004.

Raheb, Mitri. *Bethlehem Besieged: Stories of Hope in Times of Trouble*. Minneapolis: Augsburg Fortress, 2004.

Black September

An armed conflict between the Jordanian army and the Palestine Liberation Organization (PLO) beginning in September 1970. The struggle did not end until July 1971, when the PLO was permanently expelled from Jordan and relocated to Lebanon.

Relations between Jordan and the PLO had steadily deteriorated during the late 1960s for two primary reasons. First, PLO attacks on Israel launched from Jordanian territory frequently resulted in disproportionate Israeli retaliation against Jordan. Second, the PLO sought to create a state within a state in northern Jordan. Tensions increased in early September when the Popular Front for the Liberation of Palestine (PFLP) forced three Western airliners to land at an abandoned air base in northern Jordan. The passengers survived the ordeal, but the aircraft did not. The planes were deliberately destroyed on September 12, 1970, in a theatrical event staged for the media. The hijackings and their aftermath, which seemed to prove that King Husayn did not have control over his own country, deeply embarrassed him.

Sensing that he now had to take strong and decisive action, Husayn ordered his army to launch an offensive against PLO guerrilla organizations. The operation began on September 17, 1970. The ensuing conflict pitted 70,000 Jordanian troops with heavy weapons against the PLO, which had approximately 12,000 regulars and 30,000 militiamen armed with light weapons. The offensive was supposed to take two days but quickly bogged down into a war of attrition because of stiff Palestinian resistance and Jordanian tactical errors. Fighting was concentrated in northern Jordan, especially around Amman and Irbid.

On September 19, 1970, Syria sent tanks and troops to assist the PLO but were repulsed in the end by Jordan's air force. Fighting between Jordan and the PLO did not come to an end until July 1971, at which point the PLO withdrew to Lebanon. Approximately 600 Jordanians died in the fighting, while more than 1,200 were wounded. Palestinian casualties ran into the thousands, but the exact figures are unknown.

Black September produced numerous aftershocks. The stressful negotiations undertaken by Egypt to resolve the matter likely precipitated President Gamal Abdel Nasser's fatal heart attack on September 28, 1970. His successor, Anwar Sadat, eventually made peace with Israel. In Syria, Minister of Defense Hafez al-Assad used the events of Black September to seize power in a bloodless coup d'état on November 13, 1970. PLO forces relocated to Lebanon, where they served as catalysts to the Lebanese civil war (1975–1990) and the 1982 Israeli invasion of Lebanon. Black September also spawned a terrorist group of the same name, whose attacks included the massacre of Israeli athletes at the 1972 Munich Olympics.

Chuck Fahrer

See also: Arafat, Yasser; Jordan; Lebanon, Israeli Invasion of; Palestine Liberation Organization

Further Reading

Cooley, John K. *Green March, Black September: The Story of the Palestinian Arabs.* London: Frank Cass, 1973.

Dobson, Christopher. *Black September: Its Short, Violent History.* New York: Macmillan, 1974.

Mishal, Shaul. *The PLO Under Arafat: Between Gun and Olive Branch.* New Haven, CT: Yale University Press, 1986.

Boycott, Divestment, and Sanctions (BDS) Movement

International campaign calling for boycotts of Israel. The Boycott, Divestment, and Sanctions (BDS) movement calls for participants to boycott Israel and Israeli products until the government of Israel concedes to four specific demands: withdrawing from the territories captured in the 1967 Six-Day War; dismantling the security barrier built around the West Bank; affording full equality to Arab citizens of Israel; and accepting the Palestinian right of return concept. The BDS movement has had significant economic and political effects, and the Israeli government spends much time and treasure combating it.

The BDS movement was created by the Palestinian BDS National Committee, a coordinating body with nearly 200 Palestinian nongovernmental organizations (NGOs) that support the BDS movement. It calls for adherents to boycott Israel, divest themselves of holdings in Israeli corporations, and push for international sanctions against the Israeli government. The BDS founders argue that this is the most sure nonviolent means to bring about freedom, justice, and equality within the region, and they point to the success of previous antiapartheid campaigns, particularly against the Republic of South Africa, as inspiration for their movement. The campaign is supported by an ongoing academic boycott of Israeli scholars and universities, which has been endorsed by the American Studies Association and some other scholarly societies. The academic boycott is led by the Palestinian Campaign for the Academic and Cultural Boycott of Israel.

Proponents of the BDS movement argue that it is a nonviolent means of forcing the Israeli government to cease illegal activity aimed at harming Palestinians. They seek to influence individuals, organizations, and governments directly to change their behaviors regarding personal links to Israel and its businesses. To the leaders of the BDS movement, the Israeli government, and by extension Israeli society, are guilty of enormous human rights violations on a daily basis. In particular, the erection of physical barriers and security checkpoints have served to block Palestinians from gainful employment and deny their access to schools and medical facilities. The supporters also argue that many Israeli employers hire Palestinians at wages well below the legal minimum established by Israeli law, although said wages still tend to be much higher than anything available within the Palestinian-controlled areas of the West Bank.

Opponents of the BDS movement tend to liken it to the anti-Semitic boycotts of the twentieth century, particularly those perpetrated by Nazi Germany. They argue that Israel is being unfairly targeted by the sanctions, which are not employed against other governments with similar behaviors, laws, and backgrounds. Some critics insist that the goal of BDS is to delegitimize the only Jewish state in the world, and thus it is anti-Semitic. To bolster their case, they point to the statements of some prominent BDS supporters, which have called for attacks upon Jews living inside and outside Israel. Some critics argue the hardest-hit individuals from the economic effects of BDS activities tend to be Palestinian workers of Israeli-owned businesses operating in and around the West Bank.

The BDS movement has had a significant impact within the academic community. Israeli scholars have found it increasingly difficult to be published outside Israel, to participate in academic conferences, and to be accepted as members of scholarly organizations. Critics insist that academics should not be blacklisted because of their nationality, and doing so stifles academic debate and contradicts the purpose of higher education.

Few national governments outside the immediate region have expressed open support for the BDS movement, and many within the Middle East that have done so already have bans in place blocking trade with Israel. Within the United States, both the Democratic and Republican parties have condemned the BDS movement, and about half the state legislatures have passed laws limiting government agencies from contracting with, or investing in, companies and individuals suspected of supporting BDS. Some state governors have used executive orders to the same effect.

At the federal level, some lawmakers (supported by certain elements of the pro-Israel community and with the encouragement of the Israeli government) have repeatedly proposed various bills that would make it a federal crime to support BDS, prevent federal monies to go to BDS supporters, and help protect state legislatures passing anti-BDS legislation from lawsuits. These anti-BDS efforts have been widely criticized by free speech advocates, and so far, none of the federal bills have made it into law. The governments of many Western countries have similarly criticized the BDS movement, even though many citizens have joined.

The BDS movement has frequently pressured artists who consider performing in Israel. At times, it has caused performers to cancel shows or avoid playing in Israel. However, many prominent entertainers have criticized the BDS movement and have performed in Israel.

Israel's Ministry of Foreign Affairs and Ministry of Strategic Affairs spearhead that country's official efforts to undermine the BDS movement. Israel spends tens of millions of dollars every year combating BDS via lobbying efforts, public diplomacy campaigns, arranging "solidarity visits" to Israel by influential opinion makers, participating in social media, and coordinating pro-Israel groups around the world. Israel also shares intelligence on BDS activities with law enforcement and security organizations in foreign countries.

Israeli government officials insist that elements of the BDS movement have ties to the Palestinian terror group Hamas. Proponents of BDS argue that these efforts demonstrate that Israel cannot tolerate even nonviolent resistance. In 2017, Israel began barring BDS supporters from entering the country, focusing most closely on key activists, mayors, and other higher-profile supporters. Israel also maintains a list of organizations that are blacklisted from entry. As of late 2018, there were twenty on the list, including the left-wing Jewish Voice for Peace and the Quaker organization American Friends Service Committee, which was awarded the Nobel Peace Prize in 1947 for its role in rescuing Jews from Nazis. In September 2019, Israel refused to allow two Democratic congresswomen, Ilhan Omar and Rashida Tlaib, to enter Israel because of their public stance in support of BDS.

Paul J. Springer and Robert C. DiPrizio

See also: Israeli Occupations; Israelis; Palestinian Refugees; Palestinians; Right of Return; West Bank

Further Reading
Barghouti, Omar. *Boycott, Divestment, Sanctions: The Global Struggle for Palestinian Rights.* Chicago: Haymarket Books, 2011.
Dawson, Ashley. *Against Apartheid: The Case for Boycotting Israeli Universities.* Chicago: Haymarket Books, 2015.
Lim, Audrea. *The Case for Sanctions Against Israel.* Brooklyn: Verso, 2012.
Nelson, Cary, ed. *Dreams Deferred: A Concise Guide to the Israeli-Palestinian Conflict and the Movement to Boycott Israel.* Bloomington: Indiana University Press, 2016.

Breaking the Silence

A nonprofit organization made up of veteran Israeli soldiers. Breaking the Silence works to generate opposition to the occupation through meaningful discourse and debate among the Israeli public. In particular, it aims to bring an end to the occupation through raising awareness about the reality of young Israeli soldiers controlling a Palestinian civilian population on a daily basis. The organization was founded in 2004 by a group of soldiers who served in the Palestinian city of Hebron. Today, the nongovernmental organization has twelve core staff members and is led by its executive director, Avner Gvaryahu. One of Breaking the Silence's primary activities involves gathering public testimonies from soldiers about their military service in the occupied territories. Based on over 1,000 testimonies, Breaking the Silence organizes lectures and other public events to raise awareness about the price that Israeli society pays for maintaining the occupation through the voices of its own soldiers. By focusing on the perspectives of Israelis who have witnessed the impacts of their military service firsthand, Breaking the Silence aims to facilitate open dialogue around the moral costs of continued occupation. The organization also offers tours to the Hebron region for both Israelis and internationals. These tours reveal the consequences of maintaining an Israeli military presence in the heart of one of the largest Palestinian cities in the West Bank. These tours have been shown to facilitate political transformations and greater awareness of Israel's military occupation.

Emily Schneider

See also: Israel Defense Forces; Israeli Occupations; West Bank

Further Reading
Breaking the Silence. *Our Harsh Logic: Israeli Soldiers' Testimonies from the Occupied Territories, 2000–2010.* New York: Picador, 2012.

Sasson-Levy, O., Y. Levy, and E. Lomsky-Feder. "Women Breaking the Silence: Military Service, Gender, and Antiwar Protest." *Gender & Society*, 25, no. 6 (2011): 740–763.

British Mandate for Palestine

The period from 1922 to 1948 when Great Britain assumed control over the territory known as Palestine as a League of Nations mandate. The area that became the British Mandate for Palestine had been part of the Ottoman Empire until the end of 1917. Beginning in the 1920s, Palestine became increasingly subject to violent clashes between Arabs and Jews, as both groups claimed the territory as their homeland. Complicating matters was the fact that both groups believed that Britain had promised Palestine to them.

The region now known as Palestine has, at one time or another, been home to the Canaanites, Philistines, and other tribes, but also has been under the authority of the Egyptians, the Jews, the Assyrians, the Persians, the Hellenic Empire, the Roman Empire, the Byzantine Empire, the Arab-Islamic Empire, Crusader Europeans, the Turkish or Ottoman Empire, the British, and, since 1948, the Jews again. According to biblical lore, the various Hebrew tribes in Palestine created a unified

Winston Churchill with Bishop MacInnes of Jerusalem at a memorial service in the British Military Cemetery on Mt. Scopus, March 26, 1921. Over 3,000 soldiers are buried on Mt. Scopus, casualties of Britain's campaign in 1916–1917 to conquer Palestine from the Ottoman Empire. (Library of Congress)

kingdom of Israel around 1050 BCE. It lasted only about seventy years before internal strife tore it in two. Within a few hundred years, both Jewish kingdoms had been conquered by invading empires, which took turns dominating the Middle East. Under imperial rule, Jews in Palestine were allowed varying degrees of autonomy until about 70 CE, when the Romans forced most of them to flee as punishment for one too many rebellions.

The Palestinians are descended from the land's original inhabitants, who either converted to Islam or retained their Christian faith, as well as tribes that were part of or followed the Islamic conquests of the seventh century. In the late nineteenth century, the Arabs in Palestine numbered about 446,000 people, representing 90 percent of the total population. There were also some 60,000 Jews. Although the notion of returning to Palestine had been a Jewish dream for centuries, it did not find serious consideration until the late nineteenth century with the rise of the Zionist movement. A significant increase in anti-Semitism during that time, particularly in Eastern Europe, ignited the movement. Zionism was committed to settling Jews in Palestine and establishing a Jewish homeland there. The Holocaust significantly increased the appeal of Zionism, as many Jews came to believe that their survival could be assured only by the creation of a country of their own.

During World War I, the British government took great interest in Zionism. During the war, Britain sought Jewish support to secure its aims, one of which was control of certain Ottoman territories in the Middle East after the end of the war. British leaders recognized that support for Zionism would bring Jewish support for Britain's Middle Eastern imperial ambitions. Meanwhile, Chaim Weizmann, a leading Zionist in Britain, lobbied the British government to support Zionism and skillfully exploited London's desire to curry favor with Jews. On November 2, 1917, British foreign secretary Arthur Balfour wrote to Lord Walter Rothschild, another prominent Zionist figure in Britain, pledging British support for Zionism. Balfour declared that London viewed "with favor the establishment in Palestine of a National Home for the Jewish people and will use [its] best endeavors to facilitate the achievement of this object." Yet seemingly in contradiction to this pledge, Balfour went on to say that "it being clearly understood that nothing shall be done which may prejudice the civil and religious rights of existing non-Jewish communities in Palestine"—namely, the Arabs.

At the same time, Britain also sought help from the Arabs, who were agitating for independence from the Ottoman Empire. This it accomplished with pledges of support for independence and self-rule in exchange for Arab support for Britain during World War I. Thus, while promising a homeland for Jews in Palestine, the British also promised independence to the Arabs, including those living in Palestine. While this may have been a shrewd wartime strategy, it would later prove impossible for the British to deliver on both sets of promises and satisfy both Arabs and Jews.

Following the end of World War I, the British and the French refused to let the Arabs rule themselves and assumed control of present-day Lebanon, Jordan, Iraq, and Syria. They called them "mandates," which were given legitimacy by the League of Nations. In each mandate, the European powers pledged to grant Arabs independence when they were deemed ready for self-government. At the San Remo conference in April 1920, Palestine was placed under British authority, defined for the first time to consist of the present-day countries of Israel and Jordan. The British then divided Palestine and turned the territory east of the Jordan River into the state of Transjordan and announced that the Balfour Declaration did not apply there.

The Arabs of Palestine were intensely opposed to the Jewish pursuit of a state in Palestine and were unwilling to compromise with either the British or the Jews. The British Mandate government in Palestine during 1922–1948 failed to keep the peace between the Arabs and Jews. The escalating violence between the two was the result of a British policy that sought to achieve mutually exclusive goals: implementing the Balfour Declaration while safeguarding the interests and rights of the majority-Arab population. Much of the tension arose over the numbers of Jewish immigrants admitted to the country. In response to Arab violence and riots, the British considered suspending Jewish settlements and Jewish land purchases in Palestine, which were often from wealthy, absentee Arab landowners but then led to the eviction of Arab peasants. But London relented in the face of strong Jewish opposition.

In 1920, Palestinian Arabs began sporadically attacking Jewish settlements, and in response, Jews formed a clandestine defense organization known as Haganah in 1921. To encourage cooperation between Arabs and Jews, the British in 1922 and 1923 attempted to create a legislative council, but Arabs refused to participate. Indeed, they not only suspected British manipulation and Jewish favoritism, but also believed that their participation would signal their acceptance of the British Mandate and recognition of the Balfour Declaration.

Violence between Arabs and Jews throughout 1929 led the British to halt all Jewish settlement in Palestine. But in the face of outcries by Jews in Palestine and Zionists in London, the British government quickly reversed its policy. By 1936, the Jewish population of Palestine was approximately 400,000, or 30 percent of the total population. That same year, the British resurrected the idea of a legislative council, but this time both Arabs and Jews rejected the idea. Also in 1936, a full-fledged Arab rebellion began that lasted until 1939. This forced Britain to dispatch 20,000 troops to Palestine. The Arab Revolt led to a temporary collaboration between the British and Jews against the Arabs to suppress the rebellion.

In 1937, the British recommended partitioning Palestine into separate Arab and Jewish states, but a year later, they rejected partition as not feasible. By the end of the Arab Revolt in 1939, some 5,000 Arabs had been killed and thousands more wounded or arrested. That same year, the British announced that Palestine would become an independent state within ten years. They also seemingly repudiated the Balfour Declaration by severely limiting future Jewish immigration and also restricting the sale of land to Jews.

By 1939, with the threat of world war looming again, Britain sought to secure its Middle East interests by placating the Arabs. For the first time, the Jews found themselves marginalized and ignored by the British. As a result, some Jews began taking up arms against the British administration in Palestine. There was a temporary lull in fighting between Arabs and Jews owing to the German threat in the Middle East, but by the end of 1942 and the looming defeat of the Axis in North Africa, the Arabs and Jews resumed fighting. At the same time, Jewish groups stepped up their attacks against the British.

News of the Holocaust gradually became public knowledge in 1942, and Zionists became increasingly impatient in their demands not just for more Jewish settlement in Palestine, but also for the immediate creation of a Jewish state there. At the same time, some Jewish groups, such as Lohamei Herut Israel (also known as Lehi, or the Stern Gang) and the Irgun Tsvai Leumi (National Military Organization), were increasingly resorting to violence. The Holocaust facilitated the creation of Israel by further legitimizing Zionism and by uniting Jews around the idea that they needed a state of their own. The employment of terrorism and guerrilla warfare by armed Zionist groups in Palestine against the British throughout the 1940s became a major factor in Britain's decision to relinquish control of Palestine in 1948.

As for the Arabs, they took the view that because they neither caused nor were responsible for the Holocaust, they should not be forced to make up for it by accepting the creation of a Jewish state in Arab territory. Many Arabs regard Israel's creation as a product of Western shame over the Holocaust. At the end of World War II, European governments struggled with what to do with more than 250,000 displaced Jews who were survivors of the Holocaust.

Britain resisted Zionist demands that they be allowed to settle in Palestine, especially while experiencing mounting terrorist violence there perpetuated by Jewish groups. This included the bombing by Irgun of the British military headquarters at the King David Hotel in Jerusalem on July 22, 1946, which killed about ninety people. Between November 1945 and July 1946, Jewish terrorism increased, with some forty British soldiers and police killed by Irgun and Lehi, along with the sabotage of infrastructure. Britain resented Jewish efforts to embarrass London by sending ships of Jewish refugees from Europe to Palestine, only to have them intercepted by the Royal Navy. Meanwhile, the terrorist violence only reinforced Britain's uncompromising position.

British unwillingness to allow at least some of these displaced European Jews to settle in Palestine encouraged even more anti-British sentiment among Jews and further attacks by militant Jewish organizations. On February 14, 1947, seeking to extricate itself from Palestine, Britain gave the newly created United Nations (UN) the responsibility of solving the Palestinian problem. On August 31, 1947, the UN Special Commission on Palestine (UNSCOP) recommended the termination of the British Mandate for Palestine and the granting of Palestinian independence. A majority of UNSCOP members agreed to partition Palestine into Arab and Jewish states, with Jerusalem remaining an international city. Although the Arab population was 1.2 million and the Jewish population just 600,000, the Arab state would have constituted only about 43 percent of the land of Palestine, and the Jewish state would take up about 56 percent. Jews already owned 6–8 percent of the total land area.

While not getting as much as they had hoped for, Jews supported the partition plan. But the Arabs of Palestine and elsewhere rejected it as unjust. The newly created Arab League threatened war if the United Nations implemented partition. Desperate to quit Palestine, the British government announced that it would accept the UN recommendation and declared that the British Mandate would terminate on May 14, 1948. In November 1947, the United Nations officially approved the partition of Palestine, triggering the six-month-long Arab-Jewish Communal War. On the day that the British Mandate ended, Israel declared independence. The very next day, the Arab armies of Egypt, Lebanon, Jordan, Syria, and Iraq invaded, thus sparking the 1948 Arab-Israeli War.

Stefan Brooks

See also: Arab-Israeli War, 1948; Arab-Jewish Clashes in Palestine, Pre-1947; Arab-Jewish Communal War, 1947; Arab Revolt, 1936; Balfour Declaration; Haganah; Irgun Tsvai Leumi; McMahon-Husayn Correspondence; Stern Gang; UN Partition Plan for Palestine

Further Reading
Dowty, Alan. *Israel/Palestine*. Malden, MA: Polity, 2005.
Kamrava, Mehran. *The Modern Middle East*. Berkeley: University of California Press, 2005.
Sachar, Howard M. *A History of Israel: From the Rise of Zionism to Our Time*. 3rd ed. New York: Knopf, 2007.
Shepherd, Naomi. *Ploughing Sand: British Rule in Palestine, 1917–1948*. New Brunswick, NJ: Rutgers University Press, 1999.
Yapp, M. E. *The Making of the Modern Near East 1792–1923*. London: Longman, 1987.

British White Paper

A British government policy statement that sought to mollify mounting Arab anger over increasing Jewish immigration into Palestine. British efforts to formulate a partition plan for Palestine met staunch opposition both from Arab leaders, who were adamantly opposed to partition, and from Zionist leaders, who objected to the small amount of land assigned to the proposed Jewish state. On May 17, 1939, the British government issued a White Paper spelling out its Palestine policy.

In the White Paper, the British government stated that 450,000 Jews had settled in Palestine and that, as a consequence, the British government had fulfilled its pledges under the Balfour Declaration of 1917 to establish a Jewish national home in Palestine. It called for the establishment of an independent Palestine state within ten years, to be governed jointly by Arabs and Jews. The British government held that it was not the intention of the Balfour Declaration that Palestine be converted into a Jewish state against the will of its Arab population, and that London had an obligation to the Arabs to prevent that from happening.

The White Paper sharply restricted Jewish immigration to 75,000 people over the next five years, with immigration thereafter to be entirely contingent on Arab agreement. It also noted that land sales by Arabs to Jews risked sharply reducing the Arab standard of living, and therefore it invested the British high commissioner in Palestine with full authority to prohibit and regulate transfers of land.

The White Paper represented a tilt to the Arab position—an about-face that Jews in Palestine bitterly resented. The immigration restrictions were particularly onerous, given the persecution of Jews in Germany and in Poland. Arabs also opposed the White Paper, though. The Arab Higher Committee (AHC), representing the Palestinian Arabs, opposed any new immigration of Jews to Palestine and the establishment of a state there, in which the Jews would have a joint governing role. The

Arab side sought a complete repudiation of the principle of a Jewish national home in Palestine.

Implementation of the White Paper proceeded slowly, and when Winston Churchill became prime minister of Britain in May 1940, it was dropped. Nonetheless, the British government was anxious to maintain Arab support during World War II and worked to prevent wide-scale Jewish immigration to Palestine, turning Jews away from there even after full knowledge of the Holocaust came out.

Spencer C. Tucker

See also: Arab Higher Committee; Arab Revolt, 1936; Balfour Declaration; British Mandate for Palestine

Further Reading

Bethell, Nicholas. *The Palestine Triangle: The Struggle for the Holy Land, 1935–48.* New York: Putnam, 1979.

Hurewitz, J. C. *The Struggle for Palestine.* New York: Schocken, 1976.

Sachar, Howard M. *A History of Israel: From the Rise of Zionism to Our Time.* 3rd ed. New York: Knopf, 2007.

Camp David Accords

A peace agreement reached between Egypt and Israel at the U.S. presidential retreat at Camp David, in rural Maryland. During 1977 and 1978, several remarkable events took place that set the stage for peace negotiations. In autumn 1977, Egyptian president Anwar Sadat indicated his willingness to visit Israel, something that no Arab leader had done before. On November 19, 1977, Sadat addressed the Israeli Knesset (parliament) and called for peace. The Israelis welcomed Sadat's bold initiative but took no immediate steps to end the state of belligerency, instead agreeing to ministerial-level meetings in preparation for final negotiations.

In February 1978, President Jimmy Carter and congressional leaders hosted Sadat, hailing him as a statesman and courageous leader. American adulation for Sadat led to greater cooperation by the Israelis, who agreed to a summit in September at Camp David. When negotiations began, Israeli prime minister Menachem Begin insisted on separating the Palestinian issue from the peace talks, something no Arab leader had been willing to do before. Israel also demanded that Egypt negate any former agreements with other Arab nations that called for war against Israel.

Sadat bristled at Begin's demands, which led to such acrimony between the two men that they met in person only once during the entire negotiation process. Instead, Carter shuttled between them in an effort to moderate their positions. After several days of little movement and accusations of bad faith (directed mostly at Begin), Carter threatened to break off the talks. Faced with the possibility of being blamed for the failure of the negotiations, Begin returned to the table ready to deal. He agreed to dismantle all Jewish settlements in the Sinai Peninsula and return all of it to Egypt. For his part, Sadat agreed to put the Palestinian issue aside and sign an agreement separate from the other Arab nations. On September 15, 1978, Carter, Sadat, and Begin announced that an agreement had been reached.

In reality, there were still many details to work out. Carter and his secretary of state, Cyrus Vance, made numerous trips to the Middle East over the next several months to finalize the agreement. One guarantee that Carter made was to organize an international peacekeeping force to occupy the Sinai following the Israeli withdrawal. It still operates to this day. The United States also promised $2 billion to pay for the relocation of an airfield from the Sinai to Israel and made guarantees of economic assistance to Egypt in exchange for Sadat's signature. Egypt received about $2 billion in annual military and economic aid for the next thirty years.

Finally, on March 26, 1979, in a White House ceremony Sadat and Begin signed a permanent peace treaty normalizing relations between their two countries. When the accord was reached, all sides believed that other Arab states, particularly the pro-Western regimes in Jordan and Saudi Arabia, would follow Egypt's lead. They were mistaken. Sadat was denounced for having sold out the Arab cause, and Egypt was expelled from the Arab League. Several Middle Eastern states broke off diplomatic relations with Cairo, and Sadat was soon assassinated by members of his own military.

Brent Geary

See also: Arab-Israeli War, 1973; Arab League; Begin, Menachem; Egypt; Israel; Sadat, Anwar

Further Reading

Carter, James E. *Keeping Faith: Memoirs of the President.* New York: Bantam Books, 1982.

Quandt, William. *Camp David: Peacemaking and Politics.* Washington, DC: Brookings Institution, 1986.

Camp David Summit, 2000

A two-week summit in which U.S. president Bill Clinton hosted Israeli prime minister Ehud Barak and Yasser Arafat, chairman of the Palestinian Authority (PA), in a failed effort to negotiate a final settlement agreement. Clinton brokered the meeting in the hope of building on the monumental success of the Oslo Accords several years earlier. Oslo had established mutual Israeli-Palestinian recognition and a greater role for Palestinian governance, but it was only intended as a transition agreement. Clinton's aim for the summit, therefore, was to reach a final status agreement on all major issues, including the sovereignty of Jerusalem, final borders of a new Palestinian state, Israeli settlements in Palestinian territory, Palestinian refugees and their claim to a right of return, and Israeli security. This all-or-nothing approach proved impossible to manage in a dispute with so many potential spoilers. In addition, the summit was hastily organized. Clinton had only six months left in office and wanted to leave his mark on the Israeli-Palestinian conflict with a peace deal. Moreover, he wanted to help Barak stay in power because his main rival, Ariel Sharon, was opposed to the Oslo Accords.

Barak promoted compromise with the Palestinians, but many Israelis opposed making territorial concessions. Indeed, just a few years earlier, another prime minister, Yitzhak Rabin, had been assassinated by an Israeli Jew for his participation in the Oslo peace process. Barak concluded that his best chance for political survival was to deliver a peace deal with the Palestinians that did not include major concessions. He made numerous offers at Camp David, but all were rejected by Arafat as woefully unacceptable.

Barak's last offer was his most generous, but it was presented by Clinton as an American proposal that was a take-it-or-leave-it proposition. When Arafat asked for clarification on vague language regarding sovereignty over the Temple Mount and Palestinian refugees, the talks collapsed. None of the offers made by Barak at Camp David were written down and were made contingent on Arafat's acceptance. But Arafat feared assassination if he compromised on key issues like East Jerusalem without first gaining support from other Arab leaders on specific proposals.

At the conference's conclusion, the summit's participants signed a Trilateral Statement, dated July 25, 2000, in lieu of a negotiated settlement. The statement outlined principles for further negotiation, including an indictment of unilateral actions and a commitment to the principles of UN Security Council Resolutions 242 and 338. Further negotiations occurred in Jerusalem in September, in Washington in December, and then at Taba in January 2001, but these talks were overtaken by events.

Not long after Camp David, Sharon visited the Temple Mount with hundreds of security personnel in tow to declare Israel's sovereignty. Palestinians protested his arrival with widespread demonstrations that included rock throwing and tire burnings. Israeli security personnel responded with live ammunition, killing many of the protesters. The violence soon spiraled into the extremely bloody Second Intifada. The Likud Party won parliamentary elections that were held soon after violence erupted, and Sharon became prime minister.

Sean P. Braniff and Robert DiPrizio

See also: Arafat, Yasser; Haram al-Sharif/Temple Mount; Intifada, Second; Oslo Accords; Rabin, Yitzhak; Sharon, Ariel; Two-State Solution; UN Security Council Resolution 242; UN Security Council Resolution 338

Further Reading
Bickerton, Ian J., and Carla L. Klausner. *A History of the Arab-Israeli Conflict.* 7th ed. Boston: Pearson Books, 2015.
Eisenberg, Laura Zittrain, and Neil Caplan. *Negotiating Arab-Israeli Peace: Patterns, Problems, Possibilities.* 2nd ed. Bloomington: Indiana University Press, 2010.

Canaanites

Inhabitants of Canaan in Palestine, or ancient Israel, during the time of the Old Testament. The word *Canaan* might come from a Hebrew word meaning "low," and some scholars have taken that to mean that the original land of Canaan was the low land near the sea in Palestine. It may also be a reference to the reddish-purple dye made in Canaan. According to the Old Testament, the Canaanites were believed to be the descendants of Canaan, son of Ham and grandson of Noah.

According to the Book of Genesis, the descendants of Canaan formed themselves into several tribes that settled in western Palestine. Scholars do not know very much about those tribes, though they appear to have moved into the area between 3000 and 2000 BCE. The main groups were the Amorites, who settled in the inland areas, and the Canaanites, who settled on the coast and in the lowlands, but there were no clear lines between them. Instead, they seem to have been fractured into a number of kingdoms that occasionally fought with one another. They also seem to have been subject to the pharaohs of Egypt, sending tribute to the Egyptian rulers. The Canaanites built several large cities with massive walls and filled with iron chariots; Jericho was the most famous of these. They worshipped the deities Astarte, Baal, and Moloch and were said to sacrifice their children on stone altars. Historians believe that the Canaanites were the first to use an alphabet.

The Canaanites lived in Phoenicia and Palestine. The land of Canaan seems to have encompassed at least most of western Palestine, from the Mediterranean Sea to the Jordan River, and south to the land of Judah. Their territory might also have encompassed the land of the Philistines. The name *Canaanite* eventually became synonymous with the term *trader* because the people of Phoenicia were known for their trading prowess. The Phoenician people sometimes referred to themselves as descendants of Canaan.

During the Israelite invasion of Canaan, led by Joshua sometime c. 1400 BCE, the Israelites attacked the Canaanite cities and conquered many of them. Solomon later issued orders making all Canaanites slaves of the Hebrews.

Amy Hackney Blackwell

See also: Israelite Conquest of Canaan; United Kingdom of Israel

Further Reading
Golden, Jonathan M. *Ancient Canaan and Israel: An Introduction.* Oxford: Oxford University Press, 2009.
Killebrew, Ann E. *Biblical Peoples and Ethnicity: An Archaeological Study of Egyptians, Canaanites, Philistines, and Early Israel 1300–1100 B.C.E.* Atlanta: Society of Biblical Literature, 2005.
Schreiber, Mordecai, ed. *The Shengold Jewish Encyclopedia.* Rockville, MD: Schreiber Pub., 2003.

Cave of the Patriarchs Massacre

Terror attack by an Israeli settler on Palestinian worshippers. On February 25, 1994, American-born Baruch Goldstein (1956–1994) attacked hundreds of Muslim worshippers praying during Ramadan at the Cave of the Patriarchs, located in Hebron, West Bank. Goldstein wore an Israel Defense Forces (IDF) uniform and used an Israeli-made Galil assault rifle in the attack, which he opened by hurling a hand grenade into a crowd of prostrate worshippers. He fired 140 rounds, killing 29 people and wounding more than 125 before being overwhelmed, disarmed, and beaten to death by the crowd.

Goldstein was a member of the Kach Movement, a far-right political movement founded by Rabbi Meir Kahane. He may have been motivated by the assassination of Kahane in 1990 by a Muslim attacker in New York City. Goldstein believed that the Israeli government should eject all Arabs from the nation as a security measure, and a final confrontation was imminent.

In the aftermath of the attack, violence erupted between Palestinians and Israelis, largely in retaliatory actions. Two Hamas suicide bombers attacked targets inside Israel, killing fourteen and wounding eighty-five, at the end of the forty-day mourning period for the victims.

Paul J. Springer

See also: Hebron; Intifada, First; Kahane, Meir

Further Reading
Inbari, Motti. *Messianic Religious Zionism Confronts Israeli Territorial Compromises.* Cambridge: Cambridge University Press, 2012.
Sprinzak, Ehud. "Extremism and Violence in Israeli Democracy." *Terrorism and Political Violence* 12, no. 3–4 (Autumn–Winter 2000): 209–236.

Christian Zionism

The belief among some Christians that the creation of Israel is in accordance with biblical prophecy. The term *Christian Zionist* is generally used to describe those who, on the basis of their Christian beliefs, support the existence of a Jewish state in some portion of the biblical Promised Land.

Christian Zionism arose out of a theological movement known as *premillennial dispensationalism,* which was systematized in the eighteenth century by Anglo-Irish theologian John Nelson Darby and American evangelists such as Dwight Moody and Cyrus I. Schofield. Premillennial dispensationalism, unlike other Christian eschatology, asserts that human history will unfold in specific stages that will culminate in the return of Jesus Christ to establish the millennium—a 1,000-year reign of peace attested to in the Book of Revelation. These stages include the return of all Jews to their land, the so-called Rapture (ascension) of the faithful directly into heaven, and an escalating series of upheavals that culminate in the battle of Armageddon.

Most Christian Zionists believe that the establishment of the state of Israel in 1948 was the beginning of the fulfillment of biblical prophecy that Jews would be returned to their land. The next step for which Christian Zionists advocate is the rebuilding of the temple on the Temple Mount, currently home to two Islamic holy sites: the Dome of the Rock and al-Aqsa Mosque. Many Christian Zionists believe that Jews also must convert to Christianity for biblical prophecy to be fulfilled. Others eschew dispensationalism, instead anchoring their support for Israel on biblical passages that identify Jews as God's "chosen" people and Palestine as their Promised Land, and threaten to smite those who curse the Jews.

There are tens of millions of Christian Zionists in the United States. It is a particularly popular ideology among evangelicals. Christian Zionist organizations like Christians United for Israel and the National Christian Leadership Conference for Israel contribute tens of millions of dollars per year in charitable donations to Israel, and also lobby state and federal government officials to adopt what they see as pro-Israel policies.

Deonna Neal

See also: Christianity; Haram al-Sharif/Temple Mount; U.S. Aid to Israel; Zionism

Further Reading

Clark, Victoria. *Allies for Armageddon: The Rise of Christian Zionism*. New Haven, CT: Yale University Press, 2007.

Goldman, Samuel. *God's Country: Christian Zionism in America*. University Park: Penn State University Press, 2018.

Weber, Timothy P. *On the Road to Armageddon: How Evangelicals Became Israel's Best Friend*. Grand Rapids, MI: Baker Academic Press, 2004.

Christianity

An Abrahamic, monotheistic religion with over 2 billion adherents. Christianity teaches that Jesus of Nazareth was the long-awaited messiah (Christ) foretold by the Jewish scriptures. He was born between 6 and 4 BCE and lived for thirty-three years. His followers believe in his moral teachings, baptism, communion, and resurrection of the dead, with a missionary imperative to spread his message. Churches were established throughout the Middle East and parts of Europe, Africa, India, and elsewhere in Asia within the first century CE.

Christianity was initially viewed by the Romans as a schismatic sect of Judaism, and Christians were persecuted until the conversion of the emperor Constantine in 312. He issued the Edict of Milan, legalizing Christianity, and moved the imperial capital to Byzantium (renamed Constantinople). Church leaders convened ecumenical councils to address competing theologies, which produced statements of faith or *creeds* that outlined orthodoxy. Many believed that the establishment of the church adulterated its message and escaped to the deserts of Egypt and Syria, giving birth to the monastic movement. Those who disagreed with the council of Nicaea (325) regarding the nature of Christ broke away to form the Jacobite (Syrian Orthodox), Coptic, Ethiopian, Armenian, and Nestorian (Church of the East) confessions.

Eastern Christians populated large portions of Asia and Africa and much of what is now considered the Middle East. These communities remained the dominant religion of the Middle East until the Arab conquests of the seventh century. Christianity continued to flourish for decades, building many churches around holy sites, but it eventually declined in the region as a result of persecution and conversion. Most Middle Eastern churches disappeared by the mid-twentieth century. Some Eastern churches (Melkites) continued to support the orthodox confession following the council of Chalcedon (451).

The Roman Catholic and Eastern Orthodox confessions developed in the West. Barbarians sacked Rome, while the imperial church maintained power in Constantinople. Following the decline of the Roman Empire, church leaders (known as *popes*) emerged as de facto rulers by providing leadership and order. Charlemagne eventually restored the Western Empire in 800, recognizing the pope as the ecclesiastical head of the Holy Roman Empire. The papacy eventually weakened, however, due to competing claimants and ecclesiastical abuses such as the selling of church offices and indulgences. Priests and bishops mediated worship for the church.

Throughout the fifth century, many invaders converted to Christianity, spreading its growth throughout Europe. The pope split with the Orthodox patriarchs over theology and questions of primacy in 1054. The Eastern Orthodox Church expanded into Russia in the tenth century.

In the eleventh century, the Roman church responded to the rapid advance of Islam with a series of eight Crusades lasting two centuries. Christians from Europe sought to liberate the holy land, while protecting holy sites, pilgrimages, and Constantinople. The Crusades included the killing of women, children, Jews, Arabs, and other Christians. Ottoman Turks captured Constantinople in 1453, and they made the imperial church (Hagia Sophia) there into a mosque.

Printing presses permitted the distribution of Christian scripture in local vernaculars. This gave birth to dissenting movements seeking to reform the church and eventually known as *Protestantism*. Protestants emphasized the authority of Scripture, salvation by grace, personal conversion, and the priesthood of all believers. Initially, principalities throughout Europe defined themselves religiously according to the confession of their rulers. In some areas, Christians persecuted or warred against those who belonged to rival churches. At the conclusion of the Thirty Years' War, the Peace of Westphalia (1648) gave birth to the modern secular state.

As European powers developed shipbuilding, they expanded across the oceans, taking Christianity with them. Spain and Portugal exported Catholicism to South America and Africa. Protestants, escaping persecution in England, came to North America to form colonies in New England. Spiritual renewal movements, focusing on individual conversion and experience, produced the Great Awakening revivals of the eighteenth century—which doubled American Protestant congregations. Evangelical churches emerged, which promoted individual expressions of faith over clergy-mediated worship.

The Industrial Revolution resulted in a growing divide between church and state. The poor were marginalized in overcrowded slums and substandard living conditions. Protestant churches developed programs to educate children and alleviate suffering, including the Young Men's Christian Association (YMCA), Sunday school, and the Salvation Army. Renewed Christian activism eventually fueled the abolitionist movement in England. Protestantism divided along racial lines in the United States with the growth of several black churches resulting from segregation and discrimination. These churches became instrumental in the civil rights movements of the twentieth century.

Following the two world wars, some Christians expected Christ's imminent return. Believing that this could not occur without a Jewish state, many Protestants called for its creation. While Zionism was embraced by many in the evangelical and fundamentalist movements, other Christians opposed it. Mainline Protestants and Roman Catholics saw the formation of the state of Israel as a move that would produce conflict and ongoing hatred for the West. Some in the modern church, especially evangelicals, see the state of Israel as evidence of biblical prophecy and actively support it. Other Christians decry Israel's inhumane treatment of Arabs.

Christian expansion has been characterized by both oppressive colonialism and liberation movements. In the Middle East, Catholics often sought to bring Eastern churches under their authority, while Protestants looked to aid them in renewal. While the percentage of Christians in Europe is in decline, exponential growth is predicted in the Global South. Analysts predict that by 2025, sub-Saharan Africa will emerge as the nexus of global Christianity. However, the Christian population living in the Holy Land today is small (about 200,000) and is likely to continue to dwindle. Most Christians in this area are Palestinians. Many live under occupation, but Israel is home to a small number of Palestinian Christians and a small number of Christians from the former Soviet Union who came over with Jewish family members in the 1990s. Palestinian Christians trace their roots to the earliest days of the religion. The West Bank town of Bethlehem, the birthplace of Jesus, is home to over 30,000 Palestinian Christians.

David R. Leonard

See also: Bethlehem; Christian Zionism; Church of the Holy Sepulcher; Crusades in the Holy Land; Jerusalem; Jerusalem, Old City of

Further Reading

Gonzalez, Justo L. *The Story of Christianity, Vol. 1: The Early Church to the Dawn of the Reformation,* New York: HarperOne, 2010.

Jenkins, Philip. *The Lost History of Christianity: The Thousand-Year Golden Age of the Church in the Middle East, Africa, and Asia—and How It Died.* New York: HarperOne, 2009.

Jenkins, Philip. *The Next Christendom: The Coming of Global Christianity.* New York: Oxford University Press, 2007.

Merkley, Paul Charles. *Christian Attitudes Towards the State of Israel, 1948–2000.* Montreal: McGill-Queens University Press, 2001.

Church of the Holy Sepulcher

Significant Christian holy site in Jerusalem. The Church of the Holy Sepulcher, also known as the *Church of the Resurrection,* is located in the northwest quarter of the Old City of Jerusalem, now occupied by Israel. The church sits atop the site believed since the third century CE to be that of Jesus Christ's crucifixion (Golgotha) and the tomb out of which Jesus arose.

The Via Dolorosa (Italian for "Trail of Tears") is a street in the Old City of Jerusalem that is the alleged path that Jesus trod with his cross to Golgotha. The final five stations of this path are contained within the walls of the church. Constantine I, the first Christian Roman emperor, directed Bishop Makarios of Jerusalem

The Church of the Holy Sepulcher in the Old City of Jerusalem was first established by order of the Roman emperor Constantine I in 330 CE. Believed to be built on the site where Jesus was crucified, buried, and resurrected, the church is considered one of the holiest sites in Christianity. (Corel)

(builder of the Church of the Nativity in Bethlehem) to construct the church. It was completed in 335 CE, only to be razed and rebuilt numerous times by Jerusalem's conquerors.

The building was first divided among its primary custodians, the Greek Orthodox, the Armenian Apostolic, and Roman Catholic churches, in 1767. A status quo document was signed in 1852, making the divisions permanent and assigning lesser custodial responsibilities to the Coptic Orthodox, the Ethiopian Orthodox, and the Syriac Orthodox churches that also share the building. Disagreements among all the custodians continue into the twenty-first century despite this document.

The main entrance to the church is a single door controlled by the Nuseibeh and Joudeh families, two neutral neighboring Muslim families given this responsibility by Saladin in 1192, after defeating the Crusaders. The door is unlocked on a rotating schedule agreed upon by the various religious communities. Common areas of worship within the building are used on an agreed-upon schedule. The building also serves as the headquarters of the Orthodox patriarch of Jerusalem and the Catholic archpriest of the Basilica of the Holy Sepulcher.

Richard M. Edwards

See also: Christianity; Crusades in the Holy Land; Roman Conquest of Judea

Further Reading

Clark, Victoria. *Holy Fire: The Battle for Christ's Tomb.* New York: Macmillan, 2005.

Mansour, Atallah. *Narrow Gate Churches: The Christian Presence in the Holy Land Under Muslim and Jewish Rule.* Carol Stream, IL: Hope Publishing House, 2004.

Poole, Karen, ed. *Jerusalem and the Holy Land.* New York: Dorling Kindersley, 2007.

Closed Military Zones

Areas into which the Israeli military prohibits entry without explicit permission. There are many closed military zones in the Occupied Palestinian Territories (OPT), which restrict the presence of Palestinians. Some of these zones are established for limited durations to manage flare-ups, but others remain in place indefinitely. Closed military zones have been set up around many Israeli settlements and between the security barrier and the Green Line. Palestinians can tend land that they own inside these zones with a special permit—but Israel rarely grants these permits. Israeli settlers sometime establish their own exclusion zones around settlements. These are created ostensibly for security reasons, but the exclusion zones are often used by settlers for cultivation or other activities. Israeli authorities rarely interfere with such activities.

Closed firing zones are a separate but related category. These are established ostensibly for military training purposes, even though some are rarely used in this manner. Access to these areas is strictly controlled by the Israeli military. Sometimes Palestinian residents are allowed to remain, sometimes not. About 15 percent of the West Bank is designated as closed firing zones. While Israel insists these zone restrictions are necessary for security purposes, critics insist that they are methods by which Israelis expand their control over Palestinian territory.

Robert C. DiPrizio and Tom Dowling

See also: Israeli Occupations; West Bank

Further Reading
Association for Civil Rights in Israel. *Info-Sheet: The 12 Villages of Firing Zone 918 in the South Hebron Hills.* Updated February 21, 2016. https://law.acri.org.il/en/2016/02/21/firing-zone-918-infosheet.
United Nations, Office for the Coordination of Humanitarian Affairs. *The Humanitarian Impact of Israeli-Declared "Firing Zones" in the West Bank.* August 2012; https://www.ochaopt.org/sites/default/files/ocha_opt_firing_zone_factsheet_august_2012_english.pdf.

Crusades in the Holy Land

A long, protracted conflict between Christian Europe and the Islamic Near East over the land and holy sites of modern-day Palestine. It amounted to several aggressive attempts by European nobility, at the behest of successive popes, to reinforce the Latin kingdom or regain territory lost to Islam, but it gave the appearance of multiple invasions.

During the seventh and eighth centuries, Islam swept out of the Near East, across North Africa, and into Spain, where it began to encroach on central Europe. During the tenth century, European Christianity went on the offensive, and by the eleventh century, the tide began to turn against Islam. Christian Europe hoped to expel Muslim rule from Europe and recover Jerusalem for Christianity.

Italian city-states exercised naval and commercial dominance, and the German empire was on the rise. Christianity was spreading into northern Europe, and the number of pilgrimages to the Holy Land and other sacred sites increased. The desire to spread the gospel was mixed with the desire to open new markets and conquer new territories. Despite the opportunity for war with the Muslims, the feudal barons of central Europe engaged in private wars with one another. The need for peace compelled the pope to declare the Peace of God, and later the Truce of God, in a vain attempt to limit such conflict.

Image from an illuminated manuscript depicting the capture of Jerusalem in 1099 during the First Crusade. Once in control of the city, Crusaders massacred many of its Muslim, Christian, and Jewish inhabitants. (Library of Congress)

POPE URBAN II AND THE FIRST CRUSADE

By 1095, the power and influence of the papacy, as well as the sanctity of the majority of the clergy, were waning, while the power and influence of the German empire were on the rise. Pope Urban II, fearing that the Catholic Church would lose what little influence it had, and horrified at the results of continued infighting among the Christian nobility, sought a way to unite Christendom in a common cause. At the Council of Clermont, he preached the First Crusade. It was a mixture of propaganda concerning the alleged cruelty of Muslims to Christian pilgrims, a request for aid by Byzantine emperor Alexius I Comnenus, a call for a display of righteous action toward the recovery of Jerusalem, and an offer of remission of sins for those who participated.

The effect was overwhelming. Not only did the nobility—his prime audience—heed Urban's call, but so did many peasants and the poor in the cities. Others also took to preaching the Crusade, most notably Peter the Hermit, whose call went mostly to peasants and street rabble. The nobility were led by Godfrey of Bouillon, Raymond I of Toulouse, and Bohemund I. Along with the peasants and rabble, they made up six hosts of 100,000 to 200,000 *cruciata*, or cross-signed, who traveled to meet in Constantinople before continuing on to Jerusalem.

The so-called Peasants' Crusade, led by Peter the Hermit, consisted primarily of peasants and petty criminals. It preceded the main contingents of nobility and men-at-arms and turned into a binge of pillage, thievery, and eventual widespread murder of innocent Jews. Many of Peter's "army" died at the hands of the Turks; only a few reached Constantinople.

THE NOBILITY AND THEIR ARMIES IN THE FIRST CRUSADE

The main forces under command of the nobility reached Constantinople in 1096. The leaders were required to swear allegiance to Alexius, emperor of the Byzantine Empire, in return for immediate gifts and a promise of future help (neither of which was ever forthcoming). Alexius's main objective was to get the Crusaders to help him regain territories lost to the Turks. Before they were allowed to leave for Jerusalem, however, the Crusaders were coerced into helping Emperor Alexius capture the city of Nicaea in 1097.

The Muslim world was totally unprepared for the Christian invasion; the strength and power of the mounted knights, as well as the bravery of the common foot soldiers, were more than a match for the Muslim cavalry. The march to Palestine was marked by a decisive victory at the Battle of Dorylaeum and the conquest of Tarsus by Baldwin I and Tancred. The Crusaders and their camp followers were not prepared, however, for the arduous march through the Black Mountains toward Antioch. This journey killed of many through hunger, thirst, and heat.

Antioch fell to the Crusaders in 1098 after eight months despite poor provisions and ill health among the besiegers. The Crusaders' confidence in the leadership of their God and the righteousness of their cause helped them to overcome numerous attempts by the inhabitants to break the siege and defeat reinforcements attempting to relieve the city. Antioch finally fell, after betrayal by one of its citizens. The Crusaders spent the next several months in Antioch recuperating, making local conquests, and repelling Turkish attempts to regain the city. Bohemond finally secured Antioch for himself as the others continued to Jerusalem.

Tales of the seeming invincibility of the Christian army preceded it, and the march toward Bethlehem and Jerusalem was without incident. The Crusaders reached Jerusalem in 1099 and immediately put it under siege. It fell to Godfrey and Raymond on July 15. For several days, any Muslims found were put to death. After the 1099 Siege of Jerusalem and the securing of the surrounding territory, most of the Crusaders returned home, believing that they had done what was required of them by their God and their pope. Only the adventurers stayed to establish the four Crusader States. These four states, the Kingdom of Jerusalem and the vassal states of the County of Edessa, Principality of Antioch, and eventually the County of Tripoli, were islands of Christianity in a hostile sea of Islam.

MUSLIMS, CHRISTIANS, AND THE SECOND CRUSADE

The Muslim world was now much more aware of the Crusaders' presence and purpose, their strengths and weaknesses. Muslims wasted little time in trying to regain what had been taken from them. Communications between the four Crusader States was difficult, if not impossible, and the Christians' only hope of survival lay in reinforcements from Europe.

The Second Crusade was preached by the pope and Bernard of Clairvaux after the fall of Edessa in 1144 to Zangi, governor of Mosul. This Crusade was led by Louis VII of France and Conrad III of Germany during 1147–1149. The two armies were unable to cooperate and were separately defeated in Asia Minor. An attempt to capture Damascus failed, and the Crusaders returned home.

THE THIRD CRUSADE AND MUSLIM MILITARY RESURGENCE

Muslim power was consolidated under Zangi, his son, Nur al-Din, and later Saladin, who sought a holy war with Christianity. In 1187, Saladin's army captured Jerusalem. This caused the pope to preach the Third Crusade of 1189–1192, which was led by Philip Augustus of France, Richard the Lionhearted of England, and Holy Roman Emperor Frederick I (Frederick Barbarossa). Frederick drowned in Asia Minor, and Philip and Richard were unable to work together because of jealousy. Philip returned home and left Richard in the Holy Land; Richard won the Siege of Acre but was unable to recapture Jerusalem. The best he could manage was a treaty with Saladin to allow safe passage for pilgrims visiting Jerusalem.

THE FOURTH, FIFTH, SIXTH, AND SEVENTH CRUSADES

In 1198, Pope Innocent III's influence finally brought peace to the feuding nobility of Europe, and he tried to reestablish the Fourth Crusade as a holy cause.

This Crusade was led mainly by the Venetians, whose only goal was to expand their trading empire by destroying the influence of Constantinople. This they did with the sacking of Constantinople in 1204 by the Crusaders, whom the Venetians had starved into compliance after they could not afford passage to the Holy Land.

In 1215, Innocent III proclaimed the Fifth Crusade of 1218–1221. Emperor Frederick II of Germany obtained the title of king of Jerusalem by marriage in 1225 but was excommunicated in 1227 for delaying his start of the Crusade. In 1228, Frederick finally went to the Holy Land in the Sixth Crusade, gaining Jerusalem, Bethlehem, Nazareth, and a connecting strip of land to Acre—by treaty, not by conquest.

In 1244, Jerusalem fell to the Muslims, and a new Crusade was proclaimed by Innocent IV in 1245. This Seventh Crusade was led by Louis IX of France during 1248–1254. Although he invaded Egypt and captured Damietta, Louis was taken prisoner, and Damietta was lost. Egypt revolted, and a new Muslim movement called for the recovery of Syria. Within the next few years, all remaining Christian possessions in Syria were recaptured.

SUBSEQUENT CRUSADES

The Crusades effectively came to an end after the Seventh Crusade, but some continued to fight. In 1269, King James of Aragon in Spain reluctantly launched the Aragonese Crusade under pressure from the pope. James was driven off by heavy storms and failed in his attempt to land in Asia Minor. In 1270, Louis IX renewed his Crusade with the Eighth Crusade. Instead of going to the Holy Land directly, he sailed to Tunis, on the mistaken information that the ruler there was interested in converting to Christianity. Louis laid siege, and an epidemic killed much of the invading force, including Louis. His brother negotiated some tribute and left.

Peter I of Cyprus began a Crusade in 1365 that lasted until 1369. He harassed the Muslim Mediterranean coast, and in 1365, he captured Alexandria. It ended with Peter's assassination. In 1396, Pope Boniface IX called for the Crusade of Nicopolis, to halt Muslim expansion in the Balkans. French knights made up the bulk of the force that responded, but they were soundly defeated by the Turks at Nicopolis in Bulgaria.

THE FINAL CRUSADE

The Last Crusade was fought during 1443–1444. King Ladislas of Poland organized a group of Hungarians, Poles, Bosnians, Wallachians, and Serbians to expel the Muslims under Murat II from the Balkans. A Venetian fleet was to ferry the Crusaders from Varna to Constantinople and stop any Muslim reinforcements from crossing the Bosporus. The fleet failed, and Murat's army crushed the Crusaders at the Battle of Varna.

EVALUATING THE CRUSADES: GOALS AND RESULTS

The major military goals of the Crusades—driving Muslims from the Holy Land and imposing Western culture on the captured territory—were never accomplished.

On the contrary, the Crusades strengthened and united the Islamic world and weakened the Byzantine Empire until it was overcome by the Turks in the fifteenth century. They succeeded, however, in accomplishing Pope Urban II's original goals of returning the papacy to its previous position of power and influence and eventually ending feudal warfare.

The long-term consequences of the Crusades for the West were generally negative, as the high cost of foreign warfare impoverished the aristocracy. The population of Europe was depleted, and the Catholic Church lost much of its stature after successive defeats. In spite of its decreasing influence over the Crusaders, however, the Catholic Church enjoyed a power rarely exercised before or since. But that power corrupted. The sale of indulgences and the exaction of tithes (church taxes) led away from spirituality and into worldliness, which people like Martin Luther would later use as justification for the Protestant Reformation.

There were some positive aspects for Europe, however. A sense of unity prevailed for a time under the banner of the Church. France, a struggling set of dukedoms and principalities, began unifying into a single country, although it would be fought over by internal and external factions for years to come. Although the Knights Templar and Knights Hospitaller suffered a severe decline, the Teutonic Knights (another military order of monks) began fighting the Church's enemies in Eastern Europe, and in so doing laid the foundations for the countries of both Poland and Germany. Also, Italian merchants were able to establish trading privileges in the major ports of Acre and Tyre. By controlling the Mediterranean Sea, they provided Muslim merchants with access to European goods while remaining the sole distributors of Asian goods to the West. Italian traders were able to move and work freely in dedicated districts of these cities and gained some legal control over citizens and visitors within those districts.

The Crusades had a profound effect on commerce and trade, both inside and outside Europe. Feudalism and serfdom disintegrated. A money economy began to predominate, which stimulated a need for banks. Spheres of influence were set up in port cities of Palestine by the trading powers of Venice, Genoa, and Pisa, providing easier acquisition of goods from both the Near and Far East. Navigation and shipbuilding improved with the increased need for transportation of people and goods. But many of the developments attributed to the Crusades were merely the end result of changes that had begun before Pope Urban's call to retake the Holy Land. The Crusades served only to facilitate and accelerate them.

Thomas E. Davis

See also: Christianity; Church of the Holy Sepulcher; Hattin, Battle of; Islam; Jerusalem; Saladin

Further Reading

Armstrong, Karen. *Holy War: The Crusades and Their Impact on Today's World.* New York: Anchor Books, 2001.

Bronstein, Judith. *The Hospitallers and the Holy Land: Financing the Latin East, 1187–1274.* Woodbridge, UK: Boydell, 2005.

Phillips, Jonathan. *The Crusades: 1095–1197.* New York: Longman, 2002.

Dahlan, Mohammed

Palestinian politician in both Fatah and the Palestinian Authority (PA). Mohammed Dahlan was born September 29, 1961, in the Khan Yunis Refugee Camp in the Gaza Strip. His family had fled Hammama, Palestine (now Nitzanim, Israel). Dahlan became politically active as a teenager in Khan Yunis, recruiting youngsters for civic projects. As a college student in Gaza, he created a youth organization that became the Fatah Youth Movement in 1981.

By age 25, Dahlan had been arrested by the Israeli authorities eleven times. He spent six years in prison, where he learned Hebrew. One of the leaders of the First Intifada, in which the Fatah Youth Movement was very much involved, Dahlan was again arrested by the Israeli authorities in 1988 and deported to Jordan. He then went to Tunis, where he worked with the leaders of the Palestine Liberation Organization (PLO).

A protégé of PLO chairman Yasser Arafat, Dahlan returned to Gaza with him in 1994 and was appointed head of the Preventive Security Service (PSS) for the Gaza Strip. With a police force of 20,000 men, Dahlan became the most powerful figure in Gaza. To enforce his authority, his associates reportedly used strong-arm methods, including torture. As with many other Fatah leaders, he became very wealthy through PLO monopolies over commodities like oil and cement and through kickbacks on building contracts.

As head of the PSS in Gaza, Dahlan met regularly with Israeli security officials and U.S. Central Intelligence Agency (CIA) representatives to coordinate security issues. Dahlan negotiated with Israeli officials on a variety of issues, including at Wye River (1998), Camp David (2000), and the Taba negotiations (2001).

Enjoying support from the George W. Bush administration, Dahlan fancied himself as the successor to Arafat but lost out to Mahmoud Abbas. In early 2007, in the wake of the victory of Hamas at the polls, President Abbas appointed Dahlan chief of the reformed security forces in Gaza. He received weapons, funding, and training from the United States, reportedly as part of a plan to overthrow Hamas in Gaza. But Hamas struck first and drove PA forces out of the Strip. Many in Fatah blamed Dahlan for the easy Hamas victory, pointing out that he and his key lieutenants were absent from Gaza at the time. In the course of the fighting, Dahlan's Gaza residence—which many Palestinians had come to view as a symbol of Fatah corruption—was demolished by Hamas militants.

Viewing Dahlan as a political threat, President Abbas expelled him from West Bank in 2011 amid allegations that he played a role in Arafat's 2004 death. He lives in the United Arab Emirates and has close relations with the ruling family. He has reportedly met with leaders in Egypt, the United States, Israel, and Gaza in an effort to build support for his bid to become the next PA president. He remains a controversial figure within the Palestinian community.

Spencer C. Tucker

See also: Abbas, Mahmoud; Arafat, Yasser; Palestinian Authority; Palestinians

Further Reading

Pappe, Ilan. *A History of Modern Palestine: One Land, Two Peoples*. Cambridge: Cambridge University Press, 2003.

Parsons, Nigel. *The Politics of the Palestinian Authority: From Oslo to Al-Aqsa*. London: Routledge, 2005.

David

Second king of ancient Israel, noted for uniting all the Israelite tribes into one kingdom. David was born in Bethlehem in the eleventh century BCE. As a youth, he was anointed by the prophet Samuel as the successor of Saul, the first king of Israel. David distinguished himself in battle with the Philistines, and according to the Old Testament, he slew the Philistine Goliath with a mere slingshot. As David's popularity grew, King Saul became jealous and plotted to kill him. However, David fled to southern Judah and Philistia until Saul's demise.

David gained support from the people of Judah by protecting them from raiders and regaining their stolen property. He returned to Hebron around the age of thirty, when Saul and all but one of his sons were killed in battle with the Philistines. David was quickly recognized as the king of Israel in Hebron, Judah, and other neighboring areas.

After seven-and-a-half years in Hebron, David conquered the city of Jerusalem from the Jebusites, moving the capital of Israel there. Beginning at about 1000 BCE, he reigned in Jerusalem for about thirty-three years. David was a skillful military leader, and from Jerusalem, he commanded the Israelites to victories over the Philistines and other small kingdoms, including Ammon, Edom, and Moab. He also ordered the building of several public works, including highways for trade and travel. Under David's rule, Israel prospered economically and socially.

Before David's reign, most of Israel consisted of loose tribal unions. In an effort to keep the tribes united, he married women from each of the various kingdoms, hoping to build a familial relationship that could serve as a model for all of Israel.

David continued to conquer the surrounding regions and put down occasional revolts in Israel. One of his greatest achievements was his reacquisition of the Ark of the Covenant from the Philistines. The ark was a rectangular wooden box that housed the Ten Commandments tablets and other sacred Israelite relics. David placed the ark in a tabernacle in Jerusalem built especially for it. The Ark of the Covenant was carried in public feast processionals, pilgrimages, and during battle to demonstrate God's presence with his people.

About the time of the recovery of the Ark of the Covenant, David committed adultery with Bathsheba. When he found out she was pregnant, he had her soldier husband sent to the front lines of battle, where he was killed. Although the infant died, Bathsheba later conceived another child by David: Solomon. Upon David's death (c. 962 BCE) in Jerusalem, Solomon became king and continued his father's policy of a united Israel.

David is one of the most important figures in the history of Judaism and Christianity. In the Jewish tradition, the house of David became a symbol of God's relationship with his chosen people. The word *messiah* is derived from the Hebrew *hameshiach* ("the anointed one"), the title of the Israelite kings. By tracing Jesus' lineage back to David, early Christians determined that Jesus was the messiah—the new king—that God had promised to send from the house of David.

Christina Girod

See also: Canaanites; First and Second Temple Periods; Israelite Conquest of Canaan; United Kingdom of Israel

Further Reading
Brueggemann, Walter. *David's Truth in Israel's Imagination and Memory.* Minneapolis: Fortress Press, 2002.
Kirsch, Jonathan. *King David: The Real Life of the Man Who Ruled Israel.* New York: Ballantine Books, 2000.
McKenzie, Steven. *King David: A Biography.* New York: Oxford University Press, 2000.

Dayan, Moshe

A popular general and statesman, one of the most important founders of Israel. Distinguished by a trademark black eyepatch, Moshe Dayan was a heroic figure to many Israelis due to his service in Haganah (an underground Jewish militia in Palestine) and victories in various subsequent wars. He was born on May 20, 1915, at Degania, Palestine's first kibbutz, but grew up in Nahalal, a cooperative farm settlement. He joined the Haganah when he was a teenager and later was recruited by British authorities to help guard settlements and railways and respond to Arab guerrillas near the border with Lebanon.

However, in 1939, Britain backed away from its policy of supporting a Jewish homeland in Palestine, outlawed Haganah, and imprisoned Dayan. Dayan was released in 1941 to lead some Haganah volunteers on a reconnaissance mission in Syria against the Germans. Leading a unit ahead of the main Allied invading force, Dayan was struck by a bullet and lost his left eye.

During Israel's War for Independence in 1948, Dayan served as commander of West Jerusalem, successfully defending it against a siege and negotiating a truce with the Jordanians. He later participated in negotiations with Jordan's king that produced an armistice between Israel and Jordan. On December 6, 1954, Prime Minister David Ben-Gurion appointed Dayan chief of staff. The quiet and often diffident Dayan directed the successful invasion of the Sinai Peninsula during the 1956 Suez Canal Crisis, which made him enormously popular in Israel.

Dayan was elected to the Knesset (parliament) in 1959, representing the Israeli Labor Party coalition, Mapai. He was appointed minister of agriculture, a post he held until 1964. He resigned in a political dispute but again won election to the Knesset in 1965 as a member of Rafi, a new party headed by Ben-Gurion.

In 1967, on the brink of war, Prime Minister Levi Eshkol appointed Dayan defense minister. He and Yitzhak Rabin, chief of staff of the Israel Defense Forces (IDF), orchestrated a resounding defeat of Egypt and its Arab allies. Once again, Israelis embraced Dayan as a hero. He generated controversy, however, when he established an Open Bridges policy that permitted people and goods to journey between Jordan and the West Bank and Gaza Strip without hindrance, risking infiltration of militia and weapons. This policy also contrasted with Israel's policy of curtailing the liberties of its Arab citizens.

In 1973, Egypt and Syria launched a surprise attack on Israel. Dayan was criticized for delaying the mobilization of forces, but Prime Minister Golda Meir continued to support him as defense minister. In 1974, Prime Minister Yitzhak Rabin forced Dyan from office. Dayan became foreign minister when Menachem Begin was elected in 1977, but he resigned in 1979 after strenuously opposing Begin's plan to annex the West Bank. In 1981, Dayan formed Telem, a new political party, advocating Israel's withdrawal from all lands occupied after the 1967 Six-Day War. He died on October 16, 1981, from cancer.

ABC-CLIO

See also: Arab-Israeli War, 1948; Arab-Israeli War, 1967; Arab-Israeli War, 1973

Further Reading

Comay, Joan. *Who's Who in Jewish History After the Period of the Old Testament.* London: Weidenfeld & Nicolson, 1974.

Dayan, Moshe. *Moshe Dayan: Story of My Life.* Jackson, TN: Da Capo Press, 1992.

Deir Yassin Massacre

Massacre of Palestinians by Jewish forces in 1947. During the 1947–1948 Arab-Jewish Communal War in Palestine, Arab forces blockaded Jerusalem, cutting off access to weapons, food, and medical supplies for the Jewish inhabitants. On April 8, 1948, the Jewish paramilitary groups Irgun and Lehi (Stern Gang) attacked the Palestinian village of Deir Yassin, which sat astride the Jerusalem–Tel Aviv road. Inhabitants of Deir Yassin had signed a nonaggression pact with the neighboring Orthodox settlement, Givat Shaul. Neither side wished to become a battlefield in the ongoing conflict, and thus both guaranteed safe passage to one another and promised to inform each other if the warring sides attempted to enter their territory.

The commanders of Irgun and Lehi agreed to an ill-conceived plan to attack the village in the predawn hours, with each of the militant groups moving in from a different direction. The Irgun and Lehi commanders agreed to commence the attack with a warning over loudspeakers, telling the villagers to flee the area. However, the groups had no means of communication with one another once the attack started, and when the Lehi fighters, who had the loudspeaker, arrived late to their designated positions, the warning proved useless.

The villagers detected the advancing enemies and opened fire upon them from a number of prepared positions. The early gunfire alerted more men in the village, who began engaging targets from within the stone buildings. As a result, rather than the planned quick raid, the Irgun and Lehi members found themselves in a bloody house-to-house fight and began to take dozens of casualties. In desperation, they resorted to tossing explosives into each building, regardless of how many noncombatants might be inside. As the battle continued to go poorly for the Jewish militants, they called for assistance from Palmach units of the Haganah, who arrived with trinitrotoluene (TNT) and small mortars. This proved too much for the defenders of Deir Yassin, as the Palmach warriors were better trained and equipped than the Irgun and Lehi members.

By noon, more than 100 villagers were dead, with hundreds more wounded and fleeing the area. The fight at Deir Yassin proved a turning point in the Communal War, as both sides attempted to use the incident as a rallying point. It triggered the flight of hundreds of thousands of Palestinians, who feared that they might encounter similar treatment from Jewish armed bands. It also provoked international condemnation of Irgun and Lehi, and a refusal by Albert Einstein, among others, to support the cause of organizations that could perpetrate such an attack. The massacre created enormous pressure upon Arab states to invade Palestine in opposition to the creation of Israel—and one month later, the invasion commenced.

Paul J. Springer

See also: Arab-Jewish War, 1947; Haganah; Irgun Tsvai Leumi; Palestinian Refugees; Palmach; Right of Return; Stern Gang

Further Reading

Morris, Benny. *The Birth of the Palestinian Refugee Crisis Revisited.* New York: Cambridge University Press, 2004.

Tessler, Mark. *A History of the Israeli-Palestinian Conflict.* 2nd ed. Bloomington: Indiana University Press, 2009.

Democratic Front for the Liberation of Palestine (DFLP)

One of many Palestinian organizations dedicated to liberating Palestine and part of the Palestine Liberation Organization (PLO). In 1969, Nayef Hawatmeh and Yasser Abed Rabbo broke from the Popular Front for the Liberation of Palestine (PFLP) because they believed that the PFLP focused too narrowly on military concerns. In 1974, the new organization adopted the name *Democratic Front for the Liberation of Palestine (DFLP).* Arab nationalist and Marxist in orientation, the DFLP was known as the most intellectually oriented of the Palestinian resistance groups. It called for a unified democratic Palestinian state that would allow "both Arabs and Jews to develop their national culture." Originally, it believed that this could be achieved only through the political activation of the masses and a so-called people's war. Gradually, it moderated its stance. Although it condemned PFLP airline hijackings, the DFLP mounted a number of small-scale raids against Israeli targets, the most infamous of which was the so-called Ma'alot Massacre on May 17, 1974, which left twenty-six Israelis killed and sixty wounded.

In 1991, the DFLP split when cofounder Rabbo supported the Oslo peace process. He rejected terrorist activities in favor of negotiations and the democratization of Palestinian society. The DFLP itself opposed the Oslo Accords, claiming that they denied Palestinians their legitimate rights. It continues to support military activities but insists they be confined to targets in the occupied territories and not Israel. It argues that Palestinians should fight only against the occupation rather than against Israeli citizens.

Spencer C. Tucker

See also: Oslo Accords; Palestine Liberation Organization

Further Reading
Gresh, Alain. *The PLO: The Struggle Within.* London: Zed, 1988.
Said, Edward W. *The Question of Palestine.* New York: Vintage Books, 1992.

Demographics in Israel and Palestine

Demography is inextricably tied to the ongoing political, environmental, socioeconomic, and sociocultural interests of various perspectives in Israel and Palestine. Political and geographic boundaries depend, in part, on the ethnic and religious composition of the people within them, and this is linked to issues of policy, employment, housing, urban planning (transportation, water, waste, etc.), environmental concerns, and security. This is certainly notable in Israel and Palestine, where population numbers on the ground affect policy decisions and vice versa. To the extent that demographic trends are controllable and can be regulated, policy decisions regarding demography have the potential to escalate or improve the ongoing conflict and peace process. The conflict, any chance of a peace process, and demographics are intertwined; demography can alleviate or exacerbate the conflict or the peace process, and it will definitely play an important and unavoidable role.

"Who's who and where" is an important consideration in the context of Israel and Palestine and is more complex than the labels *Israeli* or *Palestinian*. Within both of these two categories, ethnic, religious, and political identities abound. Upon its declaration of independence in 1948, Israel became a melting pot of diaspora Jews; the main ethnic distinction was made between Ashkenazim and Mizrahim, though these terms are applied broadly to cover Jews of various ethnic backgrounds. In assessing the impact of ethnicity on education, religion, and political expression, one must consider Ashkenazi prejudice, status gains, assimilation qualifications, and an idea that Smooha coins "The Orientalization Vicious Circle." For instance, prejudice serves as a rationalization of discrimination against minorities in the labor market. Because most Mizrahim compete with Israeli-Arabs and foreign workers for low-status jobs, it is beneficial for the Mizrahim to subjugate their competition to optimize their socioeconomic opportunity, and expressing anti-Arab feelings and views helps to justify such discrimination. Israeli-Arabs, as well as other foreign workers, drive wages downward, adding an element of competition to the Mizrahi employment field; however, white-collar positions, predominantly Ashkenazim, do not compete with Israeli-Arabs or foreigners in the labor market; hence, they are less inclined to develop this sort of resentment. The reestablishment of a national Jewish homeland in historic Israel helped develop and strengthen, through "othering" and opposition, a unique Palestinian national identity as well.

After the war of 1967, when Palestinians distinguished themselves as an autonomous political entity apart from the unity of Arab nations against Israel, scholars began to classify distinctions among the Palestinian population based on their region, religion, and political affiliations. The most enduring distinction remains those divided into West Bank, Gaza Strip, or refugees abroad. As a result, three distinct ethnic groups (Ashkenazim, Mizrahim, and Israeli-Arabs) came under the jurisdiction of the Ashkenazi-led Zionist vision, the effects of which continue to lead the two subordinate groups, Mizrahim and Israeli-Arabs, to seek representation and advancement through political action.

Obscuring these primary divisions are divisions between Christian Palestinians, Druze (a distinct ethnic and religious group), black African Jews (four waves, mostly Eritrean and Ethiopian), and foreign laborers and refugees (mostly Eritrean and Sudanese). Demography threatens to disrupt peace throughout the region. In Gaza, amid already unsustainable population density in an area of only 140 square miles, a population of over 11 million is projected by 2050. Fertility and birth rates are, in general, decreasing among Palestinians in Israel and the West Bank, but growing communities resulting in intensified urbanization have created a vacuum for jobs and a strain on the economy as the shift from self-reliant agriculture to urban jobs.

Implicit in Israel's founding was the importance of a Jewish national home, therefore implying a Jewish majority; however, this creates tension with its democratic aspirations. Israel strives to be democratic and Jewish, and so intrinsic in its goals is a certain ethnic composition that affects its minority groups. Because Israel has yet to draft a formal constitution and continues to function from its Basic Laws, many civil, political, cultural, social, and economic rights are either denied or simply not specified among both the Jewish and Arab population.

The July 2018 passing of a new law that explicitly enshrines the status of Israel as the nation-state of the Jewish people further calls into question the relationship between Jewish and non-Jewish citizens of Israel. The legislation stipulates that Israel is the historic homeland of the Jewish people, and therefore Jews have an exclusive right to national self-determination in it. This caused substantial criticism from those inside and outside Israel, who insist that it is important for Israel to be democratic and just, and question what the law means for non-Jewish citizens of Israel. Furthermore, the law appears to rule out the right of return for Palestinian refugees and promote Jewish settlements in the West Bank.

Kristin Hissong

See also: Israeli Occupations; Israelis; Law of Return; Palestinian Refugees; Palestinians; Right of Return; Settlements; West Bank

Further Reading

Cohen, Y., and N. Gordon. "Israel's Biospatial Politics: Territory, Demography, and Effective Control." *Public Culture* 30, no. 2 (2018): 199–220.

Smooha, S. *Ethnicity as a Factor in the Israeli Jews' Attitudes Toward Arabs: Comparing Cultures and Conflicts.* Baden-Baden, Germany: Nomos, 2007.

Smooha, S. "The Mass Immigrations to Israel: A Comparison of the Failure of the Mizrahi Immigrants of the 1950s with the Success of the Russian Immigrants of the 1990s." *Journal of Israeli History* 27, no. 1 (2008): 1–27.

Diaspora, Jewish

Greek term meaning "dispersion"; in this context, it is generally dated from the Babylonian exile of 586 BCE. The term also describes all Jews residing outside Israel. *Diaspora* today means the dispersion of any people, including the Palestinians, but for a long time, it was applied only to the Jews.

The Jews who were deported to Mesopotamia originally thought of it as exile (*Galut* in Hebrew). When it became possible for the Jews to return to Palestine, however, only a few thousand of the Babylonian Jews did so. By the time the Romans crushed the Great Jewish Revolt of 66–70 CE, captured Jerusalem, and destroyed its temple, there were already thriving Jewish communities in Babylonia, Syria, Egypt, Asia Minor, Greece, and Rome. Nonetheless, the end of the Great Jewish Revolt and Bar Kokhba's revolt of 135 CE greatly increased the numbers of diaspora Jews. Many Jews fled, while others were sold into slavery and dispersed throughout the empire.

When the Romans expanded their empire north in Europe, Jews established new communities in those lands, and the spread of the Byzantine Empire also saw some limited Jewish communities established as well. Jews settled as far as India, Central Asia, and even China. Persecutions in one place brought new Jewish diasporas in other areas. Jews also found their way to North and South America and Australia. Indeed, as a result of the persecutions (pogroms) in Russia and Poland, the United States came to have the world's largest Jewish population.

The two key elements of Jewish consciousness came to be the diaspora and a longing for Israel, but only after the proclamation of the state of Israel in 1948 were most Jews able to return. A primary goal of Zionism was to return Jews from the diaspora home. Today, most Jews still live outside Israel, even though Israel contains the largest population of Jews, with the United States a close second.

Spencer C. Tucker

See also: Babylonian Conquest of Judah; Masada; Roman Conquest of Judea; Zionism

Further Reading

Comay, Joan. *The Diaspora Story: The Epic of the Jewish People Among the Nations.* New York: Random House, 1980.

Gold, Steven J. *The Israeli Diaspora.* Seattle: University of Washington Press, 2002.

Grant, Michael. *The Jews in the Roman World.* New York: Scribner, 1973.

Diaspora, Palestinian

Greek term meaning "dispersion," applied to the Palestinians. For a long time, the term *diaspora* was applied only to Jews living outside their ancient homeland in Palestine, but today, it is used to describe the dispersion of any people from their homeland. The Palestinian diaspora represents an unresolved problem in the Israeli-Palestinian conflict and remains a contentious issue in any discussion of its future resolution. The diaspora energizes both peaceful dialogue and violent actions. Today, many displaced Palestinians have only known life in camps in foreign countries. These refugees are not accounted for by the Palestinian Authority (PA), and most do not have citizenship within their current country of residence. Jordan contains the largest contingent of displaced Palestinians, with Lebanon, Syria, Kuwait, and Saudi Arabia all hosting large numbers. There are also notable concentrations of Palestinians in the Gulf States, Egypt, Libya, and Iraq.

In 1947, the Arab population residing in Palestine numbered 1.2 million, but in only a few years, this figure plummeted as many fled the region in search of safety. Following the United Nations (UN) General Assembly's call for a regional partition, the first exodus of Palestinians began, as the more affluent families chose to depart and establish new homes abroad. These initial migrations were made by those who had the resources to leave, but once fighting between the Haganah and the Palestinian resistance began in May 1948, many less affluent citizens also fled the violence.

The massacre in the village of Deir Yassin in 1947 dramatically increased the exodus, as fears of similar reprisals spurred families to leave their homes. Many of these uprooted families were forced to find residence in camps established in neighboring countries. By 1949, approximately 680,000 Palestinians resided in refugee camps. A second wave of refugees left Palestine after war broke out again in 1967.

The defeat of the Arab armies left many Palestinians in doubt of safety in the West Bank and Gaza as they faced the subsequent military occupation. Estimates indicate that by 1972, the number of registered refugees rose by 1.5 million. Today, the global population of Palestinians is about 13 million. Nearly 5 million live under Israeli occupation, and another 1.75 million live in Israel as citizens.

As the Palestinian-Israeli conflict escalated, many Palestinians living in camps supported guerrilla groups that struck back at Israel. Most prominent of these groups was the Palestine Liberation Organization (PLO). Either directly or indirectly, refugees sustained the PLO's countermovement against Israel. Then in 1993, Yasser Arafat signed the Oslo Accords, which laid out a blueprint of sorts for the creation of a Palestinian state in the occupied West Bank and Gaza Strip. Many diaspora Palestinians viewed Arafat's signing onto Oslo as effectively abandoning their right to return. The Boycott, Divestment, and Sanctions (BDS) movement was started largely by Palestinians living under occupation, but it has enjoyed widespread support from diaspora Palestinians because it, unlike Oslo or the Palestinian Authority (PA), insists on Israel respecting their internationally recognized right to return to their homeland. A third generation of Palestinian refugees are now growing up in foreign countries. They share a strong desire to return to their grandparents' homeland, but Israeli leaders remain steadfast that these refugees will never be allowed to return.

Sean N. Blas

See also: Boycott, Divestment, and Sanctions Movement; Deir Yassin Massacre; Lydda and Ramle; Oslo Accords; Palestinian Refugees

Further Reading

Sayre, Ward, and Jennifer Olmsted. "Economics of Palestinian Return Migration." *Middle East Report* no. 212 (1999).

Smith, Charles. *Palestine and the Arab-Israeli Conflict: A History with Documents*. 9th ed. Boston: Bedford/St. Martin's, 2017.

Smith, Pamela Ann. "The Palestinian Diaspora, 1948–1985." *Journal of Palestine Studies* 15, no. 3 (1986).

Druze

A people who adhere to a Muslim sect derived from Ismaili Shia Islam. Some other Muslims treat the Druze as an extremist sect or discredit their beliefs. The Druze number about 1 million and are most numerous in Syria (400,000–500,000) and Lebanon (300,000–400,000). Smaller communities also exist in Israel (60,000), the Golan Heights (15,000), Jordan (10,000–20,000), and elsewhere in the world (90,000). Their esoteric teachings are not revealed to all Druze, meaning that the common folk (*juhhal*) were excluded from some of the secrets of the faith possessed by the wise elders (*uqqal*).

The Druze marry within the faith and no longer accept converts. They also forgo alcohol, tobacco, and pork. Their five-pointed, multicolor star represents the five seminal principles: reason and intelligence, the universal soul, the word, historical precedence, and immanence (*al-tali'*, or the following).

In Israel, the Druze live mainly in the Galilee and Carmel regions. The Druze of the Golan Heights suffered from expulsion from their villages or actual separation of territory. In all, the Druze have seen about 80 percent of their former lands confiscated by Israel. The Israeli government treated the Druze more favorably than other Arabs as part of a policy aimed at dividing Arabs and creating loyalty to the state. The Druze routinely serve in the Israel Defense Forces (IDF) but nevertheless experience discrimination as non-Jews.

In 2013, Israel began reaching out to the Druze of the Golan Heights, hoping that they would increase the pressure on Bashar al-Assad's regime in Syria and act as a buffer during the ongoing Syrian civil war. In 2018, the Druze held massive rallies protesting Israel's Nation-State Law, which many viewed as discriminatory against non-Jewish Israelis.

Sometimes the Israeli, Syrian, and Lebanese Druze communities have tried to support one another. When the IDF attempted to establish Christian domination in Lebanon over the Shuf area, Palestinian Druze vocally opposed this policy, which may have partially prompted Israeli withdrawal from the area. Some Druze officers have, in recent years, risen to general officer rank within the IDF.

Paul G. Pierpaoli Jr. and Sherifa Zuhur

See also: Golan Heights; Israel Defense Forces; Israelis; Syria

Further Reading

Betts, Robert Brenton. *The Druze*. New Haven, CT: Yale University Press, 1990.

Dana, Nissim. *The Druze in the Middle East*. East Sussex, UK: Sussex Academic, 2003.

Rosenthal, Donna. *The Israelis: Ordinary People in an Extraordinary Land*. New York: Free Press, 2005.

E

Egypt

The most populous Arab country, situated in north Africa, which has played a central role in the Arab-Israeli conflict. Egypt gained independence form the British in 1922, but Britain remained influential in the country until the rise of Gamal Abdul Nasser. The Arab League was created in 1945 and headquartered in Cairo, both reflecting and enhancing Egypt's role as a leader in the Arab world. During the 1948 Arab-Israeli War, Egypt took control of the Gaza Strip. It supported the establishment of a Palestinian government to rule Gaza and the West Bank, but Jordan's King Abdullah I, who secretly negotiated with Zionist leaders to carve up Palestine, opposed the idea and annexed the West Bank and East Jerusalem. The Arab League then placed Egypt in charge of Palestinian affairs in Gaza, from which Palestinian guerillas (*fedayeen*) launched attacks into Israel.

Egypt's President Anwar Sadat shakes hands with Israel's Prime Minister Menachem Begin at Camp David as United States President Jimmy Carter looks on, September 5, 1978. Egypt was the first Arab state to sign a peace treaty with Israel, which ended its military occupation of the Sinai Desert in 1981. (Jimmy Carter Library)

In July 1952, a group called the Free Officers, led by Colonel Gamal Abdel Nasser, overthrew the corrupt King Farouk, who was widely seen as a stooge of the British and generally blamed for Egypt's poor performance in the 1948 war. Nasser emerged as the most charismatic Arab leader to date; he was initially immensely popular among Arabs both inside and outside Egypt. He espoused pan-Arab, anti-Israel, and anti-British sentiments. At first, the United States and Britain courted Nasser with promises of aid and assistance in the hope of moderating his policies toward the West and Israel and keeping him from allying with the Soviet Union. These efforts failed, and when Nasser nationalized the Suez Canal, Britain and France recruited Israel to launch a coordinated surprise attack in the hope of retaking the canal and removing him from power. Israel's lightning victory in the 1956 Arab-Israeli War (i.e., the Suez Crisis) left it in control of the Sinai Peninsula, but intense pressure from the United States forced Israel, France, and Britain to withdraw their forces.

In the aftermath, Israel secured a United Nations (UN) peacekeeping force in the Sinai to monitor a cease-fire and the free flow of shipping through the Straits of Tiran. However, in May 1967, Nasser forced the peacekeepers to evacuate and threatened war with Israel, which responded with a preemptive strike on June 5, decimating Egypt's air force in a matter of hours. Over the next six days, Israel captured the Sinai and Gaza Strip from Egypt, East Jerusalem and the West Bank from Jordan, and the Golan Heights from Syria.

Nasser resigned in shame, but popular support swept him back to power, and he immediately began planning to reclaim Egypt's lost territory. With assistance from the Soviets, he launched a series of attacks in 1969 on Israeli forces along the Suez Canal. Israel responded with heavy artillery and air strikes on the Egyptian military and on civilian infrastructure deep inside Egypt. Nasser appealed to Moscow for direct intervention. When the Soviets began flying missions above parts of Egypt, Israel ended its deep air strikes, although fighting along the canal continued for weeks. The so-called War of Attrition ended in August 1970 with a U.S.-negotiated cease-fire. Egypt did not reclaim any of its lost territory but did inflict enough casualties on Israeli troops to bolster Egyptian military confidence.

When Nasser died in September 1970, he was replaced by Anwar Sadat, who first sought to negotiate a return of the Sinai. Frustrated with his inability to do so, he coordinated with Syria to launch a surprise attack on Israel on October 6, 1973. Armed with more Soviet weaponry and training, Egypt quickly pushed Israeli troops back from the banks of the Suez. Many believe that Egyptian leaders were seeking a limited victory of this sort in order to convince the United States to mediate a full Israeli withdrawal from the Sinai. But because Egypt paused its advance after the first day of fighting, Israel was able to send reinforcements to the Golan Heights to reverse Syria's onslaught. Israel Defense Forces (IDF) were soon threatening Damascus. Syrian and Soviet leaders pressured Sadat to resume fighting, which he did, but soon Egypt's forces were extended beyond the cover of their Soviet-supplied air defense systems, and Israel took advantage. Within a few days, Israel turned the tide of battle in the Sinai, and the war ended with Israel reclaiming all the territory it had captured in 1973. Still, the 1973 war exposed Israel's fallibility and convinced U.S. leaders that American and Israeli national security would be enhanced by drawing Egypt away from the Soviet camp.

Over the next few years, Washington wooed Cairo. After Sadat made a historic visit to Israel, the Jimmy Carter administration brokered the 1978 Camp David Accords, which led to an Israel-Egypt peace treaty. Israel completed its withdrawal from the Sinai in 1982, and since then, the two countries have maintained a cold peace. This was a major achievement for all three countries. The United States completed its recruitment of Egypt, undermining Soviet influence in the Middle East and developing what would become a reliable regional ally. Israel no longer faced an existential threat from the Arab world because no array of Arab states could destroy it without Egypt's participation. And Egypt not only got its territory back, but also was handsomely rewarded for making peace with Israel, to the tune of $2 billion in annual U.S. military and economic aid for the next three decades. But because the treaty did not address Israel's relations with its neighbors or the Palestinians, the Arab world saw it as a betrayal. The Arab League suspended Egypt for nearly a decade, and Sadat was soon assassinated by disillusioned soldiers in his own military. He was succeeded by Hosni Mubarak, who ruled Egypt for the next thirty years.

During this time, Egyptian-Israeli relations faced periodic tensions related to Israel's military interventions in Lebanon and against the Palestinians. Overall, however, Egypt coordinated closely with Israel on many security issues, especially those relating to the Sinai and the Palestinians. While Egypt often helped negotiate agreements between the Palestinians and Israel (and among competing Palestinian groups), it also helped Israel contain Hamas, which is an offshoot of the Muslim Brotherhood, an Egyptian Islamist group that Cairo has long feared. Indeed, popular uprisings during the Arab Spring in 2011 led to the ouster of Hosni Mubarak and the rise to power of the Muslim Brotherhood.

Many feared that the new Islamist regime would adopt anti-Israel, anti-American, pro-Hamas policies, but before the Brotherhood could solidify power, the Egyptian military overthrew it. General Abdel Fattah Sisi, one of the coup plotters, was elected president in 2014 with 97 percent of the vote. He quickly returned Egypt's foreign policy toward Israel to its thirty-year norm: respecting the peace treaty with Israel (which is not particularly popular in Egypt), combating mutual security threats in the Sinai, containing the influence of Hamas, and playing peacemaker between Israel and Palestinians, as well as among competing Palestinian factions.

Robert C. DiPrizio

See also: Arab-Israeli War, 1956; Arab-Israeli War, 1967; Arab-Israeli War, 1973; Arab Spring; Camp David Accords; Gaza Strip; Hamas; Nasser, Gamal Abdel; Sadat, Anwar

Further Reading

Kirkpatrick, David D. *Into the Hands of the Soldiers: Freedom and Chaos in Egypt and the Middle East.* New York: Viking Press, 2018.

Lippman, Thomas W. *Hero of the Crossing: How Anwar Sadat and the 1973 War Changed the World.* Lincoln, NE: Potomac Books, 2016.

Quandt, William B. *Peace Process: American Diplomacy and the Arab-Israeli Conflict Since 1967.* Washington, DC: Brookings Institute, 2005.

Sabry, Mohannad. *Sinai: Egypt's Linchpin, Gaza's Lifeline, Israel's Nightmare*. Cairo: American University in Cairo Press, 2015.

Egyptian Conquest of Canaan

During the Egyptian New Kingdom (1539–1075 BCE), aggressive pharaohs sent armies north into Canaan as part of an effort to establish an Egyptian empire in the region. Egyptian armies fought against coalitions of Canaanite rulers, and around 1456 BCE, they won a decisive battle at Megiddo. This victory initiated approximately three centuries of Egyptian rule in the land of Canaan. The Egyptians built fortresses, mansions, mines, and farms to solidify their hold on Canaan. Artifacts left from these activities has provided evidence to confirm an Egyptian presence in Canaan. In addition to the discovery of stamps that bore the names of Egyptian pharaohs, including Thutmoses III (1504–1450 BCE) and Amenhotep III (1386–1349 BCE), archaeologists have discovered tombs modeled after Egyptian customs and burial goods and jewelry in line with Egyptian practices. These discoveries point to merchant activity from Egypt that brought Egyptian goods into Canaan, as well as goods being made in Judea with Egyptian cultural themes.

After conquering the region, the Egyptians used Canaan as a buffer against other northern kingdoms, as well as a source of revenue through taxes, tribute, and trade. Egyptian rule throughout the land led to cultural transfer between peoples, as Egyptians shared their poetry, music, weapons, clothing, and religion. Egyptian influence from this time period is evident from architecture and building styles in Beth Shan, Aphek, Ashdod, Gaza, and Joppa, among others.

Archaeologists have also found evidence of an Egyptian presence in Jerusalem during the Bronze Age (3300–1200 BCE), citing discoveries in the city of Egyptian temples, column capitals, a hieroglyphic stela, and two Egyptian-style alabaster vessels. These discoveries lend further support to the argument that Egyptians pharaohs established a system of imperial rule during the Bronze Age, which employed local vassal rulers to control territory that included Jerusalem and the land of Canaan. This system of Egyptian rule and its success in Canaan have been documented in the Amarna letters, which detail how Canaanite chieftains obeyed Egyptian rulers and also competed for their favor. Archaeological evidence also lends support to arguments that Egyptians controlled territory much farther north than previously understood—perhaps as far north as modern-day Tel Aviv.

This period of Egyptian rule in the land of Canaan coincides with the settlement of the Jewish patriarchs Abraham, Isaac, and Jacob (Genesis 12–50). Abraham's journey from the land of Canaan into Egypt and his interactions with Pharaoh (Genesis 12:10–20) provide further insight into Egyptian influence throughout the region. All this evidence indicates that Egypt was a powerful empire during the late Bronze Age and retained significant authority throughout the region.

Scholars argue that Egypt's influence in Canaan started to decline as the result of severe droughts that led to famines and assaults from seaborne invaders. These challenges combined to loosen Egypt's grip on Canaan, which started first in the north around 1200 BCE, and then later in the south. Scholars argue that Egyptian rule ended completely in Canaan in about 1125 BCE, when the last Egyptian military outpost, located at Jaffa, was destroyed by the second of two catastrophic blazes.

Hugh Gardenier

See also: Canaanites; Israelite Conquest of Canaan

Further Reading
Brier, Bob, and Hoyt Hobbs. *Ancient Egypt: Everyday Life in the Land of the Nile.* New York: Sterling, 2013.
Miller, Maxwell, and John Hayes. *A History of Ancient Israel and Judah.* Louisville, KY: Westminster John Knox Press, 2006.
Redford, Donald B. *Egypt, Canaan, and Israel in Ancient Times.* Princeton, NJ: Princeton University Press, 1993.

Entebbe Raid

Daring Israeli rescue of a hijacked jetliner. On June 27, 1976, terrorists commandeered Air France Flight 139, en route from Tel Aviv to Paris with 246 passengers and 12 crew aboard. The hijacking was led by the West German Red Army Faction and the Popular Front for the Liberation of Palestine (PFLP). The hijacked plane flew to Entebbe Airport in Uganda, where President Idi Amin Dada assisted the terrorists. On June 29, the hijackers issued their demands: the release of forty Palestinians held by Israel and another thirteen terrorists in France, Germany, Switzerland, and Kenya. As a sign of so-called good faith, the terrorists agreed to release some captives, but 105 Jewish passengers and the flight crew remained as hostages.

On July 3, the Israeli government authorized a rescue attempt, which was led by Lieutenant Colonel Jonathan Netanyahu, the brother of future prime minister Benjamin Netanyahu. The main assault team quickly managed to gain control of the terminal after duping guards by driving up to the building in an exact replica of President Amin's limousine. During the ensuing firefight, however, Netanyahu was fatally wounded. By midday on July 4, the rescue had succeeded. The entire operation lasted less than an hour, and around half of the Ugandan air force had been destroyed. Six terrorists and twenty to forty Ugandan soldiers supporting them were killed. Three hostages died during or shortly after the operation, and apart from the death of Netanyahu, the Israel Defense Forces (IDF) suffered only one other casualty.

Ralph Martin Baker

See also: Netanyahu, Benjamin; Palestinian Hijackings; Popular Front for the Liberation of Palestine

Further Reading
Hastings, Max. *Yoni, Hero of Entebbe.* New York: Bantam Books, 1979.
Herzog, Chaim. *Heroes of Israel: Profiles of Jewish Courage.* London: Little, Brown, 1989.
Netanyahu, Iddo. *Yoni's Last Battle: The Rescue at Entebbe.* Jerusalem: Gefen Books, 1976.

Erekat, Saeb

Palestinian academic and politician, diplomat, and peace negotiator. Born in Abu Dis in the outskirts of Jerusalem, Saeb Erekat graduated from a primary school in Jericho. He earned both bachelor of arts (1977) and master of arts degrees in international relations (1979) from San Francisco State University. He obtained a PhD in peace and conflict studies from Bradford University in the United Kingdom (1983).

Erekat has been politically active since the 1980s, teaching at An-Najah National University in Nablus as professor of political science until he joined the negotiations team of the Palestine Liberation Organization (PLO). Committed to a negotiated two-state solution, Erekat served as a vice-chair of the Palestinian delegation to the Madrid Peace Conference (1991) and the Washington negotiations (1992). Since then, he has been the lead negotiator in on-again, off-again peace talks with Israel. Erekat has urged Israel to agree to the Arab Peace Plan of 2002, stating that the two-state solution is the only sensible way forward to end the Arab-Israeli conflict.

In 1996, Erekat was elected to the Palestinian Legislative Council. He served as a minister in different Palestinian governments led by Palestinian Authority (PA) prime ministers Mahmoud Abbas and Ahmed Qurai. Erekat has published books and numerous op-eds in leading international newspapers, and he has long been one of the most prominent Palestinian spokespersons in Western media. In 2011, Erekat was humiliated by leaked documents indicating that he offered unpopular concessions to Israeli negotiators in failed negotiations. He received a lung transplant in the United States in 2017.

Erekat currently serves as secretary-general of the PLO and is sometimes mentioned as a potential successor to Palestinian president Mahmoud Abbas.

Philipp O. Amour

See also: Arab Peace Plan; Oslo Accords; Palestinian Authority; Palestine Liberation Organization

Further Reading

Ashrawi, Hanan. *This Side of Peace: A Personal Account*. New York: Simon and Schuster, 1996.

Mattar, Philip, ed. *Encyclopedia of the Palestinians*. New York: Facts on File, 2005.

Swisher, Clayton. "Ofcom's Ruling on the Palestine Papers Offers Hope to the Middle East." *The Guardian,* https://www.theguardian.com/commentisfree/2011/oct/10/ofcom-al-jazeera-palestine-papers.

Eretz Israel

Hebrew for "the Land of Israel." *Eretz Israel* is a long-held traditional name among Jews for the ancestral homeland of the Jews in the southwest Mediterranean, encompassing territory beyond Israel's present-day borders into Lebanon and across the Jordan River. Revisionist Zionists like Ze'ev Jabotinsky and Menachem Begin believed that the Jews have the right to reclaim all this land.

The term *Eretz Israel* has origins in the Torah and Old Testament. According to their accounts, Jacob, whom God renamed Israel, received the covenant land of his grandfather, Abraham, and his father, Isaac. Israel in turn had twelve sons, one of whom, Judah, became the namesake for the Jewish people. For centuries, Eretz Israel was home to the Jews' ancestors, at times politically united and at others with significant internal political rifts, but always viewed through the lens of a religious birthright. Upon the Jewish emigration from the region under harsh Roman governance in the first century AD, Eretz Israel took new meaning, encapsulated by the later aspirational refrain among the Jewish diaspora of "Next year in Jerusalem."

The rise of political Zionism in the late nineteenth century brought with it a renewed focus on a political home for the Jews in Eretz Israel. The First Zionist Congress, held in Basel, Switzerland, in 1897, called for a Jewish home in Palestine. Waves of Jewish immigration through the late 1800s and early 1900s provided a demographic base upon which future third-party political actions, such as the Balfour Declaration and the later United Nations (UN) partition recommendation, were built. While Eretz Israel still inspires some extremists to claim that Israel has the right to expand its borders into Lebanon and Jordan, its mainstream use is as a rallying cry for Jews who think Israel should control all the West Bank indefinitely.

Sean P. Braniff

See also: Aliya; Begin, Menachem; Diaspora, Jewish; Jabotinsky, Ze'ev; Zionism

Further Reading

Morris, Benny. *Righteous Victims: A History of the Zionist-Arab Conflict, 1881–2001.* New York: Vintage Books, 2001.

Troen, Ilan, and Shay Rabineau. "Competing Concepts of Land in Eretz Israel." *Israel Studies* 19, no. 2 (2014): 162–186.

F

Fatah

A highly influential political and military faction within the Palestine Liberation Organization (PLO). Fatah, whose name means "victory" or "conquest" in Arabic, was founded in the late 1950s by Yasser Arafat, Salah Khalaf, Khalil al-Wazir (Abu Jihad), and Khalid Hassan. Since the late 1960s, Fatah has been the leading faction within the PLO, the umbrella organization of Palestinian national liberation groups.

For much of the group's official history, Arafat (who also was PLO chairman from 1969 until his death in 2004) served as the leader of Fatah. It operated out of Jordan until 1970, when King Husayn expelled it in a violent clash known as "Black September." Fatah and the PLO relocated to Lebanon until an Israeli invasion in 1982 forced them to relocate again, this time in Tunisia, where they remained for the next decade.

Early on, Fatah embraced armed confrontation as the primary means of achieving a unified, independent Palestine. But by the mid-1970s, many leaders concluded that armed conflict was not moving them any closer to their goal of a Palestinian state. By 1988, Arafat explicitly accepted the idea of a two-state solution and recognized Israel's right to exist.

The 1993 Oslo Accords and the 1994 creation of the Palestinian Authority (PA) heralded the relocation of the PLO and Fatah to Gaza and the West Bank, finally centering the Palestinian power base in Palestine after almost fifty years of transience. However, by this time, the Palestinians were no longer entirely represented by the Tunisian old guard of Fatah. Younger leaders were frustrated with the policies of the longtime exiles, as well as with major financial difficulties and corruption. Also, Islamist organizations such as Islamic Jihad of Palestine and Hamas had begun to attract support from the Palestinian population. Arafat clung to power, still being recognized for his many years of devotion to the Palestinian cause. In January 1996, he was elected as the PA's first president, making him leader of the PLO, PA, and Fatah simultaneously.

Fatah essentially controlled the PA bureaucracy, although the fissures within the organization began to grow. While Fatah attempted to advance the Oslo peace process, certain members began to sabotage Arafat. Now the group was divided by hardliners versus peace proponents, old guard versus the young, and bureaucrats versus revolutionaries. The Second Intifada, which broke out in September 2000, created more divisions. Fatah member Marwan Barghouti organized a militia called al-Tanzim, whose goal was attacking Israeli forces. In 2002, another Fatah-aligned faction, the al-Aqsa Martyrs Brigades, began launching major attacks against Israeli forces as well. To punish the PA for suicide bombings in the spring of 2002, the Israelis reoccupied much of the West Bank. Arafat was trapped in his own headquarters, and much of the West Bank's infrastructure was destroyed. Israeli officials were periodically launching campaigns against Arafat's leadership, and these were now revived.

In April 2003, under enormous pressure from Israel and the United States, Arafat reluctantly agreed to appoint Mahmoud Abbas to the newly created post of prime minister. However, Abbas resigned only a few months later, after much infighting. Arafat died on November 11, 2004, and this threw Fatah and the PA into more turmoil. Days later, Fatah named an opponent of the peace process, Farouk Qaddumi, as its leader. Meanwhile, Abbas succeeded Arafat as PLO chairman. For the first time, Fatah and the PLO were not controlled by the same person (and this was the case until Abbas became Fatah chairman in 2009).

After bitter political machinations, Fatah nominated Abbas as its presidential candidate in the January 2005 election. Abbas faced a strong challenge from Barghouti, who vowed to run as an independent candidate from a jail cell in Israel. But Barghouti bowed out after coming under intense pressure, opening the way for Abbas's victory in January 2005.

Abbas's victory, however, was not a harbinger of a resurgent and unified Fatah. In December 2005, Barghouti formed a rival political alliance, al-Mustaqbal, vowing to run a new slate of candidates for the January 2006 PA legislative elections. At the last moment, the two factions decided to run a single slate, but this temporary rapprochement couldn't prevent a stunning victory for Hamas, which won seventy-four seats to Fatah's forty-five. The election allowed Hamas to form its own government and elect a prime minister, Ismail Haniyeh, who assumed the premiership in February 2006. Israel, the United States, and some European nations cut off funding to the PA in protest of the electoral success of Hamas. This placed the PA in a state of crisis, as no civil servants could be paid and hospitals and clinics had no supplies. For more than a year, and despite an agreement between Hamas and Fatah, the U.S. government insisted that only if Hamas renounced violence in a format satisfactory to Israel would it fund the PA.

In March 2007, Abbas brokered a Palestinian unity government, with Hamas leader Haniyeh becoming prime minister. Yet in May, violence between Hamas and Fatah escalated, resulting in the Hamas takeover of Gaza. Abbas immediately dissolved the unity government, declared a state of emergency, and swore in an emergency Palestinian government. That same day, the United States ended its fifteen-month embargo on the PA in an effort to strengthen Abbas's government, which was now limited to the West Bank. Abbas cut off all ties with Hamas, pending the return of Gaza. On July 1, 2007, Israel restored financial ties to the Fatah-led PA.

As of 2018, the Fatah-Hamas split remains the defining feature of Palestinian politics. The Fatah-dominated PA is viewed by many Palestinians as corrupt, ineffective, and coopted by the Israeli "occupiers." There is no clear successor to Abbas as head of Fatah or the PA, although many believe that the still-imprisoned Barghouti is one of the few leaders popular enough to bridge the gap between Hamas and Fatah supporters.

Paul G. Pierpaoli Jr. and Sherifa Zuhur

See also: Al-Aqsa Martyrs Brigades; Arafat, Yasser; Barghouti, Marwan; Gaza Strip; Hamas; Oslo Accords; Palestine Liberation Organization; Palestinian Authority; West Bank

Further Reading

Aburish, Said K. *Arafat: From Defender to Dictator.* New York and London: Bloomsbury, 1998.

Jamal, Amal. *The Palestinian National Movement: Politics of Contention, 1967–2005.* Bloomington: Indiana University Press, 2005.

Kurz, Anat N. *Fatah and the Politics of Violence: The Institutionalization of a Popular Struggle.* Eastbourne, UK: Sussex Academic Press, 2006.

Rubin, Barry M. *Revolution Until Victory? The Politics and History of the PLO.* Cambridge, MA: Harvard University Press, 1996.

Faysal-Weizmann Agreement

An informal accord signed on January 3, 1919, between Faysal ibn Husayn, the son of Sharif Husayn of Mecca, and Dr. Chaim Weizmann, leader of the World Zionist Organization (WZO) and later the first president of Israel. It was a short-lived accord regulating Hashemite-Jewish postwar cooperation to improve their political standing during the 1919 Paris Peace Conference following the end of World War I. Weizmann promised that the WZO would support Husayn's effort to create and control a pan-Arab state based in Syria, as promised by the British and French during World War I. Husayn in turn pledged to support Jewish migration to Palestine, which was to become independent. He had been (insincerely) assured by Weizmann that the Zionists did not intend to create a Jewish government there or take supreme power. Faysal also appended a handwritten statement that made his commitment contingent upon the establishment of his Pan-Arab state based in Syria, as formulated by him for the British. Thus, the Zionist movement appeared at the Paris Peace Conference with hardly any objection from the Hashemite-led Arab national movement. When Britain and France refused to grant him claim to Syria, Faysal repudiated the Faysal-Weizmann Agreement.

Philipp O. Amour

See also: Arab Revolt, 1916; Weizmann, Chaim; World Zionist Organization; Zionism

Further Reading

Caplan, Neil. "Faysal Ibn Husain and the Zionists: A Re-Examination with Documents." *International History Review* 5, no. 4 (November 1983): 561–614.

Kimmerling, Baruch, and Joel S. Migdal. *The Palestinian People: A History.* Cambridge, MA: Harvard University Press, 2003.

First and Second Temple Periods

The First Temple Period (970–586 BCE) and the Second Temple Period (530 BCE–70 CE) are the names used to designate specific theological-political periods of time in Jewish history.

The First Temple Period corresponds roughly with the existence of the First Temple, also known as King Solomon's Temple. The construction of the First

Temple (approximately 950 BCE) in Jerusalem, the capital of the United Kingdom of Israel, was the signature accomplishment of King Solomon's reign (970–931 BCE) and was built to be the permanent residence of God, as symbolized by its housing the Ark of the Covenant, which contained the Ten Commandments.

In the ancient world, the formation of "nation-states" depended upon the idea that the nation's chief deity approved and supported the concentration of power in the hands of the few who controlled the administrative structure of that state. A temple building, as the visible symbol of a god's presence, was the most effective way for leaders of a country to communicate the fact that their god favored the political organization that was being established. The legitimizing function of a temple operated on an international level as well. For example, King Solomon's Temple in Jerusalem bore the message that the Israelite domination of nearby states had divine sanction. For the Jewish people, the establishment of the monarchy and the building of the Temple fulfilled the prophecies of the Hebrew Bible about God's favor toward the Israelites and his promise to bring them to a Promised Land. The Israelite monarchy of Judah came to an end when the First Temple was destroyed in 587–586 BCE by the Babylonians, at which time the Jewish people were taken into Babylonian captivity.

The Second Temple Period commenced with the Edict of Cyrus in 530 BCE. This edict, issued by Cyrus, king of Persia, is attested to in the biblical books of Ezra and Chronicles, which released the Jews from Babylonian captivity and encouraged them to return to the Holy Land and rebuild the First Temple, which was completed in 516 BCE. The Second Temple played a different role during this period because there was no king to sit on the throne. Hence, the legitimizing role of the temple in national life shifted to the priestly administrators of Judah, whose responsibilities became greatly enlarged as they stepped in to fill the gap left by the absence of a civil authority. The three major sects, known as the Pharisees, Sadducees, and Essenes, were formed during this period. As the temple stood alone as the center of the semiautonomous national life of a dispersed community, of which many were still in exile, the monarchic role became a matter of future expectation, which Christians claim was fulfilled by Jesus of Nazareth. The Second Temple was destroyed in 70 CE during the first Jewish-Roman War and has not been rebuilt, though some Jews call for the construction of a Third Temple on the Temple Mount in Jerusalem.

Deonna Neal

See also: Babylonian Conquest of Judah; Haram al-Sharif/Temple Mount; Israelite Conquest of Canaan; Roman Conquest of Judea; Solomon; Third Temple Movement

Further Reading

Bright, John. *A History of Israel.* 4th ed. Louisville, KY: Westminster John Knox Press, 2000.

Grabbe, Lester L. *An Introduction to Second Temple Judaism: History and Religion of the Jews in the Time of Nehemiah, the Maccabees, Hillel, and Jesus.* New York: T & T Clark International, 2010.

Na'aman, Nadev. *Ancient Israel's History and Historiography: The First Temple Period (Collected Essays), Volume 3.* University Park, PA: Eisenbrauns, 2006.

Gaza Raid, 1955

Israeli military raid of an Egyptian army outpost in Gaza on February 28, 1955. The Gaza Raid was undertaken by approximately fifty paratroopers of the Israel Defense Forces (IDF) and came as a complete surprise to the Egyptians. It resulted in the deaths of thirty-nine Egyptian soldiers and the wounding of another thirty. The attack was supposedly in retaliation for continuing fedayeen attacks on Israel, but Gaza had historically been the quietest of the Israeli frontier borders. Israeli prime minister David Ben-Gurion had come under increasing pressure from the political right, both in and out of the government, to take a more proactive stance against fedayeen attacks. Thus, he somewhat reluctantly agreed to sanction the raid.

In retrospect, the Gaza Raid was a major Israeli miscalculation. Before the February raid, the Egyptians had discouraged attacks on Israel from Egyptian soil. But afterward, outraged by the audacity of the Israeli Gaza attack, Gamal Abdel Nasser now began to sanction commando and Palestinian fedayeen raids against Israel. The Jordanians did the same. This marked the beginning of a trend of escalating violence among fedayeen forces, Israel's Arab neighbors, and Israel, which would result in many hundreds of deaths.

The Gaza Raid proved to be a political hot potato for Nasser, who now believed that he had to take extraordinary measures to counter the growing threat of Israeli incursions into Egyptian territory. The raid also convinced Nasser and his military advisers that Israel was gaining strength militarily and this buildup needed to be matched. Shortly thereafter, Nasser approached several Western nations about arms purchases. The Americans, British, and French rebuffed his inquiry, however, leading him into the arms of the Soviets. Before the year was out, he had consummated a major arms deal with the Soviet Union amounting to about $325 million (in 1955 dollars). This marked the start of a major Soviet effort to assert its influence in the Middle East. It was also the beginning of an Egyptian-Soviet alliance that would last until the mid-1970s and paved the way for similar Soviet arms deals with Syria and Iraq.

Clearly, the 1955 Gaza Raid set off a chain reaction of events that nobody imagined. The Egyptian-Soviet arms deal compelled the United States and Great Britain to pull their financial underwriting of Egypt's Aswan High Dam project. This in turn forced Nasser to nationalize the Suez Canal in 1956, which in turn precipitated the Suez Crisis of October–November 1956.

Paul G. Pierpaoli Jr.

See also: Arab-Israeli War, 1956; Ben-Gurion, David; Egypt; Gaza Strip; Israel; Nasser, Gamal Abdel

Further Reading

Jabber, Paul. *Not by War Alone: Security and Arms Control in the Middle East*. Berkeley: University of California Press, 1981.

Leng, Russell J. *Bargaining and Learning in Recurrent Crises: The Soviet-American, Egyptian-Israeli, and Indo-Pakistani Rivalries*. Ann Arbor: University of Michigan Press, 2000.

Louis, William R., and Roger Owen, eds. *Suez, 1956: The Crisis and Its Consequences*. New York: Oxford University Press, 1989.

Gaza Strip

A heavily populated costal enclave along the Mediterranean Sea, adjacent to Egypt's Sinai Peninsula. The Gaza Strip is seven miles wide and twenty-five miles long. It takes its name from its principal city of Gaza. In biblical times, the area was the home of the Philistines, from which the name *Palestine* is derived.

The Gaza Strip is home to 2 million Palestinians, most of whom are classified as refugees by the United Nations (UN). It has long faced a massive humanitarian crisis brought on by a number of factors, most notably the poor governance of Hamas, the punitive efforts of the Palestinian Authority (PA) to wrestle control of the region away from Hamas, and Israel's ongoing siege and periodic bombardment of the territory.

An Israel Defense Forces gun positioned along the Israel-Gaza Strip border. Since 2015, Israel has rapidly upgraded the security barrier it maintains around Gaza. It now includes a 20-foot tall galvanized fence, an underground concrete wall that stretches into the sea to deter tunnel and sea-born attacks, and an array of smart sensors. (Rafael Ben Ari/Dreamstime.com)

Gaza has a border of approximately 31 miles with Israel on the northeast and east and 6.6 miles with Egypt on the southwest. It has been one of the main focal points of the Arab-Israeli conflict since 1967, when it became Israeli-occupied territory. Although Gaza is now under Palestinian rule, its borders, airspace, sea lanes, and entry and exit points are all still controlled by Israel. Egypt usually coordinates its policy toward Gaza with Israel.

According to the 1947 UN partition plan, the Gaza Strip and the West Bank were to form an independent Arab state following the dismantling of the British Mandate for Palestine. Arab leaders, however, rejected the plan and instead waged war. During the 1948–1949 Israeli War of Independence, or *nakba* (catastrophe) as Palestinians call it, some 700,000 Palestinians living in what became Israel fled or were expelled into surrounding areas, including Gaza. The 1949 armistice left Egypt in control of the strip. In 1959, Egypt suspended the Palestinian government that had been operating in Gaza over the previous decade.

Despite the 1949 armistice, significant portions of the Israeli population believed that the Gaza Strip (along with the West Bank and parts of Lebanon and Syria) was part of Eretz Israel, the biblical lands of Israel, and therefore should be part of the modern Jewish state. After a failed attempt to capture the strip in the 1956 Sinai Campaign, Israel took control of Gaza during the 1967 war. UN Security Council Resolution 242 called for Israel to withdraw from territories captured in that war, but instead Israel proceeded to construct Jewish settlements. At the beginning of the twenty-first century, there were twenty-five settlements in Gaza housing some 9,000 Israeli Jews among a population of about 1.4 million Palestinians. In May 1994, the Oslo Accords transferred some governmental services of the strip to the PA, but its status remained in dispute.

A high birth rate has contributed to the Gaza Strip's ongoing poverty, unemployment, and low standard of living. Although control of Gaza's finances was given to the PA as part of the 1994 transfer, government corruption and Israeli border closures severely hindered the economy until 1998, when Israel began taking measures to ensure that border closures resulting from terrorism threats would not affect cross-border trade so adversely. However, with the outbreak of the Second (al-Aqsa) Intifada in 2000, many of these measures were reversed, and the area witnessed another economic downturn.

In 2005, Israeli prime minister Ariel Sharon's government voted to begin unilateral disengagement from the Gaza Strip, a plan that was met with mixed reactions in the international community. Although the European Union and the United States supported Sharon's plan to dismantle Israeli settlements in the area and withdraw Israeli forces from many areas, critics said that the plan did not go far enough in reestablishing Israel's pre-1967 borders and was not being thoroughly coordinated with the PA. Many Israelis opposed the plan and supported the settlers. Palestinians, while in favor of any move that increased PA jurisdiction, complained that the plan was not comprehensive. Nonetheless, many hoped that disengagement would mark a step in implementing the so-called Road Map to Peace in the Middle East, a peace plan brokered by the United States, the European Union, Russia, and the United Nations.

The Israeli government began dismantling its Gaza settlements on August 15, 2005. Although contested by the nationalist right wing within Israel, by some of the Jewish community abroad, and in some confrontational events, the Israel Defense Forces (IDF) completed the process on September 12, 2005. Israel, however, retained control of Gaza's airspace and maritime space, and most entry and exit points. At the same time, Israel withdrew from the Philadelphi Route adjacent to the strip's border with Egypt, following a pledge by Egypt that it would secure its side of the border. Following Israel's withdrawal, Palestinian militants repeatedly fired Qassam rockets from Gaza into Israeli border towns. Israel carried out several military campaigns in 2006 against Gaza, both prior to the war with Hezbollah in Lebanon and again in November.

While an optimistic attitude prevailed in Gaza in 2005, when Israel withdrew its troops and settlers, hopes were dashed by fighting among clans and criminal gangs. Clashes between Palestine's two major political factions, Hamas and Fatah, soon escalated, ultimately killing an estimated 160 people and wounding 800 more. In January 2006, Hamas unexpectedly won the PA's legislative elections, setting up a showdown with PA president Mahmoud Abbas and his Fatah party. On March 17, 2007, Abbas brokered a unity government in which Hamas leader Ismail Haniyeh became prime minister, but Israel and the United States refused to recognize any government that included Hamas members. In May, armed clashes between Hamas and Fatah escalated and by June, Hamas took over Gaza entirely and asserted its control over clashing clans and warring gangs that had plunged the region into chaos since Israel's withdrawal.

The PA responded by declaring a state of emergency and creating a government excluding Hamas, but its de facto authority was limited to the West Bank. On June 19, 2007, Abbas cut off all ties and dialogue with Hamas, pending the return of Gaza. This left Fatah, backed by the United States, the European Union, and Israel, scrambling to consolidate its control in the West Bank, while Hamas tightened its grip on Gaza and imposed its brand of religious conservatism.

With aid from the West largely cut off and Israel effectively blockading the Gaza Strip, Hamas and the people under their rule were under siege. By the end of 2007, few Gazans could leave for any reason. With the Egyptian border also closed, the economy was in a state of near-collapse. Gaza was more isolated than ever.

In early 2008, rocket attacks on Israel launched from the Gaza Strip led to an Egyptian-brokered six-month cease-fire that brought relative calm during the latter half of the year. But as the agreement's expiration approached, Israel destroyed one of the hundreds of tunnels that Hamas had dug to smuggle goods, arms, and terrorists. Vowing revenge for this purported violation of the truce, and citing Israel's continued refusal to lift its blockade, Hamas launched a barrage of rockets, to which the IDF responded with a full-scale assault, code-named Operation Cast Lead. After the deaths of more than 1,000 Palestinians and intense international pressure, Israel halted the campaign on January 18, 2009.

In November 2012, violence flared up again when Israel launched Operation Pillar of Defense, designed to punish Hamas for rocket attacks and other acts of provocation on Israeli territory. Hamas claimed that its attacks were in retaliation for the Israeli blockade of Gaza and its continued occupation of East Jerusalem and the West Bank. Israel's operation began with the targeted assassination of Ahmed Jabari, the head of Hamas's military establishment. More than 1,500 strikes occurred within the Gaza Strip, killing over 100 Palestinians. Human Rights Watch later claimed that both Hamas and Israel had violated the laws of modern warfare during the seven-day clash.

The Fatah-Hamas break was not substantially mended until early June 2014, when Abbas announced the formation of another unity government. However, unlike the 2007 government, this one did not include any Hamas members in the cabinet. Hamas agreed to support the government without direct participation in it. The United States and most of its allies cautiously backed the new setup, but Israel denounced the government because of its ties to Hamas, which it continued to view as a terrorist group (and still does to this day). A renewed conflict between Israel and Hamas in July and August 2014 resulted in substantial bloodshed, all but unraveling Abbas's unity government. On July 17, Israel escalated the conflict by sending ground forces into the Gaza Strip and using Israeli warplanes to hammer Hamas targets.

Several abortive cease-fire agreements were negotiated before a somewhat more permanent one was reached on August 26, 2014. By then, Israel had withdrawn its ground troops from Gaza and announced that it had disrupted or destroyed numerous Hamas tunnels. As many as 2,150 Gazans died during the fifty-day conflict, which Israel code-named Operation Protective Edge. The precise number of civilian deaths is contested, but the United Nations estimates that over 2,200 Palestinians were killed, at least 1,400 of them civilians, including 500 children. Meanwhile, Israel reported sixty-six soldiers and eight civilians killed. Destruction in Gaza was widespread, with over 500,000 Palestinians displaced from their homes and considerable damage to schools and other public buildings. As many as 8,000 Israeli civilians were forced from their homes in southern Israel in an effort to protect them from short-range rocket attacks that Israel's antimissile defenses could not intercept.

In 2017, another unity government agreement was struck, but both sides claim that the other has not lived up to their promises. In an effort to force Hamas to yield, the PA cut government salaries and welfare payments to Gazans, and even coordinated with Israel to cut the flow of electricity to the enclave. The humanitarian crisis there grows more severe by the day. The misery and hopelessness that Gazans face helped spark a series of mass protests in the spring and summer of 2018, known as the Great March of Return, in which over 100 Gazans were killed and thousands more were wounded by Israeli snipers and tear gas. Israel insists that its blockade is both legal and necessary to contain its most virulent enemy, Hamas. But critics insist that it is nothing less than collective punishment of and economic warfare on innocent people.

Spencer C. Tucker

See also: Abbas, Mahmoud; Arab-Israeli War, 1967; Fatah; Gaza Strip Blockade; Gaza Strip Disengagement; Great March of Return; Hamas; *Nakba;* Palestinian Authority; Palestinian Refugees; Right of Return; West Bank

Further Reading
Baconi, Tareq. *Hamas Contained: The Rise and Pacification of Palestinian Resistance.* Stanford, CA: Stanford University Press, 2018.

Oren, Michael B. *Six Days of War: June 1967 and the Making of the Modern Middle East.* New York: Oxford University Press, 2002.

Said, Edward. *The End of the Peace Process: Oslo and After.* New York: Vintage, 2001.

Smith, Charles D. *Palestine and the Arab-Israeli Conflict: A History with Documents.* 9th ed. New York: Bedford/St. Martin's, 2017.

Gaza Strip Blockade

Israeli-enforced restrictions on the flow of goods and people into and out of the Gaza Strip. In late 2005, Israel unilaterally withdrew its military forces from Gaza and evacuated its 9,000 settlers. It reinforced a barrier surrounding Gaza, which Israel had constructed a decade earlier and ever since has imposed strict control over land, sea, and air access to the overcrowded enclave. In 2006, Israel imposed limitations on the flow of goods and people into and out of Gaza and stiffened them in 2007, when Hamas forced the Palestinian Authority (PA) out of the enclave and asserted exclusive control. While Israel's restrictions have fluctuated over time, they have effectively banned Gazan exports, drastically restricted the importation of goods and building materials, largely prevented the exit of Gazans from the territory, and limited their ability to fish the Mediterranean Sea. Israel no longer controls Gaza's border with Egypt but coordinates policy with Egypt, which views Hamas with suspicion because of its ties to the Muslim Brotherhood, which Cairo considers a terrorist group. In 2017, the PA, in an effort to wrestle control of Gaza from Hamas, cut the subsidies that it normally pays for the provision of fuel and electricity, most of which comes from Israel.

The upshot of these measures has been the slow suffocation of Gaza's economy and the creation of a massive humanitarian crisis. Unemployment is over 50 percent, and Gazans lack access to clean water and fuel to power its sole electricity plant. They also suffer from medication and food shortages, underresourced hospitals and schools, soaring poverty rates, and extensive mental health challenges, especially among the traumatized youth. Gaza is also facing severe environmental degradation, including the dumping of untreated sewage and wastewater into parts of the Strip and the Mediterranean Sea, the result of damaged or limited operations of treatment facilities. Much of Gaza's infrastructure and many homes have been damaged during numerous wars with Israel and remain unrepaired, in part because of restrictions on building materials. Israel claims that these restrictions are necessary because such materials can be used by Hamas and other militant groups to build smuggling tunnels or fortify military positions.

Critics insist that Israel's blockade has turned Gaza into an enormous, open-air prison and is a form of collective punishment of the innocent. Humanitarian groups and the United Nations warn that the situation grows more hopeless by the day, and soon the enclave could become uninhabitable. For its part, Israel insists that all blame lies with Hamas, and its measures are necessary to ensure the security of Israelis living along Gaza's border, who are subject to persistent rocket attacks.

Robert C. DiPrizio

See also: Gaza Strip; Gaza Strip Disengagement; Hamas; Israeli Occupations

Further Readings
Gitlin, Martin, ed. *The Blockade of the Gaza Strip: Opposing Viewpoints.* New York: Greenhaven Press, 2019.
Migdalovitz, Carol. *Israel's Blockade of Gaza, the Mavi Marmara Incident, and Its Aftermath.* Washington, DC: Congressional Research Service, 2010.
Zurayk, Rami, and Anne Gough. *Control Food, Control People: The Struggle for Food Security in Gaza.* Washington, DC: Institute for Palestine Studies, 2013.

Gaza Strip Disengagement

A plan devised by Israeli prime minister Ariel Sharon to remove Israeli settlers from the Gaza Strip and four Jewish settlements in the northern West Bank. The Gaza Strip Disengagement officially began on August 15, 2005, and was completed on September 12, 2005. Sharon first announced his plan for withdrawal in December 2003, at the Fourth Herzliya Conference in Israel. Sharon declared that the purpose of the pullout plan was to reduce terror as much as possible and grant Israeli citizens the maximum level of security. This would be done by containing their most virulent enemy, Hamas, within the Gaza Strip. Some analysts have suggested that the withdrawal was a shrewd strategic maneuver on Sharon's part, designed to undermine Palestinian unity. As it turned out, soon after Israel withdrew, simmering tensions between Hamas and the Palestinian Authority (PA) boiled over into a brief conflict that left Hamas in control of Gaza and the PA running the West Bank.

Despite opposition from Sharon's own Likud Party, which believed that he had betrayed his previous policies supporting the Gaza settlements, the Israeli cabinet approved the disengagement on June 6, 2004. Benjamin Netanyahu, the finance minister, accused Sharon of destroying Jewish towns and villages while receiving nothing in return, and he decided to resign his post in protest.

Many Palestinians opposed the plan, as it did not call for Israel to withdraw militarily from the Gaza Strip, nor did it address any of the intolerable conditions of occupation in the West Bank. Israelis who opposed the plan joined together in nonviolent protests, such as a demonstration on July 25, 2004, in which tens of thousands of Israelis formed a fifty-mile-long human chain from the Nissanit settlement in Gaza to the Western (Wailing) Wall in Jerusalem. Other protests throughout the country occurred as well, including a symbolic war of flags (orange for those who opposed withdrawal and blue for those who favored withdrawal), until the disengagement was complete. By July 2005, polls showed that a majority of Israelis supported Sharon and the withdrawal plan.

On August 17, the forced evacuation of those Israelis who refused to leave on their own began. Israeli civilians were removed from their homes, and their residences were demolished. While there was much less violence than expected, there were some instances of Israeli troops dragging screaming Jews from their homes and synagogues in Gaza. (Israel did not destroy any synagogues during the pullout, leaving that emotionally charged act to the Palestinians.) In all, it took the Israel Defense Forces (IDF) and the Israeli police only four and a half days to forcibly evict some 5,000 settlers.

Gregory Morgan

See also: Abbas, Mahmoud; Gaza Strip; Hamas; Sharon, Ariel

Further Reading

Efrat, Elisha. *The West Bank and Gaza Strip: A Geography of Occupation and Disengagement.* New York: Routledge, 2006.

Makovsky, David. *Making Peace with the PLO: The Rabin Government's Road to the Oslo Accord.* Boulder, CO: Westview, 1996.

Gaza Wars—2008, 2012, 2014 (see Gaza Strip)

Geneva Accord, 2003

A peace agreement negotiated extragovernmentally between the Israelis and Palestinians, designed to jump-start the ongoing Middle East peace process and address long-standing roadblocks to an Israeli-Palestinian rapprochement. The Geneva Accord was formally signed on December 1, 2003. While negotiators on both sides had held high-level posts in their respective governments, they were not acting at the specific behest of those governments.

The accord agreed to the creation of an independent Palestinian state, to be located largely in the West Bank and the Gaza Strip. In return, the Palestinians were to officially recognize the state of Israel on the lands that it would subsequently inhabit. All other land claims would be abandoned. The Palestinians would also have to agree to cease all forms of violence against Israel and disarm terrorist groups. Israel would allow the settlement of a limited number of Palestinian refugees within its boundaries. Beyond that, Palestinians would waive the right of return for remaining refugees. The accord also called for Jerusalem to be divided, with much of East Jerusalem going to the Palestinians. The Palestinians would receive most of the territory captured by Israel in the 1967 Six-Day War, and Israel would annex several areas, including Gush Etzion and Ma'ale Adumim. Jewish settlers in Hebron and Ariel would be obliged to move into officially recognized Israeli territory.

Some Palestinian politicians embraced the basic tenets of the pact, for it went a considerable way toward addressing long-standing Palestinian demands, but the agreement was not well received in Israel. The Israeli government, led by the Likud Party, refused to support any part of it. The Labor Party did not reject it, but it refused to support it either. The accord received much play in the Israeli press, but it is believed that public support for it has never exceeded much more than 30 percent.

Paul G. Pierpaoli Jr.

See also: Jerusalem; Oslo Accords; Palestinian Authority; Palestinian Refugees; Settlements; Two-State Solution; West Bank

Further Readings

Lerner, Michael. *The Geneva Accord and Other Strategies for Healing the Israeli-Palestinian Conflict.* Berkeley, CA: North Atlantic Books, 2004.

Watson, Geoffrey R. *The Oslo Accords: International Law and the Israeli-Palestinian Peace Agreements.* New York: Oxford University Press, 2000.

Golan Heights

Israeli-occupied territory captured from Syria in the 1967 Six-Day War. The Golan Heights is an area of great strategic importance, as it overlooks much of northern Israel, is within easy striking distance from Damascus, and is home to important water resources and rich farming lands. Syria insists on the return of the Golan Heights as a condition for normalizing relations with Israel, and bilateral peace talks on the highly volatile issue have been unsuccessful thus far. Lebanon says that a small portion of the Heights, known as the Shebaa Farms, is part of its territory, a claim disputed by Israeli and Syrian officials.

Following World War I, the Golan Heights was included in the French Mandate of Syria, although in 1924, a small portion of the area was designated as part of the British Mandate of Palestine. When Syria became independent in 1944, it gained control of the Golan, which was known within the country as the Syrian Heights. The Heights were strategically important to Syrian because, as previously stated, it overlooks northern Israel and contains water resources.

Following the Israeli War of Independence in 1948, both Israel and Syria violated the Israel-Syrian Armistice Agreement that was established to end the war. Tensions between the two sides increased when Syria attempted to divert the tributaries that flowed out of the Golan Heights into the Jordan River, leading to large-scale Israeli air strikes on Syrian dam projects. Israel captured the Golan on June 9 and 10, 1967, in the midst of the Six-Day War. At this time, approximately 90 percent of the population (mostly Druze Syrians and Circassians) fled the area and have not been permitted to return. Israel immediately began building Jewish settlements in the Golan, with the first settlement town of Merom Golan being established in July. Today, there are about 20,000 Jewish settlers inhabiting more than thirty settlements.

In spite of Syria's refusal to make peace with Israel unless the Heights were returned, Israel continued building settlements in the area, with twelve Jewish towns set up by 1970. Tensions culminated with a surprise attack on Israel by Egypt and Syria that started a war in 1973. Syria quickly made gains in the Golan but despite being severely outnumbered (180 Israeli tanks faced 1,400 Syrian tanks), the Israel Defense Forces (IDF) was able to push the Syrians back to the 1967 border. The IDF then continued to march into Syria proper, coming within twenty-five miles of Damascus before a combined force of Jordanians, Iraqis, and Syrians forced the Israelis to withdraw. At the end of the war, more than 1,000 United Nations (UN) peacekeeping troops were stationed in the Golan, and the armed conflict between the Syrian and Israeli armies came to an end.

The Golan Heights remained under Israeli military administration until 1981, when legislation was passed subjecting the area to Israeli law and granting citizenship privileges to people living within the Heights. Although Israel did not use the word *annexation* within the legislation, much of the international community saw the move as such. The United Nations responded to the move with Security Council Resolution 497, which said that "the Israeli decision to impose its laws, jurisdiction, and administration in the occupied Syrian Golan Heights is null and void and without international legal effect." However, the United Nations also avoided calling the move an annexation.

Syria demands that Israel withdraw to the 1948 armistice line, which would place Syria's border on the shores of the Sea of Galilee. Syria claims that its demands are in keeping with UN Security Council Resolutions 242 and 338, which call for Israel to withdraw from the territories that it occupied during the 1967 Arab-Israeli War. In 1999–2000 peace negotiations, Israel proposed returning most of the Golan to Syria, save for a strip of land bordering the Sea of Galilee. Syria refused the offer, insisting on a full withdrawal.

Many Israelis insist that they must maintain control of the Golan to protect the water resources that flow through the area and to keep Israel's enemies off the plateau. Given the events of the Syrian civil war and the activity of Israel's enemies near its northern border, Israel today is even more determined to retain control of the Golan Heights. In April 2019, U.S. president Donald Trump recognized Israel's claim to sovereignty over the territory.

Jessica Britt

See also: Arab-Israeli War, 1967; Arab-Israeli War, 1973; Arab Spring; Arab Spring, Effects on Israel; Syria; UN Security Council Resolution 242

Further Reading

Lerman, Hallie. *Crying for Imma: Battling for the Soul on the Golan Heights.* San Francisco: Night Vision Press, 1998.

Moaz, Moshe. *Syria and Israel: From War to Peacemaking.* Oxford: Oxford University Press, 1995.

Rabil, Robert G. *Embattled Neighbors: Syria, Israel, Lebanon.* Boulder, CO: Lynn Rienner Publishers, 2003.

Grand Mufti of Jerusalem

The senior Sunni Muslim cleric in charge of Muslim holy sites in Jerusalem. A *mufti* is a Muslim legal expert empowered to issue fatwas or authoritative legal opinions. Under Ottoman rule, Sunni Muslim communities like Jerusalem had both a mufti and a senior religious judge known as a *qadi*. Both were members of the Hanafi branch of Sunni Islam, to which most Palestinian Muslims belong.

Originally, the mufti's authority was restricted to greater Jerusalem and was subordinate to a senior cleric in Istanbul. Over time, the power balance between qadi and mufti gradually shifted until, in 1913, the Ottomans made each mufti the leader of all Muslim clergy in his region. In 1921, the British Mandate authorities decided that a single, senior cleric for Palestine would best serve its interests. The British thus made the mufti the senior Palestinian Muslim cleric, eventually terming him the Grand Mufti of Jerusalem.

While many Grand Muftis were relatively noncontroversial, some have been outspoken antagonists of their secular counterparts. The first and most famous is Muhammad Amin al-Husayni (1895–1974). Husayni was an Arab nationalist and anti-Zionist who first followed a fairly subdued and often cooperative political approach with the British. That changed when he led the Arab Higher Committee (AHC) during the 1936–1939 Arab Revolt. The revolt was put down, and Husayni was exiled by the British. He later publicly supported the Nazis and in 1941 offered to form an Arab Legion to fight for the Germans. By 1948, his intransigence led Jordan's King Abdullah to dismiss him and forbid him from entering Jerusalem. In 2006, another mufti, Ekrima Sa'id Sabri, was dismissed by Palestinian president Mahmoud Abbas for his political activities. Since then, the position has been held by Muhammad Ahmad Husayn. Tensions between the current mufti, Israelis, and Palestinian officials continue, with periodic clashes and threats of his dismissal.

Tom Dowling

See also: Arab Higher Committee; Arab Revolt, 1936; British Mandate for Palestine; Jerusalem

Further Reading

Mattar, Philip. *Al-Hajj Amin al-Husayni and the Palestinian National Movement.* New York: Columbia University Press, 1988.

Smith, Charles D. *Palestine and the Arab-Israeli Conflict: A History with Documents.* 9th ed. New York: Bedford/St. Martin's, 2017.

Great March of Return

Long-running Palestinian rallies in Gaza demanding the right to return and the end of Israel's blockade. The Great March of Return began as a Palestinian protest on March 30, 2018, and was intended to end on May 15, although they have occurred every Friday since. The chosen dates coincided with Land Day and Nakba Day, respectively. Land Day commemorates the death of Palestinian protesters who opposed Israel's expropriation of land claimed by Palestinians, and Nakba is the day when many Palestinians mourn the formation of Israel. While open to all Palestinians, the protests were organized by Gazans, and most of the rallies have been along the Gaza-Israel border. Protesters are demanding the right to return to homes that are now part of Israel and the end of Israel's eleven-year siege of Gaza, which has contributed to shortages of food, potable water, medicines, building supplies, and widespread unemployment. They also were protesting the U.S. decision in late 2017 to recognize Jerusalem as Israel's capital and to move its embassy there.

While the protests have been largely nonviolent, some Palestinians youths have thrown Molotov cocktails, burned tires, tried to break through Israel's border fences, and flew incendiary kites into Israeli fields just over the border. The Israel Defense Forces (IDF) has responded with tear gas, rubber bullets, and lethal fire, shooting protesters that come within 100–300 meters of Israel's border, which is denoted by a barbed wire fence. On May 14, 2018, the day that U.S. and Israeli officials inaugurated the opening of the new U.S. embassy, the protests swelled and the IDF injured over 2,400 people, 60 of whom died. As of April 2019, these ongoing weekly protests have resulted in nearly 250 Palestinians dead and over 29,000 injured, including hundreds who have lost limbs. One IDF soldier has been killed as well.

Many have decried Israel's response as excessively violent and disproportionate to the threat posed by the rallies. A 2019 report from the United Nations Human Rights Council asserts there are "reasonable grounds" to believe that Israel violated international humanitarian law. Israeli officials insist that the protests are orchestrated by Hamas and are a grave threat to Israel's national security. They reject criticism of the IDF's behavior and insist that all responsibility for casualties lie with Hamas and the protesters.

Sean N. Blas

See also: Gaza Strip; Hamas; Israel Defense Forces; Israeli Occupations; *Nakba*

Further Reading
United Nations Human Rights Council. *Report of the Detailed Findings of the Independent International Commission of Inquiry on the Protests in the Occupied Palestinian Territory A/HRC/40/CRP.2.* March 18, 2019. https://www.ohchr.org/EN/HRBodies/HRC/CoIOPT/Pages/Report2018OPT.aspx.

Gush Emunim

A radical Israeli religious group that espouses the doctrine of Greater Israel. An earlier group, the Movement for the Whole Land of Israel, formed a couple of months after the 1967 Six-Day War to lobby for an expanded Israel, to include the West Bank and the Gaza Strip. Members of this group were secular Zionist intellectuals, generals, and politicians. A group of Orthodox Israelis held an exploratory meeting in February 1974 to discuss the formation of a new political bloc. Then, in March 1974, the founding meeting of Gush Emunim (Bloc of the Faithful) took place at Kfar Etzion, a West Bank settlement. Gush Emunim adopted the program of the Movement for the Whole Land of Israel and absorbed many of its members.

Adherents of Gush Emunim came from the National Religious Party (NRP), the Land of Israel Movements, Orthodox students of the Yeshiva Merkaz Harav, and members of the B'nai Akiva movement. Unlike a political party, the Gush Emunim never had an elected leader or a formal organization with dues-paying members, but it had an effective network of leaders coming out of the settlement movement. Uniting these groups was the ideology of Rabbi Zvi Yehuda Kook, who believed in the incorporation of the lands of Judea and Samaria into the state of Israel. The victory of Israel in the 1967 Arab-Israeli War was a fulfillment of his dream of a Greater Israel. His followers organized to oppose territorial concessions to the Palestinians, and they pursued a policy of acquiring territory in the West Bank, either by military action or by settlements.

Gush Emunim found itself in opposition to the policies of the Labor government. In the mid-1970s, adherents of Gush Emunim began establishing settlements in the occupied territories of the West Bank. This action brought these settlers into conflict with the Labor government of Prime Minister Yitzhak Rabin. By 1977, Gush Emunim had become a close political ally of the right-wing Likud Party. The victory of the Likud Party in 1977 allowed the new prime minister, Menachem Begin, to sanction the widespread building of new settlements. Israelis flocked to the settlements not only for new land, but also to gain government financial subsidies. Members of Gush Emunim dominated the settlers' lobby, and they have continued to push for more settlements. This is in support of their view that the occupied West Bank and Gaza Strip should be permanently incorporated into the state of Israel.

Jewish vigilante groups formed to drive Palestinians off the land, and Israeli authorities did little to curb the violence.

The radical wing of Gush Emunim formed a terrorist group. Beginning in 1980, twenty-seven of the group's members created the Jewish Underground, under the leadership of Yehudah Etzion. Over the next four years, this group exploded several bombs and engaged in shootings. However, their most ambitious plan, to blow up the Muslim Dome of the Rock on the Temple Mount in Jerusalem, was thwarted. Members of the Underground were arrested, and they received prison sentences ranging from seven to ten years. An extensive lobbying campaign by the Likud and the NRP led to their early pardon by President Chaim Herzog.

The main goal of Gush Emunim was to sabotage any attempts at an Israeli-Palestinian peace agreement that creates a Palestinian state. Its leaders opposed the Camp David Accords in 1977 because they granted Palestinians self-rule in the West Bank and Gaza. They lobbied against the agreement, and soon actions by both the Israelis and Palestinians ensured that the agreement did not result in self-rule.

The next major threat to Gush Emunim was the September 1993 Oslo Accords. Various Israeli governments had encouraged further settlements in the occupied territories. As these settlements increased in number and size, tensions increased with the Palestinians. The outbreak of the First Intifada in 1987 was the result. Civil disobedience and violence made it impossible for the Israel Defense Forces (IDF) to control the Palestinians. Vigilante actions by Gush Emunim members only made the crisis worse. In 1992, a new Labor government won office, with Yitzhak Rabin as prime minister. Rabin had a history of opposing Gush Emunim and its settlement program. Rabin's negotiations leading to the Oslo Agreements infuriated the group. Leaders of Gush Emunim declared war on Rabin, and members worked with elements in the Likud Party to attack him. This campaign of vilification led to Rabin's assassination on November 4, 1995, by Yigal Amir, a religious fanatic and an adherent of the Greater Israel movement.

Stephen E. Atkins

See also: Arab-Israeli War, 1967; Eretz Israel; Haram al-Sharif/Temple Mount; Jewish Underground; Oslo Accords; Settlements; Settler Violence

Further Reading

Friedman, Robert I. *Zealots for Zion: Inside Israel's West Bank Settlement Movement.* New York: Random House, 1992.

Lustick, Ian S. *For the Land and the Lord.* New York: Council on Foreign Relations, 1988.

Sprinzak, Ehud. *Brother Against Brother: Violence and Extremism in Israeli Politics from Altalena to the Rabin Assassination.* New York: Free Press, 1999.

Sprinzak, Ehud. "From Messianic Pioneering to Vigilante Terrorism: The Case of the Gush Emunim Underground," in David C. Rapoport, ed., *Inside Terrorist Organizations.* London: Frank Cass, 2001, 194–216.

H

Habash, George

Palestinian leader best known for founding the Arab Nationalist Movement (ANM) and the leftist Popular Front for the Liberation of Palestine (PFLP). Born on August 2, 1926, in Lydda (present-day Lod in Israel), to Eastern Orthodox Christian parents, George Habash fled with his family when Israel conquered Lydda in 1948. His sister was killed in the fighting. Habash studied medicine at the American University in Beirut, Lebanon (he became a pediatrician), where he was exposed to the Arab nationalist teachings of Constantine Zurayk and Sati al-Husari, known as the father of Arab nationalism.

In 1951, Habash formed the ANM, whose ideology was based on the ideas of Zurayk and Husari. Following the 1967 Six-Day War, he created the PFLP and turned to Marxism, primarily as a result of his imprisonment in Syria, during which he read the collected works of Karl Marx, Friedrich Engels, Vladimir Lenin, Ho Chi Minh, and Mao Tse-tung. Habash believed that Israel's devastating military defeat of Arab forces in the 1967 war necessarily required that Palestinians adopt guerrilla tactics, similar to the military tactics being used by North Vietnamese forces. In the end, revolutionary violence would lead to the creation of a democratic Palestine, where Jews and Arabs would live with equal rights.

Habash oversaw the PFLP's tactical decision to initiate a systematic campaign of airline hijackings to bring publicity to the plight of the Palestinian people. He later told a German newspaper that hijacking one plane gained more attention than killing 100 Israelis in battle. On September 6, 1970, the PFLP conducted its most famous operation, when it hijacked four airliners, flying three of them to Dawson's Field in Jordan. (The other ultimately was taken to Cairo.) The incident received widespread international media attention and greatly embarrassed King Husayn, who then expelled the Palestine Liberation Organization (PLO) from the country.

In 1972, Habash ceased hijacking operations. This, however, did not signal a softening of his stance. In 1974, he withdrew the PFLP from the PLO's Executive Committee in opposition to Yasser Arafat's moratorium on acts of terrorism outside Israel and the Occupied Palestinian Territories and his willingness to explore a Middle East settlement plan. In September 1980, Habash underwent brain surgery to remove a benign tumor. In 1992, Habash suffered a stroke. In 2000, he resigned as leader of the PFLP. Habash eventually died of a heart attack in Amman, Jordan, on January 26, 2008. He was eight-two years old.

Paul J. Smith

See also: Arafat, Yasser; Palestinian Hijackings; Palestine Liberation Organization; Popular Front for the Liberation of Palestine

Further Reading

Habash, George. "George Habash: The Future of the Palestinian National Movement." *Journal of Palestine Studies* 14, no. 4 (Summer 1985), 3–14.

Habash, George, and Mahmoud Soueid. "'Taking Stock': An Interview with George Habash." *Journal of Palestine Studies* 28, no. 1 (Autumn 1998), 86–101.

Levy, Gideon. "This Biography Makes It Clear: The Founder of the Palestinian Popular Front Was Right." *Haaretz*, April 15, 2018. https://www.haaretz.com/middle-east-news/palestinians/.premium-biography-makes-it-clear-this-palestinian-leftist-leader-was-right-1.5994244.

Haganah

Jewish underground self-defense and military organization during 1920–1948, and the precursor of the Israel Defense Forces (IDF). *Haganah* is Hebrew for "defense." The group was organized to protect the Jewish community (Yishuv) following the Arab riots of 1920 and 1921. During 1920–1929, Haganah was composed of localized and poorly armed units of Jewish farmers who took turns guarding one another's farms and kibbutzim. Its structure and role changed radically after the Arab riots of 1929. Haganah began to organize the rural and urban Jewish adult and youth populations throughout Palestine into a much larger, better-equipped, and better-trained but still primarily self-defense force. Although Haganah was able to acquire some foreign weapons, Haganah constructed secret weapon fabrication workshops for ammunition, some small arms, and grenades.

Even as the British mandatory government slowly shifted its support to the Arab population of Palestine, the leadership of the Jewish Agency for Palestine continued to attempt to work closely with it to promote the interests of the Jewish population in Palestine. Haganah supported this position through its self-defense and military strategy of *havlaga* (self-restraint), but not all of its members agreed with a restrained response to what they perceived as the British mandatory government's pro-Arab bias. This political and policy disagreement and Haganah's prevailing socialist ideology led in 1931 to the formation of a minority splinter group headed by Avraham Tehomi, known as Irgun Tsvai Leumi (National Military Organization). Irgun advocated harsh retaliation for Arab attacks and an active military campaign to end British mandatory governance of Palestine.

By 1936, the year that the Palestinian revolt known as the Arab Revolt began, Haganah had grown to 10,000 mobilized men and 40,000 reservists. Although the British mandatory government still refused to recognize Haganah, the strategy of *havlaga* seemed to bear fruit when the British security forces cooperated in the establishment of the Jewish Settlement Police, Jewish Auxiliary Forces, and Special Night Squads as Jewish civilian militia. In addition, the British and Haganah worked together to suppress the 1936 Arab Revolt and to protect British as well as Jewish interests.

Despite these perceived gains, in 1937, Haganah again split into right-wing and left-wing factions. The right-wing faction joined Irgun, and some of the members of Irgun, including Tehomi, rejoined Haganah. Irgun had been nothing more than a small and ineffective irritant until this transition changed it into an effective guerrilla force, branded as terrorists by the British and some in Haganah.

The Arab Revolt matured Haganah and taught it many lessons. Haganah improved its underground arms production capability, increased the acquisition of light arms from Europe, and established centralized arms depots and fifty strategically placed kibbutzim. Haganah also enhanced the training of its soldiers and officer corps and expanded its clandestine training of the general population.

The British White Paper of 1939 openly shifted British support away from the Jews to the Arabs. Jewish immigration, settlement, and land purchases in Palestine were severely restricted, and the British effectively retreated from its active support of an independent Jewish homeland. Even with this betrayal, Yishuv leader David Ben-Gurion asserted that the Zionists should stand against the change in policy, even while supporting the British against Nazi Germany. Haganah responded by organizing demonstrations against the British and by further facilitating illegal immigration through bases in Turkey and Switzerland under the auspices of Aliya Bet, the Organization for Illegal Immigration, created in 1938. Irgun's response was to begin bombing British installations and attacking British interests.

As World War II progressed, on May 19, 1941, Haganah created the Palmach to train young people in leadership and military skills and to help defend Palestine if the Germans invaded. The Palmach cooperated with the British during 1941–1943, fought behind the lines in Vichy-dominated Lebanon and Syria, worked with Irgun during 1945–1946 against British mandatory rule, and helped facilitate illegal Jewish immigration during 1946–1947 prior to being folded in 1948 into the IDF.

Fearing that the Germans would overrun all of North Africa, Britain negotiated a reciprocal support agreement with Haganah that provided intelligence, and even commando assistance. The British retreated from the agreement following their victory at El Alamein (al-Alamayn) in November 1942, although in 1943, they did form the Jewish Brigade and deployed its 5,000 men in Italy in September 1944 before disbanding it in 1946. Although Palestinian Jews were not allowed to enlist in the British army until 1940, more than 30,000 served in various units from the start of the war.

Haganah focused its operations after the war on the British mandatory government, attacking rail lines, bridges, and deportation ships, and even freeing immigrants from the Atlit internment camp. It also facilitated illegal immigration from Jewish displaced person camps in Europe. Immediately after partition in 1947, Haganah concentrated on defending the Yishuv against attacks by Palestinian Arabs and the neighboring Arab states.

Haganah took the offensive in the Israeli War of Independence in April 1948. Haganah and Irgun took Tiberias, Haifa, and the Arab cities of Acre and Jaffa. They went on to open a road to West Jerusalem as well. On May 28, 1948, the provisional government of the newly declared state of Israel transformed Haganah into its national military, which it called the IDF, and outlawed all other armed forces. In September 1948, the military activities of Irgun were folded into the IDF.

Richard M. Edwards

See also: Aliya Bet; Arab-Israeli War, 1948; Arab-Jewish Communal War, 1967; Deir Yassin Massacre; Israel Defense Forces; Lydda and Ramle; Yishuv; Zionism

Further Reading
Bauer, Yehuda. *From Diplomacy to Resistance: A History of Jewish Palestine, 1930–1945.* Trans. Alton M. Winters. Philadelphia: Jewish Publication Society of America, 1970.
Farris, Karl. *Growth and Change in the Israel Defense Forces Through Six Wars.* Carlisle Barracks, PA: U.S. Army War College, 1987.
Mardor, Munya M. *Haganah.* Ed by D. R. Elston; foreword by David Ben-Gurion. Trans. H. A. G. Schmuckler. New York: New American Library, 1966.

Hamas

An Islamist Palestinian organization formally founded in 1987. Hamas seeks the creation of an Islamic way of life and the liberation of Palestine through Islamic resistance. Essentially, it combines Islamic fundamentalism with Palestinian nationalism. Hamas gained about 30–40 percent support in the Palestinian population within five years because of its mobilization successes and the general desperation experienced by the Palestinian population during the First Intifada. In January 2006, Hamas won a majority in the Palestinian Authority's (PA) general legislative elections, which brought condemnation from Israel and a power struggle with PA president Mahmoud Abbas and his Fatah party.

The word *Hamas* means courage, bravery, or zeal; it is also an Arabic acronym for *Ḥarakat al-Muqāwamah al-'Islāmiyyah,* the Movement of Islamic Resistance. The growth of Islamist movements was delayed among Palestinians because of their status as a people without a state and the tight security controls imposed by Israel, which had strengthened the more secular nationalist expression of the Palestine Liberation Organization (PLO).

The Muslim Brotherhood, established in Egypt in 1928, set up branches in Syria, Sudan, Libya, the Gulf, Jordan, and Gaza. However, for two decades, the Muslim Brotherhood focused on its religious, educational, and social missions and was quiescent politically. That changed with the First Intifada (1987). The Muslim Brotherhood advocated *dawah,* which may be described as a re-Islamization of society and thought; *adala* (social justice); and an emphasis on *hakmiyya* (the sovereignty of God, as opposed to temporal rule). The Muslim Brotherhood turned to activism against Israel after Palestinian Islamic Jihad (PIJ) had accelerated its operations during 1986 and 1987. As the new organization of Hamas emerged from the Muslim Brotherhood, it was able to draw strength from the social work of Sheikh Ahmed Yassin, an influential schoolteacher who used a wheelchair.

In December 1987, Abd al-Aziz Rantisi, who was a physician at the Islamic University, and former student leaders Salah Shihada and Yahya al-Sinuwwar, chief of security for the Muslim Brotherhood, formed the first unit of Hamas. While Yassin gave his approval, as a cleric he was not directly connected to the new organization.

In February 1988, the Brotherhood granted formal recognition to Hamas, which issued its charter that same year. The charter condemns world Zionism and the efforts to isolate Palestine, defines the mission of the organization, and locates that mission within Palestinian, Arab, and Islamic elements. It does not condemn the West or non-Muslims, but it does condemn aggression against the Palestinian people, arguing for a defensive jihad. It also calls for fraternal relations with the other Palestinian nationalist groups.

Hamas is headed by a Political Bureau, with representatives for military affairs, foreign affairs, finance, propaganda, and internal security. An Advisory Council is linked to the Political Bureau; to Hamas's social and charitable groups, elected members, and district committees; and to the leadership in Israeli prisons.

Major attacks against Israel have been carried out by the Izz al-Din al-Qassam Brigades of Hamas. They also developed the Qassam rocket used to attack Israeli civilian settlements in the Negev Desert. However, much of Hamas's activity during the First Intifada consisted of participating in more broadly based popular demonstrations and locally coordinated efforts at resistance, countering Israeli raids, and enforcing the opening of businesses.

Hamas greatly expanded by 1993, and it decried the Oslo Accords between Israel and the PLO as too limited a gain. Its leadership rejected participation in the 1996 PA legislative election but didn't rule it out in the future. This gave the organization the ability to continue protesting Oslo.

During the Second Intifada, Hamas spearheaded the widespread use of suicide bombings against Israeli targets and as such became the most reviled Palestinian group among Israelis. The Israel Defense Forces (IDF) responded with targeted killings of many Hamas leaders, including Shihada (July 23, 2002), Dr. Ibrahim Al-Makadma (August 3, 2003), Ismail Abu Shanab (August 21, 2003), Yassin (March 22, 2004), and Rantisi (April 17, 2004).

Hamas funds an extensive array of social services aimed at ameliorating the plight of the Palestinians. It provides funding for hospitals, schools, mosques, orphanages, food distribution, and aid to the families of Palestinian prisoners who, as they number more than 10,000 people, constitute an important political force. Given the PA's frequent inability to meet such needs, Hamas stepped into the breach, and in so doing, endeared itself to a large number of Palestinians.

Hamas has received funding from a number of sources. Palestinians living abroad provide money, as do a number of private donors in the wealthy Gulf States. Iran has been a significant donor to Hamas, although this has largely dried up because Hamas refused to support the Bashar al-Assad regime in the Syrian civil war.

Hamas has two sets of leaders—those inside the West Bank and Gaza and those outside. The outside leaders used to be based in Damascus but have since moved to Qatar. Meanwhile, the West Bank leadership is divided along political, charitable, student, and military activities. The political leadership is usually targeted for arrests because its members can be located, unlike the secret military units. Hamas gained much popularity in the occupied territories in part because it was able to accomplish what the PA could not (namely, to provide for the everyday needs of the people and continue to resist Israeli occupation).

Hamas, which is widely seen as far less corrupt than Yasser Arafat's Fatah party, won legislative elections in January 2006, allowing it to create a new, Hamas-dominated PA. Nonetheless, the United States, Israel, and most of Europe consider

Hamas a terrorist group and refused to recognize a Hamas-dominated government. The United States, European Union, and Israel all cut aid and financial dealings with the PA, which created difficulties for ordinary Palestinians. The loss of this aid halted the delivery of supplies to hospitals and ended other services, in addition to stopping the payment of salaries. The cutoff in funds was designed to discourage Palestinian support for Hamas.

On March 17, 2007, Abbas brokered a Palestinian unity government that included members of both Hamas and Fatah, in which Hamas leader Ismail Haniyeh became prime minister. Yet in May, armed clashes between Hamas and Fatah escalated, and in June, Hamas seized control of Gaza. Abbas promptly dissolved the Hamas-led unity government and declared a state of emergency. On June 18, Abbas swore in an emergency Palestinian government. That same day, the United States ended its fifteen-month embargo on the PA and resumed aid in an effort to strengthen Abbas's government, now limited to the West Bank. On June 19, Abbas cut off all ties and dialogue with Hamas, pending the return of Gaza. Soon after, Israel restored financial ties to the PA to prop up the moderate Abbas government.

In early 2008, rocket attacks on Israel launched from the Gaza Strip led to an Egyptian-brokered six-month cease-fire agreement that brought relative calm during the latter half of the year. But as the agreement's expiration approached, Israel destroyed one of the hundreds of tunnels that Hamas had dug to smuggle goods, arms, and terrorists. Vowing revenge for purportedly violating the truce, and citing Israel's continued refusal to lift its blockade, Hamas launched a barrage of rockets, to which the IDF responded with a full-scale assault that left over 1,000 Palestinians dead. In the face of intense international pressure, Israel halted operations on January 18, 2009.

In November 2012, violence flared up again when Israel launched Operation Pillar of Defense, designed to punish Hamas for about 100 rocket attacks and other acts of provocation on Israeli territory. Hamas claimed that its attacks were in retaliation for the Israeli blockade of Gaza and its continued occupation of East Jerusalem and the West Bank. Israel's operation began with the targeted assassination of Ahmed Jabari, the head of Hamas's military establishment. More than 1,500 strikes occurred within the Gaza Strip, killing over 100 Palestinians. Human Rights Watch later claimed that both Hamas and Israel had violated the laws of modern warfare during the seven-day clash.

In June 2014, Abbas and Hamas announced the formation of another unity government. Unlike the 2007 government, this one included no Hamas members in the cabinet, but Hamas agreed to support the government without direct participation in it. The United States and most of its allies cautiously backed the new arrangement, but Israel denounced the government because of its ties to Hamas.

A renewed conflict between Israel and Hamas in July and August 2014 resulted in substantial bloodshed, all but unraveling Abbas's unity government. On July 17, Israel escalated the conflict, sending ground forces into the Gaza Strip, and Israeli warplanes continued to hammer Hamas targets. Several abortive cease-fire agreements were negotiated before a somewhat more permanent one was reached on August 26, 2014. By then, Israel had withdrawn its ground troops from Gaza and announced that it had disrupted or destroyed numerous Hamas-built tunnels linking Gaza with Israel. As many as 2,150 Gazans died during the fifty-day conflict. Israel reported sixty-six soldiers and eight civilians killed.

In 2017, another unity agreement was struck, but its implementation has stalled. In an effort to force Hamas to yield control of the Gaza Strip, the PA has cut government salaries and welfare payments to Gazans, and has even coordinated with Israel to cut the flow of electricity to the enclave. The humanitarian crisis there grows more severe by the day. The misery and hopelessness that Gazans are suffering helped spark a series of mass protests in the spring and summer of 2018, known as the Great March of Return, in which over 100 Gazans were killed and thousands more were wounded by Israeli snipers and tear gas. Hamas has since responded with more rocket attacks, and Israel with more air raids. Gazans have been flying burning kites and balloons into Israel, sparking wildfires. Israel has since tightened its embargo on Gaza in an effort to force Hamas to prevent such kite and balloon attacks.

Harry Hueston, Paul G. Pierpaoli Jr., and Sherifa Zuhur

See also: Abbas, Mahmoud; Fatah; Gaza Strip; Intifada, First; Intifada, Second; Izz al-Din al-Qassam Brigades; Katyusha Rockets; Oslo Accords; Palestinian Authority; Yassin, Sheikh Ahmed

Further Reading

Baconi, Tareq. *Hamas Contained: The Rise and Pacification of Palestinian Resistance.* Stanford, CA: Stanford University Press, 2018.

Reeve, Simon. *The New Jackals.* Boston: Northeastern University Press, 1999.

Smith, Charles D. *Palestine and the Arab-Israeli Conflict: A History with Documents.* 9th ed. New York: Bedford/St. Martin's, 2017.

Souryal, Sam. *Islam, Islamic Law, and the Turn to Violence.* Huntsville, TX: Office of International Criminal Justice, Sam Houston State University, 2004.

"Straight From the Mouth of Hamas." Jerusalem: Jerusalem Media and Communications Center, March 17, 2005.

Haram al-Sharif/Temple Mount

A hotly contested religious site in the Old City of Jerusalem. Haram al-Sharif, whose name means "noble sacred space" in Arabic, is a major Muslim religious complex containing the Dome of the Rock and the al-Aqsa Mosque built in the seventh century, as well as other historic features, such as a fountain and Umayyad-era pillars and stairs. Built above the site of the first and second Jewish Temples in Jerusalem, this thirty-five-acre site is also called the Temple Mount and, according to Judaism, is to be the future site of the third and final temple in the time of the Messiah. The remains of the second temple are the holiest site in Judaism, and Haram al-Sharif is one of the three holiest sites in Islam, the other two being Mecca and Medina.

A Muslim *waqf* (religious endowment) has encompassed the Haram al-Sharif/Temple Mount and adjacent land continuously since the seventh century. Such endowments were taken over by the Israeli state within the Green Line and managed in some instances by local councils mostly composed of Israeli Jews, with

A view of the Harem al Sharif/Temple Mount in the center of Jerusalem, Israel. This rocky outcrop is considered sacred as the place where the Biblical father Abraham prepared to sacrifice his son Isaac. It was the site of three successive Jewish temples and is now capped by the Muslim Dome of the Rock. (Tamara Johnson)

only token appointments of approved Muslim religious officials. Because of the historical renown of this particular site, it was handled differently. The legality of the waqf has been completely discounted by some Israelis, who regard Haram al-Sharif, just like all parts of Jerusalem, as sovereign Israeli territory. However, since the Oslo agreements, Palestinian security has supervised entry to Haram al-Sharif.

Under this arrangement, Jews, like other non-Muslims, are generally permitted to visit the site in tour groups or as individuals, but are not allowed to pray on the Temple Mount. Officials or Palestinian tour guides usually accompany such visitors to ensure that no prohibited Jewish prayer takes place. Israel refuses to let Palestinians of the West Bank or Gaza to worship at Haram al-Sharif, a fact that Palestinians say shows that their fundamental religious rights are being violated. But Israel insists that these prohibitions are for security reasons.

Few Israelis object to the continued Muslim presence on the Temple Mount, as the only remains of the actual temple site are within the Western (Wailing) Wall, which is below and to the side of the entrance into Haram al-Sharif. Some groups, including the Temple Mount Faithful, advocate the removal of the Dome of the Rock and the al-Aqsa Mosque and the building of the Third Temple. Members of the Gush Emunim Underground (Jewish Underground) plotted to blow up the Dome of the Rock in the mid-1980s, but they were arrested by Israeli authorities. Israeli politician Ariel Sharon's September 2000 visit to Haram al-Sharif with hundreds of security forces is credited with helping to trigger the Second (al-Aqsa) Intifada.

Moshe Terdiman and Sherifa Zuhur

See also: Jerusalem, Old City of; Jewish Underground; Sharon, Ariel; Third Temple Movement

Further Reading
Andrews, Richard. *Blood on the Mountain: A History of the Temple Mount from the Ark to the Third Millennium.* London: Weidenfeld and Nicolson, 1999.
Gonen, Rivka. *Contested Holiness: Jewish, Muslim, and Christian Perspectives on the Temple Mount in Jerusalem.* Jersey City, NJ: Ktav Publishing House, 2003.

Hattin, Battle of

A decisive defeat of the Frank armies of Outremer by the forces of Saladin on July 4, 1187, leading to the collapse of the Latin Kingdom of Jerusalem and the loss of the city of Jerusalem to the Muslims. From the 1170s on, Saladin, the most powerful Muslim ruler in the Near East, launched a series of attacks against the Kingdom of Jerusalem. In 1185, however, a truce was concluded. When Reynald of Châtillon, Lord of Transjordan, attacked a Muslim caravan traversing his territory in late 1186 or early 1187, Saladin demanded restitution. Reynald refused to comply, and Saladin raided Transjordan in May 1187. He also proclaimed jihad (holy war) and assembled 30,000 troops from his empire in Egypt, Syria, and Mesopotamia. In the same month, Guy of Lusignan, King of Jerusalem, called all able-bodied men of the kingdom to arms. They were reinforced by men drawn from the fortresses, mercenaries, and pilgrims, as well as by contingents from the principality of Antioch, the county of Tripoli, and the military orders. In June, some 1,200 knights, 4,000 light cavalry, and 11,000–14,000 infantry assembled at the springs of Saforie, some fifteen miles west of Tiberias.

On June 27, 1187, Saladin crossed the Jordan River south of Lake Tiberias. The Franks could not afford to lose a pitched battle for fear that their cities and fortresses—stripped of manpower to bolster the field army—would become easy prey for the victors if the battle were lost. Saladin, by contrast, could afford to lose substantial forces in battle, as he could easily replace them from his vast dominions. He sought to draw the Franks from their position at Saforie by laying siege to Tiberias on July 2, 1187. The city fell quickly, but the citadel held out. The besieged Franks sent an appeal for help to the Frankish army.

On the morning of July 3, the Frankish army left Saforie to relieve Tiberias. The Franks' main problem was access to water, which could be found only at the springs of Saforie, Turan, and Hattin along the way, whereas the Muslim forces could easily be supplied from Lake Tiberias. Once the Franks had passed Turan, the army was encircled by the Muslims, slowed, and continually harassed. Fighting on the march, the Franks reached Maskanah, where they spent the night. The Muslim forces, led by Saladin in person, converged on the encircled Franks.

On the morning of July 4, the Franks progressed about a mile along the road toward Tiberias. The rearguard came under heavy attack by the main body of the Muslim forces. The Frankish advance came to a halt near the Horns of Hattin, a small elevated plateau, as a result of the continuing harassment by the Muslim light cavalry and bowmen, lack of water, and smoke from the fires that had been lit by the Muslims. Raymond of Tripoli and the vanguard had become separated from the main body of the Frankish forces. He and his mounted men broke through the Muslim lines to the northeast and escaped to Saphet.

The Franks' only hope was a breakthrough along the road toward Lake Tiberias. Their forces, however, had become disordered. Against the express orders of King Guy, the Frankish infantry retreated to the relative safety of the Horns of Hattin. But there was no water on the Horns, and the infantry could not be convinced to resume the march. The mounted Franks had to retreat to the heights as well, as they could not hold their position without infantry support. From the Horns, the mounted knights launched two charges at the Muslim center, but both were repulsed. The Muslims fought their way onto the Horns against fierce resistance and captured the relic of the Holy Cross and the king's tent. When King Guy himself was captured, the battle was over. The surviving Franks surrendered. The infantry were enslaved or killed, while the secular knights were held for ransom. The knights of the military orders, however, were purchased by Saladin from their captors and decapitated. The only secular knight to share their fate, at Saladin's personal behest, was Reynald of Châtillon.

After the crushing defeat of the Franks, the Kingdom of Jerusalem collapsed for lack of defenders. Most of the fortified places in the kingdom surrendered to Saladin or were captured soon after the battle; Jerusalem surrendered on October 2, 1187.

The loss of Jerusalem brought about the Third Crusade (1189–1192), which resulted in the recapture of Acre in 1191 and the reconstitution of the Kingdom of Jerusalem (although with greatly reduced territory and without the city of Jerusalem) under Guy, who meanwhile had been released from captivity. But the Franks were never able to recover fully from the defeat at Hattin, nor could they regain a territorial basis that would enable them to perpetuate their hold on the East.

Martin Hoch

See also: Crusades in the Holy Land; Saladin

Further Reading

Ehrenkreutz, Andrew S. *Saladin*. Albany: State University of New York Press, 1972.

Lyons, Malcolm C., and D. E. P. Jackson. *Saladin: The Politics of the Holy War*. Cambridge: Cambridge University Press, 1982.

Nicolle, David. *Hattin 1187: Saladin's Greatest Victory*. Oxford, UK: Osprey, 1993.

Prawer, Joshua. *Crusader Institutions*. Oxford: Oxford University Press, 1980.

Hebron

West Bank city in the mountains of southern Judea. Hebron is located some twenty-three miles south-southwest of Jerusalem. With a total estimated population of approximately 170,000 people, including some 600 Jewish settlers, Hebron has been the site of considerable violence between Arabs and Jews over the past century. The city is an important urban and agricultural center. With its narrow, winding streets, Hebron is known for its grapes, pottery making, leather tanning, and glass blowing, a craft that has been practiced there for 6,000 years.

One of the world's oldest cities and oldest continuously inhabited sites, Hebron was probably established around 3500 BCE. Hebron is a holy site for Christianity, Islam, and Judaism. To Jews, it is second only to Jerusalem, for Hebron is the location of the Tomb of the Patriarchs. Here, the prophets Abraham, Isaac, and Jacob and their wives, Sarah, Rebecca, and Leah, are believed to be buried. The Talmud also identifies Hebron as the resting place of Adam and Eve. Muslims venerate the site as well because they also claim ancestry through Abraham.

Hebron played an important role in early Jewish history. It was the residence of the patriarchs, and David was anointed king there and made it his capital. The city has also been identified as one of the locations to which Jews exiled to Babylon returned. A small Jewish community continued in Hebron thereafter. Herod the Great constructed a wall around the Tomb of the Patriarchs. In the sixth century CE, the Byzantine emperor Justinian I erected a Christian church over the tomb, only to be destroyed by the Sassinid Persians in the early seventh century. Decades later, Arab Muslims built the al-Ibrahimi (Abraham) mosque over ruins of the church. Still later, Jews were permitted to build a synagogue near the site.

Godfrey de Bouillon, Duke of Lorraine, who led the First Crusade, took Hebron in 1099 and converted the mosque and synagogue into a Christian church. The Crusaders also expelled the Jews from Hebron. The city changed hands a number of times thereafter. In 1266, under Mamluk rule, Christians and Jews were prohibited from visiting the Tomb of the Patriarchs. Following the imposition of Ottoman rule during 1516–1517, there was a pogrom in Hebron, in which Jewish property was seized and Jews were murdered. Another pogrom occurred in Hebron in 1834.

The Tomb of the Patriarchs, Hebron. This holy site, important to Muslims and Jews alike, was the site of a massacre in 1994 when an Israeli settler shot to death twenty-nine Palestinian worshippers. (Peter Spiro/iStockPhoto.com)

In 1820, Habad Hasidim established the first Ashkenazic Jewish community in Hebron, and during the Arab riots of 1929 in Hebron, sixty-eight Jews were killed and another fifty-eight were wounded. British authorities evacuated the remaining Jews from the city. Some of the Jews returned to Hebron in 1931, but they left again with the Arab Revolt of 1936.

The UN partition plan of 1947 assigned Hebron to the proposed Arab state. Forces of the Arab Legion held the area during the 1948 Arab-Israeli War. As a result, Jews could not access Hebron until June 1967, when Israel Defense Forces (IDF) captured the entire West Bank. It has been under Israeli control ever since. In 1968, Jewish settlers arrived in Hebron and reestablished the Jewish community there.

In May 1980, Palestinian terrorists killed six Jewish students and wounded another twenty as they returned from worship at the Tomb of the Patriarchs. Then, in February 1994, Jewish settler Baruch Goldstein opened fire on Muslims in the tomb, killing twenty-nine Palestinians and wounding another 125 people. Three years later, the United Nations established an unarmed international observer force in Hebron in an effort to keep the peace there. In January 2019, after twenty-two years, Israel forced this observation group to cease operations.

According to the 1993 Oslo Accords, Israeli forces were to redeploy from West Bank cities. While this redeployment occurred in other cities in 1995, the Israeli army did not leave Hebron, claiming that to do so would endanger the lives of the Jews living there. In 1997, the city was divided into two zones, H1 and H2, under the terms of the Hebron Protocol of January 15. H1 contains about 80 percent of the area and the bulk of the population, is exclusively Palestinian Arab, and came under the control of the Palestinian Authority (PA). H2, in the center of the city, contains about 20 percent of the area and originally was home to some 30,000 Arabs and 500 Jews. The Arab population in H2 is believed to now number only about 10,000 people, the consequence of harassment from settlers and other Arabs, as well as restrictions placed on them by the IDF. Maintaining the presence of a small community of committed Jewish settlers in the city center remains an ongoing flashpoint between Israelis and Palestinians.

Spencer C. Tucker

See also: Crusades in the Holy Land; Oslo Accords; Palestinian Authority; West Bank

Further Reading

Lochery, Neill. *The Difficult Road to Peace: Netanyahu, Israel and the Middle East Peace Process*. Reading, UK: Ithaca, 1999.

Murphy-O'Connor, Jerome. *The Holy Land: An Oxford Archeological Guide from Earliest Times to 1700*. New York: Oxford University Press, 1998.

Shahin, Mariam. *Palestine: A Guide*. Northampton, MA: Interlink, 2005.

Herod the Great

Longtime ruler of Judea. Famous for his remarkable contribution to the architectural treasures of biblical-era Palestine, Herod the Great became one of the most illustrious and controversial provincial rulers in Roman history. Herod was born to an Edomite (a Semitic people) father and a Nabataean (an Arabic people) mother in 73 BCE in southern Palestine. His father, Antipater, was a wealthy man, and his mother, Cyprus, came from a powerful family in Petra. Thus, Herod began life in a privileged social position, which he would maintain throughout his life. By his tenth birthday, Herod's family had aligned itself with the expanding and powerful Roman Republic, which brought more wealth and power into its grasp. Antipater, who had thrown his support behind the Roman Conquest of Judea in 63 BCE, was rewarded by Julius Caesar, who granted Roman citizenship to the family in 47 BCE. In addition, Caesar bestowed the powerful position of procurator of Judaea on Antipater.

Meanwhile, by sixteen years of age, Herod had become close friends with Mark Antony, who would exert a powerful influence on him. Also around that time, he married Doris, and together they had one son. When Antipater was appointed procurator of Judaea, he granted Herod the governorship of Galilee, and by forty-one, Antony had appointed him as tetrarch of the region. The stable position, however, quickly disintegrated as civil war and invasion swept through Galilee in 40 BCE.

As a result, Herod fled to Rome, where he made an unforgettable impression on the Roman senate. With his dynamic personality and intimate connections with such elites as Antony and Caesar, Herod won many fans, and the Senate granted him the title of king of Judaea. In 37 BCE, Herod returned to Palestine with the Roman army and solidified his rule over Judaea. Herod wanted to show a strong tie to the native people of the land, and so he divorced Doris and married a Hasmonean princess named Mariamne. The marriage not only brought peace between Herod and the Hasmoneans (Maccabees), but also encouraged Herod to practice Judaism. Although his father was a practicing Jew, his mother had not been; thus, the marriage solidified his identity as a Jew. Herod and Mariamne, who had a passionate love for one another, had two sons rather quickly after their union.

The period between Herod's return to Palestine and 31 BCE was politically tempestuous. Herod sided with his old comrade Antony, who was feuding with Octavian, the future emperor Augustus. However, once Antony was defeated during the Battle of Actium in 31 BCE, Herod had to make peace with Octavian to keep his position as ruler of Judaea. After Herod swore his allegiance, Octavian reconfirmed him to the throne of Judaea. Over the next decade, Herod, who fostered relationships with Octavian and his family, was rewarded with expanded territory. Indeed, by 20 BCE, Herod's kingdom grew far beyond Judaea and encompassed territories east of the Jordan River and north of the Golan Heights into Lebanon.

Throughout his kingdom, Herod became renowned for his patronage of the arts, his support of the Olympic Games, and his sponsorship of tremendous architecture. To honor those of Jewish descent, Herod rebuilt the Temple of Jerusalem, which was the focus of Jewish worship in Palestine until its destruction in 70 CE. He also supported the building of the massive structure marking the Cave of the Patriarchs in Hebron. Moreover, he commissioned the amazing cities of Sebaste, in Samaria, and Caesarea Palaestinae, on the Mediterranean coast. The latter would eventually become the Roman capital in the region. In addition, Herod contributed to the creation of pagan and Jewish monuments in territories of the Roman Republic that he did not rule, including sites in Rhodes, Antioch, and Damascus.

Herod's vast land holdings, coupled with profits from investments and his familial wealth, made him extremely rich. However, in his final years, he became notoriously cruel and suffered ill health. He turned against his wife, Mariamne, who he believed had committed adultery, and had her killed. He also killed his two children, Mariamne's mother, her brother, and her grandfather. He even killed his first son and heir, Antipater, and revised his will to benefit his other eleven children, whose mothers were from his household. The Christian New Testament notes that Herod's proclamation called for the killing of male babies in an effort to destroy the child Jesus of Nazareth. Although the veracity of that event is debated among historians, the reference to Herod's cruelty is a reminder of his reputation in his later years.

In either March or April of 4 BCE, Herod died at his ornate palace in Jericho. With his death, the large kingdom he had ruled was divided among his remaining sons: Archelaus, Herod Antipas, and Philip. Despite his amazing contributions, Herod's legacy was forever tainted by his bizarre and sinister behavior in his later life.

Nancy Stockdale

See also: First and Second Temple Periods; Haram al-Sharif/Temple Mount; Jerusalem, Old City of; Roman Conquest of Judea

Further Reading

Grant, Michael. *Herod the Great*. New York: American Heritage Press, 1971.
Gross, William. *Herod the Great*. Baltimore: Helicon Press, 1962.
Knoblet, Jerry. *Herod the Great*. Lanham, MD: University Press of America, 2005.

Herzl, Theodor

Cofounder of modern Zionism, the nationalist movement that sought to create a Jewish state in Palestine. Theodor Herzl was born in Budapest on May 2, 1860, to secular Jewish parents who moved the family to Vienna in 1878. His father was a successful businessman and provided his family with a comfortable life. After earning a law degree at the University of Vienna, Herzl served as the Paris correspondent for a prestigious Viennese newspaper. Despite being integrated into European society, he was well aware of the widespread anti-Semitic currents in the region. Many believe that the seminal event that led him to abandon his assimilationist ways and take up the Zionist cause was the Dreyfus Affair. In 1895, a Jewish French officer named Alfred Dreyfus was unjustly convicted of treason, and Herzl was there to cover the trial and associated events. He concluded that anti-Semitism was so deeply rooted in Europe that the only long-term solution was for the Jewish people to create a state of their own. In 1896, he published *Der Judenstaat* (The State of the Jews), which established him as a preeminent leader of the world Zionist movement.

Other strands of Zionism had been developing independently elsewhere, especially in Eastern Europe. In 1897, Herzl organized the First Zionist Congress in

Basel, Switzerland, which established the World Zionist Organization (WZO) and kickstarted the modern Zionist movement that would eventually result in the creation of the state of Israel in 1948. Herzl hoped to receive broad support from Western Jews, but most attendees of the congress were from Eastern Europe. These Zionists faced more extreme forms of anti-Semitism and were committed to an ethic of self-help within the Jewish community.

Herzl's *Der Judenstaat*, on the other hand, appealed to wealthy Western Jews to fund the purchase of land and convince European statesmen to support the cause. At first, Herzl preferred accepting empty territory that might be offered by European governments, but most members of the WZO (of which he served as president from its inception until his death) insisted that Palestine was the only suitable territory for the new Jewish state because it had been the ancient homeland of the Jewish people.

Herzl dedicated the rest of his life to promoting the Zionist cause, but with mixed results. Many religious Jews opposed the movement, insisting that only God could return them to Zion. Many Western secular Jews opposed the Zionist movement because they feared that it would jeopardize their position as assimilated citizens of their respective countries. (Zionism would not be widely embraced by the broader Jewish community until the 1940s.) In 1898, he made his only visit to Palestine, which had been ruled by the Ottoman Empire for the past 400 years. He failed to convince Ottoman leaders to support the creation of a Jewish homeland in Palestine in exchange for Zionists paying off Ottoman debts.

His lobbying efforts in Britain were more successful. In 1902, British colonial secretary Joseph Chamberlain offered Zionists land in Uganda (now part of Kenya), which Herzl tentatively supported as a temporary solution to the plight of Europe's Jews; but the idea was eventually rejected by the WZO. Also in 1902, Herzl published *Altneuland* (Old-New Land), a novel envisioning a utopian Jewish society in Palestine. He died of heart disease in July 1904 in Edlach, Austria, at the age of forty-four.

Despite his mixed results in garnering broad support for Zionism and the tensions that existed between Herzl and his Eastern European colleagues, there is no doubt that the eventual creation of the state of Israel was made possible by his successes in inspiring and organizing the world Zionist movement. Indeed, Israel's Declaration of Independence refers to Herzl as "the spiritual father of the Jewish State."

Robert C. DiPrizio

See also: Israel; Pale of Settlement; World Zionist Organization; Zionism

Further Reading

Avineri, Shlomo. *Herzl's Vision: Theodor Herzl and the Foundation of the Jewish State*. New York: Bluebridge, 2014.

Robertson, Ritchie, and Edward Timms. *Theodor Herzl and the Origins of Zionism*. Edinburgh, UK: Edinburgh University Press, 1997.

Smith, Charles D. *Palestine and the Arab-Israeli Conflict: A History with Documents*. 9th ed. New York: Bedford/St. Martin's, 2017.

Hezbollah

A Lebanese radical Shia Islamist organization. Founded in Lebanon in 1984, Hezbollah is a major political force in Lebanon and, along with the Islamic Amal movement, a principal political party representing the Shia community in Lebanon. It also operates a number of social service programs, schools, hospitals, clinics, and housing assistance programs for Lebanese Shiites.

In the midst of the ongoing civil war in Lebanon, a Shia resistance movement developed in response to Israel's invasion in 1982. Israel's first invasion of southern Lebanon had occurred in 1978, but the invasion of 1982 was more devastating to the region, with huge numbers of casualties, prisoners taken, and peasants displaced. On the grounds of resistance to Israel and its Lebanese proxies, Islamic Amal (a militarist offshoot of the pro-Shia Amal Party) made contact with Iran's ambassador to Damascus, Akbar Muhtashimi, who had once found refuge as an Iranian dissident in the Palestinian camps in Lebanon. Iran sent between 1,000 and 1,200 Revolutionary Guards to the Bekáa Valley to aid an Islamic resistance to Israel. At a Lebanese army barracks near Baalbek, the Revolutionary Guards began training Shia fighters identifying with the resistance, or Islamic Amal. In early 1995, an association of Lebanese Shia resistance groups formed Hezbollah.

Another militant Shia group operating in Lebanon in the early 1980s was the Organization of the Islamic Jihad, led by Imad Mughniya. It was responsible for the 1983 bombings of the U.S. and French peacekeeping forces' barracks and the U.S. embassy and its annex in Beirut. Hezbollah, however, is accused to this day of bombings committed by Mughniya's group. While it had not yet officially formed, the degree of coordination or sympathy between the various militant groups operative in 1982 can be ascertained only on the level of individuals. Hezbollah stated officially that it did not commit the bombing of U.S. and French forces, but it also did not condemn those who did. Regardless, Hezbollah's continuing resistance in the south earned it great popularity with the Lebanese, whose army had split and had failed to defend the country against the Israelis.

With the Taif Agreement, the Lebanese civil war should have ended, but in 1990, fighting broke out, and the next year, Syria mounted a major campaign in Lebanon. The Taif Agreement did not end sectarianism or solve the problem of Muslim underrepresentation in government. Militias other than Hezbollah disbanded, but because the Lebanese government did not assent to the Israeli occupation of southern Lebanon, Hezbollah's militia remained in existence.

The leadership of Hezbollah changed over time and adapted to Lebanon's realities. The multiplicity of sects in Lebanon meant that an Islamic republic there was impractical, and as a result, Hezbollah ceased trying to impose the strictest Islamic rules and focused more on gaining the trust of the Lebanese community. The party's Shura Council was made up of seven clerics until 1989; from 1989 to 1991, it included three laypersons and four clerics, and since 2001, it has been entirely composed of clerics. An advisory Politburo has from eleven to fourteen members. Secretary-General Abbas al-Musawi took over from Subhi al-Tufayli in 1991. Soon after the Israelis assassinated Musawi in February 1992, Hassan Nasrallah, who had studied in Najaf and briefly in Qom, took over as secretary-general.

In 1985, as a consequence of armed resistance in southern Lebanon, Israel withdrew into the so-called security zone. Just as resistance from Hezbollah provided Israel with the ready excuse to attack Lebanon, Israel's continued presence in the south funded Lebanese resentment of Israel and support for Hezbollah's armed actions. In 1996, the Israelis mounted Operation Grapes of Wrath against Hezbollah in south Lebanon, pounding the entire region from the air for a two-week period.

In May 2000, after suffering repeated attacks and numerous casualties, Israel withdrew its forces from southern Lebanon, a move that was widely interpreted as a victory for Hezbollah and boosted its popularity hugely, both in Lebanon and throughout the Arab world. Hezbollah disarmed in some areas of the country but refused to do so in the border area because it contests the Jewish state's control of the Shaba Farms region.

Some Israeli and American sources charge that Iran directly conducts the affairs of Hezbollah and provides it with essential funding. While at one time Iranian support was crucial to Hezbollah, the Revolutionary Guards have withdrawn from Lebanon for some time. The party's social and charitable services claimed independence in the late 1990s. They are supported by a volunteer service, provided by medical personnel and other professionals, and by local and external donations. Iran has provided weapons to Hezbollah. Some, apparently through the Iran-Contra deal, found their way to Lebanon, and Syria has also provided freedom of movement across its common border with Lebanon, as well as supply routes for weapons.

Since 2000, Hezbollah has disputed Israeli control over the Shaba Farms area, which Israel claims belongs to Syria but Syria says belongs to Lebanon. Meanwhile, resentment of Syrian influence in Lebanon built up over the years. A turning point was the assassination of Lebanese prime minister Rafik Hariri in February 2005. This led to significant international pressure on Syria to withdraw from Lebanon, although pro-Syrian elements remained throughout the country.

Hezbollah now found itself threatened by a new coalition of Christians and Hariri-supporting Sunnis who sought to deny its aim of greater power for the Shia in government. The two sides in this struggle were known as the March 14 Alliance, for the date of a large anti-Syrian rally, and the March 8 Alliance, for a prior and even larger rally supporting Syria, consisting of Hezbollah and Christian general Michel Aoun. These factions have been sparring since 2005, and in some ways since the civil war.

Demanding a response to the Israeli campaign against Gaza in the early summer of 2006, Hezbollah forces killed three Israeli soldiers and kidnapped two others, planning to hold them for a prisoner exchange as has occurred in the past. The Israel Defense Forces (IDF) responded with a massive campaign of air strikes throughout Lebanon, not just on Hezbollah positions. Hezbollah responded by launching missiles into Israel, forcing much of that country's northern population into shelters.

In this open warfare, the United States backed Israel. At the conflict's end, Sheikh Nasrallah's popularity surged in Lebanon and in the Arab world, and even members of the March 14 Alliance were furious over the destruction of the fragile peace in post–civil war Lebanon. Hezbollah offered cash assistance to the people of southern Lebanon displaced by the fighting and those in the southern districts of Beirut who had been struck there by the Israelis. They disbursed this aid immediately. The government offered assistance to other Lebanese, but this assistance was delayed.

After this conflict, the United Nations bolstered its peacekeeping force, the United Nations Interim Force in Lebanon (UNIFIL), which has been deployed in southern Lebanon since 1978. Its mission, however, is not to disarm Hezbollah, but to monitor the cessation of hostilities between it and Israel.

In 2008, when a unity government took hold in Lebanon, Hezbollah and its allies captured eleven of thirty cabinet seats, giving the coalition the power to veto. Beginning in 2012, amid the ongoing Syrian civil war, Hezbollah decided to aid Bashar al-Assad's government in its fight against antigovernment rebels, an unpopular move among many Sunni Arabs in Lebanon and neighboring states. Hezbollah's involvement in the Syrian civil war has raised concerns that the conflict might further destabilize Lebanon.

Israel has launched numerous air strikes against weapons convoys bound for Hezbollah fighters. In 2011, Hezbollah brought down the Lebanese government; similarly, it also brought down the replacement government in 2013, following a disagreement over the makeup of country's security forces. Hezbollah and its allies won the largest block of seats in the 2018 legislative elections. As the war in Syria winds down and Hezbollah forces return home, Lebanon's political future is unclear.

Harry Hueston and Sherifa Zuhur

See also: Arab Spring; Arab Spring, Effects on Israel; Israel Defense Forces; Israel-Hezbollah War, 2006; Lebanon; Lebanon, Israeli Invasion of; Syria

Further Reading

Blanford, Nicholas. *Warriors of God: Inside Hezbollah's Thirty-Year Struggle Against Israel*. New York: Random House, 2011.

Norton, Augustus Richard. *Hezbollah: A Short History*. Princeton, NJ: Princeton University Press, 2014.

Ranstorp, Magnus. *Hizb'allah in Lebanon: The Politics of the Western Hostage Crisis*. New York: St. Martin's, 1997.

Worrall, James, Simon Mabon, and Gordon Clubb. *Hezbollah: From Islamic Resistance to Government*. Santa Barbara, CA: Praeger, 2016.

Holy War Army (HWA)

An irregular force of Palestinian fighters organized and led by Abd al-Qadir al-Husayni and Hasan Salama during the 1947–1948 Arab-Jewish Communal War, and the 1948 Arab-Israeli War. Husayni and Salama sought to use the Holy War Army (HWA) to secure an independent Palestinian state. The HWA used guerrilla activities to blockade the Jewish sectors of Jerusalem, especially by attacking convoys on the road to Tel Aviv. It was incapable of large-scale, coordinated actions of a conventional nature.

At its height, the HWA had 50,000 Palestinian fighters, although most served only in local defense roles. Approximately 20 percent of the HWA was willing and able to serve away from their homes and engage in offensive operations against Jewish militias such as Irgun, Lehi, and Haganah, as well as the nascent Israel Defense Forces (IDF). In October 1948, the HWA was disbanded and disarmed by the Arab League, a coalition of Arab nations cooperating to fight the creation of an Israeli state, which also hated the idea of an independent Palestine.

Paul J. Springer

See also: Arab-Israeli War, 1948; Arab-Jewish Communal War, 1947

Further Reading

DuPuy, N. Trevor. *Elusive Victory: The Arab-Israeli War, 1947–1974.* New York: Harper & Row, 1978.

Herzog, Chaim, and Shlomo Gazit. *The Arab-Israeli Wars: War and Peace in the Middle East.* 3rd ed. New York: Vintage Books, 2010.

Husayn ibn Ali, Sharif of Mecca

Sharif of Mecca and king of the Hejaz. Born in Constantinople sometime around 1856 into the Hashemites, traditionally held as descendants of Muhammad and therefore referred to with the honorific title of *Sharif*, Husayn ibn Ali studied in Mecca from age eight. Upon the death of his uncle, Abdullah, in 1908, Turkish authorities appointed Husayn Sharif of Mecca. Husayn had long hoped for an independent Arab kingdom under his rule. World War I provided that opportunity.

As early as February 1914, Husayn was in communication through his son Abdullah with British authorities in Cairo. Abdullah met with then–British high commissioner in Egypt Lord Kitchener and told him that the Arabs were prepared to revolt against Constantinople if the British would pledge their support for such a move. The British remained skeptical until the Ottoman Empire's entrance into the war in October 1914. Husayn then entered into active negotiations with Sir Henry McMahon, who had become high commissioner in Egypt in 1915. Husayn promised to declare war on the Ottoman Empire and raise an Arab army to assist Britain in return for British support for him as king of a postwar Pan-Arab state. On June 5, 1916, Husayn initiated the Arab Revolt. His four sons were in command of its forces, and they were aided by the British officer T. E. Lawrence, an expert on irregular warfare.

Throughout the revolt, Husayn worried about the ambitions of Ibn Saud, a tribal ruler from Najd, today in the central portion of Saudi Arabia. McMahon's pledge to Husayn preceded by just six months the Sykes-Picot Agreement among the British and French governments. Husayn was profoundly upset when he learned of the Sykes-Picot Agreement, which effectively divided the Middle East between Britain and France. This happened just weeks after Britain announced the Balfour Declaration, supporting the creation of a Jewish homeland in Palestine. Husayn considered both to be breaches of the promises made to the Arabs.

Husayn's son Faysal had led the revolt to liberate Syria, where he established a government and was generally well received by the Syrian people, but he was deposed by the French in August 1920. He then became king of Iraq under British protection. Meanwhile, Abdullah became king of the newly created Transjordan.

Husayn abdicated as king of the Hejaz to his son Ali when Ibn Saud conquered most of the Hejaz. Husayn went into exile in Cyprus and died in Amman, Transjordan, on June 4, 1931.

Spencer C. Tucker

See also: Arab Revolt, 1916; Balfour Declaration; Lawrence, T. E.; McMahon-Husayn Correspondence; Sykes-Picot Agreement

Further Reading

Adelson, Roger. *London and the Invention of the Middle East: Money, Power, and War, 1902–1922.* New Haven, CT: Yale University Press, 1995.

Hourani, Albert. *A History of the Arab Peoples: With a New Afterword.* Boston: Belknap Press, 2010.

Tauber, Eliezer. *The Arab Movements in World War I.* London: Cass, 1993.

Husayn, King of Jordan

Third king of Jordan. Born in Amman on November 14, 1935, into the Hashemite family that claims direct descent from the Prophet Muhammad's clan, Husayn ibn Talal was the son of Prince Talal ibn Abdullah. Husayn was educated in Jordan, and then at Victoria College in Alexandria, Egypt, before transferring to the prestigious Harrow School in Britain. He was with his grandfather, Abdullah, when the king was assassinated in 1951.

Husayn's father was crowned king but was forced to abdicate the throne on August 11, 1952, because of mental illness. He was proclaimed king as Husayn I and returned from Britain to take up the throne at age seventeen. He formally ascended the throne on May 2, 1953.

His country's stability was threatened by a large influx of Palestinian refugees on the West Bank, which recently had been annexed by Jordan in a move that was not popular with the Israelis, the Palestinians, or other Arab states. After some hesitation, he linked his country with Egypt and Syria in their 1967 war against Israel, permitting Jordanian long-range artillery fire against Jewish areas of Jerusalem and the suburbs of Tel Aviv. The war was a disaster for Jordan, which lost the entire West Bank and its air force and suffered some 15,000 casualties.

In 1970, after an assassination attempt on Husayn and the hijacking of four British airliners by the Popular Front for the Liberation of Palestine (PFLP) and their destruction in Jordan, the king decided to take action against the Palestine Liberation Organization (PLO), operating in his country. In what became known as *Black September,* Husayn launched a military campaign to force the PLO out. Although he achieved this goal, his actions were criticized by many Palestinians and other Arabs in the region. Husayn regained favor in the Arab world when he rejected the 1979 Israel-Egypt peace treaty. Decades later, after the breakthrough at Oslo between Israelis and Palestinians, he signed a peace treaty with Israel in July 1994.

On the domestic front, Husayn was a popular but autocratic leader who guided his nation to relative prosperity. He saw to it that more Jordanians had access to running water, proper sanitation, and electricity. He also actively promoted education and dramatically increased the literacy rate. In the late 1960s, he oversaw the construction of a modern highway system in the kingdom. In 1992, Husayn was diagnosed with pancreatic cancer. He died in Amman on February 7, 1999. Beloved by Jordanians for his attention to their welfare, Husayn had strengthened Jordan's position in the Arab world and contributed to the foundations of peace in the region.

Spencer C. Tucker

See also: Arab-Israeli War, 1967; Black September; Jordan; Palestinian Refugees

Further Reading

Dallas, Roland. *King Husayn: A Life on the Edge*. New York: Fromm International, 1999.

Dann, Uriel. *King Husayn and the Challenge of Arab Radicalism: Jordan 1955–1967*. Oxford: Oxford University Press, 1997.

Robins, Philip. *A History of Jordan*. Cambridge: Cambridge University Press, 2004.

Intifada, First

A spontaneous uprising by Palestinians against Israeli occupation. The First Intifada began in December 1987, and it ended in 1993 with the signing of the Oslo Accords and the creation of the Palestinian Authority (PA).

The founding of Israel in 1948, and Israel's capturing of the West Bank and Gaza in 1967, created a situation in which Israel now ruled all of Palestine. Israel's existence and expansion would remain the most contentious issue in the region for decades, and it intensified an emerging Palestinian national consciousness that called for the destruction of Israel. The anti-Israeli sentiment was generally shared by the Arab world at large. Years of active discontent among Palestinians near or inside Israel led to the establishment of draconian civil and criminal enforcement practices in Israeli-controlled territory against Palestinians. These included torture, summary executions, mass detentions, collective punishments, and the destruction of property and homes.

The already badly strained relations between Israelis and Palestinians under occupation were pushed to the limit on October 1, 1987, when Israeli soldiers ambushed and killed seven Palestinian men from Gaza who were alleged to have been members of the terrorist organization Palestinian Islamic Jihad (PIJ). Days later, an Israeli settler shot a Palestinian schoolgirl in the back. With violence against Israelis by Palestinians also on the increase, a wider conflict may have been inevitable.

The tension mounted as the year drew to a close. On December 4, an Israeli salesman was found murdered in Gaza. On December 6, an Israel Defense Forces (IDF) truck struck a van, killing its four Palestinian occupants. That same day, sustained and heavy violence involving several hundred Palestinians occurred in the Jabalya refugee camp, where the four Palestinians who died in the traffic accident had lived. The unrest spread quickly and eventually involved other refugee camps. By the end of December, violence was occurring in Jerusalem. The Israelis reacted with a heavy hand, which fanned the flames of Palestinian outrage. On December 22, 1987, the UN Security Council officially denounced the Israeli reaction to the unrest, which had taken the lives of scores of Palestinians.

The escalating spiral of violence resulted in the First Intifada, a series of Palestinian protests, demonstrations, and ad hoc attacks whose manifestations ranged from youths throwing rocks at Israeli troops to demonstrations by women's organizations. Along with general strikes and boycotts, these caused such disruption to the Israeli state that the government responded with military force.

The violence soon escalated. While the Palestinians had initially relied on rocks, they started hurling Molotov cocktails and grenades. In the meantime, Israeli defense minister Yitzhak Rabin exhorted the IDF to "break the bones" of the demonstrators. Rabin's tactics brought more international condemnation and strained ties with the United States. Moshe Arens, who succeeded Rabin in 1990, seemed better able to understand both the root of the uprising and the best ways of subduing it. Indeed, the number of Palestinians and Israelis killed declined during the period 1990–1993. However, the intifada itself seemed to be running out of steam after 1990, and violence among Palestinians themselves was on the increase.

In the early 1990s, the Palestine Liberation Organization (PLO) officially abandoned the goal of destroying Israel. Despite continued violence on the part of Hamas, on September 13, 1993, Rabin (now prime minister) and PLO chairman Yasser Arafat signed the historic Oslo Accords in Washington, D.C. The accords, which brought both Rabin and Arafat the Nobel Peace Prize in 1994 (along with Israeli foreign minister Shimon Peres), called for a five-year transition period, during which the Gaza Strip and the West Bank would be jointly controlled by Israel and the PA, with power eventually to be turned over to the Palestinians.

The First Intifada caused both civil destruction and humanitarian suffering but also produced gains for the Palestinian people. First, the intifada solidified and brought into focus a clear national consciousness for the Palestinian people, and made statehood a clear national objective. Second, the intifada cast Israeli policy toward Palestine in a negative light internationally, especially with the killing of Palestinian children, and thus rekindled public and political dialogue on the Arab-Israeli conflict across other Middle Eastern states, as well as Europe and the United States. Third, the intifada helped to bring the PLO out of its Tunisian exile. Finally, the intifada cost Israel hundreds of millions of dollars in lost imports and tourism.

By the time the Oslo Accords were signed in September 1993, the six-year-long First Intifada had resulted in the deaths of some 1,160 Palestinians, of which 241 were children. On the Israeli side, 160 died, 5 of whom were children. Clearly, the IDF's inexperience in widespread riot control had contributed to the high death toll, for in the first thirteen months of the intifada alone, more than 330 Palestinians were killed. Indeed, the policies and performance of the IDF split Israeli public opinion and invited international scrutiny. In late 2000, as the Oslo peace process stalled, a new wave of violent Palestinian protest broke out, which eventually would become known as the Second (al-Aqsa) Intifada.

Paul G. Pierpaoli Jr.

See also: Arafat, Yasser; Gaza Strip; Hamas; Intifada, Second; Israel Defense Forces; Israeli Occupations; Oslo Accords; Rabin, Yitzhak; West Bank

Further Reading

Peretz, Don. *Intifada: The Palestinian Uprising.* Boulder, CO: Westview, 1990.

Said, W. Edward. *Intifada: The Palestinian Uprising Against Israeli Occupation.* Boston: South End Press, 1989.

Schiff, Ze'Ev, and Ehud Ya'Ari. *Intifada: The Palestinian Uprising—Israel's Third Front.* New York: Simon and Schuster, 1990.

Smith, Charles D. *Palestine and the Arab-Israeli Conflict: A History with Documents.* 9th ed. New York: Bedford/St. Martin's, 2017.

Intifada, Second

Palestinian uprising and period of enhanced Israeli-Palestinian hostilities during 2000–2005. The Second Intifada followed the collapse that summer of the Camp David peace talks to resolve the Palestinian issue. The Second Intifada is also known as the al-Aqsa Intifada because it began at the al-Aqsa Mosque in the Old City of Jerusalem.

On September 28, 2000, Israeli leader Ariel Sharon, accompanied by a party delegation and 1,500 security personnel, entered the Haram al-Sharif complex where the al-Aqsa mosque and the Dome of the Rock are located. The enclave is one of Islam's three holiest sites and is sacred to Jews as well. Sharon claimed that he was investigating Israeli complaints that Muslims were damaging archaeological remains below the surface of the Temple Mount. By agreement, at the time, this area was supervised by Palestinian rather than Israeli security.

Palestinians held that Sharon's action demonstrated Israeli contempt for limited Palestinian sovereignty and for Muslims in general. Soon riots and demonstrations erupted. Israeli troops launched attacks in Gaza, and on September 30, television footage showed the shooting of an unarmed twelve-year-old boy, Muhammad Durrah, hiding behind his father as Israeli forces attacked. Muslim protests now grew more violent and involved Israeli Arabs as well as Palestinians.

Thousands of Israelis also attacked Arabs, destroying Arab property in Tel Aviv and Nazareth over the Jewish holiday of Yom Kippur. On October 12, two Israeli reservists were lynched by a mob at the Ramallah police station, further inflaming Israeli public opinion. Israel responded with a series of air strikes.

On October 17, Israeli and Palestinian officials signed the Sharm el-Sheikh agreement to end the violence, but it continued nevertheless. Sharon's election as prime minister in February 2001 heightened Israel's hardline tactics toward the Palestinians, such as the use of U.S.-supplied F-16 aircraft for the first time. Both Palestinians and Israelis admitted that the high hopes of the Oslo period were over. Some Palestinians characterized their response as the warranted resistance of an embittered population who had received no positive assurances of sovereignty from years of negotiations. Others began or encouraged suicide attacks, as in the June 1, 2001, attack on Israelis waiting to enter a Tel Aviv discotheque and another attack on a Jerusalem restaurant on August 9, 2001. While various Palestinian organizations laid claim to some of the attacks, the degree of organizational control over the bombers and issues such as payments to families of the martyrs remain in dispute.

The attacks in public places terrified Israelis. Most malls, movie theaters, stores, and children's centers hired security guards. Israeli authorities soon began a heightened campaign of targeted assassinations of Palestinian leaders. Some political figures began to call for complete segregation, or separation, of Arabs and Israelis, even within the Green Line (the 1967 border). This would be enforced by a security wall and even population transfers, which would involve evicting Arab citizens from Israel in some areas and forcing them to move to the West Bank.

A virulent campaign against Yasser Arafat, Palestine Liberation Organization (PLO) chairman and president of the Palestinian Authority (PA), began in Israel with American approval, complicating the negotiations between the two sides.

Israelis charged Arafat with corruption and with supporting the intifada. Some Israelis argued that he had actually planned it. The anti-Arafat campaign intensified when, in May 2001 and again in January 2002, Israel intercepted arms shipments to the Palestinians.

The regional response to the intifada consisted of cautious condemnation by Egypt and Jordan, which had concluded peace agreements with Israel, and calls of outrage from other more hardline states such as Syria. In February 2002, Crown Prince Abdullah of Saudi Arabia called for Arabs to fully normalize relations with Israel in return for that country's withdrawal from the occupied territories. This plan was formally endorsed at an Arab League summit in Beirut in March, although Israeli authorities prohibited Arafat from attending it. Israeli authorities rejected the proposal.

Instead, in response to a suicide bomber's attack on the Netanya Hotel on March 28, 2002, in which thirty Israeli civilians died, the Israel Defense Forces (IDF) began a major military assault on the West Bank. The PA headquarters was targeted, and international negotiations became necessary when militants took refuge in the Church of the Nativity in Bethlehem. Investigation of charges of a massacre in an IDF assault on Jenin revealed a smaller-than-claimed death count of fifty-five.

The IDF response to the intifada did not convince Palestinians to relinquish their aims of sovereignty; indeed, it seemed to spark more suicide attacks rather than discouraging them. In March 2003, Mahmoud Abbas became the first Palestinian prime minister of the PA because the United States refused to recognize or deal with Arafat. On April 30, 2003, the European Union, the United States, Russia, and the United Nations announced the so-called Road Map for Peace, a plan that was to culminate in an independent Palestinian state.

The plan did not unfold as designed, however, and in response to an Israeli air strike intended to kill Abd al-Aziz al-Rantisi, the leader of Hamas, militants launched a bus bombing in Jerusalem. At the end of June 2003, Palestinian militants agreed to a truce, which lasted for seven weeks (and longer on the part of certain groups). There was no formal declaration that the intifada had ceased, and additional Israeli assassinations of Palestinian leaders continued, as did suicide attacks. Nevertheless, since 2004, Hamas has respected the cease-fire, and the issues of Israeli withdrawal from Gaza, Arafat's November 2004 death, Palestinian elections, and the Israeli response to their outcome took the spotlight in late 2004 and 2005.

Casualty numbers for the Second Intifada are disputed, but approximately 1,000 Israelis died and 6,700 more were wounded; and over 3,300 Palestinians were killed, while nearly 30,000 were wounded. Israel's tourism sector suffered considerably, at a time when inflation and unemployment were already problematic.

One outcome of the Second Intifada, in the global context of the September 11, 2001, terror attacks on the United States, was that Israeli officials have tended to brand all Palestinian resistance—indeed, all activity on behalf of Palestinians—as terrorism. The intifada also served to strengthen the ranks of those Israelis who call for separation rather than integration of Israelis with Arabs. There was thus widespread support for the construction of a security barrier, which effectively cut off thousands of West Bank Palestinians from their daily route to work or school.

The Second Intifada dismayed Israeli peace activists and discouraged independent efforts by Israelis and Palestinians to engage in meaningful dialogue. It also had deleterious effects on Palestinians who had hoped for normalcy in the West Bank, particularly because 85 percent of those in Gaza and 58 percent in the West Bank lived in poverty. This was abetted by the IDF's destruction of housing units, although only 10 percent of the individuals involved were in fact implicated in violence or illegal activity. Another outcome of the Second Intifada was its highlighting of intra-Palestinian conflict, especially between the Tunis PLO elements of the PA and the younger leaders who emerged within the Occupied Territories, and also between Fatah and Hamas.

Sherifa Zuhur

See also: Al-Aqsa Martyrs Brigades; Fatah; Gaza; Hamas; Israel Defense Forces; Israeli Occupations; Israeli Security Barrier; Jerusalem, Old City of; Settlements; Sharon, Ariel; Suicide Bombings; West Bank

Further Reading

Baroud, Ramzy. *The Second Palestinian Intifada: A Chronicle of a People's Struggle*. London: Pluto, 2006.

Bucaille, Laetitia. *Growing up Palestinian and the Intifada Generation*. Trans. Anthony Roberts. Princeton, NJ: Princeton University Press, 2004.

Smith, Charles D. *Palestine and the Arab-Israeli Conflict: A History with Documents*. 9th ed. New York: Bedford/St. Martin's, 2017.

Irgun Tsvai Leumi

Right-wing, paramilitary, Zionist, underground insurgent movement operating in Palestine during 1931–1948. Irgun Tsvai Leumi was known for launching immediate and harsh retaliatory attacks on persons or organizations initiating violence against the Jewish community in Palestine, and also for its advocacy of military action against the British, who controlled Palestine under a League of Nations mandate until May 1948. The British categorized Irgun as a terrorist organization.

Even as the British slowly shifted their support to Palestine's Arab population in the 1930s, the leadership of the Jewish Agency for Palestine, in particular David Ben-Gurion, continued to work closely with the British to promote the interests of the Jewish population. Haganah, the Jewish self-defense organization, supported this position through its military strategy of *havlaga*, or self-restraint. Some Haganah members rejected this approach, however, given Britain's increasingly pro-Arab bias. A minority left Haganah in 1931 and formed Irgun.

Irgun was based on premises formulated by Ze'ev Jabotinsky, leader of the Jewish Legion, which had fought with the British against the Ottoman Turks in Palestine during World War I (1914–1918). Jabotinsky held that swift retaliatory action would forestall Arab attacks on the Jewish community. By 1936, Irgun was largely controlled by Jabotinsky's extremist nationalist Revisionist Zionists, which had seceded from the World Zionist Organization (WZO) and advocated the creation by force of a Jewish homeland spanning both banks of the Jordan River.

When Arab attacks during the Arab Revolt of 1936–1939 killed a number of Jews, Irgun retaliated with car bombs in areas of high Arab congregation. These endured until the beginning of World War II and killed as many as 250 Arab civilians. Irgun also directed acts of terrorism and assassination against the British. When the British White Paper of 1939 severely restricted Jewish immigration, settlement, and land purchases in Palestine, the group focused on attacking British military installations and interests.

During 1941–1943, Irgun suspended its attacks on British interests and supported the Allies against Germany and its Arab allies in the Middle East. However, a small group known as *Lohamei Herut Israel* (Fighters for the Freedom of Israel), also known as Lehi or the Stern Gang, separated from Irgun in 1941 and continued to attack the British in Palestine. Led by future prime minister Menachem Begin from 1943–1948, Lehi declared war against the British in February 1944 and resumed attacks on Arab villages and British interests.

On November 6, 1944, in Cairo, Lehi assassinated Lord Moyne, the British minister of state. The murder was ostensibly in retaliation for the 1939 White Paper. At that point, the more moderate Haganah and the Jewish Agency for Palestine launched a campaign against Irgun and Lehi. The British ultimately arrested and jailed about 1,000 Irgun and Lehi members.

Irgun, Lehi, and Haganah allied during October 1944–July 1945 as the Jewish Resistance Movement to fight against British restrictions on Jewish immigration. This alliance ended in August 1945 after Irgun bombed the British military, police, and civil headquarters at the King David Hotel in Jerusalem, killing ninety-one people on July 22, 1946. Begin and Irgun claimed to have issued three warnings in an attempt to limit casualties. Nevertheless, the British arrested, tried, convicted, and hanged several members of Irgun. When Irgun responded by hanging two British sergeants, the executions stopped, although British arrests of Irgun members continued. On May 5, 1947, Haganah and Irgun combined forces to breach the wall of the British prison at Akko (Acre), freeing 251 prisoners.

In anticipation of and following the partition of Palestine, Irgun and Haganah increasingly coordinated their forces from July 1947 to June 1948. Irgun's greatest victory and largest operation was the capture of the Arab city of Jaffa. It also participated in the Deir Yassin Massacre on April 9, 1948. On May 28, 1948, the provisional government of the newly declared state of Israel transformed Haganah into its national military, the Israel Defense Forces (IDF), and outlawed all other armed forces. In September 1948, the military activities of Irgun were folded into the IDF.

Richard M. Edwards

See also: Arab Revolt, 1936; Begin, Menachem; Deir Yassin Massacre; Haganah; Jabotinsky, Ze'ev; King David Hotel Bombing; Stern Gang

Further Reading

Begin, Menachem. *The Revolt*. Los Angeles: Nash, 1972.

Bell, J. Bowyer. *Terror out of Zion: Irgun Zvai Leumi, Lehi, and the Palestine Underground, 1929–1949*. New York: St. Martin's, 1979.

Ben Ami, Yitshaq. *Years of Wrath, Days of Glory: Memoirs from the Irgun*. New York: R. Speller, 1982.

Levine, David. *The Birth of the Irgun Zvai Leumi: The Jewish Resistance Movement.* Jerusalem: Gefen Books, 1996.

Islam

A monotheistic religion that developed through the life and preaching of the prophet Abu al-Qasim Muhammad ibn Abdullah (570–632) in the Arabian Peninsula. The word *Islam* means "submission to the will of Allah" in Arabic. After someone submits, they become a Muslim. The living practice of the faith today gives preeminent importance to the Qur'an, whose name means "the recitation," consisting of revelations that Muhammad received and shared with his followers, who memorized them and eventually wrote them down. The Qur'an consists of 114 chapters called *suras,* arranged in descending length except for the short first one, which Muslims recite in full during each prayer cycle. The main tenets of Islam begin with Tawahid, meaning the "Oneness" of Allah, the Arabic name for the creator of the universe. Muslims agree on five duties, called the pillars of Islam: (1) Confession of the creed, "There is no god but Allah, and Muhammad is his prophet; (2) ritual prayer; (3) giving alms or charity to the poor; (4) fasting from food and water during daylight hours through the month of Ramadan; and (5) Hajj, a pilgrimage to Mecca once in life for those who can afford it.

Muslims derive important information for interpreting the Qur'an from anecdotes about the events in the life of Muhammad and his reactions to specific questions and circumstances, called *hadith*. The early followers of Muhammad collected as many hadith as possible to extract the habitual practice or general example of the Prophet, called the *Sunna*. Because the Qur'an does not contain much explicitly legal or political

A Muslim prays at the al-Ibrahimi Mosque (Tomb of the Patriarchs) in Hebron. According to Islamic belief, Muslims must pray five times daily. The daily prayer, or salat, is preceded by ablutions, or ritual cleansings, and is a sequence of standing, bending, kneeling, and reciting phrases in Arabic. (Rrodrickbeiler/Dreamstime.com)

guidance, Islamic scholars developed a concept of law, or sharia, from the collections of hadith and the example of the prophet.

Islam spread quickly from Arabia during the lifetime of the first four leaders following Muhammad (called the *caliphs*), eventually controlling an empire stretching from Spain to India. Islamic doctrine claims that all the prophets of Judaism and Christianity brought the same message of Islam, but then people corrupted it. Therefore, Islam is the pure truth, while Jews and Christians are practicing a form of corruption. Some parts of the Qur'an promote coexistence with, and even protection of, Jews and Christians, as "people of the book." Other parts take a stronger tone of competition and rejection.

In the early years of public preaching, Muhammad had relatively good relations with the Jewish communities he encountered, and in Medina, the Jews and Muslims formed a single political community. Later, he argued that Arabia should not have any community other than Islam. This was not carried out fully. In practice, the Arab armies that fought and conquered the Sassanids also included Arab Christian mercenaries. Although the Umayyad and Abbasid caliphates engaged in warfare against the Christian Byzantine Empire, many Christians served in government, even in high positions as administrators, as well as scribes and secretaries. The Islamic doctrine that Muslims are the best of all people has relegated non-Muslims to a protected but second-class status. However, in actual practice, conditions for non-Muslims have varied a great deal. By the year 1000 CE, the number of Christians in the area of greater Syria remained about equal to the number of Muslims, but after the Crusades, the percentage of Christians dropped to about 10 to 15 percent, where it remained until the 1880s.

SUNNI–SHI'A SPLIT

A dispute over succession between the extended family of the third caliph and those who followed the Prophet's son-in-law and cousin Ali (who became the fourth caliph) became very strong. A sharp battle resulting in the death of Ali's son Husayn, and the defeat of his supporters created a lingering grievance and a set of emotionally powerful symbols that fuel the greatest division in Islam. The losers were eventually called the "Partisans of Ali," from which we get the term *Shia*. Shia are the largest minority in Islam and are a majority of the population in Iran, Iraq, and Bahrain. The majority of Muslims in the world, however, are Sunnis. The two communities have developed contrasting political principles. The Shia believe that political and religious authority passes through the descendants of the Prophet (i.e., through Ali). They tend to favor a more formal, hierarchical structure of religious authority, requiring decades of study to advance from one level to the next. In contrast, Sunnis say that authority passed to the most qualified person, as determined by the elites of the Muslim community.

Despite long periods of coexistence in many countries, competing leaders sometimes appeal to this Sunni–Shia split to justify their pursuit of power. For example, Ismail, the first Safavid ruler, forced his armies to adopt Shia doctrine to use religion in his battles against the Sunni Ottoman Turks. He then imposed this belief on all of Iran. The 1979 Iranian Revolution gave great power to sectarian competition. The Ayatollah Khomeini threatened his Sunni neighbors and sought to export his revolution in the name of Shia Islam. The more that Iran threatens the Sunni Gulf States, the more they prefer that Israel take action against it, even if this means allowing overflight rights or providing information, but they keep their cooperation with Israel as secret as possible.

Khomeini made antagonism to Israel the banner of his credibility as an Islamic leader. This motivated him to support not only the Shia movement Hezbollah, in Lebanon, but also the Sunni Hamas organization in Gaza. Although in purely religious terms, Shia despise the Alawites of Syria for following a corrupt, pagan religion, Iran chooses to overlook this for political reasons. In 1972, Ayatollah Hasan Mehdi al-Shirazi declared that the Alawites are Shia. Iran has sent fighters to protect Shia shrines in Syria and to bolster the regime of Bashar al-Assad. It also uses Syria as a logistics channel to Hezbollah.

MUSLIM CLAIMS ON JERUSALEM

Muhammad initially directed his early disciples to pray facing the same direction that Jews and Christians did—toward Jerusalem. After the Jews rejected his religion, though, he received a revelation, called the "Night Journey," in the form of a dream in which he was taken to "the uttermost mosque," on a winged, horselike creature called Buraq. The Qur'an says very little about this, but *hadith* develop the now-accepted idea that "the outermost mosque" refers to Jerusalem, and specifically to the Temple Mount area. Various Muslim authors promote different conceptions of where Muhammad tied up Buraq while he prayed and received visions, but they generally say that it is near the present-day Western (Wailing) Wall. When the second caliph, Umar Ibn al-Khattab, conquered Jerusalem, he organized the cleaning of a rock considered both the location of the Jewish temple and the place of Mohammad's departure on his Night Journey. He ordered the construction of a small building over the rock to protect it, now called the Dome of the Rock. Muhammad also prayed in a place nearby, now commemorated by the al-Aqsa Mosque, which has been expanded and rebuilt several times. These buildings and the area around them—known as the Haram al-Sharif—hold special significance to Muslims. Because of the long tradition of Islamic visitation, it is widely considered Islam's third-holiest site.

Jonathan K. Zartman

See also: Arab-Islamic Conquest of Palestine; Muhammad, Prophet of Islam

Further Reading

Ahmed, Akbar S. *Discovering Islam: Making Sense of Muslim History and Society.* New York: Routledge, 2002.

Brown, Jonathan. *Misquoting Muhammad.* London: Oneworld Publications 2014.

Haider, Najam Iftikhar. *Shi'a Islam: An Introduction.* New York: Cambridge University Press, 2014.

Kelsay, John. *Arguing the Just War in Islam.* Cambridge, MA: Harvard University Press, 2007.

Tibawi, Abdul Latif. *Jerusalem: Its Place in Islam and Arab History*. Beirut: Institute for Palestine Studies, 1969.

Israel

Majority-Jewish state in the Middle East. Israel is a small country, containing only 8,019 square miles. As of 2019, it had 8.7 million citizens, 75 percent of whom are Jewish and 20 percent Palestinian. It borders the Mediterranean to the west, Lebanon to the north, Jordan and Syria to the east, and Egypt to the southwest. Its government is a parliamentary democracy, and the country boasts an advanced, Western-style economy.

According to the Jewish Bible, the Tanakh (known as the "Old Testament" to Christians), Jews trace their origins back some 4,000 years, to the prophet Abraham and his son Isaac. A series of Jewish kingdoms and states intermittently ruled Palestine or Israel for more than a millennium thereafter. After suppressing a series of Jewish revolts in the first century, the Romans expelled most Jews from Palestine. Beginning at the end of the nineteenth century, however, a Jewish nationalist movement known as Zionism sought to create a homeland in Palestine.

During World War I, in order to secure Jewish support for the war, the British government in 1917 issued the Balfour Declaration, which announced British support for the "establishment in Palestine of a national home for the Jewish people." After the war, Britain received a League of Nations mandate over Palestine that included a commitment to creating a Jewish homeland there. Arabs in Palestine, who outnumbered Jews twenty to one when the first Zionists arrived, opposed the Zionist project but ultimately were unable to stop it.

After World War II, the newly created United Nations (UN) voted to divide Palestine into two states: one for Jews, containing about 56 percent of the territory; and one for Arabs, containing about 43 percent. At the time, Jews were outnumbered two to one by Arabs in Palestine. Arabs in Palestine and elsewhere rejected partition, considering it unjust and partly driven by the West's guilt over the Holocaust, which killed over 6 million Jews. After the UN vote, communal violence erupted, but within months, Jewish forces gained the upper hand.

The state of Israel was declared on May 14, 1948, and the next day, Arab armies from neighboring states invaded. Israel won the war and secured more land and more defensible borders than it had been granted under the UN partition plan. As a result of the fighting, however, about 700,000 Palestinian Arabs fled or were forced to leave their homes. Israel refused to allow their return.

In 1950, Israel promulgated a law stipulating the right of any Jew, anywhere, to settle there. In 1951 alone, 687,000 Jews arrived—some 300,000 from the Arab states. Israel's early years were dominated by the great challenge of absorbing and integrating into society hundreds of thousands of Jewish immigrants from different parts of the world. The differences in terms of cultural background and socioeconomic status among these various groups of Jews initially proved a challenge for the Israeli government. Indeed, even today, Israel faces many ethnic, religious, and economic cleavages among its Jewish population.

In 1956, Egyptian president Gamal Abdel Nasser nationalized the Suez Canal, which provided the pretext for the French, British, and Israeli governments to collaborate to attack Egypt. On October 29, 1956, Israeli forces invaded the Sinai and headed for the Suez Canal; and the British and the French intervened as well. The U.S. government applied considerable pressure, and all three states agreed to withdraw by the end of the year. Israel secured the right to free navigation through the Suez Canal and on the waterways through the Straits of Tiran and the Gulf of Aqaba. The United Nations deployed a peacekeeping force between Egypt and Israel, but it was forced out by Egypt on the eve of the 1967 Arab-Israeli War.

During 1957–1967, Israel was primarily preoccupied with domestic politics, including continued agricultural and industrial development. Its border with Egypt generally remained calm, although incidents with Syria in particular increased, especially over water rights as Israel was diverting water from the Jordan River to irrigate its land. This led Syria and Lebanon to begin building water diversion projects upstream from the Jordan River. Israel's air force repeatedly struck these building sites until the projects were abandoned.

Throughout the spring of 1967, Israel faced increasing attacks along its borders from Syria and the Palestine Liberation Organization (PLO), created in 1964 to represent the Palestinians and coordinate efforts with Arab states to liberate Palestine. The PLO began mounting cross-border attacks from Jordan. By May, war seemed imminent with Syria, as Egypt and Jordan announced that they had mobilized their armies. This was in reaction to what they claimed was an Israeli mobilization.

On May 23, Egypt closed the Straits of Tiran and blockaded the Gulf of Aqaba, thereby blockading the Israeli port of Eilat. Fearing an imminent Arab attack and invasion, Israel launched a preemptive attack on June 5, 1967, crippling the air forces of Egypt, Syria, and Jordan. Five days later, Israel occupied the Sinai and the Gaza Strip from Egypt, the West Bank and East Jerusalem from Jordan, and the Golan Heights from Syria, doubling the amount of territory under its control. In the wake of its military victory, Israel announced that it would not withdraw from these captured territories until negotiations with the Arab states took place to get them to recognize Israel's right to exist. Israel almost immediately began building settlements in these occupied territories.

Israel's military victory did not lead to peace. Humiliated by their defeat, the Arab states refused to negotiate with, recognize, or make peace with Israel. The war united much of Israeli society and muted, if not silenced, most political disputes for several years.

In September 1970, President Nasser died. His successor, Anwar Sadat, sought an end to the war with Israel so as to focus on Egypt's many internal problems. Frustrated at the lack of a peace process, on October 6, 1973, on the Jewish high holy day of Yom Kippur, Egypt and Syria launched a surprise attack on Israel. After regrouping its forces and being resupplied by the United States, Israel repulsed the Egyptian and Syrian offensives and reclaimed control of the Sinai and Golan Heights. But the Yom Kippur War shook Israel's confidence and morale. Israel won the war, but only after heavy losses. Clearly, the military balance between Israel and its Arab foes had shifted, and the notion of Israeli invincibility that lingered after the Six-Day War had ended. Moreover, international opinion was growing increasingly anti-Israeli. Israel's refusal to withdraw from Arab territories seized during the Six-Day War led to the loss of much world support and sympathy, especially in Africa, which viewed Israel's occupation as a form of colonialism.

During this time, Arab states along with the PLO proved much more effective in publicizing the plight of the Palestinians. Increasing acts of terrorism by the PLO during 1970–1972 focused world attention on the Palestinian cause. On October 14, 1974, the UN General Assembly authorized the PLO to participate in a series of debates. Included was PLO chairman Yasser Arafat, who was considered a terrorist in Israel. He addressed the body, and on November 10, 1975, the General Assembly declared Zionism as racist. Israel refused to negotiate with the PLO, which it considered a terror group.

In May 1977, the right-wing Likud Party ended the Labor Party's twenty-nine-year political reign, and Menachem Begin became prime minister. Seeking to jump-start the peace process, President Sadat shocked the world by announcing his willingness to go to Jerusalem and meet with the Israelis face to face to negotiate peace. Accepting an invitation by Begin, Sadat arrived in Israel on November 19, the first Arab head of state to do so, effectively recognizing Israel's right to exist. Although every other Arab state refused to negotiate with Israel, Egypt and Israel made peace in 1979 after two years of negotiations mediated by U.S. president Jimmy Carter. Per the Camp David Accords, Israel withdrew from the Sinai in exchange for Egypt recognizing Israel. Discussions about the status of the Palestinians took place, but the two states never achieved any common ground on this issue. Sadat's assassination on October 6, 1981, effectively ended the talks.

On July 7, 1981, the Israeli air force bombed the nuclear reactor at Osirak, Iraq, thwarting Iraqi efforts to acquire nuclear weapons. The next year, Israel invaded Lebanon, which had been fighting a civil war since 1975, ostensibly to defend its northern border from terrorist attacks, but also to expel the PLO from Lebanon, which it did by capturing the capital, Beirut, and forcing the PLO to relocate to Tunisia. This came at a terrible human cost and material destruction to Lebanese civilians, however, and Israel failed to achieve its broad policy objectives of creating a stable, pro-Israel government in Lebanon. In 1983, Begin resigned and was replaced by fellow Likud member Yitzhak Shamir. Israel withdrew from most of Lebanon in 1986 but maintained a security zone there until May 2000, when it surrendered that territory as well.

A major Palestinian uprising—the First Intifada—erupted in 1987 in the Israeli-occupied territories of the West Bank and the Gaza Strip and consumed much of Israel's military resources. The images of armed Israeli soldiers battling Palestinian children and teenagers, mostly throwing rocks, led to considerable international criticism of Israel.

The United States sponsored peace talks in 1991 and 1992 among Israel, Syria, Lebanon, Jordan, and the Palestinians. Those talks paved the way for the 1993 Oslo Accords between Israel and the PLO, stipulating the beginning of Palestinian self-rule in parts of the West Bank and the Gaza Strip, and peace between Israel and Jordan in 1994. Initial Israeli support for the Oslo Accords waned following a series of terrorist attacks by Hamas, a Palestinian terrorist group founded in 1987 at the beginning of the First Intifada that opposed the Oslo Accords. On November 4, 1995, a right-wing Jewish religious nationalist assassinated Prime Minister Yitzhak Rabin for his apparent willingness to cede occupied territory in the West Bank to the Palestinians. Continued Hamas terrorism led to the election as prime minister of hardliner Benjamin Netanyahu of Likud. Netanyahu refused to pursue the land-for-peace dialogue with the Palestinians, thus stalling peace talks. In 1999, Labor's Ehud Barak became prime minister. Negotiations between Barak and Arafat the following year, mediated by U.S. president Bill Clinton, failed to produce agreement on a Palestinian state. The collapse of these talks and the visit of Likud's Ariel Sharon to the contested religious site Temple Mount, known to Muslims as the Haram al-Sharif, sparked the Second (al-Aqsa) Intifada.

In late 2005, under Prime Minister Ariel Sharon's leadership, Israel withdrew from the Gaza Strip, although it tightly controls Gaza's borders, coast, and airspace. Under Sharon, Israel also began building a series of barriers in the West Bank to deter terror attacks. Their construction has been criticized as a violation of international law and as an impediment to the establishment of any viable, independent Palestinian state. After Sharon suffered a massive stroke on January 4, 2006, Ehud Olmert became acting prime minister. He was formally elected to the post in the legislative elections of April 14, 2006.

In June 2006, after a Hamas raid killed two Israeli soldiers and captured another, Israel launched a series of attacks on Gaza. The next month, the Olmert government launched a monthlong war in Lebanon following an attack by Hezbollah on Israel that killed three Israeli soldiers and captured two others. Hezbollah is a large political party with a social and charitable wing, but it also has a militia that has received Iranian backing in the past and Syrian logistical support. This conflict, which devastated southern and central Lebanon, seemed to be a repeat of 1982, with Israel having failed to achieve its broad policy objectives and leaving Hezbollah stronger than ever.

In 2009, Netanyahu became prime minister again, and he has held that post continuously since then. Under his leadership, Israel has fought two wars against Hamas, increased coordination with Arab states against their mutual enemy Iran, and resisted efforts by the administration of U.S. president Barack Obama to promote a two-state resolution to Israel's conflict with Palestinians. Netanyahu also cultivated a close relationship with Obama's successor, President Donald Trump, who has adopted a staunchly pro-Israel stance.

The Trump administration has recognized Jerusalem as Israel's capital, moved the U.S. embassy there, defunded almost all U.S. aid programs to the Palestinians, scuttled a nuclear agreement that President Obama negotiated with Iran, and recognized Israel's claim to sovereignty over the Golan Heights—all policies advocated by Netanyahu. Israeli governments under Netanyahu have also greatly expanded settlements in East Jerusalem and the West Bank and ramped up efforts to combat the international Boycott, Divestment, and Sanctions (BDS) movement, which Netanyahu claims is anti-Semitic and seeks to destroy Israel. During both of his reelection campaigns in 2019, Netanyahu promised to annex Israel's West Bank settlements.

Stefan Brooks, Daniel E. Spector, and Spencer C. Tucker

See also: Arab-Israeli War, 1948; Arab-Israeli War, 1967; Gaza; Israel Defense Forces; Israeli Occupations; Israelis; One-State Solution; Oslo Accords; Security Barrier; Settlements; Two-State Solution; West Bank; Zionism

Further Reading
Dershowitz, Alan M. *The Case for Israel*. New York: Wiley, 2004.
Dowty, Alan. *Israel/Palestine*. Malden, MA: Polity, 2005.
Gilbert, Martin. *Israel: A History*. New York: William Morrow, 1998.
Reich, Bernard. *A Brief History of Israel*. New York: Facts on File, 2005.
Sachar, Howard M. *A History of Israel: From the Rise of Zionism to Our Time*. 3rd ed. New York: Knopf, 2007.

Israel Defense Forces (IDF)

Israel's military. *Tzava Haganah L-Yisra'il* is the official name of Israel's military establishment, known more familiarly as the Israel Defense Forces (IDF). In the relatively short period of its existence, the IDF has become one of the most battle-tested, effective, and simultaneously respected and reviled military forces in the world. The IDF consists of a regular air force, a regular coastal navy, and a small standing army with a large and well-trained reserve, an early warning capability, and efficient mobilization and transportation systems.

The IDF's approach to fighting wars is based on the premise that because Israel is so small and surrounded by so many enemies on all sides, it cannot afford to lose a single war. It emphasizes the strategic importance of surprise and first strikes, as demonstrated in 1956 and 1967, when it launched first strikes on Egypt, catching the enemy by surprise and hastening Israel's victory. Indeed, Israel's lack of territorial depth makes it imperative that the IDF take the war to the enemy's territory and determine the outcome as quickly and decisively as possible.

In seven major wars beginning with the Israeli War of Independence (1948–1949) and continuing through its 2014 Gaza War, over 22,000 Israeli military personnel have been killed in the line of duty. During that same time period, however, the IDF has inflicted many times that number of casualties on its enemies. Some observers insist this is because the IDF is better trained and equipped than their enemies, who usually field much larger armies. Others suggest the imbalance of casualties is the result of a long practiced policy of disproportionate retaliation—responding to enemy attacks with massive retaliatory strikes in an effort to deter future attacks.

The IDF continually strives to maintain a broad, qualitative advantage in advanced weapons systems, which it achieves in part due to the annual military aid it receives from the United States, which now sits at about $3.8 billion per year. Since 1948, Israel has received around $150 billion in direct U.S. assistance, the vast majority of which has been military aid. Israel now develops and manufactures many of the world's most sought-after military technologies. Its defense industry has become world renowned and is one of the nation's largest exporters, selling over $9.2 billion worth of goods in 2017.

The IDF's major strategic advantage, however, has always been the high quality, motivation, and discipline of its soldiers. The IDF is the backbone of Israel.

With the exception of most Arab Israelis (about 20 percent of the population), all Israeli citizens are required to serve in it for some length of time, and that experience forms the most fundamental common denominator of Israeli society. For most new immigrants to Israel, the IDF is the primary social integrator, providing educational opportunities and Hebrew-language training that might not have been available to immigrants in their countries of origin.

Most Israelis are inducted into the IDF at age eighteen. Unmarried women serve for two years, and all men serve for three years. Following initial service, men remain in the reserves until age fifty-one, and single women until age twenty-four. Reservists with direct combat experience may qualify for discharge at age forty-five. Most reservists serve for thirty-nine days a year, although that period can be extended during emergencies. Because older reservists in particular may have considerable mismatch between their military ranks and their positions in the civilian world, the IDF pays a reservist on active duty what he was making in his civilian position. The IDF is one of the very few militaries in the world with such an expensive policy. Indeed, more than 9 percent of Israel's gross domestic product (GDP) goes to military expenditures.

There are some exceptions to IDF service. Older immigrants may serve shorter periods or be deferred completely. Although Bedouin Arabs, Christian Arabs, Druze, Circassians, and some other Arab Israelis are permitted to serve in the IDF, most Arab Israelis are not, and this constitutes one of the principal fault lines of Israeli society. Another involves the ultra-Orthodox. Most religiously Orthodox women receive deferments, as do ultra-Orthodox men who pursue Torah studies or are enrolled in other religious studies programs. Many Israelis resent this "draft dodging," especially because most ultra-Orthodox families receive extensive government subsidies and many Hasidic men refuse to work in the public sector. Service in the IDF is only one of the many tensions that plague relations between the ultra-Orthodox and the rest of Israeli society.

Conscripts who have performed their initial IDF service successfully may apply to become career noncommissioned officers (NCOs) or officers. The recruitment process is highly selective, and the training is rigorous. There is no Israeli military academy or reserve officers' training corps (ROTC). Once an officer completes initial training, the IDF provides him or her with multiple opportunities to pursue advanced civilian education at IDF expense. IDF officers who retire or otherwise leave active duty retain reserve commissions and are subject to recall in time of war. The most famous example is Ariel Sharon, who commanded a division during the 1967 Six-Day War, retired as a major general in 1973, and was recalled only a few months later and placed in command of a division during the Yom Kippur War.

IDF generals are a major force in Israeli society. Many go into politics when they leave active duty. In fact, many Israeli prime ministers have been IDF generals, as have most Israeli defense ministers. Lieutenant general is the highest rank in the Israeli military, and it is held only by the IDF chief of staff. Until recently, all the IDF chiefs of staff had come from the army. In 2005, Lieutenant General Dan Halutz became the first air officer to head the IDF. He resigned in January 2007 after coming under widespread criticism for his handling of the 2006 war in Lebanon.

Although Israel has never formally admitted to having nuclear weapons, Mordecai Vanunu revealed the program to the world in 1986, becoming an enemy of the state as a result. The Jewish experience in the Holocaust is often cited as the justification for Israel to take any measures necessary, including nuclear weapons, to ensure its survival. With French support, Israel had constructed its first nuclear reactor at Dimona in 1960, and the IDF most probably acquired a nuclear weapons capability in the late 1960s. Most estimates today place Israel's nuclear stockpile at between 100 and 200 weapons, including warheads for the Jericho-1 and Jericho-2 mobile missiles and bombs for longer-range delivery by Israeli aircraft.

The IDF is the direct successor of the Haganah, the secret Jewish self-defense organization, whose roots go back to the 1907 formation of the Bar Giora organization, established to protect Jewish towns and settlements in Palestine. During World War I, many Jews acquired military training and experience in the British army, which formed the Zion Mule Corps in 1915 and the all-Jewish 38th, 39th, and 40th King's Fusiliers near the end of the war.

With Palestine becoming a British mandate following World War I, Haganah was formed in 1920 as a local self-defense force, although the British considered it an illegal militia. In 1931, a group of Haganah members broke away to form the far more aggressive Irgun Tsvai Leumi (National Military Organization). During the Arab Revolt of 1936–1939, the British cooperated unofficially with Haganah, with Captain Orde C. Wingate forming and training the Special Night Squads, one of Israel's first special operating forces.

In 1941, Haganah formed the Palmach as its strike force. The same year, an even more radical group broke away from Irgun to form the Lohamei Herut Israel (Lehi), also called the Stern Gang. During the course of World War II, more than 30,000 Palestinian Jews served in the British army. The Jewish Brigade served with distinction against the Germans in northern Italy during the final stages of World War II.

Following World War II, Haganah defied British rule in Palestine by smuggling in Holocaust survivors and other Jewish refugees, all the while conducting clandestine military training and defending Jewish settlements. Irgun and Lehi, which many considered little more than terrorist organizations, launched an all-out armed rebellion against the British. On July 22, 1946, under the orders of future prime minister Menachem Begin, Irgun bombed the King David Hotel, Britain's military headquarters in Jerusalem.

Immediately following the establishment of the state of Israel in 1948, the provisional government established the IDF and merged all Jewish fighting organizations under it. Although the IDF essentially absorbed the General Staff and combat units of Haganah, the integration of the other units was difficult and protracted. Lehi dissolved itself, and its members joined the IDF individually. Some battalions of Irgun joined the IDF, while others fought on independently. The turning point came when Prime Minister David Ben-Gurion ordered the IDF to sink Irgun's arms ship *Altalena* as it approached Tel Aviv in June 1948. It was a defining moment for the new state of Israel, establishing the authority of the central government. The remaining Irgun battalions finally disbanded on September 20, 1948.

The IDF is organized administratively into traditional branches of service, with the army, navy, and air force all having their own career tracks and distinctive uniform. Operationally, the IDF is organized into four joint regional commands. The Northern Command is responsible for the occupation of the Golan Heights and the security of Israel's northern border with Lebanon and Syria. The Southern Command is responsible for the occupation of Gaza and securing the porous southern border through the trackless Negev Desert. The Central Command is responsible for the occupation of the West Bank and the security of the Israeli settlements there. The Home Front Command's main role is to provide security to civilians during wars and mass disasters.

The Israeli standing ground force consists of four infantry brigades, plus several mixed-unit battalions and several special forces and counterterrorism units. The armor force has three brigades, as does the artillery force. Engineers have one brigade, and each infantry brigade has an engineer company.

The Israeli air force is one of the strongest in the Middle East, and with much justification, its pilots are considered some of the best in the world. Between 1948 and 2006, IAF pilots shot down 687 enemy aircraft in air-to-air combat. During the same period, only twenty-three Israeli aircraft were shot down in air-to-air combat, giving the air force an incredible thirty-to-one victory ratio. Thirty-nine pilots have achieved ace status by shooting down five or more enemy aircraft.

The Israeli navy was also formed in 1948. Its predecessor was Haganah's Palyam (whose name transliterates to "Sea Company"). The Palyam's primary mission had been smuggling Jewish refugees from Europe to Palestine. The Israeli navy today operates in two unconnected bodies of water. Its main base on the Mediterranean is at Haifa, and its main base on the Red Sea is at Eilat. The three principal operating units of the navy are the Missile Boats Flotilla, the Submarine Flotilla, and Shayetet 13, a naval special operations force similar to the U.S. navy's SEALs.

The IDF's Directorate of Main Intelligence (*Aman*) is a separate branch of service on the same level as the army, navy, and air force. The head of Aman is also a coequal to the heads of Shin Bet (internal security and counterintelligence) and Mossad (foreign intelligence), and together they direct all Israeli intelligence operations. The army itself has an Intelligence Corps (*Ha-Aman*) that is responsible for tactical-level intelligence but also comes under the overall jurisdiction of Aman.

David T. Zabecki

See also: Arab-Israeli War, 1956; Arab-Israeli War, 1967; Gaza Strip; Haganah; Irgun Tsvai Leumi; Israel-Hezbollah War, 2006; Israeli Occupations; Israelis; Lebanon, Israeli Invasion of; Stern Gang; U.S. Aid to Israel; West Bank

Further Readings

Heller, Charles E. *Economy of Force: A Total Army, the Israel Defense Forces Model.* Carlisle, PA: Strategic Studies Institute, 1992.

Hersh, Seymour. *The Sampson Option: Israel's Nuclear Arsenal and American Foreign Policy.* New York: Random House, 1991.

Lorch, Netanel. *Shield of Zion: The Israel Defense Forces.* Charlottesville, VA: Howell, 1992.

Van Creveld, Martin. *The Sword and the Olive: A Critical History of the Israel Defense Forces.* New York: Public Affairs, 2002.

Williams, Louis. *The Israel Defense Forces: A People's Army.* Lincoln, NE: Authors Choice, 2000.

Israel-Hezbollah War, 2006

Fighting between the Israeli military and Hezbollah fighters carried out over a thirty-two-day period in southern Lebanon and northern Israel from July 13 to August 14, 2006. The day before war erupted, Hezbollah fighters crossed the Israeli-Lebanese border into northern Israel and killed three Israel Defense Forces (IDF) soldiers and captured two others, evidently with the intent to use them for prisoner exchange purposes. This closely followed a similar recent operation mounted by Hamas in southern Israel, in which one Israeli soldier was captured and two others were killed.

Holding the Lebanese government responsible for not enforcing security in the southern part of its country, Israel imposed an air, land, and sea blockade against Lebanon on July 13. The Beirut International Airport was also bombed. Israel had a number of objectives: the return of the two captured IDF soldiers, the removal of the Hezbollah threat against Israeli territory by destroying its armaments and outposts, and the establishment of long-term stability along the northern border. Israel also hoped to strengthen the anti-Syrian and anti-Hezbollah forces within Lebanon.

Israel's operation consisted chiefly of air and naval strikes on Lebanon's infrastructure, which destroyed a total of forty-two bridges and damaged thirty-eight roads. This effort also caused extensive damage to telecommunications, electricity distribution, ports, airports, and even private-sector facilities, including a milk factory and food warehouses. Roughly 70 percent of Lebanese civilians living in southern Lebanon fled north during the conflict. For its part, Hezbollah responded by launching an average of 100 Katyusha rockets per day into northern Israel, targeting such cities as Haifa and hitting hospitals, chemical factories, military outposts, and residential areas. Although the Israeli air force tried to strike at the launchers, they were virtually impossible to find, and many of the rockets were fired from residential areas, even near mosques.

Israeli commenced a ground offensive on July 22, 2006, in the village of Marun al-Ras. IDF forces engaged Hezbollah fighters in Bint Jbayl, the largest Lebanese town near the border. One week later, Israel declared that it would occupy a strip inside southern Lebanon with ground troops. Meanwhile, four unarmed observers from the United Nations (UN) died when an errant Israeli air strike hit their observation post near the border.

U.S. secretary of state Condoleezza Rice visited the region during July 24–25 and again during July 29–31 in an effort to negotiate a cessation of hostilities. However, she opposed a cease-fire that would merely return the status quo. Meanwhile, discussions at the United Nations centered on how a negotiated solution to the conflict could prevent further violence, and how an international—or Lebanese—force might control southern Lebanon and disarm Hezbollah. Talks were also undertaken in Rome among American, European, and Arab leaders in an attempt to reach a satisfactory end to the conflict, but to no avail.

On August 11, 2006, the UN Security Council unanimously approved UN Resolution 1701 in an effort to end hostilities. The resolution, which was approved by both the Lebanese and Israeli governments, called for a cease-fire, the disarming of Hezbollah, Israel's withdrawal from Lebanon, and the deployment of the Lebanese army and an enlarged UN Interim Force in Lebanon (UNIFIL) in southern Lebanon. Nevertheless, the seventy-two hours that preceded the effective date of the cease-fire on August 14, 2006, witnessed the fiercest fighting of the monthlong conflict.

The Lebanese army began deploying into southern Lebanon on August 17, 2006. However, Israel's air and sea blockade was not lifted until September 8, 2006. On October 1, 2006, the Israeli army reported that it had completed its withdrawal from southern Lebanon, although UNIFIL denied these assertions.

The conflict killed an estimated 1,187 Lebanese civilians, as well as 44 Israeli civilians; severely damaged Lebanese infrastructure; displaced some 1 million Lebanese and 300,000 Israelis; and disrupted life across all of Lebanon and northern Israel. By September, 60 percent of the towns and villages in the south had no water or electricity. Even after the cease-fire, 256,000 Lebanese remained internally displaced, and much of southern Lebanon remained uninhabitable because of more than 350,000 unexploded cluster bombs in some 250 locations south of the Litani River. Moreover, the Lebanese coasts witnessed a tragic oil spill that resulted from Israel's bombing of fuel tanks. About 40 percent of the coastline was affected. Both Hezbollah and Israel were accused of violating international humanitarian law during the conflict.

Hezbollah launched an estimated 3,970 rockets into Israel during the conflict, and the Israeli air force carried out about 15,500 sorties, striking more than 7,000 targets in Lebanon. Between 250 and 600 Hezbollah fighters were killed, and 13 Hezbollah fighters were captured by the IDF during the conflict. The IDF reported 119 Israeli soldiers killed, more than 400 wounded, and 2 taken prisoner. The Lebanese army suffered casualties as well: 46 killed and more than 100 injured. Finally, 7 UN personnel were killed, and 12 others were injured.

None of the objectives that the IDF had set for its operation in Lebanon were realized. In a significant sense, the conflict was the result of both sides having misjudged the other. Hezbollah has stated that it would not have kidnapped IDF soldiers had it known the severity of Israel's response. Israel, meanwhile, was taken aback by the effectiveness of the Hezbollah defenses. There was sufficient anger in Israel over the results of the operation that the government was forced to appoint an investigating committee. In January 2007, IDF chief of staff Dan Halutz resigned in the face of increasing criticism of the IDF's performance in the war.

Rana Kobeissi

See also: Hezbollah; Israel Defense Forces; Lebanon; Lebanon, Israeli Invasion of

Further Reading

Allen, Lori. "Social Security: How Palestinians Survive a Humanitarian Crisis." *Middle East Report* no. 240 (Fall 2006), 12–19.

Arkin, William. *Divining Victory: Airpower in the 2006 Israel-Hezbollah War.* Montgomery, AL: Air University Press, 2011.

International Crisis Group. "Israel/Hizbullah/Lebanon: Avoiding Renewed Conflict." *The International Crisis Group Middle East Report* no. 59 (November 2006).

Schiff, Ze'ev. "The Fallout from Lebanon." *Foreign Affairs Magazine* (November–December 2006): 13–41.

Israeli Occupations

Israeli military occupations of Arab territory. In 1967, Israel captured the West Bank and East Jerusalem from Jordan, the Sinai Desert and Gaza Strip from Egypt, and the Golan Heights from Syria. It returned the Sinai to Egypt in 1982 as part of a peace treaty and removed all 5,000 of its settlers from northeastern Sinai. Israel annexed the Golan Heights in 1981. No country recognizes this annexation except the United States, which did so in March 2019. Currently, over 20,000 Israeli citizens live in settlements built on the Golan Heights. Israel also occupied much of southern Lebanon in 1982, although it did not develop settlements there and unilaterally withdrew in 2000.

Since 1967, Israel has maintained control of the Gaza Strip, East Jerusalem, and the West Bank—commonly referred to as the *Occupied Palestinian Territories (OPT)*—and has constructed hundreds of illegal settlements there. It removed its settlers from Gaza in 2005 but continues to build in East Jerusalem and the West Bank, also known as *Judea* and *Samaria,* which are the biblical terms for the region and often used to emphasize Israel's historical connection to the land. The remainder of this entry will focus on the OPT.

Many Israelis insist that the West Bank, East Jerusalem, and Gaza are not "occupied" territory and settlement construction is not illegal. There are multiple justifications for such assertions: these territories are part of the land that God bequeathed the Jewish people, who have sole claim to them; the lands were once part of ancient Israeli kingdoms and never part of an independent Palestinian state; Israel won these territories during wars thrust upon it; ownership of these territories was unsettled when Israel took control, and so they should be considered "disputed lands," to which Israel has the strongest claim based on its religious and historical connections to the land, as well as its security requirements; and because Israeli settlers are not being forcefully moved into Judea and Samaria, but volunteer to go, Israeli settlements do not transgress the Geneva Convention prohibition against the forced transfer of an occupying power's population into occupied territory.

Few in the international community are convinced by these arguments. Most consider these territories to be occupied Palestinian land and that settlement construction there is illegal.

GAZA

From 1967 to 2005, Israel maintained a direct military occupation of the Gaza Strip. It allowed the development of about twenty-one settlements in Gaza, housing about 9,000 Israeli Jews. During this time frame, it ruled Gaza much as it did the West Bank. Initially, Palestinians were allowed to travel throughout the occupied territories, and even into Israel, with few limitations. This afforded Israel a cheap source of labor and improved Palestinian living standards. For the first twenty years, Palestinians proved to be a fairly docile population for Israel to rule over, but that changed in 1987, when a generation of built-up frustrations erupted into the First Intifada. Since then, Israel introduced or intensified a series of policies tightening Israeli control over the OPT. These policies include settlement expansion, increased permit requirements, permanent and mobile checkpoints and barriers, blockades, home demolitions, collective punishments, population transfers, restrictive urban planning, and tight travel restrictions, among others.

In late 2005, Israel unilaterally withdrew its military from Gaza and evacuated all its settlers. It reinforced a barrier that it had constructed a decade earlier to surround Gaza and since has severely restricted ingress and egress via air, sea, and land. Israel does not control Gaza's border with Egypt, but for reasons of its own, Egypt coordinates its policy with Israel and has largely enforced the blockade. Israel insists that these steps are necessary to contain its most virulent Palestinian enemy, Hamas, which took control of the overcrowded enclave soon after Israel pulled out. Hamas killed hundreds of Israelis during the Second Intifada (2000–2005) with suicide bombings and other attacks. Hamas has also launched thousands of rockets into Israel since 2006, causing few casualties, but terrorizing the nearby Israeli population. Hamas has also built hundreds of smuggling tunnels into Egypt and some into Israel itself used for attacks. Simmering tensions between Hamas-dominated Gaza and Israel have spilled over into extensive violence in 2008, 2012, 2014, and 2018. Critics of Israeli policy insist that by so severely restricting who and what can go in and out of Gaza, Israel has turned it into an open-air prison and is collectively punishing 1.8 million Gazans, many (if not most) of whom are innocent.

EAST JERUSALEM

In June 1967, Israel annexed East Jerusalem and a number of surrounding Palestinian villages from the West Bank. In doing so, it intentionally incorporated underdeveloped Palestinian lands into the newly expanded borders of Jerusalem for future Jewish settlement expansion. There are now about 210,000 Jews living in this annexed territory, and about 370,000 Palestinians. Within a few days of capturing East Jerusalem, Israel took a census, and all Palestinians not present lost their residency rights. Those Palestinians that remained in the expanded municipal boundaries were afforded permanent residency status; this allows them to work and travel in Israel and apply for certain social benefits, but they cannot vote in national elections or run for mayor. They are allowed to vote in local elections and run for city council, but most refuse to because they do not want to legitimize Israeli rule. Israel allows East Jerusalem Palestinians to apply for citizenship, but for nationalist reasons, very few have. Those who do face an extensive and expensive application process that can last for years. They also must deal with ostracization within their communities for betraying the nationalist cause.

Family reunification requests can drag on for years and are usually unsuccessful, especially when involving Palestinians living in Gaza or the West Bank. Indeed, Israel passed legislation in 2003 preventing Palestinians from living with an Israeli spouse inside Israel. Ostensibly, the law is a temporary security measure that closes off another avenue that Palestinian terrorists might use to enter Israel. It has been renewed every year since its introduction.

Palestinians also face losing residency status if they cannot regularly prove Jerusalem is their "center of life," or if they live elsewhere for extended periods of time (as defined by Israeli authorities). These restrictions do not apply to Jews. Building permits for new housing construction are rarely awarded to Palestinians in East Jerusalem, which leads to "illegal" home building and overcrowding. Sometimes these homes are demolished. In 2016 alone, Israel demolished 1,093 Palestinian homes throughout the West Bank and East Jerusalem. In comparison, Jewish settlements in the city have grown steadily since 1967. Government spending on schools, hospitals, roads, and other physical infrastructure in Palestinian neighborhoods is far below that which is spent in Jewish neighborhoods. And the security barrier that Israel has constructed to impede terrorist attacks cuts off East Jerusalem from surrounding Palestinian villages and towns, disrupting economic and social relations and forcing tens of thousands of East Jerusalem Palestinians to pass through barrier checkpoints every day.

WEST BANK

In 1967, Israeli forces initially declared the West Bank a closed military zone administered by the regional military commander. In 1972, the Israeli military leader Moshe Dayan declared the "Open Borders" policy, giving Palestinians general travel permission in order to integrate them into the Israeli labor force. In 1981, the IDF established its Civil Administration for the West Bank. Palestinians enjoyed relatively free movement until the end of the second half of the 1980s. Since then, controls on Palestinians have tightened steadily.

As a result of agreements following the signing of the Oslo Accords, the West Bank was divided into areas A, B, and C. Area A contains major Palestinian cities and is governed by a Palestinian proto-government known as the Palestinian Authority (PA). Area A covers only about 18 percent of the West Bank but has most of the Palestinian population. Area B covers another 22 percent and includes most Palestinian villages strewn throughout the West Bank. This area is under Israeli military control, but the PA runs civilian affairs for Palestinian residents. Together, Areas A and B contain the vast majority of Palestinians in the West Bank, although about 300,000 Palestinians live in Area C, which is under the complete control of the IDF; the PA has no authority there. It comprises about 60 percent of the West Bank and is home to over 400,000 Israeli settlers. Unlike the other areas, Area C is contiguous, and this separates many of the 165 or so Palestinian villages and cities from one another. Area C does not include East Jerusalem, which is home to about 200,000 Jewish settlers and 300,000 Palestinians.

Since Oslo, Israel has rapidly developed settlements and infrastructure, mostly in Area C. When Oslo was signed, about 250,000 Israelis lived in the West Bank (including East Jerusalem); in 2019, nearly 700,000 settlers live there. Many see this expansion as evidence that Israel has no intention of relinquishing control of the West Bank or allowing the creation of a Palestinian state. Land use restrictions are one of the primary tools that Israel uses to tighten its grip on the West Bank and limit Palestinian development. In short, the Israeli government steadily authorizes, supports, funds, and subsidizes the construction of Jewish settlements in much of the West Bank. Even settlements unauthorized by the Israeli government are tolerated and often retroactively "legalized." In contrast, almost any type of Palestinian construction outside Area A is severely restricted by Israeli authorities.

The densely populated areas A and B afford Palestinians little space or suitable land for economic and agricultural development. Available space is often used for housing projects to ease overcrowding. By restricting Palestinian access to the open tracts of land in Area C while enabling settlement growth there, Israel strengthens its grip on large swaths of the West Bank, while simultaneously undermining Palestinian economic development.

Palestinians must obtain permits not only for construction, but for most forms of travel outside their towns and villages. Over 100 types of permits regulate Palestinian travel to the areas inside Israel and into Israeli settlements; passage between Gaza and the West Bank, to Jerusalem, and through Area C (and parts of B); and travel abroad. Tens of thousands of Palestinians who live in the "seam zone" (the land between Israel's security barrier and its 1967 border) are in constant need of permits to pass newly created permanent checkpoints.

While many roads in the West Bank are technically open to use by Palestinians, in practice, many are not. By late January 2017, about 60 kilometers of West Bank roads (mostly in Area C) were designated for exclusive, or near-exclusive, use by Israeli citizens. Within Hebron, Palestinians are further banned from even walking in some areas. Elsewhere, there are multilevel traffic systems using overpasses and underpasses to separate Arabs and Jews. Some Palestinian roads are interrupted by Israeli-only highways.

In 2010, the Israeli High Court ruled segregation of roads to be illegal. To travel certain roads, however, one must have the correct permits. For instance Route 4370 in the West Bank is a set of two-lane highways separated by a twenty-six-foot-tall barrier. One side is used primarily by Israeli settlers seeking a more direct route to Jerusalem because the road avoids the Hizma checkpoint north of the city. The other side is used primarily by Palestinians because it bypasses Jerusalem (which they are rarely allowed into) on its way to Bethlehem and Ramallah. Israeli government officials advertise the road as a way to alleviate traffic congestion for everyone in that area of the West Bank. It is one of many upcoming infrastructure projects that they say will deepen Israeli sovereignty over the West Bank while also improving the lives of Palestinians. But critics say that the new road will encourage more Israeli settlement construction east of Jerusalem and call it an apartheid road because they believe it is intended to separate the settler and indigenous populations further. Israeli officials reject the label, insisting that the word *apartheid* refers to discrimination based on race or ethnicity, while anyone with the correct permits can travel this road. But only Palestinians need such permits (Israelis are free to travel anywhere in the West Banks except Area A), and the IDF rarely grants them.

There are over 100 permanent Israel checkpoints in the West Bank, and another 100 or so temporary ones are set up monthly. Not only are travel permits difficult to get, but the IDF can cancel them anytime. Palestinian fathers are often humiliated in front of their children by Israeli soldiers manning checkpoints, many of whom are teenage conscripts. They can deny or delay passage for any reason, and Palestinians have little recourse. Because permits are so central to the daily lives of Palestinians, they are one of many leverage points used by Israel's Shin Bet to recruit informants. Many Palestinians view these collaborators as traitors. Individuals caught doing this are often killed and their families stigmatized. Collaboration tears at the fabric of Palestinian society.

Israel applies a dual legal system in the West Bank—one for Palestinians and one for settlers. Palestinians live under martial law, meaning that they are tried in an Israeli military court system under laws established by the Israel military. Israeli settlers, on the other hand, are subject to Israeli civilian law, which affords them many more legal protections. Critics insist that settler violence against Palestinians, as well as human rights abuses by IDF soldiers, are underinvestigated, rarely prosecuted, and even more rarely result in convictions. This is in stark contrast to the thousands of Palestinians arrested every year for suspected security violations. The IDF can hold Palestinians in administrative detention for 180 days without charges, and the detention is renewable indefinitely, subject to authorization by a military judge. When Palestinians are brought to trial, Israeli military courts have a 99 percent conviction rate. Israel affords Palestinians the opportunity to petition its High Court for certain issues, but these efforts rarely succeed, and in 2018, Israel's Knesset (parliament) passed a law restricting this opportunity even further.

Israeli officials insist that their various policies regulating Palestinian life in Gaza, East Jerusalem, and the West Bank are legal, humane, and required for Israel's national security.

Robert C. DiPrizio and Tom Dowling

See also: Gaza; Golan Heights; Intifada, First; Intifada, Second; Lebanon, Israeli Invasion of; Israel Defense Forces; Oslo Accords; Security Barrier; Settlements; Suicide Bombings; West Bank

Further Reading
Gordon, Neve. *Israel's Occupation.* Berkeley: University of California Press, 2008.
Hever, Shir. *The Political Economy of Israel's Occupation: Repression Beyond Exploitation.* London: Pluto Press, 2010.
Makdisi, Saree. *Palestine Inside Out: An Everyday Occupation.* London: W. W. Norton, 2010.
Smith, Charles D. *Palestine and the Arab-Israeli Conflict: A History with Documents.* 9th ed. New York: Bedford/St. Martin's, 2017.
Zertal, Idith, and Eldar, Akiva. *Lords of the Land: The War for Israel's Settlements in the Occupied Territories, 1967–2007.* Philadelphia: Nation Books, 2007

Israeli War of Independence (see Arab-Israeli War, 1948)

Israelis

Citizens of the modern state of Israel. From its earliest days of independence, Israeli society has been diverse. A total of 75 percent of the country's citizens are Jews. One of the many challenges that a young Israel faced was developing a unique Israeli national identity among Jewish immigrants from around the world. Most of the Zionists who created the institutions that would become the state of Israel were Ashkenazim (Jews from Europe). While they came from many countries, most spoke Yiddish as a common language. Zionist leaders, however, sought to promote the development of a so-called Hebrew culture that would serve as the cornerstone of a new Israeli identity. Central to this was transforming biblical Hebrew into a modern language for daily use. Today, only a small number of ultra-Orthodox Jews insist on speaking Yiddish, viewing Hebrew as a holy language reserved for religious activities. In the 1950s and 1960s, large numbers of Mizrahim (Middle Eastern and North African Jews) migrated to Israel and learned modern Hebrew. By this point, however, the Ashkenazim had already gained the commanding heights of Israel's political, economic, and cultural landscape, and the Mizrahim faced major challenges in assimilating. Ashkenazi culture was heavily influenced by nineteenth-century European ideals regarding egalitarianism, socialism, and secularism.

These values stood in stark contrast with those of the Mizrahim, who tended to be more conservative, placed significant importance on their Middle Eastern identity, and largely ignored the Zionist movement until 1948. As the Israeli government sought to quickly integrate hundreds of thousands of Mizrahim, it separated many close-knit extended families and moved them into so-called development towns and kibbutzim to meet the demand for factory workers and farmers. They quickly became Israel's lower class and suffered large disparities in almost every meaningful measure of economic, political, and cultural achievement. Stereotypes on both sides developed, with Ashkenazim being characterized as elitist, antireligious, and socialists and Mizrahim regarded as backward, poor, and inferior. These stereotypes linger today, even though disparities between the two have decreased significantly.

Unsurprisingly, Judaism has a significant influence on Israeli society, even though only about half of Israel's Jews identify as observant. The workweek in Israel is structured around the observance of the Shabbat (Sabbath), and events commonly understood to have religious meaning such as Pesach (Passover) are celebrated as national holidays. Jewish religious leaders have significant influence on food and marriage laws in Israel, and the influence of religious political parties ensures that Israeli law and society reflect Jewish religious tradition and belief. Jewish religious beliefs and traditions originate from how the Tanakh, or Hebrew Bible, is interpreted. The ultra-Orthodox hold to the most conservative interpretation of the Tanakh and strictly adhere to the food, marriage, work, and worship traditions that are accepted as central to Judaism. The other two broad Jewish religious categories, Orthodox and Reformed (also known as Conservative), are incrementally more liberal.

While only about 16 percent of Israel's Jewish population is ultra-Orthodox (or Haredim, which is Hebrew for "those who tremble in front of God"), they have an

Israelis celebrate the Jewish Holiday of Tu Bishvat by planting a tree. Seventy-five percent of Israelis are Jews and even though most identify as secular, Jewish religious traditions permeate Israeli society. (Rafael Ben Ari/Dreamstime.com)

outsized influence on Israeli politics and society. Because they tend to vote in blocs, their political parties are often kingmakers in coalition governments, which affords them political influence that far outweighs their numbers. Haredi men participate minimally in Israel's economy, receive significant government subsidies, and wield great influence over issues of marriage and divorce, Sabbath observance, and kosher laws. Many of them regard the creation of the state of Israel as apostasy because they believe the only valid way for Israel to be reestablished is by God. Many thus refuse to observe Israel's Independence Day or serve in the Israel Defense Forces (IDF), which is mandatory for other Jews.

The IDF serves double duty as defender of the state and a primary creator of the nation, as it helps mold Jews of disparate backgrounds into Israelis. It is the most exalted of public institutions, yet ultra-Orthodox men studying in religious schools are exempt from service. This policy was introduced by Israel's first prime minister, David Ben-Gurion, who thought the Haredim were a relic of diaspora Jewry that would soon vanish. But consistently high birth rates (the average Haredi family has six children) have led to the opposite: they are now the fastest-growing segment of Israeli Jews. When this exemption policy was first implemented, only about 400 Haredi students qualified. Now about 60,000 qualify every year. Many Israelis resent these religious exemptions, as well as the economic burden and outsized influence that the Haredi have on Israeli society.

Like religion, Zionist ideology also serves to unite and divide large segments of Israel's Jewish population. The idea that Jews are a people with the right to self-determination in their ancient homeland lies at the heart of Zionism. Most Israeli Jews agree that for this to happen, Israel must have a majority-Jewish population. However, Israeli Jews are torn between two other deeply held tenets of Zionism—the desire to create a just and democratic society and the desire to reclaim all of ancient Israel. The political left in Israel has generally privileged justice and democracy over the reclamation of land, and thus has been more open to a two-state solution with the Palestinians. The political right, on the other hand, opposes giving up control of Judea and Samaria (biblical terms for the West Bank) for religious, nationalist, and security reasons. The left's vision of Zionism was ascendant in the 1990s, but after the assassination of Prime Minister Yitzhak Rabin by an Israeli Jew opposed to a two-state solution, the failure of the Oslo peace process, and the eruption of the very bloody Second Intifada, right-wing coalitions have dominated Israeli politics.

While Israel is predominantly Jewish, about 25 percent of its citizenry is not. Most non-Jewish citizens are referred to as *Arab-Israelis* by the government, even though many of them prefer the term *Palestinian* or *Palestinian citizens of Israel*. Many view the creation of the state of Israel as the *nakba*, or great catastrophe, as it spoiled their dream of national self-determination in their homeland and forced hundreds of thousands to become refugees. The hundreds of thousands of Arabs who did not leave were placed under military rule until 1966. They became full citizens of Israel, but most insist they are not treated equally under the law. Indeed, numerous studies (and even some Israeli government reports) have demonstrated how certain laws and institutional practices result in persistent disparities, including in education (Jews receive more per capita spending than Arabs and are much more likely to qualify to go to college); the provision of government services (Arab cities receive subpar municipal services and have higher poverty rates); income levels (Arab-Israelis earn about 60 percent of what Jews make for the same work); housing opportunities (admissions committees in some Jewish communities are allowed to deny applicants based on "social suitability," and only about 1 percent of the 1,000 communities built in Israel since 1948 have been for Arabs); and political participation (Arab parties are never invited into ruling coalitions and are thus incapable of influencing government policies and budgets). Israel also inhibits family reunifications of Arab-Israeli families, as well as the lease of "state lands" (i.e., 93 percent of Israel) in ways that do not apply to Israeli Jews. The Israeli government affords diaspora Jews the right to return but refuses that right to diaspora Palestinians.

Critics insist that Arab-Israelis are thus forced to suffer the indignities of second-class citizenship as the price for remaining in their homeland. Most feel alienated and ostracized by the "Jewishness" of their country, which they experience, in ways big and small, as a negation of their Palestinian identity and their connection to the land. As if to emphasize the point, Israel passed the Nation-State Law in 2018, which states, among other things, that only Jews have the right to self-determination in Israel. Months later, Prime Minister Benjamin Netanyahu declared publicly that Israel is "the national state, not of all its citizens, but only of the Jewish people."

Israel is thus sometimes described by Arabs not as a Jewish democratic state, but as a democratic state for the Jews and a Jewish state for the Arabs.

While many Israeli Jews regret the inequities and estrangement of their fellow Arab citizens, others have no tolerance for *nakba* commemorators who criticize the country that protects them, exempts them from military service, and provides them with better living conditions than they would get elsewhere in the Middle East. Most insist that Israel must remain Jewish, and they have little sympathy for Arabs who complain about the Jewishness of the state and its symbols, holidays, laws, and practices. Some Jewish Israelis view Arabs as disloyal or worse. The result is a single group of people called "Israelis," but with very different identities and many cleavages yet to be resolved.

Some observers have suggested that Israeli society is so riven with tensions that it needs the specter of an existential security threat—Arab states, Palestinians, Hezbollah, or Iran—to survive. Without such a threat, these internal cleavages would tear the country apart. Others believe that such doom-and-gloom predictions are unwarranted, and these differences are simply the mark of a diverse but healthy democracy and will work themselves out in time. Indeed, despite Israel's difficult security situation and internal tensions, its economy is booming. Widely known as "the start-up nation," Israel is the site of many companies that have become world leaders in many high-tech fields. If Israel were ever to achieve normal relations with its neighbors, its highly educated citizenry and technologically advanced economy could be the engine that spurs regional economic development.

Hugh Gardenier and Robert C. DiPrizio

See also: Aliya; Demographics in Israel and Palestine; Israel Defense Forces; Israeli Occupations; Jewish Emigration from Arab Countries; Judaism; *Nakba;* Oslo Accords; Palestinians; Settlements; Zionism

Further Reading
Jorisch, Avi. *Thou Shalt Innovate: How Israeli Ingenuity Repairs the World.* Edison, NJ: Gefen Books, 2018.
Rosenthal, Donna. *The Israelis: Ordinary People in an Extraordinary Land.* New York: Free Press, 2003.
Senor, Dan, and Saul Singer. *Start-up Nation: The Story of Israel's Economic Miracle.* New York: Twelve, 2009.
Smooha, Sammy. *Arab-Jewish Relations in Israel: Alienation and Rapprochement.* Washington, DC: United States Institute for Peace, 2010.
Williams, Louis. *The Israel Defense Forces: A People's Army.* Lincoln, NE: iUniverse, 2000.

Israeli Security Barrier

A barricade separating most West Bank Palestinians from most Israelis. In 1992, Israeli prime minister Yitzhak Rabin proposed the creation of a physical barrier between Israeli and Palestinian territory in the West Bank. Rabin believed that such a barrier would improve the security situation faced by Israel, while at the same time promoting a Palestinian nationalism that would lead to the formation of an independent Palestinian state. The first elements of the barrier were constructed in 1994, following the Green Line, the demarcation of Israeli territory agreed to in 1949. The first segments separated the Jewish settlements at Bat Hefer from Palestinian territory in Tulkarm. In 2000, Prime Minister Ehud Barak agreed to finance an additional segment of the wall, although construction in earnest did not begin until 2002, when Prime Minister Ariel Sharon lent his full support to the project.

The barrier is designed to essentially encircle the West Bank. Although it ostensibly follows the Green Line, in many areas it deviates from the agreed-upon settlement line for topographical, political, or economic reasons. Critics of the barrier claim that Israel is attempting to claim territory by fiat, essentially by blocking anyone else from reaching it. Proponents of the wall, on the other hand, argue that the Israelis are effectively ceding most of the territory captured in the 1967 Six-Day War to the Palestinians, and creating a more effective means of self-governance by reducing the number of Israel Defense Forces (IDF) troops and checkpoints in the West Bank.

By 2014, approximately 70 percent of the barrier was either in place or under construction. Suicide bombings originating in the West Bank dropped precipitously after the barrier was put in place, and the areas most prone to sniping have an extra-high wall to block visual access. In most locations, the barrier consists of multiple layers of defenses, including barbed-wire fences, antivehicle ditches, intrusion-detection sensors, and concrete walls. There are a series of entry points spaced throughout the barrier; some are opened daily, while others only open up during agricultural seasons.

The wall has evoked mixed reactions. In 2003, the United States vetoed a resolution of the UN Security Council to declare the wall illegal. Although the General Assembly of the United Nations (UN) has adopted measures condemning the wall, it cannot enforce any such decrees. Palestinian residents of the West Bank have demonstrated against the enormous economic and health-care costs imposed by the barrier—but the Israelis have retorted that the Palestinian Authority (PA) refused to contain terror attacks from the West Bank, requiring the construction of the wall in the first place.

Paul J. Springer

See also: Intifada, Second; Israeli Occupations; Suicide Bombings; West Bank

Further Reading
Dolphin, Ray, and Graham Usher. *The West Bank Wall: Unmaking Palestine.* London: Pluto Press, 2006.
Kershner, Isabel. *Barrier.* Basingstoke, UK: Palgrave MacMillan, 2006.
Parry, William. *Against the Wall: The Art of Resistance in Palestine.* Chicago: Lawrence Hill Books, 2011.

Israelite Conquest of Canaan

Israelite conquest of the Holy Land, emanating from the Sinai Desert around 1400 BCE. As a religious and racial group, Jews have long believed that they are God's "chosen people" and enjoy a special covenant with Him that includes eternal possession of the land known in ancient times as Canaan (now Palestine/Israel and parts of surrounding states). Yet when the first Hebrews, led by Abraham, first migrated to the Promised Land from Mesopotamia, they were unable to conquer it. According to biblical tradition, famine forced the Hebrews to flee to Egypt, where they were enslaved for centuries until the prophet Moses (aided by divine intervention) managed to free them. Moses then led his people into the Sinai, intending to conquer Canaan, but because they lacked sufficient faith, God forced them to wander the desert for forty years. By the time the Israelites began their invasion, the number of fighting men among their ranks had dwindled from 600,000 to 40,000.

Some of the first Israelite victories described in the Old Testament came against the Amorite kingdoms of Sihon and Og, on their way to taking of the great walled city of Jericho. Before the battle of Jericho, Moses passed the mantle of leadership to Joshua, his top general, whom God had blessed with invincibility. Perched on the eastern bank of the Jordan River, just south of Jericho, Joshua instructed his people to follow the priests carrying the Ark of the Covenant into the river. The waters of the Jordan then miraculously stopped flowing, and Joshua's army passed safely to the other side.

Once across, Joshua sent spies into the city on a reconnaissance mission. He learned that the local residents were terrified of his army, in part because the populations of Sihon and Og were all killed. Indeed, to protect his people from being corrupted by idol worshippers, God commanded the Hebrews to kill everyone in the Holy Land as they conquered it. At Jericho, Joshua commanded his army to march around the city walls once a day for six days, accompanied by priests carrying the Ark of the Covenant. On the seventh day, they marched around the city seven more times and let out a roar that caused the walls to come tumbling down. All of Jericho's residents were then slaughtered, except for one family that had harbored the Israelite spies.

Joshua's next major victory was the conquest of a nearby walled city, Ai, in central Canaan. After first failing to capture it with a small force, he sent the majority of his army and tricked the city's defenders out of the city where they were ambushed. All the fighters and inhabitants of Ai were killed.

One of the few exceptions to this policy of genocide demanded by God was made around this time. Representatives of the nearby city of Gibeon, dressed in rags, convinced Joshua that their city lay outside Canaan and thus posed no threat. Joshua agreed to an alliance, but once he learned of their deceit, Joshua forced the Gibeonites into servitude.

After conquering central Canaan, Joshua turned his army south, capturing the cities of Libnah, Lachish, Eglon, Debir, and Hebron, among others. Then, marching north, he defeated an alliance led by the king of Hazor and destroyed most of the northern cities. In all, Joshua conquered thirty-one kingdoms in Canaan, which left him in control of most of the land. Still, there were some holdouts, including the Jebusites, who controlled Jerusalem, and the Philistines along the southern coastland.

It was not until the time of King David, about four centuries after Joshua's invasion, that the Israelites completed their conquest of Canaan. Even then, God's command to cleanse the land of non-Jews was incompletely fulfilled, and the Old Testament blames many of Israel's later problems on interracial marriages and idol worshipping.

For the next 1,000 years, the Israelites and their descendants exercised varying levels of control over the Holy Land until the Romans expelled them. Then, 2,000 years later, the Zionists recaptured part of ancient Canaan and established the state of Israel.

Robert C. DiPrizio

See also: Canaanites; David; Judaism; United Kingdom of Israel; Zionism

Further Reading

Alter, Robert. *Ancient Israel: The Former Prophets: Joshua, Judges, Samuel, and Kings: A Translation with Commentary.* New York: W. W. Norton and Company, 2013.

Arnold, Bill T., and Richard S. Hess, eds. *Ancient Israel's History: An Introduction to Issues and Sources.* Grand Rapids, MI: Baker Academic, 2014.

Cline, Eric H. *Jerusalem Besieged: From Ancient Canaan to Modern Israel.* Ann Arbor: University of Michigan, 2004.

Copan, Paul, and Matt Flannagan. *Did God Really Command Genocide? Coming to Terms with the Justice of God.* Grand Rapids, MI: Baker Books, 2014.

Izz al-Din al-Qassam Brigades

The armed paramilitary wing of the Palestinian group Hamas. The Izz al-Din al-Qassam Brigades were formally established in 1991 by Yahya Ayyash, the key military strategist for Hamas. Named after the militant Palestinian leader of the Black Hand organization in the 1920s, the al-Qassam Brigades have mounted numerous attacks and terror campaigns against Israelis. Ayyash claims to have established the brigades to facilitate Hamas's political goals, which include opposing the 1993 Oslo Accords.

The al-Qassam Brigades have operated amid much secrecy. They are made up of small, largely independent cells directed by the head of the organization. It is not uncommon for the various cells to be completely unaware of other cells' goals or activities. Hamas and the brigades have been the strongest in the Gaza Strip, although they try to maintain a presence in the West Bank as well. During 2004, however, strikes by the Israel Defense Forces (IDF) against brigade cells in the West Bank largely decimated the group there.

From 1992 to 2000, al-Qassam Brigades fought an intermittent guerrilla campaign against the IDF, as well as Israeli civilians. Palestinian Authority (PA) president Yasser Arafat was unable to rein in the brigades. When the Second (al-Aqsa) Intifada began in September 2000, the brigades played a role in fomenting unrest and in arming and training militants to carry out terrorist attacks (including suicide bombings) against Israel. Other attacks were organized by Palestinian Islamic Jihad (PIJ) or carried out by individuals.

Although multiple IDF attacks took a toll on the brigades' foot soldiers and leadership alike, the group continued to maintain its cohesion and attract many new recruits. Hamas accepted a truce in 2004 as part of an overall agreement between the PA and Israel. However, the organization used the time to reconstitute and rearm itself.

After the Israelis pulled out of the Gaza Strip in August 2005, the al-Qassam Brigades sought to dominate the area in the ongoing effort by Hamas to supplant Fatah. Nevertheless, the brigades decreased their activity against the Israelis by generally honoring the truce that had begun in 2004 and was reiterated in 2005. Meanwhile, the PA was under heavy pressure to disarm Hamas. That attempt failed, however, when Hamas won the 2006 legislative elections and took control of Gaza soon afterward.

In June 2006, the al-Qassam Brigades allegedly supported the capture by Hamas of an IDF soldier, Gilad Shalit, which precipitated the first of many short wars to come over the next few years between Israel and Hamas. Brigade soldiers were heavily involved in the fighting. On July 12, 2006, Mohammed Dayf, a leader of the al-Qassam Brigades, narrowly escaped an Israeli attack on a house in Gaza, in which a Hamas official and his entire family were killed.

During another flare-up in 2008, Egypt brokered a cease-fire in Gaza in June, but the agreement collapsed in November, when Israel killed six Hamas fighters in retaliation for a rocket attack on Israel. This precipitated more rocket fire into Israel. In January 2009, an Israeli air strike killed Nizar Rayan, a top Hamas leader; Israeli attacks killed at least three more Hamas/al-Qassam leaders before the year ended. Israeli air strikes in 2011, 2012, and 2014 killed three other high-ranking fighters. In early 2017, Yahya Sinwar, a former brigade leader, was appointed the political director of Hamas in Gaza.

Paul G. Pierpaoli Jr.

See also: Hamas; Intifada, First; Intifada, Second; Suicide Bombings

Further Reading

La Guardia, Anton. *War Without End: Palestinians and the Struggle for a Promised Land.* New York: Thomas Dunne, 2002.

Mishal, Shaul, and Avraham Sela. *The Palestinian Hamas: Vision, Violence, and Coexistence.* New York: Columbia University Press, 2000.

Smith, Charles D. *Palestine and the Arab-Israeli Conflict: A History with Documents.* 9th ed. New York: Bedford/St. Martin's, 2017.

Jabotinsky, Ze'ev

Writer, soldier, and founder of revisionist Zionist movement. Vladimir Yevgenyevich (Ze'ev Yina) Jabotinsky was born into a middle-class Jewish family in Odessa on October 18, 1880. He left Russia in 1898 to study law in Italy and Switzerland, and then became a highly acclaimed foreign correspondent.

In 1903, when a pogrom seemed imminent in Odessa, Jabotinsky helped form the first Zionist self-defense group. Later that year, he not only worked to organize self-defense units within the Jewish communities of Russia, but also became an outspoken advocate of full civil rights for Russian Jews. Elected a delegate to the Sixth Zionist Congress in Basle in 1903, he opposed a scheme to establish a Jewish homeland in East Africa. Soon the most important Zionist speaker and journalist in Russia, he worked to promote Jewish culture in Russia and helped establish Hebrew University in Jerusalem.

With the beginning of World War I, Jabotinsky became a war correspondent. He met Joseph Trumpeldor in Egypt, and the two men then worked to establish Jewish military units as part of the British army. Jabotinsky believed that the Ottoman Empire was doomed and Jewish support for the Allies in the war would help bring about the creation of a Jewish state in Palestine. Their efforts led to the creation of the Jewish Legion (also known as the *Jewish Battalions*). Enlisting in the 38th Battalion of Royal Fusiliers as a private, Jabotinsky was soon promoted to lieutenant and participated in the British crossing of the Jordan River and the liberation of Palestine from Ottoman rule.

After the war, Jabotinsky joined the Zionist Committee and for a while headed its Political Department. The British authorities in Palestine denied his requests that he be allowed to arm a small number of Jews for self-defense purposes. Nonetheless, he was able to arm about 600 men in secret.

During the April 1920 Arab riots in Jerusalem, Jabotinsky secured permission from the British military government to introduce 100 armed Jews into the city, but when he tried to do this, he was promptly arrested, along with 19 other Jews. The British then searched his residence and discovered arms there. Jabotinsky was tried and sentenced to fifteen years at hard labor for weapons possession. Following a public outcry over the British conclusion that Jews were responsible for the riots, Jabotinsky served only a few months of his jail term. The April 1920 Arab riots, meanwhile, led to the establishment in Palestine of Haganah, the Jewish self-defense organization.

In March 1921, Jabotinsky joined the executive council of the World Zionist Organization (WZO), headed by Chaim Weizmann. Disagreeing sharply with British policies in Palestine and with what he considered the lack of Jewish resistance to them, Jabotinsky resigned from the WZO in January 1923. That same year, he helped found and headed the Betar youth movement.

In 1925, Jabotinsky founded his own organization, the Union of Zionist Revisionists, in Paris and became its president. It called for the immediate establishment in Palestine of a Jewish state. Jabotinsky argued that this state should occupy both sides of the Jordan River, and also for continued immigration until Jews were a majority there and the establishment of a military organization to defend the new creation.

From 1925 on, Jabotinsky made his home in Paris except during 1928–1929, when he lived in Jerusalem and was director of the Judea Insurance Company and edited the Hebrew daily newspaper *Doar Hayom*. In 1929, he left Palestine to attend the Sixteenth Zionist Congress, after which the British administration in Palestine denied him reentry. For the rest of his life, he lived abroad.

When the Seventeenth Zionist Congress of 1931 rejected Jabotinsky's demand that it announce that the aim of Zionism was the creation of a Jewish state, he resigned from the WZO and founded his own New Zionist Organization (NZO) at a congress held in Vienna in 1935. The NZO demanded free immigration of Jews into Palestine and establishment of a Jewish state. Supplementing the NZO were its military arm, the Irgun Tsvai Leumi (National Military Organization), established in 1937 and commanded by Jabotinsky, and the Betar youth movement. Jabotinsky hoped that Betar might train the young Jews of the diaspora so that they could return to Palestine and fight for the establishment of a Jewish state. These organizations cooperated in abetting illegal immigration by ship to Palestine.

Deeply concerned in the 1930s about the plight of Jews in Poland, where there was rampant anti-Semitism, he called for the evacuation of the entire Jewish population of Poland and their relocation to Palestine. During 1939–1940, he traveled in Britain and the United States. He especially sought the establishment of a Jewish army that would fight on the Allied side against Nazi Germany.

Jabotinsky suffered a massive heart attack while visiting a Betar camp near Hunter, New York, and died on August 4, 1940. In 1964, his remains were reinterred in Israel. The state of Israel also created in his honor a medal to recognize distinguished accomplishment.

Spencer C. Tucker

See also: Aliya Bet; Eretz Israel; Irgun Tsvai Leumi; Jewish Legion; Jewish Underground; Zionism

Further Reading

Jabotinsky, Vladimir. *The Story of the Jewish Legion*. New York: Bernard Akerman, 1945.

Katz, Shmel. *Lone Wolf: A Biography of Vladimir Ze'ev Jabotinsky*. 2 vols. Fort Lee, NJ: Barricade Books, 1996.

Sachar, Howard M. *A History of Israel: From the Rise of Zionism to Our Time*. 3rd ed. New York: Knopf, 2007.

Shepherd, Naomi. *Ploughing Sand: British Rule in Palestine, 1917–1948*. New Brunswick, NJ: Rutgers University Press, 1999.

Jerusalem

The disputed capital city of Israel, considered sacred to Judaism, Christianity, and Islam. Jerusalem is a diverse city, tracing its origins to King David's conquest in 1004 BCE of a Jebusite citadel. It is built amid three valleys and four mountains running east to west and is located near the border of the West Bank. Jerusalem covers an area in excess of 42 square miles, with a growing population of some 850,000 (including East Jerusalem), making it the largest city in Israel. Although the demography of the Old City's Armenian, Christian, Jewish, and Muslim quarters remains steady, the modern city witnessed an ever-increasing Jewish population after East Jerusalem was captured in the 1967 Six-Day War.

Jerusalem is sacred to Christians because of its connection to the ministry, crucifixion, and resurrection of Jesus. And it is sacred to Muslims because it is the home of the third-most-sacred shrine in Islam, the al-Aqsa Mosque complex, which includes the Dome of the Rock that marks the spot from which Muhammad ascended at the end of his Night Journey. Finally, Jerusalem is sacred to Judaism because it is the City of David and the Temple Mount, on which three temples were built.

The Ottoman Turks, who ruled Palestine and Jerusalem from the early sixteenth century, allowed some Jewish settlement in the latter part of the nineteenth and early twentieth centuries, but the Zionist movement did not flourish until the British took control of the region during World War I. In 1917, Lieutenant General Sir Edmund Allenby's British troops took Jerusalem as the Turks retreated. The League of Nations granted Britain temporary mandatory control of Palestine and Jerusalem, to act on behalf of both the Jewish and non-Jewish populations in accordance with the 1917 Balfour Declaration which declared British support for the creation of a Jewish homeland in Palestine.

Although there were numerous Arab-Jewish clashes during the period of British mandatory rule, most notably in 1920, 1929, and 1936–1939, the population of the city increased and the economy grew. There were also military/terrorist actions launched against the British in Jerusalem, the most notable being the paramilitary group Irgun's bombing of the King David Hotel on July 22, 1946, killing ninety-one soldiers and civilians. On November 29, 1947, the United Nations (UN) partitioned British-ruled Palestine into an independent Jewish state and an independent Arab state and declared Jerusalem to be an international city to be administered by the UN Trusteeship Council. Jerusalem was to be neither Jewish nor Arab. However, the Arabs did not accept either the partition of Palestine or the internationalization of Jerusalem. In 1948, Israel declared its independence, with Jerusalem as its capital.

The Arab-Israeli War of 1948 ended with Jerusalem divided between the Israelis (West Jerusalem) and the Jordanians (East Jerusalem). The Israelis seized and annexed Jordanian-controlled East Jerusalem (consisting of the Old City and a few neighboring villages) and occupied the West Bank in the June 1967 Six-Day War. Israel then expanded the city's borders into surrounding West Bank villages, adding about twenty-five square miles and thus more than doubling its size. Despite international protests, Israel declared the combined city its capital.

Israeli citizenship was offered to the residents of these annexed territories, but it was conditioned on abdication of their Jordanian citizenship. Most rejected the offer, in part because they did not want to undermine the Palestinian national cause or give tacit approval of Israel's annexation. These Palestinian residents maintain "permanent resident" status today, which allows them free movement within Israel proper, but if they move out of Israel, even into the Palestinian territories, this status is terminated and their reentry denied.

Israel began constructing extensive Jewish settlements around Jerusalem and in the West Bank in the late 1970s and has continued the process to this day, despite repeated UN resolutions and international denunciations. Over 200,000 Jews now live in East Jerusalem. In 1980, Israel's Knesset (parliament) attempted to legitimize these settlements and a "complete and united" Jerusalem as the Israel's "eternal and indivisible capital" by passing the Basic Law: Jerusalem-Capital of Israel. The UN Security Council responded with UN Resolution 478, declaring this law "null and void and must be rescinded forthwith," instructing all UN member-states to withdraw their diplomatic representation from Jerusalem. The vote was 14–0–1, with the United States abstaining.

In 1988, Jordan withdrew all claims to East Jerusalem and the West Bank in favor of the claims of the Palestine Liberation Organization (PLO). The PLO remains adamant that East Jerusalem must be the capital of any future Palestinian state. Jerusalem's status continues to be a major stumbling block to any Palestinian-Israeli peace agreement.

After seizing East Jerusalem in 1967, the Israelis cleared the area in front of the Western (Wailing) Wall, creating a plaza used for prayer. Muslims have at times showered the plaza area with rocks, and the nearby al-Aqsa Mosque complex has been the target of Jewish extremists, most notably a fire started by a delusional Australian tourist in 1969 and a plot by the Gush Emunim (Jewish Underground) in 1984 to blow up the Dome of the Rock. In addition, ancient tunnels running underneath the complex were discovered in 1981, 1988, and 1996. In 1996, Israeli prime minister Benjamin Netanyahu and Jerusalem mayor Ehud Olmert opened an exit for the Western (Wailing) Wall tunnel, sparking three days of Palestinian riots in which more than a dozen Israelis and approximately 100 Palestinians died.

When Israeli prime minister Ariel Sharon visited the Temple Mount/al-Aqsa Mosque complex on September 28, 2000, with hundreds of security personnel in tow, Palestinian faithful saw it as a violation of the sacred environs. This thirty-four-minute visit and the ensuing violence marked the beginning of what is popularly known as Second Intifada, or the al-Aqsa Intifada.

All branches of the Israeli government have their primary offices and buildings located in Jerusalem, with the Knesset building being a well-known landmark. In 2000, Israeli prime minister Ehud Barak suggested that Jerusalem would eventually have to be divided into Israeli and Palestinian sectors in order to secure a durable peace. In 2014, however, Prime Minister Benjamin Netanyahu declared that the city will never be divided. In December 2017, U.S. president Donald Trump broke with decades of American foreign policy and recognized Jerusalem as Israel's capital. On May 14, 2018, the U.S. embassy was officially moved to Jerusalem.

Richard M. Edwards

See also: Arab-Israeli War, 1967; First and Second Temple Periods; Haram al-Sharif/Temple Mount; Jerusalem, Old City; Judaism; Permanent Status Issues; UN Partition Plan for Palestine

Further Reading

Armstrong, Karen. *Jerusalem: One City, Three Faiths*. Reprint ed. New York: Ballantine, 1997.

Cline, Eric H. *Jerusalem Besieged: From Ancient Canaan to Modern Israel*. Ann Arbor: University of Michigan Press, 2004.

Irving, Clifford. *The Battle of Jerusalem: The Six-Day War of June, 1967*. New York: Macmillan: 1970.

Lewis, David A., and Jim Fletcher. *The Last War: The Failure of the Peace Process and the Coming Battle for Jerusalem*. Green Forest, AZ: New Leaf, 2001.

Tamari, Salmi. *Jerusalem 1948: The Arab Neighbourhoods and Their Fate in the War*. Beirut: Institute of Palestine Studies, 1999.

Jerusalem, East (see Jerusalem; Jerusalem, Old City of; Israeli Occupations)

Jerusalem, Old City of

Portion of Jerusalem, with an approximate area of 0.35 square mile, within the imposing walls constructed by Sultan Suleiman the Magnificent (1537–1541). The Old City of Jerusalem is home to the Western (Wailing) Wall, as well as the adjoining Temple Mount (Haram al-Sharif), containing the Dome of the Rock and the al-Aqsa Mosque. The presence of sites sacred to both Jews and Muslims underlies the seemingly irreconcilable Israeli and Palestinian claims to the city as a capital. As the focus of national and religious aspirations, the Old City has been the flashpoint of repeated conflicts, including the Crusades, interethnic and communal strife under the British Mandate (1922–1948), multinational warfare between the 1948 creation of Israel and the 1967 Six-Day War, and thereafter renewed interethnic clashes.

In 1947, the Zionists reluctantly accepted the United Nations (UN) partition of Palestine and its recommendation for the internationalization of Jerusalem, whereas the Arabs rejected both. In 1948, Jordan captured and annexed the Old City. Although both Jordan and Israel tacitly preferred the division of Jerusalem to its internationalization, Jordan expelled the inhabitants of the Jewish Quarter, destroyed its synagogues, and denied Israelis access to its holy places. Thus, for Israelis, Israel's 1967 conquest of the Old City was not just a return, but a liberation. Indeed, Israelis employed this moral argument to buttress historical claims to their control over the city, as heirs to the only state to have had its capital there.

Israeli rule in the Old City, as in united Jerusalem as a whole, remains controversial in areas ranging from municipal services to demographic and cultural policies. On the one hand, Israel left Christians and Muslims in control of their holy places and established a freedom of worship that was lacking under the previous Jordanian administration. On the other hand, Israelis viewed as rectification of past injustices what Arabs saw as unacceptable changes to the status quo. Notably, the latter pointed to the reconstruction and enlargement of the Jewish Quarter and to the more controversial return of a Jewish population to the Old City (only 9 percent of the 37,000 inhabitants, but many of these were religious zealots and adherents of the political right wing), including building seizures by settlers within the Muslim and Christian quarters. Arab politicians and Islamists, for their part, have used purported Israeli threats to the Temple Mount and its mosques as a rallying cry, while dismissing Jewish claims to an ancient historical presence.

The city remained calm during the Yom Kippur War (1973), but the First Intifada (1987–1993) revealed that Jews and Arabs were still worlds apart. Ironically, tensions over symbolic issues increased with the beginning of the Oslo peace process in 1993. Also, virtually all archaeological work in the Old City has been controversial. The Likud Party leader Ariel Sharon's visit to the Temple Mount in the wake of the failed Camp David meetings in 2000 served to trigger the Second (al-Aqsa) Intifada (2000–2004).

In late 2017, U.S. president Donald Trump recognized Jerusalem as Israel's capital, and in 2018, the U.S. embassy was moved there.

James Wald

See also: Arab-Israeli War, 1967; First and Second Temple Periods; Haram al-Sharif/Temple Mount; Israeli Occupations; Jerusalem; Judaism; Settlements; UN Partition Plan for Palestine

Further Reading

Benvenisti, Meron. *City of Stone: The Hidden History of Jerusalem.* Berkeley: University of California Press, 1996.

Dumper, Michael. *The Politics of Sacred Space: The Old City of Jerusalem in the Middle East Conflict.* Boulder, CO: Lynne Rienner, 2002.

Klein, Menachem. *Jerusalem: The Contested City.* Trans. Haim Watzman. New York: New York University Press, 2001.

Jewish Agency

Zionist organization that promoted the formation of an Israeli state in Palestine. Established in 1923, the Jewish Agency for Palestine was intended to speak on behalf of the Yishuv (Jewish community in Palestine) during the British Mandate for Palestine. It operated as the quasi-government for the Yishuv until independence in 1948. It then changed its name to the Jewish Agency for Israel. The organization's goals were the promotion of Jewish immigration to Palestine, the purchase of land to be made a part of Jewish public property, the colonization of farmland to be supported by Jewish labor, the recovery of the Hebrew language, and a renewal of the Hebrew culture.

Following the 1937 Peel Commission Report, the Jewish Agency believed that an impending partition plan was in the works and accelerated Jewish land purchases and colonization along the borders of Palestine. During World War II, the British adopted an essentially pro-Arab policy toward Palestine, especially with regard to the issue of immigration. After the war, the agency shifted its stance from accommodation with the British to physical resistance. The British responded by jailing agency officials. The agency responded to World War II by helping support Haganah (a Jewish paramilitary organization) and secretly conscripting young Jews, both men and women. The agency funded Haganah, promoting military instruction and enabling the purchase of illegal weapons.

Immigration became a point of contention, in that the Jewish Agency was unwilling to back down in the face of German atrocities. The Jewish Agency sought to openly relocate Jewish refugees to Palestine regardless of British immigration quotas, believing that such a policy could take advantage of a horrible situation by demonstrating the insensitivity of British immigration policy in Palestine.

After the establishment of the state of Israel in May 1948, the newly formed Israeli government absorbed most of the Jewish Agency's departments. The agency was made independent of the Israeli government in order to continue its traditional work of absorbing and resettling Jewish refugees. The Jewish Agency also sought to market Israel abroad by promoting interest in Israel among the diaspora and marketing Israeli accomplishments and ambitions for the future.

Brian Parkinson

See also: Ben-Gurion, David; British Mandate for Palestine; Haganah; Yishuv; Zionism

Further Reading

Jewish Agency, The. *The Story of the Jewish Agency for Israel.* New York: The Jewish Agency, American Section, 1964.

Sachar, Howard M. *A History of Israel: From the Rise of Zionism to Our Time.* 3rd ed. New York: Knopf, 2007.

Stock, Ernest. *Chosen Instrument: The Jewish Agency in the First Decade of the State of Israel.* Jerusalem: Herzl, 1988.

Jewish Defense League (JDL)

Jewish nationalist organization with the stated purpose of fighting anti-Semitism. The Jewish Defense League (JDL) was formed by Rabbi Meir Kahane with Morton Dolinsky and Bertam Zweibon in New York in 1968. The Federal Bureau of Investigation (FBI) describes the JDL as "a right-wing terrorist group," while the Southern Poverty Law Center refers to it as a "hate movement" that actively propagates "anti-Arab terrorism." Initially, the JDL focused its attention on the Soviet Union and the plight of Soviet Jews, who were barred from leaving the country to emigrate and resettle in Israel if they wished to do so.

While the group mostly engaged in propaganda and lobbying efforts, it was also connected to a number of violent attacks. These included a bombing outside the Manhattan offices of Aeroflot on November 29, 1970; an attack on the Soviet Cultural Center in Washington, D.C., on January 8, 1971; and an alleged firing spree against the Soviet Union's mission to the United Nations in 1971. In 1975, U.S. authorities accused Kahane, the JDL's founder and leader, of trying to kidnap a

Russian diplomat and bomb the Iraqi embassy in Washington, D.C. He was sentenced to one year in jail for violating probation on another conviction.

Apart from the Soviets, the JDL also targeted neo-Nazis, Holocaust deniers, and other individuals and groups viewed as enemies of the Jewish people. One notable incident attributed to the group was the October 11, 1985, murder of the American-Arab Anti-Discrimination Committee regional director Alex Odah.

Following the fall of the Soviet Union in 1989, the JDL redirected the thrust of its activity toward Middle Eastern states opposed to Israel. This brought the group more squarely into the crosshairs of Arab and Palestinian militants, which culminated in November 1990, when El Sayyid Nosair, an Egyptian American, shot and killed Kahane in front of an audience at a Manhattan hotel. Nosair was later convicted to life imprisonment for the murder, as well as for participating in the 1993 bombing of the World Trade Center in New York.

In 1994, former JDL member Baruch Goldstein slaughtered 29 Palestinians while they were praying and wounded another 125 at the Tomb of the Patriarchs in the West Bank. The JDL lauded the attack, proclaiming on its website that it was "not ashamed to say that Goldstein was a charter member of the Jewish Defense League."

In 2004, the JDL had an internal dispute over legal control of the organization and split into two factions. The groups operated as independent entities for two years before reunifying under the name of B'nai Elim. Other extremist groups associated with the JDL over the years have included Kach, Eyal, Kahane Khai, the Jewish Task Force, and the Jewish Resistance Movement.

Donna Bassett

See also: Hebron; Kahane, Meir; Jewish Underground; Third Temple Movement

Further Reading

Friedman, Robert I. *The False Prophet: Rabbi Meir Kahane, from FBI Informant to Knesset Member.* Westport, CT: Lawrence Hill, 1990.

Gorenberg, Gershom. *The End of Days: Fundamentalism and the Struggle for the Temple Mount.* New York: Oxford University Press, 2000.

Kahane, Rabbi Meir. *The Story of the Jewish Defense League.* Radnor, PA: Chilton, 1975.

Jewish Emigration from Arab Countries

Large-scale immigration to Israel of Arab Jews. Focus on the Israeli-Palestinian conflict (or the broader Israeli-Arab conflict) obscures the fact that Israel is plagued by domestic factional, religious, and ethnic divides as well. One distinction that has affected the development of Israeli society and politics is between Jews of European origin, called Ashkenazim; and Jews emigrating from Middle East and North African (MENA) countries, called Sephardim (Spanish origin; i.e., Maghreb), or, more broadly, Mizrahim (Easterners or Oriental; i.e., Arab). Israel experienced two principal waves of mass immigration in the twentieth century, first in the 1950s, from the MENA region; and later in the 1990s, primarily from the former Soviet Union countries. From 1948 to 1964, 1,213,555 immigrants reached the newly declared state of Israel, 648,160 (53 percent) of whom came from predominantly

Arab and/or Muslim countries such as Yemen, Iraq, Iran, Morocco, Libya, and Tunisia.

While some Jewish migrants chose to make *aliyah* under the Law of Return, many were displaced and forced to leave their homelands because of the intensification of conflict in Israel-Palestine following the declaration of statehood in 1948. Motivated to populate the state and fulfill the Zionist aim of a Jewish homeland in historic Israel, Jewish mass immigration was welcomed. However, Mizrahi arrivals were viewed as backward, uncultured, and inferior in the eyes of the existing (European) Yishuv and other European newcomers.

This period of state development created a social gap between the Ashkenazi and Mizrahi communities resulting from unequal distribution of political power and resources that benefited active advocates of the pioneering Ashkenazi Zionists. The projected image of a universal Jewish experience was designed by, and in the image of, Ashkenazi intellectuals. Forced to leave property and valuables behind, the majority arrived with few resources, lacking the necessary material and human capital to compete in a Western, secular industrial society. As a result, a system of ethnic stratification emerged; Mizrahi immigrants were crucial for enhancing the Jewish demographic in the country, but they were not seen as active contributors to its success. This process has been labeled in Israel's diplomatic pronouncements as a spontaneous population exchange; however, as Palestinians fled or were expelled, Mizrahim underwent an associated trauma, finding themselves in a new Jewish state that viewed their Arabness as inferior. Among ideologies of ethnic and national belonging, hundreds of thousands of Israeli Jews were caught between the false contrast between Jewish and Arab.

In the twenty-first century, following multiple generations of assimilation with the Hebrew language and Israeli culture through schools, military, media, and workplaces, the image of Israeli Jews of Mizrahi origins is changing. The current Minister of Culture and Sport, Miri Regev, identifies proudly as a Mizrahi Israeli Jew and is purposely carrying out projects to celebrate Mizrahi cultural contributions across mediums of art and culture. She faces criticism for her projects, which celebrate Mizrahi Arab culture but omit Palestinian Arab contributions. Nevertheless, her efforts reflect narrowing gaps in both socioeconomic and public discourse and the increased presence of Mizrahi identities into mainstream Israeli culture more broadly.

Kristin Hissong

See also: Demographics in Israel and Palestine; Israelis; Law of Return; Zionism

Further Reading

Chetrit, S. S. *Intra-Jewish Ethnic Conflict in Israel: White Jews, Black Jews*. New York: Routledge, 2010.

Shenhav, Y. "Ethnicity and National Memory: The World Organization of Jews from Arab Countries (WOJAC) in the Context of the Palestinian National Struggle." *British Journal of Middle Eastern Studies* 29, no. 1 (2002): 27–56.

Smooha, S. "The Mass Immigrations to Israel: A Comparison of the Failure of the Mizrahi Immigrants of the 1950s with the Success of the Russian Immigrants of the 1990s." *Journal of Israeli History* 27, no. 1 (2008): 1–27.

Jewish Legion

Formation of Jewish volunteers raised by Great Britain, also known as the *Jewish Battalions,* who fought in World War I. Expelled by the Ottoman Empire, Palestinian Jews who retained citizenship with Entente countries gathered in Egypt in December 1914. Many of them, led by Ze'ev Jabotinsky and Joseph Trumpeldor, petitioned to join the British army. London initially rejected their offer but later formed the 650-man Zion Mule Corps under Colonel John H. Patterson, with Trumpeldor as his second-in-command. The Mule Corps served with distinction in the Gallipoli Campaign, carrying supplies to the front lines until it was disbanded at the campaign's conclusion.

Jabotinsky and others continued to lobby for the creation of Jewish combat units, believing that these would further the Zionist cause. In August 1917, shortly after issuance of the Balfour Declaration, British prime minister David Lloyd George and Foreign Secretary Arthur Balfour approved the formation of a Jewish regiment. Patterson, assisted by Jabotinsky, who became his aide-de-camp, recruited a battalion from Jewish refugees and Mule Corps veterans. This battalion, the 38th Royal Fusiliers (City of London Regiment), completed training in February 1918 and arrived in Alexandria, Egypt, in March. In April, Britain formed the 39th Battalion, primarily with U.S. and Canadian Jewish volunteers, and in June, it recruited the 40th Battalion with Jews who had remained in Palestine. Grouped together and attached to the Australian and New Zealand Mounted Division, the Jewish Legion forced a crossing of the Jordan River, paving the way for Lieutenant General Sir Edmund Allenby's successful autumn offensive and the capture of Damascus.

Britain also formed the 41st and 42nd Reserve Battalions from Jewish volunteers. These remained in Britain and supplied replacements for the three combat battalions. In all, about 6,500 Jews served in these five battalions, including David Ben-Gurion, who would become Israel's first prime minister. Most of these veterans settled in Palestine after the war.

Stephen K. Stein

See also: Balfour Declaration; Ben-Gurion, David; Jabotinsky, Ze'ev; Zionism

Further Readings
Jabotinsky, Vladimir. *The Story of the Jewish Legion.* New York: Bernard Akerman, 1945.
Patterson, John Henry. *With the Zionists in Gallipoli.* New York: George H. Doran, 1916.

Jewish National Fund (JNF)

A Zionist organization founded in 1901 for the purpose of buying land for Jewish settlement in Palestine. Today, the Jewish National Fund (JNF) owns 14 percent of land in Israel. Beginning in 1904, the JNF purchased many plots south of the Sea of Galilee and in central Palestine. Most of the land was purchased from Arab landowners. JNF landholdings grew steadily from 25,000 acres in 1921 to almost 90,000 acres by 1937. This made possible the creation of 108 Jewish settlements. In 1939, 10 percent of the Jewish population in Palestine lived on JNF land. In the summer of 1939, when the British prohibited the establishment of additional Jewish communities, the JNF continued to purchase land and secretly establish new settlements.

The JNF planted millions of trees over thousands of acres as it drained swamps and reclaimed land for agricultural purposes. In 1960, the management of JNF land (apart from forested areas) was transferred to the Israel Land Administration, an Israeli government agency that manages 93 percent of Israeli land. JNF policy forbids leasing land to non-Jews.

Spencer C. Tucker

See also: Absentee Landlords; Israelis; World Zionist Organization; Zionism

Further Reading
Bar-Gal, Yoram. *Propaganda and Zionist Education: The Jewish National Fund, 1924–1947*. London: Boydell and Brewer, 2003.
Lehn, Walter. *The Jewish National Fund*. London: Kegan Paul, 1988.

Jewish Revolts

Uprisings by Jewish groups against Roman rule in Palestine between 66 and 135 CE. The Jewish Revolts marked the last of the Jewish resistance to Roman rule in Palestine. Following their defeats at the hands of the Roman Empire, many Jews were expelled from their homeland.

The First Jewish Revolt, sometimes referred to as the Zealots Revolt, began in 66, but its roots had been planted several years earlier. In 64, the emperor Nero sent Gessius Florus to Judaea to serve as Roman procurator. Florus immediately encountered political crises. In Jerusalem, he angered Jews by seizing the payment of a large fine from the Temple of Jerusalem's treasury. When rioting erupted there, Florus's reprisals were brutal. However, the rebellions continued, and the Romans were soon pushed from most areas of Judaea.

In 67, Nero dispatched Vespasian to Judaea, and after being joined by his son, Titus, Vespasian laid siege to Jotapata in the Galilee region. After forty-seven days, the Jewish commander Joseph Ben Matthias surrendered, eventually becoming the Romans' historian and changing his name to Flavius Josephus. Instead of advancing directly upon Jerusalem, Vespasian cautiously continued suppressing local revolts.

Following Nero's assassination in 68, Vespasian returned to Italy to become emperor, leaving Titus in command of the Judaean legions. Titus marched on Jerusalem in the spring of 70 and captured the Temple of Jerusalem in early August. Roman victory was inevitable, despite the resistance of Eleazar ben Yair at the fortress of Masada in 72. Flavius Silva led the siege of Masada, which finally led to the capture of the fortress in 73, whereupon the defenders committed suicide.

The Second Jewish Revolt, sometimes called Bar Kokhba's Revolt after its leader, began in 132 after the Roman emperor Hadrian banned circumcision and founded a colony in Jerusalem that he renamed Aelia Capitalina. This revolt was led by a messianic figure named Bar Kokhba. In 132, Bar Kokhba expelled Tinnius Rufus, Judaea's consular governor, and struck coins in commemoration of the victory.

Hadrian soon sent a force commanded by the able Sextus Julius Severus, who employed a strategy of attrition against the Jews.

Unable to draw Bar Kokhba into open combat, Severus surrounded strongholds and starved out the rebels. In 135, after a long siege, the Romans captured the fortress of Bethar, the last refuge of Bar Kokhba, who was killed in the battle. As punishment for the rebellion, the Romans changed the name of Judaea to Palestine and expelled most of the Jews who lived there.

Stanley Sandler

See also: First and Second Temple Periods; Masada; Roman Conquest of Judea

Further Reading

Grant, Michael. *The Jews in the Roman World.* New York: Dorset Press, 1984.

Josephus, Flavius. *The Jewish War.* Trans. Geoffrey Arthur Williamson. New York: Penguin Classics, 1984.

Sandler, Stanley, ed. *Ground Warfare: An International Encyclopedia.* Santa Barbara, CA: ABC-CLIO, 2002.

Tacitus, Cornelius. *The Complete Works of Tacitus.* Ed. Moses Hadas. New York: McGraw-Hill Humanities/Social Sciences/Languages, 1964.

Jewish Underground

Jewish terrorist organization active in the early 1980s. In 1980, twenty-seven members of the radical wing of the settler organization Gush Emunim formed the Jewish Underground, under the leadership of Yehudah Etzion. Over the next four years, the Jewish Underground engaged in bombings and shootings. In June 1980, the group carried out car bombing attacks against the mayors of Ramallah and Nablus. Both men lost one or more limbs. A third bombing attempt on the mayor of El Bireh was discovered and forestalled before he started his car. Three years later, the Underground gunned down Palestinian college students in Hebron, killing three and wounded many more.

In 1984, the group's members planned to blow up multiple buses carrying Palestinians, but they were arrested by Shin Bet agents on the night of the operation after planting the bombs, but before they went off. During the ensuing investigation, it was uncovered that the group had stolen explosives from Israeli army depots and planned to blow up the Muslim Dome of the Rock, on the Haram al-Sharif/Temple Mount in Jerusalem. Members of the Jewish Underground received prison sentences ranging from seven years to life in prison, but an extensive lobbying campaign by Likud and the National Religious Party (NRP) led to reduced sentences. Even the three members convicted of murder in the Hebron shooting incident and sentenced to life in prison were pardoned by Israeli president Chaim Herzog in 1990.

Robert C. DiPrizio

See also: Gush Emunim; Haram al-Sharif/Temple Mount; Shin Bet

Further Reading

Lustick, Ian. *For the Land and the Lord: Jewish Fundamentalism in Israel.* New York: Council on Foreign Relations: 1988.

Segal, Haggai. *Dear Brothers the West Bank: Jewish Underground.* Washington, DC: Bet Shamai Pubns: 1988.

Jordan

Hashemite kingdom neighboring Israel that has played an important role in the Arab-Israeli conflict. After World War I, Britain obtained a mandate from the League of Nations to rule over Palestine, which previously had been part of the Ottoman Empire. To reward the Hashemites for supporting the Arab Revolt against the Ottomans, Britain divided its mandate in two, creating Transjordan east of the Jordan River and placing Abdullah ibn Husayn, son of Sharif Husayn of Mecca (leader of the 1916 Arab Revolt and coauthor of the McMahon-Husayn Correspondence) in charge. In 1946, Transjordan gained its independence, although Britain maintained a strong presence. King Abdullah kept close relations with the Zionist leaders in Palestine and even secretly discussed carving up Palestine. When the United Nations (UN) created a plan to divide Palestine into Jewish and Arab states in 1947, Abdullah was the only Arab leader to approve the plan, figuring that he could take control of the Arab state.

During the 1948 Arab-Israeli War, the British-trained Transjordan army was the most proficient of the Arab armies arrayed against Israel—so much so, in fact, that King Abdullah was made commander-in-chief of all Arab forces. It proved to be an empty title, however, as the Arab armies were unable to coordinate their campaigns and were defeated by the Israelis. Still, Abdullah's army took control of the Old City of Jerusalem and the West Bank, which the king then annexed. Jordan is the only country that offered Palestinian refugees full citizenship.

In April 1950, Transjordan became Jordan. The annexation of the West Bank was not popular, either in the wider Arab world or among many Palestinians, one of whom assassinated Abdullah in 1951. His grandson, Husayn, became king in 1953. King Husayn purged the Jordanian army of British influence in 1956, and in 1957, he suppressed an attempted communist coup by declaring martial law. From 1957 on, the Jordanian armed forces have acted completely in accordance with the wishes of the monarchy. The Jordanian army was even able to incorporate exclusively Palestinian units within its ranks without difficulty. For the most part, however, the senior staff of the Jordanian army is drawn from men of Bedouin background.

Jordan did not participate again in active conflict against Israel until the 1967 Six-Day War, when it was overwhelmed by the preemptive Israeli attack. Jordan abandoned Jerusalem and the entire West Bank to avoid having its army completely destroyed. False reports of Egyptian successes and the lack of promised reinforcements from Iraq, Saudi Arabia, and Syria contributed to the Jordanian debacle. King Husayn had hesitated to enter the war, but he did so primarily because if he did not participate, the expected Arab victory would have left him the odd man out in the Arab world.

Jordan subsequently abstained from open warfare with Israel and concentrated on suppressing the Palestine Liberation Organization (PLO), which by the early

1970s was threatening his grip on power. Following an assassination attempt, King Husayn ordered his military to expel the PLO, in what became known as *Black September*. In the course of this internal conflict, Jordan administered a bloody nose to Syrian forces that attempted to assist the PLO. King Husayn reportedly asked for Israeli assistance in his efforts to restrain Syria. Israel moved troops to its border with Syria and Jordan and put its air force on alert, but the conflict ended without direct Israeli interdiction. Israel has long considered Jordan a buffer state to more powerful regional enemies (especially Iraq); as such, Israel has sought to help maintain the stability and independence of the Hashemite kingdom.

Israel often looked to Jordan as a possible solution to its Palestinian problems. Some sought to create a Jordanian-Palestinian federation. Other Israelis, however, insisted that Palestinians should move to Jordan because it was already a Palestinian state, as it was carved out of the original Palestinian Mandate and half its population is Palestinian. But King Husayn abandoned any claim to the West Bank and East Jerusalem in 1988, after the First Intifada erupted.

King Husayn refused to condemn Iraqi dictator Saddam Husayn's invasion of Kuwait in August 1990, and Jordan did not participate in the anti-Saddam military coalition during the 1991 Persian Gulf War. This badly strained Jordanian's relations with its neighbors and the United States and provoked a steep decline in the nation's economy. It also encouraged King Husayn to publicly support the U.S. postwar efforts to jump-start Arab-Israeli peace negotiations. In October 1994, after the Oslo Accords were signed between Israel and the Palestinians, Jordan signed a peace treaty with Israel, thus recognizing what has long been a tacit alliance.

When King Husayn died in 1999, his eldest son, Abdullah, took the throne. Like his father before him, Abdullah II has maintained close relations with Israel and the Palestinians, often playing the role of interlocutor. The Arab Spring did not trigger in Jordan the kind of intense popular uprisings experienced in Egypt, Libya, and Syria, but the monarchy has faced popular protests and pressure for political and economic reforms. Initially, the Hashemite kingdom faced widespread unrest among some Palestinian tribes and Islamist groups protesting economic privation, governmental corruption, and Jordan's relations with Israel. Protesters have also called for more public input into the governing system.

King Abdullah II has cracked down on some dissenters while pursuing high-profile corruption cases and reshuffling his cabinet ministers numerous times. Islamist groups have become more popular in recent years, and the economy is strained by nearly a million refugees from Syria, Iraq, and Yemen.

Walter Boyne and Robert C. DiPrizio

See also: Abdullah II, King of Jordan; Arab Spring; Black September; Husayn ibn Ali, Sharif of Mecca; McMahon-Husayn Correspondence; Palestine Liberation Organization

Further Reading

Nevo, Joseph. *King Husayn and Jordan's Perception of a Political Settlement with Israel, 1967–1988*. Sussex, UK: Sussex Academic Press, 2006.

Rubin, Avshalom. *The Limits of the Land: How the Struggle for the West Bank Shaped the Arab-Israeli Conflict*. Bloomington: Indiana University Press, 2017.

Ryan, Curtis R. *Jordan and the Arab Uprisings: Regime Survival and Politics Beyond the State*. New York: Columbia University Press, 2018.

Susser, Asher. *Israel, Jordan, and Palestine: The Two-State Imperative*. Waltham, MA: Brandeis University Press, 2011.

Wilson, Mary C. *King Abdullah, Britain and the Making of Jordan*. Cambridge: Cambridge University Press, 1990.

Judaism

Religion holding that there is one all-powerful God (Yahweh) and the Jews are his chosen people. Judaism states that all Jews have a personal relationship with God, which is enacted through individual conduct. God has revealed Himself through prophets and great events. Historical events are therefore seen as crucial guides to the development and meaning of Judaism. The primary Jewish scripture, the Torah, devotes large sections to the recording of that history. Most Jews do not believe that their Messiah has come yet, but he will someday.

Judaism is a relatively small world religion, with fewer than 20 million followers worldwide. Its spread has not occurred via the conversion of nonbelievers, as is the case with other religions, but via the migration of Jews from the modern Middle East throughout much of the world, in what is called the *Jewish diaspora*. However, the relatively small number of Jews belies the religion's significance: Judaism provided the philosophical and historical foundation from which two of the world's largest religions, Christianity and Islam, sprang.

HISTORY OF JUDAISM

Judaism dates back to about 2000 BCE, when God made a covenant with Abraham that in exchange for obedience, he would become the father of a great nation that will live in "a land of milk and honey" (aka the Promised Land, the borders of which are nebulous but include what we now call *Israel/Palestine*) that will be protected by God. Drought forced Abraham's descendants to roam northern Arabia for years until they were enslaved by Egyptian pharaohs.

In the thirteenth century BCE, Moses emerged as a leader to guide the Jews out of enslavement and back to the Promised Land, which had become occupied by the Canaanites. Moses led the Jews through the Sinai Desert. At Mount Sinai, he climbed to the top of the mountain to meet with God, who initiated a covenant with the Jewish people consisting of the Ten Commandments. Because the covenant was accepted by the Jewish people, all Jewish descendants are bound to it.

The commandments are the basic ethical code of Judaism. They include pronouncements not to kill, commit adultery, steal, bear false witness, use God's name in vain, worship any likeness of God, or covet one's neighbor's possessions or wife. In addition, God invoked Jews to worship Him as the sole god, to honor one's father and mother, and to keep the Sabbath as a day of rest once a week. So long as the Jews abided by these commandments, God would protect them and assure them prosperity.

After forty years, the Jews finally crossed the Jordan River under the leadership of Joshua. Their arrival coincided with the arrival of the Philistines, a seafaring tribe that also envisioned their future in the land occupied by the Canaanites. The three groups struggled for domination for more than 200 years, until King David prevailed and established a Jewish kingdom. His son and successor, Solomon, built a great temple in Jerusalem. Before long, however, the kingdom collapsed and divided into two parts. In both of the divided kingdoms, Jews strayed from worshipping only Yahweh despite the pleas of the Jewish prophets, who condemned the occultism and illicit behaviors of their brethren. The prophets took on the responsibility for the character of the Jewish religion. They equated human conduct to ethical principles and moral obligations and claimed that good conduct was more important than fulfilling religious ceremony. They stressed the inward quality of religion as a personal relationship between the individual and God.

In the sixth century BCE, the ruling Babylonians exiled the Jews three times, the most important of which took place in 587, when the Babylonians destroyed the Temple of Solomon. Those exiles marked the beginning of the diaspora, the scattering of Jews throughout the world.

In 538, nearly fifty years after the temple was destroyed, the Persian king Cyrus the Great allowed the Jews back to Jerusalem, where they built a new temple. Under the leadership of Nehemiah and Ezra, a Jewish theocratic state was created in the fifth century BCE, which ruled according to the dictates of the Torah. It was during that time that many of the diverse practices of the Jews were consolidated into

Torahs on display in the Jerusalem Great Synagogue. The ethical tradition laid down in the Torah is the moral foundation of Judaism, Christianity, and Islam. (Corel)

a single religion. In 332 BCE, Alexander the Great conquered the region (then known as *Palestine*) and brought Greek civilization with him. The Roman general Pompey the Great entered Palestine in 63 BCE and quickly occupied it as a Roman district.

After years of repression, the Jews revolted against Rome in 66 CE but the uprisings were put down in brutal fashion. Jerusalem was destroyed and the temple burned to the ground. The Jews were exiled from Palestine and scattered throughout the Mediterranean lands.

The center of Jewish life shifted westward to Spain for several centuries until the Muslims conquered the region in the eighth century. When Christian rule returned to Spain in the fourteenth and fifteenth centuries, the Jews were expelled. By that time, they were scattered throughout Europe and under constant threat of persecution in most European and Arabic countries. In 1555, the pope authorized the containment of Jews in ghettos and placed tight restrictions on their activities. They became subject to uprisings known as *pogroms*. Nevertheless, they developed new languages, such as the Sephardim (a mixture of Hebrew and Spanish) and Yiddish (a mixture of Hebrew and German), and kept the Jewish traditions alive. Jews in Arab nations faced similar hardships. They lived in their own communities and engaged in specific occupations, like metalworking.

ELEMENTS OF JUDAISM

The Jewish Bible (known as the *Old Testament* by Christians) outlines the central components of Jewish beliefs. The Bible (which means "books" in Greek) consists of three main sections: the *Torah* (Law), *Neviim* (The Prophets), and *Ketuvim* (Writings). Those writings, which are supplemented by a collection of more modern writings called the *Talmud*, describe Jewish tradition, laws, priorities, religious ceremonies, and codes of conduct. The Torah consists of the books of Genesis, Exodus, Leviticus, Numbers, and Deuteronomy; it is considered the most significant scripture.

After the Bible, the next most important writings for Judaism comprise the Talmud, a collection of commentaries and traditions, and the Midrash, a series of interpretations of Scripture. The two are often considered as recordings of the oral version of the written Bible. Both those collections are studied in Judaism to supplement the knowledge imparted in the Bible.

Throughout the centuries, Judaism has encompassed many interpretations. At the time of Jesus of Nazareth, several sects existed. During the diaspora, as Jewish groups became scattered and isolated throughout the world, various versions of Judaism evolved. One important distinction is between Ashkenazim, or European Jews, whose culture evolved in eastern and central Europe, and Sephardim, or Oriental Jews, whose culture evolved in Spain, North Africa, and the Middle East.

David Levinson

See also: Babylonian Conquest of Judah; First and Second Temple Periods; Israelis; Israelite Conquest of Canaan; Roman Conquest of Judea; United Kingdom of Israel; Zionism

Further Reading

Dosick, Wayne. *Living Judaism: The Complete Guide to Jewish Belief, Tradition, and Practice.* San Francisco: Harper, 1995.

Robinson, George. *Essential Judaism: A Complete Guide to Beliefs, Customs & Rituals.* New York: Pocket Books/Simon and Schuster, 2001.

Silver, Daniel Jeremy. *A History of Judaism: From Abraham to Maimonides.* New York: Basic Books, 1974.

Judea and Samaria

Biblical names for the geographic regions corresponding to much of today's Israel and Palestinian territories. Lying west of the Jordan River and the Dead Sea and extending to the Mediterranean Sea, Judea and Samaria were home to the ancient Israelites. According to biblical tradition, following the division of the united Kingdom of Israel, Samaria became home to the northern kingdom, also known as the Kingdom of Israel, while Judea in the south was home to the Kingdom of Judah. Samaria takes its name from the city of Samaria, the northern kingdom's capital, while Judea's etymology is derived from the word *Judah*. These kingdoms eventually fell to Assyrian and Babylonian conquest.

During Roman rule of the region, Judea was a Roman province covering traditional Judea and Samaria and beyond. In the second century CE, the province was merged with that of Syria and renamed *Syria Palaestina.* The moniker of *Palestine* remained a common name for the region through the establishment of Israel in 1948. Today, Judea and Samaria are the preferred terms of many Israelis and their supporters when referring to the West Bank.

Sean P. Braniff

See also: Israeli Occupations; United Kingdom of Israel; West Bank; Zionism

Further Reading

Josephus. *The New and Complete Works of Josephus.* Trans. William Whiston. Commentary by Paul L. Maier. Grand Rapids, MI: Kregel Publications, 1999.

Ochsenwald, William, and Sydney Nettleton Fisher. *The Middle East: A History,* 7th ed. New York: McGraw-Hill, 2010.

K

Kahane, Meir

Rabbi and leader of a fanatical wing of the Zionist movement, and the founder of the Jewish Defense League (JDL). Meir Kahane was born August 1, 1932, in Brooklyn. His father was a staunch Zionist supporter of Ze'ev Jabotinsky, an early radical Zionist leader. When Kahane was six, Arabs massacred members of his family living in Palestine. At fourteen, he joined Betar, a right-wing Zionist youth organization. A year later, he physically attacked the British foreign minister, Ernest Bevin, in New York City. He received a suspended sentence for this assault. Kahane attended the Brooklyn Talmudical Academy and Brooklyn College, as well as the Orthodox Yeshiva Mirrer, and was ordained as a rabbi in 1957.

After his schooling, Kahane worked as a writer for the *Brooklyn Daily* and the *Jewish Press*. He also served as a spy for the Federal Bureau of Investigation (FBI), monitoring left-wing radicals. He then worked for the Central Intelligence Agency (CIA), promoting support among Orthodox Jews for the Vietnam War. He used his newspaper contacts to convince Jews to volunteer to fight in Vietnam.

Kahane became a national leader in the extremist wing of the Orthodox Zionist movement in June 1968 when he founded the JDL with Morton Dolinsky and Bertam Zweibon. The JDL was ostensibly intended to protect Jews from physical attacks by blacks on the streets of New York City; however, Kahane turned it into an organization that attacked perceived enemies of Jews using all types of tactics, including violence. Among these perceived enemies were Arabs, Palestinians, and Soviets. In May 1971, U.S government authorities imprisoned him briefly on charges of conspiracy to manufacture explosives. A Mafia boss, Joseph Columbo, bailed him out. Kahane pleaded guilty and received four years' probation. His growing friendship with Columbo allowed the JDL to obtain weapons and money. Eager to carry his ideas to Israel, and one step ahead of a federal indictment for his attacks on Soviet diplomats, Kahane emigrated to Israel in August 1971, along with a large number of his supporters.

Kahane earned a reputation in Israel as the most radical exponent of extreme Zionism. Right-wing Israeli leaders, especially Menachem Begin, welcomed his arrival. Kahane was offered leadership positions in several conservative parties, but he rejected all of them to form a JDL organization in Israel. He advocated the removal of Palestinians from all territories occupied by Israel and the settlement by Jewish settlers of these lands, including the West Bank.

Kahane based his anti-Palestinian policy on the belief that violence is justified in the name of Jewish survival. To carry out this program, Kahane formed the Kach (Only Thus) Party in 1971. He started an Israeli death squad, the Terror Against Terror (TAT), to assassinate Palestinian leaders and pro-peace Israelis.

He also plotted to blow up the Dome of the Rock in Jerusalem. For these actions, Kahane spent six months in detention in 1980. While in detention, Kahane wrote the anti-Palestinian treatise *They Must Go*. After several attempts to win a seat in the Knesset, Kahane was successful in 1984, but the Israeli government banned Kahane's Kach Party from the 1988 election for being racist and undemocratic.

Kahane often traveled back to the United States to direct JDL activities there and to conduct fund-raising tours. In 1975, he formed a JDL terrorist group, the Jewish Armed Resistance, to carry out attacks against selected U.S. and Soviet targets. After a two-year campaign of bombings in 1975 and 1976, most of those members were captured and sentenced to long prison terms. Kahane disavowed them and left them to their fate.

A gunman assassinated Kahane on November 5, 1990, in New York City. Kahane's funeral attracted most of the significant leaders of the Israeli radical right. An Egyptian-born Muslim, El Sayyid Nosair, was charged with murdering Kahane but was convicted only on assault, coercion, and weapons charges and sentenced to a fifteen-year jail term. Kahane was buried in Israel, and his grave is protected by his supporters. With his death, Kahane became a martyr to the extreme right and religious wings of the Zionist movement.

Stephen E. Atkins

See also: Jewish Defense League; Jewish Underground; Third Temple Movement; Zionism

Further Reading

Friedman, Robert I. *The False Prophet: Rabbi Meir Kahane—From FBI Informant to Knesset Member.* Westport, CT: Lawrence Hill Books, 1990.

Juergensmeyer, Mark. *Terror in the Mind of God: The Global Rise of Religious Violence.* Berkeley: University of California Press, 1999.

Kahane, Meir. *They Must Go.* 5th printing. CreateSpace Independent Publishing Platform, 2012.

Katyusha Rockets

Medium-range rockets used by Hamas and Hezbollah to attack Israel. First developed by the Soviet Union during World War II, the unguided Katyusha rocket is not particularly accurate, but it can be launched from light trucks and even human-portable launchers. Katyushas have been employed by Hezbollah and the Palestinian Islamic Jihad (PIJ) against Israel. In March 2006, a Katyusha was fired into Israel from the Gaza Strip—the first time that one had been sent into Israel from Palestinian-controlled territory. The nine-foot, two-inch BM-21 variant has a range of nearly thirteen miles and a warhead of nearly thirty-five pounds

Katyushas are much more of a worry to Israel than the short-range, homemade Qassam rockets fired by Hamas. The United States developed the Tactical High-Energy Laser (THEL) system specifically to defeat the Katyusha during flight. Hamas fired numerous Katyushas into Israel during the 2012 and 2014 conflicts with Israel; many were intercepted and destroyed by Israel's Iron Dome missile defense system. In recent years, Iran has reportedly been supplying Hezbollah with sophisticated guiding systems to retrofit its Katusha rockets.

Spencer C. Tucker

See also: Hamas; Izz al-Din al-Qassam Brigades; Syria

Further Reading

Bellamy, Chris. *Red God of War: Soviet Artillery and Rocket Forces.* London: Brassey's, 1986.

O'Malley, T. J. *Artillery: Guns and Rocket Systems.* Mechanicsburg, PA: Stackpole, 1994.

Khartoum Resolution

A joint resolution passed on September 1, 1967, in Khartoum, Sudan, by eight member-states of the Arab League: Algeria, Egypt, Iraq, Jordan, Kuwait, Lebanon, Sudan, and Syria. Coming in the immediate wake of the stunning Israeli success of the June 1967 Six-Day War, the heads of eight Arab countries convened in Khartoum during August 29–September 1, 1967, with the express purpose of establishing a united front against Israel. As a result of the recent war, the Israelis had seized the Sinai Peninsula, the West Bank, the Gaza Strip, and the Golan Heights.

The Khartoum Resolution—actually a series of resolutions—not only established official Arab positions vis-à-vis Israel and the Arab-Israeli conflict, but also acted as a vehicle by which Arab nations drew closer together and helped them put aside their differences. Perhaps most notable in this regard was Egyptian president Gamal Abdel Nasser's pledge to cease and desist from his ongoing attempts to destabilize the Middle East and topple Arab monarchies in the Persian Gulf. In return, Egypt was promised economic incentives, which it sorely needed at the time. The idea of supranational Arab unity, then, took a back seat to national and regional stability.

The Khartoum Resolution stressed seven principles. First, warfare against Israel would continue. Second, the oil boycott enacted against the West during the Six-Day War was to end. Third, the Yemeni civil war should be ended. Fourth, economic aid packages for Egypt and Jordan would commence as soon as was practical. Resolutions 5 through 7, soon to be known as the "three nos," stated unequivocally that there would be no peace with Israel, no recognition of Israel, and no negotiations with the Israelis.

The Khartoum Resolution seemed to close the door to any potential peace deal between Arabs and Israelis and lent credence to hardliners in the Israeli government, who were arguing that peace initiatives with the Arabs were pointless. Over the subsequent years, several of the countries involved in the Khartoum Resolution backed away from its positions, beginning with Egypt after the 1973 Yom Kippur War.

Paul G. Pierpaoli Jr.

See also: Arab League; Arab-Israeli War, 1967; Arab-Israeli War, 1973; Nasser, Gamal Abdel

Further Readings

Bickerton, Ian J., and Carla L. Klausner. *A Concise History of the Arab-Israeli Conflict*. 8th ed. New York: Praeger Press, 2017.

Schulze, Kirsten E. *The Arab-Israeli Conflict*. New York: Longman, 1999.

Kibbutz

A Jewish communal settlement in Palestine/Israel. The kibbutz (pl. *kibbutzim*) is a uniquely Israeli farming, industrial, or tourist community. These were first founded in 1909 as a means of settling Jews in Palestine on land leased from and purchased by the Jewish National Fund (JNF) with coins dropped by Jews worldwide into special "Blue Boxes." Kibbutzim combined Zionism and communism at a time when the harsh environment and dangers of Palestine made individual farming impractical. Joseph Baratz founded the first kibbutz, Degania, at the southern end of the Sea of Galilee.

All kibbutzim played defensive roles in the creation of Israel, but some were founded for the specific, strategic purpose of defining, expanding, and protecting the borders of the Jewish community in Palestine both before and after the partition of Palestine by the United Nations. Kibbutzim were started in the 1930s by those anticipating partition rather than the formation of a binational government. These kibbutzim were intended to expand the land area to be incorporated into Israel by establishing a Jewish presence well before the boundaries of partition were

A kibbutz in Israel. These uniquely Zionist communal settlements contributed both to the economic development and security of the Jewish community in Palestine. (Wing Travelling/Dreamstime.com)

determined. In addition, some kibbutzim, called *Tower and Stockade kibbutzim,* were established overnight in the years prior to partition for the specific purpose of enhancing land claims antecedent to partition. A dozen of these kibbutzim, for example, were erected overnight in the northern Negev in 1946. This trend of establishing strategic kibbutzim for establishing, stabilizing, and enhancing the defensive perimeters continued through the 1960s under the Nahal group of the Israel Defense Forces (IDF).

The role of the kibbutzim in the defense of Israel is illustrated by the casuality figures from the 1967 Six-Day War. Israel lost 800 soldiers, but even though kibbutzniks numbered less than 4 percent of the total Israeli population at the time, 200 of these deaths were kibbutzniks.

Richard M. Edwards

See also: Aliya; Arab-Israeli War, 1948; Arab-Jewish Communal War, 1947; Haganah

Further Reading
Gavron, Daniel. *The Kibbutz.* Lanham, MD: Rowman & Littlefield, 2000.
Leviatan, Uriel, Hugh Oliver, and Jack Quarter, eds. *Crisis in the Israeli Kibbutz: Meeting the Challenges of Changing Times.* Events of the Twentieth Century series. Haverhill, MA: Praeger, 1998.
Near, Henry. *The Kibbutz Movement: A History.* 2 vols. London: Vallentine Mitchell, 1997.

King David Hotel Bombing

A Jewish terror attack on a Jerusalem hotel. On July 22, 1946, a bomb exploded in the basement of the King David Hotel, which at the time housed the headquarters of the British army and the secretariat of the Palestinian government. The blast killed ninety-one people, including seventeen Jews, and injured forty-five others. It was the deadliest terrorist act directed at the British during the Mandate era (1920–1948).

The Irgun Tsvai Leumi (known as Irgun for short) claimed responsibility, declaring that the attack was in retaliation for a June 29, 1946, British raid on the Jewish Agency for Palestine. That sweep had netted a large quantity of information detailing the agency's operations and links with violent groups, and this material was then taken to the King David Hotel.

The immediate British response was to declare martial law and initiate a house-to-house search that resulted in the detention of 133 men and 10 women. The British government then enacted widely unpopular restrictions on the civil liberties of Jews in Palestine, which included military curfews, roadblocks, and mass arrests. The measures shifted British public opinion further against the Mandate system and alienated the Jewish populace, which had been Irgun leader Menachem Begin's intention from the beginning.

Donna Bassett

See also: British Mandate for Palestine; Irgun

Further Reading
Boyer Bell, J. *Terror out of Zion: Irgun Zvai Leumi, Lehi, and the Palestine Underground, 1929–1949.* New York: St. Martin's, 1979.

Clarke, Thurston. *By Blood and Fire: July 22, 1946: The Attack on Jerusalem's King David Hotel*. New York: Putnam's Sons, 1981.

Kingdom of Israel

The northern of two kingdoms, composed of ten of the twelve tribes descending from the patriarch Jacob that lived in Palestine after the united monarchical period of David and Solomon. The Kingdom of Israel split from the Kingdom of Judah around 928 BCE and lasted until conquered by the Assyrians between 732 and 721 BCE. The people in this territory accepted Phoenician influence and assimilated to the religious practices of their neighbors. According to the biblical narrative, a total of nineteen kings ruled during this time period. With three-quarters of the combined population of the two kingdoms, and most of the territory, Israel was stronger than Judah militarily and economically.

At one point, Jehoash, king of Israel, thoroughly defeated Judah's king (Amaziah; 797–768 BCE) and armies. Archaeologists claim that the northern kingdom consisted of rural, poorly unfortified settlements until the sixth king, Omri (884–873 BCE), embarked on a monumental building campaign. The Assyrian records referred to this kingdom by reference to Omri, who established a new religious system to compete with that of the southern Kingdom of Judah. The second most significant king, Jeroboam II, ruled for approximately forty years (788–747 BCE) and conquered significant territory, including Damascus, from his neighbors. The kingdom suffered from a number of coups and insurrections, as well as military pressure from the rulers of Damascus, before the conquest by Sargon II, the Assyrian emperor in 722 BCE. The annals of Sargon report that he took over 27,000 people captive—approximately 5 percent of the population.

Jonathan K. Zartman

See also: Assyrian Conquest of Israel; Israelite Conquest of Canaan; Judaism; Kingdom of Judah; United Kingdom of Israel

Further Reading

Finkelstein, Israel. *Forgotten Kingdom: The Archeology and History of Northern Israel*. Atlanta: Society of Biblical Literature, 2013

Kramer, Gudrun. *A History of Palestine: From the Ottoman Conquest to the Founding of the State of Israel*. Trans. Graham Karman and Gudrun Kramer. Princeton, NJ: Princeton University Press, 2008.

Kingdom of Judah

The southern of two kingdoms, initially composed of two tribes—Judah and Benjamin—of the twelve tribes descending from Jacob living in Palestine, after the united monarchical period of David and Solomon. After the Kingdom of Israel split from the Kingdom of Judah around 928 BCE, the latter kingdom endured until conquered by the Babylonians in 586 BCE. Because the leaders of the competing Kingdom of Israel actively promoted a different religious system, significant numbers of the tribe of Levi moved south to continue their leadership function in

Jewish, monotheistic temple worship. Some members of the other tribes also moved to the Kingdom of Judah to participate in its religious practices, rather than those adopted in the Kingdom of Israel.

The Kingdom of Judah survived for almost a century and a half after the demise of the northern Kingdom of Israel. In the biblical record, it had a total of eighteen kings and one queen, all descendants of David. Six of these kings followed monotheism, two had a mixed record, and the rest promoted the competing religious practices of Assyria and neighboring states. As a buffer state between competing great powers of Assyria and Egypt, foreign interference promoted a great deal of intrigues and competing internal political pressures. Although the mountainous terrain offered some defensive advantages, the position of Judah could potentially threaten the lines of communication on the coastal trade and invasion route, as well as along the Jordan River. As such, the kings of Judah sometimes felt compelled to offer tribute to one side or the other, while also facing threats from the lesser powers of Moab and Ammon on the east side of the river. As the power of Assyria declined, Egypt tried to offer aid to prevent the Chaldeans from replacing them.

In 605 BCE, the Chaldeans under Nebuchadnezzar defeated Egypt at the Battle of Carchemish on the Euphrates River. Nebuchadnezzar chased the Egyptians back to their border, and in returning to Babylon, attacked Jerusalem and took some captives and loot, but did not conquer the whole kingdom. Later, the Chaldeans pushed the Aramaeans, Moabites, and Ammonites against Judah for refusing to pay tribute. In 597 BCE, Nebuchadnezzar conquered Jerusalem and took 10,000 leading men and their families captive, in what is called the *first Babylonian captivity*. Jews calculate the Babylonian captivity from this date due to the large number of people and their high status.

After a few years of submission, under pressure from Egypt, King Zedekia refused to pay tribute. The Chaldeans invaded again in 589 and conquered the whole region, with the possible exception of the territory of Benjamin and the area around Bethlehem, which may have surrendered and were thus spared destruction. In 586, the Chaldeans took another large cohort of captives to Babylon, which included members of every tribe.

Jonathan K. Zartman

See also: Babylonian Conquest of Judah; Diaspora, Jewish; Judaism; Kingdom of Israel; United Kingdom of Israel

Further Reading

Kramer, Gudrun. *A History of Palestine: From the Ottoman Conquest to the Founding of the State of Israel*. Trans. Graham Karman and Gudrun Kramer. Princeton, NJ: Princeton University Press, 2008.

Learsi, Rufus, *Israel: A History of the Jewish People*. Cleveland: World Publishing Company, 1949.

Knesset

Israel's parliament. The Knesset is the supreme legislative body of the Israeli state. The first Knesset was elected on January 25, 1949, as a constituent assembly to draw up a constitution for the newly born Israeli state. On June 13, 1950, having disagreed on creating a whole constitution immediately, the constituent assembly called for the gradual creation of a constitution for the state, chapter by chapter, in the form of a series of basic laws.

The Knesset is a unicameral legislature comprised of 120 Members of the Knesset (MKs). MKs are elected every four years according to the electoral system of proportional representation: the number of seats that every party list obtains in the Knesset is proportional to the number of people who voted for it. (Potential candidates are selected within the framework of party lists, which are determined by either the party leadership or party primaries.) The only limitation is the 3.25 percent qualifying threshold. Given the difficulty of obtaining a clear majority, governments are formed through multiparty coalitions under the leadership of the prime minister (usually the leader of the largest party in the Knesset).

In addition to passing legislation and setting the government's budget, the Knesset elects the president, who has limited powers. Also, with a majority of at least sixty-one MKs, the Knesset can remove the prime minister from government and bring about new elections. While Arab-Israeli parties usually earn seats in the Knesset, Israeli political culture excludes them from coalitions.

Sergio Catignani

See also: Israel; Palestinians

Further Reading

Arian, Asher. *The Second Republic: Politics in Israel*. Chatham, NJ: Chatham House, 1998.

Mahler, Gregory. *Politics and Government in Israel: The Maturation of a Modern State*. Lanham, MD: Rowan and Littlefield, 2016.

Kook, Avraham Yitzhak

A controversial and influential Orthodox rabbi. Considered one of the pioneers of religious Zionism, Avraham Yitzhak Kook was a mystic, poet, philosopher, and communal leader. Born in 1865, in what is now Latvia, Kook lived in London prior to World War I, where he cultivated popular support for the Balfour Declaration, which committed Britain to supporting the creation of a Jewish homeland in Palestine. In 1921, he was appointed chief rabbinate of the Jewish population in Palestine. Kook believed that the spirit of God and spirit of the Jewish people were one and the same, and thus support for Zionism was an expression of support for God.

Kook died on September 1, 1935, but his ideas lived on through the teachings of his son, Rabbi Zvi Yhuda Kook, who helped usher in a revival of religious Zionism following Israel's victory in the Six-Day War. The younger Kook emphasized the conservative elements of his father's religious views and his nationalist fervor. He professed that the messianic process of Jewish redemption began when Zionists started to migrate to Palestine, grew with the founding of the state of Israel, and gained momentum with the capture of the West Bank. The views of the Kooks informed the thinking of many adherents to Gush Emunim, a religious group committed to reclaiming all the land that God gave the Jews. Many followers of the Kooks have since organized to oppose territorial concessions to the Palestinians and to settle the West Bank. For many of them, patriotism and religiosity are intertwined.

Robert C. DiPrizio

See also: Eretz Israel; Gush Emunim; Judea and Samaria; Settlements; Third Temple Movement

Further Reading
Mirsky, Yehuda. *Rav Kook: Mystic in a Time of Revolution.* New Haven, CT: Yale University Press, 2014.
Schwartz, Ari Ze'ev. *The Spiritual Revolution of Rav Kook.* Edison, NJ: Gefen Books, 2018.

L

Labor Party

Israeli social-democratic political party. While the Labor Party initially embraced many members who had hawkish outlooks, it has since become more centrist. The party was formed in 1968 by the joining of Mapai, formed in the 1930s as the most moderate of Israeli socialist parties; Ahdut Ha'avodah, a moderate leftist party that had split with the more extreme leftist Mapam Party in 1954; and Rafi, a group that had split from Mapai only three years earlier.

During Israel's first three decades of existence, all Israeli prime ministers came either from the Labor Party or the parties that eventually formed it. David Ben-Gurion, who formed Rafi in 1951 and facilitated the split with Mapai, became the first prime minister of Israel in 1948. He pursued rapid economic development and efforts to increase Israel's Jewish population. Ben-Gurion remained prime minister until 1963, when he resigned the post. When the Labor Party formed in 1968, Levi Eshkol, the Mapai leader, became prime minister. Golda Meir, the first and only female prime minister to date, succeeded Eshkol. Other major Labor leaders have included Yitzhak Rabin and Shimon Peres, who negotiated the Oslo Accords and both served as prime minister; and Ehud Barak, who also served as prime minister and presided over Israel's withdrawal from southern Lebanon in 2000.

Concerning the Arab-Israeli conflict, the modern Labor Party has generally supported a two-state solution, in contrast to its nemesis, the Likud Party. Still, leaders have adopted differing approaches. Some support unconditional peace negotiations with the Palestinians, while others insist that negotiations should proceed only after the current Palestinian leadership is replaced. Others are even less compromising, deemphasizing withdrawal from the West Bank and justifying the targeted killings of Palestinian terrorists. Labor's influence in Israeli politics has greatly declined over the past couple of decades as the electorate has moved right. In the April 2019 Knesset elections, Labor won only 4.5 percent of the vote.

Gregory Morgan

See also: Ben-Gurion, David; Oslo Accords; Peres, Shimon; Rabin, Yitzhak

Further Reading

Ben-Gurion, David. *Israel: A Personal History.* Trans. Nechemia Meyers and Uzy Nystar. New York: Funk and Wagnalls, 1971.

Blumberg, Arnold. *The History of Israel.* Westport, CT: Greenwood, 1998.

Inbar, Efraim. *War and Peace in Israeli Politics.* Boulder, CO: Lynne Reinner, 1991.

Lavon Affair

An Israeli plan to have Jewish-Egyptians attack U.S. and British interests in Egypt, with the aim of alienating the United States and Britain from the regime of Egyptian president Gamal Abdel Nasser. The Lavon Affair of 1954 involved Israel's military intelligence branch, Aman, organizing, training, and funding a group of Egyptian Jewish saboteurs. The operation was named after then-Israeli defense minister Pinhas Lavon, but was the brainchild of Aman chief Colonel Benyamin Gibli.

Aman activated the ring in the spring of 1954, during which they bombed post offices, a railway terminal, two U.S. Information Agency libraries, and a British theater. Egyptian authorities arrested ring member Robert Dassa when his bomb prematurely ignited in his pocket. On October 5, 1954, the Egyptians announced the arrest of an eleven-person spy ring and put them on public trial on December 11. Two of the defendants were acquitted, five received sentences ranging from seven years to life imprisonment, and two were hanged. Two had already committed suicide in prison. Because the Israeli government refused to acknowledge the operation during the trial, the Israeli public remained uninformed, and the Jewish press characterized the trial as an outrageous, anti-Jewish frame-up.

The operation later caused a scandal in the Israeli government, and both Lavon and Gibli were forced to resign their positions. The Lavon Affair also damaged Israel's relations with the United States and Great Britain. Not surprisingly, the operation's tactics caused deep-seated suspicion of Israeli intelligence methods, both in the Middle East and around the world.

Paul J. Magnarella

See also: Arab-Israeli War, 1956; Nasser, Gamal Abdel

Further Reading

Golan, Aviezer. *Operation Susannah*. New York: Harper and Row, 1978.

Hirst, David. *The Gun and the Olive Branch: The Roots of Violence in the Middle East*. 2nd ed. New York: Nation Books, 2003.

Law of Return

Law passed by the first Knesset (Israeli parliament) in July 1950 governing the return of Jews to Israel. The law stated that Israel was a homeland not only for Jews then residing there, but also for Jews everywhere in the world. The law was intended to encourage Jewish settlement in Israel in the long shadow of the Holocaust. Moreover, although Israel had emerged victorious over its Arab neighbors in its War for Independence, Israelis worried both about their small numbers vis-a-vis their far more populous Arab neighbors and the possible return of Palestinians forced from their homes during the war.

The Law of Return was designed to fulfill Theodor Herzl's Zionist vision of a state that would protect all Jews. It affords qualifying Jews nearly automatic citizenship. Excluded from the law are most non-Jews and Jews who are considered an imminent danger to public health, state security, or the Jewish people as a whole.

Jewish migrants arriving at Ben-Gurion International Airport. Israel's Law of Return allows Jews from around the world to attain nearly instantaneous citizenship when they step foot in the country. (Rafael Ben Ari/Dreamstime.com)

In 1970, the Knesset amended the Law of Return to allow additional immigration, especially from the United States. It offered the right of immigration not only to Jews (a Jew was defined as a person born of a Jewish mother or who had converted to Judaism), but also to the children and grandchildren of Jews, to the non-Jewish spouses of Jews, to the non-Jewish spouses of children of Jews, and even the non-Jewish spouses of non-Jewish grandchildren of Jews.

Since the mid-1980s, tensions in the Middle East and the influx of East European Jews into Israel have challenged the efficacy of the law. By December 1994, the large influx of Jews from the former Soviet Union placed an economic, social, and cultural strain on Israel. The Israeli government attempted to ease the crisis by creating temporary settlements in the West Bank, but this led to a military confrontation with the Palestinians.

One major issue has been that of who has authority over the validity of conversions to Judaism in order to emigrate to Israel and be eligible for citizenship. In a decision that angered Orthodox leaders, in March 2005 the Israeli Supreme Court ruled 7–4 that all conversions to Judaism conducted outside Israel would be ruled as valid under the Law of Return.

Jaime Ramón Olivares and Spencer C. Tucker

See also: Herzl, Theodor; Israelis; Judaism; Knesset; Zionism

Further Reading
Cohe, Michael J., ed. *The Rise of Israel, 1938–1945*. New York: Garland Publishing, 1987.

Friedman, Isaiah. *The Rise of Israel. From Precursors of Zionism to Herzl*. New York: Garland Publishing, 1987.

Harris, Ron. *The History of Law in a Multi-Cultural Society: Israel 1917–1967*. Aldershot, UK: Ashgate, 2002.

Lawrence, T. E.

British army officer who assisted the Arab Revolt against the Ottoman Empire. Born on August 15, 1888, in Wales, Thomas E. Lawrence was educated at Jesus College, Oxford. Upon the outbreak of World War I, Lawrence was sent to Cairo and served as an intelligence officer concerned with Arab affairs. In October 1916, he accompanied a mission to the Hejaz, where Husayn ibn Ali, Sharif of Mecca, had proclaimed a revolt against the Turks. The following month, Lawrence was ordered to join as liaison officer to Husayn's son, Faysal, commanding an Arab force southwest of Medina. He was instrumental in acquiring considerable material assistance from the British army for the Arab cause. Recognizing that the key to Turkish control lay in the Damascus-Medina railway, Lawrence accompanied Faysal and his army in a series of attacks on the railway.

On July 6, 1917, Lawrence led a force of Huwaitat tribesman in the capture of the port of Aqaba, at the northernmost tip of the Red Sea. It became the base for Faysal's army. From there, he attempted to coordinate Arab movements with the campaign of General Sir Edmund Allenby, who was advancing from Jerusalem in southern Palestine.

Lawrence was never a leader of Arab forces; command always remained firmly in the hands of Emir Faysal. He was, however, an inspirational force behind the Arab Revolt, a superb tactician, and a highly influential theoretician of guerrilla warfare. During the last two years of the war, Lawrence's advice and influence effectively bound the Arab nations to the Allied cause, thereby tying down about 25,000 Turkish troops who would otherwise have opposed the British army. Despite his efforts, Lawrence witnessed the defeat of his aspirations for the Arabs when their seemingly incurable factionalism rendered them incapable of becoming a nation. Upon returning to England, Lawrence lobbied vainly against the detachment of Syria and Lebanon from the rest of the Arab countries as a French mandate.

Lawrence became an almost mythic figure in his own lifetime. His reputation was to an extent self-generated through his own literary accounts, including his war memoir *The Seven Pillars of Wisdom* (1922), and lecture tours, assisted by his postwar election to a research fellowship at Oxford University. He died at Bovington Camp Hospital on May 19, 1935, following a motorcycle accident.

James H. Willbanks

See also: Arab Revolt, 1916; British Mandate for Palestine; Husayn ibn Ali, Sharif of Mecca

Further Reading

Korda, Michael. *The Life and Legend of Lawrence of Arabia*. New York: Harper, 2010.

Lawrence, Thomas E. *The Seven Pillars of Wisdom: A Triumph*. Garden City, NY: Doubleday, Doran, 1935.

Schneider, James. *Guerrilla Leader: T. E. Lawrence and the Arab Revolt*. New York: Bantam, 2011.

League of Nations

A supranational organization formed in the aftermath of the Paris Peace Conference held at the end of World War I. Article 22 of the League of Nations Covenant called for the creation of a mandate system that transferred the former colonies of Germany and the former territories of the Ottoman Empire to the custody of the League of Nations. Nations or regions falling under a mandate would be administered by a third-party nation upon the approval of the League of Nations. The former colonies and territories of Germany and the Ottoman Empire were distributed among the victorious Allied powers. Britain and France benefited the most, acquiring the majority of these territories as mandates. The French administered mandates in Syria and Lebanon, while the British Dominions of Australia and New Zealand were given mandates as rewards for their service in the war. For its part, Britain gained a mandate over Palestine, which the League defined as including the territories of modern-day Israel, the Occupied Palestinian Territories (OPT), and Jordan. Britain immediately divided the mandate in two, creating the state of Transjordan east of the Jordan River, and lands west of the Jordan River remained the British Mandate for Palestine, which ended on May 14, 1948.

Dino E. Buenviaje

See also: Arab Revolt, 1916; British Mandate for Palestine

Further Reading

Nothedge, F. S. *The League of Nations: Its Life and Times 1920–1946*. Leicester, UK: Leicester University Press, 1986.

Ostrower, Gary B., and George Lankevich, eds. *League of Nations, 1919*. New York: Putnam, 1996.

Lebanon

A small country on the Mediterranean Sea bordering Israel and Syria. Since its formal independence in 1943, Lebanon has been plagued by sectarian violence and civil war, often made worse by its involvement in Arab-Israeli conflicts. The very makeup of Lebanese society lends itself to conflict: among the population are the Sunni, Shia, and Druze sects of Islam, as well as five separate Christian denominations: Maronite, Greek Orthodox, Greek Catholic, Armenian Orthodox, and Syriac. The diverse nature of the Lebanese population means that various—and quite different—cultures coexist side by side. Until the late 1960s, when Muslims began to outnumber Christians, there were separate educational systems based on religion. The government has remained divided along religious lines. This badly fractured Lebanese society and led to an increasingly ineffective government.

After the 1948 Arab-Israeli War, some 100,000 Palestinians sought refuge in Lebanon, virtually guaranteeing that it would become involved in the

Israeli-Palestinian conflict. Soon, some Palestinians living in Lebanon began staging raids into Israel. Many more Palestinians took up residence in the late 1960s and early 1970s, resulting in a growing Muslim presence in Lebanon. This also increased tensions among the various religious groups in the country. The ultimate outcome of these developments was the Lebanese civil war, which began in 1975 and endured until 1990. The conflict commenced in earnest on April 13, 1975, when an unknown gunman opened fire on a Christian church in East Beirut; four people died in the attack. Later that same day, members of the Christian Lebanese Phalanges Party, in an apparent retaliatory move, murdered twenty-seven Palestinians on a bus in Ayn ar Rummanah. In December 1975, four Christians died in an attack in East Beirut. The violence only escalated, and during early 1976, Muslim militias and Phalangists killed at least 600 Muslim and Christian civilians at checkpoints throughout the country.

Sectarian combat in Lebanon during April 1975–November 1976 alone killed at least 40,000 and wounded 100,000 others; many of the victims were civilians. By 1976, both Israel and Syria had become involved in the civil war. Syrian troops intervened, entering Lebanon and imposing a short-lived cease-fire. On January 20, 1976, when the predominantly Christian town of Damour fell to Muslim forces, at least 300 citizens were massacred. On August 12, in response to the incursion of Syrian troops, Christian militias perpetrated a horrific massacre of at least 2,000 Palestinians at Tal al-Zaatar, the site of a huge Palestinian refugee camp outside Beirut. Other residents were raped, beaten, or tortured. By the end of 1976, Lebanon was divided militarily. The Christians controlled East Beirut and part of Mount Lebanon, while the Palestinians and allied Muslims controlled southern Lebanon and western Beirut.

In March 1978, Palestinian militants raided northern Israel and commandeered a bus, resulting in the deaths of thirty-four Israelis and six militants. Outraged, Israel invaded Lebanon on March 15. Some 2,000 Lebanese died during the invasion, and another 100,000 were displaced before Israel withdrew. However, Palestinian and allied guerilla groups frequently rocketed and raided northern Israel. In July 1981, Israeli jets bombed Palestinian positions in a suburb of West Beirut in retaliation for rocket attacks. About 200 people died in the bombardment, and another 600 were wounded, most of them civilians. Palestinian retaliation killed six Israeli civilians and wounded fifty-nine others.

In June 1982, Israel invaded southern Lebanon in a bid to destroy Palestinian bases there. Israeli forces then moved further into Lebanon, laying siege to Beirut. During this operation, 6,700 Christian civilians in East Beirut were killed, the victims not of Israeli bombs, but rather of Palestinian and Muslim bombs. One of the worst atrocities to unfold in Lebanon occurred on September 16–18, 1982, when Christian militias massacred at least 2,000 Palestinians at the Sabra and Shatila refugee camps; this massacre unfolded in clear view of Israeli troops, who did virtually nothing to stop the carnage.

Various attempts by neighboring nations, as well as the international community, to stop the civil war all failed, including an ill-fated U.S. military mission to Lebanon that was suddenly halted after the October 23, 1983, truck bombing of a barracks in Beirut. That attack killed 241 U.S. marines and 58 French troops and wounded scores of others. In the so-called War of the Camps in 1985–1986, several thousand Palestinians died in refugee camps. The Taif Accords of 1989 finally set the stage for an end to the bloody civil war, and by October 1990, a fragile peace was in place.

This did not, however, end the violence in Lebanon. In 1993, and again in 1995, Israel attacked Palestinian strongholds in southern Lebanon, killing hundreds and displacing several hundred thousand civilians. The attacks were an attempt to stop Palestinian rocket attacks. In 2006, another war erupted after Hezbollah, a militant Shia Islamic group in Lebanon founded during Israel's 1982 invasion, raided a border village and captured two Israeli soldiers. The Israelis retaliated, and the monthlong conflict resulted in the deaths of as many as 700 soldiers and militants in Lebanon and 1,187 Lebanese civilians. Up to 1 million Lebanese civilians were displaced. Israel reported forty-four civilian deaths, the result of rocket attacks by Hezbollah.

After more infighting within Lebanon following the short summer war with Israel, the country seemed ready to embrace some semblance of normalcy. Lebanon remains a tinderbox of sectarian and political strife, however, and Hezbollah's refusal to disarm raises doubts that the war-torn nation will be able to secure a lasting stability or peace with Israel. Indeed, in the years following the 2006 war, Hezbollah acquired many thousands more rockets and missiles from Syria and Iran. By 2011, its arsenal was larger and more lethal, and the next round of fighting with Israel promised to be deadlier than ever. But Hezbollah spent the next seven years fighting in support of the Bashar al-Assad regime in the Syrian civil war.

Israel has launched hundreds of air strikes into Syria to disrupt the delivery of weapons to Hezbollah, knowing that in time, Hezbollah forces will return home and increase Israel's level of insecurity. Indeed, recent discoveries of newly constructed tunnels from Lebanon into Israel have put Israeli security professionals on edge. So has the knowledge that Iran is supplying Hezbollah with sophisticated targeting systems for its missile arsenal.

Paul G. Pierpaoli Jr.

See also: Assad, Bashar al-; Hezbollah; Israel; Israel Defense Forces; Lebanon, Israeli Invasion of; Palestine Liberation Organization; Syria

Further Reading

Achcar, Gilbert, and Michel Warschawski. *33-Day War: Israel's War on Hezbollah in Lebanon and Its Consequences.* New York: Routledge, 2016.

Fisk, Robert. *Pity the Nation: Lebanon at War.* Oxford: Oxford University Press, 2001.

Hovespian, Nubar, ed. *The War on Lebanon: A Reader.* Northampton, MA: Olive Branch, 2008.

Rabil, Robert. *Embattled Neighbors: Syria, Israel, and Lebanon.* Boulder, CO: Lynne Rienner, 2003.

Lebanon, Israeli Invasion of

The Israeli invasion and occupation of southern Lebanon beginning in 1982. The Israeli invasion of Lebanon, code-named "Operation Peace for Galilee," began on

June 6, 1982, when Defense Minister Ariel Sharon, acting in full agreement with instructions from Prime Minister Menachem Begin, ordered Israel Defense Forces (IDF) troops into south Lebanon to destroy the Palestine Liberation Organization (PLO) there.

In 1977, Begin had become the first Israeli prime minister from the right-wing Likud Party. He sought to maintain Israel's hold over the West Bank and Gaza, but Begin also had a deep commitment to Eretz Israel, the ancestral homeland of the Jews that embraced territory beyond Israel's borders and into Lebanon and across the Jordan River. Sharon, also a prominent member of the Likud Party, shared Begin's ideological commitment to Eretz Israel. Indeed, he played an important role in expanding Jewish settlements in the West Bank and Gaza. Sharon took a hardline approach toward the Palestinians, endeavoring to undermine PLO influence in the West Bank and Gaza. He was also influential in the formation of Israeli foreign policy.

In June 1978, under heavy U.S. pressure, Begin withdrew Israeli forces that had been sent into south Lebanon to remove PLO forces there. The United Nations Interim Force in Lebanon (UNIFIL) then took over in south Lebanon and was charged with confirming the Israeli withdrawal, restoring peace and security, and helping the Lebanese government reestablish its authority in the area. The Israeli failure to remove PLO bases in southern Lebanon was a major embarrassment for the Begin government.

UNIFIL proved incapable of preventing PLO forces from operating in southern Lebanon and striking Israel, which led to Israeli reprisals. Attacks back and forth across the Lebanese-Israeli border killed civilians on both sides, as well as some UNIFIL troops. Israel, meanwhile, provided weapons to the South Lebanon Army, a pro-Israeli Christian militia in south Lebanon, which used them against the PLO.

In July 1981, the Ronald Reagan administration of the United States sent the Lebanese-American diplomat Philip Habib to the area in an effort to broker a truce. On July 24, Habib announced agreement on a cease-fire, but it was in name only. The PLO repeatedly violated the agreement, and while Israel conducted both air strikes and commando raids across the border, it was unable to prevent a growing number of PLO personnel from going there. PLO rocket and mortar attacks regularly forced thousands of Israeli civilians in northern Galilee to seek protection in bomb shelters.

On June 3, 1982, three members of a Palestinian terrorist organization connected to Abu Nidal attempted to assassinate Israeli ambassador to Britain Shlomo Argov in London. Although Argov survived the attack, he remained paralyzed until his death in 2003. Abu Nidal's organization had been linked to Yasser Arafat's PLO in the past, and the Israelis retaliated by bombing Palestinian targets in West Beirut and other targets in south Lebanon during June 4–5, 1982. The PLO responded by attacking Israeli settlements in the Galilee with rockets and mortars. It was this PLO shelling of the settlements, rather than the attempted assassination of Argov, that provoked the Israeli decision to invade Lebanon.

Operation Peace for Galilee began on June 6, 1982. It took its name from the Israeli intention to protect its vulnerable northern region of Israel from the PLO rocket and mortar attacks launched from southern Lebanon. The Israeli mission had three principal objectives. First, Israeli forces sought to destroy the PLO in south Lebanon. Second, Israel wanted to evict the Syrian army from Lebanon and bring about the removal of its missiles from the Beqaa Valley. Although Sharon perceived Syrian forces in Lebanon as a major security threat to Israel, he maintained that the IDF would not attack them unless it was first fired upon.

Finally, Israel hoped to influence Lebanese politics. It sought to ally itself with the Maronite Christians, led by Bashir Gemayel, the leader of the Phalange (al-Kataeb) and commander of the Lebanese Forces. While the Phalange was mainly a political association, the Lebanese Forces were an umbrella military organization comprised of several Christian militias. Gemayel had carried out a series of brutal operations to destroy the autonomy of the other Christian militias and had incorporated them into his Lebanese Forces. He was opposed to relinquishing the power held by the Maronites in this traditionally Christian-dominated Arab state to the Sunni and Shia Muslims of Lebanon. To this end, Gemayel maintained a close relationship with Israel. As did the Israelis, he harbored intense opposition to a Syrian presence in Lebanon.

The PLO was not only entrenched in the southern part of the country, but was also well established in West Beirut. Understandably, the Israeli cabinet was loath to place its troops into an urban combat situation that was bound to bring heavy civilian casualties and incur opposition from Washington and Western Europe. Begin and Sharon informed the cabinet that the goal was merely to break up PLO bases in south Lebanon and push back PLO and Syrian forces some twenty-five miles, beyond the rocket range of Galilee.

Once the operation began, however, Sharon quickly changed the original plan by expanding the mission to incorporate Beirut, which was well beyond the twenty-five-mile mark. Many in the cabinet now believed that Begin and Sharon had deliberately misled them. The IDF advanced to the outskirts of Beirut within days. Tyre and Sidon, two cities within the twenty-five-mile limit, were both heavily damaged in the Israeli advance. The PLO withdrew to West Beirut. Sharon now argued in favor of a broader operation that would force the PLO from Beirut altogether, and for some ten weeks, Israeli guns shelled West Beirut, killing both PLO fighters and civilians.

Fighting also occurred with Syrian forces in the Beqaa Valley. By June 10, the Israeli air force had shot down dozens of Syrian jets. The Israelis employed U.S.-supplied *Cobra* helicopter gunships to destroy dozens of Syrian armored vehicles and trap Syrian forces in the Beqaa Valley. Israel was on the verge of severing the Beirut-to-Damascus Highway on June 11, when Moscow and Washington brokered a cease-fire.

In Beirut, meanwhile, Sharon hoped to join up with Gemayel's Lebanese Forces. He wanted the Lebanese Forces to bear the brunt of the fighting in West Beirut, but Gemayel feared that such a move would harm his chances to become the president of Lebanon. Begin's cabinet was unwilling to approve an Israeli assault on West Beirut because of the probability of high casualties. Meanwhile, the United States had been conveying ambiguous signals regarding its position in the conflict. This only encouraged Arafat to entrench himself and the PLO in the West Beirut.

Sharon disregarded cabinet opposition and placed the western, predominantly Muslim, part of the city under siege from air, land, and sea. He hoped that this might convince the citizens to turn against the PLO. The bombing and shelling resulted in mostly civilian casualties, however, provoking denunciations of Israel in the international press. The PLO believed that it could hold out longer under siege than the Israelis could under international pressure; this intransigence led Israel to intensify its attack on Beirut in early August. Believing that there was an impending full-scale assault, the PLO then consented to an arrangement brokered by the United Nations (UN), whereby American, French, and Italian peacekeeping forces, known as the Multinational Force in Lebanon, would escort the PLO fighters out of Lebanon by the end of the month. (The PLO relocated to Tunis.) Habib assured the PLO that the many refugees in camps in Lebanon would not be harmed.

On August 23, 1982, Gemayel was elected president of Lebanon. But he was dead shortly thereafter, the victim of assassination on September 14 by a member of the pro-Damascus National Syrian Socialist Party. Some suspected an Israeli conspiracy to kill Gemayel owing to his recent attempts to disassociate himself from Israel.

Following the assassination of Gemayel, Israeli forces occupied West Beirut. This was in direct violation of the UN agreement calling for the evacuation of the PLO and protection of the Palestinian refugees who remained behind. With the PLO removed, the refugees had virtually no defense against the Israelis. In September 1982, once Israel had control of the Palestinian refugee camps, Sharon invited members of the Phalange to enter the camps at Sabra and Shatila to clean out the Palestinian "terrorists." The Phalange militia, led by Elie Hobeika, then slaughtered more than 1,000 refugees in what he claimed was retaliation for Gemayel's assassination.

Estimates of casualties in the Israeli invasion and subsequent occupation vary widely, although the numbers may have been as high as 17,826 Arabs killed and approximately 675 Israelis. Israel had achieved a number of goals, including expelling the PLO from Lebanon and temporarily destroying its infrastructure. It had also weakened the Syrian military, especially its air force. The Israelis also supported the establishment of the South Lebanon Army, an allied militia.

However, the invasion had negative repercussions as well. Much of Beirut lay in ruins, with damage estimated as high as $2 billion, and the tourist industry was a long time in recovering. Operation Peace for Galilee also became an occupation. In May 1983, with assistance from the United States and France, Israel and Lebanon reached an agreement calling for the staged withdrawal of Israeli forces, although the instruments of this agreement were never officially exchanged; and in March 1984, under Syrian pressure, the Lebanese government repudiated it. In January 1985, Israel began a unilateral withdrawal to a "security zone" in southern Lebanon, which was completed in June 1985. Not until June 2000 did Israel finally withdraw all its forces from south Lebanon.

Rather than producing a stable, pro-Israeli government in Beirut, the occupation led to the rise of contentious new resistance groups, most notably Hezbollah, which has become one of Israel's most virulent enemies. There was also considerable unrest in Israel. A protest demonstration in Tel Aviv that followed the Sabra and Shatila massacre drew a reported 300,000 people. Responding to the furor within Israel over the war, the government appointed the Kahan Commission to investigate the massacre. It found that Israeli officials were indirectly responsible, and Sharon was forced to resign as minister of defense. Begin's political career also suffered greatly. Disillusioned by the invasion and the high Israeli casualties, Begin resigned as prime minister in 1983, withdrawing entirely from public life.

Brian Parkinson and Spencer C. Tucker

See also: Assad, Hafez al-; Begin, Menachem; Lebanon; Hezbollah; Israel; Israel Defense Forces; Palestine Liberation Organization; Sharon, Ariel; Syria

Further Reading

Blanford, Nicholas. *Warriors of God: Inside Hezbollah's Thirty-Year Struggle Against Israel*. New York: Random House, 2011.

Cleveland, William L. *A History of the Modern Middle East*. San Francisco: Westview Press, 1994.

Rabinovich, Itamar. *The War for Lebanon, 1970–1985*. Rev. ed. Ithaca, NY: Cornell University Press, 1986.

Smith, Charles D. *Palestine and the Arab-Israeli Conflict: A History with Documents*. 9th ed. New York: Bedford/St. Martin's, 2017.

Likud Party

A right-wing political party in Israel. Likud was formed as a coalition of parties before the 1973 elections. Likud, whose name is the Hebrew word for "consolidation," has been either the ruling party or the leading opposition party since its creation. Its first leader was Menachem Begin, who also became the first Likud prime minister in 1977, when the coalition defeated the ruling Labor Party. Yitzhak Shamir became party leader and prime minister when Begin retired in 1983. In 1988, Likud's factions were formally dissolved, and it began to operate as a single party. Likud was defeated in 1992, and Benjamin Netanyahu replaced Shamir as party leader. In 1996, Netanyahu became prime minister, but a number of its leaders, including Benny Begin (Menachem Begin's son) and former prime minister Yitzhak Shamir, left Likud because they felt that it had become too moderate.

When Ehud Barak defeated Netanyahu in the prime minister election in 1999, Ariel Sharon became the Likud Party leader. Sharon then defeated Barak in 2001. Likud experienced a significant internal split in 2006, when Sharon left to form the Kadima Party. But under the leadership of Benjamin Netanyahu, Likud staged a dramatic political comeback in the 2009 elections, winning enough seats to form a new coalition government. Netanyahu thus became prime minister again in March 2009 and has kept that post ever since.

Likud holds hawkish views on security matters, strongly supports settlement construction, and largely opposes a two-state solution to Israel's conflict with the Palestinians. Netanyahu has flip-flopped on the two-state issue as matter of political expediency. In late 2017, the Likud Central Committee passed a nonbinding resolution calling for its leaders to pursue annexation of Israeli settlements in the West Bank. In April 2019, just days before being reelected again, Netanyahu publicly promised to annex Israeli settlements in the West Bank. Critics complain that a decade of Netanyahu-led coalition governments have ushered in an era of right-wing extremism in Israeli politics. Still, supporters keep returning him and the Likud Party to power.

John David Rausch Jr. and Robert C. DiPrizio

See also: Begin, Menachem; Netanyahu, Benjamin; Shamir, Yitzhak; Sharon, Ariel

Further Reading

Ahren, Raphael. "AIPAC Rekindles Old Debate: Does Israel Seek a Two State-Solution." *Times of Israel*, March 6, 2018. https://www.timesofisrael.com/aipac-rekindles-old-debate-is-israel-in-favor-of-a-two-state-solution-or-not/.

Arian, Alan. *The Second Republic: Politics in Israel*. Chatham, NJ: Chatham House, 1997.

Shindler, Colin. *Israel, Likud and the Zionist Dream: Power, Politics and Ideology from Begin to Netanyahu*. London: Tauris, 1995.

Lydda and Ramle

Palestinian Arab towns conquered and emptied by the Israel Defense Forces (IDF). The 1947 UN Palestine Partition Plan placed Lydda and Ramle in the boundaries of what was supposed to become the Arab state, but they were near the border with the proposed Jewish state and only a few miles southeast of Tel Aviv. They also overlooked important lines of communication, including major roads, rail lines, and Palestine's only international airport. Clashes between villagers and Jewish forces had been ongoing since the United Nations voted for partition, but when Israel declared independence on May 14, 1948 the armies of the surrounding Arab states invaded, and 125 or so Jordanian regulars soon reached the Lydda and Ramle area to butress the capabilities of the local volunteers. From these villages, this small contingent of Arab forces disrupted vital lines of communication. On May 8, Prime Minister David Ben-Gurion authorized Operation Dani to capture Lydda and Ramle.

The IDF initiated the offensive with limited air strikes and a lightning-quick advance on the ground. After intense fighting, Lydda and Ramle were subdued. In Lydda, thousands of Palestinian civilians were confined in the Great Mosque. The following night, a small skirmish precipitated into a widespread firefight that put many civilians in the crossfire. With only 400 Israeli troops securing the two towns, and fearing attack from the approaching Jordanian army, soldiers were ordered to shoot anyone on the street. Fighting lasted only thirty minutes but resulted in 250 Palestinian deaths. When news of the situation reached Ben-Gurion, he ordered the expulsion of the Arab residents. Yitzhak Rabin, a future prime minister of Israel, issued the written order, "The inhabitants of Lydda must be expelled quickly, without regard to age." The next day, Israeli commanders suggested to Arab city leaders that large-scale massacres could be avoided only if they evacuated the city. The next day, the residents of Lydda, along with those of Ramle and surrounding villages, fled their homes with what little they could carry.

The capture of Lydda and Ramle was a major IDF victory in the War for Independence and ultimately helped expand Israel's border. This expansion served the dual purpose of giving an additional buffer to vital lines of communication (especially to what would become the Ben-Gurion Airport) and offering space for new Jewish immigrants to live. The IDF's actions also removed 70,000 or so Palestinians from the center of what became the state of Israel. For Palestinians, the events in Lydda and Ramle were a microcosm of the broader catastrophe they suffered in 1948.

Sean N. Blas and Robert C. DiPrizio

See also: Arab-Israeli War, 1948; *Nakba;* Palestinian Refugees; Right of Return; UN Partition Plan for Palestine

Further Reading

Morris, Benny. "Operation Dani and Palestinian Exodus from Lydda and Ramle in 1948." *Middle East Journal* 40, no. 1 (Winter 1986), 82–109.

Shavit, Ari. *My Promised Land: The Triumph and Tragedy of Israel.* New York: Spiegel and Grau, 2013.

Smith, Charles. *Palestine and the Arab-Israeli Conflict: A History with Documents.* 9th ed. Boston, Bedford/St. Martin's, 2017.

M

Madrid Conference

Conference held in Madrid, Spain, during October 30–November 1, 1991, which brought together for the first time Syrian, Lebanese, Jordanian, Palestinian, and Israeli officials with the aim of beginning the process of securing a comprehensive Middle East peace settlement. The United States and the Soviet Union cosponsored the meeting. Also in attendance were officials from Egypt, the European Union, and the Gulf Cooperation Council.

The Madrid Conference came in the immediate aftermath of the 1991 Persian Gulf War and the waning days of the Cold War. Many Arab leaders who just joined a U.S.-led coalition to oust Saddam Husayn from Kuwait pressed President George H. W. Bush to begin peace negotiations between them and Israel. His administration had to pressure Israel's right-wing leader, Yitzhak Shamir, to secure his participation. Syrian president Hafiz al-Assad refused to attend, but sent high-ranking officials. It was understood by attendees that the resultant peace process should be guided by the land-for-peace formula first promulgated by UN Security Council Resolution 242. In approaching the Palestinian-Israeli dilemma, the congress was to begin a two-stage process, which included the establishment of interim self-government for the Palestinians, followed by the creation of a permanent Palestinian government that would ultimately lead to an autonomous Palestinian state.

Follow-on multilateral talks focused on five major concerns: water allocation, environmental preservation, refugee issues, economic development, and regional arms control. Negotiations went nowhere quickly, although bilateral negotiations between Israel and Jordan lead to a historic peace treaty in October of 1994. Several attempts to negotiate an Israeli-Syrian peace treaty over the next few years failed. But the guidelines set up at Madrid pertaining to the Israel-Palestinian conflict became the basic framework for the Oslo Accords, which were first negotiated in secret but finalized quite publicly in a dramatic September 13, 1993, signing ceremony on the White House lawn. The Oslo peace process ultimately failed to produce the two-state solution, but as part of the process, Palestinians were allowed to set up a governing entity, the Palestinian Authority (PA), which had limited powers over certain areas of the West Bank and Gaza Strip. Perhaps the biggest winner in all of this was Israel, as the process that had begun in Madrid resulted in several key nations finally recognizing that state. These included India and the People's Republic of China, as well as Tunisia, Morocco, Qatar, and Oman. The Arab economic boycott of Israel also began to loosen.

Paul G. Pierpaoli Jr.

See also: Oslo Accords; Palestinian Authority; UN Security Council Resolution 242

Further Reading

Brown, Nathan J. *Palestinian Politics After the Oslo Accords: Resuming Arab Palestine.* Berkeley: University of California Press, 2003.

Watson, Geoffrey R. *The Oslo Accords: International Law and the Israeli-Palestinian Peace Agreements.* New York: Oxford University Press, 2000.

Weinberger, Peter. *Co-opting the PLO: A Critical Reconstruction of the Oslo Accords, 1993–1995.* New York: Rowman and Littlefield, 2006.

Masada

A fortress overlooking the Dead Sea in the eastern Judean Desert, in which Jewish Zealots stood against a Roman siege at the end of the First Jewish Revolt. The term *masada* is a Latin transliteration of the Hebrew name *Metzada*, meaning "fortress." Masada's eastern cliffs rise some 1,350 feet (150 feet above sea level) above the Dead Sea, with the more vertical western cliffs rising 300 feet above the floor of the Dead Sea Valley. The plateau comprised an area of some 1,200 feet by 900 feet. Access was limited to four very difficult and quite steep approaches: the Snake Path from the east, still used by some tourists today; the White Rock ascent from the west; and one approach each from the south and north. Three large cisterns collected rainwater, and numerous storehouses dotted the site.

Roman soldiers were garrisoned at Masada when it was captured by Jewish forces in 66 CE, at the beginning of the First Jewish Revolt. Except for the Zealots

Ruins of the ancient Masada fortress in Israel where Jewish Zealots succumbed to a Roman siege at the end of the Jewish Revolt. Various elements of the Israel Defense Forces hold their swearing-in ceremonies on this site commemorating Jewish resolve and courage. (VanderWolfImages/Dreamstime)

at Masada, Jewish resistance ended when the Romans captured Jerusalem and destroyed its temple in September of 70 CE. The Romans laid siege to Masada in 72, with a force of 10,000–15,000 men. The Jewish defenders and family members numbered between 1,000 and 1,500 people.

After surrounding the fortress with eight military camps, the Romans oversaw in a nine-month period the construction by Jewish slave labor of an assault ramp to the top of Masada. On the verge of defeat, the Zealots burned their personal belongings and selected by lot ten defenders to kill the general population. These ten then killed each other in turn, leaving only a final defender to commit suicide. Two women and five children survived by hiding in one of the cisterns.

Masada emerged as a symbol of Jewish and Zionist resolve and courage and became a widely visited pilgrimage site for many Zionist youth groups and Haganah in the years prior to Israel's formation in 1948. The Star of David flag of Israel was raised over Masada following the end of the Israeli War of Independence in 1949, and the site continues to be used by various units of the Israel Defense Forces (IDF) and contemporary youth movements for swearing-in ceremonies that conclude with the oath that "Masada shall never fall again." Masada is accessible today both by foot, on the arduous Snake Path, and by aerial tramway.

Richard M. Edwards

See also: Diaspora, Jewish; First and Second Temple Periods; Herod the Great; Jewish Revolt; Roman Conquest of Judea

Further Reading

Ben-Yehuda, Nachman. *Sacrificing Truth: Archaeology and the Myth of Masada*. Amherst, NY: Humanity Books, 2002.

Yadin, Yigael. *Masada: Herod's Fortress and the Zealots' Last Stand*. New York: Welcome Rain, 1998.

McMahon-Husayn Correspondence

Correspondence in the form of ten letters exchanged between Sir A. Henry McMahon, the British high commissioner for Egypt, and Husayn ibn Ali, emir of the Arabian Hejaz and Sharif of Mecca. Many Arabs have viewed the exchange as Britain's commitment to Arab autonomy and independence in the Middle East, including the entire area of Palestine. The exchange began with a letter from Husayn to McMahon, translated into English and read by McMahon on July 14, 1915. The last letter was one from McMahon to Husayn on March 10, 1916. The ambiguities in McMahon's proposals, combined with subsequent British policies that flew in the face of the McMahon-Husayn correspondence, have been a constant source of contention in the Middle East.

Husayn's initial letter to McMahon outlined the conditions of Arab participation in the British struggle against the Ottoman Turks during World War I. Essentially, he pledged Arab support for the fight against the Turks in exchange for British concessions, most specifically those relating to Arab independence. In an October 24, 1915, letter, McMahon assured Husayn that Great Britain would recognize and support independence for Arabs residing in areas outlined by Husayn. The territories affected included the Arabian Peninsula, Greater Syria, Palestine, Lebanon, and Transjordan. Naturally, many Arabs saw in this promise a British commitment to independence, either right away or in the immediate wake of World War I.

At the same time, Britain and France were drawing up the secret 1916 Sykes-Picot Agreement, which would divide the Middle East into French and British spheres of influence once the war ended. These spheres incorporated much of the land that McMahon and Husayn had agreed would be subject to Arab autonomy. Not until December 1917 did Husayn learn the full details of the agreement, which had been leaked to him by the Turkish government in the hope that it would drive a wedge in the Anglo-Arab alliance.

Even before the leak, the November 1917 Balfour Declaration clearly demonstrated the British duplicity. The declaration committed Britain to support the creation of a Jewish homeland in Palestine. This, in the eyes of Husayn and other Arab leaders, was a patent violation of the promises that McMahon had made to Husayn. The British claimed that the McMahon correspondence did not apply to Palestine, and so the Balfour Declaration did not contradict any earlier pledges made to the Arabs. Indeed, McMahon's letter of October 25, 1915, had not explicitly mentioned Palestine. Nonetheless, Palestine had always been included in historic Syria.

From the Arab perspective, because these areas were not specifically excluded from the Arab sphere, they understood that they would come under Arab control. But McMahon and Husayn had agreed that land not purely Arab in makeup was to be excluded from the understanding. The British argued that because Palestine was neither completely Arab nor Muslim, it was not part of the agreement. The Arabs, however, argued that Palestine was overwhelmingly Arab and therefore should be part of Arab-controlled areas.

The final insult, in the eyes of the Arabs, was the League of Nations mandate that granted the British de facto control over Palestine. It is certainly easy to see how the McMahon-Husayn correspondence would buoy the spirits of Arab nationalists, and that its aftermath sowed the seeds of a deep-seated distrust and enmity toward the West.

Paul G. Pierpaoli Jr.

See also: Arab Revolt, 1916; Balfour Declaration; British Mandate for Palestine; Husayn ibn Ali, Sharif of Mecca; League of Nations

Further Reading

Kent, Marian, ed. *The Great Powers and the End of the Ottoman Empire.* 2nd ed. Portland, OR: Cass, 1996.

Smith, Charles D. *Palestine and the Arab-Israeli Conflict: A History with Documents.* 9th ed. New York: Bedford/St. Martin's, 2017.

Tauber, Eliezer. *The Arab Movements in World War I.* London: Cass, 1993.

Meir, Golda

A prominent Israeli political leader and prime minister. Born in Kiev, Russia, on May 3, 1898, Golda Mabovitch was one of eight children. Her family emigrated to the United States in 1906. In 1917, she married Morris Meyerson, and they moved to Palestine in 1921. The Meyersons worked on a kibbutz, and Golda became active in the Histadrut, Israel's labor movement.

Shortly before Israel's 1948 War of Independence, Golda Meyerson twice met secretly with Jordan's King Abdullah. While unsuccessful in averting a Jordanian invasion of the Jewish state, these secret contacts proved useful in limiting Jordanian participation in the war, and secret meetings became the norm in Israeli-Jordanian relations. During the war, she traveled to the United States, where she raised $50 million for Israel from private citizens.

Following the war, Israel's first prime minister, David Ben-Gurion, sent her to Moscow as Israel's ambassador. At his urging, she adopted the Hebrew surname *Meir*, which means "to burn brightly."

In 1949, Meir was appointed minister of labor by Ben-Gurion. Her greatest task was resettling the hundreds of thousands of Jewish refugees who emigrated to Israel during these years. The new arrivals, 685,000 of whom arrived in her first two years in office, lived in large tent cities, while Meir marshaled the new state's scant resources to construct housing for them, teach them Hebrew, and integrate them into Israeli society.

Ben-Gurion, who once called Meir "the only man in my cabinet," forced the moderate Moshe Sharett to resign as foreign minister on June 18, 1956, and appointed Meir in his place. Meir held that post until 1965, gaining international fame as one of the few women to hold a prominent position in international affairs. As foreign minister, Meir worked to improve U.S.-Israeli relations that had been damaged by the 1956 Suez Crisis, but she met a generally cold reception from the Dwight D. Eisenhower administration. The next U.S. administration proved different, though, and Meir developed a particularly good relationship with President John F. Kennedy. In a conversation with Meir in December 1962, Kennedy first referred to a "special relationship" between Israel and the United States that resembled the relationship between the United States and Great Britain.

Along with Israeli ambassador Abba Eban, Meir convinced Kennedy to sell sophisticated Hawk antiaircraft missiles to Israel. This sale ended the U.S. embargo of arms sales to Israel and opened the door to further arms transfers. The Lyndon B. Johnson and Richard M. Nixon administrations both increased arms sales to Israel, and after the 1967 Six-Day War, the United States displaced France as Israel's primary arms supplier. On February 26, 1969, the ruling Labor Party appointed Meir prime minister following the death of Levi Eshkol. Meir, the fourth prime minister in Israel's brief history, faced daunting challenges, including Israeli national security imperatives and Middle Eastern instability.

Tensions with Egypt and Syria increased steadily until the morning of October 6, 1973, when Israel's director of intelligence warned of an imminent attack. Concerned about Israel's international reputation, Meir rejected proposals to launch a preemptive attack, as Israel had done in 1967. That afternoon, while Meir met with her cabinet, Egyptian and Syrian forces invaded the Sinai and Golan Heights, driving back the surprised and outnumbered Israeli army. Following a series of early defeats, Israeli counteroffensives finally defeated both Arab forces. A U.S.-imposed cease-fire ended the war on October 24.

Although the war was won, the early setbacks, surprise of the invasion, heavy casualties, and rumors that she had considered using nuclear weapons during the first days of the war tarnished Meir's administration. Meir resigned on June 3, 1974, and Yitzhak Rabin succeeded her as prime minister. She returned to private life. Meir died of leukemia in Jerusalem on December 8, 1978.

Stephen K. Stein

See also: Arab-Israeli War, 1973; Ben-Gurion, David; Israel; U.S. Aid to Israel

Further Reading

Mann, Peggy. *Golda: The Life of Israel's Prime Minister*. New York: Coward, McCann & Geoghegan, 1971.

Martin, Ralph G. *Golda Meir, the Romantic Years*. New York: Scribner, 1988.

Meir, Golda. *My Life*. New York: Putnam Books, 1975.

Middle East Quartet

A diplomatic mission of states and intergovernmental organizations (the United States, Russia, the United Nations, and the European Union) charged with promoting the peace process between Israel and the Palestinians. The Quartet was set up after the outbreak of the deadly Second or al-Aqsa Intifada in 2000, which featured an escalation of mutual violence and extensive Israeli military intrusions into the Occupied Palestinian Territories (OPT). The first meeting of the Quartet representatives took place in Madrid in 2002. The Quartet's mandate is to help mediate Arab-Israeli peace talks and promote Palestinian economic growth and institution-building in preparation for eventual statehood.

Among its most known initiatives is the introduction in 2003 of the Road Map for Peace to resolve the Israeli-Palestinian conflict. The principles of the road map include the end of violence; termination of Israel's settlement activity; acceptance of Israel's right to exist; and the establishment of a viable, sovereign Palestinian state. The peace plan went nowhere fast, and the Quartet has proved to be unable to move the parties down a path to peace. Despite the Quartet's inability to affect peace negotiations, the Office of the Quartet continues to promote Palestinian capacity-building projects in the areas of water, energy, and the rule of law.

Philipp O. Amour

See also: Intifada, Second; Oslo Accords; Permanent Status Issues; Two-State Solution

Further Reading

Musu, Costanza. "The Middle East Quartet: A New Role for Europe?" in *European-American Relations and the Middle East: From Suez to Iraq*, ed. Daniel Möckli and Victor Mauer. New York: Routledge, 2010, 124–139.

Tocci, Nathalie. "The Middle East Quartet and (In)effective Multilateralism." *Middle East Journal* 67, no. 1 (2013): 29–44.

Mishal, Khalid

Palestinian politician and the former political chief of Hamas. Khalid Mishal is among the more moderate leaders of Hamas and has played an important role in recent years in transforming the movement. Mishal was born in Silwad in the West

Bank. His family later moved to Kuwait, where he completed his high school education. While studying physics at the University of Kuwait, he became increasingly active in politics. When Iraq invaded Kuwait, Mishal moved to Jordan.

Mishal rose to prominence soon after he became the head of the political bureau of Hamas in 1996. During his administration, he was active in expanding the movement's foreign relations with Syria, Iran, Qatar, and later Turkey. He also promoted the fundraising activities of Hamas, which contributed to its weight in socioeconomic and paramilitary terms. He is one of the cofounders of Hamas and is known for supporting the right of the Palestinians for self-defense and resistance. He survived an Israeli assassination attempt in 1997, when he was living in Jordan. He was exiled from Jordan in 1999, and by 2001, he took up residence in Syria, where he lead Hamas's external leadership. When the civil war in Syria erupted, Mishal moved to Qatar and supported the opposition.

In recent years, Mishal played an important role in transitioning Hamas from mainly a resistance movement to a political one, winning Palestinian parliamentary elections in 2006. He has also led efforts to moderate Hamas positions toward Israel and the Palestine Liberation Organization (PLO). During his term, Hamas revised its charter, introducing language and content with more moderate stances toward Israel. He articulated his readiness to accept a two-state solution in return for a permanent treaty with Israel. In 2017, Hamas held internal elections. Due to term limits, Mishal stepped down and was replaced as Hamas's supreme leader by Gazan native Ismail Haniyeh.

Philipp O. Amour

See also: Gaza Strip; Hamas; Mossad; Palestine Liberation Organization

Further Reading
McGeough, Paul. *Kill Khalid: The Failed Mossad Assassination of Khalid Mishal and the Rise of Hamas.* New York: The New Press, 2010.
Rabbani, Mouin. "Khalid Mishal: The Making of a Palestinian Islamic Leader." *Journal of Palestine Studies* 37, no. 3 (Spring 2008): 59–73.

Mossad

The Israeli organization responsible for intelligence and special operations outside Israel. The Central Institute for Intelligence and Special Missions, or Mossad (whose name means "institute" in Hebrew), was formed in April 1951 by Prime Minister David Ben-Gurion. The agency reports directly to the prime minister to this day. Within two months of its inception, Mossad had worked out an agreement with the U.S. Central Intelligence Agency (CIA) concerning the sharing of information between the two organizations.

The many operations that Mossad has carried out include securing a copy of Soviet leader Nikita Khrushchev's secret speech to the Twentieth Communist Party Congress on February 25, 1956, in which he denounced Joseph Stalin's policies. Mossad also recruited successful agents in Egypt and in Syria. The agency also hunted down former Nazis who had been in hiding since the end of World War II. The most significant such capture was that of Adolf Eichmann, living in Argentina in 1960. Eichmann was transported to Israel and later tried for war crimes, found guilty, and executed.

Prior to the 1967 Six-Day War, Mossad, along with the army's intelligence agency, collected information on neighboring Arab countries. This intelligence was an important factor in Israel's lightening victory. Mossad was not successful, however, in warning the government prior to the 1973 Yom Kippur War. Mossad operatives were fairly certain that Egypt and Syria were planning an offensive against Israel sometime in late 1973. This time, however, army intelligence concluded that these Arab states were indeed not going to attack Israel, and therefore dismissed Mossad's information. The result was a stunning reversal for Israel in the early stages of the conflict.

In 1973, following the murders of eleven members of the Israeli sporting contingent at the 1972 Munich Olympics, Mossad tracked down and assassinated twelve of the Palestinians involved in that operation. The agency also played a key role in helping to collect information in support of the successful Israeli raid on Entebbe Airport in 1976, and it was also responsible for the destruction in April 1979 of two nuclear cores in France that were bound for the Iraqi nuclear power reactor, Tammuz I. In June 1980, Mossad engineered the assassination of an Egyptian nuclear physicist who was working with the Iraqis. Then, in June 1981, Mossad agents helped plan the Israeli air raid on Iraq's nuclear facility at Osirak, near Baghdad.

In more recent years, Mossad reportedly has been responsible for the assassinations of numerous Hezbollah and Hamas militants, allegedly has been operational in Syria (particularly after the civil war began there in 2011), and has been accused of killing several Iranian scientists in connection with Iran's disputed nuclear weapons program.

Dallace W. Unger Jr.

See also: Arab-Israeli War, 1967; Arab-Israeli War, 1973; Munich Olympics

Further Reading

Black, Ian, and Benny Morris. *Israel's Secret Wars: A History of Israel's Intelligence Services*. New York: Grove Weidenfeld, 1991.

Polmar, Norman, and Thomas B. Allen. *Spy Book: The Encyclopedia of Espionage*. New York: Random House, 1997.

Steven, Stewart. *The Spymasters of Israel*. New York: Macmillan Publishing Co., 1980.

Mubarak, Hosni

Longtime president of Egypt. Muhammad Hosni Said Mubarak was born on May 4, 1928, in Kafr-al Meselha. He graduated from the Egyptian Military Academy in 1949 and the Egyptian Air Force Academy in 1950. He then attended advanced flight training in the Soviet Union and finished his military training at the Soviet General Staff Academy in Moscow. Mubarak quickly rose through the ranks, becoming chief of staff of the Egyptian air force from 1967–1972 and deputy minister of war from 1972–1975. In 1975 he was elevated to vice president.

Mubarak became president following the assassination of Egyptian president Anwar Sadat on October 6, 1981. He mediated the dispute among Morocco, Algeria, and Mauritania concerning the future of Western (Spanish) Sahara, and he maintained sufficient neutrality in the Israeli-Palestinian conflict to mediate some of the elementary disputes of the Second Intifada and the bilateral agreement between Israel and the Palestine Liberation Organization (PLO) in 1993.

Even though Mubarak supported Egypt's peace treaty with Israel in 1979, Egypt's relations with the other Arab countries improved during his presidency. He organized the Arab League's opposition to Iraq's invasion of Kuwait and contributed approximately 38,500 Egyptian troops to the coalition in the Persian Gulf War (1991), but none to the U.S.-led ouster of Saddam Husayn in 2003. Although Mubarak's stated policy was "positive neutrality" between the United States and Russia, refusing to side with either, the United States remained Egypt's primary benefactor, providing about $2 billion a year in aid.

In early 2011, dissatisfaction among many young Egyptians over high unemployment and government corruption erupted into massive street protests in Cairo and other cities, in what became known as the Arab Spring. Mubarak was forced to resign on February 11. He and his sons were put on trial for numerous crimes, including corruption, but by 2017, they were all free men.

Richard M. Edwards

See also: Arab Spring; Camp David Accords; Egypt; Sadat, Anwar

Further Reading

Kirkpatrick, David D. *Into the Hands of the Soldiers: Freedom and Chaos in Egypt and the Middle East.* New York: Viking Press, 2018.

McDermott, Anthony. *Egypt from Nasser to Mubarak: A Flawed Revolution.* London: Routledge Kegan & Paul, 1998.

Tripp, Charles, and Roger Owen. *Egypt Under Mubarak.* London: Routledge, 1990.

Muhammad, Prophet of Islam

The Prophet of Islam, who established the first community of Muslims in the Arabian Peninsula in the seventh century. Muhammad ibn Abdullah ibn Abd al-Mutallib, always referred to by Muslims as the Prophet Muhammad, was at once a military, political, and religious leader who effectively united the disparate tribes of the region into a single empire. As a prophet of Allah (God), he received a series of orally transmitted revelations, the Message, that were eventually transcribed as the Qur'an. The Prophet Muhammad is called the Seal of Prophecy, which means that he, following the earlier prophets of the Bible and Jesus, was the last and final prophet. Unlike Jesus, the Prophet Muhammad is not considered to be a divine figure, but he is revered by Muslims as the Beautiful Model because his Sunna (Way) provided the example for future generations of Muslims.

Muhammad was born in approximately 570 CE into a branch of an important clan, the Banu Hashim of the Quraysh tribe, in Mecca, located on the western Arabian Peninsula area of the Hejaz. Prior to his birth, his father died. Thus, Muhammad was, in the terms of that era, an orphan. As an infant, he was sent as was the custom to a wet nurse, Halima, a tribal woman. Muhammad's mother died when he was six years old, and his grandfather, Abd al-Mutallib, died just two years later. Muhammad then came under the guardianship of his uncle, Abu Talib, who was an influential merchant. Muhammad soon began accompanying his uncle on trading journeys during the pilgrimage season. On one journey to Bosra, Syria, he was greeted by a monk named Buhaira, who hailed Muhammad as a future prophet.

As an adult, Muhammad entered the employ of Khadija (555–619), a wealthy, forty-year-old widow, and managed her caravans, earning a reputation for honesty such that he was known as *al-Amin* (the faithful one). Khadija subsequently proposed to him. The two married in 595, and Muhammad remained devoted to her until her death in 619. The number of children born to the marriage remains in dispute. Some accounts argue that the pair had four daughters—Zaynab, Ruqayya, Umm Kulthum, and Fatima—and one or two sons who died. In any case, only Fatima was still living after her father's death. Muhammad married other women after Khadija's death, and he had a son by one of these wives, who also died before the son was two years old. Of Muhammad's other wives, Aysha was said to be his favorite.

According to Muslim tradition, Muhammad received his first revelation in the year 610 while fasting in the cave of Hira, near Mecca. He heard the voice of the archangel Gabriel, who commanded him to recite verses of Scripture, which Gabriel spoke to Muhammad. At first, Muhammad did not know how to respond to his experience, but Khadija regarded his words as proof of a new revelation and thus became the first formal convert to Islam. For the remainder of his life, Muhammad continued to receive revelations. Within a few years of his initial revelations, he began to preach to any who would listen to his message about the One God, Creator, and Judge of the World. As the Meccans then worshiped a pantheon of gods and goddesses, they were not very impressed with his message and later became increasingly hostile toward him.

As Muhammad's group of followers grew, they became perceived as a threat by the leadership of Mecca, including his own tribe. Some of the early converts to Islam came from the disaffected and disadvantaged segments of society. Most important, the Muslims' new set of beliefs implicitly challenged the Meccans' and the Quraysh tribe's guardianship over the Kaaba, the holy site dedicated to the gods and goddesses of the area that hosted an annual pilgrimage. The city's leading merchants attempted to persuade Muhammad to cease his preaching, but he refused. In response, the city leadership persecuted Muhammad's followers, and many fled the city. In 619, Muhammad endured the loss of both Khadija and Abu Talib, while the mistreatment of his followers increased.

The following year, Muhammad undertook two miraculous journeys with the archangel Gabriel. The first, called the *Isra*, took Muhammad from Mecca to Jerusalem, where he ascended to the site of today's Dome of the Rock in the al-Aqsa Compound in Jerusalem. The second, called the *Miraj*, included a visit to heaven and hell. During the Miraj, Muhammad spoke with earlier monotheistic prophets, including Abraham, Moses, and Jesus, and saw Allah. Muhammad asked Allah for forgiveness for his *ummah*, the Muslim community, and Allah accepted his intercession (*shafa*). Allah assigned Muhammad the task of making fifty daily prayers for Muslims, and Moses advised Muhammad to return to Allah and request that the number of prayers be reduced (to five), which he did. The Isra and Miraj were accomplished in a single night. Scholars have presented the travels as both a spiritual vision and an actual physical experience.

In 622, Muhammad decided to leave the city of his birth at the invitation of groups residing in the city of Yathrib. Yathrib was located at a major oasis, and there, Muhammad hoped to firmly establish a new community of Muslims free from the persecution of the Meccans. The immigration to Yathrib, called the *Hijra*, marks the beginning of the Muslim calendar. When Muhammad arrived in Yathrib, he found a city divided by competing tribes, the Aws and the Khazraj. Both soon converted to Islam, uniting under Muhammad after a century of fighting. Yathrib later took the name of *Madinat al-Nabi*, or City of the Prophet. With the exception of a sizable Jewish community divided into three clans, the city of Medina was entirely under Muhammad's control by 624. At Medina, the rituals of Islam were established.

After Muhammad and most of his followers departed Mecca for Yathrib, the Meccans confiscated all Muslim property that had been left behind. In March 624, Muhammad led an abortive raid on a Meccan caravan. In retaliation, 1,000 Meccan warriors marched on Medina. Not content to await the attack, Muhammad led a force of approximately 300 warriors to meet the invading army. The armies collided at Badr, and Muhammad's followers achieved a decisive victory, inflicting more than 100 casualties at a cost of only fourteen Muslims and driving off the Meccan army.

In 625, a Meccan army of 3,000 returned to menace Medina. Emboldened by his victory at Badr, Muhammad marched his army out of the city to face the enemy. At the Battle of Uhud, the Muslims were defeated, but the Meccan leader, Abu Sufyan, chose to withdraw his army rather than raze Medina. Two years later, Abu Sufyan again attacked Medina but failed to destroy Muhammad's army at the Battle of the Trench. In 628, Muhammad led a band of 1,400 followers to Mecca, ostensibly as a pilgrimage (hajj). They were refused entry to the city, although the differences between the Meccans and the Muslims were formally abolished in the Treaty of Hudhaybiyya. The truce lasted only two years. Renewed skirmishing led Muhammad to attack Mecca directly.

Eight years of converting other client tribes on the Arabian Peninsula provided Muhammad with an army of more than 10,000 followers, far too numerous for the Meccans to withstand. The polytheistic statuaries in Mecca were destroyed, and the majority of the populace converted to Islam. Following the conquest, Mecca became the heart of the Muslim empire, which rapidly unified the competing tribes of the region.

Muhammad did not live long after consolidating his power. In 632, he fell ill in Medina, and after several days of pain and weakness, he died and was buried in a plot adjacent to his house. His followers quickly moved to expand his legacy, moving out of the Arabian Peninsula to challenge the Sassanians and the client tribes of the Eastern Roman (Byzantine) Empire. Eventually, they conquered lands stretching from Central Asia to the Iberian Peninsula. However, political divisions coupled with external threats created competing dynasties rather than a united Muslim empire, and also led to the growth of religious sects and varying intellectual trends within the religion and Muslim culture.

In nearly all these sects, the Prophet Muhammad is honored to this day. His birthday is celebrated, and he has been a favorite subject of Muslim poets. The stories of his deeds and words, collected into the Hadith, remain an important source of religious law and history. Modern Islam is one of the largest religions in the world, with approximately 1.3 billion adherents spanning across the globe.

Paul J. Springer and Sherifa Zuhur

See also: Arab-Islamic Conquest of Palestine; Islam; Jerusalem, Old City of

Further Reading
Cook, M. A. *Muhammad*. New York: Oxford University Press, 1983.
Haykal, Muhammad Husayn. *The Life of Muhammad*. Trans. Isma'il R. al-Faruqi. Indianapolis: North American Trust Publications, 1976.
Schimmel, Annemarie. *And Muhammad Is His Messenger: The Veneration of the Prophet in Islamic Piety*. Chapel Hill: University of North Carolina Press, 1985.
Weinberger, Eliot. *Muhammad*. New York: Verso, 2006.

Munich Olympics

Site of an infamous Palestinian terror attack on Israeli athletes and coaches. Early on the morning of September 5, 1972, eight Palestinian terrorists, dressed as athletes, entered the Olympic Village, five of them by scaling a fence. Carrying their weapons in gym bags, they sought out the apartment building housing the Israelis. The terrorists called themselves "Black September" to mask their Fatah identity, but the Fatah leader Yasser Arafat had ordered the operation.

The terrorists shot dead two Israeli athletes and took nine others hostage. They demanded that Israel free 234 Arab prisoners and that West Germany release two German terrorist leaders. Negotiations failed to secure the release of the hostages. A rescue mission was launched by German security forces on September 6, but the terrorists killed all the hostages. In all, the incident claimed the lives of eleven Israelis, five terrorists, and one German policeman. Three terrorists were captured alive and imprisoned, but they were released two months later in response to the hijacking of a Lufthansa jet.

Israeli prime minister Golda Meir and her cabinet, meanwhile, approved a top-secret operation by Mossad (the Israeli intelligence services) to track down and kill those responsible for the Munich atrocity. Mossad's success in this operation and its moral implications are the subject of the 2005 film *Munich* by Steven Spielberg.

Spencer C. Tucker

See also: Arafat, Yasser; Fatah; Meir, Golda; Mossad; Palestine Liberation Organization

Further Reading
Espy, Richard. *The Politics of the Olympic Games*. Berkeley: University of California Press, 1979.
Hill, Christopher. *Olympic Politics*. 2nd ed. Manchester, UK: Manchester University Press, 1996.

N

Nakba

The Arabic word for "catastrophe," which Palestinians use to describe the creation of Israel in 1948, an event that suspended their hopes for statehood and resulted in 700,000 displaced Palestinians. These refugees were not allowed to return to their homes in Israel and were never fully incorporated into neighboring Arab states.

Prior to 1948, Palestinians saw their relative power vis-à-vis Jewish settlers gradually shift in favor of the Zionists. When Zionists began emigrating to Palestine in the late nineteenth century in hopes of establishing a Jewish state there, the region fell under the authority of the Ottoman Empire. During World War I, in an effort to gain both Arab and Jewish support, Britain made seemingly contradictory promises. The McMahon-Husayn Correspondence appeared to promise Arabs independence and self-determination, while the Balfour Declaration clearly expressed British support for the creation of a Jewish homeland in Palestine.

After the Ottomans were defeated, Britain took control of Palestine and favored the Zionists until 1939, when it put down an Arab revolt in Palestine. Soon thereafter, Britain abandoned its goal of creating a Jewish homeland in Palestine and strictly limited Jewish immigration. Britain's about-face was in part an attempt to bolster Arab support on the eve of World War II, but its actions were too little too late to assuage anti-British sentiment among Arabs in Palestine and was viewed as a betrayal by Zionists. Facing increased levels of violence from Zionist groups in Palestine, Britain referred the matter of Palestine's future to the newly formed United Nations (UN), which decided to partition Palestine.

Although Arabs had a two-to-one population advantage over Jews at the time and land ownership considerably favored Arabs, the UN partition plan allocated roughly 43 percent of the land to Palestinians and 56 percent to Jews. Much of the desirable land of the coastal plains went to the Jews. Jerusalem was to become an international city, controlled by neither state. Palestinians rejected the partition, and large-scale communal fighting erupted. The initial months of war favored the Palestinians, but Jewish forces rebounded by April 1948 and thereafter made significant advances.

Following the Jewish victory over the Palestinians, the leaders of the Jewish governing body declared Israeli independence on May 14, 1948. The next day, armies from the surrounding Arab states invaded. Israel's victory over its Arab neighbors was not certain prior to the war—Israel was outmanned and lacked the Arabs' artillery and armor—but in retrospect, the reasons for its battlefield successes are evident. The stakes of the combatants, for example, were very different. While Israel was fighting what it saw as an existential conflict, its opponents fought for a variety of reasons, none matching the urgency of Israel's cause. Jordan sought to gain territory, especially Jerusalem, for itself. Egypt and Syria, fearful of losing status to Jordan, fought as much to limit Jordan's gains as to defeat Israel. Furthermore, the Arab coalition lacked a unified command structure, while Israel had already tested its command and control during the civil conflict with the Palestinians. When the guns fell silent, Israel had control of 78 percent of Palestine, including most of Jerusalem. Jordan controlled the Old City of Jerusalem and what became known as the West Bank, while Egypt controlled the Gaza Strip.

Why so many Palestinians left their homes in 1947 and 1948 has been a contentious question. Some, including Israel, have argued that Palestinians left their homes willingly, following advice from their own political leaders. Others have argued that the source of Palestinian flight was Israeli coercion. It is clear from the historical record that both Israelis and Palestinians forced population expulsions as they took territory.

The Israelis, however, were the ultimate victors, and by the end of the 1948 war, hundreds of thousands of Palestinians were displaced. Israel refused to allow the displaced Palestinians to return to their homes, a decision that it justified largely through the lens of the expulsion of Jews from many Arab countries. Palestinian refugees settled throughout the West Bank, Gaza, Lebanon, Syria, and Jordan. The United Nations (UN) established an assistance agency in 1949, the UN Relief and Works Agency for Palestine Refugees in the Near East (UNRWA), which continues to operate today. The UNRWA provides health care, education, and other services for Palestinian refugees who now number more than 5 million. The abovementioned territories and states are home to fifty-eight refugee camps, which are administered by the host governments.

The legacies of 1948 endure today. The Palestinian national movement was shattered in 1948, creating a Palestinian diaspora. It was not until the late 1960s that the Palestine Liberation Organization (PLO) reenergized the Palestinian nationalist movement, although it has achieved only limited success so far. Other legacies of 1948 also continue. The final status of Jerusalem and the boundaries between Israel and a possible Palestinian state have been consistent spoilers to possible Israeli-Palestinian reconciliation. Many Palestinians view Israeli settlement building as slowly establishing new facts on the ground in the West Bank that further remove Palestinians from any historical claim to the territory. That historical memory of territory lost is central to the Palestinian conceptualization of the *Nakba*. A meaningful symbol in Palestinian nationalist discourse is that of a house key, symbolizing for many the homes that they or their families left in 1948 and to which they feel they have the right of return.

Sean P. Braniff

See also: Arab-Israeli War, 1948; Arab-Jewish Communal War, 1947; Palestinian Refugees; Palestinians; Right of Return; UN Partition Plan for Palestine; UN Relief and Works Agency for Palestinian Refugees in the Near East

Further Reading

Collins, Larry, and Dominque Lapierre. *O Jerusalem: Day by Day and Minute by Minute, The Historic Struggle for Jerusalem and the Birth of Israel.* New York: Touchstone, 1988.

Morris, Benny. *1948: A History of the First Arab-Israeli War*. New Haven, CT: Yale University Press, 2008.

Sa'di, Ahmad H., and Lila Abu-Lughod, eds. *Nakba: Palestine, 1948, and the Claims of Memory*. New York: Columbia University Press, 2007.

Nasser, Gamal Abdel

Egyptian nationalist president. Born in Beni Mor, Egypt, on January 16, 1918, the son of a civil servant, Gamal Abdel Nasser at an early age developed great antipathy toward Britain's rule over Egypt. Nasser was commissioned into the Egyptian military in 1936. While stationed at a post in the Sudan, he became friends with future Egyptian president Anwar Sadat. Based on their mutual dislike of the British, they eventually formed the foundation for a secret anti-British organization that came to be called the *Free Officers*.

The Free Officers recruited Egyptian military officers who wished to bring about an end to British colonial rule and to oust King Farouk II. After months of painstaking planning, the Free Officers fomented a revolt against Farouk's government on July 23, 1952. Three days later, the king abdicated and fled Egypt. Nasser and his faction soon consolidated their hold on power, and Nasser became president in 1955. Britain withdrew from Egypt in 1956.

In addition to seeking land reform and following quasi-socialist economic policies, Nasser sought to modernize Egyptian infrastructure. His public works projects included the building of a massive dam at Aswan, for which he received promises of financial support from the United States and Great Britain. Nasser also approached the Americans about purchasing arms. When the United States refused this request, Nasser turned to the Soviet Union, whereupon the United States and Britain withdraw their support for the Aswan Dam project. Seeing an additional opportunity to gain more influence with the Egyptians, the Soviet Union quickly offered to help Nasser with the Aswan Dam.

Nasser used the loss of Western financial support as a pretext to nationalize the Suez Canal on July 26, 1956. In response, France, Britain, and Israel launched a surprise attack against Egypt. The United States put great pressure on the Israelis, French, and British to withdraw, which they soon did. Far from being defeated, Nasser was vindicated by the Suez Crisis, and he shrewdly used this victory to further consolidate his rule at home and to promote pan-Arabism throughout the Middle East. The Suez Crisis turned Nasser into a hero of Middle East nationalism.

In pursuit of his pan-Arab vision, Nasser established the United Arab Republic with Syria in February 1958. The republic fell apart when Syria withdrew on September 28, 1961. Nevertheless, Nasser continued to promote Arab nationalism and his vision of a pan-Arab union.

Nasser signed a defense pact with Syria in November 1966. In early 1967, Nasser had peacekeepers from the United Nations removed from the Sinai, blocked the Gulf of Aqaba, and moved troops to the Sinai. On June 5, 1967, Israel attacked Egypt, Syria, and Jordan. The war lasted only six days and proved to be a humiliating defeat for Nasser. Nasser's miscalculation eroded his support in Egypt and blemished his reputation throughout the Middle East. In March 1969, he launched sporadic attacks on Israeli forces in the Sinai, which resulted in many more Egyptian than Israeli casualties. In July 1970, Nasser agreed to a cease-fire arrangement put forward by U.S. secretary of state William Rogers to end the so-called War of Attrition. Now in deteriorating health, Nasser died on September 28, 1970 in Cairo.

Dallace W. Unger Jr.

See also: Arab-Israeli War, 1956; Arab-Israeli War, 1967; Egypt; War of Attrition

Further Reading

DuBius, Shirley Graham. *Gamal Abdel Nasser, Son of the Nile.* New York: Third Press, 1972.

Dupuy, Trevor N., Curt Johnson, and David L. Bongard. *Harper Encyclopedia of Military Biography.* New York: HarperCollins, 1992.

Lacouture, Jean. *Nasser, A Biography.* New York: Knopf, 1973.

Netanyahu, Benjamin

Soldier, diplomat, and prime minister of Israel. Benjamin "Bibi" Netanyahu was born in Tel Aviv, Israel, on October 21, 1949. He spent much of his youth in the United States, where his father worked as a university history professor. Netanyahu joined the Israel Defense Forces (IDF) in 1967, serving in an antiterrorist unit. He was wounded during the Ehud Barak–led rescue of hijacked Sabena Airlines hostages at Ben-Gurion Airport on May 8, 1972, and served during the 1973 Arab-Israeli War. He returned to the United States soon after and earned undergraduate and graduate degrees from the Massachusetts Institute of Technology.

Netanyahu served as deputy to Moshe Arens, the Israeli ambassador to the United States, from 1982–1984, and then as Israeli ambassador to the United Nations from 1984–1988. A member of the right-wing Likud Party, he won election to the Knesset in 1988 and served as deputy foreign minister from 1988–1991 and as the Israeli spokesman during the Persian Gulf War (1991).

Netanyahu assumed leadership of the Likud from Yitzhak Shamir in 1993, in part because of his opposition to the Oslo Accords, which afforded the Palestinians autonomy in parts of the West Bank and Gaza Strip. Using the campaign slogan "Netanyahu—making a safe peace," Netanyahu narrowly defeated the Labor Party's Shimon Peres for the post of prime minister of Israel in May 1996 following the assassination of the Labor Party prime minister Yitzhak Rabin and a series of Palestinian suicide bombings that killed thirty-two Israeli citizens. Netanyahu was the youngest person ever to be elected prime minister in Israel.

Netanyahu's tenure was marked by worsening relations with Syria, which led to the posting of Syrian troops in Lebanon that remained until 2005. Relations with the Palestinians also deteriorated when he and Jerusalem mayor Ehud Olmert in September 1996 opened ancient tunnels under the Western (Wailing) Wall and the al-Aqsa Mosque complex. His position weakened within the Likud when he agreed to reposition troops from Hebron in the West Bank in 1997. His attempt to restore that support by increasing Israeli settlements in the West Bank, promoting Jewish housing in predominantly Arab East Jerusalem in March 1997, and decreasing the amount of land to be ceded to the Palestinians served only to provoke Palestinian violence and impede the peace process.

Netanyahu again angered the conservative wing of Likud when he agreed in the Wye Memorandum of 1998 to relinquish control of as much as 40 percent of the West Bank to the Palestinians. Netanyahu again reversed himself and suspended the accords in December 1999. He resigned as chairman of Likud after he was defeated as prime minister by Labor's Ehud Barak in May 1999. Netanyahu accepted the position of minister of foreign affairs in November 2002, and after the 2003 elections, he became finance minister under Prime Minister Ariel Sharon, a post that he held until 2005.

From 2006 until 2009, Netanyahu was leader of the opposition in the Knesset. He returned as Israeli prime minister in 2009 and has stayed in that position since. Critics complain that he has helped push Israeli society to the extreme right, undermined U.S.-Israel relations during the Barack Obama administration, actively undermined peace efforts, and has exaggerated Iran's nuclear threat. Supporters insist that Netanyahu has made Israel safer and wealthier than ever and that he has dramatically improved relations with Washington by cultivating close ties to the Donald Trump administration. He has been plagued by longstanding accusations of corruption, and he and his wife are the targets of ongoing criminal investigations. In February 2019, Israel's attorney general announced that he intended to indict Netanyahu for fraud, bribery, and breach of trust. Despite this, Netanyahu won reelection in April 2019 to a fifth term and is now poised to become Israel's longest-serving prime minister. Also in April 2019, he publicly promised to annex Israeli settlements in the West Bank.

Richard M. Edwards and Robert C. DiPrizio

See also: Entebbe Raid; One-State Solution; Oslo Accords; Rabin, Yitzhak; Settlements; Shamir, Yitzhak; Two-State Solution

Further Reading

Caspit, Ben, and Ilan Kfir. *Netanyahu: The Road to Power.* Trans. Ora Cummings. New York: Birch Lane, 1998.

Lochery, Neill. *The Difficult Road to Peace: Netanyahu, Israel and the Middle East Peace Process.* Reading, UK: Ithaca, 1999.

Shindler, Colin. *Israel, Likud and the Zionist Dream: Power, Politics and Ideology from Begin to Netanyahu.* London: Tauris, 1995.

Noble Sanctuary (see Haram al-Sharif/Temple Mount)

Occupied Palestinian Territories (see Israeli Occupations)

October War (see Arab-Israeli War, 1973)

One-State Solution

A proposed resolution to the enduring conflict between Israelis and Palestinians, which entails the creation of a single state combining Israel, the West Bank, and the Gaza Strip. Conventional wisdom holds that the only viable resolution to the Israeli-Palestinian conflict is for the parties to trade land for peace. In practice, this would require Israel to end its fifty-two-year occupation and allow the creation of a Palestinian state in the West Bank and Gaza, in exchange for an end to Palestinian violence against Israelis. But confidence in the two-state orthodoxy is wavering in many quarters. Indeed, an increasing number of advocates on both ends of the conflict spectrum insist that that option is neither possible nor preferable.

Some insist that a two-state solution is not possible because Israel lacks the political will to make it happen, as evidenced by its extensive colonization of East Jerusalem and the West Bank, which has created so many facts on the ground favoring Israel that no conceivable partition plan could satisfy both Israelis and Palestinians. A two-state solution is also undesirable because it cannot address the grievances of the Palestinian nation as a whole. Before the creation of the state of Israel in 1948, nearly all Palestinians lived within Palestine. Since then, however, hundreds of thousands fled or were forced to leave, creating a large Palestinian diaspora. More Palestinians now live outside the occupied territories than within them.

The argument goes that justice demands that the Palestinians' internationally recognized right to return home must be respected. Affording Palestinians control over 22 percent or less of their historic homeland would do little to rectify the injustices that diaspora Palestinians have suffered; nor would it do anything to ameliorate the discriminatory treatment that Palestinian citizens of Israel endure. As an alternative, it has been proposed that a single binational, democratic state should be created, encompassing Israel, the West Bank, and Gaza, in which all Jews and Palestinians enjoy full citizenship and equal treatment under the law, and Jews and Palestinians worldwide enjoy the right to return to their historic homeland. Once all the discriminatory laws, structures, and practices that now define their relationship are rectified, Jews and Palestinians can live side by side in peace in one country.

To be sure, many critics of Israel's occupation insist that a one-state solution already exists because the Israeli government rules, directly or indirectly, over everyone from the Jordan River to the Mediterranean Sea. This state, in their view, is an apartheid-like, discriminatory one that needs to be drastically reformed through a nonviolent civil rights movement (complemented by international pressure) that demands full citizenship and equal treatment of all people subject to Israeli rule.

Most Zionists and their supporters consider this type of one-state solution a nonstarter because sooner or later, Jews would be a minority. While Israeli Jews disagree about a great many things, most believe that Israel must always be a Jewish state, which in turn requires a Jewish majority. Most also believe the kind of post-Zionist one-state solution described here is really a thinly veiled strategy for destroying the state of Israel and preventing Jewish self-determination. Indeed, some in the pro-Israel community in the United States have not only disparaged the idea but have actively sought to squelch its public discussion. Still, a growing number of right-wing Israelis have embraced the idea of a one-state solution—albeit not a post-Zionist one.

To these Zionists, the two-state solution is a bipartisan pipe dream advocated by naive Westerners as a sort of panacea for a conflict that is really about the right of Jews to self-determination in their ancient homeland, and about Israel's right to protect itself from terrorism. Palestinians are not interested in peace with Israel—just the opposite, in fact. The so-called peace process has failed because of insincere negotiation efforts on the part of the Palestinians, who continue to teach their children to hate Jews. Anti-Israeli violence is not rooted in the occupation, but in Palestinian opposition to Israel's existence and their anti-Semitism. Moreover, Palestine is not even a real nation, and Arabs' claim to Palestine is baseless because that land rightfully belongs to the world's oldest nation, the Jews.

From this viewpoint, Jews are not occupiers, colonists, or settlers of Palestine; rather, they are the only true indigenous people. For an increasing number of Zionists, the best solution to breaking the status quo of continuous Palestinian terrorism and unfair international criticism of Israel is to extend Israeli sovereignty over all or part of the West Bank (while leaving the status quo in the Gaza Strip). Some versions of such a so-called Israeli solution would annex up to 80 percent of the West Bank and create autonomous enclaves around major Palestinian cities. Others would annex all the territory and force or encourage Palestinians to leave. Still others would afford Palestinians in the newly annexed territories permanent residency and the right to apply for citizenship.

What all these proposals have in common is a desire to effectively annex the West Bank, while maintaining the current political structures ensuring that Israel remains a Jewish state. During both his campaigns for reelection, Prime Minister Benjamin Netanyahu promised to annex Israeli settlements in the West Bank. In the most recent elections held in September 2019, Netanyahu came in second to Benny Gantz of the Blue and White Party, and negotiations to put together a coalition government were continuing.

Robert C. DiPrizio

See also: Arab-Israeli War, 1948; Boycott, Divestment, and Sanctions Movement; Diaspora, Palestinian; Israelis; Permanent Status Issues; Settlements; Two-State Solution; Zionism

Further Reading

Abunimah, Ali. *One Country: A Bold Proposal to End the Israeli-Palestinian Impasse.* New York: Metropolitan Books, 2006.

Glick, Caroline. *The Israeli Solution: A One-State Plan for Peace in the Middle East.* New York: Crown Forum. 2014.

Makdisi, Saree. *Palestine Inside Out: An Everyday Occupation.* New York: W. W. Norton & Company, 2008.

Remnick, David. "The One-State Reality." *The New Yorker*, November 17, 2014. https://www.newyorker.com/magazine/2014/11/17/one-state-reality.

Operation Cast Lead (see Gaza Strip)

Operation Nickel Grass

A U.S. military airlift aimed at resupplying Israel during the 1973 Arab-Israeli War. The war involved a massive expenditure of ammunition and weaponry, and Israel appealed to the United States for assistance. The Israeli request was not immediately answered, despite pressure from Secretary of State Henry Kissinger. Only after the Soviet Union began to resupply Syria and Egypt did the United States decide to send weapons and other military supplies to Israel.

On October 14, 1973, the first U.S. aircraft began deliveries, and by November 15, about 23,000 tons of supplies were delivered. In addition to the airlift, the United States sent supplies by sea. Israel received hundreds of different kinds of missiles, jet aircraft, tanks, armored personnel carriers, helicopters, antitank weapons, and M-16 assault rifles. The United States also sent tank and artillery ammunition.

Operation Nickel Grass proved vital to Israel during the war, especially in light of Israeli ammunition shortages. Much of the aircraft and tank support, however, arrived after the cease-fire had taken effect.

Tal Tovy

See also: Arab-Israeli War, 1973; U.S. Aid to Israel

Further Reading

Aker, Frank. *October 1973: The Arab-Israeli War.* Hamden, CT: Archon Books, 1985.

Allen, Peter. *The Yom Kippur War.* New York: Charles Scribner, 1982.

Blum, Howard. *The Eve of Destruction: The Untold Story of the Yom Kippur War.* New York: Harper, 2003.

Operation Peace for Galilee (see Lebanon, Israeli Invasion of)

Operation Pillar of Defense (see Gaza Strip)

Operation Protective Edge (see Gaza Strip)

Oslo Accords

An interim peace and autonomy agreement between Israel and Palestinians. The Oslo Accords, formally known as the Declaration of Principles on Interim Self-Government Arrangements, was signed on September 13, 1993, in Washington between Israeli prime minister Yitzhak Rabin, Palestine Liberation Organization (PLO) chairman Yasser Arafat, and U.S. president Bill Clinton. In the agreement, the PLO—the Palestinians' de facto government-in-exile—formally recognized Israel's right to exist and Israel's sovereignty over 78 percent of historic Palestine, as well as pledging to end military actions against Israel. Israel, while failing to recognize Palestinian statehood, did recognize Palestinian nationhood, including the right of self-determination, and the PLO's role as the Palestinians' legitimate representatives.

The document spelled out ways in which the Palestinians could achieve a degree of autonomy in parts of the West Bank and Gaza Strip, which had been occupied by Israel since the 1967 Six-Day War. The hope was that by Palestinians demonstrating competent self-governance and control of anti-Israel violence, Israelis would gain the confidence to make a phased withdrawal from the occupied territories and

President Bill Clinton (center) watches as Israeli prime minister Yitzhak Rabin (left) and Palestine Liberation Organization leader Yasser Arafat (right) shake hands at the ceremony for the signing of the historic Israeli-Palestinian Declaration of Principles (also known as as the Oslo Accords) on September 13, 1993. (William J. Clinton Presidential Library)

grant the Palestinians an independent state alongside Israel. Similarly, it was hoped that the removal of foreign occupation forces from certain areas, increasing levels of self-government, and the prospects of a viable independent state would give the Palestinian population confidence to end the violence and live in peace with the Israelis. The interim period was to be completed by 1998, at which time a permanent peace agreement would be signed.

Although the U.S. government became the guarantor of the Oslo Accords, the United States had little to do with the agreement itself. Soon after the election of a more moderate Israeli government in 1992, direct talks began in secret between representatives of Israel and the PLO, first initiated by Norwegian nongovernmental organizations (NGOs), and later with the assistance of the Norwegian foreign ministry. This apparently took place without the knowledge of U.S. officials, who still took the position that the PLO should not be allowed to take part in the peace process, excluding them from the stalled peace talks then going on in Washington. As the secret negotiations in Norway progressed during the summer of 1993, the Clinton administration put forward what it called a compromise proposal for Palestinian autonomy—which was actually less favorable to the Palestinians than what was then being put forward by the Israelis in Norway.

The U.S. role in the Oslo process began with a historic signing ceremony on the White House lawn that September. Given the ambiguities in the agreement, both parties agreed that the United States should be its guarantor. The Israelis saw the U.S. government as the entity most likely to support its positions on outstanding issues, and the Palestinians saw it as the only entity capable of forcing Israel to live up to its commitments and push the occupying power to compromise.

Peace talks resumed in Washington in the fall of 1993 within the Oslo framework. Over the next seven years, the United States brokered a series of Israeli-Palestinian agreements that led to the withdrawal of Israeli forces from most of the Gaza Strip and parts of the West Bank. By the end of the decade, about 40 percent of the West Bank and Gaza Strip was placed under the rule of the new Palestinian Authority (PA), headed by Arafat, and the land was divided into dozens of noncontiguous zones wherein for the first time, the Palestinians could exercise some limited autonomy.

During this period, the Israeli government severely limited the mobility of Palestinians within and between the West Bank and Gaza Strip, dramatically expanded its expropriation of land in the occupied territories for colonization by Jewish settlers, and refused to withdraw from as much territory as promised in the U.S.-brokered disengagement agreements. In addition, the United States tended to side with the Israelis on most issues during talks regarding the disengagement process, even after a right-wing coalition that had opposed the Oslo Accords came to power in Israel in 1996. This alienated many Palestinians from the peace process and hardened anti-Israeli attitudes.

Meanwhile, much of the PA proved itself to be rather inept, corrupt, and autocratic, alienating much of the Palestinian population and making it difficult to suppress the growth of radical Islamic groups. On more than two dozen occasions between 1994 and 2000, Islamic extremists from the Occupied Palestinian Territories (OPT) engaged in a series of terrorist attacks inside Israel that killed scores of Israeli civilians, thereby hardening anti-Palestinian attitudes.

The Palestinians had hoped that the United States would broker the negotiations based upon international law, which forbids the expansion of any country's territory by military force and prohibits occupying powers from transferring their civilian population into occupied land, as well as a series of specific UN Security Council resolutions demanding that Israel honor these principles. From the Palestinians' perspective—as well as that of the United Nations (UN), most U.S. allies, and most international legal experts—the impetus was on Israel, the occupying power, to make most of the compromises to achieve peace. The Clinton administration, however, argued that these UN resolutions were no longer relevant and saw the West Bank and Gaza Strip simply as disputed territories, thereby requiring both sides to compromise. This gave the Israelis (by far the more powerful of the two parties) a clear advantage in the peace process.

The Palestinians, in signing the Oslo Accords, worked on the assumption that the agreement would result in concrete improvements in the lives of those in the occupied territories, that the interim period would be no more than five years, and that the final settlement would be based on UN Security Council Resolutions 242 and 338, which called upon Israel to withdraw from the territories seized in the 1967 war. For their part, the Israelis had hoped that the Oslo Accords would lead to the emergence of a responsible Palestinian leadership and greater security. None of these, however, have come to pass.

In late 2000, negotiations at Camp David between the Israelis, Palestinians, and Americans failed. Opposition leader Ariel Sharon then visited the Temple Mount/Haram al-Sharif, with hundreds of security personnel, in what was clearly meant to be a provocation. Palestinians responded with the Second (al-Aqsa) Intifada.

The Oslo peace process was never revived. Indeed, because there has been no progress in negotiations, Palestinian leaders have declared that they are no longer bound by the Oslo Accords and have taken unilateral action to earn international recognition, including repeated (unsuccessful) attempts to gain full member-state status at the United Nations. Successive Israeli governments have declared support for a negotiated two-state solution, but also have allowed hundreds of thousands of Israeli Jews to settle in the occupied territories. When the Oslo Accords were signed, there were about 250,000 Israeli settlers living in East Jerusalem and the West Bank; today, there are over 630,000. In 2015, on the eve of a tight reelection campaign, Israeli prime minister Netanyahu declared that Palestinian independence would not occur under his watch. In 2019, during both his reelection campaigns, Netanyahu promised to annex Israeli settlements in the West Bank.

Stephen Zunes

See also: Arafat, Yasser; Intifada, Second; Netanyahu, Benjamin; Permanent Status Issues; Settlements; Rabin, Yitzhak; Two-State Solution

Further Reading

Bauck, Peter, and Mohammed Omer, eds. *The Oslo Accords: A Critical Assessment*. Cairo: American University in Cairo, 2017.

Enderlin, Charles. *Shattered Dreams: The Failure of the Peace Process in the Middle East, 1995–2002*. New York: Other Press, 2003.

Khalidi, Rashid. *Brokers of Deceit: How the U.S. Has Undermined Peace in the Middle East*. Boston: Beacon Press, 2013.

Peres, Shimon. *The New Middle East*. New York: Henry Holt and Company, 1993.

Ottoman Conquest of Palestine

In 1517, Salim I (1512–1520), the ninth Ottoman sultan, went to war against the Mamluk dynasty, which had controlled Egypt and Syria since defeating the Fatimids in 1250 and the Mongols in 1260. After the Ottomans gained control over the Anatolian Peninsula, conquered Constantinople, expanded into the Balkans, and beat back challenges from the Shia Safavid Empire of Iran, the sultan turned his attention south to the Mamluks. The Ottomans justified their expansion west as Muslim *ghazis* (warriors) fighting Christian infidels, and to the east as war against heretical Shia. Salim accused Mamluk governors of conspiring to aid the Safavids, and on this basis gained authorization from a council of Muslim leaders to wage war against the orthodox Sunni Mamluks.

The Ottomans met the Mamluk army in the Battle of Marj Dabiq, north of Aleppo, and defeated it resoundingly. Although the Mamluks enjoyed greater numbers and superior cavalry, the Ottoman grand vizier Sinan Pasha employed the infantry creatively to aid the cavalry. The Ottoman infantry had greater numbers and quality of firearms, as well as greater practice using them, learned from Jewish exiles from Spain. The Mamluks had only just begun to adopt gunpowder technology, and they had few cannons or muskets. The Mamluk governor of Aleppo defected to the Ottomans. Later, it became clear that he had been an Ottoman secret agent for some time.

Damascus surrendered without fighting, and in Jerusalem, Sultan Salim visited the Muslim holy places. During this time, Muslims considered Palestine the southern part of Bilad al Sham, in Greater Syria. Then the Ottomans defeated a Mamluk army at the Battle of Yaunis Khan south of Gaza. Finally on January 23, 1517, only a week after leaving Damascus, the Ottomans defeated a Mamluk army at Raydaniyya, outside Cairo. Although Sultan Salim briefly entered Cairo, he had to leave due to resistance. Only after a later defeat of the Mamluk commanders at the end of March did their victory become complete. As a result of this conquest, the Ottomans gained greater legitimacy as guardians of the holy places of Mecca and Medina and protectors of pilgrims. They gained control of land and sea trade routes, as well as grain from Egypt, and became recognized as the central power of the Muslim world, which would last for almost 400 more years.

Jonathan K. Zartman

See also: Absentee Landlords; Haram al-Sharif/Temple Mount; Jerusalem, Old City of

Further Reading

Finkel, Caroline. *Osman's Dream: The History of the Ottoman Empire*. New York: Basic Books, 2005.

Goldschmidt, Arthur, Jr., and Lawrence Davidson. *A Concise History of the Middle East*. 8th ed. Boulder, CO: Westview Press, 2006.

Schmuelevitz, Aryeh. "Capsali as a Source for Ottoman History, 1450–1523." *International Journal of Middle East Studies* 9 (1978): 339–344.

P

Pale of Settlement

The western border region of imperial Russia, within which Jews were expected to reside. In the late nineteenth century, some 40–50 percent of the world's Jews lived in Russia. The 5 million Russian Jews differed from the great majority of the Russian population not only in terms of religion, but also in language and social customs, and as a consequence, the government and many ordinary Russians suspected their loyalty. During the 1880s and 1890s, a number of anti-Jewish measures legally restricted the Jews regarding their residence, educational opportunities, political rights, and economic status.

All Jews were expected to live within the Pale region. Created by Czarina Catherine II (the Great) in 1791 as an alternative to the expulsion of the Jews from Russia, it comprised a wide swath of western Russia running north from the Black Sea to the Baltic and comprising present-day Ukraine, Moldavia, Poland, Belarus, Lithuania, and part of western Russia. Within the Pale, Jews were generally compelled to live in small provincial towns, where they could be kept under government surveillance.

The government sharply restricted Jewish political rights. Jews could not vote for the representative assemblies in the cities; instead, the government appointed their representatives. In education, Jews were limited to a fixed percentage of the total student body in any particular school. Jews could also not legally buy or lease land in rural districts. Government approval was required for a Jew to become a lawyer, and Jews were not permitted to be civil servants. Government regulations also sharply limited the number of Jewish stockholders in industrial corporations. And while Jews were required to serve in the Russian army, they could not be officers in it. Finally, no Christian could legally marry a Jew. As a result of these regulations, many Jews became of necessity moneylenders, bankers, or retail merchants. In these capacities, they were often hated by the peasants because of the high interest charged for loans.

Conversion to Russian Orthodoxy would remove all restrictions. The anti-Jewish laws were not always and everywhere enforced, and with the low salaries paid to local officials, corruption was rampant. Still, anti-Jewish riots, known as *pogroms*, often broke out, with the full approval of the authorities. Jews were systematically subjected to beatings, or even killed, and their property might be plundered or destroyed as the police looked on. Such pogroms occurred throughout Russia, especially during 1881–1883 and 1903–1906. Both the anti-Jewish legislation and pogroms led many Jews to emigrate, most of them to the United States but a number to Palestine.

The Pale officially ceased to exist in 1917, when two revolutions swept the czarist regime out of power. Yet it had contributed substantially to the alienation of the

Jewish community from Russian society at large, and thus it indirectly advanced Zionism.

Spencer C. Tucker

See also: Aliya; Judaism; Zionism

Further Reading

Gitelman, Zvi Y. *A Century of Ambivalence: The Jews of Russia and the Soviet Union, 1881 to the Present.* New York: Schocken, 1988.

Klier, John Doyle. *Russia Gathers Her Jews: The Origins of the "Jewish Question" in Russia, 1772–1825.* De Kalb: Northern Illinois Press, 1986.

Palestine

Homeland of the Palestinian people. In modern parlance, the term *Palestine* (derived from the word *Philistine,* referring to a people that lived in the coastal parts of Canaan prior to the creation of the United Jewish Kingdom) is most often used in reference to either the geographic region that encompasses the modern state of Israel and the Occupied Palestinian Territories (OPT) of the Gaza Strip and West Bank, or in reference to the declared state of Palestine, which claims sovereignty over Gaza and West Bank, with its capital in East Jerusalem.

After World War I, Britain wrestled control of Palestine away from the Ottoman Empire and ruled it as a League of Nations mandate until 1948. For most of this period, it actively assisted Zionists seeking to establish a Jewish state in Palestine, which the Palestinian Arab majority opposed. The ensuing struggle to control Palestine was often violent, and after World War II, Britain referred the matter to the newly formed United Nations (UN). In 1947, the United Nations voted to partition Palestine into two states: one for Arabs and one for Jews. Jerusalem was to become an international city. Although the Arab population was 1.2 million and the Jewish population just 600,000, the Jewish state would take up about 56 percent of Palestine. Arabs in Palestine and the surrounding countries rejected the partition, and war raged until early 1949. By then, the new state of Israel had gained control of 78 percent of Palestine, while Egypt took over the Gaza Strip and Jordan controlled the West Bank and East Jerusalem.

During the Arab-Israeli War of 1967, Israel occupied Gaza, East Jerusalem, and the West Bank. It immediately annexed East Jerusalem and parts of the West Bank and began building settlements. Unlike 1948, when over 80 percent of the Palestinian population fled or were forced out of what became Israel, the vast majority of Palestinians remained in Gaza and the West Bank in 1967. Today, the Palestinian population under occupation is about 5 million—2 million in Gaza and 3 million in the West Bank and East Jerusalem.

In the early 1960s, the Palestine Liberation Organization (PLO) was created with the stated goal of liberating all of Palestine, but within a generation, it accepted the concept of a two-state solution, in which an independent Palestine would exist side by side with Israel. In 1988, the PLO declared Palestine to be an independent state, with sovereignty over the West Bank and Gaza Strip and East Jerusalem as its capital. Although dismissed as hyperbole by some, many developing states recognized Palestine, and the PLO has since sought to expand international recognition.

Prospects for moving from a de jure to a de facto independent Palestinian state were boosted dramatically in 1993 with the signing of the Oslo Accords. Follow-on agreements led to the redeployment of Israeli troops from major Palestinian population centers and the creation of the Palestinian Authority (PA), a proto-government with varying levels of control over the Palestinian population in the occupied territories. The PA has responsibility for security, public education, health, social welfare, taxation, tourism, and judicial matters throughout Area A in the West Bank, which includes the major Palestinian cities and towns. This covers about 20 percent of the West Bank. On the outskirts of these cities and towns, known as Area B, Israel and the PA coordinate on security matters. In Area C, which constitutes 60 percent of the West Bank, the PA has no authority. The PA had similar limited authority in the Gaza Strip until Israel pulled out of the enclave in 2005. The Palestinian Islamist group Hamas and the PA fought a brief civil war in 2007, which left Hamas in control of Gaza and limited the PA's authority to the West Bank. The PA has no authority in East Jerusalem, which Israel annexed in 1967.

Since the signing of the Oslo Accords, opponents of partition on both sides have worked to undermine peace negotiations. Hamas and other Palestinian groups have carried out numerous terror attacks and suicide bombings, while Israelis expanded settlements and rallied behind politicians opposed to partition. Some Israeli Jews also carried out terror attacks against Palestinians, and one of them assassinated Prime Minister Yitzhak Rabin. Intermittent negotiations over the past twenty-five years have all failed.

In 2011, Palestinian officials unsuccessfully sought full membership in the United Nations. Full membership requires the approval of the UN Security Council, but the United States is one of five nations with veto power on the Security Council and has vowed to block any effort that doesn't meet with Israel's approval. The United States and Israel insist that Palestinian statehood can come about only as a result of direct negotiations between the PA and Israel. For their part, Palestinians argue that over fifty years of occupation and twenty-five years of failed negotiations have proved that Israel is unwilling to negotiate a two-state solution, and unilateral action is the only option left for establishing an independent Palestine.

In November 2012, 138 member-states voted in the UN General Assembly to grant "non-Member observer status" to Palestine. The United States and Israel were two of only nine member-states that opposed the measure. Palestine is a member of the Arab League, Organization of Islamic Cooperation, the International Criminal Police Organization, the International Olympic Committee (IOC), International Federation of Association Football (FIFA), and the International Criminal Court (ICC). It also flies its flag at the United Nations.

Palestinian officials have used membership in international organizations like the ICC, IOC, and FIFA to exert international pressure on Israel. They have requested, for example, that the ICC investigate purported Israeli war crimes in the state of Palestine. The United States and Israel have retaliated by cutting or withholding funds and building more settlements.

While Palestinians have made some headway in gaining international recognition of a notional Palestine, they are no closer to achieving actual independence. For that, Israel would have to end its occupation, remove large numbers of settlers, and give up security control of the West Bank. None of this is likely.

Israel's settlement population has grown from about 250,000 when the Oslo Accords were struck to nearly 700,000 today, and settlements have expanded deep into the West Bank. Indeed, Israel's right-wing parties, emboldened by U.S. president Donald Trump's pro-Israel policies, are calling for annexation of the West Bank. Just days before being reelected in April 2019, Israeli prime minister Benjamin Netanyahu publicly promised to begin annexing Israeli settlements. Moreover, the Trump administration is proposing a final settlement that does not include Palestinian independence. Combined with ongoing divisions between Hamas and the PA, the prospects for Palestinian statehood are dimming.

Robert C. DiPrizio

See also: Arafat, Yasser; Gaza; Jerusalem; Netanyahu, Benjamin; Oslo Accords; Palestine Liberation Organization; Palestinian Authority; Permanent Status Issues; West Bank

Further Reading

Khalidi, Rashid. *Palestinian Identity: The Construction of Modern National Consciousness*. New York: Columbia University Press, 2010.

Kimmerling, Baruch, and Migdal, Joel S. *The Palestinian People: A History*. Cambridge, MA: Harvard University Press, 2003.

Shapira, Anita. *Israel: A History*. Waltham, MA: Brandeis University Press, 2012

Smith, Charles D. *Palestine and the Arab–Israeli Conflict: A History with Documents*. 9th ed. New York: Bedford/St. Martin's Press, 2017.

Palestine Liberation Army (PLA)

Military organization established by the first Palestinian National Congress in 1964. Proposed by Ahmad Shukeiri, the Palestine Liberation Army (PLA) was created to serve as the conventional military arm of the Palestine Liberation Organization (PLO). The PLO was originally a forum for traditional, influential Palestinian notables. Its leadership did not consider guerrilla or commando activities at that time. Instead, they established the PLA as a force of three brigades, totaling some 20,000–30,000 men, to be hosted and trained in Egypt, Iraq, and Syria, that would fight alongside these Arab armies under their command.

Although nominally under PLO direction, in practice, the PLA has always been firmly under the control of its host nations, and PLA units have been incorporated into their military establishments. Thus, the Ayn Jalut Brigade in Gaza came under Egyptian control, the Hittin Brigade came under Syrian control, and the Qadisiyya Brigade came under Iraqi control. In Jordan, where much larger numbers of Palestinians resided, Shukeiri had to promise King Husayn that Palestinians would not arm or organize Palestinians there. Later, however, the Yarmuk Brigade formed with defectors from the Jordanian army. The presence of Palestinian troops has proved a convenient circumstance on a number of occasions, particularly for Syria, which utilized PLA troops during its armed actions in Jordan and Lebanon.

The 1967 Six-Day War made it impossible for the Egyptian government to oppose commando activities. Hence, Gamal Abdel Nasser met with Fatah leaders and arranged to help arm and train them. Shukeiri was overthrown as PLO leader and replaced by Yahya Hammuda in 1967, and then by Yasser Arafat in 1969. This period saw a displacement of the PLO leaders who had emphasized politics and diplomacy in favor of those who wanted more independent Palestinian military activities. Arafat, who had opposed the creation of the PLA out of concern that it would be dominated by its host nations, argued that it hurt the recruitment of Palestinian fighters. This lack of unity demonstrated the inherent weakness of the PLO, which had never maintained even rudimentary control over its military wing. In 1970 Arafat was named the head of the PLA at the Seventh Palestinian National Council (PNC), but the commander of the PLA, Uthman Haddad, refused to recognize Arafat's supremacy and remained in power. In a face-saving gesture, Haddad was renamed the PLA's chief of staff, and in this position, he continued his policy of maintaining PLA autonomy from Arafat's control.

By the mid-1980s, the PLA had grown to a peak strength of approximately 14,000 permanent forces, divided into eight brigades. After the signing of the Declaration of Principles and the Cairo Agreement on May 4, 1994, some of the PLA was redeployed into the autonomous area to serve as the police force of the Palestinian Authority (PA).

The Syrian brigade, which is autonomous in principle, as it is staffed entirely by drafted Palestinian refugees, is in fact controlled by Syria. It organizes pro-Syrian events to demonstrate Syrian solidarity with the Palestinian cause. Since the start of the Syrian civil war in March 2011, the brigade of the PLA controlled by the Syrian government has been involved in combat against antigovernment rebels. In these conflicts, it has reportedly suffered numerous casualties, including the death of a general, Anwar al-Saqa.

Paul J. Springer, Spencer C. Tucker, and Sherifa Zuhur

See also: Palestine Liberation Organization; Palestinian Authority Security Forces

Further Reading
Amos, John W. II. *Arab-Israeli Military/Political Relations: Arab Perceptions and the Politics of Escalation.* New York: Pergamon, 1979.
Brand, Laurie. *Palestinians in the Arab World: Institution Building and the Search for State.* New York: Columbia University Press, 1988.
Khouri, Fred. *The Arab-Israeli Dilemma.* Syracuse, NY: Syracuse University Press, 1985.

Palestine Liberation Front (PLF)

A militant Palestinian group labeled a terrorist organization by the United States and some European nations. The Palestine Liberation Front (PLF) was first founded in 1959 by Ahmed Jibril, with Syrian backing. In 1967, it merged with two other organizations, the Heroes of the Return and the Youth of the Revenge Group, to form the Popular Front for the Liberation of Palestine (PFLP), led by George Habash. In 1968, however, Jibril split off part of the membership to form the Popular Front for the Liberation of Palestine–General Command (PFLP-GC), which supported

Syria in doing battle with the Palestine Liberation Organization (PLO) in 1976 during the Lebanese civil war.

The PFLP-GC action led to the reestablishment of the PLF in April 1977 under Abu Abbas (Muhammad Zaidan) and Talat Yaqub. PLF leaders were angry that the PFLP-GC did not oppose Syrian support for the Phalangists against the PLO in Lebanon. Some fighting occurred thereafter between the PLF and the PFLP-GC, including the bombing of PLF headquarters in August 1977, in which some 200 people died.

Following the 1983 Israeli invasion of Lebanon, the PLF split into three factions. The two principal groups were a pro-Syrian faction, led by Yaqub, and a larger, pro-Iraqi group, led by Abbas. Both kept the same name and claimed to represent the original organization. Yaqub died in November 1988, and only then did his group rejoin that led by Abbas.

Reportedly receiving some Libyan funding, the PLF believed strongly in armed struggle against Israel in the form of terrorist attacks, most of them mounted along Israel's northern border with Lebanon. The most notorious of its terrorist actions was the hijacking of the Italian cruise ship *Achille Lauro* on October 7, 1985. It also mounted an unsuccessful attack on Nizamim Beach, near Tel Aviv, on May 30, 1990. The attack was designed to kill both Israelis and tourists in the hopes of torpedoing any move toward peace talks between the PLO and Israel. Abbas came under heavy criticism from within the PLO leadership for this, and he was forced to resign from the PLO Executive Committee.

Following the 1993 Oslo Accords, the PLF accepted the PLO policy of halting terrorist activities against Israel. Abbas was captured by U.S. troops in Iraq in 2003 as he was trying to seek refuge in Syria. In March 2004, Abbas died while still in American custody. The PLF campaigned in the 2006 Palestinian elections under the name of Martyr Abu Abbas, but it failed to win any seats.

Spencer C. Tucker

See also: Habash, George; Palestine Liberation Organization

Further Reading

Alexander, Yonah. *Palestinian Secular Terrorism*. Ardsley, NY: Transnational Publishers, 2003.

Bohn, Michael K. *The Achille Lauro Hijacking: Lessons in the Politics and Prejudice of Terrorism*. Dulles, VA: Potomac Books, 2004.

Nassar, Jamal R. *The Palestine Liberation Organization: From Armed Struggle to the Declaration of Independence*. New York: Praeger, 1991.

Palestine Liberation Organization (PLO)

A political and military organization founded in 1964 and dedicated to protecting the human and legal rights of Palestinians and creating an independent state for Palestinian Arabs in Palestine. Since the 1960s, the Munazzamat al-Tahrir Filastiniyyah (in English, the Palestine Liberation Organization, PLO) has functioned as the official mouthpiece for the Palestinian people. Numerous factions and organizations fall loosely under the PLO's umbrella. In addition to Fatah, which is the largest and most influential of these groups, the PLO has encompassed the Popular Front for the Liberation of Palestine (PFLP), the Democratic Front for the Liberation of Palestine (DFLP), the Palestinian People's Party, the Palestine Liberation Front (PLF), the Arab Liberation Front, al-Saiqa (Syrian Baathists), the Palestine Democratic Union, the Palestinian Popular Front Struggle, and the Palestinian Arab Front. Two groups no longer associated with the PLO include the Popular Front for the Liberation of Palestine–General Command (PFLP-GC) and the Fatah Uprising. The PLO is comprised of centrist-nationalist groups (such as Fatah), rightist groups, leftist groups (including communists), militant groups, and nonmilitant groups. It has purposely eschewed embracing any one political philosophy, so as to be as inclusive as possible in its membership. The PLO is funded mostly by donor-states from the Arab world.

The PLO was founded in 1964 by the Arab League and Egypt. Its first president was Ahmad Shukeiri. The stated purpose of the PLO was the liberation of Palestine, condemnation of Zionist imperialism, and the dissolution of Israel through the use of armed force. Throughout its existence, the PLO has often used violence to express its viewpoints and attract international attention. This has earned it the reputation of being a terrorist group, although Palestinians and many international observers dispute that characterization. In 1988, PLO chairman Yasser Arafat—who led the organization from 1969 to 2004—renounced violence as a means to achieve Palestinian goals, but a number of PLO groups did not follow this decree and have continued to mount terrorist attacks in Israel and elsewhere.

Although the PLO has been reorganized many times since its inception, its leading governing bodies have been the Palestinian National Council (PNC), the Central Council, and the Executive Committee. The PNC has 300 members and functions as a nominal legislature. The Executive Committee has fifteen members elected by the PNC and holds the PLO's real political and executive power.

The PLO has always represented a variety of viewpoints, some more radical and prone to violence than others, and Egyptians dominated the organization in its first years. As the 1960s wore on, fedayeen organizations (groups that existed expressly to take up armed struggle against the Israelis) became more powerful. These groups used guerrilla and paramilitary tactics to resist the encroachment of Israelis on what they considered Palestinian territory.

In 1968, Fatah took control of the PLO's activities after Arafat appeared on the cover of *Time* magazine as the leader of the Palestinian movement. On February 3, 1969, the PNC in Cairo officially appointed Arafat the PLO chairman. Over the next four years, Arafat consolidated power over the PLO, which he based in Jordan.

In 1968 and 1969, the PLO functioned as a well-organized, unofficial state within Jordan, with its uniformed soldiers acting as a police force and collecting their own taxes. In 1968, King Husayn of Jordan and the PLO signed an agreement by which the latter agreed that its members would stop patrolling in uniform with guns, stop searching civilian vehicles, and act as Jordanian civilian citizens. The PLO did not comply with this agreement, however, and attacks on civilians and clashes between Palestinians and Jordanian soldiers increased. By 1970, Husayn decided that the Palestinians threatened national security and ordered his army to evict them. This led to several months of violence, during which Syria aided the Palestinians and the United States aided Jordan. The events of Black September (including an attempt on Husayn's life), several airliner hijackings by the PFLP, and a declaration of martial law in Jordan culminated with the PLO agreeing to a cease-fire on September 24 and promising to leave the country.

Arafat relocated the PLO to Beirut, where Palestinians moved into existing refugee settlements. The Lebanese government tried to restrict the PLO's movements, which led to tension, but the Palestinians used their position to launch periodic attacks across the Israeli border. Lebanese Muslims and some Druze supported the Palestinian cause, seeing the Palestinians as allies in their struggle against certain Christian factions that dominated the government and the Lebanese Forces (Maronite militias). The latter disliked the PLO presence and wanted to drive the Palestinians out by force.

During the early 1970s, Arafat and the various groups that comprised the PLO often came into conflict over the proper means of achieving the organization's goals. Although Arafat agreed that a certain amount of violence against Israel was necessary to accomplish the PLO's purposes, he believed that diplomacy and compromise were also key to gaining international support. After 1968, the more politically radical groups, such as the PFLP, the DFLP, and other smaller factions, strongly disagreed because it seemed apparent that the Arab countries could not defeat Israel militarily. Such groups gained notoriety for carrying out airplane hijackings in the late 1960s and early 1970s, in Europe and the Middle East. These attacks were intended to advance efforts to destroy Israel and create a socialist, secular Arab society in its stead. Arafat himself condemned these overseas attacks because he believed (correctly) that they hurt the PLO's international image.

When the radical Black September organization killed several Israeli athletes and coaches at the Olympic Games in Munich in 1972, Arafat promptly stated that the PLO was not responsible for those attacks. Arafat closed down the Black September organization in 1973, and in 1974, he ordered the PLO to restrict its violent attacks to Israel, the Gaza Strip, and the West Bank.

In 1974, the Arab Summit recognized the PLO as the sole representative of the Palestinian people. Arafat appeared before the United Nations (UN) that same year as the official representative of the Palestinians. Speaking before the UN General Assembly, he condemned Zionism and said that the PLO would continue to operate as freedom fighters, but he also said that he wanted peace. This was the first time the international community had heard directly from the PLO, and many international observers praised Arafat and came to support the Palestinian cause. The UN granted the PLO "non-Member observer status" on November 22, 1974; after 1988, it transferred that status to Palestine. In 2012, the UN General Assembly recognized Palestine as a non-member state observer.

Also in 1974, the leaders of Fatah, in the guise of the PNC, created a Ten-Point Program that set forth the PLO's goals. This program called for a single secular state in Israel and Palestine that would welcome both Jews and Arabs and provide all citizens with equal rights regardless of religion, race, or gender. It also called for the creation of the Palestinian Authority (PA) on free Palestinian territory. Israel rejected the Ten-Point Program. Meanwhile, the radical guerrilla groups the PFLP and the PFLP-GC, which had earlier split from the PFLP, departed from the PLO in protest of its attempt to negotiate with Israel.

In 1975, the Lebanese civil war broke out. Israel supported the Maronite militias who opposed the Palestinians. The PLO and Fatah joined forces with the National Front, a more left-wing coalition of Muslims, Druze, and Christians. Syria intervened on behalf of Muslim forces at first, but later came to the aid of the Maronites; in the 1980s, it also supported the Shia militias.

On January 12, 1976, the UN Security Council voted to grant the PLO the right to participate in Security Council debates. The PLO became a full member of the Arab League that same year.

During the late 1970s, PLO members continued to enter Lebanon and maintain positions in Beirut, from which they exchanged attacks with Israel. On July 24, 1981, the PLO and Israel agreed to a cease-fire within Lebanon and on the border between Lebanon and Israel. Arafat interpreted the cease-fire agreement literally, and thus he continued to allow the PLO to attack Israel from Jordan and the West Bank. For their part, the Israelis violated the cease-fire numerous times, bombing PLO targets in Beirut. That autumn, Israeli prime minister Menachem Begin and Defense Minister Ariel Sharon planned an invasion into Lebanon to occupy southern Lebanon and territory all the way up to Beirut, where they planned to destroy the PLO. Israeli troops invaded, occupied much of southern Lebanon, and rounded up much of the male population of the area.

On August 12, 1982, the two sides agreed to another cease-fire, in which both the PLO and Israel would leave Lebanon. As a result, about 15,000 Palestinian militants left Lebanon by September 1. The Israelis, however, claimed that PLO members were still hiding in Beirut and returned to the city on September 16, killing several hundred Palestinians, none of whom were known PLO members. Sharon resigned as defense minister after these Sabra and Shatila massacres, which were carried out by Lebanese Christian militias with Israeli foreknowledge and approval.

Arafat and many surviving PLO members spent most of the 1980s in Tunisia rebuilding the organization, which had been severely damaged by the fighting in Beirut. During this time, Iraq and Saudi Arabia donated substantial sums of money to the organization. But relations between the PLO and Israel remained intractably bad. The Israel Defense Forces (IDF) bombed the PLO headquarters in Tunis in 1985, an attack that killed seventy-three people.

In December 1987, the First Intifada broke out spontaneously in the West Bank and Gaza, surprising Israelis with its intensity. On November 15, 1988, the PLO officially declared the formation of the state of Palestine. That December, Arafat spoke before the United Nations again, promising to end terrorism and to recognize Israel in exchange for Israel's withdrawal from the occupied territories, according to UN Security Council Resolution 242. This was a distinct change from the PLO's previous position of insisting on the destruction of Israel. The PNC elected Arafat president of the new Palestinian state on April 2, 1989, in a symbolic vote.

Arafat and the Israelis began conducting peace negotiations at the Madrid Conference in 1991. Over the next two years, the two parties held a number of secret discussions. These negotiations led to the 1993 Oslo Accords, in which Israel agreed to Palestinian self-rule in the Gaza Strip and parts of the West Bank and Arafat officially recognized the existence of the state of Israel. Despite the condemnation of many Palestinian nationalists, the peace process appeared to be progressing apace. Israeli troops withdrew from the Gaza Strip and Jericho in May 1994.

In 1994 the PLO established a Negotiations Affairs Department in Gaza to implement the Interim Agreement. Mahmoud Abbas, then secretary-general of the PLO Executive Committee, headed the department until April 2003, when the Palestinian Legislative Council chose him as the first prime minister of the PA. He was replaced as PLO secretary-general by Saeb Erekat. The Gaza office handled Israeli affairs, agreements between Israel and Palestine, and refugees. It also kept careful track of Israeli expansion into Palestinian territory. The department also opened an office in Ramallah to handle the implementation of the Interim Agreement and prepare the Palestinian position for negotiations toward permanent status.

In 1996, the PNC agreed to remove from the PLO charter all language calling for armed violence aimed at destroying Israel, and Arafat sent U.S. president Bill Clinton a letter listing the language to be removed, although the PLO dragged its feet on actually doing this. The organization claims that it is waiting for the establishment of the Palestinian state, when it would replace the charter with a constitution.

Arafat was elected leader of the new PA in January 1996. The peace process began unraveling later that year, however, after rightist hardliner Benjamin Netanyahu was elected prime minister of Israel. Netanyahu distrusted Arafat and condemned the PLO as a terrorist organization responsible for numerous suicide bombings on Israeli citizens. The accord collapsed completely in 2000 after Arafat and Israeli prime minister Ehud Barak failed to come to an agreement at a Camp David meeting facilitated by Clinton. After that, the Second (al-Aqsa) Intifada began.

Arafat died on November 11, 2004. There was much dissension over the succession, but Abbas eventually came to represent the PLO's largest faction, Fatah. In December 2004, he called for an end to the Second Intifada. In January 2005, he was elected president of the PA but has struggled to keep the PLO together and prevent Fatah from losing its political and financial clout. In the January 2006 PA parliamentary elections, Abbas and Fatah were dealt a serious blow when Hamas captured a significant majority of seats. An even greater setback came in June 2007, when Hamas seized control of Gaza. Since then, Hamas has been involved in numerous military confrontations with Israel, most notably in 2008–2009, 2012, and 2014.

The Fatah-Hamas split has become a defining feature of Palestinian politics. Numerous attempts have been made by Egypt and others to mend relations, but none have succeeded. Abbas holds three of the most powerful positions in Palestinian society—president of the PA, chairman of the PLO, and head of Fatah. His health is deteriorating, and there is no clear plan of succession for any of those positions.

Amy Hackney Blackwell

See also: Abbas, Mahmoud; Arafat, Yasser; Black September; Fatah; Gaza Strip; Hamas; Oslo Accords; Palestine; Palestinians; Palestinian Authority; Two-State Solution; West Bank

Further Reading

Abbas, Mahmoud. *Through Secret Channels: The Road to Oslo.* Reading, UK: Garnet, 1997.

Aburish, Said K. *Arafat: From Defender to Dictator.* New York and London: Bloomsbury, 1998.

Al-Hout, Shafiq. *My Life in the PLO: The Inside Story of the Palestinian Struggle.* New York: Pluto Press, 2011.

Khalidi, Rashid. *Under Siege: PLO Decisionmaking During the 1982 War.* New York: Columbia University Press, 2014

Saleh, Moshen Moh'd, and Na'eem Jeenah, eds. *The PLO: Critical Appraisals from the Inside* Johannesburg: Afro Middle East Center, 2018.

Palestinian Authority (PA)

The governing council of the Palestinian people in the Palestinian Autonomous Region, which is the area ceded to the Palestine Liberation Organization (PLO) under the 1993 Declaration of Principles on Interim Self-Government Arrangements between Israel and the PLO. As a result of that agreement, which came out of the Oslo Accords, the Israeli government turned over to the Palestinian Authority (PA) responsibility for security, public education, health, social welfare, taxation, tourism, and judicial matters throughout Area A in the West Bank, which includes the major Palestinian cities and towns. This covers about 20 percent of the West Bank. On the outskirts of these cities and towns, known as Area B, Israel and the PA coordinate on security matters. In Area C, which constitutes 60 percent of the West Bank, the PA has no authority.

The PA has the power to levy taxes on Palestinians under its control. It solicits foreign aid for the implementation of its programs, but such appeals for assistance are the only foreign contact the PA is allowed. The authority operates the civilian Palestinian Police Force to maintain order and security in the autonomous regions; it works closely with Israel's security forces to repress armed resistance to the occupation. The Palestinian Police Force has been attacked by liberal Palestinians for alleged civil rights violations almost from the moment the PA was created, even as Israel has criticized it for failing to halt terrorist attacks originating from within the occupied territories.

The first members of the PA were selected by PLO chairperson Yasser Arafat on May 28, 1994. The PA held elections for the Palestinian Legislative Council (PLC) in 1996. By then, Arafat had begun to receive criticism from some Palestinians that he was running the PA in a despotic manner.

On January 20, 1996, Arafat was officially elected president of the PA in the first-ever Palestinian elections. After the eruption of the Second Intifada in September 2000, however, a public perception emerged that Arafat's influence over the Palestinians was decreasing, and PLO faction leaders began to criticize him openly. In June 2002, Arafat named a new, smaller cabinet as a result of strong calls for reform from both Western governments and local Palestinians, but the violence—and the criticism of Arafat—continued.

In early 2003, with the latest cycle of violence showing no signs of abating, a besieged Arafat was finally convinced of the need to appoint a prime minister. On April 29, 2003, PLO secretary-general Mahmoud Abbas (also known as Abu Mazen) was confirmed as the first prime minister of the PA. In addition, the PLC approved a new, reform-minded PA cabinet. The next day, U.S. ambassador to Israel Daniel Kurtzer delivered a U.S.-backed Road Map to Peace in the Middle East to both Israel and the Palestinians. Although Abbas secured a cease-fire a little more than a month after taking office, the plan for peace was undermined by the resumption of violence in August and Abbas's falling out with Arafat and his subsequent resignation on September 6, 2003.

Arafat died in November 2004. In January 2005, Abbas, who had already succeeded Arafat as head of the PLO, was elected president of the PA. Abbas attempted to pursue peace with Israel, but various radical Palestinian groups (most notably Hamas) made his efforts difficult. Nevertheless, in 2005, Abbas managed to reach a consensus on some issues, and that same year, Israel began a unilateral withdrawal from the Gaza Strip. Abbas and his Fatah faction were dealt a crippling blow in the 2006 parliamentary elections, however, when Hamas won a majority of seats and established its own government within the PA, although Abbas remained president. This development led many nations to withhold aid to the PA because they considered Hamas a terrorist organization. This only ramped up tensions between Hamas and Fatah. In the meantime, Hamas began solidifying its influence in the Gaza Strip, and it precipitated a crisis with Israel when it kidnapped an Israeli soldier, Gilad Shalit. Israel responded with a major offensive into Gaza and the capture of numerous Hamas leaders. Shalit was not released until 2011, as part of a prisoner exchange.

In early 2007, Abbas cobbled together a unity government that included Hamas members. However, in June, Hamas fighters seized control of Gaza, and Abbas dissolved the government, declaring a state of emergency. Then he quickly formed a new government that did not include Hamas; the United States and other Western nations thus began aiding the PA again. Abbas, who only controlled the West Bank at this point, declared that his government would have no contact with Hamas until Gaza was relinquished. To strengthen Abba's position, Israel resumed aid to the PA in July 2007. It also blockaded Gaza.

Despite attempts to reconcile Hamas and Fatah, the political stalemate continued. Meanwhile, Palestinians in the Gaza Strip began to suffer deprivation because of Israel's blockade and a dearth of foreign aid. By the spring of 2014, both sides agreed to a power-sharing arrangement, but the unity government was quickly undermined by a new crisis between Hamas and Israel, which began in early July 2014. The confrontation was precipitated by Hamas rocket launches into Israel, which responded with another ground incursion into Gaza. Since then, repeated efforts to heal the Hamas-PA split have failed.

President Abbas is in in his mid-eighties and in poor health. So far, he refuses to step down, allow presidential elections, or lay out a clear process for selecting a successor. While a moderate who supports nonviolence and a negotiated two-state solution, Abbas is often criticized for tolerating immense corruption, closely cooperating with Israeli occupation forces, and ruling the PA in an autocratic fashion.

The impending struggle to control Abbas's most important political positions—PA president, PLO chairman, and Fatah leader—could destabilize Palestinian politics for years.

ABC-CLIO

See also: Abbas, Mahmoud; Arafat, Yasser; Fatah; Gaza Strip; Hamas; Intifada, Second; Oslo Accords; Palestine Liberation Organization; Permanent Status Issues; West Bank

Further Reading

Bauck, Peter, and Mohammed Omer, eds. *The Oslo Accords: A Critical Assessment*. Cairo: American University in Cairo, 2017.

Brown, Nathan J. *Palestinian Politics After the Oslo Accords: Resuming Arab Palestine*. Berkeley: University of California Press, 2003.

Smith, Charles D. *Palestine and the Arab-Israeli Conflict: A History with Documents*. 9th ed. New York: Bedford/St. Martin's, 2017.

Watson, Geoffrey R. *The Oslo Accords: International Law and the Israeli-Palestinian Peace Agreements*. New York: Oxford University Press, 2000.

Palestinian Authority Security Forces (PASF)

The domestic security organization of the Palestinian Authority (PA), which currently is made up of eight branches. The contemporary structure has evolved dramatically since it was first conceived in the early stages of the Oslo peace process. A series of agreements between the Israelis and Palestinians in the mid-1990s allowed for the PA to create a security apparatus to provide for public order and domestic security in designated areas. The Palestinian General Security Services (GSS), as it was originally termed, was to consist of seven organizations: Civil Police, Public Security, Intelligence, Presidential Guard, Preventive Security, Emergency Services and Rescue, and a Coastal Police Unit. They were not to exceed 30,000 personnel, and Israel imposed strict limits on weapons procurement and training.

Within a few years, however, PA president Yasser Arafat had proliferated the number and size of the security organizations operating in PA territory and established direct control over most. By some counts, Arafat oversaw thirteen different security organizations and nearly 90,000 personnel. Many organizations had overlapping authorities, most competed for Arafat's favor, and some spied on each other. These organizations helped Arafat identify and undermine potential threats to his rule, but they also served as a massive jobs program, which helped him manage tensions between outsiders (i.e., members of the PLO who lived outside the West Bank and Gaza), who were Arafat loyalists and received plum positions in the PA when it was established; and insiders (i.e., Palestinians from the West Bank and Gaza), who ignited the First Intifada and maintained local power bases.

From the Israeli perspective, job one for the GSS was "counterterrorism" (i.e., limiting Palestinian violence against Israelis) and "security cooperation" (i.e., coordinating its actions and sharing its intelligence with the Israel's military). On both these scores, the GSS performed unevenly. Arafat sometimes had GSS elements crack down on Hamas, Palestinian Islamic Jihad (PIJ), and others who perpetrated violence against Israelis. They did so through a mix of direct force, arrests, intelligence sharing with Israel, or political maneuvers. At other times, the GSS would do less than Israel demanded or overtly undermine previous counterterrorism measures by releasing members of Hamas or PIJ months after arresting them. Many are convinced that Arafat never fully abandoned violence as a tool against Israeli occupation, and the evidence is clear that at times, he tolerated—if not outright supported—terror attacks during his time as president.

Not only were Israelis concerned with how unevenly the GSS handled its counterterrorism responsibilities, they also worried that the GSS might turn their guns on the Israel Defense Forces (IDF), which happened sporadically. But in late 2000, when the Second Intifada erupted, many Palestinian security officers actively fought the IDF. In 2002, following a Hamas terror attack that killed thirty Israelis, Israel launched Operation Defensive Shield, invading and reestablishing direct control of Palestinian cities and towns in the West Bank. With helicopters, tanks, and warplanes, the IDF largely destroyed the physical infrastructure of the GSS and decimated its operational capabilities. When Israel redeployed its forces, the PA's security forces were largely incapable of providing public order. Much of the West Bank and Gaza descended into lawlessness as militias affiliated with Fatah, Hamas, the PIJ, and others competed for influence.

It was not until Arafat died in November 2004 and the more moderate Mahmoud Abbas became president in 2005 that the Second Intifada wound down. Abbas quickly embarked on an effort to reform the GSS by replacing Arafat appointees and reorganizing its branches into a new Palestinian Authority Security Forces (PASF). Abbas's efforts were aided by the George W. Bush administration, which appointed a U.S. Security Coordinator for Israel and the Palestinian (USSC) in 2005. Its goal is to help reform and professionalize the PSAF through better equipping, training, and advising. (All USSC actions are cleared first with Israel.) When Hamas won parliamentary elections in 2006, the United States stepped up its assistance to the PASF. But this assistance and Abbas's reforms were not enough to defeat Hamas forces during the brief civil war in 2007.

The PASF's inglorious defeats at the hands of the Israelis and Hamas spurred PA leaders to double their efforts to rebuild and reform the forces. In June 2007, Abbas appointed Salam Fayyad as prime minister in order to spearhead extensive governmental reforms, including in the security sector.

The newly reconstituted PASF consists of seven branches. The National Security Force (NSF) is the largest, with about 10,500 personnel. It serves as a kind of national gendarmerie and supplements the other security services when needed. It is also responsible for patrolling the borders of Area A, those Palestinian cities and towns in which the PA has security responsibilities according to the Oslo Accords. Special units within the NSF are tasked with high-risk arrest operations and hostage rescues when necessary. The USSC has spent much of its training and equipping efforts on the NSF, which reports directly to the PA president.

The Palestinian Civil Police, with about 8,000 personnel, carries out traditional policing activities, like enforcing public order, fighting crime, and controlling traffic. It also participates in riot control and oversees the PA prison system. Like the NSF, its activities are largely restricted to Area A. It receives training and equipping assistance from the European Union and is considered one of the least-politicized branches of the PASF. It reports to the interior minister.

The Presidential Guard, with about 2,700 members, is responsible for protecting the president and other top officials, important government infrastructure, and visiting dignitaries. It reports directly to the president and is considered the elite branch of the PASF. The USSC has worked extensively with the PG.

The General Intelligence (GI) branch has about 3,200 plainclothes officers, and it is charged with external intelligence operations. It works with Palestinian embassies around the world, in Palestinian refugee camps, and covertly throughout the occupied territories (and reportedly even in Israel). It also carries out countersubversion operations against internal threats to the PA. The USCC has worked extensively with the GI, which maintains relations with many intelligence agencies around the world. Its longstanding and close relationship with the U.S. Central Intelligence Agency (CIA) dates back to its inception in early days of the Oslo peace process. This relationship is reportedly one of the few conduits of communication left between the PA and the Donald Trump administration. The GI reports directly to the PA president.

The primary responsibility of the Preventive Security (PS) branch of the PASF is to provide domestic intelligence and security. It is tasked with rooting out government corruption, combating illegal militias, counterespionage, and countersubversion operations. But its primary responsibility is to track, infiltrate, and undermine Hamas and PIJ in the West Bank. It has a force of about 3,400 plainclothes officers, runs a secret prison system, and has been repeatedly accused of human rights violations, including the use of torture. Western intelligence agencies are known to help Preventive Security in its counterterrorism operations against Hamas and PIJ. It reports to the interior minister.

Military Intelligence operates as a kind of "internal affairs" division within the PASF. It is one of the smallest branches (about 1,700 officers), and its core tasks are to vet prospective PASF hires for criminal backgrounds, involvement with terrorism, collaboration with Israel, or other serious crimes. It reports directly to the president.

The District Coordination Office (DCO) facilitates Israeli-Palestinian security cooperation. There are eight DCOs throughout PA-controlled territory staffed by about 300 officers who work closely with IDF District and Coordination Liaison representatives on such issues as returning Israeli civilians who stray into Area A, returning stolen vehicles to Israel, reporting Israeli settler violence against Palestinians, coordinating PASF activities outside Area A, and handling advanced warnings from the IDF about incursions into Area A (making sure that PA security forces do not interfere with such IDF operations).

Civil Defense is the emergency services branch of the PASF, charged with responding to natural disasters, firefighting, and search-and-rescue missions. It has about 1,200 active-duty personnel and 3,000 reserves. It has received training and equipment from the USSC and has trained openly with its Israeli emergency services, even contributing personnel to help fight fires in Israel. Because of the humanitarian nature of its mission, the Civil Defense branch is the least politicized of all PASF branches. It reports to the interior minister.

By most accounts, including Israeli security officials, the PASF is more professionalized and effective than ever before. Indeed, the USSC has indicated that the bulk of its mission to "train and equip" has been successful, and now it will focus on "advising and assisting" to solidify the gains made in building PASF institutions.

Still, the PASF faces much criticism, especially from Palestinians who complain about its abuses of power, including the stifling of public dissent and criticism of the PA. However, what threatens the PASF the most is its lack of progress in ending the Israeli occupation. While most Palestinians appreciate the public goods that the PASF provides, many see it as subcontractors of their Israeli occupiers. Indeed, the more effective the PASF is, the easier it is for Israel to maintain its control of Palestinian territory. The PASF are thus stuck between a rock and a hard place—providing a level of public security for the general welfare of the Palestinians living under Israeli occupation, while at the same time helping to perpetuate that occupation. This situation cannot be sustained indefinitely.

Robert C. DiPrizio

See also: Fatah; Hamas; Oslo Accords; Palestinian Authority; Palestine Liberation Army; Palestine Liberation Organization; West Bank

Further Reading

Cordesman, Anthony. *Palestinian Forces: Palestinian Authority and Militant Forces.* Washington, DC: Center for Strategic and International Studies, 2006.

Hunter, Robert E., and Seth G. Jones. *Building a Successful Palestinian State: Security.* Santa Monica, CA: RAND, 2006.

Luft, Gal. "The Palestinian Security Services: Between Police and Army." *Middle East Review of International Affairs* 3, no. 2 (June 1999): 1–3.

RAND Palestinian State Study Team. *Building a Successful Palestinian State.* Santa Monica, CA: RAND, 2005.

Zilber, Neri, and Al-Omari, Ghaith. *State with No Army, Army with No State: Evolution of the Palestinian Authority Security Forces 1994–2018.* Washington, DC: Washington Institute for Near East Policy, 2018.

Palestinian Hijackings

Spate of airline hijackings by Palestinian groups, intended to attract attention. An airline hijacking consists of the use or threat of force to seize control of an aircraft while it is in flight. From the late 1960s until the mid-1980s, Palestinian nationalist groups used hijackings to call attention to their cause, raise funds, and demand the release of prisoners sympathetic to their cause. They proved so adept that it became almost a cliché during that period to assume that a hijacker was of Palestinian origin.

On July 23, 1968, three members of the Popular Front for the Liberation of Palestine (PFLP) attacked the crew of an El Al flight from Rome to Tel Aviv, in the only successful takeover of an El Al aircraft. The hijackers diverted the aircraft to Algiers, where the Algerian government impounded the airplane and a standoff commenced. After a one-day delay, all non-Israeli passengers were removed from the aircraft and flown to France, leaving twelve Israeli passengers and ten crewmembers to undergo a forty-day ordeal, confined within the aircraft. In exchange for their return, the Israeli government released sixteen Arab prisoners from prison.

In September 1970, members of the PFLP managed to hijack five aircraft almost simultaneously. The initial plan was to seize control of three aircraft, demand that they be flown to Dawson's Field, near Zarqa, Jordan, and then use the passengers as hostages. TWA Flight 741 from Frankfurt and Swissair Flight 100 from Zurich were both seized on September 6, and the crews agreed to fly to Dawson's Field to avoid further violence. Two intended hijackers were denied boarding El Al Flight 219 from Amsterdam. Their remaining coconspirators, Patrick Arguello and Leila Khaled, decided to continue their attempt, but despite holding firearms and hand grenades, they could not persuade the pilots to open the cockpit door. Instead, the lead pilot put the aircraft into a steep dive, disorienting the attackers and allowing them to be subdued by fellow passengers. Arguello was killed by an Israeli security officer, and Khaled was turned over to British authorities when the plane landed in London. The two PFLP members denied boarding by El Al immediately purchased tickets on Pan Am Flight 93, and they managed to hijack it instead of their original target. The plane flew first to Beirut, and then to Cairo, but did not join the others at Dawson's Field.

On September 9, a PFLP member hijacked BOAC Flight 775 and forced it to divert to Dawson's Field, joining two other hijacked aircraft at what the PFLP dubbed "Revolutionary Airport." After releasing the non-Jewish passengers, the PFLP negotiated to trade the aircrews and Jewish passengers for the return of Leila Khaled and three PFLP members held by the Swiss. On September 30, the remaining prisoners were exchanged and recovered from their holding locations throughout Amman, Jordan.

On February 22, 1972, five PFLP operatives seized Lufthansa Flight 649 from Delhi to Athens. They initially attempted to divert it to an airstrip deep in the Arabian Desert, but later ordered it to land at Aden International Airport in South Yemen. Once on the ground, they released all women and children from the plane and then demanded a ransom of $5 million from Lufthansa. The state-run airline agreed to the payout, after which the hijackers released the passengers and crew and surrendered to South Yemeni law enforcement, which quietly released them without charges.

On October 29, 1972, Palestinian hijackers seized Lufthansa Flight 615 and threatened to destroy it with explosives unless West Germany agreed to free three members of Black September who had been captured during the Munich Olympics Massacre. The Germans complied with the demands, releasing the men and allowing the aircraft to proceed to Tripoli. Once there, the attackers freed the hostages and were allowed to quietly disappear into Libya. On October 13, 1977, four Palestinian hijackers seized Lufthansa Flight 181 and diverted it to multiple airports for refueling before ending in Mogadishu, Somalia. There, they demanded the release of ten Red Army Faction members and two Palestinian prisoners, plus a $15 million ransom. Rather than negotiate, the German government claimed to be complying, while secretly it dispatched a cadre of GSG-9, its elite antiterrorism military unit. The GSG-9 troopers staged a diversion, stormed the aircraft, and rescued the hostages, killing three hijackers in the process.

One of the deadliest hijackings in history occurred on November 23, 1985, when three members of the Abu Nidal organization hijacked EgyptAir Flight 648. They forced it to divert to Malta, where they threatened to execute hostages every fifteen minutes unless the airplane received fuel. Britain, France, and the United States all offered to send antiterrorism commandos to address the situation, but the Maltese government refused permission, before finally relenting and allowing an Egyptian commando unit to fly in. On the second day of the incident, the Egyptians stormed the plane, in an attack that killed fifty-four of eighty-seven passengers and two of the hijackers.

Forensic analysis showed that the Egyptian team placed more emphasis upon killing the hijackers than saving the passengers, and their use of explosives triggered a fire in the main cabin. Although the incident proved exceptionally deadly, it also illustrated the diminishing returns of airline hijackings, and the tactic was essentially abandoned by Palestinian groups after 1985.

Paul J. Springer

See also: Palestine Liberation Organization; Palestinian Liberation Front; Popular Front for the Liberation of Palestine

Further Reading

Baum, Philip. *Violence in the Skies: A History of Aircraft Hijacking and Bombing.* Chichester, UK: Summersdale, 2016.

Carlton, David. *The West's Road to 9/11: Resisting, Appeasing, and Encouraging Terrorism Since 1970.* New York: Palgrave Macmillan, 2006.

Koerner, Brendan I. *The Skies Belong to Us: Love and Terror in the Golden Age of Hijacking.* New York: Crown Publishers, 2013.

Raab, David. *Terror in Black September: The First Eyewitness Account of the Infamous 1970 Hijackings.* New York: Palgrave Macmillan, 2007.

Palestinian Islamic Jihad (PIJ)

A militant nationalist Palestinian group. Harakat al-Jihad al-Islami fi Filastin, known in English as the Palestinian Islamic Jihad (PIJ), was established by Fathi Shiqaqi, Sheikh Abd al-Aziz al-Awda, and others in the Gaza Strip during the 1970s. While in Egypt in the 1970s, Shiqaqi, al-Awda, and the current director-general of the PIJ, Ramadan Abdullah Shallah, embraced an Islamist vision similar to the Egyptian Muslim Brotherhood group. But they rejected that organization's moderation and distinguished itself from secular nationalists and antinationalist Islamists in calling for grassroots organization and armed struggle to liberate Palestine as part of the Islamic solution.

Shiqaqi returned to Palestinian territory, and the PIJ began to express its intent to wage jihad (holy war) against Israel. Israeli sources claim that the PIJ developed the military apparatus known as the Jerusalem Brigades (Saraya al-Quds) by 1985, and this organization carried out attacks against the Israeli military, including an attack known as Operation Gate of Moors at an induction ceremony in 1986. The PIJ also claimed responsibility for the suicide bombing in Beit Led, near Netanya, Israel, on January 22, 1994. Nineteen Israelis were killed and another sixty injured.

The PIJ emerged prior to Hamas. The two organizations were rivals despite the commonality of their nationalist perspectives, but Hamas gained a much larger popular following than the PIJ, whose estimated support is only 4–5 percent of the Palestinian population in the territories. The PIJ has a following among university students at the Islamic University in Gaza and other colleges, and it became very active in the Second (al-Aqsa) Intifada, which began in September 2000.

In the Palestinian territories, the PIJ continues to differ with Hamas. Hamas largely ceased attacks against Israel beginning in 2004 and instead pursued politics, successfully capturing a majority in the Palestinian elections of January 2006. Hamas moderates have also considered the recognition of Israel and a two-state solution. The PIJ, in contrast, called for Palestinians to boycott the 2006 elections and has refused any accommodation with Israel. It continued to sponsor suicide attacks after 2004 in retaliation for Israel's military offensives and targeted killings of PIJ leaders, including Louay Saadi in October 2005. The PIJ claimed responsibility for two suicide attacks that year.

The PIJ has continued to launch periodic attacks against Israeli citizens and interests. Because the group controls a number of religious groups and humanitarian groups aimed at helping Palestinians, its following has increased in recent years, even with the PA's efforts to shut down these organizations. In 2014, as tensions between Hamas and Israel erupted into war, the PIJ took advantage of the situation by enlarging its base and clout among Palestinians and by appealing to Iran for more funding. In May 2019, PIJ and Hamas launched hundreds of rockets from Gaza into Israel in another spate of violence that left twenty-five Palestinians and four Israelis dead.

Sherifa Zuhur

See also: Hamas; Intifada, Second; Israeli Occupations; Oslo Accords; Suicide Bombings

Further Reading

Abu-Amr, Ziad. *Islamic Fundamentalism in the West Bank and Gaza: Muslim Brotherhood and Islamic Jihad.* Bloomington: Indiana University Press, 1994.

Knudsen, Are. "Islamism in the Diaspora: Palestinian Refugees in Lebanon." *Journal of Refugee Studies* 18, no. 2 (2005): 216–234.

Levitt, Matthew. *Hamas: Politics, Charity, and Terrorism in the Service of Jihad.* Washington, DC: Washington Institute for Near East Policy, 2006.

Shallah, Ramadan 'Abdallah, and Khalid al-'Ayid. "The Movement of Islamic Jihad and the Oslo Process: An Interview with Ramadan Abdullah Shallah." *Journal of Palestine Studies* 28 (1999): 61–73.

Palestinian National Council (PNC)

The legislative body of the Palestine Liberation Organization (PLO). The Palestinian National Council (PNC) is essentially the Palestinian parliament in exile. Ostensibly, it represents all Palestinians—those under occupation and in the diaspora. In practice, it has been dominated by Fatah. The PNC is supposed to set the policies and approve the budgets of the PLO, but these activities are largely done by the PLO's Executive Committee, which leads the PNC when not in session. The

Executive Committee is selected by the PNC, and it was intended to meet annually but has met only sporadically, and rarely since the creation of the Palestinian Authority (PA). The PNC presently has its headquarters in Amman and a branch office in Ramallah.

The PNC was effectively displaced by the Palestinian Legislative Council (PLC), which was first elected in 1996 by Palestinians living in the West Bank and Gaza. The PLC has enjoyed few powers, however, as PA presidents Yasser Arafat and Mahmoud Abbas have maintained strict control over real policymaking. In May 2018, the PNC met in regular session in the West Bank for the first time since 1996. Israeli travel restrictions limited participation by Hamas and other groups, leaving Mahmoud Abbas and his Fatah Party free to dominate proceedings.

Spencer C. Tucker

See also: Abbas, Mahmoud; Arafat, Yasser; Palestine Liberation Organization; Palestinian Authority

Further Reading

Khalidi, Rashid. *The Iron Cage: The Story of the Palestinian Struggle for Statehood.* Boston: Beacon Press, 2007.

Nassar, Jamal R. *The Palestine Liberation Organization: From Armed Struggle to the Declaration of Independence.* New York: Praeger, 1991.

Palestinian Refugee Camps

Refugee encampments for Palestinians who fled their homes during the 1948–1949 Israeli War of Independence. The United Nations (UN) defines a Palestinian refugee as a person (or his or her descendants) whose primary residence was Palestine for a minimum of two years prior to May 1948. Originally, these Palestinian refugees numbered 750,000 (out of a total population of 1.5 million Palestinians). After 1948, the Israelis barred their return. Today, there are more than 5 million registered Palestinian refugees, residing in numerous countries and territories (Syria, Jordan, Lebanon, the West Bank, and Gaza).

On December 11, 1948, the United Nations adopted General Assembly Resolution 194, which recognized the Palestinians' right of return to their homes, provided that they live in peace with their neighbors. They were also to be compensated for their lost property upon their return.

Refugee camps were originally intended to be temporary. They appeared in Syria, Lebanon, Jordan, the Gaza Strip, the West Bank, and Egypt. In time, however, they became permanent because the ongoing Arab-Israeli conflict remained unresolved. The UN Relief and Works Agency for Palestine Refugees in the Near East (UNRWA) was established in December 1949 to administer the camps, but it took about two years to get up and running. In the meantime, Palestinian charitable associations brought food, clothing, and tents to these areas.

According to the 1966 Casablanca Protocol of the Arab League, host countries were expected to grant refugees unrestricted residency rights and the freedom to travel and seek employment. These governments were also expected to maintain Palestinian national identity until their repatriation. The UN High Commission on

Refugees (UNHCR), created in 1951, does not include the Palestinians in its mandate.

Many Palestinians initially sought refuge in Jordan because it controlled the West Bank and extended citizenship rights. About 370,000 refugees still inhabit ten camps. The Jordanian camps were eventually supervised by teachers of UNRWA schools who came from the ranks of the refugees and played a pivotal role in enhancing their national identity. The Jordanian refugee camps were also briefly involved in the 1970 Jordanian civil conflict, which resulted in the expulsion of Palestine Liberation Organization (PLO) fighters from that country.

Prior to the civil war in Syria, about half a million Palestinian refugees lived in nine camps, mostly near Damascus. Most camps are homogenous neighborhoods reflecting the refugees' original towns and villages, which has helped strengthen their national identity. In 1956, Syria's Law 260 granted the refugees equal rights with Syrian citizens in the areas of employment, commerce, and military service. They were also allowed to join trade unions, reside outside the camps, and reenter the country without a visa. But to discourage their permanent settlement in Syria, refugees are prohibited from owning land. Syria's Palestinian refugees have come under increasing threat as a result of the Syrian civil war that began in 2011. Over 400,000 have been displaced, either internally or to neighboring countries.

Palestinian refugees faced particularly difficult conditions in the camps in Lebanon prior to 1970 and during the Lebanese civil war. The camps bore the brunt of Israeli military actions because of raids staged from Lebanon by the PLO. Yet even before the PLO arrived in the Lebanese camps in 1970, the refugees were subject to police harassment and surveillance. The Palestinian camps were located in southern Lebanon, in Beirut's southern slum areas, and in the Bekáa Valley at Anjar, as well as in some other areas. Today, Lebanon recognizes twelve camps, although others were destroyed during the civil war. There were some 450,000 refugees in Lebanon today.

The Lebanese civil war, in combination with Israeli invasions in 1978 and 1982, resulted in the loss of at least 50,000 Palestinian lives. The situation in the Lebanese camps deteriorated badly after the 1982 Israeli invasion of Lebanon, culminating in the massacres at the Sabra and Shatila camps at the hands of local militias, with the tacit collusion of the Israeli army. Following the PLO's withdrawal from Lebanon in 1982, the refugees there were embroiled in the so-called War of the Camps against the Amal militia. Lebanon bars Palestinian refugees from many professions and from owning land.

Nineteen refugee camps are located in the Palestinian territories. Around 27 percent of the West Bank's population and 70 percent of Gaza's population are comprised of refugees. About half of the refugees in Gaza live in camps, while that number is only a quarter in the West Bank. The largest camp is Jabalya in Gaza (housing about 110,000 refugees in 2016). It often suffers from incursions by the Israeli military. A camp located within the Jerusalem area, Shufat, has been affected by the encirclement of expanding Israeli settlements such as Pisgat Zeev. Palestinian refugees in Gaza have suffered considerably since Hamas seized control in 2007 and Israel blockaded the area. Multiple major conflicts between Hamas and Israel (the latest occurring in the summer of 2014) brought more peril and disruption to Gaza refugees.

Palestinian refugees continue to suffer from extraordinarily poor conditions in camps. In the West Bank and Gaza, these conditions led to stronger support from camp residents for militant slogans and recruitment. Jordan is the only country to offer refugees full citizenship, although they made no effort to form a Palestinian state in the West Bank when they controlled it. Neither did Egypt when it controlled Gaza.

In an effort to remove from the negotiation table the Palestinian refugee issue, and to encourage Palestinians to support his proposed resolution to the Israeli-Palestinian conflict, President Donald Trump has cut off all funding of UNWRA and is pressing the United Nations to reduce drastically the number of Palestinians that it recognizes as refugees.

Ghada Hashem Talhami

See also: Arab-Israeli War, 1948; Arab-Jewish Communal War, 1947; *Nakba;* Palestinian Refugees; Right of Return

Further Reading

Aruri, Naseer Hasan, ed. *Palestinian Refugees: The Right of Return.* London: Pluto, 2001.

Morris, Benny. *The Birth of the Palestinian Refugee Problem, 1947–1949.* Cambridge: Cambridge University Press, 1990.

Sayigh, Rosemary. *Too Many Enemies: The Palestinian Experience in Lebanon.* London: Zed, 1994.

Talhami, Ghada Hashem. *Palestinian Refugees: Pawns to Political Actors.* Happauge, NY: Nova Science Publishers, 2003.

Palestinian Refugees

Palestinians displaced from their homes in the 1948 and 1967 Arab-Israeli wars. Palestinian refugees owe their origin to the conflict that accompanied the establishment of the state of Israel. The first half of the twentieth century saw a significant demographic shift in Palestine as Jewish immigrants settled in the region. Zionist immigration became especially high in the 1930s and 1940s as Jews fled the anti-Semitism that evolved into the horrors of the Holocaust. Following World War II, the United Nations took stewardship of the Palestinian question and proposed a partition of the region in 1947. Conflict between Palestinians and Jews immediately followed. Jewish forces were on the defensive against Palestinian fighters for several months, but the tide turned in April 1948. By May, the Palestinians were routed and Zionist leaders declared Israel's independence. Israel then mounted an effective defense against invasion from its Arab neighbors. Israel's civil conflict with Palestinians and interstate conflict with the Arab coalition, known as the War of Independence to Israelis and as al-Nakba ("the catastrophe") to Palestinians, resulted in the displacement of hundreds of thousands of Palestinians.

The immediate cause of this displacement—whether Palestinians left willingly, were encouraged by Palestinian and other Arab leaders, or were violently driven away at the hands of Israelis—has been the source of much historical debate. While the Israeli state held that Arab population transfers were not the result of Israeli coercion, evidence from the period suggests a more complicated reality. The Peel Commission of 1937, in which the British government proposed a territorial partition, suggested the possibility of population transfer, an idea that seems to have been internalized among both Zionist and Palestinian leaders. After fighting broke out in 1947, forced expulsions occurred as both Palestinians and Zionists gained territory. The Zionists, however, won the day, so it was the Palestinians who were disproportionately displaced from their homes. Israel refused to allow the displaced Palestinians to return after the war's conclusion, a situation complicated by the failure of Arab states to absorb Palestinians into their societies.

The Palestinian refugee crisis spurred the creation of the UN Relief and Works Agency for Palestine Refugees in the Near East (UNRWA) in 1949. UNRWA provides education, health care, food, and additional assistance (including capital investment and loans) for Palestinians displaced through the 1948 and 1967 Arab-Israeli wars. The UNRWA mission initially supported the 700,000 Palestinians of the 1948 war, but today, they and their descendants account for 5 million Palestinians who are eligible for registration. In 2018, the Donald Trump administration announced that the United States would no longer provide financial assistance to UNRWA, requiring the agency to look elsewhere to replace the one-third of its budget typically covered by U.S. support. In announcing the reasons for its decision, the Trump administration cited its criticism of UNRWA's management and its belief that only those initially displaced in 1948—and not their descendants—should be considered refugees.

Palestinian refugee camps are located not only in the West Bank (nineteen camps) and Gaza (eight camps), but in nearby Jordan (ten camps), Syria (nine camps), and Lebanon (twelve camps). While the camps began essentially as tent cities, they have developed into concrete communities but continue to face a litany of challenges, including high unemployment rates, overcrowding, sanitation and sewage problems, and unstable power grids. Most refugees in these countries do not reside in camps, and the camps themselves are not administered by UNRWA, but rather by the host governments. According to the UNRWA, there are 2.2 million Palestinian refugees in Jordan, 1.3 million in Gaza, 810,000 in the West Bank, 438,000 in Syria, and 450,000 in Lebanon.

The presence of refugees in host countries has presented challenges for both the refugees and their hosts. In Jordan, for example, some of the country's most significant political challenges have resulted from complications in accommodating its Palestinian residents. The country's first king, Abdullah I, was assassinated by a Palestinian, and tensions between Jordan and the Palestine Liberation Organization (PLO) in 1970 resulted in the violence known as *Black September*. After Jordan expelled the PLO, it found a home in Lebanon and played a role in the Lebanese civil war that began in 1975. Today, although refugees account for 10 percent of the Lebanese population, they are not afforded citizens' rights and are barred from many professions, making them some of the poorest refugees in the region. In Syria, some Palestinian refugees have been further displaced as a result of the ongoing civil war.

The status of Palestinian refugees has been and remains a significant barrier to Israeli and Palestinian reconciliation. Many Palestinians maintain that they have a right of return to their ancestral homes, in areas that have been under Israeli control since 1948 or 1967. The image of a key has become a compelling symbol among Palestinians claiming a right of return, signifying to them the keys to the homes that they or their families fled. Some maintain that while an absolute right of return may be unfeasible, the Israeli state owes reparations to Palestinian refugees. The possibility for reparations, however, has become increasingly problematic as the number of refugees has grown through the generations.

Sean P. Braniff

See also: Arab-Israeli War, 1948; Arab-Jewish Communal War, 1947; *Nakba;* Palestinian Refugee Camps; Permanent Status Issues; Right of Return; UN Relief and Works Agency for Palestine Refugees in the Near East

Further Reading
Bickerton, Ian J., and Carla L. Klausner. *A History of the Arab-Israeli Conflict.* 7th ed. Boston: Pearson Books, 2015.
Farsoun, Samih K., and Naseer Aruri. *Palestine and the Palestinians: A Social and Political History,* 2nd ed. Boulder, CO: Westview Press, 2006.
Morris, Benny. *1948: A History of the First Arab-Israeli War.* New Haven, CT: Yale University Press, 2008.
Pappé, Ilan, ed. *The Israel/Palestine Question: A Reader*, 2nd ed. New York: Routledge, 2007.

Palestinians

Distinct nation of Arabs who claim Palestine as their homeland. Under Ottoman authority, partially autonomous notables and clan leaders governed Palestine. These notables created a system of government that enabled the establishment of certain Arab families as the local elites. These elite families occupied the region's religious, legal, and government leadership positions. Even after the Ottomans made sweeping changes following the 1908 restoration of the Constitution, the same local elites were able to maintain their influence over Palestinian society. The restored Ottoman Constitution attempted to enact liberal Western changes to government, but Constantinople did not drive change for the people of Palestine. Instead, local notable families established the parameters of the new reforms. So while Palestinian identity was diluted, there existed a uniqueness among those living in Palestine. Palestinian Arabs, while considering themselves Ottoman subjects, viewed their region as distinct from the rest of the empire.

The Zionist movement catalyzed the development of Palestinian nationalism. As it gained momentum, Palestinian identity became an increasingly salient frame for oppositional consciousness toward Zionism. As the idea of a Palestinian national identity independent of the broader Arab identity grew, so did the internal power struggle for influence over the Palestinian nationalist movement. This infighting hindered the formation of a unified front against Zionism. The al-Nashashibi and al-Husayni clans were two of the most influential families vying to be the voice of Palestinians; the latter were less accommodating of Zionists and British Mandate rulers. In particular, Haj Amin al-Husayni, the Grand Mufti of Jerusalem and head of the Supreme Muslim Council (SMC), was an ardent Palestinian nationalist and advocate of active opposition to Zionism. Political infighting among these notable families subsided in the 1930s as Palestinians sought to curb the loss of their land and livelihood to Zionist immigrants. The deteriorating Palestinian economic situation was a leading cause of the 1936 Arab Revolt, which encouraged feuding factions to join forces, at least temporarily.

By 1939, the British crushed the revolt, and Palestinian nationalist movement was in tatters. Much of its leadership was killed, arrested, or exiled, which left Palestinians at a grave disadvantage against the strong leadership that Zionists enjoyed in the runup to the creation of the state of Israel in 1948. Palestinians refer to this event as the *nakba*, or "catastrophe," which deprived them of their homeland, created hundreds of thousands of refugees, and left the Palestinian nation fractured and stateless. When Israel conquered East Jerusalem, the West Bank, and Gaza Strip in 1967, it completed the takeover of Palestine, and the Palestinian nationalist movement reached its nadir.

For a moment, some Palestinians put their faith in Nasser's pan-Arabism, but humiliating military defeats against Israel in 1967 and 1973 convinced many Palestinians to redefine the Arab-Israeli conflict in terms of Palestinian national ambitions. This gave rise to the Palestine Liberation Organization (PLO) and the reinvigoration of the Palestinian national movement. But when the PLO failed to produce results (which some defined as the destruction of Israel and reclaiming of all of Palestine, while others defined as the end of Israel's occupation and creation of a Palestinian state on the West Bank and Gaza), Palestinians under occupation took matters into their own hands and launched the First Intifada in 1987. The PLO quickly asserted control over the uprising, but some Palestinians disillusioned by the secular PLO's failures turned to Hamas, which seeks to advance an Islamic form of Palestinian nationalism.

As the PLO made concessions to Israel under the 1993 Oslo Accords but failed to gain much in return, Hamas grew in popularity. After PLO chairman Yasser Arafat's death in November 2004, a power struggle between Hamas and the PLO-dominated Palestinian Authority (PA) resulted in another fracturing of Palestinian society, as Hamas took control of Gaza and the PA was left in charge of the West Bank. The charismatic Arafat had dominated the PLO and Palestinian politics for decades and is widely credited with reorganizing and reinvigorating the Palestinian nationalist movement after the shock of the *nakba*. But since his death, Palestinians have struggled with disunity brought on by Hamas and the PLO's competing visions of Palestinian nationalism, as well as geographic dispersion.

Prior to 1948, most Palestinians lived in Palestine. Today, they are spread throughout the region and beyond. A total of 2 million live in the Gaza Strip under an Israeli siege, another 3 million are in the West Bank under Israeli military rule, 300,000 live in East Jerusalem under Israeli civilian rule but without citizenship rights, another 2 million or so live in refugee camps-turned-slums in neighboring states without citizenship rights, and nearly 2 million enjoy citizenship in Israel. A couple million more Palestinians live in Europe and the Americas. Being dispersed into so many different locations and living under such diverse legal, political, and economic circumstances has undermined the Palestinian nationalist movement but not Palestinian national identity, which has only strengthened over the decades since 1948.

Much of the rhetoric surrounding the Israeli-Palestinian conflict involves mutual efforts to deny the legitimacy of each other's national identity. Many Palestinians insist that Jews are a religious group, not a national one. Those Zionists who moved to Palestine to create Israel were simply German Jews, Russian Jews, Polish Jews, and other nationalities. The implication is that Zionism is not a legitimate national movement, Israel is not a legitimate state, and that Israeli Jews should "go home."

Similarly, many Israelis insist that there is no such thing as a Palestinian because no such state ever existed, as Prime Mister Golda Meir asserted to the *Sunday Times* in 1969. Indeed, in reference to Palestine, early Zionists coined the slogan, "A land without a people for a people without a land." So-called Palestinians are simply Arabs that can be incorporated into any of the surrounding Arab countries. And to the extent that a Palestinian identity has developed over the years, some critics assert that its defining feature is opposition to Zionism (i.e., Jewish self-determination). The implication of this line of thinking is that Palestinian national identity is artificial, inferior to the more authentic Israeli identity, or even anti-Semitic.

But as described here, a national identity developed among the Arabs of Palestine sometime between the end of the nineteenth and the beginning of the early twentieth century. To be sure, the process was catalyzed by opposition to the Zionist project; but Israeli national identity, which also developed over the same time frame, was similarly catalyzed by Zionism's confrontations with Palestinian Arabs. In many ways, Palestinian and Israeli national identities have developed in a coconstitutive manner. That is, they evolved into what they are today as a result of constant interaction, each national group seeking to control the same small piece of land to which they and their ancestors have been connected to—in one way or another—for centuries. Still, their respective developments faced very different hurdles. Zionists had to forge a new, distinctly Israeli identity from a melting pot of German, Russian, Polish, Iraqi, Ethiopian, and British Jews who spoke different languages, belonged to different cultures, and practiced their religion differently. Palestinians struggled to overcome competing tribal, clan, and local identities while navigating supranational Arab and Islamic identities.

Tribes, clans, and local identities still matter in parts of the West Bank and Gaza, but they are not serious impediments to Palestinian nationalism, which remains fervent yet divided along two major axes. One is the previously mentioned division between Hamas (which promotes a nationalism infused with political Islam) and the PLO (which promotes secular democracy). The other axis is between supporters of a one-state versus a two-state solution to the Israeli-Palestinian conflict. The latter sees Palestinian nationalism as culminating in the creation of an independent Palestinian state in the West Bank and Gaza, with East Jerusalem as its capital. The former envisions the creation of one state covering all of historic Palestine (Israel, Gaza, and the West Bank), in which Palestinians and Israelis enjoy full citizenship and equal rights. The two-state vision has been dominant for the past thirty years, but support for a one-state solution is growing, especially among

Palestinians living in the diaspora and in Israel. How these tensions within Palestinian society will be resolved is an open question.

Sean N. Blas and Robert C. DiPrizio

See also: Diaspora, Palestinian; Fatah; Hamas; *Nakba;* Palestine; Palestine Liberation Organization; Palestinian Authority; Zionism

Further Reading

Gelvin, James L. *The Israel-Palestine Conflict: One Hundred Years of War.* 3rd ed. New York: Cambridge University Press, 2014.

Khalidi, Rashid. *Palestinian Identity: The Construction of Modern National Consciousness.* New York: Columbia University Press, 2010.

Kimmerling, Baruch. *Clash of Identities: Explorations in Israeli and Palestinian Societies.* New York: Columbia University Press, 2008.

Smith, Charles. *Palestine and the Arab-Israeli Conflict: A History with Documents.* 9th ed. Boston: Bedford/St. Martin's, 2017.

Suleiman, Yasir. *Being Palestinian: Personal Reflections on Palestinian Identity in the Diaspora.* Edinburgh: Edinburgh University Press, 2016.

Palmach

A Jewish fighting force numbering at its height a few thousand soldiers. The Palmach (the Hebrew abbreviation for "strike force") was created jointly by the British and the Jewish Haganah in 1941. Haganah was a Jewish underground self-defense and military organization formed in 1920, the precursor of the Israel Defense Forces (IDF). Haganah leaders realized the need for a permanently mobilized military organization to defend Jewish settlements that came under harassment from Arab bands from time to time. More important to the British, if Axis forces ever entered British Mandatory Palestine, the Palmach would assist in fighting them.

The new elite Palmach was trained and equipped by the British and dispersed throughout Palestine. The Palmach eventually grew to twelve assault teams that initiated scouting and sabotage missions, as well as preemptive strikes into Syria and Lebanon. Some of the Palmach's more notable members were Yigal Allon, Moshe Dayan, Yitzhak Rabin, Chaim Bar-Lev, Uzi Narkiss, and Ezer Weizman (Chaim Weizmann's nephew).

Haganah converted the Palmach into an underground commando force in 1942 and its platoons to various kibbutzim that provided the Palmachniks (Palmach members) with food, shelter, and other supplies. In return, the Palmach protected the kibbutz to which they were assigned, worked in the agricultural enterprises of the kibbutz, and participated in Zionist education programs.

The role of the Palmach was not limited to the protection of the Yishuv. By 1943, the Palmach had organized itself into six regular companies and a like number of special units. The Ha-Machlaka Ha-Germanit (German Department) operated against the Nazi infrastructure in the Middle East and the Balkans. The Ha-Machlaka Ha-Aravit (Arab Department, known also as the Arab Platoon because members often dressed in Arabic attire) fought Arab militias. After the formation of Israel, they formed the basis of the Border Police and IDF infiltration units. The

Pal-Yam was the sea force of the Palmach, and it focused on facilitating the illegal entry of Jewish refugees from Europe, in violation of the British White Paper of 1939, which limited Jewish immigration to Palestine.

The Palmach's Sabotage Units eventually formed the nucleus of the IDF Engineering Corps. The Palmach Air Force consisted of British-trained Jewish pilots, but it had no planes until 1948, when it commenced observation and scouting operations. In addition, Zionist youth movement participants aged eighteen to twenty were formed into Nahal (the Hebrew acronym for *noar halutzi lohem*, meaning "fighting pioneer youth") or nucleus groups. They were trained by Palmachniks and eventually formed the basis of the Nahal settlements, created as strategic strongholds in case of war.

When it was clear following World War II that the British were unwilling to create a Jewish state or allow the immigration of large numbers of Jewish refugees into Palestine, the Palmach attacked British infrastructure such as bridges, railways, radar stations, and police stations during 1945 and 1946. These attacks stopped when the British arrested en masse many of the Palmach and Haganah leadership on June 19, 1946, a date known in Israeli history as the *Black Sabbath*.

Palmach units assumed the responsibility for protecting the Jewish settlements from Arab militias when the 1948 Israeli-Arab War erupted following the partition of Palestine and the formation of the state of Israel. These Palmach units persevered until Haganah relieved them. The Palmach was then formed into two units of the newly created IDF, the Negev Brigade and the Yiftah Brigade. These units stopped the Egyptian army in the Negev and then seized the Gaza Strip and Sharem al-Sheikh.

Richard M. Edwards

See also: Haganah; Israel Defense Forces; Kibbutz; Yishuv; Zionism

Further Reading

Bar-On, Mordechai, ed. *A Never-Ending Conflict: A Guide to Israeli Military History*. Westport, CT: Praeger, 2004.

Creveld, Martin van. *The Sword and the Olive: A Critical History of the Israel Defense Forces*. New York: Public Affairs, 1998.

Goldstein, Yaacov N., and Dan Shomron. *From Fighters to Soldiers: How the Israel Defense Forces Began*. Brighton, UK: Sussex Academic, 1998.

Peace Now

Nongovernmental organization (NGO) and activist group that advocates for a two-state solution to the Israeli-Palestinian conflict. Founded in 1978, Peace Now is the oldest and largest Israeli organization of its kind. Through public campaigns and political pressure, it aims to keep the issue of normalized diplomatic relations with Israel's Arab neighbors at the forefront of the government's agenda and Israeli public discourse. For example, in 1988, Peace Now organized a demonstration of 100,000 people that called upon the Israeli government to negotiate with the Palestine Liberation Organization (PLO). Peace Now continues to organize demonstrations as well as lectures, debates, tours, and other public campaigns.

Peace Now is at the forefront of the fight against Israeli settlement expansion in the West Bank, which it identifies as one of the largest obstacles to the two-state solution. Through initiatives such as Settlement Watch, it tracks, analyzes, and publicizes current settlement activity in an effort to curtail further Israeli confiscation of Palestinian land. Peace Now has been on the receiving end of numerous right-wing attacks and smear campaigns. On account of its antisettlement activity, Peace Now has been the target of so-called "Price Tag" attacks, including death threats against the organization's leaders. On the other hand, Peace Now has enjoyed support from many prominent figures in Israeli society, such as renowned Israeli authors David Grossman and Amos Oz. Such support has played into accusations that Peace Now has an elitist, anti-Mizrahi, antireligious orientation.

Emily Schneider

See also: Israeli Occupations; Settlements; Two-State Solution

Further Reading

Feige, Michael. "Peace Now and the Legitimation Crisis of 'Civil Militarism'." *Israel Studies* 3, no. 1 (1998): 85–111.

Shohat, E. "Sephardim in Israel: Zionism from the Standpoint of Its Jewish Victims." *Social Text* No. 19/20 (Autumn, 1988): 1–35.

Peres, Shimon

Former prime minister and president of the state of Israel. Shimon Peres (Perski) was born August 16, 1923, in Wolozyn, Poland (now Valozhyn, Belarus). His family emigrated to Palestine in 1934. In 1947, Peres joined Haganah and came under the political mentorship of David Ben-Gurion. As prime minister, Ben-Gurion put the twenty-four-year-old Peres in charge of Israel's navy after the War of Independence of 1948–1949. From 1953–1959, he served as the general director for procurement for the defense ministry, developing a close relationship with the French government that led to the acquisition of the advanced Dassault Mirage III French jet fighter, the establishment of Israel's avionics industries, the procurement of a nuclear reactor, and planning for the 1956 Sinai Campaign.

Peres increased indigenous weapons production while serving as the deputy defense minister (1959–1965), and he also started Israel's nuclear-research program and further developed foreign military alliances. In 1967, Peres helped create the modern-day Labor Party and served for many years as its deputy secretary-general. He also served in various ministerial positions, including as defense minister from 1974–1977.

Peres became acting prime minister in 1977 upon the resignation of Yitzhak Rabin. The same year, he led Labor to its first defeat in a general election in thirty years. In 1988, Likud and Labor formed another coalition government, enlisting Peres to serve as deputy prime minister and minister of finance. Rabin assumed the leadership of Labor from Peres in February 1992 and went on to become Israel's prime minister in July 1992, making Peres his minister of foreign affairs. Peres and Rabin negotiated with Yasser Arafat, chairman of the Palestine Liberation Organization (PLO), to work out the 1993 Oslo Accords. A peace treaty with

Jordan followed in October 1994. In November 1995, Peres became prime minister and minister of defense when Rabin was assassinated, positions he held jointly until he was defeated by Likud's Benjamin Netanyahu in the May 1996 elections, which followed a series of Palestinian suicide bombings and a brief and ineffective operation against Hezbollah.

Peres served as minister of foreign affairs and deputy prime minister in Ariel Sharon's National Unity government (March 2001–October 2002), and as vice premier (January 2005) following his support at the end of 2004 for Sharon's disengagement from Gaza. In 2007, the Knesset elected him to the largely ceremonial position of president of Israel, which he held until July 2014. Peres died on September 28, 2016.

Richard M. Edwards

See also: Oslo Accords; Rabin, Yitzhak

Further Reading

Bar-Zohar, Michael. *Phoenix: Shimon Peres and the Secret History of Israel*. Tel Aviv: Magal Books, 2016.

Golan, Matti. *The Road to Peace: A Biography of Shimon Peres*. New York: Warner, 1989.

Ziv, Guy. *Why Hawks Become Doves: Shimon Peres and Foreign Policy Change in Israel*. Albany: State University of New York, 2014.

Permanent Status Issues

Major stumbling blocks to a two-state solution. The Oslo Accords labeled some particularly difficult to resolve matters as "permanent status issues," to be negotiated as part of a permanent resolution to the Israeli-Palestinian conflict. Most observers understood such a permanent resolution to involve the creation of an independent Palestinian state in the occupied territories. The most important and thorny permanent status issues are Jerusalem, refugees, settlements, security arrangements, and borders.

JERUSALEM

Palestinians insist that East Jerusalem must be the capital of their new state, while Israelis insist Jerusalem will always remain united and under Israeli sovereignty. This ancient city holds great religious significance for both Muslims and Jews. The Old City in East Jerusalem is home to what Muslims refer to as the *Haram al-Sharif,* a thirty-five-acre compound housing two of Islam's holiest structures, the Dome of the Rock shrine and the al-Aqsa Mosque. Completed in 691 by Arab rulers who conquered the region decades earlier, the Dome of the Rock commemorates the point from which the Prophet Mohamed made his famous Night Journey to heaven. The nearby al-Aqsa Mosque was first built a few years after the Dome of the Rock, and then it was rebuilt and expanded a number of times thereafter. For a brief time, Jerusalem was the *qibla,* or direction of prayer for Muslims. For these reasons and more, Jerusalem is widely considered the third-holiest city in Islam, second only to Mecca and Medina. Jerusalem is also part of the reason why the Israeli-Palestinian conflict resonates with Muslims around the world.

For Jews, Jerusalem is the holiest city on Earth because it is home to the ancient ruins of the great temples. What Muslims refer to as the Haram al-Sharif is known to Jews as the Temple Mount. This is where many believe Abraham went to sacrifice his son Isaac, and it is the spot where King Solomon built the first temple to house the Ark of the Covenant. The temple was also home to what Jews call the *Holy of Holies*, a sanctum in which dwells the presence of God. Finished around 950 BCE, the temple made Jerusalem the spiritual center of Judaism. The Babylonians destroyed it in 586 BCE, but it was rebuilt a few years later and remained standing until the Romans destroyed it again in 70 CE. Many believe that part of the wall on the western side of the Temple Mount is the only aboveground remains of the Second Temple complex. As such it is revered by Jews and has become a site of pilgrimage and prayer. Many believe that someday, in connection with the arrival of the Messiah, a Third Temple will be rebuilt where the Dome of the Rock and al-Aqsa Mosque now sit.

SETTLEMENTS

Since Israel conquered East Jerusalem, the West Bank, and the Gaza Strip in 1967, it has settled nearly 700,000 of its Jewish citizens in these occupied territories. For a number of reasons, settlement activity was less extensive in Gaza, so when Israel withdrew in 2005, it had to remove only about 9,000 settlers. After conquering East Jerusalem, Israeli officials expanded the city's borders and annexed it to create a unified Jerusalem. Since then, they have settled nearly 300,000 Jews there, while simultaneously imposing administrative rules and regulations aimed at constraining the growth of the Palestinian population in the city. In the West Bank, Israel has moved about 400,000 more of its Jewish citizens into 200 or so settlements dotted all over the territory. While many settlers are lured by government incentives and more affordable cost of living, others are driven by nationalist and/or religious fervor. The settlement movement has enjoyed support from Jewish parties all along the political spectrum, but it has increasingly aligned with the right wing and has become very powerful influence in Israeli politics. For religious, nationalist, and security reasons, it opposes giving up control of the West Bank.

Palestinians oppose the establishment of settlements. They insist that continued settlement growth undermines the chances of peace because it reduces the size and contiguity of the land left over for a Palestinian state. They also believe the more Israel invests in settlements, the less likely future governments will be to uproot them. So every building that Israel erects creates facts on the ground that will handicap Palestinians in any future negotiations. Indeed, many Palestinians see Israel's continuous settlement expansion as evidence that it is not serious about negotiating a fair two-state solution.

Israeli settlements are considered illegal under international law, in contravention of the Geneva Conventions, which prohibit occupying powers from permanently transferring its citizens into occupied territory. For its part, Israel insists the West Bank and East Jerusalem are not occupied territories: The latter is sovereign

Israeli territory, and the former is disputed because its ownership has never been legally determined, and so the Geneva Conventions do not apply to either.

What would become of this growing population in the advent of a negotiated solution? No Israeli government will be willing to evacuate hundreds of thousands of their own people. Israel has already declared that it intends to annex at least the largest settlements as part of any peace deal. These settlements almost completely surround Jerusalem. Previously, negotiators have suggested land swaps—Israel annexes some settlements, and Palestinians annex some Israeli territory in exchange—but the amounts and locations of such a swap are contested. And what of the settlers that are not annexed? Would they be removed by Israel or be allowed to live within the new Palestinian state? These are all unresolved issues.

BORDERS

If the two sides were to agree to a two-state solution, what would be the new Palestinian state's borders? This issue is closely tied to the settlement and security concerns. Israel insists that it will never return to its pre-1967 borders because it would be required to relinquish East Jerusalem and hundreds of settlements, and doing this would undermine its national security. Palestinians insist that the borders of their new state must include East Jerusalem and that any deviations from the pre-1967 borders have to be agreed upon and include equal territorial swaps.

SECURITY

Many Israelis worry that the creation of a Palestinian state would undermine their security. Pulling back to the pre-1967 borders would leave Israel only nine miles wide at its narrowest point. The West Bank affords Israel some level of strategic depth, protecting it from external attack from the east. While Jordan is currently a friendly neighbor, it may not remain so. Also, the new Palestinian state could become a safe haven for terrorist attacks or could be taken over by extremists. Relinquishing control of the West Bank reduces the IDF and Shin Bet's ability to counter threats to Israeli security.

To reassure Israel, many observers have suggested deploying an international security force to help the new Palestinian state stabilize itself and prevent terror attacks. Others have argued that the bulk of Palestinian violence against Israelis is motivated by the occupation and that a fair two-state solution would assuage the majority of Palestinians, leaving only a minority looking to continue the fight. These rejectionists would soon find themselves alienated within Palestinian society because the majority would be focused on the state-building process and on providing a better future for their children. Every attack on Israel would bring international condemnation, disrupt the flow of international aid and investments, and even threaten Palestine's newly gained independence because Israel's military could easily retake the territories. In short order, these rejectionists would lose domestic support and become tantamount to a criminal nuisance, as opposed to a serious security threat to Israel. Even so, many Israelis feel that while the status quo is not the optimal situation, ending the occupation is too risky.

PALESTINIAN REFUGEES

Another major stumbling block to a negotiated two-state solution is the Palestinian refugee issue. Israel's establishment in 1948, known as the *nakba* (catastrophe) in Arab circles, created hundreds of thousands of Palestinian refugees; some fled the war zone in fear, while others were forced out by Israeli troops. Refugee camps were set up in neighboring Egypt, Jordan, Syria, Lebanon, the Gaza Strip, and the West Bank. Another wave of Palestinians flooded these camps following the 1967 Six-Day War. While some refugees integrated into neighboring countries and others made their way to places outside the region, a large number remained in camps, many of which have turned into slum cities.

The Palestinian refugee population has grown from nearly 1 million in 1950 to 5 million today. Many Palestinians cling to the hope that someday they will return to their homes in Israel. Palestinian leaders have insisted upon this right of return during peace negotiations, but most Israelis considers it a nonstarter. They fear that if millions of Palestinian refugees were allowed to return home, Jews would quickly become a minority and Israel would cease being a Jewish state. While there are many things that Jewish Israelis disagree about, this is not one of them: most of them want Israel to remain a Jewish state. Indeed, Israeli officials have repeatedly insisted that Palestinian leaders publicly recognize Israel as a Jewish state before negotiations can proceed.

Negotiators have offered compromises on all these issues, but so far, no combination of compromises has been acceptable to both sides. After twenty-five years of failed peace talks, many are losing hope for a two-state solution to the Israeli-Palestinian conflict.

Robert C. DiPrizio

See also: Arab-Israeli War, 1967; Israeli Occupations; Jerusalem; Jerusalem, Old City of; Oslo Accords; One-State Solution; Palestinian Refugees; Settlements; Two-State Solution

Further Reading
Gordon, Neve. *Israel's Occupation.* Berkeley: University of California Press, 2008.
Hever, Shir. *The Political Economy of Israel's Occupation: Repression Beyond Exploitation.* London: Pluto Press, 2010.
Makdisi, Saree. *Palestine Inside Out: An Everyday Occupation.* London: W. W. Norton and Co., 2010.
Selengut, Charles. *Our Promised Land: Faith and Militant Zionism in Israeli Settlements.* Maryland: Rowan and Littlefield, 2015.
Vickery, Matthew. *Employing the Enemy: The Story of Palestinian Labourers on Israeli Settlements.* London: Zed Books, 2017.

Persian Conquest of Palestine

At the end of 603, the Persians began to systematically conquer the Roman defensive line of fortified cities, working northward along the Euphrates, across the southern part of present-day Turkey, and down the coast of Syria toward Palestine, eventually conquering Alexandria in Egypt. During this war, the Persians had to respond to attacks by Turkish nomads to the north, while the Romans faced severe attacks by the Avars and Slavs from the plains of Hungary.

The Persians exploited the resentment of Jews against the discrimination and persecution that they had suffered from Christians after Emperor Constantine gave Christianity official state recognition. In 608, the Sassanid emperor Khusrau II placed the Jewish leader Nehemiah ben Hushiel in a position of symbolic leadership within the army of Shahrbaraz and encouraged Jews to join the army. The Persian Empire also gave refuge to Nestorian Christians persecuted after the Council of Chalcedon in 451.

The Persians exploited the internal turmoil of a Roman military coup, which provoked rebellion by the leading generals of Africa and Syria. Heraclius, the son of the governor of Africa, sailed to Constantinople, and he was crowned emperor in October 610, while his younger cousin, Nicetas, took control of Egypt. Because of the rebellion in North Africa, Roman troops shifted from Syria and Palestine to Egypt, and from Armenia to Antakya, leaving the way open for the Persian advance. During 611, the Persians defeated a major counterattack in 613 outside Antioch, led by Heraclius, and then advanced without meaningful opposition to conquer Jerusalem in 614, Alexandria in 619, and Egypt in 621.

Among the large number of Jews that set out from Syria with the army of the Persian general Shahrbaraz, a wealthy man called Benjamin of Tiberias raised a Jewish force from Nazareth and Galilee, later joined by Jewish Arabs. The Judeo-Persian army conquered Jerusalem after a siege of three weeks. According to the historian Antiochus Strategos, the Jews took out their animosity against Christians in a large-scale riot, killing tens of thousands. Because the Sassanids controlled the situation, later scholars have doubted the high numbers as reflecting the anti-Jewish bias of the writer. Archaeological evidence shows mass graves in seven locations outside the walls of the Old City clearly identified with this time period, but not evidence of mass destruction.

The Persians deported a number of people, including the patriarch Zachariah, and took a famous relic called "the true cross." The fall of Jerusalem, followed by a direct attack on Constantinople by Persian forces from the east while their allies, the Avars, attacked from the west, damaged Byzantine morale. However, Roman forces under Heraclius conducted a methodical campaign through Armenia and down into the heartland of the Sassanian Empire, to the point of threatening their capital. The Persian forces eventually collapsed in 628 after Khosrau's son, Kavadh II, killed his father and ended the war. Scholars conclude that this war exhausted both empires, leaving them vulnerable to the Arab invasions that followed ten years later.

Jonathan K. Zartman

See also: Arab-Islamic Conquest of Palestine; Jerusalem; Roman Conquest of Judea

Further Reading

Avni, Gideon. "The Persian Conquest of Jerusalem (614 C. E.)—An Archeological Assessment." *Bulletin of the American Schools of Oriental Research* no. 357 (February 2010): 35–48.

Crawford, Peter. *The War of the Three Gods: Romans. Persians and the Rise of Islam*. Barnsley, UK: Pen and Sword Books, 2013.

Greatrex, Geoffrey, and Samuel N. C. Lieu, eds. and compilers. *The Roman Eastern Frontier and the Persian Wars Part II AD 363–630: A Narrative Sourcebook.* London and New York: Routledge, 2002.

Pinsker, Leon

Nineteenth-century Zionist writer. Leon Pinsker was the chair of Hovevei Zion, a coalition of groups responding to anti-Jewish pogroms and an early organizational boon to the Zionist movement. He was born Tomaszów Lubelski in modern-day Poland in 1821 and lived much of his life in Odessa in modern-day Ukraine. A trained physician, Pinsker developed his views based on his lived experience; for much of his life, he advocated for Jewish assimilation within wider society, but rising anti-Semitism in his later years convinced him that Jewish integration was not the answer. The Odessa pogrom of 1881 was especially formative on his outlook.

Pinsker's 1882 pamphlet *Auto-Emancipation* argued that Jews could not wait for enlightenment within their host nations to liberate them from their troubles; rather, they required a Jewish nation upon its own soil. Further, he argued that the road to such a solution was one of self-help and would need to come from within Jewish society. This emphasis on the Jews' national homelessness was all the more meaningful coming from Pinsker, who had supported Jewish assimilation for so many years.

Although Pinsker did not achieve the organizational or political success of Theodor Herzl, he is remembered for his early articulation of Zionist principles. In the years after his death, his place in early Zionism was often compared to that of Herzl; where Herzl was a leader, Pinsker was a teacher. He died in 1891, and his remains were later taken to Israel.

Sean P. Braniff

See also: Herzl, Theodor; Zionism

Further Reading
Reinharz, Jehuda, and Anita Shapira, eds. *Essential Papers on Zionism.* New York: New York University Press, 1996.
Shimoni, Gideon. *The Zionist Ideology.* Hanover, NH: Brandeis University Press, 1995.

Plan Dalet

Haganah military plan that aimed to clear Palestinians from territory allocated to Israel under the United Nations (UN) partition plan. The extent to which the Plan Dalet itself and the Israeli military in general were guilty of forcing Palestinians from their homes or of greater atrocities has been a matter of heated historical debate.

Haganah was a Jewish paramilitary organization and the precursor to the modern Israel Defense Forces (IDF). When hostilities broke out in the 1948 War, also known as Israel's War of Independence, Haganah joined with other paramilitary organizations, including Irgun Tsvai Leumi and Lehi (the Stern Gang), in fighting first against Palestinians, and then against a coalition including Egypt, Syria, Transjordan, and Iraq. The Plan Dalet represented a shift in Israeli military posture away from a defensive stance. By April 1948, Haganah went on the offensive, though dispersed battalion and brigade commanders were likely unaware that they were implementing the Plan Dalet, which had been formulated the previous month.

Key to the plan was securing the major roads between Jewish areas and the consolidation of Jewish control over territory. Historical debate centers around the degree to which military commanders felt that it was their imperative to expel Palestinians whether they were hostile or not. The Deir Yassin Massacre and expulsion of Arabs from Lydda and Ramle were outgrowths of the Plan Dalet and became symbols for its critics.

Sean P. Braniff

See also: Arab-Jewish Communal War of 1947; Deir Yassin Massacre; Haganah; Lydda and Ramle

Further Reading

Morris, Benny. *1948: A History of the First Arab-Israeli War*. New Haven, CT: Yale University Press, 2008.

Sa'di, Ahmad H., and Lila Abu-Lughod, eds. *Nakba: Palestine, 1948, and the Claims of Memory*. New York: Columbia University Press, 2007.

Pogroms (see Pale of Settlement)

Popular Front for the Liberation of Palestine (PFLP)

A Marxist-Leninist organization founded in 1967 that seeks to create a socialist state for Palestinians. The Popular Front for the Liberation of Palestine (PFLP) was founded by George Habash in 1967. Habash believed the destruction of Israel was necessary for purging the Middle East of Western capitalist influences. He believed much the same about many Arab regimes.

The group soon became known for its airliner hijackings. In 1973, Habash agreed that the PFLP would cease terrorist activities abroad, on the advice of the Palestinian National Council (PNC), but the organization withdrew from the Palestine Liberation Organization (PLO) the next year, complaining that it was no longer interested in destroying Israel.

The PFLP remained fairly active during the First and Second Intifadas. Habash stepped down as leader in 2000 and was replaced by Abu Ali Mustafa, who was killed by Israeli commandos in 2001. The PFLP retaliated by killing Rehavam Zeevi, the Israeli minister of tourism. Days earlier, Ahmed Sadat became general secretary of the organization. Sadat was subsequently arrested by the Palestinian Authority (PA) in 2004, and then imprisoned by Israel. Since then, PFLP attacks have fallen significantly, perhaps a reflection of the organization's loss of Sadat as its day-to-day leader.

Amy Hackney Blackwell

See also: Habash, George; Palestinian Hijackings

Further Reading

Popular Front for the Liberation of Palestine (PFLP). *A Radical Voice from Palestine: Recent Documents from the Popular Front for the Liberation of Palestine.* Oakland, CA: Abraham Guillen Press, 2002.

Smith, Charles D. *Palestine and the Arab-Israeli Conflict: A History with Documents.* 9th ed. New York: Bedford/St. Martin's, 2017.

Pro-Israel Lobby (see American Israel Public Affairs Committee; Christian Zionism; U.S. Aid to Israel)

Qassam, Izz al-Din al-

An Arab nationalist and militant credited with helping to instigate the 1936 Arab Revolt. Born in Jaballah, Syria, in 1882, Izz al-Din al-Qassam was sent at age fourteen to Cairo to study at al-Azhar University. He returned to Syria in 1903, and then returned to Alexandria, Egypt, to try to create an armed force to fight the Italians in Libya. He also studied sharia (Islamic law). In 1922, he moved to Haifa in the British Mandate for Palestine. He led a mosque and taught militant and charismatic religious leaders who believed in the necessity of armed struggle. He was also a representative of the Naqshabandi Sufi order and was elected the head of the Young Men's Muslim Association in 1928. He was then made a registrar for the Islamic court in the Haifa area. Al-Qassam attracted many followers, particularly from among the lower classes, and believed in both Arab and Muslim solidarity.

Al-Qassam argued for the immediate departure from Palestine of both the British and the Jews. When Mufti Haj Amin al-Husayni rejected al-Qassam's plan to transfer funds dedicated to mosque repairs in order to purchase weapons, al-Qassam proceeded to organize a military effort on his own in response to the British firing on a crowd of Palestinian demonstrators. Leading a group against the British at Ya'bud outside the town of Jenin, he was killed on November 20, 1935.

Palestinian militants regard al-Qassam as a hero and martyr. His followers, the Qassamiyun, or Izz al-Din al-Qassam Brigades, fought in the 1936–1939 Arab Revolt. Hamas calls its military fighters the Izz al-Din al-Qassam Brigades and employs what it calls Qassam rockets.

Spencer C. Tucker

See also: Arab Revolt, 1936; British Mandate for Palestine; Hamas; Izz al-Din al-Qassam Brigades

Further Reading

Nafi, Basheer M. "Shaykh 'Izz Al-Din Al-Qassam: A Reformist and a Rebel Leader." *Journal of Islamic Studies* 8, no. 2 (1997): 185–215.

Sherman, A. J. *Mandate Days: British Lives in Palestine, 1918–1948*. Baltimore: Johns Hopkins University Press, 2001.

Wasserstein, Bernard. *The British in Palestine: The Mandatory Government and Arab-Jewish Conflict*. London: Blackwell, 1991.

R

Rabin, Yitzhak

Israeli army general, diplomat, and prime minister of Israel. Born in Jerusalem on March 1, 1922, Yitzhak Rabin moved with his family to Tel Aviv the following year. He attended the Kadoori Agricultural High School, graduating in 1940. He then went to work at the Kibbutz Ramat Yochanan, where he joined the Palmach, an elite fighting unit of Haganah, the Jewish self-defense organization that ultimately became the Israel Defense Forces (IDF).

In 1944, Rabin was second-in-command of a Palmach battalion and fought against the British Mandate authorities. He was arrested by the British in June 1946 and spent six months in prison. Rabin spent the next twenty years fighting for Israel as a member of the IDF. On January 1, 1964, he became IDF chief of staff and held this position during the Six-Day War in 1967. Following the Israeli capture of the Old City of Jerusalem, he was one of the first to visit it, delivering what became a famous speech on the top of Mount Scopus at Hebrew University.

On January 1, 1968, Rabin retired from the army and shortly thereafter was named Israeli ambassador to the United States. He held this position until the spring of 1973, when he returned to Israel and joined the Labor Party. He was elected to the Knesset (Israeli parliament) in December 1973. Prime Minister Golda Meir appointed Rabin to her cabinet as minister of labor in April 1974. Meir resigned as prime minister in May 1974, and Rabin took her place.

As prime minister, Rabin sought to improve relations with the United States, which played a key role in mediating disengagement agreements with Israel, Egypt, and Syria in 1974. In 1975, Israel and the United States signed their first Memorandum of Understanding (a large, multiyear U.S. aid package to Israel). The best-known event of Rabin's first term as prime minister was the July 3–4, 1976, rescue of passengers on Air France Flight 139 held hostage at Entebbe, Uganda.

In March 1977, Rabin was forced to resign as prime minister following the revelation that his wife, Leah, held bank accounts in the United States, which was at that time against Israeli law. Between 1977 and 1984, Rabin served in the Knesset as a member of the Labor Party and was minister of defense in the national unity governments between 1984 and 1990. In 1985, he proposed that IDF forces withdraw from Lebanon and establish a security zone to protect the settlements along the northern border of Israel.

Rabin became prime minister for the second time in July 1992. The next year, he signed the Oslo Accords with Palestine Liberation Organization (PLO) chairman Yasser Arafat. This agreement created the Palestinian Authority (PA) and gave it some control over the West Bank and the Gaza Strip. Rabin, Arafat, and Shimon Peres shared the 1994 Nobel Peace Prize for their efforts to achieve peace. In 1995,

Rabin continued his negotiations, signing an agreement with Arafat expanding Palestinian autonomy in the West Bank.

A number of ultraconservative Israelis believed that Rabin had betrayed the nation by negotiating with the Palestinians and relinquishing control of land that they considered Jewish. On November 4, 1995, a right-wing extremist, Yigal Amir, shot Rabin after a peace rally in Kings of Israel Square in Tel Aviv (afterward renamed Yitzhak Rabin Square in the prime minister's honor). Rabin died of his wounds soon afterward. November 4 has since become a national memorial day for Israelis. Numerous squares, streets, and public foundations have been named for Rabin, who is revered by many for his efforts on behalf of peace.

Amy Hackney Blackwell

See also: Arafat, Yasser; Entebbe Raid; Intifada, First; Oslo Accords; Peres, Shimon

Further Reading

Freedman, Robert Owen, ed. *Israel Under Rabin.* Boulder, CO: Westview, 1995.

Rabin, Yitzhak. *The Rabin Memoirs.* Berkeley: University of California Press, 1996.

Tessler, Mark. *A History of the Israeli–Palestinian Conflict.* 2nd ed. Bloomington: Indiana University Press, 2009.

Ramadan War (see Arab-Israeli War, 1973)

Ramallah

A Palestinian city of 32,000 residents on the West Bank, in which the Palestinian Authority (PA) is headquartered. One of the first Palestinian newspapers, *The Mirror*, was published in Ramallah beginning in 1919. During the Arab-Jewish Communal War of 1947–1948, many Arab refugees crowded into the city, more than doubling its population. A number of refugee camps were established around Ramallah. Al-Jalazon, Kalandia, al-Amari, and Kadura today house some 30,000 refugees. The Jordanian Arab Legion took control of the Ramallah area during the 1948 Arab-Israeli War. Ramallah was relatively peaceful during the years of Jordanian control (1948–1967), but that changed when Israel captured the West Bank in 1967.

Resistance to Israel's occupation was subdued at first but intensified in the 1980s, culminating in the First Intifada (1987–1993). Because of violent clashes between Palestinians and the Israel Defense Forces (IDF), businesses were open only sporadically and schools were closed by order of the IDF. Many students lost an entire year of education during 1988–1989, but the schools reopened after much international pressure. The IDF arrested many Palestinians, and public services were sharply curtailed. In December 1995, the IDF withdrew from the city center and the new PA took over, in accordance with the Oslo Accords. Between 1995 and 2000, Ramallah saw general peace and prosperity. Some residents who had previously emigrated to the United States returned to open businesses. Unemployment remained high, however. IDF forces remained on the outskirts of the city, and residents had no access to nearby Jerusalem without work permits, which were difficult to secure.

When the Second Intifada erupted, Ramallah became a flashpoint. On October 12, 2000, it was targeted by Israel when two Israeli army reservists were killed by a mob. A number of suicide bombers came from the city or from its surrounding refugee camps. In 2002, the IDF, which had already destroyed most of the PA buildings in the city, reoccupied Ramallah. Conditions steadily deteriorated, and there were confirmed instances of looting by Israeli soldiers. Most of the expatriates who had returned departed once again. Making matters worse, large sections of the Israeli Security Barrier erected near the city hindered the mobility of its residents. Ramallah was plagued in 2004–2005 with inter-Palestinian violence and rivalries, but it remains an important commercial center, and as home to Birzeit University and various political parties, it has a lively atmosphere.

Ramallah is known for the Muqataa, a series of governmental buildings dating to the British Mandate for Palestine and located on high ground. They serve as the governmental headquarters of the PA. The city remains isolated owing to the presence of the Israel Security Barrier and the general dearth of permits for Palestinians who seek work in nearby areas controlled by Israel.

Spencer C. Tucker

See also: Palestinian Authority; West Bank

Further Reading

Hass, Amira. *Reporting from Ramallah: An Israeli Journalist in an Occupied Land.* Cambridge, MA: MIT Press, 2003.

Shehadeh, Raja. *When the Birds Stopped Singing: Life in Ramallah Under Siege.* South Royaltown, VT: Sheerforth, 2003.

Right of Return

An internationally recognized principle that holds that an ethnic, religious, or national group has the right to settle in—or become a citizen of—the country that it considers to be its homeland, regardless of national changes that may have occurred there. Usually, the right of return involves ethnically dispersed peoples. In the Middle East, it applies to Palestinians who were driven from their homes and homeland during the various Arab-Israeli wars since 1948. The Palestinians' right of return to lands now controlled by Israel has been a perennial sticking point in Arab-Israeli relations, and it continues to present a major impediment to a lasting peace in the region.

At present, there are an estimated 5 million Palestinian refugees living in refugee settlements throughout the Middle East, in addition to a much larger number of Palestinians dispersed throughout the world. Most of these refugees live in the Gaza Strip, West Bank, Lebanon, Syria, Egypt, Iraq, and Jordan. The vast majority of these refugees were displaced from their ancestral homeland (lands now controlled by Israel) during the 1948–1949 Israeli War of Independence and the 1967 Six-Day War. This number also includes the children (and even grandchildren) of those first displaced in 1948 and 1967. Palestinians believe that these refugees and their offspring have an inalienable right to return to their homes. In fact, many of them retain legal documents, deeds, and even keys to homes and businesses that they had owned prior to the diaspora.

Indeed, the Palestinians' belief that they have an absolute right to return to areas now controlled by Israel is far from unfounded. United Nations (UN) Resolution 194 (specifically Article 11), passed by the General Assembly on December 11, 1948, calls for the return of all refugees from the conflict "at the earliest practicable date." The United Nations made no distinction between Israeli and Palestinian refugees. Naturally, the Palestinians have used this resolution as the linchpin of their right of return. Over the years, the United Nations has also specified that the right of return applies to both Palestinians and their direct descendants. This stands in contrast to its normal policies regarding refugees, which usually hold that only those actually displaced have a right of return, and the right does not extend to descendants. To bolster their claims further, Palestinians also point to the Universal Declaration of Human Rights, which the United Nations adopted on December 10, 1948, just one day prior to UN Resolution 194. That document holds that an individual has the right to "leave any country, including his own, and to return to his country."

But while the Palestinian right of return seems justified based upon the various UN dictates, the issue is far more complicated to put into practice, especially in that so many years have passed since the creation of the Palestinian diaspora. From the Israeli perspective, the issue raises several critical concerns. First, Israel maintains that as a sovereign nation, it must be the sole arbiter of its immigration policy. Arguing that every nation has the right to set its own policies in this regard, the Israelis insist that to surrender to the right of return would involve giving up a piece of their sovereignty. Second, and perhaps more important, the Israeli government claims that allowing as many as 5 million Palestinians to return to Israel would threaten the very survival of the nation and seriously alter the ethnic and national identity of the state. It has repeatedly been argued that relatively few of the 5 million would even want to return. However, Israel refused to discuss this issue, even with its inclusion in the Oslo Accords, and otherwise liberal negotiators argued that it was Palestinians who were unreasonable to advance such a position. Many of the property rights that predate the founding of Israel have actually been argued in court and settled in favor of Palestinians, but the government has refused to honor these rulings.

Besides Israeli concerns, there are other potential roadblocks with the right of return. One is certainly determining the Palestinians who became refugees in 1948 and 1967. Another is determining the exact circumstances of their departure. Still, there are fairly accurate figures for Palestinian refugees that have been kept by the United Nations over the years. In 1951, for example, the United Nations determined that there were approximately 860,000 Palestinians who lost their homes, livelihoods, or both as a result of the Arab-Israeli conflict that began in 1948. After Israel annexed the West Bank and the Gaza Strip in 1967, there were an additional 300,000 Palestinians who left their homeland. Most went to neighboring Jordan.

Most Israelis see the right of return as a fundamental issue that is not to be implemented, for to agree to do so would lead to the end of Israel as a Jewish state. But the likelihood that anything like 5 million Palestinians would stream into Israel if the right of return were granted is small. A recent survey of Palestinians living in

Jordan, Lebanon, the Gaza Strip, and West Bank indicated that only about 10 percent would actually attempt to return to their homes if allowed. The vast majority preferred to stay where they were or wait for the creation of a bona fide Palestinian state. Thus, the number of likely Palestinian refugees returning to Israel would be far less than 5 million, perhaps numbering only in the hundreds of thousands. This blunts Israeli assertions that the right of return would drastically alter or destroy their nation. Still, the influx of only several hundred thousand Palestinians would be enormously expensive and would stress Israel's infrastructure, housing, education, and health-care systems.

In the final analysis, the right of return continues to stand as a contentious and outstanding issue. The Donald Trump administration has cut all U.S. funding to the UN organization charged with supporting Palestinian refugees. It also calls on the United Nations to restrict refugee status only to the generation of Palestinians that actually lost their homes, not their descendants. This would reduce the Palestinian refugee community to only tens of thousands. These efforts have delighted many Israelis and their supporters, but they have been widely denounced by the rest of the international community.

Paul G. Pierpaoli Jr.

See also: Boycott, Divestment, and Sanctions Movement; *Nakba;* One-State Solution; Palestinian Refugees; Two-State Solution; Zionism

Further Reading

Aruri, Naseer Hasan, ed. *Palestinian Refugees: The Right of Return.* London: Pluto, 2001.

Bowker, Robert. *Palestinian Refugees: Mythology, Identity, and the Search for Peace.* Boulder, CO: Lynne Rienner, 2003.

Ginat, Joseph, Edward J. Perkins, and Hassan bin Talal, eds. *Palestinian Refugees: Traditional Positions and New Solutions.* Norman: University of Oklahoma Press, 2002.

United Nations. *The Right of Return of the Palestinian People.* New York: United Nations, 1979.

Roman Conquest of Judea

Judea was a region of the Levant stretching from Caesarea Philippi in the north to Gaza in the south, roughly corresponding with modern Israel and Palestine. In 67 BCE, Pompey was granted a three-year commission to eradicate the Cilician pirates, a task that took only three months to complete. He retained his commission for its duration to subdue the eastern Mediterranean seaboard. After annexing Pontus in the Third Mithridatic War (66 BCE) and Syria (64 BCE), he entered Judea, where a bloody civil war was being fought between the brothers Aristobulus and Hyrcanus of the Hasmonean dynasty, following the death of their mother, Alexandra Salome (67 BCE). Aristobulus, who was besieged in the temple by his brother and Aretas III of Petra, enticed Pompey with a golden vine of 500 talents, which Pompey sent to the Temple of Jupiter Optimus Maximus in Rome. Pompey first sent his tribune, Amelius Scaurus, who drove out Aretas. However, Aristobulus charged Scaurus with extortion, leading Pompey to intervene in person. He placed Judea under the control of Hyrcanus, although the followers of Aristobulus, the Sadducees, still held the temple. Pompey laid siege to the temple and is said to have entered the Holy of Holies, a sanctum in which Jews believe dwells the presence of God. He returned to Rome, having appointed Hyrcanus high priest of the temple. Judea, though remaining autonomous, became a tributary and client kingdom of Rome.

During the civil war between Pompey and Julius Caesar (49–45 BCE), Hyrcanus and his adherent, Antipater of Idumea, sided with Caesar, and power was transferred to Antipater, who was named regent of Judea. After the assassination of Caesar (44 BCE), Octavian and Antony declared war on his killers, Brutus and Cassius, the latter of whom fled to the east to raise an army. During the ensuing campaign, Antipater was forced to support Cassius, who was demanding heavy tribute of the eastern provinces to finance his campaign. While struggling to raise the money in the face of local opposition, Antipater was killed and succeeded by his son Herod.

After the defeat of Caesar's assassins at Philippi (42 BCE), Herod gained the support of Antony and was named tetrarch of Galilee, sharing the rule of Judea with his brother Phasael, tetrarch of Jerusalem. During Rome's war against the Parthians, Herod, who had struggled to win the support of his subjects because his mother was Arabian and not Jewish, was driven out by Antigonus, the son of Aristobulus, and fled to Rome. After defeating the Parthians, the Romans besieged Jerusalem and sacked the city despite Herod's attempts to restrain them. Herod was restored now as sole ruler of Judea, with the title *basileus* (king). Following the defeat of Antony by Octavian at Actium (31 BCE), Herod met with Rome's new leader, assured him of his allegiance, and, winning Octavian's support, secured his hold on the throne.

The Arch of Titus in Rome, commemorating the Roman victory over Jewish rebels in Judea in 71 CE. (William Perry/Dreamstime.com)

Following the death of Herod the Great (4 CE), Augustus allocated Judea to his three sons: Herod Antipas was appointed tetrarch of Galilee and Perea, Philip was tetrarch of Golan-Heights, and Herod Archelaus was ethnarch of Judea. An inept ruler, Archelaus was removed (6 CE), and Judea, with its new capital at Caesarea, became attached to the Roman province of Syria and was placed under the rule of a prefect. P. Sulpicius Quirinius, governor of Syria, reorganized the tax system of Judea, forcing the inhabitants to pay in coin rather than kind. The locals revolted under Judas of Galilee, but they were quickly defeated. The next sixty years were a period of relative peace and tranquility in the region, though some tensions surfaced during the reign of Caligula.

The Great Jewish Revolt began in 66 CE as a result of the heavy taxation of the Jewish populace and rising religious tension between the Jews and Romans. The conflict escalated into all-out war, in which a group of Jews known as the *Sicarians*, led by Menehem, seized a cache of arms at the fortress of Masada, defeated the Roman garrison of Jerusalem, and executed the high priest of the temple. After Menehem was killed, the Sicarians returned to Masada, where they continued the war by employing guerilla tactics. The Romans recaptured Galilee but were defeated by the Zealots, who captured the legion's standard. The following year, the emperor Nero appointed Vespasian as commander of the Roman forces in charge of quelling the rebellion. Vespasian, with his son Titus, entered Galilee and besieged Jotapata. After taking the city, the commander of the Jewish forces, Joseph, son of Matthias (the future historian Josephus), predicted (in accordance with a Messianic prophecy) that Vespasian would rule Rome. By 68 CE, the Jews in Jerusalem were embroiled in an internal struggle between the Zealots and the Sadducees.

In 69 CE, the death of Nero plunged the Roman Empire into civil war, causing Vespasian to leave Judea. By the end of the year, he emerged as emperor of Rome, fulfilling the prophecy uttered by Josephus. Vespasian then charged his son Titus with putting down the revolt. During Passover in 70 CE, Titus besieged Jerusalem with a massive army comprised of four legions and numerous auxiliaries. He took the city after a seven-month siege in which the Romans looted and burned the temple, leaving Jerusalem in ruins. Titus returned to Rome in triumph, bringing untold wealth and numerous sacred artifacts from the temple, including the Menorrah. The scene of these objects being paraded through Rome was celebrated on the interior relief of the Arch of Titus at the entrance to the Roman Forum.

Vespasian used this new influx of wealth to build the Flavian Amphitheater (the Colosseum) and the Forum of Vespasian (Temple of Peace). After stabilizing the region, the Romans marched against the fortress at Masada, the last remaining stronghold of the rebels, where under Eleazer, son of Yair, nearly 966 Sicarians, including women and children, had taken refuge. The Romans entered the fortress unopposed and found the bodies of 960 people (one woman and five children remained), who had committed suicide rather than surrender. Judea was placed under the rule of a praetor, and a legion was stationed at Caesarea. Another period of calm would follow, this one lasting 40 years.

In 115 CE, the emperor Trajan was near the end of his successful campaign in the Middle East against the Parthians and Armenians when Messianic revolts broke out among several Jewish populations in Cyrenaica, Egypt, and Cyprus, before ultimately spreading to Judea in what would become known as the Kitos War. Lusius Quietus was charged with restoring order in Judea. He besieged Lydda, where the Jewish rebels had assembled under the joint command of Julian and Pappas. Quietus took the city, and in the aftermath, he executed a great number of Jewish rebels, including Julian and Pappas. Quietus was named governor of Judea and began a program of Hellenization among the local population, leading rabbis in defiance to urge men not to teach their children Greek. After the death of Trajan (117 CE), Hadrian came to power and abandoned Rome's recently acquired territories in Mesopotamia and brought an uneasy peace to Judea that would last only fifteen years.

In 130, Hadrian ordered Jerusalem, still in ruins since the destruction by Titus, to be rebuilt as a Roman city called Aelia Capitalina, with a temple to Jupiter on the Temple Mount. In 132, he may have banned circumcision, but modern scholars dispute this. The final incident that led to the outbreak of revolt was the collapse of the tomb of Solomon during the construction of the Temple of Jupiter, which the Jews took as an omen.

The revolt was led by Simon Bar Kosiba, later known as Simon Bar Kokhba ("Son of the Star"), who was deemed the Messiah by many after meeting with early success in liberating parts of Judea. Hadrian sent Julius Severus with at least six legions and auxiliaries to put down the revolt. During the fighting, Christian Jews who did not support the cause were targeted and persecuted by the rebels. Simon used guerilla tactics with great success, inflicting numerous casualties upon the Romans. The Jews employed numerous caves, often interconnected by a series of tunnels, to wage their war and shelter families from the Romans. At the height of the conflict, there were up to twelve Roman legions fighting in Judea. The Romans gradually gained the advantage under Julius Severus until the Roman army besieged the last remaining Jewish stronghold of significance at Betar in 135. After a lengthy siege, the Romans took the city and massacred the remaining inhabitants, effectively ending the revolt, although a few minor skirmishes followed.

After the revolt, the Temple of Zeus was erected where the temple once stood, and a statue of Hadrian was placed in the Holy of Holies. In an attempt to eradicate, or severely curtail, Judaism, Hadrian banned the teaching of Mosaic Law and the Hebrew calendar. He also barred all Jews from Jerusalem, now known as the pagan city Aelia Capitalina, and renamed the region Syria Palestina. This brought about the end of the Jewish state until the twentieth century.

Andrew Nichols

See also: Diaspora, Jewish; Jewish Revolts; Masada

Further Reading

Campbell, Duncan. "Capturing a Desert Fortress: Flavius Silva and the Siege of Masada." *Ancient Warfare* 4, no. 2 (2010): 28–35.

Eck, Werner. "The Bar Kokhba Revolt: The Roman Point of view." *Journal of Roman Studies* 89 (1999): 76–89.

Faulkner, Neil. *Apocalypse: The Great Jewish Revolt Against Rome*. Gloucestershire, UK: Tempus Publishing, 2004.

McDonnell-Staff, Paul. "A War of Logistics: The Siege of Jerusalem, 66 AD." *Ancient Warfare* 4, no. 2 (2010): 36–41.

S

Sabra and Shatila Massacre (see Lebanon, Israeli Invasion of)

Sadat, Anwar

President of Egypt from 1970–1981. Born in the Tala District of Egypt on December 25, 1918, Anwar Sadat attended the Royal Egyptian Military Academy, graduating in 1938. His first assignment was in the Sudan, where he met Gamal Abdel Nasser. From their mutual dislike of the British, they formed a secret nationalist organization in the army eventually known as the Free Officers.

The Free Officers sought to expel the British from Egypt, along with their puppet, King Farouk. The revolt took place on July 23, 1952. Farouk abdicated and left Egypt three days later. The British withdrew from Egypt early in 1956. Egypt was declared a republic in June 1953, and Nasser became president the next year. During this time, Sadat held a number of posts until he was named vice president in 1964. Upon Nasser's death in 1970, Sadat became president.

On October 6, 1973, the Egyptians and Syrians attacked Israel, catching the Israelis by surprise. The war went well for the Syrians and Egyptians at first. But the Israelis regrouped and counterattacked, even managing to cross the Suez Canal. The United States and Soviet Union became concerned about the balance of power in the Middle East and stepped in to secure a cease-fire that restored the prewar boundaries between Egypt and Israel. The peace agreement was a personal victory for Sadat.

Sadat concluded that the only way to secure concessions from the Israelis was to work with the Americans. In March 1976, he broke the Treaty of Friendship between Egypt and the Soviet Union and wooed U.S. support. In 1977, Sadat went to Israel to speak before the Knesset, which led to the eventual signing of the Camp David Accords in 1978. While the accords were good for Egypt, many in the Arab world saw them as Egypt selling out. Sadat was seen as a traitor to the Arab world. On October 6, 1981, he was assassinated by Muslim fundamentalists while he was at a military review commemorating the October 1973 war.

Dallace W. Unger Jr.

See also: Arab-Israeli War, 1973; Begin, Menachem; Camp David Accords; Egypt

Further Reading

Hirst, David. *Sadat*. London: Faber and Faber, 1981.

Sadat, Anwar. *In Search of Identity: An Autobiography*. New York: Harper & Row, 1978.

Saladin

Vizier (1169–1171) and sultan of Egypt (1174–1193), the main Muslim opponent of the Franks of Outremer in the fourth quarter of the twelfth century. His original name was Yusuf ibn Ayyub; the name *Saladin* is a European corruption of his honorific Arabic title, *ala al-Din* ("goodness of the faith").

Saladin was a Kurd who was born at Tikrit in 1138. His family originated in Dvin in the Caucasus, but employment opportunities brought members of the family to Iraq. Saladin's father, Najm al-Din Ayyub, and uncle, Asad al-Din Shirkuh, served as governors of Tikrit on behalf of the Seljuk sultan Muammad ibn Malik Shah. However, in 1138, they had to flee Tikrit following a murder committed by Shirkuh. They both found employment at the court of Imad al-Din Zangi, emir of Mosul. For some years, the careers of the two brothers took separate courses, but from 1154 onward, they were both in Damascus in the service of Zangi's son Nur al-Din, ruler of Muslim Syria. Saladin spent his formative years in Damascus: for a short period, he served as chief of police, but he was mostly known as Nur al-Din's highly skilled polo-playing companion.

Between 1164 and 1169, Nur al-Din found himself obliged to intervene militarily in Egypt to counter invasions mounted by the Franks of Jerusalem in alliance with the Byzantines. Saladin accompanied the expeditionary force commanded by Shirkuh, gaining his first military experience at the Battle of Babayan and the defense of Alexandria (1167).

On the death of Shirkuh (March 26, 1169), Saladin became commander of Nur al-Din's forces in Egypt and was also appointed as vizier, governing in the name of the Fatimid caliph al-'Āḍid li-Dīn Allāh. The period from this point up to the death of the caliph (September 1171) saw the consolidation of Saladin's power, the undermining of the Fatimid state, and the growth of tension with Nur al-Din. Saladin bought the loyalty of the officers of the Syrian army in Egypt by rewarding them with rural and urban property. His personal standing was much strengthened with the arrival of his father and older brothers from Damascus. His brother, Turan Shah, fought and destroyed the Fatimid infantry regiments in Cairo, thus curtailing the ability of the Fatimid regime to oppose Saladin. His father, Najm al-Din Ayyub, governed provinces of Egypt, and his nephew, Taqi al-Din, emulated Saladin by establishing educational and religious institutions that emphasized the new Sunni character of Egypt. In the struggle against the Fatimid state, Saladin was assisted by Sunni Muslims within the Fatimid administration, who had a deep dislike for the incompetent and religiously abhorrent Shiite regime. Among these, the cooperation of Qai al-Fail, head of the Fatimid chancery, proved invaluable.

The death of al-Aid in 1171 brought the tension between Saladin and Nur al-Din into the open: Nur al-Din now realized that Saladin and his Ayyubid kinsmen had developed a taste for power in Egypt, but he found himself unable to enjoy the fruits of the military investment he had made in sending his armies there. This tension, although it did not explode into open conflict, continued until the death of Nur al-Din in 1174.

Following the death of his formal overlord, Saladin set out to remove Syria from the hands of Nur al-Din's young heirs. This intra-Muslim war was presented in

Qai al-Fail's propaganda as having a different motive: the desire to wage holy war on the Franks. Damascus, Homs, and Hama came under Saladin's rule in 1174. However, it was only after two battles against Zangid forces, in 1175 and 1176, that Saladin was able to conquer Aleppo in 1183. Mosul remained a Zangid possession, while recognizing Saladin's sovereignty and contributing forces to his campaigns (1186). Other victories by Saladin included the conquest of the Artuqid towns of Mayyafariqin, Mardin, and the fortress of Amida in 1183. Saladin's expansion at the cost of other Muslim dynasties took place intermittently, interspersed with wars against the Franks of Outremer and clashes with the Assassins, who were regarded as Muslim heretics.

In 1177, Saladin suffered a disastrous defeat at the hands of the Franks in the Battle of Mont Gisard, in southern Palestine. However, he was able to recover from this and successfully fought the Battle of Marj Uyun (1179). Special animosity developed between Saladin and the lord of Transjordan, Reynald of Châtillon, who intercepted pilgrim caravans to Arabia and launched a naval raid in the Red Sea aimed at the holy city of Mecca, which was defeated by Saladin's forces in Egypt. Saladin's invasions of the Kingdom of Jerusalem in 1182 and 1183 were quite futile; in 1183, for example, the refusal of the Franks to be dragged into an all-out battle led to a stalemate and forced him to withdraw from the kingdom.

The campaign of 1187 was marked by Saladin's vast numerical superiority and tactical mistakes committed by the Franks. On June 27, Saladin rounded the southern tip of Lake Tiberias, and on June 30, he took up a position to the northwest at Kfar Sabt. This well-watered place controlled one of the roads from Saforie, where the Franks had concentrated, to Tiberias. On July 2, Saladin left most of his army at Kfar Sabt and attacked Tiberias with his personal guard. The town was quickly taken, but Eschiva of Galilee, the wife of Raymond III of Tripoli, held out in the strongly fortified citadel. On July 3, the Franks left Saforie in an attempt to relieve Tiberias. Saladin's army seized the springs of Turan as they left, cutting the Franks off from water supplies; the nearest springs were at the Horns of Hattin, but these had also been seized by Saladin's troops.

Saladin made effective use of his numerical superiority, attacking the rear of the Frankish army, held by the Templars, from the high ground of Turan. At this point, King Guy of Jerusalem decided to establish a camp, and the Franks endured a night of thirst on the arid plateau (July 3–4). In the ensuing battle, Raymond of Tripoli and some of his troops were able to escape the Muslim encirclement, but the Frankish army, although it fought gallantly, finally collapsed, with the majority of the Franks killed or taken prisoner. Saladin spared King Guy, but executed Reynald of Châtillon, along with the Templar and Hospitaller captives. Vast numbers of prisoners were sent to Damascus.

Saladin took full advantage of this victory and went on to capture the city of Jerusalem (October 20, 1187) and numerous other territories held by the Franks in Palestine and Syria in intense campaigns in 1187–1189, which occasionally continued into the winter months as well. Only Tyre and Tripoli remained in Christian hands, but this was enough for the Franks, aided by Crusader forces, to begin their attempt at reconquest.

During the Third Crusade (1189–1192), one of Saladin's major problems—the lack of adequate naval power—came to the fore. Saladin built a fleet, but it was much smaller than the European fleets operating in the eastern Mediterranean and performed poorly in combat, notably at Tyre in 1187. This naval shortcoming contributed greatly to Saladin's failure in the Siege of Acre from September 1189 to July 1191.

Although the Third Crusade failed to reconquer Jerusalem, Saladin suffered further military setbacks, losing the port of Jaffa and being defeated at the Battle of Arsuf (September 7, 1191). Fearing for the safety of Egypt, he decided to dismantle the fortifications of Ascalon. The truce of September 2, 1192, known as the Treaty of Jaffa, confirmed what the Franks held and gave the two sides a much needed respite, but events had taken a heavy toll on Saladin's health: he died on March 3, 1193, after an illness lasting only a few days.

Yaacov Lev

See also: Arab-Islamic Conquest of Palestine; Crusades in the Holy Land; Jerusalem

Further Reading

Gibb, Hamilton, A. R. *The Life of Saladin*. Oxford, UK: Clarendon, 1973.

Humphreys, R. Stephen. *From Saladin to the Mongols: The Ayyubids of Damascus, 1193–1260*. Albany: State University of New York Press, 1977.

Lev, Yaacov. *Saladin in Egypt*. Leiden, Netherlands: Brill, 1999.

Sivan, Emmanuel. *L'Islam et la Croisade*. Paris: Maisonneuve, 1968.

Saul

The first of the Hebrew kings. Saul served as king of Israel from about 1021–1000 BCE. His story is told in the Old Testament book of 1 Samuel. Few details, beyond those related in the Old Testament, are known of Saul's life. The son of Kish of the tribe of Benjamin, he became king after the Hebrews had been in Israel for about 200 years; they had been led there from Egypt by the prophet Moses.

The Hebrews had not been very successful at colonizing the land in Israel. They were ruled loosely by judges and the occasional prophet, but their organizational structure, which was composed of separate tribes, was too weak to be effective. They constantly feared invasion by outsiders, and their religious beliefs were sometimes shaky. Therefore, the Hebrews decided that they needed a more permanent form of leadership. They wanted their government to take charge of political and military matters. Their neighbors—the Egyptians, Canaanites, Philistines, and Moabites—all had kings, and the Hebrews decided that they needed one as well. They went to the prophet Samuel, who told them that a monarchy was against the desire of their god, Yahweh, and they would suffer if they submitted to the rule of a king. However, the Hebrews insisted, and Samuel finally relented.

Samuel chose Saul, as he had supposedly received a message from Yahweh that Saul would save the Hebrews from oppression by the Philistines. In the biblical account, before the Hebrews cast lots for their king, Samuel anointed Saul with oil and announced that Saul was Yahweh's choice for king. The Hebrew people then selected Saul as their king by popular acclaim, casting lots tribe by tribe. Saul functioned primarily as a military leader. He led the Hebrews to war against all their enemies: Moab, the Ammonites, Aram, Bethrehob, Zobah, and the Philistines. The Old Testament does not mention him acting as an Eastern king accustomed to royalty would. He was still a fairly simple leader of a tribal people and did not possess unusual wealth. He was a fairly effective military leader, but he eventually fell into difficulties. The Bible attributes those difficulties to his disobedience of Yahweh's orders; Samuel continued to function as the spokesman of Yahweh, and Saul often refused to follow Samuel's orders.

As king, Saul and his son Jonathan immediately led the Hebrews to war against the Philistines. He won his first major battle but then failed to follow the orders of Yahweh, delivered by Samuel: he performed sacrifices when he was not supposed to. During a major battle, he took an oath that none of his people would be allowed to eat anything until sunset. His own son, Jonathan, did not know about that oath and ate a bit of honey; when his soldiers reproached him, he said that Saul's oath had been unwise. Saul would have had Jonathan killed, but the soldiers refused to allow that to happen.

In a war against Amalek, Samuel ordered Saul to kill everyone—men, women, children, and animals. Saul had the humans killed but kept the best livestock. Samuel reproved him for his disobedience to Yahweh; when Saul claimed that he had taken the livestock in order to sacrifice it to Yahweh, Samuel informed him that obedience was more important than burnt offerings.

The Philistines then returned to fight the Hebrews and brought with them their champion, the giant Goliath. Goliath came out in front of the ranks of the Philistines and paraded back and forth while shouting challenges to the Hebrews. Saul was afraid to fight him. David, Saul's personal assistant, offered to fight Goliath in single combat, and Saul accepted his offer. Saul first dressed David in his own armor, but David refused to wear it. He used a slingshot to throw stones at Goliath, knocked him unconscious, and then killed him with Goliath's own sword.

Saul continued to love David, entrusted him with all his errands, and put him in charge of the whole army; that favor did not last for long, though. The Hebrew people adored David, and the women sang for him in the streets. That adoration made Saul jealous, and he attempted to kill David. Later, Saul's daughter Michal asked to marry David, and Saul agreed—but first he sent him on a military mission, where he hoped David would be killed. However, David succeeded, and Michal married him. Saul continued to hate him.

Eventually, David fled, and Saul pursued him with soldiers. They found him hiding in the desert. David berated Saul for hating him, which made Saul feel very guilty; he even announced that David would be king one day.

The Philistines continued to attack Israel, and finally the battle went wrong for Saul. All his sons were killed, and he was hit in the stomach with an arrow. He asked his armor-bearer to stab him so that he would not be captured by the Philistines; however, the man refused, so Saul fell on his own sword and died. The Hebrews found Saul's body and brought it back to the city of Jabesh, where they cremated him. David succeeded him as king.

Amy Hackney Blackwell

See also: David; Israelite Conquest of Canaan; Judaism; United Kingdom of Israel

Further Reading

Edelman, Diana Vikander. *King Saul in the Historiography of Judah.* Sheffield, UK: Sheffield Academic Press, 1991.

Green, Barbara. *King Saul's Asking.* Collegeville, MN: Liturgical Press, 2003.

Sanford, John A. *King Saul, the Tragic Hero: A Study in Individuation.* New York: Paulist Press, 1985.

Soggin, J. Alberto. *A History of Ancient Israel,* trans. by John Bowden. Philadelphia: Westminster Press, 1984.

Settlements

Residential communities built in the areas occupied by Israel after the June 1967 Six-Day War. These areas include the Golan Heights, the Sinai Peninsula, the Gaza Strip, East Jerusalem, and the West Bank. Settlements comprise one of the "permanent status" issues that remain unresolved in the Israeli-Palestinian conflict. Because of the size of the settlements, some of which, such as Ma'ale Adumim, are cities of 45,000 or more residents, critics argue that they are irreversible facts on the ground that pose a roadblock to a two-state solution. The settlements are illegal according to international law because they are in occupied territory under a military administration. Yet Israel does not recognize the applicability of the Fourth Geneva Convention, claiming that the land is disputed and that settlements are built on state land.

Israel's security barrier separating a Jewish settlement and Palestinian village in the West Bank. Close to 700,000 Jewish Israelis live in territory Israel occupied during the 1967 Arab-Israeli war. (Brian Maudsley/Dreamstime.com)

There are approximately 700,000 Jewish settlers living in the West Bank and East Jerusalem, the latter of which is also occupied territory according to international law but has been annexed by Israel. Settlers are Israeli citizens, with all the rights, responsibilities, and services therewith, including infrastructure services (roads, water, electricity) and military and police protection. Settlers are governed by Israeli civil law, whereas the Palestinians among whom they live are governed by a combination of Israeli military law, Ottoman law, British Mandate law, and a mixture of Palestinian and Jordanian laws.

Some Israeli settlers live or lived in the West Bank, Gaza (until 2005), and the Golan Heights for economic reasons. Housing in the settlements is highly subsidized by the government, and the communities are advertised as suburbs of Tel Aviv and Jerusalem because of the road network that has been constructed for the use of settlers (the use of much of which is prohibited to Palestinians). Others move to settlements on ideological grounds and believe that they are redeeming the land by settling on it in accordance with Jewish scripture. Most of these religious settlements are found in areas of biblical significance. One example is Kiryat Arba, which is near the Cave of Machpelah in Hebron, where Abraham, Isaac, Rachel, and Rebecca are believed buried.

While there are more than 120 official settlements consisting of permanent dwellings, schools, shops, and even some universities in the West Bank (excluding East Jerusalem), there are also about 100 outposts. These are usually small communities that have been erected without official government sanction, and they involve a few individuals or families living in mobile homes. Although these outposts are deemed illegal under Israeli law and the government has committed to evacuating them at various times, the construction of new housing units, permanent buildings, and infrastructure projects continues apace. Indeed, outposts are often built with tacit Israeli approval, are rarely permanently removed, and often obtain legally sanctioned eventually.

Jewish settlements (deemed such because Arab and Druze Israelis are not generally permitted to live in these communities) are often found on hilltops, strategically placed along the main aquifers in the West Bank, and ringing the city of Jerusalem. Israeli policy regarding the settlements has evolved since 1967. The construction of settlements has been pursued for a variety of reasons, including defense, religious beliefs, leverage in the Arab-Israeli conflict, and domestic political expedience.

The Allon Plan, which was prepared shortly after the 1967 Six-Day War, proposed Jewish settlement in strategic areas such as the Jordan Valley, East Jerusalem, and the Judean Desert. After the 1977 Likud Party victory, settlement activity turned toward areas in the central West Bank, where the majority of the Palestinian population was located. At times, Gush Emunim (Bloc of the Faithful) established new settlements. Gush Emunim is a religious group ideologically committed to the building of settlements throughout the West Bank, which they call "Judea" and "Samaria." The government recognized them only after several years of struggle.

Although elected government officials have been involved in articulating settlement policy over the years, much of the work has been designed and carried out by officials in a wide range of ministries, the civil administration, and the settler councils in the West Bank. The Settlement Division of the World Zionist Organization (WZO), whose full budget comes from the Israeli treasury, has worked with the Israeli government in establishing settlements. However, according to one recent government report, this group often acts without official authorization from elected officials.

Both of the major Israeli parties—Labor and Likud—have supported and encouraged the building of settlements, although Labor has traditionally advocated the use of settlements as a bargaining chip with the Palestinians. The Likud Party, meanwhile, has been committed to settlement expansion for ideological reasons as well. Neither party, however, envisions dismantling major settlement blocs, such as Ariel, Gush Etzion, or Ma'ale Adumim, and instead each advocates a land swap with the Palestinians.

Many Israeli peace groups, such as Peace Now, object to Israel's settlement policy, arguing that it prevents the emergence of a viable Palestinian state and therefore challenges Israel's existence as a Jewish and democratic state. They also argue that the presence of settlers and Israeli military personnel deep in the West Bank reduces Israeli security by instigating Palestinian anger and by diluting defense forces. Several groups have said that the route of the Israeli Security Barrier has been designed to incorporate not only current settlements, but also future settlement growth; by that argument, it therefore results in a poor line of defense, as it is twice the length of the 1949 Green Line.

Officially sanctioned settlements have been dismantled by the Israeli government in two historical cases: the withdrawal from the Sinai Peninsula after the signing of the 1979 Camp David Accords with Egypt, and the unilateral Gaza disengagement in September 2005. In April 2006, Israeli prime minister Ehud Olmert formed a new government with the vision of a convergence or consolidation plan that called for the withdrawal of some 60,000 Israeli settlers from smaller settlements in the eastern portion of the West Bank. The plan also called for the consolidation of settlers into major settlement blocs. This plan was shelved, however, after the war with Hezbollah in the summer of 2006. Subsequent right-wing Israeli governments have increased the rate of settlement expansion and have repudiated peace initiatives that involve removing settlers.

Many observers, especially Palestinians, view Israel's continued expansion of settlements as evidence that it is not seriously interested in a two-state solution. As a result, some have begun advocating an alternative: combining Israel and the Occupied Palestinian Territories (OPT) into one state, in which all Jews and Palestinians are granted full citizenship and equal rights. This idea is anathema to most Israelis, even though many fear that some form of a one-state solution will become a reality as settlements expand.

Maia Carter Hallward

See also: Gaza Strip; Golan Heights; Gush Emunim; Israeli Security Barrier; Israeli Occupations; Jerusalem; One-State Solution; Permanent Status Issues; Two-State Solution; West Bank

Further Readings

Efrat, Elisha. *The West Bank and Gaza Strip: A Geography of Occupation and Disengagement*. New York: Routledge, 2006.

Gorenberg, Gershom. *The Accidental Empire: Israel and the Birth of the Settlements, 1967–1977*. New York: Times Books, 2006.

Lein, Yehezkel. *Land Grab: Israel's Settlement Policy in the West Bank*. Jerusalem: B'Tselem, 2002.

Zertal, Idith, and Eldar, Akiva. *Lords of the Land: The War for Israel's Settlements in the Occupied Territories, 1967–2007*. Philadelphia: Nation Books, 2007

Settler Violence

Violence perpetrated by Israeli settlers, predominantly against Palestinians under occupation. Violence between settlers and Palestinians is a constant feature of life in the West Bank. Destruction of olive groves, crops, and property are commonly intermixed with rock throwing, occasional gunfire, and Molotov cocktails. One analysis of the period 2005–2015 identified four broad categories of settler attacks on Palestinians: violence against individuals (35 percent), attacks on property (46 percent), seizure of land (14 percent), and other attacks (5 percent). From 2005–2017, Palestinians filed 1,212 cases against Israelis with Israeli police. By the end of this period, however, 91 percent of these cases were closed without indictments. The Israeli human rights organization Yesh Din concluded that 82 percent of those cases were closed in circumstances indicating police investigative failure. For example, critics argue that closure on the grounds of "offender unknown" or "insufficient evidence" demonstrates that the police had determined that an offense had been committed but failed to identify any suspects or collect and consolidate sufficient evidence for prosecution.

So-called price tag attacks are acts of vandalism, assaults, hate crimes, and worse offenses committed by Israeli ultraextremists (usually settlers) against Palestinians, ostensibly in response to Palestinian violence or Israeli government policies deemed at odds with the settler movement. Price tag assaults have hit not just Palestinian individuals, but churches, mosques, Israeli police stations, government offices, and even military bases. The idea is to force Palestinians and moderate Israelis to pay a price for policies and actions that harm the settler movement.

Israeli authorities have struggled to control these attacks, which are often carried out by so-called hilltop youth, young settlers who set up illegal (even by Israeli law) outposts on hilltops throughout the West Bank in an effort to expand Jewish control of the disputed land. Settlers often claim that their violence is in retaliation to Palestinian attacks.

Israeli settlers are provided security either by the Israeli Defense Forces (IDF) or private security firms. They insist that such protection is necessary due to Palestinian violence. Settlers are often well armed and sometimes take matters into their own hands, especially since the Second Intifada. Palestinian police are prohibited from protecting Palestinians from settler violence, and while Israeli police and military forces are bound by international law to protect occupied civilians, they rarely intercede to protect Palestinians from settlers' harassment and attacks. Some international organizations escort children on their walks to school in an effort to document (and hopefully deter) settler harassment and attacks. Israeli settler children sometimes spit, verbally abuse, and throw stones at Palestinian schoolchildren in the presence of Israeli security forces that are often slow to respond, if at all.

Human rights organization charge that Israeli police and security forces routinely ignore their obligation under international law to protect Palestinians in the West Bank from these attacks. Critics allege that Israeli security forces (the IDF, the Border Police, and private security firms hired by settlers) not only allow settlers to harm Palestinians and their property, but often provide the perpetrators with escorts and backup, and sometimes they even actively participate in the attacks. Allegations of favoritism toward settlers are neither new nor confined to immediate, on-the-ground support.

Human rights organizations and official state reports demonstrate the low chances of a settler indictment for anti-Palestinian violence, whereas Palestinian violence against Israeli settlers almost always leads to disciplinary action. According to Yesh Din, 90–95 percent of all cases opened against Palestinians for anti-Israeli violence are brought to trial, and the Israeli government has a 99 percent success rate of such prosecutions. Conversely, only 8.5 percent of all cases opened against Israelis for anti-Palestinian violence are ever brought to trial. In fact, only 1.9 percent of police complaints filed by Palestinians resulted in the conviction of Israeli civilians. This disparity is in part due to a number of factors: settlers enjoy the legal protections of Israeli civil law, while Palestinians live under military rule; Israeli forces are reluctant to confront settler violence; and Palestinians find it difficult to avail themselves of the few legal protections theoretically available to them.

In response to an uptick in the number of settler attacks, IDF forces, including an attack in 2011 on a military base, the Israeli government authorized the IDF to arrest and detain suspects of settler violence. In June 2017, the Israeli Ministry of Justice outlined measures adopted to reduce settler violence and achieve higher levels of accountability. However, an October 2018 report from the United Nations found a 175 percent increase in Israeli settler violence in the West Bank since 2016.

In one case that received international attention, an Israeli teenager is accused of killing a Palestinian mother in December 2018 when he threw a rock through her car's windshield. The suspect is awaiting trial while under house arrest. But many observers have asserted that this case demonstrates a blatant double standard, pointing out that a Palestinian youth accused of the same crime would be in prison and his family's house would be destroyed as part of a collective punishment policy that Israel insists is necessary to deter future attacks.

Tom Dowling

See also: B'Tselem; Hebron; Settlements; Shin Bet

Further Reading

Breiner, Josh, and Yotam Berger. "Fearing Anti-Arab Attacks, Israeli Security Forces Up Presence in Settlements." *Haaretz,* May 29, 2018.

UN Office for Coordination of Humanitarian Affairs (OCHA). "Increase in Settler Violence During the First Four Months of 2018." *Monthly Humanitarian Bulletin,* May 2018.

Yesh Din, *Law Enforcement on Israeli Civilians in the West Bank*. Monitoring Update 2005–2017, December 2017.

Shamir, Yitzhak

A Zionist militant and right wing Israeli politician. Yitzhak Shamir (originally Yitzhak Jazernicki) was born October 15, 1915, in Poland. He was a member of the Polish Beitar Zionist youth movement. He emigrated in 1935 to the British Mandate of Palestine, where he ultimately enrolled in Jerusalem's Hebrew University. Shamir joined the Irgun Tsvai Leumi (National Military Organization, or Irgun), a right-wing paramilitary Zionist underground movement in Palestine known for using violence against Palestinians and members of the British mandatory government. When Irgun split in 1940, Shamir affiliated himself with the more militant Lohamei Herut Israel (Israel Freedom Fighters), a group classified by the British as a terrorist organization. It became known as the Stern Gang after its founder, Avraham Stern. Shamir was arrested by the British in 1941 but escaped in 1943. He became one of the leaders of the Lohamei Herut Israel, and he reformed and renamed the group Lehi.

Shamir served as Lehi's principal director of operations until he was again imprisoned by the British in 1946, this time in Eritrea. He escaped again and returned to Israel in 1948 to reclaim command of Lehi until it was disbanded in 1949. It was under Shamir's leadership that in 1944, Lehi assassinated Lord Moyne, heir to the Guinness fortune and the British minister resident in the Middle East, and in 1948, the group assassinated Count Folke Bernadotte, the representative of the United Nations in the Middle East.

Shamir served as a Mossad operative from 1955 to 1965 and then joined Menachem Begin's Herut movement (later to become Likud) in 1973. That same year, he was elected to the Knesset as a member of the Likud. Begin became Israel's first non-Labor prime minister in 1977, and Shamir rose to be speaker of the Knesset. Shamir presided over the ratification of the Israel-Egypt peace treaty in the Knesset, with more than half of Likud Knesset members opposing it.

Shamir served as Israel's foreign minister during 1980–1981 and was elected the leader of Likud in September 1983. His failure to decrease the inflation that racked Israel's economy led to an indecisive election in July 1984 and the formation of a government of national unity that allied in leadership Likud's Shamir and Labor's Shimon Peres.

Shamir assumed Israel's premiership in October 1986, but following another indecisive election in 1988, Likud and Labor formed another coalition government that retained Shamir as prime minister. When this coalition government failed in 1990, Shamir formed a new government with members of some ultraconservative parties. This government ordered the rescue of thousands of Ethiopian Jews in Operation Solomon in 1991; did not retaliate, at the urging of the United States, for Iraqi Scud missile attacks during the First Gulf War; and participated in the Madrid Peace Conference in September 1991, under great pressure from the United States. Shamir's premiership ended in 1992 with the defeat of Likud in general elections, and he resigned from the leadership of the party in March 1993, although he retained his seat in the Knesset until 1996 and steadfastly opposed the Oslo Accords.

After suffering from Alzheimer's disease for at least six years, Shamir died in Tel Aviv on June 30, 2012.

Richard M. Edwards

See also: Bernadotte, Count Folke; Irgun Tsvai Leumi; Madrid Conference; Stern Gang

Further Reading

Brinkley, Joel. *The Stubborn Strength of Yitzhak Shamir*. New York: New York Times Books, 1988.

Enderlin, Charles. *Shamir*. Paris: O. Orban, 1991.

Mitchell, Thomas. *Likud Leaders: The Lives and Careers of Menachem Begin, Yitzhak Shamir, Benjamin Netanyahu and Ariel Sharon*. Jefferson, NC: McFarland Publishing, 2015.

Sharon, Ariel

Israeli soldier, general, politician, and prime minister. Ariel Sharon (Scheinermann) was born on February 27, 1928, in Kfar Malal, Palestine (now Israel). At the age of fourteen, Sharon joined the Gadna, Haganah's paramilitary youth organization, and during Israel's War for Independence in 1948, he commanded an infantry company. Following the war, he founded and commanded a special commando unit (Unit 101) that specialized in retaliatory raids designed to punish and deter Israel's enemies. Sharon was criticized for targeting citizens and condemned for killing more than sixty Jordanian civilians during the raid on the village of Qibya in fall 1953. He was promoted to major general just before the 1967 Six-Day War, and in 1969, he headed the Southern Command Staff. He resigned in June 1972, only to be recalled to command the armored division that crossed the Suez Canal into Egypt, ending the 1973 Yom Kippur War.

Sharon helped found the Likud Party in September 1973 and became minister of agriculture in Likud's first government, headed by Prime Minister Menachem Begin. This position allowed Sharon to promote the construction of Jewish settlements in occupied Arab territories. In June 1981, he became Begin's minister of defense and prosecuted Israel's 1982 invasion of Lebanon. The ostensible intent was to force the Katyusha rockets being fired by the Palestine Liberation Organization (PLO) out of the range of Israel's northern border, and to destroy the terrorist infrastructure that had developed there. In reality, Sharon intended to march into Beirut and help install a Christian Lebanese government that would be pro-Israel. Israel made it to the outskirts of Beirut before U.S. pressure forced it to pull back. Although the PLO was driven from Lebanon, the invasion intensified the Lebanese civil war, allowing Syria to become entrenched in the politics of its neighbor.

Sharon resigned as Begin's minister of defense when he was found to be indirectly responsible for the massacre in September 1982 of Palestinians at the Sabra and Shatila refugee camps by Israeli's Lebanese Christian Phalangist allies. After that, he served in various Israeli governments from 1983 to 1992, including as minister of construction and housing and chairman of the ministerial committee on immigration and absorption (1990–1992), which allowed him to double the number of Jewish settlements throughout the West Bank and Gaza during his time in office. His hope was that these settlements would not only provide a strategic buffer for Israel proper, but would also lessen the possibility of relinquishing these territories.

Sharon assumed the leadership of the Likud Party in 1999. Failed negotiations at the Camp David summit in 2000, coupled with the collapse of his governing coalition and the eruption of the Second Intifada, led to Labor Party prime minister Ehud Barak's resignation and his defeat by Sharon in the general election of February 2001. Palestinian violence was triggered by Sharon's visit to the Temple Mount on September 28, 2000. Sharon also angered the French when, on July 20, 2004, he urged French Jews to emigrate to Israel because of the rise in French anti-Semitic events.

In 2004, Sharon proposed disengagement or unilateral withdrawal from the Gaza Strip, a policy opposed by his own Likud Party but supported by many Israelis. He succeeded in pulling Israeli troops and settlers out of Gaza in August-September of 2005. Also during his time as prime minister, Sharon began building a wall along Israel's border with the West Bank.

On January 4, 2006, he suffered a massive stroke that left him in a deep coma. He was kept alive by machines until January 11, 2014. At the time of his stroke, Sharon was expected to head up a new government and propose unilateral disengagement from some of the occupied territories that lay west of the planned new security barrier.

Richard M. Edwards

See also: Gaza Strip; Lebanon, Israeli Invasion of; Israeli Security Barrier; Settlements

Further Reading

Finkelstein, Norman H. *Ariel Sharon*. Minneapolis: First Avenue Editions, 2005.

Gelvin, James L. *The Israel-Palestine Conflict: One Hundred Years of War*. 3rd ed. Cambridge: Cambridge University Press, 2014.

Smith, Charles D. *Palestine and the Arab-Israeli Conflict: A History with Documents*. 9th ed. New York: Bedford/St. Martin's, 2017.

Shin Bet

The Israeli counterintelligence and internal security service. Shin Bet, also known as the General Security Service, or Shabak, is the sister agency to Mossad, which handles external security and foreign intelligence, and Aman, the military intelligence branch of the Israel Defense Forces (IDF). Isser Harel, also a founder of Mossad, started Shin Bet in 1947. Originally known as the General Security Service, it was under the aegis of the IDF but later was transferred to the direct control of the prime minister's office.

Originally tasked with counterintelligence, Shin Bet was also given responsibility for monitoring Palestinians living in Israel after 1948. During the Cold War era, it focused much of its energy on the Soviet Union. Shin Bet infiltrated Soviet-backed dissident organizations in Israel during the 1950s and 1960s. In 1961, it uncovered a top Soviet spy: Dr. Israel Bar, both a lieutenant colonel in the IDF reserves and a friend of Prime Minister David Ben-Gurion, who had access to a great deal of classified information. Also in 1961, Shin Bet unmasked Kurt Sita, an operative for Czech intelligence who was working as a professor in Israel.

After the 1967 Six-Day War, Shin Bet began to focus more of its attention and resources on monitoring Arabs in the occupied territories. It enjoyed considerable leeway when dealing with suspects, and many Israelis feared that Shin Bet would become an instrument of totalitarianism. Internal checks and balances within Shin Bet have prevented this. As the lead organization tasked with combating terrorism, it nonetheless has resorted to extrajudicial methods that received great criticism in Israel and abroad.

The most notorious incident involving Shin Bet was the KAV 300 Affair; it involved the summary execution of two suspected Palestinian terrorists who participated in a bus hijacking. The KAV 300 Affair spotlighted Shin Bet and some of its more questionable activities and led to a purging of the organization and more public oversight. Avram Shalom, the head of Shin Bet at the time, was forced to resign, and the Knesset (Israeli parliament) established the so-called Landoy Committee to monitor the service's activities.

One of Shin Bet's major responsibilities was the protection of senior Israeli ministers, including the prime minister. Thus, its reputation received a further blow in 1995, when it failed to prevent the assassination of Israeli prime minister Yitzhak Rabin. An internal investigation actually implicated Shin Bet agents in stirring up provocations and anti-Rabin sentiment as part of its domestic counterterrorism operations, which actually may have contributed to the assassination. Another housecleaning occurred after that. Avi Dichter, a tough-minded ex-commando, was eventually placed in charge of Shin Bet in 2003. Yuval Diskin succeeded Dichter in 2005; he served until 2011. Yoram Cohen took the helm from 2011–2016, when he was replaced by Nadav Argaman, its current leader.

Shin Bet is organized into three operational departments. The Arab Affairs Department handles intelligence gathering on Arab terrorist organizations (mainly Palestinian ones) via informers and interrogations. The Non-Arab Department was formerly divided between communist and noncommunist sections and was charged with debriefing Soviet refugees and countering Soviet intelligence. Since 1991, after the collapse of the Soviet Union, its mission has changed to monitoring all non-Arab immigrants in Israel. The Protective Security Department provides uniformed personnel to secure government buildings, scientific research facilities, airports, and ports. It also provides bodyguards for Israeli dignitaries and undercover operatives for El Al Airline flights. Supporting departments include, among others, finance, logistics, personnel, and transportation.

Shin Bet relies mainly on informants and other human intelligence for its information. The organization is believed to run extensive networks of Arab informants throughout Israel and abroad. Shin Bet is also tasked with the interrogation of suspects and has received a great deal of criticism from the public and the press in Israel for its use of physical coercion and torture to extract information. The organization has also received negative press for infiltrating domestic leftists and rightist Jewish organizations and political parties. Shin Bet has been widely implicated in an assassination program conducted against Arab targets, including members of Hamas, the Palestine Liberation Organization (PLO), and Hezbollah. In 2002, Shin Bet agents assassinated Yahya Ayyash, a Palestinian terrorist known as "the Engineer" and the chief bomb maker for Hamas, by placing an explosive device in his cell phone.

Shin Bet continues to work directly with the Israeli air force to target terrorist leaders and bases and also uses commandos and trained agents to root out terror networks. In 2007, the organization launched its first public recruitment drive; in 2008, it added a blog to its official website, through which prospective recruits could read about how current officers perform their jobs. This effort was aimed at recruiting more people skilled in information technology, as Shin Bet has become increasingly involved in technological operations. In 2012, interviews with six previous heads of Shin Bet were featured in the Israeli documentary *The Gatekeepers,* which detailed many of the organization's successes and failures.

Rod Vosburgh

See also: Hamas; Israeli Occupations; Jewish Underground; West Bank

Further Reading

Bergman, Ronen. *Rise and Kill First: The Secret History of Israel's Targeted Assassinations.* New York: Random House, 2018.

Katz, Samuel M. *Soldier Spies: Israeli Military Intelligence.* New York: Presidio Press, 1992.

Sprinzak, Ehud. *Brother Against Brother: Violence and Extremism in Israeli Politics from Altalena to the Rabin Assassination.* New York: Free Press, 1999.

Thomas, Gordon. *Gideon's Spies: The Secret History of the Mossad.* New York: St. Martin's Griffin. 2000.

Six-Day War (see Arab-Israeli War, 1967)

Solomon

Third and last king of a united kingdom of Israel. Solomon, or Shlomo as he is known in Hebrew, was a historical figure who is also the subject of legend. Solomon was the son of King David, the leader of the Israelites and founder of the Judaean dynasty. Although he had older brothers, Solomon was anointed by David to succeed him as king of Israel.

To eliminate threats to his power, Solomon first killed all of his enemies and anyone else who threatened his rule, and then he installed his own allies in governmental and military positions throughout his empire. Second, he created a very large harem for himself, composed of the daughters and sisters of his allies and neighbors, through which he was able to strengthen his military and commercial ties with such neighbors as Egypt, as well as to garner alliances against his enemies, including the Canaanites.

Throughout his empire, Solomon supported the establishment of colonies of Israelites to consolidate his kingdom's influence and presence in the region. He was particularly interested in controlling the caravan trade routes going east, and he used them as a pretext to encourage the creation of new Israelite settlements. Megiddo is perhaps the best-known example of one of Solomon's new Israelite cities.

Solomon ordered the construction of a city wall and an elaborate royal palace, but his most significant project was that of the Temple of Jerusalem, which was accomplished using forced labor, first from the subject Canaanites, and then by the Hebrews themselves. Despite resentment that built up in some segments of the population due to the brutal forced labor imposed on them, Solomon's temple became the central location for Hebrew religious life.

Solomon was highly acclaimed for his wisdom. Perhaps the most notable story told about him was an event in which two women laid claim to the same baby. Solomon threatened to cut the baby in half; when he saw the horrified reaction of one of the women, he knew she was the real mother. The Book of Proverbs is filled with sayings attributed to Solomon, and the apocryphal work, the *Wisdom of Solomon,* has also been credited to him.

Many Israelites and subject peoples resented the high taxes he charged, which were often exacted in labor. The increase of wealth in Israelite society was also unevenly distributed, resulting in conflicts between rich and poor. Moreover, Solomon perpetually favored the tribe of Judah, to which he belonged, breeding resentment in the northern tribes. Such resentment spelled disaster for Solomon's empire. After his death, his son and successor, Rehoboam, was unable to prevent the northern tribes from rebelling and establishing their own realm, the Kingdom of Israel.

Nancy Stockdale

See also: First and Second Temple Periods; Judaism; Kingdom of Israel; Kingdom of Judah; United Kingdom of Israel

Further Reading

Pritchard, James, ed. *Solomon and Sheba.* London: Phaidon, 1974.

Ryken, Philip. *King Solomon: The Temptation of Money, Sex, and Power.* Wheaton, IL: Crossway, 2011.

Tomoo, Ishida, ed. *Studies in the Period of David and Solomon and Other Essays.* Winona Lake, IN: Eisenbrauns, 1982.

Stern Gang

Paramilitary Zionist group established in June 1940 by Avraham Stern. The Stern Gang is the common name for Lehi (Lohamei Herut Israel, or Fighters for the Freedom of Israel). The group aimed to force the British out of Palestine. Despite its terrorist activities, Israel granted amnesty to jailed Lehi members on February 14, 1949.

In 1940, while the British were still at war with Nazi Germany, Stern was a senior member of the Irgun Tsvai Leumi (National Military Organization), another paramilitary group fighting to terminate the United Kingdom's mandate in Palestine. When this movement announced a temporary truce with the British, Stern left and formed Lehi, insisting that armed struggle was the only way to secure a Jewish state.

Soon after forming Lehi, Stern was captured and killed. One of the organization's new leaders was Yitzhak Shamir, a future prime minister of Israel. Because Lehi never had more than a few hundred members, it emphasized small-scale operations. These involved targeted killings of British soldiers, police officers, and Jews who purportedly collaborated with the British; parcel bombs sent to British politicians through the mail; and the sabotage of critical infrastructure such as bridges, railroads, and oil refineries. Funding for these activities came from private donations, extortion, and bank robbery.

On November 6, 1944, Lehi assassinated Lord Moyne, London's highest-ranking British official in the region. The murder infuriated British prime minister Winston Churchill, who made capturing the killers a top priority. The assassins were captured, tried, and executed. In 1975, their bodies were returned to Israel and given a state funeral.

Some of Lehi's attacks resulted in significant casualty counts. On January 12, 1947, a truck bombing of a police outpost in Haifa left four people dead and another 140 injured. A year later, the group mined the railroad north of Rehovot killing twenty-eight British soldiers and wounded thirty-five others. The next month another mine near Binyamina caused forty fatalities.

One of the most infamous events involving Lehi was a night attack on April 9, 1948, against Deir Yassin, a strategic village occupied by the Arab Liberation Army (ALA). During the attack, over 100 people were killed, most of whom were civilians. There were also widespread claims of rapes and mutilations. The massacre contributed to the mass exodus of Palestinians from the lands conquered by Israel.

On September 16, 1948, the Stern Gang assassinated the United Nations' chief mediator in Palestine, Count Folke Bernadotte because he was seen as a pawn of the British. The organization was soon disbanded, with some members moving on to political careers.

Donna Bassett

See also: Bernadotte, Count Folke; Deir Yassin Massacre; Irgun Tsvai Leumi; Shamir, Yitzhak

Further Reading
Boyer Bell, J. *Terror out of Zion: Irgun Zvai Leumi, Lehi, and the Palestine Underground, 1929–1949.* New York: St. Martin's, 1979.
Clarke, Thurston. *By Blood and Fire: July 22, 1946: The Attack on Jerusalem's King David Hotel.* New York: Putnam's Sons, 1981.
Marton, Kati. *A Death in Jerusalem.* New York: Random House, 1996.

Suez Crisis (see Arab-Israeli War, 1956)

Suicide Bombings

Bomb attacks meant to kill others, by persons intending to die in the attacks themselves. Suicide bombings have been common in the Middle East since the late 1970s, when they were employed in Syria by the Islamic resistance against the Baathist government. In November 1982, in response to Israel's invasion of Lebanon, a suicide bomber killed seventy-six Israelis in Tyre. Militant Islamist groups including Hezbollah, as well as numerous Christians, carried out another fifty suicide attacks between 1982 and 1999. A massive bombing in October 1983 forced U.S. and French troops from Lebanon. The belief that such attacks bring martyrdom has encouraged suicide bombings all over the world.

Palestinians began suicide bombings in the early 1990s. The inspiration for the attacks was the so-called War of the Knives, a battle between Palestinians and Jews praying at the Western (Wailing) Wall that took place on October 8, 1990. Eighteen Palestinians were killed in the melee, and the radical Islamist group Hamas called for a jihad (holy war). Omar abu Sirhan took this call literally. He walked to a neighborhood in Jerusalem and killed three people with a butcher knife. Abu Sirhan believed that he would die during his killing spree. Hamas declared him a hero. Hamas and Palestinian Islamic Jihad (PIJ) preached to their faithful that martyrdom actions or suicide attacks were a righteous act because jihad was individually required of Muslims under Israeli occupation.

The first Palestinian suicide bombing that killed Israelis occurred in Afula in April 1994, purportedly in retaliation for a massacre weeks earlier by an Israeli settler, which killed twenty-nine Palestinians praying in a mosque. There have been around 150 attacks since, killing nearly 800 Israelis. The vast majority of attacks and casualties occurred during the Second Intifada (2000–2005), and usually within Israel's pre-1967 borders. Although suicide bombings comprised only a small percentage of actual attacks launched by Palestinians against Israelis, they accounted for perhaps half the Israelis killed between 2000 and 2002.

Although most Lebanese suicide bombers were Christians, most Palestinians have been Muslims. Their motivation is often nationalist. Families of suicide bombers are often extremely proud of their loved ones and praise them publicly as heroes. Further, these families acquire higher status in their communities. Some Palestinians were at one time receiving financial support from Iraqi leader Saddam Husayn, and in this way, the bombers were able to provide for their dependents. Successful suicide bombers believe that they will be remembered as popular heroes.

Some bombers are motivated by religion. For many young Muslims, the temptation of martyrdom, with its promise of rewards in paradise, is irresistible. They are taught by radical religious leaders that martyrdom cleanses them of sins and that they will have special power to intercede on behalf of their relatives and close friends on the Day of Judgment. In actuality, Islam forbids suicide and engaging recklessly in jihad so as to obtain martyrdom. There are set rules regarding who may participate in jihad, and these exclude young people, those with dependents, and women.

The main religious justification is that jihad is really a defense of Islam and is required of believers under Israeli occupation, who need not wait for jihad to be formally declared as would be the case under normal circumstances. Religious authorities who decry the linkage of Islam with suicide and the killing of innocent people try to convince their audiences that the greater jihad, the striving to be a good Muslim in every possible aspect of life, can be substituted for jihad as armed struggle, or that if armed struggle is necessary, it should not involve attacks of this type.

Another major motivation of many suicide bombers is revenge. Suicide bombers have left statements explaining their actions, in which they list specific victims of Israeli attacks, particularly women, children, and the elderly. Suicide attackers convince themselves that they are not killing innocent victims. They often argue that all Israelis serve in the military, at least as reserves, and therefore are combatants, not really civilians. Some Hamas members made such arguments in the past, but the organization itself observed a truce on such attacks from 2005. Many suicide attacks during the Second Intifada were carried out by the al-Aqsa Martyrs Brigades, an offshoot of the Palestinian nationalist Fatah party. Indeed, a competition of sorts between Hamas, Palestinian Islamic Jihad (PIJ), and the Brigades for street credibility was one reason why the Second Intifada was so much more deadly than the First Intifada.

A large proportion of Palestinians support armed resistance to Israeli occupation, and some even support suicide attacks, but many consider such attacks on civilians reprehensible. Some analysts point out that using suicide bombers is an inexpensive method for Palestinians to wage war against Israel, making it an extreme form of asymmetric warfare. The ingredients for the explosives cost little, and many bombers even recycle the shrapnel from Israeli munitions so they can kill Israelis with the same shrapnel that killed Palestinians. Palestinian critics argue that it is impossible to put a price on human capital, and that Palestinians are not only losing their youth, but are paying a very high public relations cost.

The majority of Palestinian attackers have been young, unmarried men who grew up in refugee camps. Recruits were chosen for their psychological predispositions—not to suicide, but rather to suggestibility. Whenever possible, they were prevented from contacting friends and family.

Suicide bombings are enormously upsetting to potential civilian victims. Victims and bystanders are taken completely by surprise. They are often civilians and children sometimes make up a sizable percentage of those killed. Because the bomber has no concern for his or her own life, it is difficult to prevent such attacks.

In Israel, many businesses have hired security guards who are specially trained to spot potential bombers. Israel has also built security barriers along its borders with the West Bank and Gaza Strip to prevent Palestinian attacks. As with all acts of terror, the fact that such bombings spread fear among the Israeli population is as valuable to the radicals' cause as actually killing Israelis.

Amy Hackney Blackwell and Sherifa Zuhur

See also: Hamas; Hezbollah; Intifada, Second; Israeli Security Barrier; Palestinian Islamic Jihad

Further Reading
Aboul-Enein, Youssef H., and Sherifa Zuhur. *Islamic Rulings on Warfare.* Carlisle Barracks, PA: Strategic Studies Institute, 2004.
Friedman, Lauri S. *What Motivates Suicide Bombers?* Farmington Hills, MI: Greenhaven, 2004.
Khosrokhavar, Farhad. *Suicide Bombers: Allah's New Martyrs.* Trans. David Macey. London: Pluto, 2005.
Skaine, Rosemarie. *Female Suicide Bombers.* Jefferson, NC: McFarland, 2006.

Supreme Muslim Council (SMC)

The institution in Palestine charged with managing Muslim religious affairs. Established in December 1921 by the British authorities ruling Palestine, the Supreme Muslim Council (SMC) afforded Palestinian Arabs control over their religious affairs, particularly *awaqf* (Islamic religious trusts) and sharia courts. The Mufti of Jerusalem, Haj Amin al-Husayni, was elected president and used his position both to initiate an Islamic cultural revival in Palestine and to consolidate his position as the unquestioned leader of the Palestinian nationalist movement.

The SMC renovated religious buildings and mosques, including those in the Haram al-Sharif. It also established an orphanage, supported schools and health clinics, and oversaw the appointment of religious positions in Palestine's Islamic community. Being both the head of the SMC and Grand Mufti of Jerusalem, al-Husayni bolstered both his religious authority and his influence as a political leader. He spearheaded SMC efforts to keep the Western (Wailing) Wall under Muslim control in the face of Zionist attempts to purchase it, and led the 1936 Arab Revolt against British Mandate rule. British authorities dissolved the SMC in 1937, and al-Husayni fled to avoid arrest.

Robert C. DiPrizio

See also: Arab Revolt, 1936; Grand Mufti of Jerusalem

Further Reading

Mattar, Philip. *The Mufti of Jerusalem: Al-Hajj Amin al-Husayni and the Palestinian National Movement*. New York: Columbia University Press, 1992.

Smith, Charles D. *Palestine and the Arab-Israeli Conflict: A History with Documents*. 9th ed. New York: Bedford/St. Martin's, 2017.

Sykes-Picot Agreement

An agreement reached among the British, French, and Russian governments regarding claims of territory belonging to the Ottoman Empire in the Middle East. In the spring of 1915, Sir Henry McMahon, the British High Commissioner in Egypt, promised to Sharif Husayn of Mecca British support for an Arab state under Husayn, in return for Arab military support against the Ottoman Empire. Confident in British support, Husayn proclaimed the Arab Revolt in June 1915.

Aware of the British agreement with Husayn, Paris pressed London for recognition of its own claims in the Ottoman Empire. Sir Mark Sykes and François Georges Picot were appointed by their respective governments to conduct the negotiations. Because discussions of the future of Asiatic Turkey also affected the Russians, the two proceeded to Petrograd in the early spring of 1916 and presented their draft agreement there. After securing Russian support, the agreement was officially concluded on May 16, 1916.

The Sykes-Picot Agreement provided extensive territorial concessions to all three powers, at the expense of the Ottoman Empire. Russia was to receive the provinces of Erzurum, Trebizond, Van, and Bitlis (known as Turkish Armenia), as well as northern Kurdistan from Mush, Sairt, Ibn Omar, and Amadiya to the border with Persia (Iran). France would secure the coastal strip of Syria, the vilayet of Adana, and territory extending in the south from Aintab and Mardin to the future Russian border, to a northern line drawn from Ala Dagh through Kaisariya Ak-Dagh, Jidiz-Dagh, and Zara to Egin-Kharput (the area known as *Cilcia*). For its part, Britain would secure southern Mesopotamia with Baghdad, as well as the ports of Haifa and Acre in Palestine.

The zone between the British and French territories would be formed into one or more Arab states, but this was to be divided into British and French spheres of influence. The French sphere would include the Syrian hinterland and the Mosul province of Mesopotamia, while the British would have influence over the territory from Palestine to the Persian border. The agreement also provided that Alexandetta would become a free port, while Palestine would be internationalized.

Husayn did not learn of the Sykes-Picot Agreement until December 1917, when the new Bolshevik government of Russia revealed the plan and the Turks relayed it to Husayn, hoping that he would change his pro-British stance, but in vain. Nevertheless, at the 1919 Paris Peace Conference, the British jettisoned the Sykes-Picot Agreement. Tensions with France were not resolved until the 1920 San Remo Conference, where the British and French governments reached agreement on mandates in the Middle East. Britain received Palestine and Iraq, while France secured Lebanon and Syria. Arab self-determination was thus rejected.

Spencer C. Tucker

See also: Arab Revolt, 1916; Balfour Declaration; British Mandate for Palestine; McMahon-Husayn Correspondence

Further Reading
Kent, Marian, ed. *The Great Powers and the End of the Ottoman Empire*. 2nd ed. New York Frank Cass, 1996.
MacMillan, Margaret. *Paris, 1919: Six Months That Changed the World*. New York: Random House, 2002.
Tauber, Eliezer. *The Arab Movements in World War I*. London: Cass, 1993.

Syria

An Arab country along the Mediterranean Sea, important to the Arab-Israeli conflict. Syria has a population of about 26 million, covers about 71,000 square miles, and borders Lebanon and the Mediterranean to its east, Israel and Jordan to its south, Iraq to its west, and Turkey to its north. Once part of the Ottoman Empire, it became a French mandate following World War I and gained independence in 1946. Syria spearheaded the development of the Arab Liberation Army (ALA), whose volunteers fought against Israel during the 1948 Arab-Israeli War. Governance in Syria was markedly unstable until 1970, when Defense Minister Hafez al-Assad seized control. The Assad family still rules the country today.

Syria and the Soviet Union developed close relations during the 1960s, which played an important role in triggering the Six-Day War. In 1966, the more radical wing of Syria's Baathist rulers took power and aggressively supported Palestinian attacks on Israel. Syria and Israel also repeatedly clashed over mutual transgressions of their 1949 armistice agreement. When Israel began redirecting for irrigation purposes the water flowing out of Syria, Syria attempted to divert the water flow upstream, triggering Israeli air strikes on Syrian diversion projects. The Soviets grew concerned that Syria was vulnerable, and Egyptian president Gamal Abdel Nasser's remilitarization of the Sinai in 1967 was in part an effort to deter Israel from a possible attack on Syria.

During the Six-Day War, Israel conquered the Golan Heights from Syria and has maintained control over it ever since. About forty kilometers from Damascus, the Golan is a plateau that overlooks northern Israel and is home to important freshwater resources. Israel has established many settlements there and effectively annexed it in 1981. In October 1973, Syria joined Egypt in launching a surprise attack on Israel, but it failed to regain the Golan. Syria insists that there can be no peace with Israel until it returns all of the Golan Heights.

Syria participated in the 1991 Madrid Peace Conference and subsequent multilateral and bilateral negotiations with Israel, but no agreements were reached, in part because Israel refused to pull back to the pre-1967 border for what it says are security reasons. Hafez al-Assad and his son Bashir, who succeeded him in 2000, have been careful to keep their border with Israel quiet, opting instead to use Palestinian and Lebanese proxies to harass Israel. Most notably, Syria has supported numerous Palestinian groups, including hosting Hamas leaders, until 2011. It also supports Hezbollah, which has repeatedly clashed with Israel since its inception in the wake of the latter's 1982 invasion of Lebanon.

In the summer of 2006, Israel and Hezbollah fought a short war that left much of southern Beirut decimated. With help from Syria and Iran, Hezbollah rebuilt many destroyed neighborhoods and rearmed with thousands more missiles. Most observers believed that a more destructive round of fighting was only a matter of time, but events soon took a different turn.

In 2011, as the Arab Spring was in full bloom, mass protests demanding economic and political reforms broke out in Syria. Bashir al-Assad violently repressed these demonstrations. Within weeks, a full-blown civil war erupted, pitting the Assad regime (whose core supporters come from the country's minority Alawites) against a mishmash of opposition forces ranging from secularists to radical Islamists.

After nearly eight years of fighting, Assad is poised to retain power. His success was made possible by the active military support of Hezbollah, Iran, and Russia. In time, the Islamic State of Iraq and Syria (ISIS) became the most formidable opposition force threatening Assad's regime. When ISIS established control over a large section of Syria and Iraq and established a caliphate, the United States and others joined the fray to defeat ISIS. This improved Assad's ability to stay in power. But Syria's longstanding relations with Hezbollah and Iran, which have grown more intense during the civil war, have made it a target of Israeli attacks. Iran has built military bases and stationed troops and missile systems throughout Syria. It has also supplied Hezbollah with more capable weapons for use in Lebanon. Indeed, Israel has launched hundreds of air strikes into Syria over the past couple of years to disrupt the delivery of material to Hezbollah and to degrade Iran's growing military presence.

Under the leadership of Prime Minister Benjamin Netanyahu, Israel has developed close relations with Russian president Vladimir Putin, who has sought to protect Russia's extensive security interests in Syria by propping up the Assad regime. Israel has sought Putin's assistance to curtail Iran's activities in Syria, but it is unclear how much Russia can and is willing to do about the matter. Assad has even less control than Putin over Iran's presence in Syria, and for the moment, he still needs Tehran's support to survive.

Many Israelis are relieved that previous negotiations with Syria over the Golan Heights failed, not only because there are 20,000 Jewish settlers there and because it is home to vital freshwater sources, but because the Syrian civil war has allowed Israel's enemies (including Iran, Hezbollah, and Islamist groups like ISIS) a foothold near the Golan. Israel cannot countenance the presence of any military forces on this strategic plateau, which overlooks much of northern Israel. Indeed, Israeli government officials lobbied U.S. president Donald Trump to recognize Israel's annexation of the Golan Heights publicly, which he did in early 2019.

For the past thirty years, the focus of the Arab-Israeli conflict has been on the internal struggle between Israel and the Palestinians over whom it rules. Since Egypt and Israel made peace in 1979, relations between Israel and its Arab neighbors have been stable, except for periodic flare-ups with Hezbollah in Lebanon. But recent events in Syria may undermine this stability. Tensions over the Golan Heights, Hezbollah, and Iran are sure to define Syria's relations with Israel for years to come. It is quite possible that those relations will become more unstable and violent than they have been since 1973, refocusing attention on the international dynamics of the Arab-Israeli conflict.

Robert C. DiPrizio

See also: Arab-Israeli War, 1967; Arab-Israeli War, 1973; Arab Spring; Golan Heights; Hezbollah; Lebanon; Lebanon, Israeli Invasion of

Further Readings

Kaufman, Asher. *Contested Frontiers in the Syria-Lebanon-Israel Region: Cartography, Sovereignty, and Conflict*. Baltimore, Maryland: Johns Hopkins University Press, 2014.

Matar, Linda, and Ali Kadri. *Syria: From National Independence to Proxy War*. London: Palgrave Macmillan, 2019.

Rabil, Robert G. *Embattled Neighbors: Syria, Israel, Lebanon*. Boulder, CO: Lynne Rienner Publishers, 2003.

Reilly, James A. *Fragile Nation, Shattered Land: The Modern History of Syria*. Boulder, CO: Lynne Rienner Publishers, 2018.

T

Tanzim

A militant faction of the Fatah political party that was a central player in the run-up to the 2000 Second (al-Aqsa) Intifada. It was composed of young street activists led by Marwan Barghouti, one of the founders of Shabiba, the Fatah youth organization. The activists in the youth, social, and political organizations that operated in the occupied Palestinian territories before and during the First Intifada constituted the core personnel of the Tanzim. Yasser Arafat started the organization as a way to counteract the growing popularity of competing Islamic organizations, such as Hamas and Palestinian Islamic Jihad (PIJ). However, the older core Palestine Liberation Organization (PLO) leadership—whom Israel allowed back into Palestine from exile in Tunis (known as the "outsiders") as part of the 1993 Oslo Accords—developed a disdain for Barghouti, who also was exiled in Tunis from 1986 until April 1994. The Tanzim Fatah deputies led a campaign against the corruption and mismanagement of the Palestinian Authority (PA). The Tanzim organized protests against the security forces of the outsiders, who abused Fatah activists.

The older Fatah West Bank intifada leadership had initiated a process of democratic reform in the name of the Fatah Higher Council, led by General Secretary Barghouti. In this way, the Tanzim became relatively independent from the PA, to the point that observers speculate on the severity of the rift. In the meantime, Barghouti built good relations with the Israeli left to shape Israelis' perceptions of Palestinian grievances. The Tanzim sought to mobilize Palestinians to confront the Israeli government by exploiting their rising discontent with the consequences of Oslo. Their protests and demonstrations as part of the Second Intifada initially used only rock throwing and Molotov cocktails. However, in competition with Hamas and PIJ, Tanzim began using suicide car bombings and shootings as well. This shift to terrorism destroyed the dialogue with the Israeli peace movement.

Members of the Tanzim differ in their political strategies and goals, but they agree in rejecting the Oslo Accords, security cooperation with Israel, and the U.S.-led negotiations. They seek to develop a broader national coalition of factions and to gain recognition and intervention by the United Nations on behalf of Palestinian independence. While Barghouti was arrested in 2002 and sentenced to five life sentences for murder, in 2006, he initiated—with other prisoners—the National Concordance Document, which established a basis for common political action by all Palestinian factions, except the PIJ. He is often mentioned as one of the few Palestinians possibly capable of mending the Fatah-Hamas split and reenergizing the Palestinian national movement. Many believe that Barghouti could win the next election for PA president, despite his incarceration.

Jonathan K. Zartman

See also: Arafat, Yasser; Barghouti, Marwan; Fatah; Intifada, Second; Oslo Accords; Palestinian Authority; Suicide Bombings

Further Reading

Chen, Hillel. "Palestinian Armed Struggle, Israel's Peace Camp, and the Unique Case of Fatah-Jerusalem." *Israel Studies*, 18. no. 1 (Spring 2013): 101–123.

Inbari, Pinhas, "Will There Be a Palestinian Civil War?" *Jerusalem Issue Brief* 5, no. 27 (June 25, 2006). https://www.jcpa.org/brief/brief005-27.htm.

Usher, Graham. "Fatah's Tanzim: Origins and Politics." *Middle East Research & Information Project Middle East Report* 30, no. 217, Part 4 (2000): 6–15.

Tel Aviv

The second-most-populated city in Israel. Home to approximately 450,000 Israelis, Tel Aviv was founded on the outskirts of Jaffa as a neighborhood of sixty Jewish families in 1909. Modeled after the great European cities, Tel Aviv's planners intended from the start to create a modern city, in contrast with the rural Arab villages that surrounded Jaffa. The etymology of the name *Tel Aviv* reflects the goal to combine the past with the modern—*Tel* means "ancient manmade mound" and *Aviv* means "spring," and so the name literarily means "ancient hill of spring." The name *Tel Aviv* is referenced in both Ezekiel 3:15 in the Hebrew Bible and the Hebrew title of Theodore Herzl's book *Altneuland* ("Old New Land").

In line with its planners' ambitions, Tel Aviv grew quickly from a small neighborhood to the first all-Jewish city. This was primarily a result of the Second Aliya and Tel Aviv's proximity to the port of Jaffa, which proved attractive to European Jews immigrating into Palestine. However, rapid growth and significant ideological differences between Jewish socialists and local Arabs led to tensions that provoked the Jaffa riots in 1921, in which more than 200 Arabs and Jews died. Despite this friction, Tel Aviv continued to grow rapidly as European Jews continued to immigrate through the port of Jaffa. When war broke out in 1947, Tel Aviv's population was more than double that of Jaffa (230,000 to 100,000, respectively). A siege of Jaffa and its fall in 1948 resulted in the mass exodus of the Arab population and made possible Jaffa's annexation, at which point the city became formally known as *Tel Aviv-Yafo*.

During Israel's first year, Tel Aviv was the capital, but in 1949, the capital transitioned to Jerusalem. However, many embassies remained in Tel Aviv due to ongoing disputes regarding the disposition of Jerusalem between Israel and Jordan. Politically liberal since its founding, Tel Aviv continues to strongly support the left end of the Israeli political spectrum and is also seen as the economic and technological center of Israel, in part due to the large influx of Russian Jews in the 1990s. Tel Aviv is also known for its diverse culture, relatively large lesbian, gay, bisexual, and transgender community and twenty-four-hour nightlife, all of which make it a popular international tourist destination.

Hugh Gardenier

See also: Aliya; Israel; Zionism

Further Reading

Azaryahu, Maoz. *Tel Aviv: Mythography of a City*. Syracuse, NY: Syracuse University Press, 2006.

Rotbard, Sharon. *White City, Black City: Architecture and War in Tel Aviv and Jaffa*. Cambridge, MA: MIT Press, 2015.

Temple Mount (see Haram al-Sharif/Temple Mount)

Third Temple Movement

A small but increasingly influential movement that seeks to establish Israel's sovereignty over the Temple Mount in Jerusalem and to build a Third Temple there. The architectural plans for this Third Temple are most notably spelled out in chapters 40–47 in the Book of Ezekiel. Israel prohibits Jews from praying on the Temple Mount, in accordance with Jewish religious law. This restriction is also intended to limit tensions with Muslims.

The Third Temple Movement is made up of a number of groups, including the Temple Mount Faithful, founded by the former Israel Defense Forces (IDF) officer Gershon Salomon in 1967. This group has consistently advocated for the Jewish takeover of the Temple Mount. Their requests to enter the Temple Mount to pray and conduct services on major Jewish holidays have been repeatedly denied. Other Temple Mount groups include the Movement for the Establishment of the Temple, the Temple Institute, and the Temple Mount Heritage Foundation. A former leader of the latter two groups, Yehuda Glick, was shot in 2014 but survived and is now a Likud politician.

Some Third Temple activists call for the destruction of the Muslim holy sites, while others suggest that the Holy Temple can exist alongside them. The Third Temple Movement was once on the fringes in Israel, but its goal of expanding Jewish access to the Temple Mount has become more mainstream.

Deonna Neal

See also: Christian Zionism; Eretz Israel; First and Second Temple Periods; Jewish Underground

Further Reading

Inbari, Motti. *Jewish Fundamentalism and the Temple Mount: Who Will Build the Third Temple?* Trans. Shaul Vardi. Albany, NY: SUNY Press, 2009.

Ramon, Amnon. "Delicate Balances at the Temple Mount, 1967–1999," in *Jerusalem: A City and its Future*, eds. Marshall J. Berger and Ora Ahimeir. Albany, NY: SUNY Press, 2002, 296–332.

Two-State Solution

A proposed solution to the Israeli-Palestinian conflict, which entails the creation of a Palestinian state on all or part of the West Bank and Gaza Strip. For the past few decades, efforts to negotiate a resolution to conflict between Israelis and Palestinians have focused on a two-state solution. Many states and international organizations have publicly supported this goal, including the United States, the European Union, the United Nations (UN), the Palestine Liberation Organization (PLO), and, at times, Israel. In practice, this would require Israel to end its occupation and allow the creation of a Palestinian state in the West Bank and Gaza Strip, in exchange for the Palestinians ending all violence and dropping further claims against Israel. The idea of trading land for peace dates back at least to UN Security Council Resolution 242. Although the Oslo Accords did not specifically declare that Palestinian statehood was the intended outcome of negotiations, most participants and observers assumed this to be the case. Over the past twenty-five years, however, Israelis and Palestinians have failed to come to such an agreement.

There are many reasons for this continued failure. Some insist that there is not enough consensus in Israel for a two-state solution, as evidenced by continuous settlement expansion and the assassination of Prime Minister Yitzhak Rabin, who had spearheaded the Oslo peace process. Others insist that Israel has no good-faith partner to negotiate peace with because a large portion of Palestinians support the Islamic terror group Hamas, which rejects Israel's right to exist—to the point of giving it an electoral majority in the Palestinian government. Other explanations focus on the imbalance of power between occupier and occupied, which skews negotiations in favor of the former. Many argue that because Israel is so much more powerful than the Palestinians, it can absorb any costs of occupation that Palestinians can impose. The United States often serves as an interlocutor, in part to help manage this imbalance, but even former U.S. negotiators lament the American tendency to serve as "Israel's lawyer" in negotiations. Indeed, Palestinians consistently complain about Washington's pro-Israel bias, and most recently, their leadership refuses to meet with U.S. president Donald Trump and his administration's officials because of their overwhelmingly pro-Israel, anti-Palestinian attitude and behavior.

The political dynamics in both Israel and Palestine push negotiators to adopt maximalist, inflexible positions, and negotiators on both sides have been criticized for intransigence. Israeli leaders insist that they have made many generous offers to Palestinians, but all have been rejected because Palestinians are either unrealistic in their demands or simply bent on the destruction of Israel. In contrast, Palestinians contend that Israel has refused to even offer—never mind agree to—a fair two-state solution, instead using negotiations as political cover for its colonization of East Jerusalem and the West Bank.

The latest round of ineffective negotiations ended in 2014. There is good reason to believe that Prime Minister Benjamin Netanyahu is not interested in a two-state solution. During his reelection campaign in 2015, he declared that a Palestinian state would not be created while he was in office. In early 2019, he also promised to begin annexing settlements in the West Bank. Few observers believe Mahmoud Abbas, the unpopular president of the Palestinian Authority (PA), has the credibility to make a deal anyway.

Even if leaders on both sides negotiated in good faith, they would have to overcome a number of stumbling blocks to achieve a two-state solution. One is agreeing on the future of Jerusalem: Israel insists that it will always remain united and under Israeli control, while Palestinians insist that East Jerusalem must be the capital of their new state. Jerusalem is of great religious importance to both sides, which makes sharing or splitting control problematic. The borders of a new Palestinian state is another vexing issue. Israel says that it will never pull back to its 1967 borders and would have to maintain control of the border with Jordan, while Palestinians contend that any changes to the 1967 borders have to be agreed upon, must include one-for-one land swaps, and Palestine must have sovereign control of its borders.

Another issue to resolve involves the Israeli settlements. Israel asserts that it would have to annex major settlement blocks, which almost completely surround East Jerusalem. Palestinians insist on the evacuation of many more settlements than Israeli leaders countenance. Moreover, what happens to the settlements that are not annexed by Israel? Should they be removed or be allowed to exist in the newly created Palestine?

On the security front, Israelis fear that the new Palestinian state could become a haven for terrorists, be taken over by radical leaders, or ally itself with Israel's enemies. As a hedge against these threats, Israel demands concessions on Palestinian sovereignty that most Palestinian leaders consider unacceptable. Finally, Palestinians insist that Palestinian refugees be allowed to return to their homes in Israel, while Israelis insists this is completely unacceptable because doing so would dilute or overturn the Jewish majority that now dominate the country.

Israel's occupation has gone on for more than half a century, and twenty-five years of intermittent peace talks have failed. Few analysts hold out much hope for a two-state solution. Indeed, participants on both sides of the conflict spectrum are embracing the idea of a one-state solution, albeit very different versions. On one end of the spectrum are those that advocate for the creation of a binational state controlling Israel, the West Bank, and Gaza Strip, in which Jews and Palestinians receive full citizenship and equal treatment under the law. On the other end are advocates of a so-called Israeli solution, in which Israel annexes all or most of the West Bank (leaving the Gaza Strip as it is).

Even though these ideas are gaining ground, the two-state solution is still more popular on both sides of the conflict, at least conceptually. The devil is in the details, though, and so far, negotiators have been unable or unwilling to negotiate an agreement acceptable to majorities of Israelis and Palestinians.

Robert C. DiPrizio

See also: Gaza Strip; Israel; Netanyahu, Benjamin; Occupation; One-State Solution; Oslo Accords; Palestinian Authority; Permanent Status Issues; Settlements; West Bank

Further Reading

Abunimah, Ali. *One Country: A Bold Proposal to End the Israeli-Palestinian Impasse.* New York: Metropolitan Books, 2006.

Faris, Hani. *The Failure of the Two-State Solution: The Prospects of One State in the Israel-Palestine Conflict.* London: I. B. Tauris and Co., 2013.

Glick, Caroline. *The Israeli Solution: A One-State Plan for Peace in the Middle East.* New York: Crown Forum. 2014.

O'Malley, Padraig. *The Two-State Delusion: Israel and Palestine—A Tale of Two Narratives.* New York: Penguin Books, 2015.

United Kingdom of Israel

A unified kingdom of Israelite tribes that lasted about seventy years before splitting into two. Biblical tradition dates the establishment of a united Israelite kingdom to about 1000 BCE. Saul was the first king of the Israelites, but it was David who is believed to have unified all the Hebrew tribes and conquered Jerusalem and its environs. David moved the capital of his kingdom to Jerusalem and built a tabernacle to house the Ark of the Covenant, which he recaptured from the Philistines. The ark housed the Ten Commandments tablets and other sacred Israelite relics. It was carried into battles to demonstrate God's presence with his people.

Solomon succeeded David and established a far-flung empire throughout much of Canaan. He is best known for constructing a city wall, elaborate palace, and the first temple in Jerusalem. The temple was built with forced labor, first using subjugated peoples and then his own Hebrew subjects. His brutality and tendency to favor his own tribe, Judah, led to the rebellion of the northern tribes upon his death. Thus, the United Kingdom of Israel split into two pieces—the Kingdom of Israel in the north and Kingdom of Judah in the south.

Robert C. DiPrizio

See also: David; Israelite Conquest of Canaan; Judaism; Kingdom of Israel; Kingdom of Judah; Saul; Solomon

Further Reading

Grabbe, Lester. *Ancient Israel: What Do We Know and How Do We Know It?* New York: Bloomsberry, 2008.

McKenzie, Steven. *King David: A Biography.* New York: Oxford University Press, 2000.

Miller, Maxwell, and John Hayes. *A History of Ancient Israel and Judah.* Louisville, KY: Westminster John Knox Press, 2006.

UN Partition Plan for Palestine

United Nations (UN) plan to divide Mandate Palestine into Arab and Jewish states. On April 2, 1947, the British delegation to the United Nations requested a special session of the General Assembly to establish a committee to study the matter of Palestine.

Over the following months, the UN Special Commission on Palestine (UNSCOP) gathered information in Europe and in Palestine, where it met with representatives of both the Jewish Agency and the Arabs, hearing thirty-four witnesses and holding thirteen public meetings and eighteen closed sessions. It also toured Palestine. The Arab Higher Committee (AHC), created in 1936 to represent Palestinian Arab interests with the British, decided to boycott the hearings, so most of the testimony came from the Jewish Agency and Palestinian government officials. At the same time, militant Arab groups staged anti-Zionist demonstrations in the cities. UNSCOP then went to Lebanon, where it met with representatives of the Arab governments. Then a subcommittee visited certain displaced persons camps in Austria and Germany.

UNSCOP spent most of August debating alternative solutions. Its final report was signed in Geneva on August 31, 1947. The committee could not reach a unanimous opinion, so both majority and minority reports were released. A majority of the representatives (Canada, Czechoslovakia, Guatemala, the Netherlands, Peru, Sweden, and Uruguay) voted for the partition of Palestine into two separate states, one Arab and the other Jewish, to be joined in an economic union. Following a transition period of two years, both states were to be completely independent, provided that they adopted a constitution, guaranteed minority and religious rights, and made provision for the protection of holy places. Jerusalem would be placed under a UN trusteeship.

Three of the representatives (India, Iran, and Yugoslavia) objected to the majority report and produced a minority report. It called for a brief transition period and then the creation of a federal state of Palestine. It would have both a Jewish and an Arab state within it, with two federal legislative bodies—one on the basis of proportionate representation and the other with equal representation by Arabs and Jews. The Australian delegate refused to endorse either plan.

On September 23, 1947, at its regular fall session, the UN General Assembly referred the reports of the committee to the Special Committee on the Question of Palestine, which had representatives of all member-states. It was before this committee that the Jewish Agency representative declared a willingness to accept partition. On October 11, the U.S. delegate stated his government's support for the partition plan. Two days later, the Soviet Union followed suit.

Nonetheless, the committee continued its deliberations. It divided into two subcommittees. Subcommittee No. 2 worked on the minority report, and Subcommittee No. 1 worked on the majority report. The major stumbling block in the latter was over the territorial arrangements for partition. The investigating committee had come up with a map of three Jewish and three Arab sections and additional enclaves. The Jewish Agency pressed for an additional 200,000 acres for the Jewish state for future settlement and defensible borders. On the other hand, the United States initially sought a reduction in the area allocated to the Jewish state, and it was because of this that the port and city of Jaffa became an Arab enclave and most of western Galilee was assigned to the proposed Arab state. Also disappointing to the Jewish Agency was the committee's decision to internationalize the city of Jerusalem.

The Jewish state was awarded the Bet Ntofa Valley and Lydda (Lod) Airport, as well as gains in Lower Galilee, the Beit She'an Valley, and the Gilboa area of the Jezreel Valley. Also, thanks to a last-minute visit by Chaim Weizmann with President Harry Truman, Israel was awarded the sparsely populated but large Negev region, which the Jews hoped to use for future settlement. The plan also included the Arab-Jewish economic union. Thus, of the some 10,000 square miles of Mandate Palestine, the final report awarded the Jewish state 5,579 square miles.

This area also contained an estimated Arab population of 397,000 people, or 46.5 percent of the total there.

On November 25, 1947, the committee voted on the two reports. The minority report from Subcommittee No. 2 was rejected by 29 to 12 votes, with 16 abstentions. The majority report of Subcommittee No. 1 was accepted in a vote of 25 to 13, with 17 abstentions and 2 members absent. This was 1 vote short of the two-thirds that would be required in the final General Assembly vote.

The General Assembly voted on November 29, 1947. There were 33 votes for partition, 13 opposed, 10 abstentions, and 1 absent (Siam). The Truman administration helped corral votes for partition, while the United Kingdom abstained. The Jewish Agency accepted the vote, but the Arabs did not. Immediately on learning of the UN decision, Arabs in Palestine began attacking Jewish settlements. This marked the beginning of the Arab-Jewish Communal War.

Spencer C. Tucker

See also: Arab-Israeli War, 1948; Arab-Jewish Communal War, 1947; British Mandate for Palestine; Lydda and Ramle; *Nakba;* Palestinian Refugees; Zionism

Further Reading

Sachar, Howard M. *A History of Israel: From the Rise of Zionism to Our Time.* 3rd ed. New York: Knopf, 2007.

Shepherd, Naomi. *Ploughing Sand: British Rule in Palestine, 1917–1948.* New Brunswick, NJ: Rutgers University Press, 1999.

Smith, Charles D. *Palestine and the Arab-Israeli Conflict: A History with Documents.* 9th ed. New York: Bedford/St. Martin's, 2017.

UN Relief and Works Agency for Palestine Refugees in the Near East (UNRWA)

The principal provider of education, health, relief, social services, and other basic services to more than 5 million Palestinian refugees and their descendants who have been displaced by Arab-Israeli wars from 1951 to the present. Although most refugees fall under the purview of the Office of the United Nations High Commissioner for Refugees (UNHCR), headquartered in Geneva, Switzerland, most Palestinian refugees are the responsibility of the UN Relief and Works Agency for Palestine Refugees in the Near East (UNRWA). The responsibility for all Palestinian refugees within Israel fell to UNRWA from 1951 until it was appropriated by Israel in 1952.

UNRWA began operations on May 1, 1951. Its mandate must be renewed periodically by the General Assembly. UNRWA had an initial budget of $50 million, but by 2014, it was the largest UN undertaking in the Middle East, employing more than 30,000 people in over 900 facilities in the Gaza Strip, the West Bank, Jordan, Lebanon, and Syria, and with a budget of about $1 billion per year.

The United Nations created UNRWA when it became clear that there would not be a quick resolution of the situation of the displaced Palestinians. It was originally was headquartered in Beirut (1950–1978), and then Vienna (1978–1996), before moving to Gaza in the Palestinian territories in 1996. More recently, its headquarters are split between Amman, Jordan and Gaza.

Although the fact that large numbers of Palestinians fled or were expelled from Jerusalem during the Israeli War of Independence (1948–1949) is well documented, the number of refugees is disputed. The numbers range from the Israeli estimate of 400,000 to the Arab and Palestinian estimate of 950,000–1 million, with an official UN estimate of 711,000. The United Nations originally included in the definition of Palestinian refugees a person and his or her descendants whose "normal place of residence was Palestine between June 1946 and May 1948 and who lost both their homes and means of livelihood as a result of the 1948 Arab-Israeli conflict," but the definition was expanded to include those displaced by the 1967 Six-Day War as well. The designation of "Palestinian refugee" applies only to those meeting this definition and residing in the Gaza Strip, the West Bank, Jordan, Lebanon, and Syria, whether or not they reside in a refugee camp.

UNRWA provides direct relief services to the approximately 1.5 million Palestinian residents in the refugee camps but does not participate in the administration or governance of these camps. Half of its budget and two-thirds of its staff are committed to operating 703 elementary and secondary schools, 9 vocational training centers, 2 educational science facilities, and 3 teacher-training institutes. UNRWA also operates 138 primary health centers and provides environmental health services for the refugee camps. The agency develops infrastructure for the camps and provides loan assistance for enterprise development for all Palestinian refugees.

The majority of UNRWA funding is derived from the voluntary contributions of donor-states. The largest donors traditionally have been the United States, the European Union, the United Kingdom, Japan, Canada, the Gulf Arab states, and the Scandinavian countries. The United Nations funds over 100 UNRWA staff positions, and UNESCO and the World Health Organization (WHO) fund some of the staff positions in UNRWA education and health programs. Other funding comes from nongovernmental organizations (NGOs), private individuals, and refugee copayments and participation fees. UNRWA has operated in the red since 2000, despite reducing its annual expenditure per registered refugee to roughly $110, from its 1970s average of $200.

In recent years, the UNRWA has faced a number of new and daunting challenges. These include the Syrian civil war, which began in early 2011. That conflict has imperiled Palestinian refugees in Syria and resulted in increased staffing needs. Periodic fighting between Hamas (which has occupied Gaza since 2007) and Israel has also caused many difficulties. In July 2014, which witnessed a major Hamas-Israel conflict, a school operated by UNRWA was hit by Israeli mortar fire, resulting in the deaths of sixteen Palestinian civilians and the wounding of many others.

In September 2018, the Donald Trump administration announced that it no longer would provide assistance to UNRWA. The United States had been providing about a third of the organization's annual funding. Administration officials have also indicated that they want to drastically reduce the number of Palestinians recognized as refugees in an effort to remove the Palestinian refugee issue from the negotiations. Increased aid from the Gulf states and the European Union made up most of UNWRA's $400 million budget shortfall in 2018.

Richard M. Edwards

See also: Arab-Israeli War, 1948; Arab-Jewish Communal War, 1947; *Nakba;* Palestinian Refugees; Palestinian Refugee Camps; Right of Return

Further Reading

Dumper, Michael, ed. *Palestinian Refugee Repatriation: Global Perspectives.* New York: Routledge, 2006.

Grobman, Alex. *Nations United: How the United Nations Undermines Israel and the West.* Green Forest, AR: Balfour, 2006.

Pappe, Ilan. *A History of Modern Palestine: One Land, Two Peoples.* Cambridge: Cambridge University Press, 2003.

UN Security Council Resolution 242

A United Nations (UN) resolution calling on Israel to return lands it occupied in 1967 in exchange for peace. UN Security Council Resolution 242 was designed to pave the way for a comprehensive Middle East peace settlement. It was unanimously adopted by the Security Council on November 22, 1967, months after Israel's decisive victory in the Six-Day War, which had led to its capture and occupation of the Sinai Peninsula and the Gaza Strip from Egypt, the West Bank and East Jerusalem from Jordan, and the Golan Heights from Syria.

Resolution 242 expressed concern over the "grave situation in the Middle East," emphasized the "inadmissibility of the acquisition of territory by war," and stressed the need for "a just and lasting peace in which all states in the region could live in peace and security." It also emphasized that all member-states of the United Nations had accepted the UN Charter and undertaken to live in accordance with its Article 2. The resolution specifically called for the "withdrawal of Israeli armed forces from territories occupied in the recent conflict [and the] termination of all claims or states of belligerency and respect for and acknowledgment of the sovereignty, territorial integrity and independence of every State in the area and their right to live in peace within secure and recognized boundaries free from threats or acts of force."

The resolution went on to "affirm the necessity" for guaranteeing free navigation of all international waterways in the region, called for a just solution to the Palestinian refugee problem (although it did not explicitly say "Palestinian"), and a guarantee of "the territorial inviolability and political independence" of states in the area.

The resolution's most important feature was the so-called land for peace formula: an Israeli withdrawal from occupied Arab territories in exchange for peace with its neighbors, along with "the termination of all claims or states of belligerency" between the warring parties. The resolution imposed obligations on both the Arab states and Israel, and yet the warring parties refused to comply unless the other side went first. The Arab states were only willing to give tacit recognition of Israel in exchange for its complete withdrawal from the occupied territories, while Israel was only willing to make a partial withdrawal after the Arab states officially recognized it. Moreover, some insist that Resolution 242 does not require Israel to withdraw to its 1967 borders because the resolution calls for "a withdrawal from territories," not from "all" or "the" territories occupied in the war.

In 1973, following another Arab-Israeli war, the UN Security Council reaffirmed Resolution 242 when it passed Resolution 338. Resolution 242 has yet to be implemented to the satisfaction of the international community.

Stefan Brooks and Spencer C. Tucker

See also: Arab-Israeli War, 1967; Golan Heights; Israel Occupations; Khartoum Resolution; Two-State Solution

Further Reading

Mansfield, Peter. *A History of the Middle East.* Ed. Nicolas Pelham. New York: Penguin, 2004.

Said, Edward W., and Christopher Hitchins, eds. *Blaming the Victims: Spurious Scholarship and the Palestinian Question.* London: Verso, 2001.

Smith, Charles D. *Palestine and the Arab-Israeli Conflict: A History with Documents.* 9th ed. New York: Bedford/St. Martin's, 2017.

UN Security Council Resolution 338

A United Nations (UN) Security Council resolution passed during the October 1973 war. On October 6, 1973, on the Jewish holiday of Yom Kippur and during the Muslim monthlong fast of Ramadan, Egypt and Syria launched a surprise attack on Israel. The primary goal for the attack was to reclaim land captured by Israel in the 1967 Six-Day War, or at least to oblige the United States and the Soviet Union to bring that about through diplomacy. Israel suffered initial heavy losses in the first few days of the war. By the time of the resolution, however, it had regained the initiative, repulsed the Egyptian and Syrian attacks, and occupied even more Arab territory, in Egypt across the Suez Canal and in Syria approaching Damascus.

International efforts to halt the fighting intensified, and U.S. secretary of state Henry Kissinger flew to Moscow on October 20 to meet with Soviet leaders. Two days later, on October 22, the UN Security Council adopted Resolution 338 by a vote of 14–0, with the People's Republic of China abstaining.

UN Resolution 338 contained three provisions. First, it called for all parties to cease fighting and terminate all military activity. Second, it called for immediate implementation of UN Resolution 242, which had been passed on November 22, 1967, following the Six-Day War. Third, the resolution stated that "immediately and concurrently with the cease-fire, negotiations [would] start between the parties concerned under appropriate auspices aimed at establishing a just and durable peace in the Middle East." "Appropriate auspices" was assumed to refer to the United States, the patron and principal ally of Israel, and the Soviet Union, the patron and ally of the Arab states, rather than to the United Nations.

U.S.-led diplomacy resulted in an armistice in March 1974 between Egypt and Israel. Two months later, an armistice was negotiated between Syria and Israel. Impatient at the slow progress of the negotiations, Egyptian president Anwar Sadat took the unprecedented step of visiting Israel in November 1977, becoming the first Arab head of state to do so, and thus implicitly recognizing Israel. Sadat's visit jump-started the peace process with Israeli prime minister Menachem

Begin, and following mediation by U.S. president Jimmy Carter, it led to the Camp David Accords in 1978, whereby Israel withdrew from the Sinai in exchange for diplomatic relations and peace with Egypt. Egypt thus became the first Arab state to make peace with Israel and recover its territory occupied by Israel in 1967.

Stefan Brooks

See also: Arab-Israeli War, 1973; Golan Heights; Israeli Occupations; Two-State Solution; UN Security Council Resolution 242

Further Reading

Mansfield, Peter. *A History of the Middle East.* Ed. Nicolas Pelham. New York: Penguin, 2004.

Rabinovich, Abraham. *The Yom Kippur War: The Epic Encounter That Transformed the Middle East.* New York: Schocken, 2005.

Said, Edward W., and Christopher Hitchins, eds. *Blaming the Victims: Spurious Scholarship and the Palestinian Question.* London: Verso, 2001.

U.S. Aid to Israel

Military, economic, and financial aid given to Israel by the United States. The aid relationship between the United States and Israel is unlike any other in the world. In sheer volume, it is the most generous country-to-country foreign aid program in history, totaling at least $135 billion (not adjusted for inflation) as of 2018. One unusual aspect of this aid program is that Israel, like its benefactor, is an advanced, industrialized, technologically sophisticated country, as well as a major arms exporter.

U.S. aid to Israel began in the early 1950s, with small grants, and expanded modestly over the next decade to include loans from the Export-Import Bank of the United States, Food for Peace aid, and general economic loans. Military loans began only after the 1967 Six-Day War. These were replaced exclusively by grants in 1985. U.S. economic aid increased greatly in subsequent years, and grants replaced loans for economic assistance in 1981.

Over the past twenty years, the annual U.S. subsidy for Israel has been approximately $3 billion in military and economic grants, in addition to more than $500 million from other parts of the budget or outside the budget. Unlike most U.S. recipients of economic aid, which are required to use the bulk of the money for specific projects, such as buying certain U.S. agricultural surpluses or finished goods, most U.S. aid to Israel goes directly into the government's treasury to use as it sees fit. In every other country, officials of the U.S. Agency for International Development officials oversee the actual programs, either administered directly, through nongovernmental organizations (NGOs), or under cosponsorship with a government agency. Since 1971, however, Israel has been the exception: the U.S. government sets the level, and the funding simply becomes cash transfers to the Israeli government. Economic aid to Israel was phased out in 2008 but matched dollar for dollar in increases in military aid. Unlike any other country that receives U.S. military aid, Israel is allowed to spend 26.3 percent of its annual assistance on purchasing from the Israeli defense industry, although this particular perk is scheduled to be phased out by 2028.

Unlike other countries, which receive aid in quarterly installments, aid to Israel since 1982 has been given in a lump sum at the beginning of the fiscal year, leaving the U.S. government to borrow from future revenues. Israel even lends some of this money back through U.S. Treasury bills and collects the additional interest. This special arrangement costs the U.S. government approximately $50 million each year. Congress also mandates that these annual lump-sum deposits from the U.S. Treasury are placed into interest-bearing accounts with the Federal Reserve Bank. Israel can then collect the accrued interest. Since 1992, the United States has also provided Israel loan guarantees so it could purchase lower-cost loans totaling over $20 billion. Israel has never defaulted, but the U.S. government has to set tens of millions of dollars aside for each loan to cover that possibility. Because the U.S. government spends more money every year than it takes in through taxes, it borrows to meet its obligations. These costs to the U.S. taxpayer, and the benefits they provide Israel, are not normally included when calculating U.S. aid to Israel.

In addition, more than $1.5 billion in private U.S. funds goes to Israel annually ($1 billion in private, tax-deductible donations and $500 million in Israeli bonds). The ability of Americans to make what amounts to tax-deductible contributions to a foreign government, made possible through a number of Jewish charities, does not exist with any other country.

Annual U.S. aid to Israel is approximately one-third of the foreign aid budget, even though Israel consists of just one-tenth of 1 percent of the world's population and already has one of the world's higher per capita incomes. In 2016, of the approximately $5.65 billion that the U.S. government set aside for foreign military aid, Israel received $3.1 billion—more than 50 percent of the entire military aid budget.

The United States also stockpiles up to $2 billion worth of military equipment in Israel, which that country can tap into in emergency situations; it did this in 2006 and 2014, when fighting against Hezbollah and Hamas, respectively. Israel is the first international operator of the cutting-edge U.S. F35 fighter jet.

U.S. aid to Israel was quite small during the first two decades of Israel's existence, when its democratic institutions were strongest and its strategic situation most vulnerable. By contrast, as Israeli military power grew dramatically and its repression against Palestinians in the occupied territories increased, U.S. aid has also increased. Indeed, 99 percent of U.S. military assistance to Israel has taken place after the 1967 Six-Day War, when Israel proved itself to be far stronger than any combination of Arab armies and after Israeli occupation forces became the rulers of a large Palestinian population. Currently, Israel has both a major domestic arms industry and an existing military force far more powerful than any conceivable combination of opposing forces, including a sizable arsenal of biological, chemical, and nuclear weapons and long-range missiles.

U.S. assistance to Israel is not limited to tangible aid. The United States regularly uses its outsized influence in global forums to protect Israel from international condemnation. The United States has vetoed nearly fifty Security Council resolutions critical of Israel and derailed countless others. It has similarly helped keep the International Atomic Energy Agency from investigating Israel's nuclear weapons program and regularly tries to limit criticism of Israel's human rights record by UN agencies. In 2018, the United States withdrew from the UN Human Rights Council, claiming it is anti-Israel.

Laws passed by Congress mandate that the U.S. government must help ensure Israel's qualitative military superiority over its neighbors. This is done not only through providing large amounts of aid to Israel and selling it cutting-edge technologies, but by conditioning any arms sales to Middle East countries on the administration's determination that the sale will not adversely affect Israel's regional military superiority. Unlike many foreign aid programs, which are often criticized by both conservative Republicans skeptical of foreign aid and liberal Democrats concerned about supporting human rights violators, U.S. aid to Israel receives widespread bipartisan support on Capitol Hill and is rarely the subject of debate.

There are a number of leading explanations for what drives U.S. governments to provide Israel so much support. Some argue that Israel serves as a strategic asset, combating Soviet influence during the Cold War, containing rogue states like Iran and Saddam Husayn's Iraq, and fighting terrorism. Others insist that Israel is the only democracy in the region, that the United States and Israel share common Judeo-Christian values, and that the United States did not do enough during World War II to protect Jews from the Holocaust. For these reasons, the United States is obligated to ensure Israel's survival.

Critics however, insist that Israel is more of a strategic liability than an asset, that it often acts in direct opposition to U.S. interests in the region, and that the special relationship with Israel has contributed to widespread anti-American sentiment in the Middle East. They also argue that Israel's existence is no longer in doubt, that it is the military superpower in the region, and that its occupation of Palestinians is both illegal and immoral. Many insist the U.S. special relationship with Israel is not driven by strategic calculations or moral arguments, but instead by the influence of Jewish and Christian Zionist pro-Israel lobby groups in the United States.

In the aftermath of the Iran nuclear deal (July 2015), which the Israeli government bitterly denounced, Barack Obama's administration voiced its readiness to increase military aid to Israel, which soon asked for $5 billion per year. Israeli and U.S. negotiators settled on a ten-year agreement awarding Israel $3.8 billion per year in military assistance beginning in the 2019 fiscal year.

Stephen Zunes and Robert C. DiPrizio

See also: American Israel Public Affairs Committee; Christian Zionism; U.S. Involvement in Israeli-Palestinian Affairs

Further Reading

Mearsheimer, John J., and Steven Walt. *The Israel Lobby and U.S. Foreign Policy.* New York: Farrar, Straus and Giroux, 2007.

Sharp, Jeremy M. *U.S. Foreign Aid to Israel.* Washington D.C.:Congressional Research Service, April 10, 2018.

Zunes, Stephen. "The Strategic Functions of U.S. Aid to Israel." *Middle East Policy* 4, no. 4 (October 1996), pp. 90-101.

U.S. Involvement in Israeli-Palestinian Affairs

The U.S. involvement in the Israel-Palestine dispute began following World War II. The United States emerged from that conflict as the sole Western superpower, but prior to the war, Britain served as the key arbiter in the region of greater Palestine, having established mandate authority over the area after World War I. The British Mandate for Palestine operated through the interwar years, but after World War II, the United Kingdom referred the question of Palestine's political future to the newly established United Nations. The United Nations proposed a partition plan in 1947 that the United States eventually supported. President Harry S. Truman backed the plan in part to buoy the organization at a critical moment in its history.

This decision was at odds with recommendations from the U.S. national security establishment. The Department of Defense worried about the commitment of American troops to secure a peaceful partition, while the State Department was concerned about consequences on American relations with Arab states, especially in light of the growing competition between the United States and the Soviet Union. The Truman administration actively lobbied UN member-states to support the partition plan. After Israel declared its independence in 1948, Truman quickly recognized the new state, angering some in the State Department and the U.S. delegation to the United Nations for failing to notify them of his decision before it was announced.

During the next twenty years, American policy in the Middle East was only tangentially concerned with the Israeli-Palestinian question because the dominant

Egyptian President Anwar Sadat and Israeli Prime Minister Menachem Begin acknowledge applause during a Joint Session of Congress in which President Jimmy Carter announced the results of the Camp David Accords. The accords were the high water mark of U.S. peacemaking efforts in the Arab-Israeli conflict. (Library of Congress)

logic for the United States in the region was limiting Soviet influence. It was not until the Six-Day War of 1967 that the question of Israel and Palestine was brought into stark relief again for the United States.

The growing tensions between Israel and its Arab neighbors that led to the 1967 war took on a Cold War flavor but were not caused by it. The global superpowers took sides and provided support, yet the conflict was not a proxy war. Rather, it was the result of palpable local conflicts of interest. Israel initiated conflict on June 5, surprising Egypt and destroying most of its air force within hours. After six days of fighting, Israel had roundly beaten its Arab neighbors and gained territory in the Sinai, the Golan Heights, and the West Bank. The latter, gained from Jordan, put millions of Palestinians under Israeli authority, laying the foundation for many of the political complications that would follow.

Egypt, Syria, and Jordan rebounded in the 1973 Yom Kippur War, a conflict that brought the United States into greater alignment with Israel. Although President Richard Nixon felt that his predecessor, Lyndon Johnson, was too close to Israel in 1967, Cold War dynamics spurred him to provide significant U.S. military support for Israel in 1973. While the 1967 conflict had been one-sided and decisive, the fighting in October 1973 proved to be just the opposite. Surprised by the ferocity of the violence, and worried that the conflict could drag the United States and the Soviet Union into conflict, Secretary of State Henry Kissinger worked through formal and informal channels to arrange a cease-fire. His subsequent so-called shuttle diplomacy, in which he traveled between regional capitals brokering compromise, improved relations between the United States and Egypt and laid the foundation for President Jimmy Carter's later success in the Camp David Accords.

The Camp David negotiations did not include Palestinian representation, but the Palestinian question was central to the talks. In the end, however, the Palestinian issue was left at the status quo. Israel retained authority over the West Bank, East Jerusalem, and the Gaza Strip, and all major issues of the Palestinian dispute remained unresolved. These questions include the demarcation of mutually recognized borders delineating Israel and Palestine, the Palestinian claim of a right of return to family homes held prior to the 1948 war, and the final status of Jerusalem.

The end of the Cold War shifted the central logic with which American administrations had considered the Middle East for decades. No longer constrained by fear of Soviet action among potential client-states, the United States saw more possibility for American influence in the region than ever before. In no way was this optimism more manifest than in Secretary of State James Baker's efforts to establish a comprehensive Middle East peace through the Madrid Conference in 1991. Baker worked tirelessly to bring all relevant parties together, making nine trips to the Middle East to set up the conference. The conference brought together Israel, Egypt, Syria, Lebanon, and a joint Jordanian-Palestinian delegation and began with Camp David's Framework for Peace in the Middle East as a starting point, emphasizing the principles of land for peace under UN Resolution 242 and the importance of direct negotiations under UN Resolution 338. Three separate bilateral tracks—between Israel and Syria, Israel and Lebanon, and Israel and Jordan/Palestine—were joined by five multilateral working groups. In the end, though, process eclipsed peace, and five rounds of talks over nine months eventually failed to resolve any substantive issues.

Although the Madrid process failed to produce any meaningful political outcomes, subsequent changes within Israel and the Palestine Liberation Organization (PLO) raised the possibility of substantive bilateral talks. In Israel, the Likud Party lost its long-held control of Israeli politics when elections in 1992 brought a Labor-led coalition into power and established Yitzhak Rabin as prime minister. The rise of Labor was especially promising for peace prospects because a chief policy difference between Likud and Labor was each party's stance on Palestine, with Labor holding more centrist views on the issue than Likud. Changing dynamics among Palestinians likewise had implications for renewed peace talks. Hamas was rising as a competitor to the PLO, incentivizing Israel to work with the PLO to discredit Hamas and empower the PLO at the bargaining table.

Secret talks between Israel and the PLO began in January 1993. Representatives held fourteen meetings over the next seven months, hosted by Norway, which had good relations with both parties and provided the necessary secrecy to ensure that talks could be spared political posturing for outside audiences. Substantial progress had been made by the time the story broke in August, allowing the United States to step in as chief mediator as a signal of great power endorsement. The resulting Oslo Accords, intended as a transition agreement, provided for mutual recognition and limited Palestinian autonomy.

Although the negotiations were a breakthrough for Israeli-Palestinian dialogue—garnering the PLO's Yasser Arafat, Israeli prime minister Yitzhak Rabin, and Israeli foreign minister Shimon Peres the Nobel Peace Prize—the familiar issues of borders, refugees, and Jerusalem remained unresolved. The talks were advanced through the Taba Agreement (or Oslo II), signed in September 1995. The peace process, however, was tragically derailed by violent malcontents on both sides. Palestinian terrorism signaled the PLO's inability to deliver on its promise of peace, and the assassination of Yitzhak Rabin at the hands of an Israeli extremist killed Israel's greatest advocate for peace and allowed for the return to power of Likud a few months later under prime minister Benjamin Netanyahu, who opposed the Oslo Accords.

The Oslo Accords remain the high-water mark of Israeli-Palestinian negotiations. But little progress was made following the election of Netanyahu. It was only the return of a Labor-led coalition under Ehud Barak that allowed U.S. president Bill Clinton to attempt in his last year to achieve the type of diplomatic success that Carter had had between Egypt and Israel. Walking in the literal footsteps of that earlier accord, Clinton hosted Barak and Arafat at Camp David. Clinton aimed for a comprehensive settlement that included all major issues, but the talks went nowhere. Barak lacked negotiating strength, as threats to dissolve his shaky governing coalition tied his hands. Arafat further spoiled the negotiations by threatening a unilateral declaration of independence.

George W. Bush's administration likewise aimed to bring Israel and Palestine together, but like Madrid before it, Bush's Road Map for Peace was more process than peace. The Road Map was the product of a U.S.-led quartet that included the European Union, the United Nations, and Russia. It laid out three phases in the peace process, beginning with an end to violence and ending with a permanent status agreement. A summit in 2003 in Jordan between Bush, Israeli prime minister Ariel Sharon, and new Palestinian Authority (PA) prime minister Mahmoud Abbas was not enough to keep the Road Map on track, as Palestinians became more split than ever as a result of the growing influence of Hamas and Israel's refusal to freeze settlement building. Although the principles of the Road Map were reconfirmed at summits in Sharm el-Sheikh in 2005 and Annapolis in 2007 (with Ehud Olmert now Israeli prime minister), the 2008–2009 Israel-Gaza War spoiled any remaining hopes for success.

President Obama saw a clear role for the United States in arbitrating Israeli-Palestinian peace, but his intentions were not matched by favorable conditions in the region. One of Obama's first acts upon entering office was the appointment of diplomat and former U.S. senator George Mitchell as Special Envoy for Middle East Peace. Although Mitchell had found success in mediating the Good Friday Agreement while Special Envoy for Northern Ireland more than a decade earlier, his task in the Middle East proved more difficult. The Israel-Gaza War remained a point of severe contention between Israel and the PA. Furthermore, Obama's insistence on an Israeli settlement freeze fostered a strained relationship with Israeli prime minister Benjamin Netanyahu.

Obama hosted Netanyahu and Abbas in Washington in September 2010—along with Egyptian president Hosni Mubarak and Jordan's King Abdullah II—but meaningful negotiations never developed. Mitchell resigned from his position in May 2011. During his second term, Obama authorized Secretary of State John Kerry to pursue a negotiated settlement, but it too failed. In testimony to Congress, Kerry broke with U.S. diplomatic tradition and publicly blamed the Israeli government's refusal to curb settlement construction for the breakdown in negotiations.

U.S. president Donald Trump expressed an interest in brokering Israeli-Palestinian peace shortly after taking office, although after two years, a specific strategy has yet to be announced. Trump placed responsibility for renewed talks on his son-in-law, Jared Kushner. Kushner made early visits to Netanyahu and Abbas, but further steps toward structured negotiations did not follow. Trump has demonstrated a willingness to break diplomatic norms, having recognized Jerusalem as Israel's capital and having cancelled nearly all forms of U.S. aid to Palestinians in an effort to force them to accept his so-called deal of the century (not yet announced), which appears to offer Palestinians something far less than independence. These actions have led many to argue that the United States is too pro-Israel to serve as an honest broker in peace talks with Palestinians.

Sean P. Braniff

See also: American Israel Public Affairs Committee; Madrid Conference; Oslo Accords; Permanent Status Issues; Two-State Solution; U.S. Aid to Israel

Further Reading

Eisenberg, Laura Zittrain, and Neil Caplan. *Negotiating Arab-Israeli Peace: Patterns, Problems, Possibilities.* 2nd ed. Bloomington: Indiana University Press, 2010.

Miller, Aaron David. *The Much Too Promised Land: America's Elusive Search for Arab-Israeli Peace.* New York: Bantam Books, 2008.

Rabinovich, Itamar. *Yitzhak Rabin: Soldier, Leader, Statesman.* New Haven, CT: Yale University Press, 2018.

Takeyh, Ray, and Steven Simon. *The Pragmatic Superpower: Winning the Cold War in the Middle East.* New York: W. W. Norton & Company, 2016.

USS Liberty

A U.S. navy ship sunk by Israel during the 1967 Arab-Israeli War. On June 7, 1967, during the Six-Day War, Israeli warplanes and torpedo boats attacked the USS *Liberty*, an intelligence-gathering vessel being used by the National Security Agency for collecting signals that was operating off the coast of the Sinai Peninsula. The ship was in international waters, flew an American flag, and had proper markings identifying its country of origin, but ostensibly the Israelis mistook it for an Egyptian destroyer known to be operating in the region.

The attack nearly sank the ship, killing 34 crew members and wounding 171. The Israelis immediately apologized and offered compensation to the victims and their families. Significant controversies abound, including questions of how the ship could have been misidentified, whether the Israelis knew they were attacking an American vessel, and why an order to move the ship farther from the coast as a precautionary measure was not received until after the attack. Commander William L. McGonagle earned the Congressional Medal of Honor for his actions in response to the attack.

Paul J. Springer

See also: Arab-Israeli War, 1967

Further Reading

Ennes, James N., Jr. *Assault on the* Liberty: *The True Story of the Israeli Attack on an American Intelligence Vessel.* New York: Random House, 1987.

Scott, James. *The Attack on the* Liberty: *The Untold Story of Israel's 1967 Assault on a U.S. Spy Ship.* New York: Simon & Schuster, 2009.

War of Attrition

An inconclusive war, mainly between Israeli and Egyptian forces, along the Suez Canal. After the 1967 Six-Day War, the Arab states made it clear that they would seek the return of lands lost to the Israelis. The Soviets started to arm and train their Arab allies in Egypt and Syria almost immediately after the war. By late 1968, Egyptian president Gamal Abdel Nasser declared the cease-fire with Israel null and void and began low-level attacks on Israeli forces along the Suez Canal. Nasser also encouraged Syrian and Palestine Liberation Organization (PLO) attacks on Israel's northern and eastern borders, but the bulk of fighting was between Egypt and Israel. A cease-fire was soon arranged, while both sides fortified their defenses with aid from the Soviet Union and United States, respectively.

In March 1969, Egypt broke the cease-fire with a series of artillery and air strikes on Israeli forces in the Sinai, marking the beginning of the War of Attrition. Israel launched heavy reprisals not only on Egyptian military forces, but on infrastructure deep inside Egypt. Nasser appealed to the Soviets, who agreed to intervene directly. When Soviet pilots began flying missions over parts of Egypt, Israel ended its deep air strikes. Conflict continued along the Suez Canal for many more weeks until August 1970, when the United States brokered a cease-fire.

In the end, the results of the war were inconclusive. Israel maintained control of all the territory it captured in 1967 and inflicted many more casualties on the enemy than it suffered. Still, by inflicting significant casualties on the Israel Defense Forces (IDF), with over 1,000 troops killed, Egypt began to chip away at the sense of Israeli invincibility.

Robert C. DiPrizio

See also: Arab-Israeli War, 1967; Nasser, Gamal Abdel; Palestine Liberation Organization

Further Reading

Ginor, Isabella, and Gideon Remez. *The Soviet-Israeli War, 1967–1973: The USSR's Military Intervention in the Egyptian-Israeli Conflict.* Oxford: Oxford University Press, 2017.

Kober, Avi. *Israel's Wars of Attrition: Attrition Challenges to Democratic States.* New York: Routledge, 2009.

Water Security

An enduring struggle between Israelis and Palestinians over water rights and resources. In a land of limited resources and inequitable distribution, water is nearly as powerful a polarizing force as religion. Israel has controlled the lion's share of water since 1948, and since that time, both Jews and Arabs have argued over who owns which resources and who is using them irresponsibly. The main problem is uneven water distribution. Although experts insist that there is enough water for all the current inhabitants, Israel has controlled most of the water resources available to Palestinians living under occupation since 1967, and Palestinians claim that Israel routinely denies them access to their fair share.

Water is naturally scarce in the region due to the arid climate, and available resources cannot accommodate all proposed uses. The main water source for Israel is the Jordan River drainage basin, which includes the Sea of Galilee. The Jordan River originates in headwaters in northern Israel, in the Golan Heights, and in southern Lebanon. These waters feed Lake Tiberias (i.e., the Sea of Galilee). Runoff from the West Bank, Syria, and Jordan adds water to lower Jordan. Israel uses all the water from the Jordan River—Palestine does not receive any of it, though geographically the Palestinians are riparian. In fact, only 30 percent of the water in Palestine comes from surface sources, with the rest coming from underground aquifers. The Mountain or West Bank Aquifer system supplies most of the water to the West Bank, while the water in Gaza comes from the Gaza Strip Aquifer, which is part of the Coastal Aquifer. Because the Gaza Strip Aquifer has been overpumped for many years, the water table can no longer recharge. The water has been contaminated with so much seawater that it is no longer drinkable, representing a major water crisis for the area.

In 1953, Israel's foreign minister, Moshe Sharett, insisted on Israel's right to use the waters from the Jordan as it wished, for hydroelectric power, agriculture, and other needs. He claimed that Israel was willing to engage in negotiations with Jordan, Syria, and Lebanon to come up with a just apportionment of regional resources, but that the neighboring countries had refused to convene with Israel. Israel therefore felt justified in treating the waters of the Jordan as its own and in using these waters for development in the north and elsewhere. Between 1953 and 1965, U.S. ambassador Eric Johnston traveled between Israel and neighboring Arab states, attempting to divide water rights equitably. Experts from the affected nations agreed on a plan to divide and exploit existing resources, but the Arab League rejected the plan because it did not want to imply recognition of Israel.

Palestinians and others accuse Israel of mismanaging the region's water, in part because many Israelis live a consumer-oriented lifestyle that depends on ample water. Green lawns and swimming pools are common, and Israelis have continuously developed the land for the past 100 years, building homes, kibbutzim, and farms. Further, the government subsidizes water for Israelis, which discourages conservation. In 1995, the Ministry of Agriculture recommended ending subsidies to agriculture, but the Water Commissioner's office rejected this idea.

Almost half of the land in Israel is irrigated for agricultural purposes, and agriculture uses nearly 60 percent of the nation's water resources. In the 1960s, Israel was on the forefront of research into drip irrigation, which greatly reduces the amount of water needed to grow crops, but most of this experimentation ended after it took control of more water resources in 1967. Critics note that agriculture supplies only 6 percent of Israel's gross domestic product (GDP) and suggest that the scarce water resources might be better used to nourish nonirrigated traditional crops.

Since 1967, Palestinians living in the West Bank have been prevented from digging new wells, while Israelis have been exploiting the water resources underlying land inhabited by Arabs. Palestinians pay between three and eight times more for water than Israelis do, and each Israeli uses more than 3.5 times the amount of water used by each Palestinian. Palestinians living in the occupied territories receive on average about 70 liters of water per day, far less than the 150 liters daily water allotment recommended by the World Health Organization (WHO).

Palestinians have learned to conserve water, saving rainwater in rooftop cisterns and recycling water used for cooking and cleaning. Under international law, water resources should be shared equitably, but inequity has been the rule since the state of Israel was established. Israel insists that its people simply need more water to meet the demands of its advanced economy and to support their living standards, which are higher than those of West Bank Palestinians.

The Sea of Galilee and the Coastal Aquifer are both entirely within Israel's pre-1967 borders, and Israel completely claims them. Israel also notes that most of the water from the Western Aquifer emerges from springs in Israel, and that it has used the Western Aquifer's water since the early 1950s. Israelis argue that Palestinians are in fact benefiting from Israeli water because Palestinian settlements in the West Bank use water sources developed by Israel. Under the 1994 peace agreement between Israel and Jordan, Israel and Jordan agreed to share the Jordan River, and Israel agreed to supply a large amount of water to Jordan.

By 2014, Israel had virtually eliminated its water-access issues through stringent conservation efforts, the use of recycled wastewater (which provides the agricultural sector with 90 percent of its water needs), and the construction of desalination plants. In 2018, 70 percent of Israel's drinking water was supplied through desalination.

Amy Hackney Blackwell

See also: Arab-Israeli War, 1967; Golan Heights; Israeli Occupations; Settlements; West Bank

Further Reading

Isaac, Jad. "A Sober Approach to the Water Crisis in the Middle East." *Applied Research Institute—Jerusalem.* http://www.arij.org/pub/sober.htm (accessed May 26, 2005).

Siegel, Seth M. *Let There Be Water: Israel's Solution for a Water-Starved World.* New York: St. Martin's Press, 2017.

Smith, Charles D. *Palestine and the Arab-Israeli Conflict: A History with Documents.* 9th ed. New York: Bedford/St. Martin's, 2017.

Weizmann, Chaim

An important Zionist leader. Born in the Russian village of Motol near Pinsk on November 27, 1874, Chaim Weizmann studied chemistry and biochemistry in Germany and Switzerland and received his doctorate with honors in 1899 from the University of Freiburg. While working in Germany, he developed a fermentation process that produced acetone, a vital material in producing cordite for explosives, from maize. During World War I, Weizmann's work in this field proved critical for

British munitions production, and this led to his becoming close friends with British minister of munitions David Lloyd George. From 1916 to 1919, Weizmann directed the Admiralty laboratories and used his political connections to lobby for Zionism, a cause in which he had become active.

Weizmann is most famous for helping to persuade British secretary for foreign affairs Arthur Balfour to issue the Balfour Declaration in 1917, calling for the establishment of a "Jewish homeland" in Palestine. In 1920, the World Zionist Organization (WZO) elected Weizmann its president, and he served in that capacity during 1920–1930, and again in 1935–1946. During and after World War II, he actively lobbied for the creation of a Jewish state. He worked to secure passage of the United Nations (UN) partition plan for Palestine on November 29, 1947, and he helped convince U.S. president Harry Truman to recognize Israel.

In recognitions of his great accomplishments on behalf of the Jewish state, in 1949 Weizmann became Israel's first president (a mostly ceremonial position, but an honor nevertheless). He died in office on November 9, 1952, following a long illness, at his home in Rehovot, Israel.

Stephen K. Stein

See also: Balfour Declaration; British Mandate for Palestine; World Zionist Organization

Further Reading

Reinharz, Jehuda. *Chaim Weizmann: The Making of a Statesman*. New York: Oxford University Press, 1993.

Reinharz, Jehuda. *Chaim Weizmann: The Making of a Zionist Leader*. New York: Oxford University Press, 1987.

West Bank

Territory that lies west of the Jordan River and south of the Sea of Galilee. It is also known by its biblical names of *Judea* in the south and *Samaria* in the north. Today, about 40 percent of the area and 98 percent of the Palestinian population is under the jurisdiction of the Palestinian Authority (PA), although Israel, which has occupied the territory since the 1967 Six-Day War, has settlements in and controls through military force the remainder. East Jerusalem, although located in the West Bank, was annexed by Israel (a step not recognized by most of the international community) and is usually treated as a separate issue in peace negotiations. In 2017, U.S. president Donald Trump recognized Jerusalem as Israel's capital.

Until the end of World War I, the West Bank was part of the territory of the Ottoman Empire, after which it was part of the British Mandate for Palestine. The West Bank was captured by Jordanian forces in the Israeli War of Independence, despite the fact that it had been designated as part of a proposed Palestinian state by the United Nations (UN) in 1947. Following that war, the boundary separating Israel and Jordanian-occupied territory became known as the *Green Line*. Palestinian Arab refugees from Israel flooded into the area. Jordan annexed the West Bank in 1950, although only Britain recognized the move.

Israeli forces moved into and occupied the West Bank during the 1967 Arab-Israeli War. UN Security Council Resolution 242 of 1967 called for the withdrawal

Israel's West Bank security barrier near Ramallah. Israel has maintained a military occupation of the West Bank since 1967. It is home to nearly three million Palestinians. (Giovanni De Caro/Dreamstime.com)

of Israeli forces from the territories occupied in the Six-Day War, which included East Jerusalem, the West Bank, the Gaza Strip, the Golan Heights, and the Sinai Peninsula. Israel refused to comply with the resolution, though, and throughout the 1970s, it established Jewish settlements in all the occupied territories, with the most being in the West Bank.

After almost twenty years of Israeli occupation and the expanding encroachment of Palestinian land by the settlements, the First Intifada started in 1987. The following year, Jordan's King Husayn relinquished all claims to the West Bank, partly to support Palestinian claims and partly to reinforce Jordanian national identity.

The Palestine Liberation Organization (PLO) proclaimed the West Bank independent in 1988, but this act was largely symbolic because Israel did not recognize either the area's independence or the PLO as a legitimate governing body. The promise of a breakthrough came with the 1993 Oslo Accords, when Israel and the Palestinians agreed to a conditional withdrawal of Israeli troops from some West Bank areas. The accords, however, stipulated that the status of the territory would not be determined finally until both sides entered into a permanent agreement.

The Oslo Accords divided the West Bank (but not East Jerusalem) into three parts. In Area A, which contained the major cities and villages in which most Palestinians lived, the newly created PA was granted almost complete autonomy. In Area B, which encompassed much of the territory surrounding Palestinian cities, the PA had limited autonomy and was required to cooperate with Israel's military on security issues. Areas A and B each constituted about 20 percent of the West Bank. The remaining 60 percent was deemed Area C, and Israel maintains complete control of this territory, where the majority of Israeli settlers live. This division of governing responsibility is still in place today. Despite this agreement, Israel's military regularly operates in Areas A and B, ostensibly for security reasons.

Frustrated by the torturously slow peace process and the ever-encroaching Israeli settlements, Palestinian patience ran out in 2000 when Likud Party leader Ariel Sharon enraged the Palestinian public by visiting the al-Aqsa Mosque area of the Haram al-Sharif with a large number of Israeli security forces. This triggered the Second (al-Aqsa) Intifada, which was far more violent than the First Intifada. The Palestinian attacks and suicide bombings of the Second Intifada initially led Israel to send large military forces back into the West Bank.

Convinced that they had no reliable negotiating partner on the Palestinian side who could make agreements and deliver on them, the Israelis initiated steps that were intended to lead to a unilateral disengagement from Gaza and parts of the West Bank. In 2002, the Israelis began constructing the controversial security barrier around the West Bank. But rather than conforming to the boundary of the pre-1967 Green Line, the planned line of the barrier cut deep into the West Bank in various sectors to encompass Israeli settlements that had been established since 1967. The Palestinians, along with much of the rest of the world, condemned the Israeli move as a blatant land grab.

In 2005, Sharon (now prime minister) unilaterally withdrew all Israeli settlements from the Gaza Strip, as well as four smaller settlements in the West Bank. Meanwhile, the Israelis have continued to expand some of their larger settlements in the West Bank, resettling some settlers evicted from Gaza. Settlement expansion in the West Bank has often been cited by Palestinian and U.S. officials as impeding the peace process. Indeed, critics say that one goal of the settler movement is to create facts on the ground that reduce the chances of an Israeli withdrawal.

In 2018, the West Bank was home to about 2.8 million Palestinians and 400,000 Israeli settlers. Another 230,000 settlers live in East Jerusalem. About 30 percent of the Palestinians in the West Bank are refugees from the 1948 Arab-Israeli War or their descendants. Among the more populous Palestinian cities of the West Bank are East Jerusalem, Nablus, Ramallah, Bethlehem (home to a large number of Palestinian Christians), Hebron, Tulkarem, and Qlaquilla. In 2019, Israeli prime minister Benjamin Netanyahu pledged to begin annexing Israeli settlements in the West Bank.

David T. Zabecki

See also: Israeli Occupations; Oslo Accords; Palestinian Authority; Permanent Status Issues; Settlements; Two-State Solution

Further Reading

Said, Edward. *The End of the Peace Process: Oslo and After.* New York: Vintage, 2001.

Smith, Charles D. *Palestine and the Arab-Israeli Conflict: A History with Documents.* 9th ed. New York: Bedford/St. Martin's, 2000.

Zertal, Idith, and Akiva Eldar. *Lords of the Land: The War for Israel's Settlements in the Occupied Territories, 1967–2007.* New York: Nation Books, 2007.

World Zionist Organization (WZO)

An international organization created to establish a Jewish state in Palestine. In 1897, the First Zionist Congress held in Basel, Switzerland, created the Zionist Organization to help raise money and buy land in Palestine for Jewish settlement. Theodor Herzl was its first president. The organization spent the next fifty-two years purchasing land and creating governmental procedures for the new Israeli state. It was renamed the World Zionist Organization (WZO) in 1960.

All Jews were allowed to join the Zionist Organization. People came from all over the world to the group's congresses, which were held biennially from 1897 to 1939 but did not meet again until 1946. Since then, it has met on a semiregular basis every four to five years. The Thirty-Seventh Congress was held in 2015 in Jerusalem.

The organization established the Jewish Colonial Trust to handle financial matters. The Jewish National Fund (JNF), created in 1901, took responsibility for purchasing land. The Anglo-Palestine Bank, established in 1903, provided financial services for settlers. And Keren Hayesod, established in 1920, helped raise funds for Zionist projects. Gradually, the Zionist Organization created an infrastructure necessary for a Jewish state.

In 1922, the League of Nations called for the creation of a Jewish Agency in its Palestine mandate that would serve as the representative of the Jewish people to the British mandatory government and cooperate with it establishing the Jewish national homeland. The Zionist Organization initially served in the capacity of the Jewish Agency. A more comprehensive and somewhat autonomous Jewish Agency was established in 1929 by the Zionist Organization at its Sixteenth Zionist Congress. Dr. Chaim Weizmann, then president of the organization, was elected president of the new Jewish Agency. The agency became a quasi-Jewish government in Palestine under David Ben-Gurion's leadership (1935–1948) prior to the creation of Israel.

The primary goal of the Zionist Organization changed after the formation of the state of Israel. The organization's status was redefined by the Knesset (Israeli parliament) in 1952, making it responsible for immigration (*aliya*) and immigrant assimilation and settlement. The WZO, the Jewish Agency, and the government of Israel again redefined their relationship in 1979, making the Jewish Agency responsible for all issues related to immigration in Israel, while the WZO assumed responsibilities relating to diasporic Jewry.

Richard M. Edwards

See also: British Mandate for Palestine; Herzl, Theodor; Weizmann, Chaim; Zionism

Further Reading

Brenner, Michael. *Zionism: A Brief History*. Trans. Shelley Frisch. Princeton, NJ: M. Wiener, 2003.

Laqueur, Walter. *A History of Zionism*. New York: Holt, Rinehart and Winston, 1972.

Y

Yassin, Sheikh Ahmed

Spiritual leader and cofounder of the militant Palestinian group Hamas. Sheikh Ahmed Yassin was born in 1937 in a village outside Ashkelon in British Mandate Palestine. His family fled to Gaza during the 1948 Arab-Israeli War. At the age of twelve, he suffered a spinal cord injury that left him a quadriplegic. Homeschooled, he became a schoolteacher and popular preacher in Gaza. He married in 1960 and fathered eleven children. He became involved in the Muslim Brotherhood and established an Islamic charity in the early 1970s. He cofounded Hamas in 1987 during the First Intifada, serving as its spiritual leader. Israel jailed Yassin in 1989 but then released him in 1997 as part of a deal with King Husayn of Jordan after Israel's Mossad bungled an assassination attempt on another Hamas leader in Amman.

Hamas gained popularity in part because of its social welfare activities in Gaza and the West Bank, running schools, libraries, and hospitals. It also gained support by actively resisting Israel's occupation. Hamas is deemed a terrorist group by Israel, the United States, and Europe and is responsible for numerous deadly attacks on Israeli civilians, especially during the Second (al-Aqsa) Intifada. While many argue that Sheikh Ahmed Yassin did not directly plan or execute operations, Israeli government officials insist that he was responsible for many attacks. He survived a targeted assignation attempt in September 2003 when Israel dropped a half-ton bomb on a building where Hamas leaders were meeting. In March 2004, Israel succeeded in killing Yassin via a missile strike while exiting a mosque in Gaza City.

Robert C. DiPrizio

See also: Gaza Strip; Hamas

Further Reading

Baconi, Tareq. *Hamas Contained: The Rise and Pacification of Palestinian Resistance.* Stanford, CA: Stanford University Press, 2018.

Hroub, Khaled. *Hamas: A Beginner's Guide.* New York: Pluto Press, 2006.

Yishuv

The prestate Jewish community in Palestine. The Yishuv, which is Hebrew for "settlement," consisted of an ethnically and ideologically diverse group of Zionists (Jews seeking to establish a Jewish state in Palestine), and grew from a relatively small number in the 1880s to 583,000 in 1945. Before 1882, Jews in Palestine concentrated in Hebron, Jerusalem, Safed, and Tiberias. Most had come from various parts of the Ottoman Empire, descendants of Jews expelled from Spain and

Portugal, called *Sephardim*. Many devoted their time to religious studies and held a conservative religious perspective.

The first major wave of Zionists to Palestine in 1882–1891—called the *First Aliyah* (ascension, or "going up")—came primarily from Russia and Ukraine in response to severe persecution. The Second, Third, and Fourth Aliyah also consisted primarily of Ashkenazi Jews from Eastern Europe, many of whom sought to create a socialist state. The Fifth Aliyah (1929–1939) consisted largely of people fleeing Nazi Germany. The Ottomans restricted Jewish migration when they controlled Palestine. The British initially allowed large-scale Zionist migration, but by World War II, they reversed course to placate Arab opinion. Regardless, Jewish migrants found ways around British restrictions.

In addition to the socialist vision of the dominant Labor Party, other segments of the Yishuv promoted a cultural vision in which settlement enabled the promotion of the distinctively Jewish culture. These two groups accommodated the development of a secular state, in contrast to a third, religious perspective: those who saw their settlement as the means to promote a Messianic future. The fourth major ideological current, the Revisionist Party, emphasized developing a muscular, nationalist community capable of self-defense. The socialist, cultural, and revisionist perspectives agreed on the necessity of increasing immigration. All four groups promoted the development of Hebrew as a living language and cultural bond that could bridge the religious versus secular, Ashkenazi versus Sephardim, and traditional versus modern divisions, as well as enabling interethnic communication. By 1948, the Yishuv had created an extensive array of proto-government institutions that became the building blocks of the Israeli state.

Jonathan K. Zartman

See also: Ben-Gurion, David; British Mandate for Palestine; Jewish Agency; Zionism

Further Reading

Edelheit, Abraham J. *The Yishuv in the Shadow of the Holocaust: Zionist Politics and Rescue Aliya, 1933–1939.* Boulder, CO: Westview, 1996.

Weinstock, Nathan. "The Impact of Zionist Colonization on Palestinian Arab Society Before 1948." *Journal of Palestinian Studies* 2, no. 2 (Winter 1973): 49–63.

Yom Kippur War (see Arab-Israeli War, 1973)

Z

Zealots

A radical Jewish sect that resisted Roman occupation. Although the Romans rarely did anything to hamper the Jews of Palestine in the practice of their religion, their religious practices offended many Jews. This included the Zealots, who were not only politically active against Roman rule, but were fundamentalist in their interpretation of the Jewish law. A small faction of them (the Sicarii) became assassins, attacking not only Romans, but also Jews who cooperated with them. Despite these tensions, Jewish uprisings against Roman rule were limited until the appointment of Gessius Florus as procurator for Israel in 67 CE. Florus was unusually corrupt and was tone-deaf to Jewish sensibilities. His high-handed activities, coupled with a division within the Jewish ranks over how to respond, led to the violent Jewish Revolts.

By 70 CE, the Romans had captured Jerusalem and razed much of it. The Zealots continued to hold out in the fortresses at Macherus and Masada. Macherus resisted until its commander, Eleazer ben Jair, was taken prisoner. Eleazer was scourged and prepared for crucifixion within sight of his garrison, which offered its surrender in return for its leader's life. The Romans agreed, but then proceeded to slaughter 1,700 men and boys among the surrendered garrison and sell the women and children into slavery.

According to Josephus, the 1,000 Zealots at Masada resisted to the very end and then committed mass suicide rather than submit to Roman captivity. That story has been challenged by many scholars, who point out that the Zealots were fundamentalists and that one of the greatest sins in the Jewish faith is suicide. Suicide or not, the Roman conquest was costly for the Jews, who suffered 600,000 dead (nearly one-quarter of their population). Perhaps another quarter was sold into slavery.

Paul K. Davis and Allen Lee Hamilton

See also: Diaspora, Jewish; Jewish Revolts; Masada; Roman Conquest of Judea

Further Reading

Graetz, Heinrich, *History of the Jews,* Vol. II, 1893.

Soggin, J. Alberto. *A History of Ancient Israel,* trans. by John Bowden. Philadelphia: Westminster Press, 1984.

Yadin, Yigael. *Masada: Herod's Fortress and the Zealots' Last Stand.* New York: Random House, 1966.

Zionism

A Jewish national movement. Zionism holds that Jews constitute a nation, with the right to self-determination. As a political movement, it supports the creation of a homeland for the Jewish people. Zionism began in the late nineteenth century, arising out of the general rise of nationalism in Europe and increased anti-Semitism. It soon became a well-organized and -funded settlement movement focused on Palestine, which many Jews believed was the ancient homeland granted them by God. Zionism eventually led to the formation of the state of Israel and continues to affect politics in Israel.

The word *Zionism* comes from *Zion*, the name of a hill in Jerusalem. The term was first used in 1890 by the Austrian Jewish writer Nathan Birnbaum. Zionists found justification for their movement in the Old Testament account of God giving the land of Israel to the Israelites in perpetuity, and from the longstanding belief of diaspora Jews that they would return to the Holy Land one day. Since the sixth century BCE, Jews had looked at the Holy Land as their own property, a homeland that they had left temporarily but still belonged to them.

Zionism also grew out of the rise of nationalism in the nineteenth century, as various European nations developed national identities and political systems. Many Jews at that time had a secular view of their Judaism; they abandoned their religious practices but embraced the concept of Jews as a people and a nation that deserved a homeland. The growing specter of anti-Semitism persuaded many Jews that they would be safer in a state of their own.

Although other locations were suggested, Palestine quickly became the focus of most Zionists. In 1862, Moses Hess wrote *Rome and Jerusalem*, which urged Jews to settle in Palestine in an agrarian socialist state. Hess and other writers such as Ber Borochov and Nahum Syrkin believed that Jews had become weak and

Theodor Herzl speaks at the Second Zionist Congress in Basel, Switzerland. One of the founding fathers of the modern Zionism, Herzl organized the first Zionist Congress a year earlier which formed the World Zionist Organization. (Singer, Isadore, ed. *The Jewish Encyclopedia*, 1901)

downtrodden as a result of their centuries of working as merchants and pawnbrokers, and they needed to redeem themselves through healthful outdoor labor and socialism. Zionism and socialism often went hand in hand in the late 1800s and early 1900s. Many Jews looked at the creation of a Jewish state as their opportunity to build an ideal society—a religious community founded on the principles of socialism. This belief coalesced in a movement known as *Labor Zionism,* which held that the creation of a Jewish state must necessarily be part of a class struggle in which Jews would become agriculturists, living on collective socialist farms known as *kibbutzim.*

In the late 1870s through 1882, some Russian Jews went to Palestine (then a part of the Ottoman Empire) to establish small farms in a migration wave that became known as the *First Aliya.* Beginning in 1882, thousands of Russian Jews emigrated to Palestine, fleeing pogroms and Tsar Alexander III's 1882 anti-Semitic May Laws. These settlers called themselves *Biluim* (singular *Bilu*), after a verse from the Book of Isaiah. Their goal was to establish a Jewish national homeland in the land they called *Israel.* These first settlers nearly starved during their attempt to support themselves on land without adequate fresh water, and many of them left. Baron Edmond James de Rothschild provided the remaining settlers with money to establish a winery, which became successful in a few years' time. The settlers also used his money to found the town of Zichron Yaakov.

In 1894, the Dreyfus Affair persuaded European Jews that anti-Semitism was a growing problem, even in the supposedly enlightened Western European nations such as France. Theodor Herzl, an Austrian journalist, became a staunch supporter of Zionism after this incident. He wrote *Der Judenstaat* (The Jewish State) in 1896, in which he stated that the Jews must create their own homeland, either in Palestine or in Argentina. The following year, he organized the First Zionist Congress in Switzerland, which created the Zionist Organization, the goal of which was to raise money and buy land in Palestine so that Jews could settle there. Herzl was the group's first president. The organization spent the next fifty-two years purchasing land and creating governmental procedures for the new Israeli state. It was renamed the World Zionist Organization (WZO) in 1960.

All Jews were allowed to join the Zionist Organization. People from countries all over the world came to the group's congresses, which were held every two years between 1897 and 1946. Members assembled delegations according to ideology instead of geographic origin. Some Zionists were ardent socialists or communists. Many were vehemently secular, or even atheists, while others had more religious leanings. The Zionist Organization organized the Jewish Colonial Trust to handle financial matters. The Jewish National Fund (JNF), created in 1901, took responsibility for purchasing land. The Anglo-Palestine Bank, established in 1903, provided financial services for settlers. Gradually, the group created an infrastructure for the Jewish homeland that made the process of settling in Palestine easier than it had been in the 1800s.

In the early years of the twentieth century, Zionists debated whether Palestine was the ideal location for the Jewish homeland. In 1903, the British government proposed a Jewish homeland in modern Kenya, called the British Uganda Program. Herzl suggested this to the Sixth Zionist Congress as a temporary safe haven for

Russian Jews, but the Russian Jews themselves disliked the idea, and the Seventh Zionist Congress abandoned it in 1905. The Jewish Territorialist Organization wanted to create a Jewish homeland wherever it could, but it disbanded in 1917. In the 1930s, the Soviet Union created a Jewish Autonomous Republic in the Far East, but few Jews wanted to move there. For the most part, Palestine remained the sole focus of the Zionist movement.

During the early 1900s, many small groups of settlers went to Palestine. Many arrived there after the 1905 Revolution in Russia. Leaders such as Joseph Baratz and other settlers pooled their money, added to it contributions from Jews all over the world, and founded kibbutzim on plots of land that they lived on and farmed collectively. By 1914, there were kibbutzim throughout Palestine. Residents shared all work and all profits and governed themselves democratically.

Cultural Zionists looked on the settlement movement as an opportunity to create a unique Jewish culture. Many Jews were quite critical of Jewish culture in the late nineteenth century, which they saw as downtrodden and weak after centuries of diaspora. Some Zionist thinkers such as Asher Ginsberg and Eliezer Ben Yehudah thought that Palestine would be the ideal place to revive the Hebrew language and culture, allowing Jews to replace their Germanic Yiddish language and speak to one another in a uniquely Jewish language that would unite diverse groups of Jews. Herzl wanted German to be the official language of Palestine, but most settlers and Zionists overwhelmingly supported the use of Hebrew. Tel Aviv, founded in 1909, was the first city to make Hebrew its official language.

The United Kingdom was an important ally in the creation of the Jewish state. Jews were generally made welcome in Britain in the early twentieth century, and many British people appreciated Jewish culture. The British government also sought to mobilize the support of Jews for the war effort, and in 1917, British foreign secretary Arthur Balfour issued a statement (known as the Balfour Declaration) in favor of establishing a Jewish homeland in Palestine.

The Balfour Declaration said that a Jewish homeland should not harm the civil rights of non-Jewish people already living in Palestine. Zionists realized that the Muslim Arabs already living in Palestine would become a source of conflict, but many of them chose to ignore the issue or to suggest that Jewish immigration could only benefit the current residents. Zionist leaders such as Israel Zangwill concocted slogans such as "A land without a people, for a people without a land," which deliberately glossed over the presence of people already on the land in question.

In the early days of settlement (the 1880s and earlier), Arabs did not object to the incursion of Jews. The first Jewish settlers had been unable to farm successfully, so they ended up hiring Arab laborers to work their farms. In the 1890s, however, as Arabs began to realize what the Zionists intended, they grew concerned about losing their farmland and water. The socialist agrarian settlers of the early 1900s did not employ Arabs because their whole raison d'etre was to get Jews working the land themselves. This, along with the Balfour Declaration and the partitioning of Palestine in 1918, made Palestinian Arabs feel threatened. Palestinian Arabs began agitating for a state of their own around this time. Some Zionists suggested that Palestinian Arabs should either be expelled from the country or forced to accept the Jewish presence through armed aggression.

In the early 1920s, the Zionist Organization decided that Jewish settlement in Palestine would be socialist, having reached the conclusion that socialism was the only way to distribute available economic resources among a rapidly growing group of Jewish immigrants. During the 1920s, David Ben-Gurion was one of the leaders of the Histadrut, the Jewish Labor Zionist trade union that dominated Jewish Palestine in prenational days. He publicly opposed the use of force against Arabs, claiming that it would be unnecessary because Arabs would soon decide that Zionism was good for them. In private, however, he said that conflict was inevitable because Arabs would never accept Zionist settlement. In the late 1930s, Ben-Gurion and the Labor Zionists supported the idea of a Jewish state with no Arabs in it, the existing Arabs having been removed forcibly.

Zionism became somewhat more popular after the creation of the British Mandate over Palestine in 1922. Increasing numbers of Jews moved to Palestine, as the Zionist Organization and other Zionist groups raised money and lobbied the British government not to allow the Palestinian Arabs to create their own state. Palestinian nationalism also increased during this time, as the Arabs saw their land and livelihood increasingly threatened by Jewish newcomers.

Not all Jews supported the Zionist movement. Some socialist Jews disliked the idea of a state because it smacked of unsocialistic nationalism. Communist Jews in Russia also rejected the idea of a Jewish state in Palestine. Many Jews believed that there was no need for a Jewish homeland because Jews could live perfectly well in other nations, such as the United States. American Jews argued that the United States was already the Jewish homeland. Many religious Jews rejected Zionism too, insisting that only God could return them to the Promised Land.

All these arguments changed after Adolf Hitler came to power in 1933 in Germany. The United States, formerly so welcoming to Jews, closed its doors to Jewish immigrants. Increasing numbers of Jews moved to Palestine in the 1930s, but this angered Palestinian Arabs. After an Arab uprising that lasted from 1936–1939, the British government restricted Jewish immigration to Palestine. Jews living there armed themselves and began fighting the Arabs and launching attacks on British targets.

After World War II, when news of the Holocaust reached the world, Zionism experienced a huge upsurge of popularity and support. The United States was one of the strongest backers of the formation of a Jewish state in Palestine. Jews themselves were almost unanimous in their support for the creation of Israel. In 1947, the United Nations (UN) voted to create two states within Palestine, one Arab and one Jewish, with Jerusalem as a shared possession. The Jewish leaders in Palestine declared the independent state of Israel on May 14, 1948.

Once the Jewish homeland was established, Israeli leaders turned their attention to expelling Arab agitators, welcoming a new influx of Jewish settlers, and organizing the Israel Defense Forces (IDF). Since Israel captured territory from its Arab neighbors, much of Israeli politics have been marked by competition between those who think Zionism's success requires control of Eretz Israel (the lands of biblical Israel) and those who disagree. Some critics of Zionism contend that it is a racist form of nationalism, while others insist that Jews have the right to self-determination like all other nations.

Amy Hackney Blackwell

See also: Arab-Israeli War, 1948; Arab-Israeli War, 1967; Arab-Jewish Communal War, 1947; Balfour Declaration; British Mandate for Palestine; Eretz Israel; Israel; Israeli Occupations; Israelis; Judea and Samaria; Settlements

Further Reading

Hertzberg, Arthur, ed. *The Zionist Idea: A Historical Analysis and Reader*. Philadelphia: Jewish Publication Society, 1997.

Herzl, Theodor. *The Jewish State*. Mineola, NY: Dover Publications, 1989.

Laqueur, Walter. *A History of Zionism: From the French Revolution to the Establishment of the State of Israel*. Reprint ed. New York: Schocken, 2003.

Pappe, Ilan. *A History of Modern Palestine: One Land, Two Peoples*. Cambridge: Cambridge University Press, 2003.

Rose, John. *The Myths of Zionism*. London: Pluto Press, 2004.

Zionist Organization of America (ZOA)

A pro-Zionist association founded in 1897. Headquartered in New York City, the Zionist Organization of America (ZOA) currently has a paid membership of more than 25,000 people and maintains chapter offices in numerous cities around the country from which it conducts its lobbying efforts. Billed as the oldest Zionist organization in the United States, the ZOA has been affiliated with a sister organization, Hadassah (Women's Zionist Organization of America).

The ZOA was at the vanguard of the Zionist movement in the United States. Among its many prominent leaders was U.S. Supreme Court justice Louis D. Brandeis. The ZOA also served as the principal American liaison to the World Zionist Organization (WZO). Prior to the establishment of Israel in May 1948, the ZOA helped rally public support for Israel and maintained close contacts with the U.S. Congress and the executive branch to keep the pressure on for the creation of a Jewish homeland.

Today, the ZOA's mission is more diverse. It sponsors educational and public affairs activities aimed at strengthening the bond between the United States and Israel. The ZOA works to promote pro-Israeli legislation in Congress and combat anti-Jewish bias and anti-Semitism in the media, on college campuses, and even in instructional textbooks. Masada, the youth arm of the ZOA, funds the largest program in the country that sends Jewish youths to Israel for educational purposes.

The organization also funds cultural and educational programs throughout Israel. In Tel Aviv, the ZOA House is among the top cultural centers in the city. Near Ashkelon, Israel, the ZOA has established a large campus for the education and vocational training of new immigrants to Israel.

In recent years, the ZOA has built its Campus Activism Network and Center for Law and Justice, which promotes activism and Jewish causes via the U.S. court system. It also publishes a wide array of newsletters, reports, and periodicals.

The ZOA openly criticized President Barack Obama's policies toward Israel and actively lobbied Congress to impose tighter sanctions on Iran over its alleged nuclear program. The organization subsequently voiced its great dismay with the July 2015 nuclear deal with Iran, terming it a "truly terrible nuclear agreement." The ZOA encouraged President Donald Trump to scuttle the deal, which he did in 2018. It also supported Trump's recognition of Israeli claims of sovereignty over Jerusalem and the Golan Heights.

Paul G. Pierpaoli Jr.

See also: U.S. Aid to Israel; Zionism

Further Reading

Cohen, Naomi W. *The Americanization of Zionism, 1897–1948*. Waltham, MA: Brandeis University Press, 2003.

Klieman, Aaron S. *From Many, One: The Zionist Organization of America*. London: Routledge, 1991.

Bibliography

Abunimah, Ali. *The Battle for Justice in Palestine*. Chicago: Haymarket Books, 2014.

Abunimah, Ali. *One Country: A Bold Proposal to End the Israeli-Palestinian Impasse*. New York: Metropolitan Books, 2006.

Adwan, Sami, Dan Bar-On, Eyal Naveth, and the Peace Research Institute in the Middle East, eds. *Side by Side: Parallel Histories of Israel–Palestine*. New York: New Press, 2012.

Ahlstrom, Gosta W. *The History of Ancient Palestine*. Minneapolis: Fortress Press, 1993.

Alam, M. Shahid. *Israeli Exceptionalism: The Destabilizing Logic of Zionism*. New York: Palgrave Macmillan, 2010.

Aly, Abdel Monem Said, Shai Feldman, and Khalil Shikaki. *Arabs and Israelis: Conflict and Peacemaking in the Middle East*. New York: Palgrave, 2013.

Armstrong, Karen. *Holy War: The Crusades and Their Impact on Today's World*. New York: Anchor Books, 2001.

Armstrong, Karen. *Jerusalem: One City, Three Faiths*. New York: Ballentine Books, 1996.

Asbridge, Thomas. *The Crusades: The Authoritative History of the War for the Holy Land*. New York: Ecco, 2010.

Baltzer, Anna. *Witness in Palestine: A Jewish-American Woman in the Occupied Territories*. Boulder, Colorado: Paradigm Publishers, 2007.

Bard, Mitchell G. *Will Israel Survive?* New York: Palgrave Macmillan, 2007.

Barghouti, Omar. *Boycott, Divestment, Sanctions: The Global Struggle for Palestinian Rights*. Chicago: Haymarket Books, 2011.

Beinart, Peter. *The Crisis of Zionism*. New York: Picador, 2012.

Ben-Ami, Shlomo. *Scars of War, Wounds of Peace: The Israeli–Arab Tragedy*. New York: Oxford University Press, 2006.

Ben-Eliezer, Uri. *War over Peace: One Hundred Years of Israel's Militaristic Nationalism*. Berkeley: University of Californian Press, 2019.

Benvenisti, Meron. *City of Stone: The Hidden History of Jerusalem*. Berkeley: University of California Press, 1996.

Bickerton, Ian J., and Carla L. Klausner. *A Concise History of the Arab–Israeli Conflict*. 8th ed. New York: Routledge, 2018.

Boyle, Francis Anthony. *Palestine, Palestinians, and International Law*. Atlanta: Clarity, 2003.

Bregman, Ahron. *Elusive Peace: How the Holy Land Defeated America*. New York: Penguin Books, 2005.
Caplan, Neil. *The Israel–Palestine Conflict: Contested Histories*. New Jersey: John Wiley & Sons, 2011.
Cattan, Henry. *The Palestine Question*. London: Saqi Books, 2000.
Chomsky, Noam. *The Fateful Triangle: The United States, Israel, and the Palestinians*. Rev. ed. Boston: South End Press, 1999.
Chomsky, Noam, and Ilan Pappé. *On Palestine*. Chicago: Haymarket Books, 2015.
Cypel, Sylvain. *Walled: Israeli Society at an Impasse*. New York: Other Press, 2007.
Danahar, Paul. *The New Middle East: The World After the Arab Spring*. New York: Bloomsbury Press, 2015.
Dawson, Ashley. *Against Apartheid: The Case for Boycotting Israeli Universities*. Chicago: Haymarket Books, 2015.
Dershowitz, Alan. *The Case for Israel*. New York: John Wiley & Sons, 2004.
Dershowitz, Alan. *The Case Against Israel's Enemies: Exposing Jimmy Carter and Others Who Stand in the Way of Peace*. New Jersey: John Wiley and Sons, 2008.
Dowty, Alan. *Israel/Palestine*. 4th ed. Cambridge, UK: Polity Press, 2017.
Enderlin, Charles. *Shattered Dreams: The Failure of the Peace Process in the Middle East, 1995–2002*. New York: Other Press, 2003.
Finkelstein, Norman. *Beyond Chutzpah: On the Misuse of Anti-Semitism and the Abuse of History*. Berkeley: University of California Press, 2005.
Finkelstein, Norman. *Image and Reality of the Israel–Palestine Conflict*. 2nd ed. Brooklyn: Verso, 2003.
Friedman, Thomas L. *From Beirut to Jerusalem*. New York: Anchor, 1990.
Fromkin, David. *A Peace to End All Peace: The Fall of the Ottoman Empire and the Creation of the Modern Middle East*. 20th anniversary ed. New York: Henry Holt Company, 2009.
Gabbay, Shaul M., and Kazak, Amin. *One Land: Two Stories*. New York: Livingston Publishing House, 2012.
Gelvin, James L. *The Israel–Palestine Conflict: One Hundred Years of War*. 3rd ed. Cambridge: Cambridge University Press, 2014.
Gerner, Deborah J. *One Land, Two Peoples: The Conflict over Palestine*. 2nd ed. Boulder, CO: Westview Press, 1994.
Gil, Moshe. *A History of Palestine 634–1099*. Cambridge: Cambridge University Press, 1997.
Glick, Caroline. *The Israeli Solution: A One-State Plan for Peace in the Middle East*. New York: Crown Forum, 2014.
Goldschmidt, Arthur, Jr., and Lawrence Davidson. *A Concise History of the Middle East*. 8th ed. Boulder, CO: Westview Press, 2006.
Gordon, Neve. *Israel's Occupation*. Berkeley: University of California Press, 2008.
Grinberg, Lev Luis. *Movements of Resistance: Politics, Economy and Society in Israel/Palestine 1931–2013*. Boston: Academic Studies Press, 2014.
Guyatt, Nicholes. *The Absence of Peace: Understanding the Israeli–Palestinian Conflict*. London and New York: Zed Books, 2001.
Hadawi, Sami. *Bitter Harvest: A Modern History of Palestine*. New York: Olive Branch Press, 1989.

Hertzberg, Arthur, ed. *The Zionist Idea: A Historical Analysis and Reader*. Philadelphia: Jewish Publication Society, 1997.

Hirst, David. *The Gun and the Olive Branch*. 3rd ed. London: Faber and Faber, 2003.

Hourani, Albert. *A History of the Arab Peoples: With a New Afterword*. Boston: Belknap Press, 2010.

Karmi, Ghada. *Married to Another Man: Israel's Dilemma in Palestine*. London: Pluto Press, 2007.

Karsh, Efraim. *Arafat's War: The Man and His Battle for Israeli Conquest*. New York: Grove Press, 2003.

Kennedy, Hugh. *The Great Arab Conquests: How the Spread of Islam Changed the World We Live In*. Boston: Da Capo Press, 2007.

Khalidi, Rashid. *Palestinian Identity: The Construction of Modern National Consciousness*. New York: Columbia University Press, 2010.

Kimmerling, Baruch, and Joel S. Migdal. *The Palestinian People: A History*. Cambridge, MA: Harvard University Press, 2003.

Kovel, Joel. *Overcoming Zionism: Creating a Single Democratic State in Israel/Palestine*. London: Pluto Press, 2007.

Lustick, Ian S. *For the Land and the Lord: Jewish Fundamentalism in Israel*. Washington, DC: Council on Foreign Relations, 1988.

Makdisi, Saree. *Palestine Inside Out: An Everyday Occupation*. London: W. W. Norton and Co., 2010.

Masahla, Nur. *Palestine: A Four Thousand Year History*. London: Zed Books, 2018.

Mearsheimer, John J., and Stephen M. Walt. *The Israel Lobby and U.S. Foreign Policy*. New York: Farrar, Straus and Giroux, 2007.

Merrill, Eugene H. *Kingdom of Priests: A History of Old Testament Israel*. 2nd ed. Grand Rapids, MI: Baker, 2008.

Miller, Aaron David. *The Much Too Promised Land: America's Elusive Search for Arab-Israeli Peace*. New York: Bantam, 2008.

Moore, Megan Bishop, and Brad E. Kelle. *Biblical History and Israel's Past*. Grand Rapids, MI: Eerdmans, 2011.

Morris, Benny. *1948: A History of the First Arab-Israeli War*. New Haven, CT: Yale University Press, 2008.

Morris, Benny. *Righteous Victims: A History of the Zionist–Arab Conflict, 1881–2001*. New York: Vintage Books, 2001.

Nelson, Cary R., ed. *Dreams Deferred: A Concise Guide to the Israeli-Palestinian Conflict and the Movement to Boycott Israel*. Bloomington: Indiana University Press, 2016.

Ochsenwald, William, and Sydney Nettleton Fisher. *The Middle East: A History*. 6th ed. New York: McGraw-Hill, 2004.

Oren, Michael B. *Six Days of War: June 1967 and the Making of the Modern Middle East*. Oxford: Oxford University Press, 2002.

Pappé, Ilan. *The Biggest Prison on Earth: A History of the Occupied Territories*. London: One World Publications, 2017.

Pappé, Ilan. *The Ethnic Cleansing of Palestine*. 2nd ed. London: One World Publishing, 2006.

Pappé, Ilan. *A History of Modern Palestine: One Nation, Two Peoples*. 2nd ed. Cambridge: Cambridge University Press, 2006.

Quandt, William B. *Peace Process: American Diplomacy and the Arab-Israeli Conflict Since 1967.* 3rd ed. Washington, DC: Brookings Institution Press, 2005.

Quandt, William B. *Camp David: Peacemaking and Politics.* Washington, DC: Brookings Institution Press, 2016.

Rosenthal, Donna. *The Israelis: Ordinary People in an Extraordinary Land.* New York: Free Press, 2005.

Ross, Dennis. *The Missing Peace: The Inside Story of the Fight for Middle East Peace.* New York: Farrar, Straus and Giroux, 2005.

Rotberg, Robert I., ed. *Israeli and Palestinian Narratives of Conflict: History's Double Helix.* Bloomington: Indiana University Press, 2006.

Rubin, Barry M. *Israel: An Introduction.* New Haven, CT: Yale University Press, 2012.

Sachar, Howard M. *A History of Israel: From the Rise of Zionism to Our Time.* 3rd ed. New York: Knopf, 2007.

Said, Edward W. *The Question of Palestine.* New York: Vintage Books, 1992.

Salinas, Moises. *Planting Hatred, Sowing Pain: The Psychology of the Israeli–Palestinian Conflict.* Westport, CT: Praeger Publishers, 2007.

Sand, Shlomo. *The Invention of the Jewish People.* London: Verso, 2009.

Segev, Tom. *One Palestine, Complete: Jews and Arabs Under the British Mandate.* New York: Henry Holt and Company, 2000.

Shapira, Anita. *Israel: A History.* Waltham, MA: Brandeis University Press, 2012.

Sharif, Bassam Abu. *Arafat and the Dream of Palestine: An Insider's Account.* New York: St. Martin's Press, 2009.

Shlaim, Avi. *The Iron Wall: Israel and the Arab World.* London: Penguin Books, 2000.

Smith, Charles D. *Palestine and the Arab–Israeli Conflict: A History with Documents.* 9th ed. New York: Bedford/St. Martin's Press, 2017.

Spangler, Eve. *Understanding Israel/Palestine: Race, Nation, and Human Rights in the Conflict.* Boston: Sense Publishers, 2015.

Swisher, Clayton E. *The Truth About Camp David.* New York: Nation Books, 2004.

Tauber, Eliezer. *The Arab Movements in World War I.* London: Frank Cass, 1993.

Terry, Janice. *U.S. Foreign Policy in the Middle East: The Role of Lobbies and Special Interest Groups.* London: Pluto, 2005.

Tessler, Mark. *A History of the Israeli–Palestinian Conflict.* 2nd ed. Bloomington: Indiana University Press, 2009.

Thrall, Nathan. *The Only Language They Understand: Forcing Compromise in Israel and Palestine.* New York: Metropolitan Books, 2017.

Tilley, Virginia. *The One-State Solution.* Ann Arbor: University of Michigan Press, 2005.

Wasserstein, Bernard. *Israelis and Palestinians.* New Haven, CT: Yale University Press, 2003.

White, Ben. *Cracks in the Wall: Beyond Apartheid in Palestine/Israel.* London: Pluto Press 2018.

Worth, Robert F. *A Rage for Order: The Middle East in Turmoil, from Tahrir Square to ISIS.* New York: Farrar, Straus and Giroux, 2016.

About the Editor and Contributor List

EDITOR

ROBERT C. DIPRIZIO is an associate professor at the U.S. Air Force's Air Command and Staff College at Maxwell Air Force Base, Alabama, where he teaches courses on international security and Arab-Israeli conflict. Dr. DiPrizio is the author of numerous articles, as well as the book *Armed Humanitarians: U.S. Interventions from Northern Iraq to Kosovo* (2002).

CONTRIBUTORS

Stephen E. Atkins
Adjunct Professor of History
Texas A&M University

Dr. Philipp O. Amour
Assistant Professor, International
 Relations and Middle East Studies
Sakarya University, Turkey

Ralph Martin Baker
Independent Scholar

Donna Bassett
Senior Manager
The Information Project

Walter F. Bell
Reference Librarian
Aurora University

Amy Hackney Blackwell
Independent Scholar

**Lieutenant Colonel
Sean N. Blas**
Air Command and Staff College
U.S. Air Force

Dr. Sean P. Braniff
Assistant Professor of International
 Security Studies
Air War College
U.S. Air Force

Walter Boyne
Independent Scholar

Jessica Britt
Independent Scholar

Dr. Stefan Brooks
Professor of International Relations
 and Diplomacy
Norwich University

Dr. Dino E. Buenviaje
Visiting Assistant Professor
Riverside City College

Dr. Sergio Catignani
Senior Lecturer in Security and
    Strategic Studies
University of Exeter, United
    Kingdom

Dr. Paul K. Davis
Military Historian

Thomas E. Davis
Independent Scholar

Dr. Robert C. DiPrizio
Associate Professor of International
    Security Studies
Air Command and Staff College
U.S. Air Force

Tom Dowling
Independent Scholar

Dr. Richard M. Edwards
Senior Lecturer
University of Wisconsin Colleges

Dr. Chuck Fahrer
Professor of Geography
Georgia College and State University

Lieutenant Colonel Hugh Gardenier
Air Command and Staff College
U.S. Air Force

Brent Geary
Ohio University

Christina Girod
Independent Scholar

Dr. Maia Carter Hallward
Associate Professor
Kennesaw State University

Allen Lee Hamilton
Professor of Texas and American
    History
St. Phillip's College

Dr. Kristin Hissong
Assistant Professor of Regional and
    Cultural Studies
Air Force Culture and Language
    Center
Air University

Martin Hoch
Independent Scholar

Dr. Jonathan M. House
Professor Emeritus of Military
    History
U.S. Army Command and General
    Staff College

Dr. Harry Hueston
Professor of Criminal Justice
West Texas A&M University

Rana Kobeissi
Katholieke Universiteit Leuven,
    Belgium

Keith A. Leitich
Instructor
North Seattle Community College

Major David R. Leonard
Instructor
Air Command and Staff College
U.S. Air Force

Dr. Yaacov Lev
Professor of Middle Eastern
    Studies
Bar-Ilan University

David Levinson
President
Norwalk Community College

Dr. Paul J. Magnarella
Professor and Director of Peace and Justice Studies
Warren Wilson College

Dr. Eugene H. Merrill
Distinguished Professor Emeritus of Old Testament Interpretation
Southern Baptist Theological Seminary

Gregory Morgan
University of Southern Mississippi

Dr. Deonna Neal
Chair, Department of Leadership, Ethics, and the Profession of Arms
Air University
U.S. Air Force

Dr. Andrew Nichols
Adjunct Lecturer of Classics
University of Florida

Dr. Jaime Ramón Olivares
Professor of History
Houston Community College–Central

Dr. Peter Overlack
Independent Scholar

Brian Parkinson
Chair, Department of History
Georgia Southwestern State University

Dr. Paul G. Pierpaoli Jr.
Fellow
Military History, ABC-CLIO

Dr. John David Rausch Jr.
Teel Bivins Professor of Political Science
West Texas A&M University

Dr. Stanley Sandler
Command Historian
U.S. Army's Special Operations Command

Dr. Emily Schneider
Visiting Assistant Professor
Colorado College

Paul J. Smith
Professor, National Security Affairs
U.S. Naval War College

Dr. Daniel E. Spector
Historian
U.S. Army Chemical Corps

Dr. Paul J. Springer
Full Professor of Comparative Military Studies
Chair, Department of Research
Air Command and Staff College
U.S. Air Force

Dr. Stephen K. Stein
Associate Professor
Department of History
University of Memphis

Dr. Nancy Stockdale
Associate Professor
Department of History
University of North Texas

Dr. Ghada Hashem Talhami
D. K. Pearson Professor of Politics, Emerita
Lake Forest College

Dr. Moshe Terdiman
Director, Islam in Africa Project
Senior Research Fellow, PRISM
Gloria Center, IDC

Dr. Tal Tovy
Assistant Professor
Bar-Ilan University

Dr. Spencer C. Tucker
Senior Fellow
Military History, ABC-CLIO

Dallace W. Unger Jr.
Independent Scholar

Dr. Bryan Vizzini
Professor of History
West Texas A&M University

Rod Vosburgh
Independent Scholar

Dr. James Wald
Associate Professor of History
Hampshire College

Tim J. Watts
Humanities Librarian
Kansas State University

Dr. James H. Willbanks
Director
Department of Military History
U.S. Army Command and General
    Staff College, Fort Leavenworth

Dr. David T. Zabecki
Major General
Army of the United States,
    Retired

Dr. Jonathan K. Zartman
Associate Professor of
    Security Studies
Air Command and Staff College
U.S. Air Force

Dr. Sherifa Zuhur
Research Professor of Islamic and
    Regional Studies
U.S. Army War College, Strategic
    Studies Institute

Dr. Stephen Zunes
Professor
University of San Francisco

Index

Abbas, Mahmoud, **1–2**
    and Fatah, 104, 110, 123, 246, 248–249
    and the Palestine Liberation
        Organization, 104, 246, 248–249
    and the Palestinian Authority, 1–2, 86,
        101, 104, 110–111, 117, 123, 125, 144,
        246, 248–249, 250, 256, 309, 323
    and the Palestinian National Council,
        256
Abdullah (Crown Prince of Saudi Arabia),
    144
Abdullah I (King of Jordan), 16, 35, 94,
    138, 185, 186, 217
    assassination of, 139, 185, 259
Abdullah II (King of Jordan), **2**, 39, 42,
    186, 323
Abraham, 99, 102, 127, 130, 150, 170, 187,
    207, 222
Absentee landlords, **3**
Abu Abbas (Muhammad Zaidan), 242
Abu Bakr, 15
Abu Nidal, 207, 254
Abu Sirhan, Omar, 300
Abu Talib, 222
Achille Lauro, 242
Actium, Battle of, 132
Adalah, **4**
Agriculture, 326
Ahdut Ha'avodah, 200
Airline hijackings, 62, 90, 100, 120, 139,
    224, 244, 252–254, 272
Al-Aqsa Intifada. *See* Intifada, Second
Al-Aqsa Martyrs Brigades, **4–5**, 55, 103,
    301
Al-Aqsa Mosque, xv, 5, 76, 143, 149,
    176, 177, 222, 266. *See also* Haram
    al-Sharif/Temple Mount
Al-Awda, Abd al-Aziz, 254
Alawites, 38, 39, 48, 149

Alexander II (Czar), 6
Alexander III (Tsar), 336
Alexander the Great, 189
Alexandra Salome, 279
Alexius I Comnenus, 82
Al-Fail, Qai, 284–285
Ali (King of Transjordan), 35, 139
Ali (son-in-law of Prophet), 148
Al-Ibrahimi mosque, 130
Aliya, **5–8**
    First Aliya, 6–7, 181, 331, 333, 336
    Second Aliya, 6–7, 307, 333
    Third Aliya, 7, 333
    Fourth Aliya, 7, 333
    Fifth Aliya, 7, 333
Aliya Bet, **8**, 122
Al-Kataeb, 208
Allāh, al-'Āḍid li-Dīn (Fatimid caliph), 284
Allenby, Edmund, 35, 175, 182, 203
Allon, Yigal, 8–9, 263
Allon Plan, **8–9**
Al-Mustaqbal party, 55, 104
Allon Plan, 289
Al-Saiqa, 243
Altalena, 156
Amal Party, 135
Aman, 201
Amelius Scaurus, 279
Amenhotep III, 99
American Christian Palestine Committee
    (ACPC), 12
American Friends Service Committee, 65
American Israel Public Affairs Committee
    (AIPAC), **9–11**, 273
American Jewish Congress (AJC), **11–12**
American Palestine Committee (APC),
    12–13
American-Arab Anti-Discrimination
    Committee, 179

Amir, Yigal, 119, 276
Anatolia, 33
Anglo-Palestine Bank, 331
Antiochus Strategos, 270
Antipater of Idumea, 132, 280
Anti-Semitism, xvi, 6, 7, 35, 39, 133, 174, 179, 231, 271, 295, 335, 339
Aoun, Michel, 136
Arab boycott of Israel, **13**, 32
Arab Higher Committee (AHC), **14**, 70, 116, 311
Arab Higher Front, 14
Arab League, **31–32**
   and the Arab Higher Committee (AHC), 14
   and the Arab Peace Plan, 32, 144
   and the Arab-Israeli War, 1948, 16
   Ashrawi as media commissioner for, 47
   and the boycott of Israel, 13, 32
   Casablanca Protocol, 256
   Egypt's expulsion from, 73, 98
   Egypt's involvement in, 96
   and the Holy War Army, 138
   and the Khartoum Resolution, 193
   media commissioner for, 47
   opposition to Iraq's invasion of Kuwait, 221
   opposition to partition, 69
   Palestine as member of, 239
   peacekeeping in Lebanon, 49
   and the PLO, 32, 243, 245
   rejection of plan to share water rights, 326
   and the United State of Palestine, 16
   See also Arab Higher Committee (AHC)
Arab-Islamic conquest of Palestine, **14–15**
Arab-Israeli conflict
   beginning of, xv–xvi
   following Israel's independence, xvi
   in the 1980s, xvi
Arab-Israeli War, 1948, xvi, **15–19**, 70, 109, 115, 137, 175, 225–226, 277, 303, 314
Arab-Israeli War, 1956, **19–20**, 97
Arab-Israeli War, 1967, xvi, **20–24**, 114, 118, 120, 151, 185, 220, 227, 238, 241, 277, 318, 321, 324
Arab-Israeli War, 1973, **24–28**, 97–98, 151, 178, 217, 220, 316, 321. *See also* Operation Nickel Grass

Arab-Jewish clashes in Palestine, Pre-1947, **28–30**
Arab-Jewish Communal War, 1947, xvi, **30–31**, 70, 137, 276, 313
Arab Legion, 117
Arab Liberation Army (ALA), 17, 18, 30, 299, 303
Arab Liberation Front, 243
Arab Nationalist Movement (ANM), 120
Arab Peace Plan, **32–33**, 101
Arab Revolt, 1916, 14, **33–35**, 138, 185, 203, 302
Arab Revolt, 1936, 14, 15, 29, **35–37**, 68, 116, 121, 122, 131, 146, 156, 225, 261, 274, 302. *See also* British Mandate for Palestine
Arabs
   Christian, 148
   exodus from Tel Aviv, 307
   expulsion from Lydda and Ramle, 272
   in Hebron, 131
   in Israel, 167–168
   in Palestine, 67, 68–69, 92, 262
   Palestinian, 337–338
   See also Palestinians
Arab Spring, **37–38**
   in Bahrain, 38
   in Egypt, 38, 41, 98, 186, 221
   in Jordan, 2, 38, 42, 186
   in Kuwait, 38
   in Libya, 38, 186
   in Oman, 38
   in Palestine, 38, 41
   in Saudi Arabia, 38
   in Syria, 38, 40, 42, 48, 186, 304
   in Tunisia, 37
Arab Spring, effects on Israel, **38–41**
Arab Spring, effects on Palestine, **41–43**
Arab Summit (1974), 244
Arafat, Yasser, **43–46**
   and Abbas, 1, 104, 144, 248, 256
   and the Camp David Summit, 73–74, 153, 246, 322
   campaign against, 143–144
   death of, 45–46, 86, 144, 246, 248, 250, 261
   and Fatah, 103, 104, 124, 224, 243
   Israeli campaign against, 143–144
   Israeli negotiations with, 265
   at the Madrid Conference, 45, 245
   and the Munich Olympics, 223
   Nobel Peace Prize, 142, 275, 322

and the Oslo Accords, 94, 103, 142, 233, 245–246, 265, 275, 322
and the Palestinian Authority, 1, 45, 47, 103–104, 171, 234, 245, 246, 247–248, 249, 256
and the Palestinian National Council, 256
and the PLA, 241
and the PLO, 44–45, 46, 207, 208, 241, 243, 244, 245, 261
renouncing terrorism, 120, 243, 245
and Tanzim, 306
as terrorist, 45, 152, 171, 207, 224, 250
U.S. refusal to deal with, 144
See also Palestine Liberation Organization (PLO)
Aragonese Crusade, 84
Archelaus, 133
Arens, Moshe, 142, 228
Aretas III of Petra, 279
Argaman, Nadav, 296
Argov, Shlomo, 207
Arguello, Patrick, 253
Aristobulus, 279
Ark of the Covenant, 87, 106, 267, 311
Armageddon, Battle of, 76
Armenia, 302
Armenian Orthodox church, 77, 80, 204
Ashrawi, Hanan, **46–47**
Assad, Bashar al-, 38, 39, 40, 42, **47–48**, 137, 149, 206, 304
Assad, Hafez al-, 26, **48–49**, 62, 213, 303, 304
Assassinations
  of Abbas al-Musawi, 135
  of Abdullah I, 139, 185, 259
  of Ahmed Tabari, 125
  of André Serot, 60
  of Anwar Sadat, 73, 98, 152, 221, 283
  of Arafat (rumored/suspected), 46, 73
  attempt on Husayn I, 139, 186
  attempt on Khalid Mishal, 219
  attempt on Shlomo Argov, 207
  of Count Folke Bernadotte, 18, 60, 293, 299
  of Czar Alexander II, 6
  of Gemayel, 209
  by Irgun, 146
  of Julius Caesar, 280
  by Lehi, 60, 146
  of Lord Moyne, 146, 293, 299
  of Meir Kahane, 75, 192
  by Mossad, 220, 332
  of Nero, 183
  by Night Squads, 36
  of Palestinian leaders, 143, 144, 191
  of Palestinian terrorists, 220
  of Peter I, 84
  of Rafik Hariri, 48, 136
  by Shin Bet, 297
  by the Stern Gang, 18, 60, 146, 293, 299
  of Yahya Ayyash, 297
  of Yitzhak Rabin, 73, 119, 153, 167, 228, 239, 266, 296, 309
  by Zealots, 334
Assassins, 285
Assyrian conquest of Israel, **49–50**, 52
Aswan High Dam project, 107, 227
Augustus, 281
Aysha (wife of Muhammad), 222
Ayyash, Yahya, 171, 297
Ayyub, Najm al-Din, 284
Ayyub, Yusuf ibn. *See* Saladin

Baathists, 303
Babayan, Battle of, 284
Babylonian captivity, 188, 197
Babylonian conquest of Judah, **51–53**
Bahrain, 38
Baker, James, III, 47, 321
Baldwin I (crusader), 82
Balfour, Arthur James, 53–54, 67, 182, 328, 337
Balfour Declaration, xvi, 29, **53–54**, 58, 68, 70, 138, 150, 175, 182, 198, 216, 225, 328, 337
Bar, Israel, 296
Bar Giora, 156
Bar Kokhba, Simon, 282
Bar Kokhba's Revolt, 183–184, 282
Barak, Ehud
  and the Camp David Summit, 45, 55, 73–74, 153, 246, 322
  on the division of Jerusalem, 176
  and the Israeli Security Barrier, 169
  as prime minister, 45, 200, 210, 229, 295, 322
  rescue of airline hostages, 228
  withdrawal from Lebanon, 200
Baratz, Joseph, 194, 337
Barghouti, Marwan, 5, **54–55**, 103–104, 306
Bar-Lev, Chaim, 263

Index

Bar-Lev Line, 24
Basic Law, 176
Bathsheba, 87
BDS National Committee, 63
Bedouins, 4, **56**
Begin, Benny, 210
Begin, Menachem, **56–57**
   and the Camp David Accords, 57,
      72–73, 96, 152, 316–317, 320–321
   and Eretz Israel, 207
   and Herut, 57, 293
   and the invasion of Lebanon, 207, 208,
      209–210, 245
   and Irgun Tsvai Leumi, 57, 146, 156, 195
   and Kahane, 191
   and the King David Hotel bombing,
      57–58, 146, 156, 195
   and Lehi, 146, 156
   and the Likud Party, 210
   plan to annex West Bank, 89, 207
   as prime minister, 57, 89, 118, 152,
      207–210, 293, 294
   on settlements, 118
   and the Zionist movement, 56, 58, 101
Beitar, 293
Ben Hushiel, Nehemiah, 270
Ben Matthias, Joseph, 183
Ben Yair, Eleazar, 183
Ben Yehudah, Eliezer, 337
Ben-Ali, Zine, 37
Ben-Gurion, David, **57–59**
   airline hostage rescue, 228
   as defense minister, 58
   forming Mossad, 219
   and the Gaza Raid, 107
   and Golda Meir, 217
   and Histadrut, 338
   and the King David Hotel bombing, 58
   military service, 182
   and Operation Dani, 211
   as prime minister, 58, 59, 88, 107, 156,
      166, 200, 265, 296
   pursuing Jewish statehood, 145, 331
   and Rafi, 59, 88, 200
   sinking the *Altalena*, 156
   as Zionist, 57–58, 122
Benjamin of Tiberias, 270
Ben-Yehuda, Ben-Zion, 60
Ben-Yehuda, Eliezer, **59–60**
Berihah, 8
Bernadotte, Count Folke, **60**
   assassination of, 18, 60, 293, 299

Bernard of Clairvaux, 83
Betar youth movement, 174, 191
Bethlehem, **61–62**
   Christians in, 78
   under the Palestinian Authority, 61
Bevin, Ernest, 191
Bible, 189
Biluim, 336
Birnbaum, Nathan, 335
Black Hand, 171
Black Sabbath, 264
Black September (conflict in Jordan),
   62–63, 103, 139, 186, 244, 259
Black September (terrorist organization),
   45, 62, 224, 244, 253
Blue and White Party, 231
Blum, Léon, 8
B'nai Akiva, 118
Bohemond (crusader), 83
Boniface IX (pope), 84
Border issues, 268
Borochov, Ber, 335
Bouazizi, Mohamed, 37
Boycott, Divestment, and Sanctions (BDS)
   movement, **63–65**, 94, 153
Brandeis, Louis D., 12, 53
Breaking the Silence, **65–66**
Brezhnev, Leonid, 27
British Mandate for Palestine, **66–70**
   and the Arab Revolt, 35–37, 54, 68, 302
   British rule, xvi, 15, 145, 185, 238, 320
   expiration of, 16, 69–70, 109
   interethnic and communal conflict
      under, 28, 68, 177
   and the Jewish Agency for Palestine,
      178, 331
   and the Jewish homeland, 18, 150, 238
   opposition to, 14, 195, 216, 275, 298
   partition of, 69–70, 185, 186, 204,
      311–313
   pro-Jewish stance of, 16
   terrorism during, 195
   and the West Bank, 328
   See also Arab Revolt, 1936
British Uganda Program, 336
British White Paper, 37, **70–71**, 122, 146
Brutus, 280
Bryan, William Jennings, 53
B'Tselem, **51**
Bush, George H. W., 11, 213
Bush, George W., 86, 250, 322–323
Byzantine Empire, 15, 85, 148, 223

Cairo Agreement, 241
Caligula, 281
Camp David Accords, 32, 57, **72–73**, 96, 119, 152, 283, 290, 316–317, 320–321
Camp David Summit, 45, 55, **73–74**, 143, 153, 178, 235, 295, 322
Campus Activism Network, 339
Canaan
    Egyptian conquest of, 99–100
    Israelite conquest of, 169–171, 188
Canaanites, **74–75**
Carter, James Earl "Jimmy," 57, 72–73, 94, 98, 152, 317, 320–321
Casablanca Protocol, 256
Cassius, 280
Catherine II (the Great; Czarina of Russia), 237
Cave of the Patriarchs Massacre, **75**
Center for Law and Justice, 339
Central Institute for Intelligence and Special Missions. *See* Mossad
Central Intelligence Agency (CIA), 86, 191, 219, 251
Chaldeans, 197
Chamberlain, Joseph, 134
Charlemagne, 77
China, 16, 93, 213, 316
Christian Council on Palestine (CCP), 12
Christian Zionism, xvi, 10, **76**
Christianity, **76–79**
    in Hebron, 130
    premillennial dispensationalism, 76
    Protestant, 77–78, 85
    See also Christians; Crusades in the Holy Land
Christians
    Arab, 148
    Armenian Orthodox, 77, 80, 204
    Coptic, 77, 80
    Eastern Orthodox, 77
    Ethiopian Orthodox, 77, 80
    in greater Syria, 148
    Greek Catholic, 204
    Greek Orthodox, 61, 80, 204
    in the Holy Land, xv
    leaving Bethlehem, 61
    in Lebanon, 208
    Maronite, 204, 208, 244, 245
    Nestorian, 77, 270
    in Palestine, 78, 92
    as people of the book, 148
    Syriac, 80, 204
    See also Christianity
Christians United for Israel, 76
Church of the Holy Sepulcher, **79–80**
Church of the Nativity, 61, 144
Church of the Resurrection. *See* Church of the Holy Sepulcher
Churchill, Winston, 66, 71, 299
Clinton, William Jefferson "Bill"
    aid to Israel, 11
    and the Camp David Summit, 45, 73–74, 153, 246, 322
    and the Oslo Accords, 233
Closed firing zones, 80
Closed military zones, **80–81**
Coastal Aquifer, 326, 327
Cohen, Yoram, 296
Colonialism, 16, 48, 78, 152
Columbo, Joseph, 191
Communal War. *See* Arab-Jewish Communal War, 1947
Conrad III (King of Germany), 83
Constantine I (Emperor), 77, 79, 270
Coptic Orthodox Church, 77, 80
Council of Chalcedon, 77, 270
Council of Clermont, 82
Council of Nicaea, 77
Crusade of Nicopolis, 84
Crusades in the Holy Land, xx, 61, 77, **81–85**, 285–286
    First Crusade, 82–83, 130
    Second Crusade, 83
    Third Crusade, 83, 129, 286
    the Fourth, Fifth, Sixth, and Seventh Crusades, 83–84
    final crusade, 84
    goals and results, 84–85
Cyrus the Great (King of Persia), 52, 106, 188
Czechoslovakia, 17, 31

Dada, Idi Amin, 100
Dahlan, Mohammed, **86–87**
Damascus-Medina (Hejaz) Railway, 33–34, 203
Darby, John Nelson, 76
Dassa, Robert, 201
David, 61, **87–88**, 130, 170–171, 175, 188, 196, 197, 287, 297, 311
Dayan, Moshe, **88–89**, 162, 263
Dayf, Mohammed, 172

Declaration of Principles on Interim Self-Government Arrangements. *See* Oslo Accords
Deir Yassin Massacre, **89–90**, 94, 146, 272, 299
Democratic Front for the Liberation of Palestine (DFLP), **90–91**, 243, 244
Demographics in Israel and Palestine, **91–92**
Diaspora, Jewish, 59, **93**, 167, 179, 187, 189, 331, 337
Diaspora, Palestinian, **93–95**, 230, 263, 278
Dichter, Avi, 296
Directorate of Main Intelligence, 157
Diskin, Yuval, 296
Document of National Reconciliation of Palestinian Prisoners, 55
Dolinsky, Morton, 179, 191
Dome of the Rock, xv, 76, 119, 143, 149, 175, 176, 177, 184, 192, 222, 266. *See also* Haram al-Sharif/Temple Mount
Dreyfus, Alfred, 133, 336
Dreyfus Affair, 133
Druze, 92, **95**, 204, 244, 245, 289
Durrah, Muhammad, 143

Eastern Orthodox Church, 77
Eban, Abba, 21, 217
Edict of Cyrus, 106
Egypt, **96–99**
    Arab Spring in, 38, 41, 98, 186, 221
    and the Arab-Israeli War, 1948, 17–19, 226
    and the Arab-Israeli War, 1967, 20–22
    and the Arab-Israeli War, 1973, 24–26, 27
    and the Camp David Accords, 32, 72–73
    and the Canaanites, 74
    expelled from Arab League, 73, 98
    and Gaza, 238
    hostilities with Israel, xvi, 172
    invasion of Sinai and Golan Heights, 217
    and the Khartoum Resolution, 193
    and the Lavon Affair, 201
    at the Madrid Conference, 213, 321
    nationalization of the Suez Canal, 19, 107, 151, 227
    Palestinian refugees in, 256, 277
    peace treaty with Israel, xvi, 39, 98, 221
    and the PLO, 243
    relationship with Israel, 41, 98, 317
    relationship with Soviet Union, 283, 325
    and the United Arab Republic, 227
    See also Egyptian conquest of Canaan; Gaza Strip; Mubarak, Hosni; Nasser, Gamal Abdel; Sadat, Anwar; Sinai Desert; Sinai Peninsula; Suez Canal; Suez Crisis
Egyptian conquest of Canaan, **99–100**
Egyptian New Kingdom, 99
Eichmann, Adolf, 219–220
Eisenhower, Dwight D., 10, 217
El-Ad, Hagai, 51
Eleazer, son of Yair (Eleazer ben Jair), 281, 334
Engels, Friedrich, 120
Entebbe Raid, **100**, 220, 275
Erekat, Saeb, **101**, 246
Eretz Israel, **101–102**, 109, 207, 338
Eritrea, 92
Eschiva of Galilee, 285
Eshkol, Levi, 22, 59, 89, 200, 217
Ethiopia, 92
Ethiopian Orthodox Church, 77, 80
Etzion, Yehudah, 119, 184
European Union
    at the Madrid Conference, 213
    and the Middle East Quartet, 218
    and the Road Map for Peace, 322–323
    support for two-state solution, 309
Export-Import Bank of the United States, 317
Eyal, 180
Ezra, 188

Farouk (Faruq) (king of Egypt), 19, 95
Farouk II (king of Egypt), 227, 283
Fatah, **103–105**
    Abbas's involvement in, 1, 104, 123, 125, 246, 248, 249, 256
    and the Arab-Israeli War, 1967, 241
    Arafat and, 44, 103–104, 124, 224
    Barghouti's involvement in, 54–55
    and Black September, 224
    Dahlan's involvement in, 86
    in the Gaza Strip, 103, 110, 250
    vs. the IDF, 44
    and the Martyrs Brigades, 5, 103, 301
    and the Palestinian National Council, 255–256
    and the PLO, 242–246

split with Hamas, 41, 42, 55, 104, 110–111, 145, 172, 246, 248, 306
and Tanzim, 306
in the West Bank, 103, 250, 306
See also Palestine Liberation Organization (PLO)
Fatah Uprising, 243
Fatah Youth Movement, 86
Fatima (daughter of Muhammad), 222
Faysal (king of Iraq), 16, 35, 138
Faysal (son of Husayn), 203
Faysal, Emir, 34
Faysal-Weizmann Agreement, **105**
Fayyad, Salam, 250
Fedayeen, 96, 107, 243
First Aliya, 6–7, 333, 336
First and Second Temple Periods, **105–106**
First Gulf War, 293
First Jewish Revolt, 214
First Zionist Congress, xvi, 133–134, 331, 335, 336
Food for Peace, 317
Fourth Herzliya Conference, 113
Framework for Peace in the Middle East, 321
Frankfurter, Felix, 12
Frederick I (Frederick Barbarossa; Holy Roman Emperor), 83
Frederick II (emperor of Germany), 84
Free Officers, 95, 227, 283
French Mandate of Syria, 115

Gadhafi, Muammar, 38
Gadna, 294
Gantz, Benny, 231
Gaza Raid, 1955, 19, **107–108**
Gaza Strip, **108–112**
and the Al-Aqsa Martyrs Brigades, 4
annexation of, 278
and the Arab-Israeli War, 1967, 23
under Egypt, 226, 238
and Gush Emunim, 118
under Hamas, 1, 171, 246, 248, 261
Israeli occupation of, xvi, 151, 160–161, 193, 207, 238, 261, 267–268, 314
and the Palestinian Authority, 213, 234
Palestinian refugees in, 41, 94, 256–258, 259, 277, 279
Palestinian self-rule in, 45, 245
Palestinian state in, 230
as part of historic Palestine, 238
PLO in, xvi–xvii, 103

settlements in, 109, 113, 160–161, 164, 207, 267, 289, 295, 330
and the two-state solution, 308
withdrawal from, 153, 246
See also Egypt; Gaza Strip blockade; Gaza Strip disengagement; Occupied Palestinian Territories (OPT)
Gaza Strip blockade, 110, **112–113**
Gaza Strip disengagement, 109–110, **113–114**, 153, 161, 172, 295, 330
Gaza wars—2008, 2012, 2014. *See* Gaza Strip
Gemayel, Bashir, 208, 209
General Security Service, 295. *See also* Shin Bet
General Union of Palestinian Students, 46
General Union of Palestinian Women, 46
Geneva Accord, **114**
Geneva Conventions, 160, 267–268, 288
Gessius Florus, 183, 334
Gibeonites, 170
Gibli, Benjamin, 201
Ginsberg, Asher, 337
Glick, Yehuda, 308
Godfrey de Bouillon (Duke of Lorraine), 83, 130
Golan Heights, **115–116**
annexation of, 160, 305
and the Arab-Israeli War, 1967, 23, 24, 40
Druze in, 94
Israeli claim to, xvi, 11, 40, 153, 304, 340
occupation of, 151, 157, 193, 314, 321
settlements in, 115, 160, 289, 304
Trump recognizing Israel's claim to, 116, 153, 305
See also Syria
Goldstein, Baruch, 75, 131
Goliath, 287
Grand Mufti of Jerusalem, **116–117**, 260–261, 302. *See also* Husayni, Hajj Amin al-
Great Jewish Revolt, 281
Great March of Return, 111, **117–118**, 126
Great Revolt. *See* Arab Revolt, 1936
Greater Israel movement, 119
Greek Orthodox Church, 61, 80
Green Line, 80, 126, 143, 169, 290, 328, 330
Grossman, David, 265
Gulf Cooperation Council, 213

Gush Emunim, **118–119**, 127, 176, 184, 198, 289
Gush Etzion, 114, 290
Guy of Lusignan (King of Jerusalem), 128–129, 285
Gvaryahu, Avner, 65

Habash, George, **120–121**, 241, 272
Habib, Philip, 207, 209
Hadassah, 339
Haddad, Uthman, 241
Hadrian, 183–184, 282
Haganah, **121–123**
   and the Arab Revolt, 1936, 36, 122
   and the Arab-Jewish Communal War, 30–31
   Ben-Gurion and, 58, 145, 265
   Dayan's service in, 88
   founding of, 7, 58, 68, 156, 173, 263
   and Gadna, 294
   British attitude toward, 16, 121
   vs. Holy War Army, 138
   and the IDF, 17, 146, 156
   and the Israeli War of Independence, 122
   and the Jewish Defense League, 179
   and the Jewish Resistance Movement, 146
   and the Palestinian resistance, 94
   merge with Berihah, 8
   Peres and, 265
   pilgrimages to Masada, 215
   and Plan Dalet, 271–272
   Rabin and 275
   Sharon and 294
   See also Palmach
Hagia Sophia, 77
Halutz, Dan, 155, 159
Hamas, **123–126**
   assassination program against, 220, 297
   and the BDS movement, 64
   call for jihad, 300
   cease-fire with Israel, 144
   Egypt's support for, 98
   fighting with Israel, 125, 153, 246, 314, 318
   and the First Intifada, 123, 124, 332
   in the Gaza Strip, 108, 110, 112, 113, 124–126, 149, 171–172, 239, 246, 248, 257, 261
   and the Great March of Return, 118
   vs. the GSS, 249–250
   vs. the IDF, 158, 172
   and the Martyrs Brigades, 5, 301
   Mishal's involvement in, 218–219
   and the Palestinian Authority, 1, 45, 86, 104, 108, 110–111, 112, 113, 123, 124–126, 172, 239–240, 246, 248, 249–250, 261
   vs. Palestinian Islamic Jihad, 255, 301
   vs. the PLO, 142, 219, 262, 322
   rocket attacks against Israel, 110–111, 112, 124, 125, 161, 172, 192–193, 248, 255, 274
   and the Second Intifada, 124, 161, 332
   social services, 124, 332
   split with Fatah, 104, 110–111, 246, 248, 306
   suicide bombings by, 75, 124, 239, 300
   support from Palestinians, 103, 123, 261, 306, 323
   Syrian support for, 304
   as terrorist organization, 1, 5, 64, 124, 152–153, 239, 248, 250, 309, 332
   in the West Bank, 124, 171–172, 251, 261
   Yassin and, 332
   See also Izz al-Din al-Qassam Brigades; Muslim Brotherhood
Hammuda, Yahya, 241
Haniyeh, Ismail, 104, 110, 125, 219
Harakat al-Jihad al-Islami fi Filastin. *See* Palestinian Islamic Jihad (PIJ)
Haram al-Sharif/Temple Mount, xv, 5, 76, 119, **126–128**, 149, 175, 177, 184, 266, 302
   call for construction of third temple on, 106, 127, 267, 308
   Sharon's controversial visit to, 4–5, 74, 127, 143, 153, 176, 178, 235, 330
   Third Temple Movement, 308
   See also al-Aqsa Mosque; Dome of the Rock
Harel, Isser, 295
Hariri, Rafik, 48, 136
Hashemites, 105, 185
Hasmoneans, 132, 279
Hassan, Khalid, 103
Hattin, Battle of, **128–129**, 285
Hawatmeh, Nayef, 90
Hebrew language, 6–7, 59–60, 155, 165, 178, 189, 217, 337
Hebron, **129–131**, 163
Hebron Massacre, 130–131

Hebron Protocol, 131
Hejaz region, 33, 138–139
Heraclius (Byzantine emperor), 15, 270
Herod Antipas, 133, 281
Herod Archelaus, 281
Herod the Great, 130, **131–133**, 281
Heroes of the Return, 241
Herut Party, 57, 293
Herzl, Theodor **133–134**, 201, 307, 331, 335, 336, 337
Herzog, Chaim, 119, 184
Hess, Moses, 335
Hezbollah, **135–137**
   assassinations by Mossad, 220
   dispute over Shaba Farms, 136
   increased capabilities of, 40
   as inspiration for Martyrs Brigades, 5
   Iranian support for, 39–40, 42, 136
   Israeli operations against, 266
   Khomeini's support for, 149
   in Lebanon, 137, 206, 209
   rockets used by, 192–193
   as security threat for Israel 168, 209, 305
   suicide attacks by, 300
   support for Assad, 38, 39, 48, 49, 137, 304
   support for Lebanese people, 136–137, 304
   Syrian support for, 304
   war with Israel, 110, 136, 153, 158–159, 206, 290, 304, 318
Histadrut, 217, 338
Hitler, Adolf, 7, 338
Ho Chi Minh, 120
Hobeika, Elie, 209
Holocaust, 69, 156, 201, 319, 338
Holy Land. *See* Crusades in the Holy Land; Palestine
Holy War Army (HWA), **137–138**
Hoshea (king), 50
Hovevei Zion, 271
Husari, Sati al-, 120
Husayn (son of Ali), 148
Husayn, Abdullah bin. *See* Abdullah II (King of Jordan)
Husayn, Faisal ibn, 103
Husayn, King of Jordan, **139–140**
   alliance with Egypt and Syria, 21
   and the Allon Plan, 9
   and the Arab-Israeli War, 1973, 26
   attacking West Jerusalem, 22
   attempted assassination of, 139, 186, 244
   evicting the PLO, 44, 62, 103, 120, 139, 186, 243–244
   as king, 185–186
   and the PLA, 240
   releasing Yasser from jail, 332
   relinquishing claims to West Bank, 329
Husayn, Muhammad Ahmad, 117
Husayn, Muna, 2
Husayn, Saddam, 213, 221, 300, 319
Husayn ibn Ali, Sharif of Mecca, **138–139**
   and the Arab Revolt 1916, 138, 203, 302
   correspondence with McMahon, 34, 54, 215–216, 225, 302
   as king of the Hejaz, 33, 34, 35
   and the Sykes-Picot Agreement, 138, 302–303
Husayni, Abd al-Qadir (al-Kadr) al-, 31, 137
Husayni, Haj Amin al-, 13, 36, 260–261, 274, 302. *See also* Grand Mufti of Jerusalem
Husayni, Mohammed Abdel Raouf Arafat al-Qudwa al-. *See* Arafat, Yasser
Husayni, Muhammad Amin al-, 116–117
Huwaitat tribesmen, 203
Hyrcanus, 279–280

Ibn Saud, 35, 138
Immigration
   from Arab countries, 180–181
   illegal, 8, 122, 156
   to Israel, 5–7, 278–279, 331, 332–333
   Jewish, 5–7, 29, 70, 102, 156, 178–181, 201–202, 258, 278–279, 331, 332–333
   and the Jewish National Fund (JNF), 8
   to Palestine, 8, 54, 68
   restrictions on, 37, 70, 225
   Zionist, 258
   See also Aliya
India, 213
Innocent III (pope), 83–84
Innocent IV (pope), 84
International Atomic Energy Agency, 319
Intifada, First, **141–142**
   Arafat's approval of, 45
   creating criticism of Israel, 152
   Dahlan as leader of, 86
   and Hamas, 123, 124, 332
   inception of, xvi, 119, 245, 249, 250, 261, 276, 329

Intifada, First (*cont.*)
   opposing the Oslo Accords, 153, 178
   and the PFLP, 272
   and the PLO, 261
   resulting in harsher policies by Israel, 161
Intifada, Second, **143–145**
   Abbas's call for an end to, 246, 250
   and the al-Aqsa Martyrs Brigades, 4–5, 55, 301, 330
   and the al-Qassim Brigades, 121
   in Bethlehem, 62
   following Camp David Summit collapse, 45, 246
   and Hamas, 124, 161, 332
   Mubarak's mediation, 221
   negative effects on Palestinians, 109, 144, 145, 291
   and Palestinian Islamic Jihad, 255
   and the PFLP, 272
   and the PLO, 246, 247
   in Ramallah, 277
   results in Israeli politics and policies, xvii, 167, 218, 295, 330
   and Sharon's visit to Temple Mount, 4–5, 74, 127, 143, 153, 176, 178, 235, 330
   suicide bombings, 161, 300, 301, 330
   Tanzim and, 55, 103, 306
Iran
   and Hamas, 219
   nuclear deal with, 40, 42, 220, 340
   Shia Safivid Empire of, 236
   support for Syria, 39–40, 42
Iran-Contra deal, 136
Iranian Revolution, 149
Iraq
   Palestinian refugees in, 277
   refugees from, 2, 42
   support for PLO, 45
   U.S. invasion of, 40
Irgun Tsvai Leumi, **145–147**
   during the Arab Revolt, 146
   attacks on the British, 16, 57, 69, 122, 146, 156, 175, 195
   under Begin, 57, 146, 195
   and Ben-Gurion, 58
   disbanding of, 156
   and the Israel Defense Forces, 17, 122, 146, 156
   as Jewish resistance movement, 146
   and the NZO, 174
   as offshoot of Haganah, 30, 121, 145, 156, 271–272
   vs. Palestinians, 89–90, 122, 138
   and the Revisionist Zionists, 145
   Shamir as member, 293
   Stern as member, 298
   as terrorist organization, 145, 146
   during World War II, 146
   See also Deir Yassin Massacre; King David Hotel bombing; Stern Gang
Iron Dome missile defense system, 192–193
Isaac, 99, 102, 127, 130, 150, 267
Islam, **147–150**
   Druze, 92, 95, 204, 244, 245, 289
   fundamentalist, 36
   in Hebron, 130
   in Lebanon, 204–205, 206, 208–209
   Muslim claims on Jerusalem, 149–150
   Shia, 42, 94, 135, 204, 206, 208, 284
   Sunni, 42, 116, 136, 204, 208, 284
   Sunni-Shi'a split, 148–149
   See also Alawites; Muhammad, Prophet of Islam; Muslims
Islamic Amal, 135
Islamic Jihad, 103. *See also* Palestinian Islamic Jihad (PIJ)
Islamic State, 2
Islamic State of Iraq and Syria (ISIS), 38, 48, 304
Ismail (Safavid ruler), 148–149
Israel, **150–154**
   agreement with PLO, 221
   agriculture in, 326
   and the Allon Plan, 8–9, 289
   Arab boycott of, 13, 32
   armistice agreement with Syria, 115
   declaration of independence, xvi, 16, 175, 225
   demographics in, 91–92
   effects of Arab Spring on, 38–40
   Entebbe Raid, 100, 220, 275
   Eretz Israel, 101–102, 209, 207, 338
   fighting with Hamas, 125, 153, 246, 314, 318
   formation of, 13
   government in, 197–198
   Jewish immigration to, 5–7, 29, 70, 102, 156, 178–181, 201–202, 258, 278–279, 331, 332–333
   at the Madrid Conference, 45, 101, 213, 245, 304, 321–322

military campaigns against Gaza,
    110–111
Ministry of Agriculture, 326
Operation Peace for Galilee, xvii,
    206–208, 209
opposition to occupation, 65
peace talks with PLO, 322
peace treaty with Egypt, xvi, 38–39, 98,
    221
peace treaty with Jordan, 139, 213
recognition by other nations, 213
relationship with Egypt, 98, 317
relationship with Russia, 40, 305
relationship with U.S., 319
U.S. aid to, 317–319
war with Hamas, 318
Water Commissioner, 326
withdrawal from Gaza, 153, 246
withdrawal from Jericho, 246
withdrawal from Lebanon, 209
See also Arab boycott of Israel; Arab-Israeli War, 1948; Arab-Israeli War, 1956; Arab-Israeli War, 1967; Arab-Israeli War, 1973; Arab-Jewish Communal War, 1947; Boycott, Divestment, and Sanctions (BDS) movement; Camp David Accords; Camp David Summit; Closed military zones; Gaza Strip blockade; Gaza Strip disengagement; Knesset; Lebanon, Israeli invasion of; Oslo Accords
Israel Defense Forces (IDF), **154–158**
    and the Arab-Israeli War, 1948, 17–18
    and the Arab-Israeli War, 1967, 20, 22,
        24–27, 89
    and the Arab-Israeli War, 1973, 27, 97
    attacks on Lebanon, 136
    under Ben-Gurion, 58
    Druze serving in, 94, 155
    and the Entebbe Raid, 100
    vs. Fatah, 44
    and the First Intifada, 141–142
    and the Gaza Raid, 107
    and the Gaza Strip, 110, 113
    in the Golan Heights, 115
    and the Great March of Return, 117
    Haganah as precursor of, 121
    and Hamas, 124, 125
    vs. the Holy War Army, 138
    and the invasion of Lebanon, 208–209
    in Lydda and Ramle, 211–212
    mandatory service in, 166
    Netanyahu's participation in, 228
    organization of, 338
    and the Palestinian General Security
        Services, 250
    and the PLO, 245
    providing security in the settlements,
        291–292
    in Ramallah, 276–277
    and the War of Attrition, 325
    war with Hezbollah, 158–159
    in the West Bank, 131, 144, 169
    See also Palmach
Israel-Gaza War, 323
Israel-Hezbollah War, 2006, **158–160**, 304,
    318
Israeli Information Center for Human
    Rights in the Occupied Territories
    (B'Tselem), 51
Israeli navy, 157, 265
Israeli occupations, **160–164**
    East Jerusalem, 160, 161–162, 228, 230,
        238, 261, 267–268
    Gaza, 151, 160–161, 193, 207, 238, 261,
        267–268, 314
    West Bank, 151, 157, 160, 162–164, 176,
        191, 193, 198–199, 207, 228, 230, 235,
        238, 240, 261, 265, 267–268, 314, 321,
        329
Israeli Security Barrier, 61, **168–169**, 277,
    288, 290, 301, 329, 330
Israeli War of Independence. *See* Arab-Israeli War, 1948
Israelis, **165–168**
    Arab, 155, 289
    conflict with Palestinians, xv–xvi
    in the diaspora, 93
    Druze, 289
    evacuation from occupied territories,
        113, 114
    killed in the Intifadas, 142–145
    mandatory military service for, 155
    massacre of (Ma'alot Massacre), 90
    non-Jewish, 167–168
    See also Diaspora, Jewish; Jews
Israelite conquest of Canaan, **169–171**
Israel-Syrian Armistice Agreement, 115
Izz al-Din al-Qassam Brigades, 124,
    171–172, 274

Jabareen, Hassan, 4
Jabari, Ahmed, 110

Jabotinsky, Ze'ev, 58, 101, 145, **173–174**, 182, 191. *See also* Zionism
Jacob, 49, 99, 102, 130, 196
Jacobite (Syrian Orthodox) Church, 77
Jaffa Massacre, 29
James of Aragon (king), 84
Jebusites, 170
Jehoahaz, 52
Jehoiachin, 52
Jehoiakim, 52
Jerusalem, **175–177**
   as capital of Israel, 11, 153, 175–176, 328
   as capital of United Kingdom of Israel, 106
   captured by Rome, 215
   as Christian holy city, xv, 175
   division of, 175
   Egyptian presence in, 99
   first Babylonian captivity, 188, 197
   Grand Mufti of, 116–117, 260–261, 302
   as international city, xvi, 177, 312
   Israeli claim to, 340
   as Jewish holy city, xv, 175, 267
   Kingdom of, 128–129, 285
   Muslim claims on, 149–150
   as Muslim holy city, xv, 14, 175, 266–267
   Nebi Musa riots, 28
   occupation of, 175–176
   permanent status issues, 266–267
   Roman capture of, 334
   settlements in, 30, 31, 153, 160, 161–162, 164, 176, 238, 257, 267, 268, 289, 310
   and the two-state solution, 309
   U.S. embassy in, 176, 178
   See also Crusades in the Holy Land; Jerusalem, East; Jerusalem, Old City of; Jerusalem, West
Jerusalem, East, xvi, xvii, 175
   annexation of, 161
   under Jordan, 238
   occupation of, 160, 161–162, 228, 230, 238, 261, 267–268
   Palestinians in, 41
   See also Israeli occupations; Jerusalem; Jerusalem, Old City of; Occupied Palestinian Territories (OPT)
Jerusalem, Old City of, 9, 22, 175, **177–178**, 185, 226
   permanent status issues, 266–267
   See also al-Aqsa Mosque; Haram al-Sharif/Temple Mount
Jerusalem, West, 122
Jerusalem Brigades (Saraya al-Quds), 254
Jesus Christ (Jesus of Nazareth), 61, 76–77, 78, 79, 88, 106, 133, 175, 189, 221, 222
Jewish Agency, 36, 121, **178–179**, 195, 331
Jewish Autonomous Republic, 337
Jewish Auxiliary Forces, 121
Jewish Battalions, 173, 182. *See also* Jewish Legion
Jewish Brigade, 122, 156
Jewish Colonial Trust, 331, 336
Jewish Defense League (JDL), **179–180**, 191–192
Jewish Emigration from Arab Countries, **180–181**
Jewish Legion, 173, **182**. *See also* Jewish Battalions
Jewish National Fund (JNF), 3, **182–183**, 194, 331, 336
Jewish Resistance Movement, 180
Jewish Revolts, **183–184**, 334
Jewish Settlement Police, 121
Jewish Task Force, 180
Jewish Territorialist Organization, 337
Jewish Underground, **184–185**
Jews
   Arab, 180
   in Arab countries, 189
   Ashkenazim, 91–92, 131, 165, 180, 181, 189, 333
   black African, 92
   British, 262
   communist, 338
   displaced by Holocaust, 69
   Ethiopian, 262, 293
   German, 262, 333
   as God's "chosen" people, 76, 169–170
   Hasidic, 155
   in Hebron, 130, 131
   in the Holy Land, xv
   Iraqi, 262
   in Jerusalem, 175
   from MENA regions, 180
   Mizrahim, 91–92, 165, 180, 181
   from Muslim countries, 181
   Orthodox, 118, 165, 191, 198
   in Palestine, 67, 182
   as people of the book, 148
   Polish, 7, 93, 174, 262
   Reformed (Conservative), 165
   Russian, 6, 7, 93, 173, 237–238, 262, 307, 333, 336–338

secular, 335
Sephardim, 180, 189, 332–333
in Spain, 189
Ukrainian, 333
ultra-Orthodox (Haredi), 59–60, 155, 165–166
in the United States, 53, 93, 202, 217, 338
Yishuv, 181
See also Diaspora, Jewish; Israelis; Zionists
Jibril, Ahmed, 241
Jihad, 36, 124, 128, 254, 300. *See also* Palestinian Islamic Jihad (PIJ)
Johnson, Lyndon B., 21, 23, 217, 321
Johnston, Eric, 326
Jonathan (son of Saul), 287
Jordan, **185–187**
under Abdullah II, 2
and the Allon Plan, 8–9, 289
Arab Spring in, 38, 186
and the Arab-Israeli War, 1948, 226
and the Arab-Israeli War, 1967, 20–22
and Black September, 62
claims to East Jerusalem and West Bank, 176, 186
Druze in, 94
at the Madrid Conference, 213
Palestinian refugees in, 94, 256–257, 259, 277, 278–279
peace treaty with Israel, 139, 213
protests in, 41
war with Israel, xvi
water sharing agreements with Israel, 326
and the West Bank, 238
See also West Bank
Jordan River, 20, 115, 151, 173, 182, 188, 326, 327
Josephus, 281, 334
Joshua, 170
Josiah, 52
Judah. *See* Kingdom of Judah
Judaism, **187–190**
conversion to, 202
elements of, 188
First Temple Period, 105–106
in Hebron, 130
history of, 187–188, 279–282, 311
in Israel, 165
Second Temple Period, 105–106

Judea and Samaria, **190**
and the doctrine of Greater Israel, 118, 167
Roman conquest of, 279–282
settlements in, 160, 289
See also West Bank
Julius Caesar, 132, 280
Julius Severus, 282
Justinian I (Byzantine emperor), 130

Kach Movement/Party, 75, 180, 191, 192
Kahan Commission, 210
Kahane, Meir, 75, 179–180, **191–192**
Kahane Khai, 180
Katyusha rockets, 158, **192–193**, 294
KAV 300 Affair, 296
Kavadh II (Sassanid emperor), 270
Keating, Kenneth, 26
Kenen, I. L. "Si," 9
Kennedy, John F., 217
Kenya, 336
Keren Hayesod, 331
Kerry, John, 323
Khadija (wife of Muhammad), 222
Khalaf, Salah, 103
Khaled, Leila, 253
Khalidi, Husayn al-, 14
Khartoum Resolution, 32, **193–194**
Khattab, Umar Ibn al-, 149
Khomeini, Ayatollah Ruhollah, 149
Khrushchev, Nikita, 219
Khusrau II (Sassanid emperor), 270
Kibbutz, 6, 7, **194–195**, 336, 337
King David Hotel bombing, 58, 146, 156, 175, **195–196**
King Solomon's Temple, xv, 52, 105–106, 183, 188–189, 215, 267, 281, 298, 311. *See also* Third Temple Movement
Kingdom of Israel, **196**
formation of, 190, 196, 298, 311
twelve tribes of, 49
See also United Kingdom of Israel
Kingdom of Jerusalem, 128–129, 285. *See also* Jerusalem
Kingdom of Judah, **196–197**
Babylonian conquest of, 51–52, 196–197
split from United Kingdom of Israel, 49, 196, 311
King's Fusiliers, 156, 173, 182
Kissinger, Henry, 27, 232, 316, 321
Kitchener, Horatio, 34, 138
Kitos War, 282

Knesset, 57, 59, 72, 88, 164, 176, 192, **197–198**, 200, 201, 202, 228, 229, 266, 275, 283, 293, 294, 296, 331
Knights Hospitaller, 85, 285
Knights Templar, 85, 285
Kook, Avraham Yitzhak, **198–199**
Kook, Zvi Yehuda, 118, 198
Kurdistan, 302
Kushner, Jared, 323
Kuwait, 38, 94, 213

Labor Party, 59, 88, 114, 118, 152, **200**, 217, 228, 265, 275, 290, 322, 333
Ladislas (king of Poland), 84
Land Day, 117
Land of Israel Movements, 118
Landoy Committee, 296
Lavon, Pinhas, 201
Lavon Affair, 19, 59, **201**
Law of Return, **201–203**. *See also* Right of Return
Lawrence, T. E., 34, 138, **203–204**
League of Nations, **204**
 and Palestine, xvi, 35
 See also British Mandate for Palestine
Leah, 102, 130
Lebanese civil war, 62, 135, 205–206, 245
Lebanese National Front, 45
Lebanon, **204–206**
 Druze in, 94
 as French mandate, 203
 gaining independence, 16
 Islam in, 204–206, 208
 and the Israel-Hezbollah War, 158–159
 Israeli withdrawal from, 209
 Israel's relationship with, 39
 at the Madrid Conference, 213, 321
 Palestinian refugees in, 94, 256–257, 259, 277, 279
 PLO in, 44–45, 103, 244–245
 Shiites in, 135
 and the Sykes-Picot Agreement, 170
 Syrian involvement in, 49
 See also Lebanese civil war; Lebanon, Israeli invasion of
Lebanon, Israeli invasion of, xvi, xvii, 10, 62, 136, 152, 205, **206–210**, 245, 294
Legal Center for Arab Minority Rights in Israel. *See* Adalah
Lehi (Lohamei Herut Israel). *See* Stern Gang
Lenin, Vladimir, 120

Libya, 38
Lie, Trygve, 16
Likud Party, 45, 57, 74, 113, 118, 119, 152, 153, 184, 207, **210–211**, 228–229, 265, 290, 293, 294–295, 322
Lloyd George, David, 182, 328
Lohamei Herut Israel (Lehi). *See* Stern Gang
London Round Table Conference, 14
Louis VII (King of France), 83
Louis IX (King of France), 84
Luther, Martin, 85
Lydda and Ramle, 120, **211–212**, 272, 282, 312

Ma'ale Adumim, 114, 290
Ma'alot Massacre, 90
Maccabees, 132
MacInnes, Bishop, 66
Madrid Conference, 45, 101, **213–214**, 245, 304, 321–322
Makadma, Ibrahim Al-, 124
Makarios, Bishop, 79
Mamluk dynasty, 236
Mandates, 67–68. *See also* British Mandate for Palestine
Mao Tse-tung, 120
Mapai, 59, 88, 200
Mapam Party, 200
March 14 Alliance, 136
Marj Dabiq, Battle of, 236
Marj Uyun, Battle of, 285
Mark Antony, 132, 280
Maronites, 204, 208, 244, 245
Marx, Karl, 120
Marxism, 90, 120
Masada, **214–215**, 281, 334
May Laws, 336
Mayer, Daniel, 8
McGonagle, William L., 324
McMahon, Henry, 34, 54, 138, 302
 correspondence with Husayn ibn Ali, 215–216, 225, 302
McMahon-Husayn correspondence, **215–216**, 225, 302
Mecca, xv, 33, 34, 126, 147, 221, 222, 223, 236, 267, 285. *See also* Husayn ibn Ali, Sharif of Mecca
Medina, xv, 33, 34, 126, 223, 236, 267
Medo-Babylonian War, 49
Meir, Golda, **216–218**
 and the American Jewish Congress, 12

and the Arab-Israeli War, 1973, 26–27
as foreign minister, 217
as minister of labor, 217
as prime minister, 26–27, 89, 200, 217–218, 224, 262, 275
Melkites, 77
Menehem, 281
Merodach-Baladan, 52
Merom Golan, 115
Mesopotamia, 93, 128, 170, 282, 303
Meyerson, Morris, 216–217
Michal (daughter of Saul), 287
Middle East Quartet, **218**
Miftah (Palestinian Initiative for the Promotion of Global Dialogue and Democracy), 47
Mishal, Khalid, **218–219**
Mitchell, George, 323
Moch, Jules, 8
Mont Gisard, Battle of, 285
Moody, Dwight, 76
Morocco, 213
Moses, 170, 187, 222–223, 286
Moshavim, 7
Mossad, **219–220**, 223, 293, 295, 332
Movement for the Establishment of the Temple, 308
Movement for the Whole Land of Israel, 118
Moyne, Lord, 146, 293, 299
   assassination of, 146, 293, 299
Mubarak, Hosni, **220–221**
   as mediator, 221
   negotiations hosted by Obama, 323
   resignation of, 38–39, 41, 221
   as Sadat's successor, 98, 221
Mughniya, Imad, 135
Muhammad, Prophet of Islam, **221–224**
   in Bethlehem, 61
   in Jerusalem, 149
   Night Journey to heaven, xv, 14, 149, 175
   See also Islam
Multinational Forces in Lebanon, 209
Munazzamat al-Tahrir Filastiniyyah. *See* Palestine Liberation Organization (PLO)
Munich Olympics, 45, 62, 220, **224**, 244, 253
Muqataa, 277
Murat II, 84
Musawi, Abbas al-, 135

Muslim Brotherhood, 38–39, 41, 43, 98, 123, 332. *See also* Hamas
Muslims
   in Bethlehem, 61
   Druze, 94
   in the Holy Land, xv
   in Lebanon, 204–205, 208–209
   Palestinian, 116
   See also Crusades in the Holy Land; Islam
Mustafa, Abu Ali, 272

Nakba, 15, 109, 168, **225–227**, 258, 261
Nakba Day, 117
Naqab, 4
Narkiss, Uzi, 263
Nashashibi, Fakhri al-, 36
Nasrallah, Hassan, 135, 136
Nasser, Gamal Abdel, **227–228**
   and the Arab-Israeli War, 1967, 20–22, 97
   defense pact with Syria, 20, 227
   and the Free Officers, 97, 283
   and the Gaza Raid, 107
   Israel's plan to remove, 59
   and the Khartoum Resolution, 193
   and the Lavon Affair, 201
   modernization plans, 227
   nationalization of Suez Canal, 97, 107, 151, 227
   pan-Arabism of, 32, 227, 261
   as president of Egypt, 32, 96, 227, 283
   remilitarization of the Sinai, 304
   and the Suez Crisis, 32, 19, 227
   supporting Middle East peace, 193
   and the War of Attrition, 227–228, 325
   working with Fatah, 241
   See also Egypt
National Christian Leadership Conference, 76
National Front, 245
National Religious Party (NRP), 118, 119, 184
National Syrian Socialist Party, 209
Nation-State Law, 167
Nebi Musa riots, 28
Nebuchadnezzar/Nebuchadnezzar II, 52, 197
Negev Desert, 9, 157, 312
Nehemiah, 188
Nero, 183, 281
Nestorian Christian Church, 77, 270

Netanyahu, Benjamin, **228–229**
  on the creation of a Palestinian state, 153, 210, 235, 309
  as finance minister, 113, 229
  on Jerusalem, 176
  on Jewish self-determination, 167
  and the Likud Party, 45, 153, 210–211, 228–229, 266, 322
  military service, 228
  as minister of foreign affairs, 229
  friction with Obama, 153, 323
  opposition to Oslo Accords, 322
  as prime minister, xxviii, 45, 153, 176, 205, 210, 228–229, 246, 266, 322
  relationship with Putin, 40, 305
  Trump's diplomatic efforts, 153, 323
  and the West Bank, 40, 153, 210–211, 229, 231, 235, 240, 309, 330
Netanyahu, Jonathan, 100
Neumann, Emanuel, 12
New Zionist Organization (NZO), 174
Nicetas (son of Heraclius), 270
Nixon, Richard, 27, 217, 321
Noble Sanctuary. *See* Haram al-Sharif/ Temple Mount
Nongovernmental organizations (NGOs)
  B'Tselem, 51
  funding from, 314
  Miftah, 47
  Norwegian, 234
  Peace Now, 264–265
  supporting the BDS movement, 63
Nosair, El Sayyid, 179, 192
Nuclear weapons
  in Iran, 40, 42, 220, 340
  in Israel, 156, 319
Nur al-Din, 83, 284

Obama, Barack, 153, 319, 323, 339
  Iran nuclear deal, 40, 42
Occupied Palestinian Territories (OPT), 51, 160, 204, 218, 234, 238, 290
  closed military zones in, 80
  and UN Security Council Resolution 242, 315
  See also Gaza Strip; Israeli occupations; Jerusalem, East; West Bank
Octavian, 132, 280
October War. *See* Arab-Israeli War, 1973
Odah, Alex, 179
Olmert, Ehud, 153, 176, 228, 290, 323
Oman, 38, 213

Omar, Ilhan, 65
One-state solution, **230–232**, 262–263, 290, 312
Operation Cast Lead, 110. *See also* Gaza Strip
Operation Dani, 211
Operation Defensive Shield, 250
Operation DEKEL, 18
Operation Gate of Moors, 254–255
Operation Grapes of Wrath, 136
Operation High Minarets, 25
Operation Nickel Grass, 27, **232**
Operation Peace for Galilee, xvii, 206–208, 209. *See also* Lebanon, Israeli invasion of
Operation Pillar of Defense. *See* Gaza Strip
Operation Protective Edge, 111. *See also* Gaza Strip
Operation Solomon, 293
Organization of the Islamic Jihad, 135
Osirak power plant, 57, 152, 220
Oslo Accords, **233–235**
  and Abbas, 1
  and the DFLP, 90
  Fatah's efforts, 103
  and Haram al-Sharif, 127
  and the Madrid Conference, 213, 245
  negotiations with Arafat, 142, 265, 275
  opposition to, 73, 90–91, 119, 124, 142, 152–153, 171, 228, 234, 239, 294, 306, 322
  creation of Palestinian Authority, 103, 109, 131, 141, 213, 234, 239, 247, 249–250, 251, 276
  and Palestinian autonomy, 45, 94, 152, 228, 245
  Palestinian response to, 306
  and permanent status issues, 266–269
  PLO allowed to return from exile, 103, 306
  PLO concessions, 242, 261
  prisoner exchanges, 55
  provisions for mutual recognition, 73, 322
  and the right of return, 94, 278
  signing of, xvii, 45, 94, 139, 142, 186, 200, 241
  and the two-state solution, 167, 213, 309
  and the West Bank, 131, 162, 234, 247, 329–330
  See also Camp David Summit

Oslo II (Taba Agreement), 322
Ottoman conquest of Palestine, **236**
Ottoman Empire
    Arab Revolt against, 33–35, 67, 138, 145, 203, 215
    in Bethlehem, 61
    capture of Constantinople, 77, 236
    government of Palestine under, 3, 260
    in Hebron, 130
    Jews from, 182, 332–333, 336
    loss of Palestine to Britain, 15, 28, 54, 66, 67, 173, 185, 204, 238, 302
    in Palestine and Jerusalem, xvi, 3, 6, 58, 116, 134, 173, 175, 185, 225, 236, 333
    and the Sykes-Picot Agreement, 302
    Syria as part of, 303
    in the West Bank, 328
    in World War I, 138
    See also Arab Revolt, 1916; Syria
Ottoman Land Code, 3
Oz, Amos, 265

Pale of Settlement, 6, **237–238**
Palestine, **238–240**
    absentee landlords, 3
    and the Arab League, 16
    Arab Spring in, 38, 41–43
    Arab-Islamic conquest of, 14–15
    Arab-Jewish clashes in, pre-1947, 28–30
    declaration of statehood, 45
    demographics in, 91–92
    desire for recognition, 239–240
    division of, 150
    government under the Ottomans, 3, 260
    history of, 66–67
    Israeli solution, 310
    as Jewish homeland, xvi, 335–338
    Ottoman conquest of, xvi, 3, 6, 58, 116, 134, 173, 175, 185, 225, 236, 333
    as part of Syria, 216
    Persian conquest of, 269–270
    Roman occupation of, 189
    UN partition plan for, xvi, 14, 29, 30, 311–313, 320, 328
    in the United Nations, 1
    See also British Mandate for Palestine; one-state solution; two-state solution
Palestine Democratic Union, 243
Palestine Liberation Army (PLA), 44, **240–241**
Palestine Liberation Front (PLF), **241–242**, 243

Palestine Liberation Organization (PLO), **242–247**
    Abbas's involvement in, 1
    agreement with Israel, 221
    Arab League support for, 32
    Ashrawi's support for, 46
    and Black September, 62
    Central Council, 243
    claims to East Jerusalem, 176
    creation of, 238, 242, 243, 261
    Executive Committee, 243, 255–256
    expulsion from Jordan, 120, 139, 185–186, 243–244, 259
    in Gaza, 103, 244
    vs. Hamas, 262
    in Jordan, 243
    in Lebanon, 44–45, 62, 103, 207–209, 244–245, 259
    at the Madrid Conference, 213
    Negotiations Affairs Department, 246
    and the Oslo Accords, xvii, 142, 233–235, 261
    and Palestine nationalism, xvi–xvii, 123, 226
    peace talks with Israel, 322
    relations with Jordan, 62
    support for two-state solution, 309
    support from refugees, 94
    Ten-Point Program, 244–245
    terrorism by, 152
    in Tunisia, 45, 103, 152, 209, 245, 306
    and the West Bank, xvii, 103, 176, 244, 329
    See also Arafat, Yasser; Fatah; Palestinian hijackings
Palestinian Arab Front, 243
Palestinian Authority (PA), **247–249**
    Abbas's involvement with, 1–2, 86, 101, 104, 110–111, 117, 123, 125, 144, 246, 248–249, 250, 256, 309, 323
    and the Al-Aqsa Martyrs Brigades, 5
    Arafa's involvement with, 1, 45, 47, 103, 171, 234, 245, 246, 247–248, 249, 256
    area of jurisdiction, 239
    Barghouti's critique of, 55
    Dahlan's involvement in, 86
    Erekat and, 101
    and Fatah, 103–104, 306
    formation of, 234, 244–246
    in the Gaza Strip, 110
    and Hamas, 108, 261
    in Hebron, 131

Palestinian Authority (PA) (*cont.*)
  and Izz al-Din al-Qasam Brigades, 171
  and the Oslo Accords, 103, 109, 131, 141, 213, 234, 239, 247, 249–250, 251, 276
  in the West Bank, 113, 328
  See also Palestinian Authority Security Forces (PASF)
Palestinian Authority Security Forces (PASF), **249–252**
  Civil Defense, 251
  District Coordination Office (DCO), 251
  General Intelligence (GI) branch, 251
  Military Intelligence, 251
  National Security Force (NSF), 250
  Palestinian Civil Police, 250–251
  Presidential Guard, 251
  Preventive Security (PS) branch, 251
Palestinian Campaign for the Academic and Cultural Boycott of Israel, 63
Palestinian General Security Services (GSS)
  counterterrorism responsibilities of, 249–250
  See also Palestinian Authority Security Forces (PASF)
Palestinian hijackings, 62, 90, 100, 120, 139, 224, 242, 244, **252–254**, 272, 296
Palestinian Initiative for the Promotion of Global Dialogue and Democracy (Miftah), 47
Palestinian Islamic Jihad (PIJ), 1, 123, 141, 171, 192, 249, 251, **254–255**, 300, 301, 306
Palestinian Legislative Council (PLC), 256
Palestinian National Congress, 240
Palestinian National Council (PNC), 45, 243, **255–256**, 272
Palestinian People's Party, 243
Palestinian Popular Front Struggle, 243
Palestinian refugee camps, 209, **256–258**, 269, 314. *See also* Palestinian refugees
Palestinian refugees, **258–260**
  in Egypt, 256, 277
  in the Gaza Strip, 108
  and the Jewish settlements, 269
  in Jordan, 94, 139, 256–257, 259, 277, 278–279, 328
  in Lebanon, 204–206, 209
  and the *Nakba*, 225–226
  and the Palestinian diaspora, 93–94
  permanent status of, 269
  and the Right of Return, 92, 277–279
  and the UNRWA, 313–314
  in the West Bank, 328
  See also Diaspora, Palestinian; *Nakba*; Palestinian refugee camps
Palestinians, **260–263**
  assassination of, 143, 144, 191
  conflict with Israelis, xv–xvi
  displaced, 313–314
  in East Jerusalem, 161–162
  in Gaza, 261–263
  history of, 67
  in the Holy War Army, 137–138
  in Israel, 4
  killed in the Intifadas, 141–145
  in Lebanon, 204–206
  at the Madrid Conference, 321
  national identity of, 261–262
  under occupation, 238, 252, 326
  rights of, 4, 51
  self-rule for, 245
  in the West Bank, 144–145, 162–164, 169, 261–263, 327
  See also Deir Yassin Massacre; Diaspora, Palestinian; *Nakba*; Palestinian refugee camps; Palestinian refugees
Palmach, 17, 90, 122, 156, **263–264**, 275
Palyam, 157
Pan-Arabism, 32, 105, 138, 227, 261
Paris Peace Conference (1919), 12, 105, 170
Patterson, John H., 182
Peace movement, 264–265, 290, 306
Peace Now, **264–265**, 290
Peasants' Crusade, 82
Peel, William Robert, 37
Peel Commission Report, 178, 259
People of the Book, 148
People's Republic of China, 213, 316
Peres, Shimon, **265–266**
  and the defense ministry, 265–266
  and the Labor Party, 293
  as minister of foreign affairs, 266
  Nobel Peace Prize, 142, 275, 322
  as prime minister, 200, 228, 265–266
Permanent status issues, **266–269**
  borders, 268
  Jerusalem, 266–267
  Palestinian refugees, 269
  security, 268
  settlements in, 267–268

Persian conquest of Palestine, **269–271**
Persian Gulf War, 45, 186, 213, 221, 228
Peter I (King of Cyprus), 84
Peter the Hermit, 82
Phalangists, 208, 209, 294
Phasael (tetrarch of Jerusalem), 280
Philip (son of Herod the Great), 133, 281
Philip Augustus (King of France), 83
Picot, François Georges, 302
Pinsker, Leon, **271**
Plan Dalet, **271–272**
Pogroms, 6, 130, 173, 189, 237, 271, 336. *See also* Pale of Settlement
Politburo, 135
Pompey the Great, 189, 279–280
Popular Front for the Liberation of Palestine (PFLP), **272–273**
  airline hijackings, 90, 100, 120, 139, 244, 252–253
  DFLP split from, 90
  General Command, 241–242, 243, 245
  and the PLO, 243, 244–245
Premillennial dispensationalism, 76
Preventive Security Service (PSS), 86
Pro-Israel Lobby. *See* American Israel Public Affairs Committee (AIPAC); Christian Zionism; U.S. aid to Israel
Protestant Reformation, 85
Protestantism, 77–78
Putin, Vladimir, 40, 305

Qassam, Izz al-Din al-, 36, 124, **274**
Qassam rockets, 110, 124, 192, 274
Qassamiyun. *See* Izz al-Din al-Qassam Brigades
Qatar, 213, 219
Quakers, 64–65
Quietus, Lusius, 282
Quirinius, P. Sulpicus, 281
Qurai, Ahmed, 101
Qur'an, 147–148, 149

Rabbo, Yasser Abed, 90
Rabin, Yitzhak, **275–276**
  as ambassador to U.S., 275
  assassination of, 73, 119, 153, 167, 228, 239, 266, 276, 296, 309, 322
  as defense minister, 142
  and the First Intifada, 142
  and the IDF, 89, 211
  and the Labor Party, 118, 119, 200, 265, 322
  Nobel Peace Prize, 142, 275, 322
  and the Oslo Accords, 119, 200, 233, 265, 275–276, 322
  in Palmach, 263, 275
  as prime minister, 89, 118, 119, 142, 218, 265, 275, 322
  proposal of West Bank barrier, 168
  resignation of, 265, 275
Rachel, 289
Rafi party, 59, 200
Ramadan War. *See* Arab-Israeli War, 1973
Ramallah, **276–277**
Rantisi, Abd al-Aziz, 123, 124, 144
Rapture, 76
Rayan, Nizar, 172
Raymond of Tripoli, 83, 129
Raymond III of Tripoli, 285
Reagan, Ronald, 10, 207
Rebecca, 130, 289
Red Army (West Germany), 100
Refugees
  Eritrean, 92
  from Iraq, 186
  Jewish, 93, 156
  in Jordan, 139, 186
  Lebanese, 159
  in Lebanon, 204–206, 209
  Sudanese, 92
  from Syria, 186
  from Yemen, 186
  See also Palestinian refugees
Regev, Miri, 181
Rehoboam, 298
Republic of China (Taiwan), 16
Revisionist Party, 333
Reynald of Châtillon (Lord of Transjordan), 128, 285
Rice, Condoleezza, 158
Richard the Lionhearted (King of England), 83
Right of Return, 5–6, 117, 150, **277–279**
  for Palestinians, 226, 230, 256, 277–279
  See also Law of Return
Road Map for Peace, 109, 144, 218, 322–323
Rogers, William, 228
Roman Catholic Church, xv, 61, 77, 80. *See also* Christianity; Crusades in the Holy Land
Roman conquest of Judea, 132, 190, **279–282**

Roman empire
  Jewish revolts against, 183–184
  rule in Judea and Samaria, 132, 190, 279–282
  See also Roman conquest of Judea
Rothschild, Edmond James de, 336
Rothschild, Walter, 67
Rothschild family, 53
Royal Fusiliers, 156, 173, 182
Rufus, Tinnius, 183
Russia
  and the Middle East Quartet, 218
  and the Pale of Settlement, 237–238
  relationship with Israel, 40, 305
  and the Road Map for Peace, 322–323
  support for Syria, 40
  and the Sykes-Picot Agreement, 302
  See also Putin, Vladimir; Soviet Union
Russian Orthodox Church, 237
Russian revolution, 53

Saadi, Louay, 255
Sabra and Shatila Massacre, 205, 209–210, 245. *See also* Lebanon, Israeli invasion of
Sadat, Ahmed, 272
Sadat, Anwar, **283**
  and the Arab-Israeli War, 1973, 26, 27, 97
  assassination of, 73, 98, 152, 221, 283
  and the Camp David Accords, 72–73, 94, 96, 98, 152, 283, 316–317, 320–321
  as president of Egypt, 97, 151
  See also Egypt
Sadducees, 279, 281
Safavids, 148–149
Saladin, **284–286**
  and the Battle of Hattin, 128–129, 285
  and the Church of the Holy Sepulcher, 80
  and the Third Crusade, 83, 286
Salama, 137
Salim I (Ottoman sultan), 236
Salomon, Gershon, 308
Salvation Army, 78
Samuel (prophet), 61, 87, 286–287
Samuel, Herbert, 53
Saqa, Anwar al-, 241
Sarah, 102, 130
Saraya al-Quds (Jerusalem Brigades), 254
Sassanid Empire, 15, 148, 223, 270
Saud, Abd al-Aziz al-, 35

Saudi Arabia
  Arab Spring in, 38
  Palestinian refugees in, 94
  support for PLO, 45
  support for rebels in Syria, 42
Saul, 87, **286–288**, 311
Schlesinger, James R., 27
Schofield, Cyrus I., 76
Sea of Galilee, 326, 327
Second Zionist Congress, 335
Security issues, 268
Seljuk Turks, xv
Serot, André, 60
Settlement Watch, 265
Settlements, **288–291**
  annexation of, 36, 210–221, 231, 235, 240, 309, 330
  attacks on, 15, 30, 36, 68, 207, 313
  and borders, 268
  defense of, 36, 58, 80, 88, 156, 157, 263, 264
  in East Jerusalem, 267
  expansion of, 1, 23, 109, 119, 151, 153, 201, 210, 239–240, 290, 309, 312, 323
  in Galilee, 30, 31, 207
  in Gaza, 109, 113, 160–161, 164, 207, 267, 289, 295, 330
  in Golan Heights, 115, 160, 289, 304
  in Jerusalem, 30, 31, 153, 160, 161–162, 164, 176, 238, 257, 267, 268, 289, 310
  in the Jordan Valley, 289
  in the Judean Desert, 289
  opposition to, 265, 267
  and Palestinian refugees, 269
  permanent status issues, 267–268, 288
  Rabin's opposition to, 119
  security issues, 268
  Sharon's support for, 294–295
  under Solomon, 298
  violence in, 291, 306
  in West Bank, 9, 36, 55, 92, 113, 118, 153, 157, 160, 162–164, 176, 191, 207, 228–229, 231, 235, 238, 267, 288, 289, 290, 295, 309, 328–330
  withdrawal of, 330
  Zionist movement for, 58, 118, 182–183, 335, 337, 338
  See also Kibbutz; Occupied Palestinian Territories (OPT)
Settler violence, **291–293**
Seventeenth Zionist Congress, 174

Seventh Zionist Congress, 337
Severus, Sextus Julius, 184
Shaba Farms, 136
Shabak, 295. *See also* Shin Bet
Shabiba, 306
Shahrbaraz (Persian general), 270
Shalit, Gilad, 172, 248
Shallah, Ramadan Abdullah, 254
Shalmaneser (king), 50
Shalom, Avram, 296
Shamir, Yitzhak, **293–294**
    in Irgun, 293
    in Lehi, 60, 293
    and the Likud Party, 152, 210, 228
    and the Madrid Conference, 213
    as prime minister, 152, 293–294
Shanab, Ismail Abu, 124
Sharett, Moshe, 217, 326
Sharia law, 148, 274, 302
Sharon, Ariel, **294–295**
    building West Bank barrier, 153, 169
    and the Camp David Summit, 295
    death of, 153, 295
    as defense minister, 45, 207–208, 210, 245, 294
    and the invasion of Lebanon, 207–210
    and the Likud Party, 74, 210, 294, 295
    military service, 155
    as minister of agriculture, 294
    and the Oslo Accords, 73
    plan for Gaza Strip disengagement, 74, 143, 153, 109, 113, 330
    as prime minister, 266, 295, 330
    and the Second Intifada, 143
    summit with Bush and Abbas, 323
    visit to Temple Mount, 4–5, 74, 127, 143, 153, 176, 178, 235, 330
Shazly, Saad el-, 25, 27
Shebaa Farms, 115
Shihada, Salah, 123, 124
Shalit, Gilad, 248
Shin Bet, **295–297**
Shiqaqi, Fathi, 254
Shirazi, Ayatollah Hasan Mehdi al-, 149
Shirkuh, 284
Shukeiri, Ahmad, 240, 243
Sicarians/Sicarii, 281, 334
Siege of Acre, 83
Silva, Flavius, 183
Sinai Campaign (1956), 265

Sinai Desert, xvi, 187
    Egypt's control over, 39
    occupation of, 160, 321
    See also Egypt
Sinai Peninsula
    and the Arab-Israeli War, 1967, 22–23, 24
    Jewish settlements returned to Egypt, 72
    occupation of, 193, 314
    See also Egypt
Sinan Pasha, 236
Sinuwwar, Yahya al-, 123
Sinwar, Yahya, 172
Sisi, Abdel Fattah Saeed Hussein Khalil El-, 38, 41, 98
Sita, Kurt, 296
Six-Day War. *See* Arab-Israeli War, 1967
Sixteenth Zionist Congress, 174, 331
Sixth Zionist Congress, 173, 336
Socialism, 6, 336
Solomon, 49, 51, 75, 87–88, 188, 196, 267, 282, **297–298**, 311
    Temple of, xv, 52, 105–106, 183, 188–189, 215, 267, 281, 298, 311
Soviet Union
    and the Arab-Israeli War, 1967, 22, 23
    and the Arab-Israeli War, 1973, 27–28
    at the Madrid Conference, 213
    recognition of Israel by, 16
    relationship with Egypt, 227, 235
    supplying arms to Egypt, 107
    supplying arms to Iraq, 107
    supplying arms to Syria, 107
    support for partition plan, 312
    See also Russia
Spain, expulsion of Jews from, 189
Special Night Squads, 36, 121, 156
Stalin, Joseph, 219
State List party, 59
Steiner, David, 11
Stern, Avraham, 60, 293, 298–299
Stern Gang (Lehi; Lohamei Herut Israel), **298–299**
    and the Arab-Jewish Communal War, 30
    assassinations by, 18, 60, 146, 293, 299
    and the Deir Yassin Massacre, 89–90
    as offshoot of Irgun, 146, 156
    vs. Palestinians, 138
    Shamir as leader of, 293
    as terrorist organization, 69
    during the War of Independence, 171–172

Suez Canal, 24–25, 32, 325
  nationalization of, 97, 107, 151, 227
  See also Suez Crisis
Suez Crisis, 10, 19, 44, 59, 88, 97, 217, 227. *See also* Arab-Israeli War, 1956; Suez Canal
Suez War, 32. *See also* Arab-Israeli War, 1956; Suez Crisis
Suicide bombings, **299–301**
  by the Al-Aqsa Martyrs Brigades, 4–5, 55
  by Hamas, 75, 124, 239
  by Hezbollah, 300
  Palestinian, 103, 228, 266, 300
  in Ramallah, 277
  during the Second Intifada, 330
  by Tanzim, 306
  in the West Bank, 169
Suleiman the Magnificent, 177
Supreme Muslim Council (SMC), **302**
Sykes, Mark, 302
Sykes-Picot Agreement, 35, 138, **302–303**
Syria, **303–305**
  Arab Spring in, 38, 48, 304
  and the Arab-Israeli War, 1948, 226
  and the Arab-Israeli War, 1967, 20
  and the Arab-Israeli War, 1973, 25–26
  Druze in, 94
  French Mandate for, 16, 115
  and the Golan Heights, 115–116, 217
  and Hamas, 219
  history of, 190, 216
  Israel's relationship with, 39–40, 115
  at the Madrid Conference, 213, 321
  Palestinian refugees in, 94, 256–257, 259, 277, 314
  and the PLA, 241
  and the PLO, 44, 244, 245
  refugees from, 2, 42
  relationship with Iran, 39–40
  Roman annexation of, 279
  and the Sykes-Picot Agreement, 303
  and the United Arab Republic, 227
  war with Israel, xvi
  See also Golan Heights
Syriac Orthodox Church, 80, 204
Syrian civil war, 48, 137, 206, 304, 314
Syrian Heights, 115
Syrkini, Nahum, 335

Taba Agreement (Oslo II), 322
Taif Accords/Agreement, 135, 206
Talmud, 189
Tancred, 82
Tanzim, 55, 103, **306–307**. *See also* Fatah
Tehomi, Avraham, 121
Tel Aviv, 5–6, **307–308**, 337
Temple Institute, 308
Temple Mount. *See* Haram al-Sharif/Temple Mount
Temple Mount Faithful, 127, 308
Temple Mount Heritage Foundation, 308
Temple of Jerusalem, 132, 183. *See also* Temple of Solomon
Temple of Solomon, xv, 52, 105–106, 183, 188–189, 215, 267, 281, 298, 311
Terror Against Terror (TAT), 191
Terrorism
  anti-Arab, 179
  Arafat blamed for, 45
  Cave of the Patriarchs Massacre, 75
  by Gush Emunim, 119
  by Hamas, 152–153, 239
  by Irgun, 57, 145–146
  Jewish, 195
  and the Jewish National Fund (JNF), 69
  Palestinian, 131, 144, 234, 249
  by the PLO, 152, 243
  renounced by PLO, 45
  See also King David Hotel bombing; Suicide bombings
Teutonic Knights, 85
Third Mithridatic War, 279
Third Temple Movement, 106, 127, 267, **308**
Thirty-Seventh Zionist Congress, 331
Thutmoses III, 99
Tilglath-Pilneser III, 50
Titus, 281
Tlaib, Rashida, 65
Tomb of the Patriarchs, 130, 147
Torah, 187–188, 189
Trajan, 281–282
Transjordan, 16, 138, 185
Treaty of Friendship, 283
Treaty of Jaffa, 286
Truman, Harry, 312, 320, 328
Trump, Donald J./Trump administration
  AJC support for, 12
  and the Iran nuclear deal, 11, 40, 42, 153, 340
  and the Israeli-Palestinian conflict, 42

moving U.S. embassy to Jerusalem, 176, 178
and the Palestinian Authority, 251
recognizing Israel's claim to Golan Heights, 116, 153, 305
recognizing Jerusalem as Israel's capital, 153, 176, 323
support for Israel, 229, 240, 309, 323
and the UNRWA, 258, 259, 314
Trumpeldor, Joseph, 173, 182
Tu Bishvat, 166
Tufayli, Subhi al-, 135
Tunisia
Arab Spring in, 37
PLO in, 45, 103, 152, 209, 245, 306
recognizing Israel, 213
Turan Shah, 284
Turkey, 219
Two-state solution, 231, 238, 255, 262, 265, 268, 288, **308–310**, 312
Abbas's support for, 1
stumbling blocks to, 266–268
Tzava Haganah L-Yisra'il. *See* Israel Defense Forces (IDF)

Uganda
proposal for Jewish homeland in, 134, 336
See also Entebbe Raid
Umar ibn Al-Khattab, 15
UN General Assembly Resolution 194, 32, 256, 278
UN Human Rights Council, 319
UN Interim Force in Lebanon (UNIFIL), 137, 159, 207
UN Partition Plan for Palestine, 14, 211, **311–313**, 328
UN Relief and Works Agency for Palestine Refugees in the Near East (UNRWA), 226, 256, 258, 259, **313–315**
UN Security Council Resolution 242, 23, 32, 74, 109, 116, 213, 235, 245, 309, **315–316**, 321, 328–329
UN Security Council Resolution 338, 32, 74, 116, 235, **316–317**, 321
UN Security Council Resolution 478, 176
UN Security Council Resolution 1701, 159
UN Special Commission for Palestine (UNSCOP), 69, 311–312
UNESCO, 314
Unit 101, 194
United Arab Emirates (UAE), 42
United Arab Republic, 227
United Jewish Kingdom, 238
United Kingdom
and the Arab Revolt, 36
British forces in Palestine, 34–35
British White Paper, 70–71
and the creation of the Jewish state, 337
Zionists in, 53, 67, 68
See also Balfour Declaration; Sykes-Picot Agreement
United Kingdom of Israel, 66–67, 106, **311**
and the Babylonian conquest of Judah, 51–52
See also Kingdom of Israel; Kingdom of Judah
United Nations
High Commission on Refugees (UNHCR), 256–257, 313
and the Middle East Quartet, 218
and the partition of Palestine, xvi
peacekeeping forces, 97, 137, 151
and the Road Map for Peace, 322–323
support for two-state solution, 309
unarmed international observer force, 131
United Nations Emergency Force (UNEF), 21
United Nations Interim Force in Lebanon (UNIFIL), 137, 159, 207
United States
aid to Egypt, 38–39
aid to Israel, 232, 317–319
aid to Jordan, 244
and the Arab-Israeli War, 1967, 27–28
invasion of Iraq, 40
at the Madrid Conference, 213
and the Middle East Quartet, 218
moving embassy to Jerusalem, 176, 178
opposing ISIS, 38
and the Oslo Accords, 233–235
recognition of Israel by, 16
relationship with Egypt, 283
relationship with Israel, 319
response to BDS movement, 64
and the Road Map for Peace, 322–323
support for partition plan, 312
support for two-state solution, 309
See also Obama, Barack; Trump, Donald J./Trump administration; U.S. aid to Israel; U.S. involvement in Israeli-Palestinian affairs

Universal Declaration of Human Rights, 278
Urban II (pope), 82–83, 85
U.S. Agency for International Development (USAID), 317
U.S. aid to Israel, 9–11, **317–319**
U.S. involvement in Israeli-Palestinian affairs, **320–324**. *See also* Camp David Accords; Camp David Summit; Oslo Accords
U.S. Security Coordinator for Israel and the Palestinian (USSC), 250
USS *Liberty*, 22, **324**

Vance, Cyrus, 72
Vanunu, Mordecai, 156
Vespasian, 183, 281
Via Dolorosa, 79
Violence
   involving Israeli settlers, 291–292
   See also Assassinations; King David Hotel bombing; Suicide bombings; Terrorism
Voice for Peace, 64

Wailing Wall. *See* Western (Wailing) Wall
War of Attrition, 97, 227–228, **325**
War of the Camps, 206
War of the Knives, 300
Water Security, **325–327**
Wazir, Khalil al- (Abu Jihad), 103
Weizman, Ezer, 263
Weizmann, Chaim, 53, 67, 105, 173, 312, **327–328**, 331
West Bank, **328–330**
   and the Al-Aqsa Martyrs Brigades, 4–5
   and the Allon Plan, 8–9
   annexation of, xvi, 40, 89, 96, 153, 185, 210–211, 229, 231, 235, 238, 240, 278, 309, 310, 319, 328, 330
   anti-Israel violence in, 1
   and the Arab-Israeli War, 1967, 22–23
   Bethlehem, 61
   under Fatah, 1
   and Gush Emunim, 118
   Israel's claim to, 40, 109, 167
   under Jordan, 226, 238
   occupation of, 151, 157, 160, 162–164, 176, 191, 193, 198–199, 207, 228, 230, 235, 238, 240, 261, 265, 267–268, 314, 321, 329
   and the Oslo Accords, 131, 162, 234, 247, 329–330
   under the Palestinian Authority, 110, 213, 234
   Palestinian refugees in, 41, 94, 256–258, 259, 277, 279
   Palestinian self-rule in, 45, 245
   Palestinian state in, 230
   as part of historic Palestine, 238
   PLO in, xvii, 103, 176, 244, 329
   settlements in, 9, 36, 55, 92, 113, 118, 153, 157, 160, 162–164, 176, 191, 202, 207, 228–229, 231, 235, 238, 267, 288, 289, 290, 295, 309, 328–330
   and the two-state solution, 308
   violence in, 291–292
   water resources in, 327
   withdrawal from, 113, 200, 330
   See also Israeli Security Barrier; Izz al-Din al-Qassam Brigades; Jordan; Judea and Samaria; Occupied Palestinian Territories (OPT)
Western (Wailing) Wall, xv, 29, 113, 127, 176, 177, 300, 302
Wilson, Woodrow, 53
Wingate, 156
Wise, Stephen, 54
Women's Zionist Organization of America, 339
World Health Organization (WHO), 314, 327
World Jewish Congress, 12
World Trade Organization (WTO), 2, 13
World War I, 28, 33, 53, 67, 105, 138, 145, 150, 156, 173, 183, 203, 204, 215, 225, 327–328
World War II, 16, 68, 69, 71, 122, 146, 156, 178–179, 319
World Zionist Organization (WZO), xvi, 105, 134, 145, 173, 328, **331**, 336
   Settlement Division, 290
   See also Zionism
Wye Memorandum, 229

Yaqub, Talat, 242
Yassin, Sheikh Ahmed, 123, 124, **332**
Yaunis Khan, Battle of, 236
Yemen, 42
   civil war in, 193
Yesh Din, 291
Yeshiva Merkaz Harav, 118
Yiddish language, 165, 189, 337
Yishuv, 6–7, **332–333**

Index

Yom Kippur War. *See* Arab-Israeli War, 1973
Young Men's Christian Association (YMCA), 78
Young Turks, 33
Youth of the Revenge, 241

Zaidan, Muhammad (Abu Abbas), 242
Zangi (governor of Mosul), 83
Zealots, 183, 214–215, 281, **334**
Zealots Revolt, 183
Zedekiah, 52
Zeevi, Rehavam, 272
Zion Mule Corps, 156, 182
Zionism, **334–339**
   and the AJC, 11
   and the American Palestine Committee (APC), 12
   and the Arab League, 32
   and the Arab Revolt, 36
   in Britain, 53, 67
   Christian attitudes toward, 78
   denunciation of, 152
   founding of, xvi, 28, 133, 150, 175
   and the Jewish diaspora, 93
   and the Jewish Legion, 182
   and kibbutzim, 194–195
   Labor, 57, 336, 338
   and land ownership, 3
   Orthodox, 191
   and the Palestinians, 260, 262
   and the PLO, 243, 244
   religious, 198
   revisionist, 57, 101, 145
   and the right of return, 5–6, 7, 181, 201
   as unifying ideology, 167
   See also Christian Zionism; Jabotinsky, Ze'ev; Jewish National Fund (JNF); Stern Gang; Weizmann, Chaim; World Zionist Organization (WZO); Zionist Congresses; Zionist Organization; Zionist Organization of America (ZOA); Zionists
Zionist Congresses
   First, xvi, 133–134, 331, 335, 336
   Second, 335
   Sixth, 173, 336
   Seventh, 337
   Sixteenth, 174, 331
   Seventeenth, 174
   Thirty-Seventh, 331
Zionist Organization, 336–338. *See also* World Zionist Organization (WZO)
Zionist Organization of America (ZOA), **339–340**
Zionists, xv, 122, 225, 259, 332–333
   and the Faysal-Weizmann Agreement, 105
   in Great Britain, 53–54, 67, 68
   Jabotinsky, Ze'ev, 58, 101, 145, 173–174, 182, 191
   Kahane, 191
   one-state vs. two-state solution, 231
   in Palestine, xvi, 15
   Pinsker, 271
   Weizmann, Chaim, 53, 67, 105, 173, 312, 327–328, 331
   See also Ben-Gurion, David; Zionism
Zurayk, Constantine, 120
Zweibon, Bertam, 179, 191

www.ingramcontent.com/pod-product-compliance
Lightning Source LLC
Chambersburg PA
CBHW082023300426
44117CB00015B/2327